ENCYCLOPEDIA of DOG BREEDS

ISBN 0-87666-285-8

E·H·HART

ENCYCLOPEDIA
of
DOG BREEDS

HISTORIES AND OFFICIAL STANDARDS

evolution, geneology, genetics,
breeding, feeding, husbandry,
training, medical care, showing

by

ERNEST H. HART

designed and illustrated
by the author

" . . . *and to the scribe she offered*
aid and more and he said to her,
'Meum et Tuum be this that I
have written herein'."

to
Kay,
my wife

Distributed in the U.S.A. by T.F.H. Publications, Inc., 211 West Syl-
vania Avenue, P.O. Box 27, Neptune City, N.J. 07753; in England by
T.F.H. (Gt. Britain) Ltd., 13 Nutley Lane, Reigate, Surrey; in Cana-
da to the book store and library trade by Clarke, Irwin & Company,
Clarwin House, 791 St. Clair Avenue West, Toronto 10, Ontario; in
Canada to the pet trade by Rolf C. Hagen Ltd., 3225 Sartelon Street,
Montreal 382, Quebec; in Southeast Asia by Y.W. Ong, 9 Lorong 36
Geylang, Singapore 14; in Australia and the south Pacific by Pet
Imports Pty. Ltd., P.O. Box 149, Brookvale 2100, N.S.W., Australia.
Published by T.F.H. Publications Inc. Ltd., The British Crown Col-
ony of Hong Kong.

CONTENTS

FOREWORD

This book was conceived as a vehicle to fill many needs. Its initial and primary purpose is to bring the reader a panoramic and entire picture of the domesticated canine species, from its beginnings in its struggle for survival in the evolutionary mists of prehistory, to its fantastic growth and multitudinous breed development at the hands of man in this modern era. Secondly, this book was designed to present to a dog-conscious readership the most complete, best illustrated and, I hope, interesting treatise on the history of the breeds (accompanied by their official and up-to-date standards) to be found in any other tome in its category. It is a book which should find favor with the novice, to aid him in selecting and caring for the dog that best suits his needs; the student of dogs, for its tracing of canine evolution and geneology; the breeder, who will find the chapters on heredity and the methods and mechanics of breeding of interest; the ordinary dog owner who can profit by perusing the material on feeding, husbandry, training and medical care; and the neophyte show enthusiast who will find much of interest, specifically in that section devoted to showing and dog shows.

Judges can use this book as a quick and pleasant refresher course on the various standards, and it should find favor with dog fanciers as a whole from a purely esthetic view, as a handsome as well as useful addition to their canine library.

A wealth of time and research has gone into this book. It was a task that seemed monumental at first, but was made much lighter and enjoyable by the help of other hands, particularly the gifted ones of my wife, Kay. She it was who did most of the typing of seemingly endless standards and deciphering and typing my long-hand, execrable scribbling and research notes from odd shaped pieces of paper written at odd times in odd corners of the globe. I must thank also those few breed club secretaries who answered my letters requesting a history of their particular breed which would be approved by their club membership. Lack of cooperation in this quarter made my job much more difficult and time consuming, for I then found myself amidst a multitude of old and dusty volumes digging out ancient historic data, often long forgotten, on breeds in focus today.

Forgive me if I have not given full credit to some one of you who have supplied me with a vital photograph or breed data. Correspondence is often mislaid during one's journeys. My grateful thanks also to Mr. John C. Neff for his gracious permission to use the official American Kennel Club breed standards.

All things have a beginning and an end and this book is finally finished. I present it now to you with the hope that you will approve of it and find it a worthwhile addition to the ever growing canine book shelf.

Ernest H. Hart

Villa Santa Emilia,
Torremolinos, Spain

SECTION 1

E·H·HART

1

EVOLUTION OF THE DOG

Through impossible-to-grasp eons of time, approximately forty million years, the genus *Canis* had been developing on a plastic, forming earth. Long before a curious, simian creature that was to become man crept from the sheltering tree limbs to the floor of the primeval world, *Miacis*, a small, climbing, tree-dwelling carnivore, common ancestor of both bear and dog, stalked its prey in the upper branches of the verdant forests of far distant prehistoric ages.

Slowly, blindly groping with ponderous, unskilled fingers, nature needed thirty million years more to crudely mold the evolutionary clay of this coming species into *Cynodictis*, a creature not yet a dog but moving ever closer to the family *Canidae*. It would take a mere ten million years more before *Tomarctus*, the prototype dog, would make his appearance on the stage of specie origin and the drama of the dog would unfold.

At first, long before even *Miacis* as time is considered in the limitless agelessness of life's beginnings, there was a yeasty stirring in the seas of the new world and then the creatures of the deep waters and the slimy pools, over untold periods of awesome time, developed legs and lungs and crawled onto the land and, in that era of monstrous change, grew to grotesque vastness to match the spinning rawness of the infant planet on which they had been spawned. The extinct giant reptiles, living nightmares of the almost unending Mesozoic era, roared and trampled and ate themselves into oblivion. But, in the process, dramatic mutations occurred within the germ plasm of a few of the smaller dinosaurs. Small skeletal changes took place, body scales changed and became rudimentary fur or feathers, certain of the reptile creatures displayed more energy than their slow moving and almost brainless kin, and some perhaps began to develop warm blood. These were the living transitional forms, precursors of various coming classes of life including Mammalia, the viviparous, milk giving, intelligent animals destined to become the dominant creatures of the whole world.

It was during the primitive Paleocene age that mammalian carnivores began to reach definition as animal entities. In the twenty million years of the Eocene age that followed the mammals, hiding furtively in the ancient forests amid the teeming, awesome animal life of a humanless earth, began to segregate and specialize. This age produced, along with rodents and cat-creatures, the doglike *Mesonyx*.

New faunas came into focus during the Oligocene epoch of the Cenozoic era (the period of time when mammals were the dominant life form on earth). A great and dramatic change took place in the teeming animal population on earth. The more primitive mammals gradually became the victims of their own simplicity and inability to cope with the changing world around them. In the evolving gene-pool of the primitive flesh eaters small, beneficial mutations

MIACIS, ancestor to several mammalian species
including the canine, was a small, stealthy,
nocturnal carnivore whose habitat and hunting
ground was the towering, frondescent trees of
that primeval time.

occurred that gave rise to varied forms or sub-species within the overall carnivorous evolutionary format, forms standing ready for natural selection through their greater capability to exist and prosper in the face of habitat change. It was from these early, selected carnivores that two great modern groups of meat eaters began to emerge into the light of easy recognition, the solitary stalking cats, and the dogs, the latter specializing in the pack pursuit of their quarry. At this time there were yet no true men on earth, but an ape-like creature of Proconsul type was emerging from the trees and attempting to stand partially erect on the danger-infested ground, and all over the world the varied hosts of animal life raced along their diverse evolutionary paths into the coming clear specie focus we know today.

In a time that ended a million years ago, the Pliocene epoch, the evolving mammals, following a pattern that had become evident in the latter phases of the Oligocene age, continued to enlarge in size. Evolutionary groping by experimenting life produced gross mistakes in some instances. The Canine-Ursine line gave birth to *Agriotherium*, an enormous bear, and *Amphicyon*, a colossus of the dog family. This canine giant, like most living things that go beyond the limits of reasonable size for their kind, marched down the corridor of that autumn of the Cenozoic era, sniffing the cold winds of the coming invasion of ice from the north, and into oblivion. In the direct evolutionary process of the true canine monstrous *Amphicyon* had no part. It might be interesting to mention that during this period, in the person of *Pleisanthropus transvaalensis*, true man began to emerge from the slime of creation.

10

The ice sheets moved slowly southward. During a million-year-old winter continental glaciers came down from the north four times and four times withdrew. The animals of the earth responded to each new wave of warmth by multiplying and increasing in size, even to giantism in some instances, as witness *Canis dirus*, a monstrous, six foot wolf, that ranged the new world continent. Drastic changes brought by the moving times of cold further eliminated animals that were unable to cope with a changing environment. And during this same era man was moving steadily away from his simian beginning toward humanness. Soon, a relative measure of time considering the millenniums that had gone before, the paths of man and dog would converge and they would stand together for over one hundred thousand years and up to the present day.

But we are moving ahead of our story, a story told in the rock stratas and pieced together, with still many gaps, by men of science, vision and patience.

The prototype dog mentioned earlier, short-legged, predatory *Tomarctus*, who lived fifteen million years ago the product of random selection from the same mammalian stock that eventually resulted in bears, cats, raccoons, hyenas and seals, was in turn the probable ancestor of the wolf, coyote, jackal, fox and like canine creatures. Also, in a direct line of prehistoric descent from the Miocene era, from *Tomarctus* and representing the most important cleavage in canine geneology, there appeared four prototype breeds. *Canis familiaris metris-optimae*, was the basis of the sheep herding breeds beginning with the early Persian herding dogs. *Canis familiaris intermedius*, was ancestor

TOMARCTUS, the prototype dog who lived fifteen millon years ago. Low to the ground, predatory, with short, furry, upright ears and a long, balancing tail, Tomartus was the probable and direct ancestor of all true canines.

to many of the hauling, hunting and toy breeds, the latter descending from the early Egyptian house dogs. The third prototype canine, *Canis familiaris leineri*, was responsible for the sight hounds, again through an Egyptian breed, the early Egyptian Greyhound. Also from *leineri* descended many of the terriers. *Canis familiaris inostranzewi*, the last of the important quartet, gave us the thick-jawed, powerful, mastiff-type animals as well as some of our water dogs.

The above categories of descent are necessarily broad in concept. So many of the most popular breeds of today are the result of the interlacing and crossing of the genetic heritage of the ancestral animals that came down from the four basic canine types.

Man's earliest association with the carnivorous canine race which would in time become his "best friend," was quite possibly not a happy one. One can, without much difficulty, envision an early, brutish ancestor stalked and pulled down by the slavering jaws of a hunting pack of primeval dogs. So, too, can we imagine Swanscombe man, two hundred and fifty thousand years ago, stealthily following a teat-dragging bitch to her lair, killing her with his flint axe or wooden spear, then cracking the heads of her whelps, delicacies to bring back to fill the bellies of his own hungry young.

In the dawn of man, the species *Homo*, insensitive, stupid, unhampered by custom or social canons, existed in an aura of animal filth. The outside of his cave, and probably also the inside to a lesser extent, was a receptacle for all manner of garbage and refuse. There came a time when a dog, unsuccessful in the hunt, or too old or injured to find and bring down prey, his hunger titillated by the scent of food rot, came to man's cave and furtively carried off what man had left or thrown away. As time passed more and more canines came to eat, to find easy sustenance at the caves, performing a service that man finally recognized and they, dog and man, developed a tolerance to each other's company.

There came a day, too, when man the hunter, tracking the milk-laden bitch to her cave, saved a pup from her litter to bring home alive for his own whelps to play with, and man and dog then dwelt together under the same roof. As man's mentality and abilities developed he came to realize the worth of the dog as a companion in the hunt, and they shared the fruits of their labor together, between them finding and bringing down more game and being able then, to subsist together better than either could alone. So they adopted each other and the dog warned against other predators, guarded the man's home and his person from the myriad deadly dangers of the time, while man in his turn fed and protected the dog in sickness, anointed his wounds and so secured this unique pact between two diverse animal races, a covenant that has survived and come down through uncountable generations to the present day.

Undoubtedly some dogs with keener scent, greater agility and more general ability in the pursuit of game, would be selected by man, the hunter, for this vital task. Such animals could probably be catalogued and selected for, due to certain recognized physical aspects, by man. Other dogs, exhibiting slightly different characteristics, man saw made better watchdogs or pets for the children. Big, powerful canines could carry packs of the master's belongings when he followed the migrating herds for food. And later, when men gathered together, domesticated and held herds of the formerly wild ungulates he had once hunted, certain dogs aided him in this endeavor and ultimately became

First there was tolerance between dog and man. Then these two diverse species adopted each other, sharing a single roof and the fruits of their collective labor. So a partnership was formed between primordial man and primitive canine that was to endure and prosper through the long ages from that incredibly ancient time until (and I am certain beyond), the present era.

13

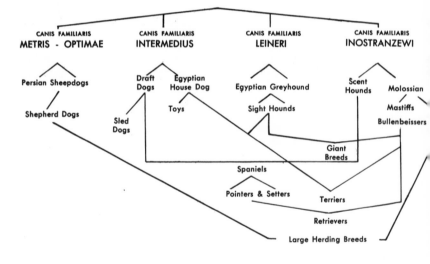

MIACIS
carnivorous mammal

CATS

CARRION EATERS

HYENAS

CYNODICTIS

TEMNOCYON
CYNODESMUS

BEARS

BEAR DOG   RACCOONS

SEALS

TOMARCTUS
WOLVES - JACKALS - WILD DOGS - FOXES
family Canidae

CANIS FAMILIARIS
METRIS - OPTIMAE

Persian Sheepdogs

Shepherd Dogs

CANIS FAMILIARIS
INTERMEDIUS

Draft   Egyptian
Dogs   House Dog

Sled   Toys
Dogs

CANIS FAMILIARIS
LEINERI

Egyptian Greyhound

Sight Hounds

CANIS FAMILIARIS
INOSTRANZEWI

Scent
Hounds   Molossian

Mastiffs

Bullenbeissers

Giant
Breeds

Spaniels

Pointers & Setters   Terriers

Retrievers

Large Herding Breeds

GENEOLOGY
OF THE
DOG

14

herding dogs. So crude selection was made for type and the species *Canine* began to form into utilitarian breeds.

The peoples of early, highly developed civilizations possessed breeds that can be recognized, from the formalized art of their time, as belonging to distinct breeds known and bred today. The ancient Assyrians, Egyptians, Macedonians, Spartans, Greeks, Romans, peoples of every clime and condition including barbarian tribes and the Mongol Huns, all developed breeds for specific purposes to aid them in the hunt, in war, as herders, household pets, and companions.

In recent years man, using the evolutionary and genetic tools handed to him by Darwin, Mendel, and their brilliant disciples, and through recognition of mutation in given directions and ruthless selection thereafter, has diversified *Canis familiaris* to such a bizarre extent that only geneological knowledge, in the case of some breeds, can assure us of the linkage between the dog and his feral ancestors.

In this book the standards and modern histories of the recognized breeds of dogs in America, as well as some unrecognized but definitely pure breeds of this and other countries, are presented. The author, traveling throughout the world, has seen many breeds specific to their locale and evidently pure bred in other countries, that are unknown to American fanciers. As time passes and the accessibility of fast, comfortable, inexpensive travel makes the world smaller, wandering dog people will certainly bring home with them, from their travels, specimens of many breeds formerly unknown to fanciers in this country but old and established in the land of their birth, to add to the growing list of dogs developed by man for his ever increasing pleasure and individual utilitarian and aesthetic needs.

There has been, down through the ages and yet today, between dog and man, a need for each other, a need that no other living creature can fill. We can didactically recite reasons for it. We can scientifically show the necessity for it. But we cannot truthfully and clearly define it, for it is of the heart and mind, of the inner being, of the spirit, in that place within man where the secret things dwell, and such matters defy definite equation.

HART

2

INHERITANCE OF THE DOG

From the time that early man first became aware of himself as an entity and probed questioningly at the world around him, he pondered the "why?" and "what?" of being.

The first interpretations given to natural phenomena by ancient man were mythological. But as early as 500 years before Christ the Greek philosopher Thales applied scientific thought to the subject and shrewdly concluded that all life originated and came from water (the Aegean Sea). Aristotle later collected and analyzed all facts and zoological data up to his time and made the initial attempt, on the basis of comparative anatomy, to classify the animal kingdom.

Down through the centuries other men of splendid and inquiring minds bent their efforts to shed more light upon the study of specie origin. But it remained for one man to find the key to the origin of species; that man was, of course, Charles Robert Darwin. He found the answer to the mystery of life in evolution, the theory that all life forms find kinship through a common and basic ancestry, and that divergence occurs to permit variety to better fit changing environment.

The decades passed with men of clear vision accepting and aiding in further formulating the principles of evolution as Darwin had advanced them initially. Science was aware that natural selection produced changes. But how did these changes come about? There seemed to be no rules, nothing that could be considered definite, no design that could be followed to an end result. There had to be a pattern of inheritance, but what was it and how did it work?

Darwin asked these questions too, but could find no answers. He did not know that while he founded his basic laws of evolution those of heredity were being developed at approximately the same time. But it would not be until the year 1900 that the laws governing inheritable linkage would be made known to the world.

Meanwhile superstition and arrogant, baseless theorizing took the place of truth in advancing so-called formulas of inheritance. The inheritance of acquired characteristics is one of the fallacious theories that was widely believed and has its disciples even today. Birthmarking is another false theory which must be discarded in the light of present-day genetical knowledge. The genes which give our dogs all their inheritable material are isolated in the body from any environmental influence. What the host does or has done to him influences them not at all. The so-called "proofs" advanced by the adherents of both these bogus theories were simply isolated coincidences.

Telegony is another of the untrue beliefs about influencing inherited characteristics. This is the theory that the sire of one litter could or would influence the progeny of a future litter out of the same bitch but sired by an entirely different stud. Telegony is, in its essence, comparable to the theory of

Throughout the world, in far and distant places of great antiquity, the author has found evidence of the close association of man and dog. In a distant time a man, dead long before the Egyptian pyramids rose from the sands of Giza, had his favorite dog buried with him in the jar that was the customary tomb of his simple civilization. Above is a bas relief sculpted by some forgotten Assyrian artist and found in the ruins of Nineveh. The animals are hunting dogs owned by the great monarch, Assur-bani-pal. Mastiff in type, used for hunting and as war dogs, here is proof again of the ancient bond between man and dog.

saturation—which is the belief that if a bitch is bred many times in succession to the same stud, she will become so "saturated" with his "blood" that she will produce only puppies of his type, even when mated to an entirely different stud. By far the strongest and most widely believed was the theory that the blood was the vehicle through which all inheritable material was passed from parents to offspring, from one generation to the next. The taint of that superstition still persists in the phraseology we employ in our breeding terms such as "bloodlines," "percentage of blood," "pure-blooded," "blue-blooded," etc.

The truth was found in spite of such a persistent theory, and in the history of science there is no more dramatic story than that of the discovery of the true method of inheritance. No, the truth was not arrived at in some fine, endowed scientific laboratory gleaming with the mysterious implements of research. The scene was instead a small dirt garden in Moravia, which is now a part of Czechoslovakia. There Johann Gregor Mendel, a Moravian monk, planted and crossed several varieties of common garden peas and quietly recorded the differences that occurred through several generations. Over a period of eight years this remarkable man continued his studies. Then, in 1865, he read a paper he had prepared regarding his experiments to the local Brunn, a society of historians and naturalists. The society subsequently published this paper in its journal, which was obscure and definitely limited in distribution.

Now we come to the amazing part of this story, for Mendel's theory of inheritance, which contained the fundamental laws upon which all modern advances in genetics have been based, gathered dust for thirty-four years, and it seemed that one of the most important scientific discoveries of the nineteenth century was to be lost to mankind. Then in 1900, sixteen years after Mendel's death, the paper was rediscovered and his great work given to the world.

In his experiments with the breeding of garden peas, Mendel discovered and identified the units of heredity. He found that when two individual plants which differed in a unit trait were mated, one trait appeared in the offspring and one did not. The trait which was visible he named the "dominant" trait, and the one which was not visible he called the "recessive" trait. He proposed that traits, such as color, are transmitted by means of units in the sex cells and that one of these units must be pure, let us say either black or white, but never be a mixture of both. From a black parent which is pure for that trait, only black units are transmitted, and from a white parent, only white units can be passed down. But when one parent is black and one is white, a hybrid occurs which transmits both the black and white units in equal amounts. The hybrid itself will take the color of the dominant parent, yet carry the other color as a recessive. Various combinations of unit crosses were tried by Mendel, and he found that there were six possible ways in which a pair of determiners (Mendel's "units") could combine with a similar pair. The Mendelian expectation chart shows how this law of Mendel's operates and the expected results. The simple Mendelian law holds true in the actual breeding of all living things —of plants, mice, humans, or dogs.

The beginning of new life in animals arises from the union of a male sperm and a female egg cell during the process of breeding. Each sperm cell has a nucleus containing one set of chromosomes, which are small packages, or units, of inheritable material. Each egg also possesses a nucleus of one set of chromosomes. The new life formed by the union of sperm cell and egg cell then possesses two sets of chromosomes—one from the sperm, one from the egg, or one set from the sire and one set from the dam. For when the sperm cell enters the egg, it does two things—it starts the egg developing and it adds a set of chromosomes to the set already in the egg. Here is the secret of heredity. For in the chromosomes lie the living genes that shape the destiny of the unborn young. Thus we see that the pattern of heredity, physical and mental, is transmitted to our dog from its sire and dam through tiny living cells called genes, which are the connecting links between the puppy and his ancestors.

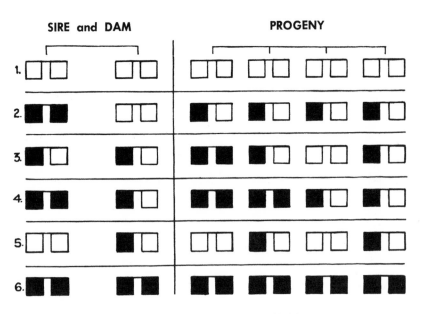

MENDELIAN EXPECTATION CHART

The six possible ways in which a pair of determiners can unite. Ratios apply to expectancy over large numbers, except in lines number 1, 2 and 6, where expectancy is realized definitely in every litter (the exception due to mutation).

These packets of genes, the chromosomes, resemble long, paired strings of beads. Each pair is alike, the partners formed the same, yet differing from the like partners of the next pair. In the male we find the exception to this rule, for here there is one pair of chromosomes composed of two that are not alike. These are the sex chromosomes, and in the male they are different from those in the female in that the female possesses a like pair while the male does not. If we designate the female chromosomes as X, then the female pair is XX. The male too has an x chromosome, but its partner is a y chromosome. If the male x chromosome unites with the female x chromosome, then the resulting embryo will be a female. But if the male y chromosome is carried by the particular sperm that fertilizes the female egg, the resulting progeny will be a

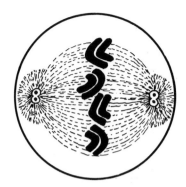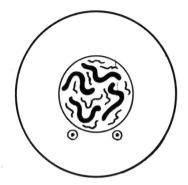

Miosis in process. A spindle covers the center of the cell, the nucleus has vanished and the centrioles have divided into separate pairs. The chromosomes have split and are preparing to separate and utilize the spindle to reach opposite sides of the cell as it prepares to divide. On the right the cell has completed division, the spindle has disappeared and there is now a complete set of chromosomes in the nucleus of the cell, and two centrioles. This cell is soon ready to divide again.

male. It is, therefore, a matter of chance as to what sex the offspring will be, since sperm is capricious and fertilization is random.

The actual embryonic growth of the puppy is a process of division of cells to form more and more new cells and at each cell division of the fertilized egg each of the two sets of chromosomes provided by sire and dam also divide, until all the myriad divisions of cells and chromosomes have reached an amount necessary to form a complete and living entity. Then birth becomes an accomplished fact, and we see before us a living, squealing puppy.

What is he like, this puppy? He is what his controlling genes have made him. His sire and dam have contributed one gene of each kind to their puppy, and this gene which they have given him is but one of the two which each parent possesses for a particular characteristic. Since he has drawn these determiners at random, they can be either dominant or recessive genes. His dominant heritage we can see when he develops, but what he possesses in recessive traits is hidden.

There are rules governing dominant and recessive traits useful in summarizing what is known of the subject at the present time. We can be reasonably sure that a dominant trait: (1.) Does not skip a generation. (2.) Will affect a relatively large number of the progeny. (3.) Will be carried only by the affected individuals. (4.) Will minimize the danger of continuing undesirable characteristics in a strain. (5.) Will make the breeding formula of each individual quite certain.

With recessive traits we note that: (1.) The trait may skip one or more generations. (2.) On the average a relatively small percentage of the individuals in the strain carry the trait. (3.) Only those individuals which carry a pair of determiners for the trait, exhibit it. (4.) Individuals carrying only one determiner can be ascertained only by mating. (5.) The trait must come through both sire and dam.

21

You will hear some breeders say that the bitch contributes 60 per cent or more to the excellence of the puppies. Others swear that the influence of the sire is greater than that of the dam. Actually, the puppy receives 50 per cent of his germ plasm from each, though one parent may be so dominant that it seems that the puppy received most of his inheritable material from that parent. From the fact that the puppy's parents also both received but one set of determiners from each of their parents and in turn have passed on but one of their sets to the puppy, it would seem that one of those sets that the grandparents contributed has been lost and that therefore the puppy has inherited the germ plasm from only two of its grandparents, not four. But chromosomal selection varies, and it is possible for the puppy's four grandparents to contribute an equal 25 per cent of all the genes inherited, or various and individual percentages, one grandparent contributing more and another less. It is even possible for the pup to inherit no genes at all from one grandparent and 50 per cent from another.

The genes that have fashioned this puppy of ours are of chemical composition and are living cells securely isolated from any outside influence, a point which we have made before and which bears repeating. Only certain kinds of man-directed radiation, some poisons or other unnatural phenomena can cause change in genes. No natural means can influence them. Environment can effect an individual but not his germ plasm. For instance, if the puppy's nutritional needs are not fully provided for during his period of growth, his end potential will not be attained; but regardless of his outward appearance,

Parent and pups are the product of their germ plasm, fashioned by a specific chromatic design that is unique to each of them as an individual.

his germ plasm remains inviolate and capable of passing on to the next generation the potential that was denied him by improper feeding.

Breeding fine dogs would be a simple procedure if all characteristics were governed by simple Mendelian factors, but alas, this is not so. Single genes are not solely responsible for single characteristics, mental or physical. The complexity of any part of the body and its dependence upon other parts in order to function properly, makes it obvious that we must deal with interlocking blocks of controlling genes in a life pattern of chain reaction. Eye color, for instance, is determined by a simple genetic factor, but the ability to see, the complicated mechanism of the eye, the nerves, the blood supply, the retina and iris, even how your dog reacts to what he sees, are all part of the genetic pattern of which eye color is but a segment.

Since they are living cells in themselves, the genes can and do change, or mutate. In fact, it is thought now that many more gene mutations take place than were formerly suspected, but that the great majority are either within the animal where they cannot be seen, or are so small in general scope that they are overlooked. The dramatic mutations which affect the surface are the ones we notice and select for or against according to whether they direct us toward our goal or away from it. Again, with the vagary inherent in all living

23

things, the mutated gene can presumably change once again back to its original form.

We see then that the puppy is the product of his germ plasm, which has been handed down from generation to generation. We know that there are certain rules that generally govern the pattern that the genes form, and that a gene which prevents another gene from showing in an individual is said to be a dominant and the repressed gene a recessive. Remember, the animal itself is not dominant or recessive in color or any other characteristic. It is the gene that is dominant or recessive, as judged by results. We find that an animal can contain in each of his body cells a dominant and a recessive gene. When this occurs, the dog is said to be heterozygous. We know that there is an opposite to the heterozygous individual, an animal which contains two genes of the same kind in its cells—either two dominants or two recessives—and this animal is said to be homozygous. The loss of a gene or the gain of a gene, or the

These German Shorthaired Pointer puppies reflect the characteristics of their breed as a whole, and the particular genetic properties which they have inherited from their sire and dam. Each parent has supplied half of the chromatic material that formed the pups into exclusive canine beings.

process of change among the genes, is known as mutation, and the animal affected is called a mutant.

Every bitch that stands before us, every stud we intend to use, is not just one dog, but two. Every living thing is a Jekyll and Hyde, shadow and substance. The substance is the dog that lives and breathes and moves before us, the animal that we see, the physical manifestation of the interaction of genotypic characters and environment—the *"phenotype."* The shadow is the dog we don't see, yet this shadow is as much a part of the dog before us as the animal we see. This shadow dog is the gene-complex, or total collection of its genes—the *"genotype."* The visual substance is easily evaluated, but the invisible shadow must also be clearly seen and evaluated, for both shadow and substance equally contribute to the generations to come. Without understanding the complete genetic picture of any particular dog, we cannot hope to successfully use that dog to accomplish specific results. In order to understand, we must delve into the genetic background of the animal's ancestry until the shadow becomes as clearly discernible as the substance and we can evaluate the dog's genetic worth as a whole; for this dog that stands before us is but the containing vessel, the custodian of a specific pattern of heredity.

With the basic concept of heredity that Mendel discovered as a foundation, other scientists went forward to fantastic new discoveries. Genetics became a major science of its own and men of intellect who studied, experimented, and dedicated their lives to this young science were called geneticists.

The units of inheritance, the genes, were examined and their behavior catalogued. Mutations were recognized and understood. But the makeup, the chemistry of the gene itself remained a mystery, though not for long.

It was discovered that there was a chemical powder (*deoxyribonucleic acid*) called DNA, and another nucleic acid named RNA (*ribonucleic acid*) in chromosomes that were, with protein, the materials of heredity. DNA, it was found, is a genetic Svengali with complete domination over all living cells and able to constantly reproduce itself, a process of startling uniqueness. So tiny it requires an enormous electron microscope to become visible, yet so omniscient that it contains within itself a creative diversity to command uncountable billions of forms; this is DNA, composed of four nucleotides which produce twenty universal amino acids, which in turn produce over 100,000 proteins, which give shape, form and substance to the infinite diversity of life forms.*

The study of genetics continues. What has already been discovered is of immeasurable importance in animal breeding. But those who breed dogs will not, in the foreseeable future, be able to use enough of this scientific knowledge to make the breeding of fine dogs a cut-and-dried matter. This is where the fascination lies, in that bit of the unknown in every breeding that makes the production of top animals a combination of science, experience, sixth-sense and deduction, and art. Add to this a touch of necessary genius and aesthetic innovation and you have the ingredients that make the study of canine inheritance and its actual application, the most fascinating hobby recipe one could wish for.

---

* For more definitive information on genetics and the art of breeding fine dogs, see the author's comprehensive book, "The Dog Breeder's Handbook."

3

METHODS OF DOG BREEDING

In today's mechanistic world, with its rushing pace and easy pleasures, much of the creative urge in man has been throttled. We who breed dogs are extremely fortunate, for in our work we have a real creative outlet—we are in the position of being able to mold beauty and utility in living flesh and blood. Our tools are the genes of inheritance, and our art, their infinite combination. We have the power to create a work of art that will show the evidence of our touch for generations to come.

If we are to achieve the greatest good from any program of breeding, there are four important traits which we must examine. It is essential that these traits should never depart from the norm.

The first is *fertility*. The lack of this essential in any degree must be guarded against diligently.

The second is *vigor*. Loss of vigor, or hardiness, and its allied ills, such as lowered resistance to disease, finicky eating, etc., will lead to disaster.

Longevity is the third important trait. An individual of great worth—who represents a fortunate combination of excellent characteristics which he dominantly passes on to his offspring—must be useful for a long time after his or her worth is recognized by the progeny produced.

The fourth is *temperament*. Here is the sum total of the dog's usefulness to man in the various categories in which he serves.

The real objective of all breeding is to raise the norm of a given breed and thereby approach always closer to the breed standard. The norm can be likened to the force of gravity, possessing a powerful pull toward itself, so that regression toward the average is strong, even though you have used, in your breeding, parents which are both above average. The same holds true for progeny bred from animals below norm, but from these you will get a lesser number which reach the mean average and a greater number which remain below norm. In the case of the better-than-average parents, some of the progeny will stay above the norm line and the majority will regress. Occasionally a dog of superior structure is produced by a poor family, but inevitably this animal is useless as a stud because he will produce all his objectionable family traits and none of the fortuitous characteristics he displays in himself. From a breeding standpoint it is far better to use an average individual from top stock than a top individual from average or below-average stock. It is also true that many times a great show dog produces average progeny while his little-known brother, obscured by the shadow of the great dog's eminence, produces many above-average young. This is not as strange as it sounds when we consider the fact that the individual animal is the custodian of his germ plasm and it is this germ plasm that produces, not the individual. In this instance, due to variation in the germ plasm, the top dog does not possess the happy genetic combinations that his average brother does and so cannot produce stock of comparative value.

Any of the various categories of breeding practice which are outlined here can be followed for the betterment of the breed if used intelligently. Regardless of which practice one follows, there generally comes a time when it is necessary to incorporate one or more of the other forms into the breeding program in order to concentrate certain genetic characters, or to introduce new ones which are imperative for over-all balance. Outcross breeding is not recommended as a consistent practice. Rather, it is a valuable adjunct to the other methods when used as a corrective measure. Yet outcross breeding does not, as would be supposed from definition, produce completely heterozygous young. The root stock of any breed is the same regardless of which breeding partners are used and much of the stock which represents what we term outcross breeding shows common ancestry within a few generations.

INBREEDING

By breeding father to daughter, half brother to half sister, son to mother, and, the closest inbreeding of all, brother to sister, stability and purity of inherited material is obtained. Specifically, inbreeding concentrates both good features and faults, strengthening dominants and bringing recessives out into the open where they can be seen and evaluated. It supplies the breeder with the only control he can have over prepotency and homozygosity, or the combining and balancing of similar genetic factors. Inbreeding does not produce degeneration, it merely concentrates weaknesses already present so that they can be recognized and eliminated. This applies to both physical and psychical hereditary transmission.

The most important phases of inbreeding are: (1.) To choose as nearly faultless partners as is possible; (2.) To cull, or select, rigidly from the resultant progeny.

Selection is always important regardless of which breeding procedure is used, but in inbreeding it becomes imperative. It is of interest to note that the most successful inbreeding programs have used as a base an animal which was either inbred or line-bred. To the breeder, the inbred animal represents an individual whose breeding formula has been so simplified that certain results can almost always be depended upon when the inbred dog is used.

It is interesting to note that genetic experiments with plants, vegetables, and animals which we consider lower in the evolutionary scale than our beloved dogs, have shown that when two intensely inbred lines of consecutive brother and sister matings are crossed (heterosis), the resultant progeny are larger than the original heterozygous stock and possess hybrid vigor such as the mongrel possesses, which enables him to exist even under environmental neglect.

It is essential that the breeder have a complete understanding of the merits of inbreeding, for by employing it skillfully results can be obtained to equal those found in other animal-breeding fields. We must remember that inbreeding in itself creates neither faults nor virtues, it merely strengthens and fixes them in the resulting animals. If the basic stock used is generally good, possessing but few, and those minor, faults, then inbreeding will concentrate all those virtues which are so valuable in that basic stock. Inbreeding gives us great breeding worth by its unique ability to produce prepotency and unusual similarity of type. It exposes the "skeletons in the closet" by bringing to light hitherto hidden faults, so that they may be selected against. We do not correct faults by inbreeding, therefore, we merely make them recognizable so they can be eliminated. The end result of inbreeding, coupled with rigid selection, is complete stability of the breeding material.

With certain strains inbreeding can be capricious, revealing organic weaknesses never suspected that result in decreased vitality, abnormalities—physical and mental—or lethal or crippling factors. Unfortunately, it is not possible to foretell results when embarking on such a program, even if seemingly robust and healthy breeding partners are used as a base. The best chance of success generally comes from the employment of animals which themselves have been strongly inbred and have not been appreciably weakened by it in any way.

An interesting development frequently found in inbreeding is in the extremes produced. The average progeny from inbreeding are equal to the average from line-breeding or outbreeding, but the extremes are greater than those produced by either of the latter methods. Inbreeding, then, is capable of producing the best and the worst, and in the same litter.

Another type of inbreeding, which is not practiced as much as it should be, is "back-crossing." Here we think in terms of the male dog, since the element of time is involved. The process involves finding a superior breeding male who is so magnificent in type that we want to perpetuate his qualities and produce,

Many breeds were fashioned from basically similar canine stock, variation occurring due to environment and special selection. The Afghan and Saluki, both gaze or sight hounds, are typical examples of this phenomenon.

as closely as we can, the prototype of this certain individual. This good male is bred to a fine bitch, and the best female pup who is similar to her sire in type is bred back again to her sire. Again, the best female pup is selected and bred back to her sire. This is continued as long as the male can reproduce, or until weaknesses become apparent (if they do) that make it impractical to continue. If this excellent male seems to have acquired his superiority through the genetic influence of his mother, the first breeding made should possibly be the mating of son to mother, and the subsequent breedings as described above. In each litter the bitch retained to backcross to her sire should, of course, greatly mirror the sire's type.

LINE-BREEDING

Line-breeding is a broader kind of inbreeding that conserves valuable characteristics by concentration and in a general sense gives us some control of type but a lesser control over specific characteristics. It creates *"strains,"* or *"families,"* within the breed which are easily recognized by their similar conformation. This is the breeding method used by most of the larger kennels, with varied success, since it is not extreme and therefore relatively safe. It is also the method the neophyte is generally advised to employ, for the same reasons.

Specifically, line-breeding entails the selection of breeding partners who have, in their pedigrees, one or more common ancestors. These individuals

Line-breeding is a form of inbreeding that results in broadly similar characteristics within the scope of the breeder's stock. This pair of Bedlington Terriers exhibit line-breeding similarity.

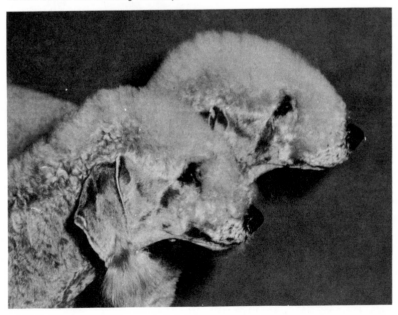

(or individual) occur repeatedly within the first four or five generations, so that it can be assumed their genetic influence molds the type of succeeding generations. It is a fact that in many breeds success has been obtained by line-breeding to outstanding individuals.

The method varies greatly in intensity, so that some dogs may be strongly line-bred, while others only remotely so. Selection is an important factor here, too, for if we line-breed to procure the specific type of a certain fine animal, then we must select in succeeding generations breeding stock which is the prototype of that individual, or our reason for line-breeding is lost.

One of the chief dangers of line-breeding can be contributed by the breeder of the strain. Many times the breeder reaches a point where he selects his breeding partners on pedigree alone, instead of by individual selection and pedigree combined within the line.

To found a strain which has definite characteristics, within the breed, the following recommendations can be used as a guide.

1. Decide what few traits are essential and what faults are intolerable. Vigor, fertility, character, and temperament must be included in these essentials.

2. Develop a scoring system and score selected virtues and faults in accordance with your breeding aim. Particular stress should be put upon scoring for individual traits which need improvement.

3. Line-breed consistently to the best individuals produced which, by the progeny test show that they will further improve the strain. Inbreeding can be indulged in if the animal used is of exceptional quality and with no outstanding faults. Outcrossings can be made to bring in wanted characteristics if they are missing from the basic stock. Relationship need not be close in the foundation animals, since wide outcrosses will give greater variation and therefore offer a much wider selection of desirable trait combinations.

Every dog used in this breeding program to establish a strain must be rigidly assessed for individual and breeding excellence and the average excellence of its relatives and its progeny.

OUTCROSS BREEDING

Outcross breeding is the choosing of breeding partners whose pedigrees, in the first five or six generations, are free from any common ancestry. With our dogs we cannot outcross in the true sense of the term, since the genetic basis of all pure breeds is based upon the germ plasm of a few selected individuals. To outcross completely, using the term literally (*complete heterozygosity*) it would be necessary to use an individual of an alien breed as one of the breeding partners.

For the breeder to exercise any control over the progeny of an outcross mating, one of the partners should be inbred or closely line-bred. The other partner should show, in himself and by the progeny test when bred to other bitches, that he is dominant in the needed compensations which are the reasons for the outcross. Thus, by outcross breeding, we bring new and needed characteristics into a strain, along with greater vigor and, generally, a lack of uniformity in the young. Greater uniformity can be achieved if the outcross is made between animals of similar family type. Here again we have a breeding method which has produced excellent individuals, since it tends to conceal recessive genes and promote individual merit. But it generally leads to a lower breeding worth in the outbred animal by dispersing favorable genetic combinations which have given us strain uniformity.

The root stock of all breeds displays the close inbreeding necessary to establish basic breed type. These Keeshonden mirror this intensive striving toward a definite type pattern as a breeding goal.

Outcross breeding can be likened to a jigsaw puzzle. We have a puzzle made up of pieces of various shapes and sizes which, when fitted together form a certain pattern. This basic puzzle is comparable to our line-bred or inbred strain. But in this puzzle there are a few pieces that we would like to change, and in so doing change the finished puzzle pattern for the better. We outcross by removing some of the pieces and reshaping them to our fancy, remembering that these new shapes also affect the shapes of the adjoining pieces, which must then be slightly altered for perfect fit. When this has been successfully accomplished, the finished pattern has been altered to suit our pleasure—we hope.

It sometimes happens that a line-bred or inbred bitch will be outcross bred to a stud possessed of an open pedigree. It would be assumed by the breeder that the bitch's family type would dominate in the resulting progeny. But occasionally the stud proves himself to be strongly prepotent, and the young instead reflect his individual qualities, not those of the bitch. This can be good or bad, depending on what you are looking for in the resultant litter.

Incidently, when we speak of corrective, or compensation, breeding, we do not mean the breeding of extremes to achieve an intermediate effect. Corrective, or compensation, breeding means the breeding of one partner which is lacking, or faulty, in any specific respect, to an animal which is normal or excellent in the particular area where the other partner is found lacking. In the resulting progeny we can expect to find some young which show the desired improvement.

To sum up briefly, we find that *inbreeding* brings us a fixity of type and simplifies the breeding formula. It strengthens desirable dominants and brings hidden and undesirable recessives to the surface where they can be recognized and possibly corrected by *outcross breeding*. When we have thus established definite improvement in type by rigid selection for wanted characteristics, we *line-breed* to create and establish a strain or family line which, in various degrees, incorporates and produces the improvements which have been attained.

In this maze of hidden and obvious genetic stirring, we must not forget the importance of the concrete essence that stands before us. The breeding partners must be examined as individuals in themselves, apart from the story their pedigrees tell us. For as individuals they have been fashioned by, and are the custodians of, their germ plasm, and mirror this fact in their being. Breedings made from paper study only are akin to human marriages arranged in youth by a third party without consulting the partners—they can be consummated but have small chance of success.

E.H HART

4

MECHANICS OF DOG BREEDING

To begin breeding we must, of necessity, start with a bitch as the foundation. The foundation of all things must be strong and free from faults or the structure upon which it is built will crumble. The bitch we choose for our foundation must, then, be a good bitch, as fine as we can possibly get, in structure, mentality, and breeding. She is the product of her germ plasm and must be closely analyzed for hidden faults for which we must compensate in breeding.

She will first come in season between six and twelve months of age according to her breed size. Though this is an indication that nature considers her old enough and developed enough to breed, it is best to allow her to pass this first heat and plan to breed her when she next comes in season. This should come within six months if her environment remains the same. Daylight, which is thought to affect certain glands, seems to occasionally influence the ratio of time between heats, as will complete change in environment. Scientific studies of the incidence of seasonal variation in the mating cycles of bitches indicates that more bitches come in heat and are bred during the months of February through May than at any other time of year. The figures might not be completely reliable, since they were assembled through birth registrations in the A.K.C., and many breeders refrain from fall and winter breedings so they will not have winter or early spring litters. Small breeds reach maturity much earlier than large breeds, and bitches of these diminutive breeds may be bred at first heat, which generally comes at a younger age.

When your bitch is approaching her period of heat and you intend to breed her, have her stool checked for intestinal parasites, and if any are present, worm her. Feed her a well-balanced diet, such as she should have been getting all along. Her appetite will increase in the preparatory stage of the mating cycle as her vulva begins to swell. She will become restless, will urinate more frequently, and will allow dogs to approach her, but will not allow copulation. Within the bitch other changes are taking place at this stage. Congestion begins in the reproductive tract, the horns of the uterus and the vagina thicken, and the luteal bodies leave the ovaries.

The first sign of blood from the vulva ushers in the second stage of the mating cycle. In some bitches no blood appears at all, or so little that it goes unnoticed by the owner, and sometimes we find a bitch who will bleed throughout the cycle. In either circumstance we must depend upon other signs. The bitch becomes very playful with animals of her own and the opposite sex, but will still not permit copulation. Congestion within the bitch reaches a high point during this period. Ova develop within the follicles of the ovaries, and, normally, the red discharge gradually turns to pink, becoming lighter in color until it becomes straw color and is no longer obvious. Her vulva is more swollen, and she becomes increasingly more playful with males.

This period is generally of about ten days' duration, but the time varies greatly with the individual. Rather than rely upon any set time period, it is best to presume that this interval reaches its conclusion when the bitch will stand for the stud and permit copulation. This generally occurs at about the tenth day, but can take place as early as the fourth or fifth day of this period or as late as the seventeenth day.

The third stage in the cycle is the acceptance period. The bitch will swing her hind end toward the dog, her tail will arch and fall to the side, and she will permit copulation. Sometimes the stud may have to tease her for a time, but she will eventually give in. The bitch may be sensitive and yelp and pull away when the stud's penis touches the lining of the vagina. If this occurs several times, it is best to wait another day, until the sensitivity has left this region. A very definite indication that the bitch is in the acceptance period is the softness and flaccidity of the vulva, from which the firmness and congestion has gone. Within the bitch the ovarian follicles have been growing ever bigger, and approximately midway in the acceptance period, some of them burst and the eggs are ready for fertilization. If the bitch has a normal mating cycle the best time to breed her is about the thirteenth or fourteenth day of the mating cycle, when ovulation has occurred. This time also varies with the individual bitch, so that until you have bred your bitch once or twice and feel that you know the best time for her, it is better to breed her on the eleventh day and every other day thereafter until her period of acceptance is over. This last, of course, is generally only possible when the stud is owned by you. One good breeding is actually all that is necessary to make your bitch pregnant, providing that breeding is made at the right time. If copulation is forced before the bitch is ready, the result is no conception or a small litter, since the sperm must wait for ovulation and the life of the sperm is limited. The acceptance period ceases rather abruptly, and is signaled by the bitch's definite resistance to male advances.

NORMAL BITCH MATING CYCLE

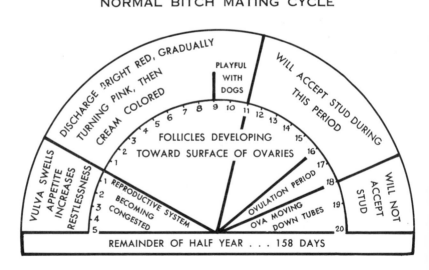

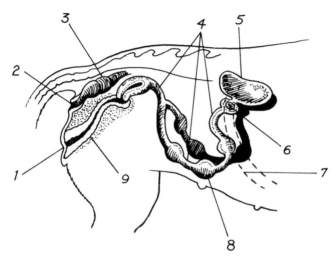

REPRODUCTIVE SYSTEM OF BITCH

1. Vulva 2. Anus 3. Rectum 4. Uterus 5. Kidney 6. Ovary 7. Ribs (indicated by broken lines) 8. Developing embryo 9. Vagina

If your bitch is a maiden, it is best to breed her this first time to an older stud who knows his business. When you bring her to the stud and if there are adjoining wire-enclosed runs, put the stud in one run and the bitch in the adjacent one. They will make overtures through the wire and later, when the stud is loosed in the run with the bitch, copulation generally occurs quickly. You may have to hold the bitch if she is flighty or reluctant, sometimes a problem with maiden bitches. If your bitch fails to conceive from a good and proper breeding, do not immediately put the blame on the stud. In most instances it is the fault of either the bitch or the owner of the bitch who has not adequately timed the mating. Many bitch owners fail to recognize the first signs of the mating cycle and so bring their bitch to the stud either too early or too late. Normal physiology of the reproductive system can be interrupted or delayed by disturbance, disease, or illness in any part of the dog's body. A sick bitch will therefore generally not come in season, though it is time to do so, until after she has completely recovered and returned to normal. Bitches past their prime and older tend to have a shorter mating cycle and so must be bred sooner than usual to assure pregnancy.

After you have returned home with your bitch, do not allow any males near her. She can become impregnated by a second dog and whelp a litter of mixed paternity, some of the puppies sired by the first dog and others sired by the second animal. Often a bitch is bred to a selected stud just before ovulation. The sperm will live long enough to fertilize the eggs when they flush down. The next day another male breeds to the bitch, the sperm of the two dogs mix within her and both become sires of the resulting litter.

Let us assume that your bitch is in good health and you have had a good breeding to the stud of your choice at the proper time in the bitch's mating cycle to insure pregnancy. The male sperm fertilizes the eggs and life begins. From this moment on you will begin to feed the puppies which will be born in about sixty to sixty-three days from ovulation. Every bit of food you give the bitch is nutritionally aiding in the fetal development within her. Be sure that she is being provided with enough milk to supply calcium, meat for phosphorus and iron, and all the other essential vitamins and minerals. A vitamin and mineral supplement may be incorporated into the food if used in moderation. She must be fed well for her own maintenance and for the development of the young *in utero*, particularly during the last thirty days of the gestation period. She should not, however, be given food to such excess that she becomes fat.

Your bitch, her run, and house or bed, should be free of worm and flea eggs. She should be allowed a moderate amount of free exercise in the pre-natal period to keep her from becoming fat and soft and from losing muscular tone and elasticity. If your bitch has not had enough exercise prior to breeding and you wish to harden and reduce her, accustom her to the exercise gradually and it will do her a great deal of good. But do not allow her to indulge in unaccustomed, abrupt, or violent exercise, or she might abort.

The puppies develop in the horns of the uterus, not in the "*tubes*" (Fallopian tubes), as is commonly thought. As the puppies develop, the horns of the uterus lengthen and the walls expand until the uterus may become as long as three and a half feet in a bitch carrying a large litter. A month before the bitch is due to whelp, incorporate fresh liver in her diet two or three times a week. This helps to keep her free from constipation and aids in the coming, necessary production of milk for the litter. If the litter is going to be small, she will not show much sign until late in the gestation period. But if the litter is going to be a normal or large one, she will begin to show distention of the abdomen at about thirty-five days after the breeding. Her appetite will have been increasing during this time, and gradually the fact of her pregnancy will become more and more evident.

Several days before she is due to whelp, the whelping box should be prepared. It should be located in a dimly lit area removed from disturbance by other dogs, or humans. The box should be large enough for the bitch's comfort, enclosed on all sides by boards, either plank or plywood. Boards of the same height must be added above these in about three weeks to keep the pups from climbing out. A few inches up from the flooring (when it is packed down), a one- by three-inch smooth wooden slat should be attached to the sides with small angle irons all around as a rail, or a pipe rail can be used. This will prevent the bitch from accidentally squeezing to death any puppy that crawls behind her. On the floor of the box lay a smooth piece of rubber matting which is easily removed and cleaned when the bedding is cleaned or changed. The bedding itself should be of rye or oat straw, and enough of it supplied so that the bitch can hollow out a nest and still leave some of the nesting material under the pups. Another method much used is to have several layers of newspapers in the bottom of the box so that they can be removed, one or two at a time, as they become soiled during whelping. After the litter is completely whelped, the straw bedding is provided and hollowed into a saucer shape so the whelps will be kept together in a limited area. The whelping box should be raised from the ground and a smaller box, or step provided, to make it easier for the bitch to enter or leave.

As the time approaches for the whelping, the bitch will become restless; she may refuse food and begin to make her nest. Her temperature will drop approximately one degree the day before she is ready to whelp, and she will show a definite dropping down through the abdomen. Labor begins with pressure from within that forces the puppies toward the pelvis. The bitch generally twists around as the puppy is being expelled to lick the fluid which accompanies the birth. Sometimes the sac surrounding the puppy will burst from pressure. If it doesn't, the puppy will be born in the sac, a thin, membranous material called the fetal envelope. The navel cord runs from the

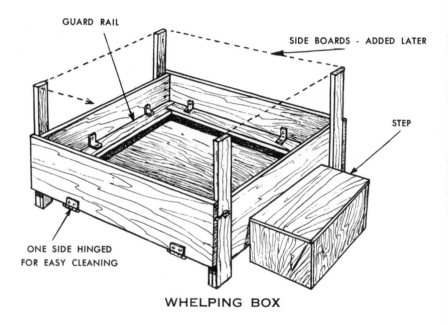

GUARD RAIL

SIDE BOARDS - ADDED LATER

STEP

ONE SIDE HINGED
FOR EASY CLEANING

WHELPING BOX

puppy's navel to the afterbirth, or placenta. If the bitch is left alone at whelping time, she will rip the fetal caul, bite off the navel cord and eat the sac, cord, and placenta. Should the cord be broken off in birth so that the placenta remains in the bitch, it will generally be expelled with the birth of the next whelp. After disposing of these items, the bitch will lick and clean the new puppy until the next one is about to be born, and the process will then repeat itself. Under completely normal circumstances, your bitch is generally able to whelp her litter and look after them without any help from you, but since the whelping might not be normal, it is best for the breeder to be present, particularly so in the case of bitches who are having their first litter.

If the breeder is present, he or she can remove the sac, cut the umbilical cord, and gently pull on the rest of the cord, assuming that the placenta has not yet been ejected, until it is detached and drawn out. Some breeders keep a small box handy in which they place each placenta, so they can, when the

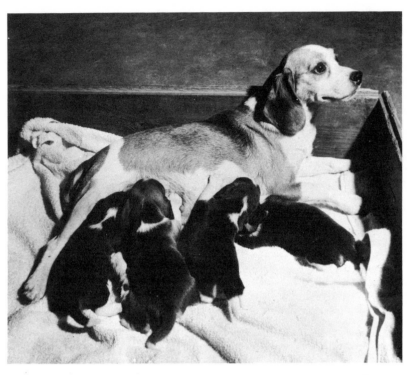

Fulfilling the destiny of her sex this Beagle bitch should be given peace and quiet. But, even if all goes well, the breeder should check both dam and whelps several times daily so that any of the myriad and incipient troubles of this period can be recognized and treated before they become grave.

whelping is completed, check them against the number of puppies to make sure that no placenta has been retained. The navel cord should be cut about three inches from the pup's belly. The surplus will dry up and drop off in a few days. There is no need to tie it after cutting. You need not attempt to sterilize your hands or the implements you might use in helping the bitch to whelp, since the pups will be practically surrounded with bacteria of all kinds, some benign and others which they are born equipped to combat.

If a bitch seems to have difficulty in expelling a particularly large puppy, you can help by wrapping a towel around your hands to give you purchase, grasping the partly expelled whelp, and gently pulling. Do not pull too hard, or you might injure the pup. The puppies can be born either head first or tail first. Either way is normal. As the pups are born, the sac broken, and the cord snipped, dry them gently but vigorously with a towel and put them at the mother's breast, first squeezing some milk to the surface and then opening their mouths for the entrance of the teat. You may have to hold them there by the head until they begin sucking.

Often several puppies are born in rapid succession, then an interval of time may elapse before another one is born. If the bitch is a slow whelper and seems to be laboring hard after one or more pups have been born, regular injections of Pitocin, at three-hour intervals (see your veterinary for dosage), can help her in delivery. Pituitrin is a similar drug and the one most often used, though Pitocin brings less nausea and directly affects the uterus. Both these drugs should be administered hypodermically into the hind leg of the bitch at the rear of the thigh. After the bitch has seemingly completed her whelping, it is good practice to administer another shot of the drug to make sure no last pup, alive or dead, is still unborn and to cause her to clean out any residue left from the whelping. Never use either of these drugs until she has whelped at least one pup.

Allow her to rest quietly and enjoy the new sensation of motherhood for several hours, then insist that she leave her litter, though she won't want to, and take her out to relieve herself. Offer her some warm milk. From then on, feed her as recommended during the gestation period, with the addition of three milk feedings per day. Sometimes milk appears in the udders before birth, but generally it comes in when the pups begin to nurse, since it is manufactured by glands, from blood, while the pups are at the breast.

Except for the removal of dew claws and tail docking, if required, the pups, if healthy, need not be bothered until it is time to begin their supplementary feeding at about three weeks. Dew claws should be removed on about the second day after birth.*

There are several ills which might befall the bitch during gestation and whelping which must be considered. Eclampsia, sometimes called milk fever, is perhaps most common. This is a metabolic disturbance brought on by a deficiency of calcium and phsophorus in the diet. If you give your bitch plenty of milk and a good diet such as we have recommended, she should not be troubled with this condition. Should your bitch develop eclampsia—evidenced by troubled shaking, wild expression, muscular rigidity, and a high temperature—it can be quickly relieved by an injection of calcium gluconate in the vein.

Should your bitch be bred by accident to an undesirable animal, your veterinarian can cause her to abort by the use of any one of several efficient canine abortifacients. He can also aid old bitches who have been resorbing their fetuses to carry them full term and whelp with the aid of stilbestrol.

Mastitis, an udder infection, is a chief cause of puppy deaths. It is generally mistaken by the uninformed for "acid milk," a condition which does not exist in dogs because the bitch's milk is naturally acid. Mastitis is an udder infection which cuts off part of the milk supply and the whelps either die of infection, contracted from the infected milk, or from starvation, due to the lack of sufficient milk. It is not necessary to massage the dam's breasts at weaning time with camphorated oil. They will cake naturally and quickly quit secreting milk if left completely alone.

Growths, infections, injuries, cysts, and other and various ailments can affect the female reproductive system and must be taken care of by your veterinarian. The great majority of bitches who have been well cared for and well fed are strong and healthy, and the bearing of litters is a natural pro-

* Unless the puppies are Briards or Great Pyrenees.

The stud dog should be strong and vigorous, the
epitome of breed maleness and exhibiting, to a
marked degree, undeniable secondary sex characteristics. This Collie, Champion Debonair of
Glenmist, definitely has the "stallion" appearance.

REPRODUCTIVE SYSTEM OF THE MALE DOG

1. Prostate 2. Rectum 3. Anus 4. Pelvis 5. Testicle 6. Scrotum 7. Bulb 8. Penis
9. Sheath 10. Vas deferens 11. Bladder

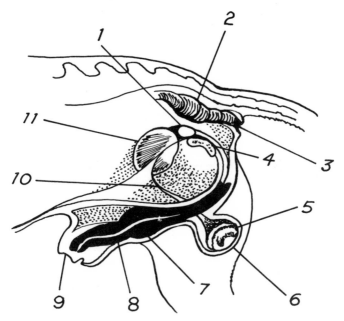

cedure—the normal function of the female of the species to bear and rear the next generation, and in so doing fulfill her precious destiny.

THE STUD DOG

If what we have said above about the unrivalled importance of the brood bitch is true, it may be difficult to understand why we pay so much attention to the male lines of descent. The reason is that stud dogs tend to mold the aspects of the breed on the whole and in any given country or locality, to a much greater extent than do brood bitches. While the brood bitch may control type in a kennel, the stud dog can control type over a much larger area. The truth of this can be ascertained by the application of simple mathematics.

Let us assume that the average litter is comprised of five puppies. The brood bitch will produce, then, a maximum of ten puppies a year. In that same year a popular, good producing, well-publicized stud dog may be used on the average of three times weekly (many name studs, in various breeds, have been used even more frequently over a period of several years).* This popular stud can sire fifteen puppies a week, employing the figures mentioned above, or 780 puppies a year. Compare this total to the bitch's yearly total of ten puppies, and you can readily see why any one stud dog wields a much greater influence over the breed in general than does a specific brood bitch.

* A prime example was the famous Cocker Spaniel stud dog, Red Brucie.

The stud dog needs a balanced diet, clean quarters, and plenty of exercise, but no special care as does the brood bitch. Though it is against most of the advice previously written on the subject, we recommend that the stud be used in breeding for the first time when he is about twelve months old. He is as capable of siring a litter of fine and healthy pups at this age as he ever will be. He should be bred to a steady, knowing bitch who has been bred before, and when she is entirely ready to accept him. Aid him if necessary this first time. See that nothing disturbs him during copulation. In fact, the object of this initial breeding is to see that all goes smoothly and easily. If you succeed in this aim the young dog will be a willing and eager stud for the rest of his life, the kind of stud that it is a pleasure to own and use.

After this first breeding, use him sparingly until he has reached sixteen or seventeen months of age. After that, if he is in good health, there is no reason why he cannot be used at least once a week or more during his best and most fertile years.

The male organs vital for reproduction consist of a pair each of: *testicles*, where the sperm is produced; *epididymis*, in which the sperm are stored; and *vas deferens*, through which the sperm are transported. The dog possesses no seminal vesicle as does man. But, like man, the male dog is always in an active stage of reproduction and can be used at any time.

When the stud has played with the bitch for a short period and the bitch is ready, he will cover her. There is a bone in his penis, and behind this bone is a group of very sensitive nerves which cause a violent thrust reflex when pressure is applied. His penis, unlike most other animals', has a bulbous enlargement at its base. When the penis is thrust into the bitch's vagina, it goes through a muscular ring at the opening of the vagina. As it passes into the vagina, pressure on the reflex nerves causes a violent thrust forward, and the penis, and particularly the bulb, swells enormously, preventing withdrawal through the constriction band of the vulva. The stud ejaculates semen swarming with sperm, which is forced through the cervix, uterus, Fallopian tubes, and into the capsule which surrounds the ovaries, and the breeding is consummated.

In most breeds the dog and bitch are tied, or "hung," and the active part of the breeding is completed. The owner of the bitch should then stand at her head and hold her by the collar. In the case of medium to large bitches the stud's owner should kneel next to the animals with his arm or knee under the bitch's stomach, directly in front of her hindquarters, to prevent her from suddenly sitting while still tied. He should talk soothingly to the stud and gently prevent him from attempting to leave the bitch for a little while. Presently the stud owner should turn the dog around off the bitch's back by first lifting the front legs off and to the ground and then lifting one hind leg over the back of the bitch until dog and bitch are standing tail to tail.*

Dogs remain in this position for various lengths of time after copulation, but fifteen minutes to a half an hour is generally average. When the congestion of blood leaves the penis, the bulb shrinks and the animals part.

The stud dog owner should keep a muzzle handy to be used on snappy bitches. Many bitches, due to temperament, environment, or fright, may cause injury to the stud by biting. If she shows any indication of such conduct,

* Some studs, generally of larger breeds, prefer to stand alongside the bitch after dismounting but while still tied.

Exercise is a necessity for the stud dog. Most sporting dogs, like this Brittany Spaniel pictured on point, are generally vigorous breeders due, in part, to their activity during the hunting season.

she should be muzzled. Should she continue to attempt to bite for any length of time, it is generally because it is either too early or too late in the estrus cycle to consummate a breeding. If the bitch is small, sinks down when mounted, or won't stand, she must be held up. In some instances her owner or the stud's owner will have to kneel next to her and, with his hand under and between her hind legs, push the vulva up toward the dog's penis or guide the stud's penis into her vulva. Straw or earth, pushed under her hind legs to elevate her rear quarters, is effective in the case of a bitch who is very much too small for the stud.

It is often a good idea to feed the dog a light meal before he is used, particularly if he is a reluctant stud. Young, or virgin, studs often regurgitate due to excitement, but it does them no harm. After the tie has broken, allow both dog and bitch to drink moderately.

If you have read this far you now have a good working knowledge of the inheritance of the dog, the methods and mechanics of breeding. If you use this knowledge well I am sure that from now on all your troubles will be little ones . . . good little ones, I hope.

45

E·H·HART·

5

FEEDING

Your dog is a carnivore, a flesh eater. His teeth are not made for grinding as are human teeth, but are chiefly fashioned for tearing and severing. Over a period of years this fact has led to the erroneous conclusion that the dog must be fed mostly on muscle meat in order to prosper. Wolves, jackals, wild dogs, and foxes comprise the family Canidae to which your dog belongs. These wild relatives of the dog stalk and run down their living food in the same manner the dog would employ if he had not become attached to man. The main prey of these predators are the various hoofed herbivorous animals, small mammals and birds of their native habitat. The carnivores consume the entire body of their prey, not just the muscle meat alone. This manner of feeding has led some zoologists to consider the dog family as omnivorous (eater of both plant and animal matter), despite their obvious physical relationship to the carnivores.

You would assume, and rightly so, that the diet which keeps these wild cousins of the dog strong, healthy, and fertile, could be depended upon to do the same for your dog. Of course, in this day and age your dog cannot live off the land. He depends upon you for sustenance, and to feed him properly, you must understand what essential food values the wild carnivore derives from his kill, for this is nature's supreme lesson in nutrition.

The canine hunter first laps the blood of his victim, then tears open the stomach and eats its contents, composed of predigested vegetable matter. He feasts on liver, heart, kidneys, lungs, and the fat-encrusted intestines. He crushes and consumes the bones and the marrow they contain, feeds on fatty meat and connective tissue, and finally eats the lean muscle meat. From the blood, bones, marrow, internal organs, and muscle meat he has absorbed minerals and proteins. The stomach and its contents have supplied vitamins and carbohydrates. From the intestines and fatty meat he gets fats, fatty acids, vitamins, and carbohydrates. Other proteins come from the ligaments and connective tissue. Hair and some indigestible parts of the intestinal contents provide enough roughage for proper laxation. From the sun he basks in and the water he drinks, he absorbs supplementary vitamins and minerals. From his kill, therefore, the carnivore acquires a well-rounded diet. To supply these same essentials to your dog in a form which you can easily purchase is the answer to his dietary needs.

BASIC FOODS AND SUPPLEMENTS

From the standpoint of nutrition, any substance may be considered food which can be used by an animal as a body-building material, a source of energy, or a regulator of body activity. From the preceding paragraphs we have learned that muscle meat alone will not fill these needs and that your dog's diet must be composed of many other food materials to provide elements necessary to his growth and health. These necessary ingredients can be found in any grocery store. There you can buy all the important natural sources of the dietary essentials listed below.

1. PROTEIN: meat, dairy products, eggs, soybeans.
2. FAT: butter, cream, oils, fatty meat, milk, cream cheese, suet.
3. CARBOHYDRATES: cereals, vegetables, confectionery syrups, honey.
4. VITAMIN A: greens, peas, beans, asparagus, broccoli, eggs, milk.
5. THIAMINE: vegetables, legumes, whole grains, eggs, muscle meats, organ meats, milk, yeast.
6. RIBOFLAVIN: green leaves, milk, *liver*, cottonseed flour or meal, egg yolk, wheat germ, yeast, beef, chicken.
7. NIACIN: milk, lean meats, liver, yeast.
8. VITAMIN D: fish that contains oil (salmon, sardine, herring, cod), fish liver oils, eggs, fortified milk.
9. ASCORBIC ACID: tomatoes, citrus fruits, raw cabbage (it has not been established that ascorbic acid is necessary for dogs).
10. IRON, CALCIUM, AND PHOSPHORUS: milk and milk products, vegetables, eggs, soybeans, bone marrow, blood, liver, oatmeal.

A well balanced diet is reflected in the appearance of your dog. Clear eyes, alertness, vigor and a quick eagerness for play, a healthy appetite, a perky and prideful mein and a coat of rich fullness, such as these fine Shetland Sheepdogs wear, are all indicative of proper and nutritious feeding.

The first three listed essentials compliment each other and compose the basic nutritional needs. Proteins build new body tissue and are composed of amino acids, which differ in combination with the different proteins. Carbohydrates furnish the fuel for growth and energy, and fat produces heat which becomes energy and enables the dog to store energy against emergency. Vitamins and minerals, in general, act as regulators of cell activity.

The main objective in combining food factors is to mix them in the various amounts necessary to procure a balanced diet. This can be done in a number of ways. The essential difference in the many good methods of feeding lies in the time it takes to prepare the food and in the end cost of the materials used. Dogs can be fed expensively and they can be fed cheaply, and in each instance they can be fed equally well.

There are various food products on the market packaged specifically for canine consumption. The quality of these foods as complete diets in themselves ranges from poor to excellent. The better *canned*, or *pudding*, foods are good but expensive for large breeds since the moisture content is high and your dog must consume a large amount for adequate nourishment. Compact and requiring no preparation, the canned foods are fine for use at shows or when traveling—though for traveling an even better diet is biscuits, lean meat, and very little water. The result is less urination and defecation, since the residue from this diet is very small. The diet is, of course, not to be fed over any extended period of time because it lacks food-value.

By far the most complete of the manufactured foods are the *grain and kibbled foods*. In such a highly competitive business as the manufacturing and merchandising of these foods, it is essential for the manufacturer to market a highly palatable and balanced ration. The better grain foods have constantly changing formulas to conform to the most recent results of scientific dietary research. They are, in most cases, the direct result of controlled generation tests in scientific kennels where their efficacy can be ascertained. A good grain food should not be considered merely a filler. Rather, it should be employed as the basic diet to which fillers might possibly be added. Since the grain food is bag or box packaged and not hermetically sealed, the fat content is necessarily low. A high degree of fat would produce quick rancidity. Therefore fat must be added to the dry food. Milk, which is one of the finest of foods in itself, can be added along with broths or plain warm water to arrive at the proper consistency for palatability. With such a diet we have a true balance of essentials, wastage is kept to a minimum, stools are small and firm and easily removed, and cost and labor have been reduced to the smallest equation possible to arrive at and yet feed well. The *pellet type* food is simply grain food to which a binding agent has been added to hold the grains together in the desired compact form.

Fat should be introduced into the dog's diet in its pure form. Proteins and carbohydrates are converted into fat by the body. Fat also causes the dog to retain his food longer in the stomach. It stores vitamins E, K, A, and D, and lessens the bulk necessary to be fed at each meal. Fat can be melted and poured over the meal, or put through the meat grinder and then mixed with the basic ration.

Just as selection is important in breeding, so ratio is important in feeding. The proper diet must not only provide all the essentials, it must also supply those essentials in the proper proportions. This is what we mean by a balanced diet. It can be dangerous to your dog's well being if the ratios of any of his dietary essentials are badly unbalanced over a period of time. The effects can be disastrous in the case of puppies. This is the basic reason for putting your faith in a good, scientifically balanced grain dog food.

In many instances kennel owners feel that their animals, for various reasons, need a supplementary boost in their diet. Some are in critical stages of growth, bitches are about to be bred or are in whelp, mature dogs are being frequently used for stud, and others are recuperating from illness. In such cases supplements can be added to the food, but in reasonable amounts.

Water is one of the elementary nutritional essentials. Considering the fact that the dog's body is approximately 70 per cent water, which is distributed in varying percentages throughout the body tissues and organs, including the teeth and bones, it isn't difficult to realize the importance of this staple to the dog's well being. Water flushes the system, stimulates gastric juice activity, brings about better appetite, and acts as a solvent within the body. It is one of the major sources of necessary minerals and helps during hot weather, and to a lesser degree during winter, to regulate the dog's temperature. When a dog is kept from water for any appreciable length of time, dehydration occurs. This is a serious condition, a fact which is known to any dog owner whose animal has been affected by diarrhea, continuous nausea, or any of the diseases in which this form of body shrinkage occurs. Water is the cheapest part of your dog's diet, so supply it freely, particularly in warm weather.

Breeders with only a few dogs can sometimes afford the extra time, expense, and care necessary to feed a varied and complicated diet. But to feed a large kennel in such fashion would take an immense amount of time, labor, and expense. Actually, the feeding of a scientifically balanced grain food as the basic diet eliminates the element of chance which exists in diets prepared by the kennel owner from natural sources, since overabundance of some specific elements, as well as a lack of others, can bring about dietary ills and deficiencies.

Caloric requirements vary with age, temperament, changes in temperature, and activity. If your dog is nervous, very active, young, and kept out of doors in winter, his caloric intake must be greater than the phlegmatic, underactive, fully grown dog who has his bed in the house. Keep your dog in good flesh, neither too fat nor too thin. You are the best judge of the amount to feed him to keep him in his best condition. A well-fed animal should always be in show "bloom"—clear-eyed, glossy-coated, filled with vim and vigor, and with enough of an all-over layer of fat to give him sleekness without plumpness.

Remember always that feeding ranks next to breeding in the influence it exerts on the growing dog. Knowledgeable breeding can produce genetically fine specimens, selection can improve the strain and the breed, but, without full and proper nourishment, particularly over the period of growth, the dog cannot attain to the promise of his heritage. The brusque slogan of a famous cattle breeder might well be adopted by dog breeders. The motto is, "Breed, feed, weed."

6

GENERAL CARE

When you own a dog, you own a dependent. Whatever pleasure one gets out of life must be paid for in some kind of coin, and this is as applicable to the pleasure we derive from our dogs as it is in all things. With our dogs we pay the toll of constant care. This animal which you have taken into your home and made a part of your family life depends completely upon you for his every need. In return for the care you give him, he repays you with a special brand of love and devotion that can't be duplicated. That is the bargain you make with your dog: your care on one side of the scale, his complete idolatry on the other. Not quite a fair bargain, but we humans, unlike our dogs, are seldom completely fair and unselfish.

Good husbandry pays off in dollars and cents too, particularly if you have more than one or two dogs, or run a semicommercial kennel. Clean, well-cared for dogs are most often healthy dogs, free from parasitic invaders and the small ills that bring other and greater woes in their wake. Good feeding and proper exercise help build strength and resistance to disease, and a sizable run keeps your canine friend from wandering into the path of some speeding car. Veterinarian bills and nursing time are substantially reduced, saving you money and time, when your dog is properly cared for.

Cleanliness, that partner to labor which is owned by some to be next to Godliness, is the first essential of good dog care. This applies to the dog's surrounding environment as well as to the dog himself. If your dog sleeps in the house, provide him with a draft-free spot for his bed, away from general household traffic. This bed can be a piece of rug or a well-padded dog mattress. It doesn't particularly matter what material is used as long as it is kept clean and put in the proper place.

Heavy aluminium feeding pans are best, since they are easily cleaned and do not chip as does agate or porcelain. Feed your dog regularly in the same place and at the same time. Establish a friendly and quiet atmosphere during feeding periods and do not coax him to eat. If he refuses the food or nibbles at it sparingly, remove his food and do not feed again until the next feeding period. Never allow a pan of food to stand before a healthy dog for more than thirty minutes under any circumstances. Should your dog's appetite continue to be off, consult your veterinarian for the cause.

If you are feeding several dogs in an outside kennel, it is good practice to remain until all are finished, observing their appetites and eating habits while you wait. Often two dogs, kenneled together and given the same amount and kind of food, show different results. One will appear thin and the other in good condition. Sometimes the reason is a physiological one, but more often observation will show that the thinner dog is a slower eater than his kennel mate; that the latter dog gulps down his own food and then drives the thin dog away from his food pan before his ration is fully consumed and finishes this extra portion, too.

Never, never, force feed a healthy dog simply because he refuses an occasional meal. Force feeding and coaxing make finicky eaters and a finicky feeder is never in good coat or condition and turns feeding time into the most exasperating experience of the day. Rather than forcing or coaxing, it is better to starve your dog, showing no sympathy at all when he refuses food. If he is healthy, he will soon realize that he will experience hunger unless he eats when the food pan is put before him and will soon develop a normal and healthy appetite. Immediately upon removing the food pans, they should be thoroughly washed and stacked, ready for the next mealtime.

Always provide water within an hour after feeding.

It has been the experience of most dog people that animals kept or kenneled outdoors, both winter and summer, are healthier and in better condition generally than their softer living housedog brethren. Light and the seasons have a great deal to do with shedding and coat condition. The outdoor dog, living in an environment approaching the natural, has regular shedding periods, after which his new coat comes in hard, strong, and glossy. Housedogs living in conditions of artificial light and heat seem to shed constantly, and seldom possess the good coat exhibited by the dog who lives outdoors. The housedog is much more susceptible to quick changes in temperature, particularly in the winter when he is brought from a warm, furnace-heated house, into the frigid out-of-doors.

Even the housedog should be provided with an outside run and house, a domain of his own to keep him in the sun and air and protect him from disturbance by children or other dogs. There, in his run, he is safe from accident, and you know he can't run away to become lost, strayed, or stolen. There, also, you can be sure he is not soiling or digging in your neighbor's newly planted lawn, a situation which can strain, to put it mildly, any "good-neighbor policy." Provide shade in some section of the run against the hot summer sun. Natural shade from trees is the ideal, of course, but artificial shade can be provided by a canvas overthrow placed strategically.

If you are building a kennel of several runs, remember that the length is more important than the width, and connecting runs in a row can be cut down in width if the length provided is ample.

The best surface for your run is a question open for argument. Here in America we favor cement runs. They are easy to clean and present a good appearance. But again, we have a porous surface into which the minute eggs of parasites can take refuge. Only by daily scrubbing with a strong disinfectant, or periodic surface burning, can concrete runs be kept free of parasitic eggs and larvae.

In removing stools from a run, never rake them together first. This practice tends to spread worm eggs over a greater area. Shovel each stool up separately, and deposit it in a container. When the run is clean, carry the container to a previously prepared pit, dump the contents and cover with a layer of dirt. Hose out the container and apply disinfectant, and the job is done with a minimum of bother.

GROOMING

Grooming should be a pleasant experience and a time of silent and delightful communication between you and your dog. Try to find the time to groom your dog once every day. It should take only a few minutes of your time with regular

Some breeds need greater coat care and grooming than others. The Poodle, that most popular of all dogs at the present time, is one of the breeds to which this statement applies. If such long-haired breeds are untended too long the hair will mat and require heroic measures to make it pliable again to brush and comb.

attention. By removing dead hair, dust, and skin scales in the daily grooming, you keep your dog's coat glossy, his appearance neat. This kind of daily grooming also eliminates the necessity of frequent bathings. For ordinary grooming use a metal comb with a handle. A comb of this sort permits you to get below the surface of the outer coat. Be careful not to irritate the skin. After combing thoroughly, go over the dog with a grooming glove or brush made specifically for your breed. During the grooming procedure, beginning skin disease can be seen and nipped in the bud. More specific grooming instructions can be had from a book on your particular breed.

BATHING

You may bathe your dog or puppy any time you think it necessary, as long as you do not think it is necessary too frequently. Be careful in chilly weather to bathe him in a warm room and make sure he is completely dry before you allow him to venture out into the cold outdoors. When you bathe your dog, you soak him down to the skin and remove the protective oils from his coat. When a dog is exposed to rain and snow, the dampness is shed by the outer coat and kept from his skin by his undercoat. Therefore he is not likely to be affected by natural seasonal conditions. Be careful, however, that he is not exposed to these same conditions directly after a bath, as there is danger of his contracting a cold. During the time of shedding, a bath once a week is not too often if the weather is warm. It helps to remove loose hair and skin scales, as does the grooming that should follow the bath when the dog is completely dry. The easiest way to insure the removal of deep dirt and odors caused by accumulated sebum is by employing a chemicalized liquid soap with a coconut-oil base. Some commercial dog soaps contain vermin poisons, but an occasional prepared vermicidal dip, after bathing and rinsing, is more effective and very much worth while. When bathing, rub the lather in strongly down to the skin, being careful not to get soap in the dog's eyes. Cover every inch of him with heavy lather, rub it in, scrape the excess off with your hands, rinse and dry thoroughly, then walk him in the sun until he is ready for grooming. There are paste soaps available that require no rinsing, or you may wish to use liquid detergents manufactured specifically for canine bathing. Prepared canned lathers, as well as dry shampoos, are all available at pet shops and are all useful in keeping your dog clean and odorless.

If your dog has walked in tar which you find you cannot remove by bathing, you can remove it with kerosene. The kerosene should be quickly removed with strong soap and water if it is not to burn and irritate the skin. Paint can be washed off with turpentine, which must also be quickly removed for the same reasons. Some synthetic paints, varnishes, enamels, and other like preparations, which are thinned with alcohol, can be removed by the same vehicle. If the paint (oil base) is close to the skin, linseed oil will dissolve it without irritation. Should your pet engage in a tête-à-tête with a skunk, wash him immediately (if you can get near him) with soap and hot water, or soak him with tomato juice, then walk him in the hot sun. The odor evaporates most quickly under heat.

A box of small sticks with cotton-tipped ends, which are manufactured under various brand names, are excellent for cleaning your animals ears. Drop into the ear a mixture of ether and alcohol, or of propylene glycol, to dissolve dirt and wax, then swab the ear clean with the cotton-tipped stick. Surplus liquid will quickly evaporate.

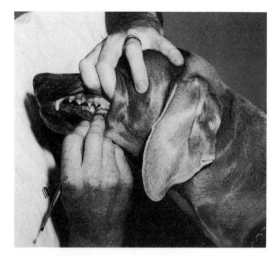

Tartar should not be allowed to form on your dog's teeth. Use an ordinary dental scraper for this purpose, or allow your veterinarian to do the chore.

CARE OF TOENAILS AND TEETH

Keep your dog's nails trimmed short. Overgrown nails cause lameness, foot ailments, spread toes, and hare feet. If your dog does a great deal of walking on cement, nail growth is often kept under control naturally by wearing off on the cement surface. Some dogs seem to possess a genetic factor for short nails which never need trimming, but the majority of our dogs need nail care. To accomplish this task with the least possible trouble, use a claw cutter specifically designed to trim canine nails and cut away only the horny dead section of the nail. If you cut too deeply, you will cause bleeding. A flashlight held under the nail will enable you to see the dark area of the blood line so you can avoid cutting into it. If you should tap the blood supply in the nail, don't be overly alarmed, simply keep the dog quiet until the severed capillaries close and the bleeding stops. Munsel's solution or a styptic pencil applied to the bleeding nail helps to hurry coagulation. After you have cut the nails, file them smooth with the use of a file made for dogs. File from above with a downward, roundning stroke. If a nail has bled from trimming, do not file it for at least twenty-four hours.

Soft rib bones or nylon or rawhide synthetic bones will help prevent tartar from forming on a large dog's teeth. His teeth pierce the bones, scraping off tooth residue in the process, keeping his teeth clean and white. If tartar should form, it can be chipped off with the same kind of instrument your dentist uses on your teeth for that purpose, or your veterinarian can clean them efficiently and without bother to you. Check your dog's mouth every other week for broken, loose, or abscessed teeth, particularly when he has passed his prime. Bad teeth must be tended by your veterinarian before they affect your dog's general health.

A periodic health check of your dog by your veterinarian can pay big mental and monetary dividends. When you take him for his examination, remember to bring with you samples of his stool and urine for analysis.

E·H·HART

7

BASIC DOG TRAINING

Responsibility for the reputation of any breed is shared by everyone who owns a specimen of that breed. Reputation, good or bad, is achieved by conduct, and conduct is the result of the molding, through training, of inherent character into specific channels of behavior.

It is a distinct pleasure, to novice, old-timer, or the public at large, to watch dogs perform which have been trained to special tasks. Here is the ultimate, the end result of the relationship between man and dog. After watching an inspired demonstration, we sometimes wonder if, under a proper training regime, our own dog could do as well. Perhaps he can if he is temperamentally fitted for the task we have in mind. No single individual of any breed, regardless of breed type, temperament, and inheritance, is fitted to cope with all the branches of specialized service. Nor does every owner possess the qualifications or experience necessary to train dogs successfully to arduous tasks. But every dog can be trained in the fundamentals of decent behavior, and every dog owner can give his dog this basic training. It is, indeed, the *duty* of every dog owner to teach his dog obedience to command as well as the necessary fundamentals of training which insure good conduct and gentlemanly deportment. A dog that is uncontrolled can become a nuisance and even a menace. This dog brings grief to his owner and bad reputation to himself and the breed he represents.

We cannot attempt, in this limited space, to write a complete and comprehensive treatise on all the aspects of dog training.* There are several worthwhile books, written by experienced trainers, that cover the entire varied field of initial and advanced training. There are, furthermore, hundreds of training classes throughout the country where both the dog and its owner receive standard obedience training for a nominal fee, under the guidance of experienced trainers. Here in these pages you will find only specific suggestions on some points of simple basic training which I feel are neglected in most of the books on this subject. I will also attempt to give you basic reasons for training techniques and explain natural limitations to aid you in eliminating future, perhaps drastic, mistakes.

The key to all canine training, simple or advanced, is control. Once you have established control over your dog, you can, if you so desire, progress to advanced or specialized training in any field. The dog's only boundaries to learning are his own basic limitations. This vital control must be established during the basic training in good manners.

Almost every dog is responsive to training. He loves his master and finds delight in pleasing him. To approach the training problem correctly, to make it a pleasant and easy intimacy rather than an arduous and wearisome task, you must first learn a few fundamentals. In the preceding paragraph we spoke of control as the paramount essential in training. To gain control over your

* See the author's book, *"How to Train Your Dog."*

dog, you must first establish control over your own vagaries of temperament. During training, when you lose your temper, you lose control. Shouting, nagging repetition, angry reprimand, and exasperation, only confuse your canine pupil. If he does not obey, then the lesson has not been learned. He needs teaching, not punishment. The time of training should be approached with pleasure by both master and dog, so that both you and your pupil look forward to these periods of contact. If you establish this atmosphere your dog will enjoy working, and a dog who enjoys his work, who is constantly trying to please, is a dog who is always under control.

Consistency is the brother of control in training. Perform each movement used in schooling in the same manner every time. Use the same words of command or communication without variance. Employ command words that are simple single syllables, chosen for their crispness and difference in sound. Don't call your dog to you one day with the command, "*Come,*" and the next day, with the command, "*Here,*" and expect the animal to understand and perform the act with alacrity. Inconsistency confuses your dog. If you are inconsistent, the dog will not perform correctly and your control is lost. By consistency you establish habit patterns which eventually become an inherent part of your dog's behavior. Remember that a few simple commands, well learned, are much better than many and varied commands only partially absorbed. Therefore, be certain that your dog completely understands a command and will perform the action it demands, quickly and without hesitation, before attempting to teach him a new command.

Before we begin training, we must first assess our prospective pupil's intelligence and character. We must understand that his eyesight is not as keen as ours, but that he is quick to notice movement. We must know that sound and scent are generally his chief means of communication with his world, and that in these departments he is far superior to us. We must reach him, then, through voice and gesture, and realize that he is very sensitive to

The long "**Down**". Two German Shepherds, owned by the author, waiting eagerly and attentively for the next command. Dogs of the so-called "working" breeds make excellent obedience animals because they are mentally geared to accept training.

60

quality change and intonation of the commanding voice. Therefore, any given command must have a definite tonal value in keeping with its purpose. The word *"No"* used in reprimand must be expressed sharply and with overtones of displeasure, while *"Good boy,"* employed as praise, should be spoken lightly and pleasantly. In early training, the puppy recognizes distinctive sound coupled with the quality of tone used rather than individual words.

All words of positive command should be spoken sharply and distinctly during training. By this we do not mean that commands must be shouted, a practice which seems to be gaining favor in obedience work and which is very much to be deplored. A well-trained, mature animal can be kept completely under control and will obey quickly and willingly when commands are given in an ordinary conversational tone. The first word a puppy learns is the word-sound of his name; therefore, in training, his name should be spoken first to attract his attention to the command which follows. Thus, when we want our dog to come to us, and his name is Bob, we command, *"Bob! Come!"*

Intelligence varies in dogs as it does in all animals, human or otherwise. The ability to learn and to perform is limited by intelligence, facets of character, and structure, such as willingness, energy, sensitivity, aggressiveness, stability, and functional ability. The sensitive dog must be handled with greater care and quietness in training than the less sensitive animal. Aggressive dogs must be trained with firmness; and an animal which possesses a structural fault which makes certain of the physical aspects of training a painful experience cannot be expected to perform these acts with enjoyment and consistency.

In referring to intelligence we mean, of course, canine intelligence. Dogs are supposedly unable to reason, since that portion of the brain which, in humans, is the seat of the reasoning power is not highly developed in the dog. Yet there have been so many reported incidents of canine behavior that seemingly could not have been actuated by instinct, training, stored knowledge,

A dog is limited in what it can learn by basic breed characteristics. A Brittany Spaniel will instinctively point game, but it would be almost impossible to teach this performance to any breeds other than those sporting dogs that are born with this specific aptitude.

61

or the survival factor, that we are led to wonder if the dog may not possess some primitive capacity for reasoning which, in essence, is so different from the process of human reasoning that it has been overlooked, or is as yet beyond the scope of human comprehension.

Training begins the instant the puppies in the nest feel the touch of your hand and are able to hear the sound of your voice. Once the pup is old enough to run and play, handle him frequently, petting him, making a fuss over him, speaking in soothing and pleasant tones and repeating his name over and over again. When you bring him his meals, call him by name and coax him to "*Come*." As time passes, he associates the command "*Come*" with a pleasurable experience and will come immediately upon command. Every time he obeys a command, he should be praised or rewarded. When calling your puppies to their food, it is good practice to use some kind of distinguishing sound accompanying the command—a clucking or "*beep*" sound. It is amazing how this distinctive sound will be retained by the dog's memory, so that years after it has ceased to be used, he will still remember and respond to the sound.

Some professional trainers and handlers put soft collars on tiny pups, with a few inches of thin rope attached to the collar clip. The puppies, in play, tug upon these dangling pieces of rope hanging from the collars of their litter mates, thus preparing the youngsters for easy leash breaking in the future. In training the pup to the leash, be sure to use a long leash, and coax, do not drag, the reluctant puppy, keeping him always on your left side. Never use the leash as an implement of punishment.

Housebreaking is usually the tragedy of the novice dog owner. Many dogs which are raised outside in a run never need to be actually housebroken, preferring to use the ground for their act and seemingly sensing the fact that the house is not to be soiled. Dogs tend to defecate in areas which they, or other dogs, have previously soiled, and will go to these spots if given the chance. Directly after eating or waking a puppy almost inevitably has to relieve himself. If he is in the house and makes a mistake, it is generally your fault, as you should have recognized these facts and removed him in time to avert disaster. If, after you have taken him out, he comes in and soils the floor or rug, he must be made to realize that he has done wrong. Scold him with "*Shame! Shame!*" and rush him outside. Praise him extravagantly when he has taken advantage of the great outdoors. Sometimes if you catch him preparing to void in the house, a quick, sharp "*No*" will stop the proceedings and allow you time to usher him out. Never rub his nose in his excreta. Never indulge in the common practice of striking the puppy with a rolled up newspaper or with your hand. If you do, you may be training your dog either to be hand shy, be shy of paper, or to bite the newsboy. Your hand should be used only in such a way that your dog recognizes it as that part of you which implements your voice, to pet and give pleasure. In housebreaking, a "*No*" or "*Shame*" appropriately used and delivered in an admonishing tone is punishment enough.

If your dog has been trained to paper and subsequently you wish to train him to use the outdoors, a simple way to teach him this is to move the paper he has used outside, anchoring it with stones. Lead the dog to the paper when you know he is ready to void. Each day make the paper smaller until it has completely disappeared, and the pup will have formed the habit of going on the spot previously occupied by the paper. Puppies tend to prefer to void on a surface similar in texture to that which they used in their first few weeks of life. Thus a pup who has had access to an outside run is easily housebroken, preferring the feel of ground under him. Smaller breeds are sometimes raised on wire-bottom pens to keep them free of intestinal parasites. Occasionally puppies so raised have been brought into homes with central heating employing an open, grate-covered duct in the floor. To the pup the grate feels similar to his former wire-bottomed pen. The result, as you can well imagine, gives rise to much profanity and such diligence that the youngster is either rapidly housebroken or just as rapidly banished to live outdoors.

If your pet is to be a housedog, a lot of grief can be avoided by remembering a few simple rules. Until he is thoroughly clean in the house, confine him to one room at night, preferably a tile- or linoleum-floored room that can be cleaned easily. Tie him so that he cannot get beyond the radius of his bed, or confine him to a dog house within the room; few dogs will soil their beds or sleeping quarters. Feed at regular hours and you will soon learn the interval between the meal and its natural result and take the pup out in time. Give water only after meals until he is housebroken. Puppies, like inveterate drunks, will drink constantly if the means is available, and there is no other place for surplus water to go but out. The result is odd puddles at odd times.

"*No*," "*Shame*," "*Come*," and "*Good boy*" (or "*girl*"), spoken in appropriate tones, are the basic communications you will use in initial training.

If your pup is running free and he doesn't heed your command to come, do not chase him—he will only run away or dodge your attempts to catch him and your control over him will be completely lost. Attract his attention by calling his name and, when he looks in your direction, turn and run away from him, calling him as you do so. In most instances he will quickly run after you. Even if it takes a great deal of time and much exasperation to get him to come to you, never scold him once he has. Praise him instead. *A puppy should only be scolded when he is caught in the act of doing something he shouldn't do.* If he is scolded even a few minutes after he has committed his error, he will not associate the punishment with the crime and will be bewildered and unhappy about the whole thing, losing his trust in you.

Puppies are inveterate thieves. It is natural for them to steal food from the table. The "*No!*" and "*Shame!*" command, or reprimand, should be used to correct this breach of manners. The same commands are employed when the pup uses your living room couch as a sleeping place. Many times dogs are aware that they must not sleep on the furniture, but are clever enough to avoid punishment by using the sofa only when you are out. They will hastily leave the soft comfort of the couch when they hear you approaching and greet you in wide-eyed innocence, models of canine virtue. Only the tell-tale hairs, the dent in the cushion, and the body heat on the fabric are clues to the culprit's dishonesty.

If the pup persists in committing this misdemeanor, we must resort to another method to cure him. Where before we used a positive approach, we must now employ a negative, and rather sneaky, method. The idea is to trick the pup into thinking that when he commits these crimes he punishes himself and that we have been attempting to stop him from bringing this punishment down upon his head. To accomplish this end with the unregenerate food thief, tie a tempting morsel of food to a long piece of string. To the string attach several empty tin cans, or small bells, eight to ten inches apart. Set the whole

contraption on the kitchen or dining-room table, with the food morsel perched temptingly on an accessible edge. Leave the room and allow the little thief to commit his act of dishonesty. When you hear the resultant racket, rush into the room, sternly mouthing the appropriate words of reproach. You will generally find a thoroughly chastened pup who, after one or two such lessons, will eye any tabled food askance and leave it strictly alone.

The use of mousetraps is a neat little trick to cure the persistent sofa-hopper. Place two or three set traps on the couch area the dog prefers and cover them with a sheet of newspaper. When he jumps up on the sofa, he will spring the traps and leave that vicinity in a great and startled hurry.

These methods, or slight variations, can be used in teaching your pup to resist many youthful temptations such as dragging and biting rugs, furniture, tablecloths, draperies, curtains, etc.

The same approach, in essence, is useful in teaching the pup not to jump up on you or your friends and neighbors. You can lose innumerable friends if your mud-footed dog playfully jumps up on the visitor wearing a new suit or dress. If the "No" command alone does not break him of this habit, hold his front legs and feet tightly in your hands when he jumps up, and retain your hold. The pup finds himself in an uncomfortable and unnatural position standing on his hind legs alone. He will soon tug and pull to release his front

The pleasure that is derived from the performance of a well-trained dog is mirrored in the expression on the face of this Doberman owner.

legs from your hold. Retain your hold in the face of his struggles until he is heartily sick of the strained position he is in. A few such lessons and he will refrain from committing an act which brings such discomfort in its wake.

Remember that only by positive training methods can you gain control which is the basis of successful training, and these tricky methods do not give you that control. They are simply short-cut ways of quickly rectifying nuisance habits, but do nothing to establish the *rapport* which must exist between trainer and dog.

During the entire puppy period the basis is being laid for other and more advanced training. The acts of discipline, of everyday handling, grooming, and feeding, are preparation for the time when he is old enough to be taught the meaning of the *Sit, Down, Heel, Stand,* and *Stay,* commands, which are the first steps in obedience training and commands which every dog should be taught to obey immediately. Once you have learned how to train your dog and have established complete control, further training is only limited by your own abilities and by the natural boundaries which exist within the animal himself.

Don't rush your training. Be patient with small progress. Training for both you and your dog will become easier as you progress. Make sure that whatever you teach him is well and thoroughly learned, and it will never be forgotten.

Let us review the few and basic truths set forth in this chapter. Remember to use simple common sense when you approach the task of training. Approach it with ease and confidence. Control yourself if you wish to control your dog, for control is the vital element in all training. Realize the limitations as well as the abilities of your dog, and the final product of your training zeal will bring you pride in accomplishment, pride in yourself and your ability, and pride in your dog.

E·H·HART

8

DOG DISEASES AND FIRST AID

Your dog, whatever his breed, is constantly exposed to innumerable diseases through the medium of flying and jumping insects, parasites, bacteria, fungus, and virus. Born into a veritable garden of disease the tiny puppy has a natural immunity to most of them during that period of babyhood when it is nursing at its mother's breast. As the puppy grows, its body develops defenses and immunities against many canine diseases, but there are many more against which he must be immunized or, if contracted, cured of, if they are not to prove fatal.

Basic health is fostered by care, good feeding and good husbandry. But, when your dog becomes ill, when the first signs of unthriftiness appear, and his appetite, attitude and general physical well-being are below normal there is only one thing to do—take him to a qualified veterinarian. He is a man qualified by years of schooling, intensive study, experimentation, intelligence and basic knowledge, in all phases of the animal medical field, to give your dog the most modern and efficacious medical care and to cope with any and all canine health problems. Upon purchase of a puppy, or even a grown dog, a thorough examination by your veterinarian is advisable. He can also, at this time, set up a program of inoculations to protect your animal from the worst of the virus and bacterial diseases.

Of course, emergencies occasionally occur which make it necessary for you to care for the dog yourself until veterinary aid is available. Quite often emergency help by the owner can save the dog's life or lessen the chance of permanent injury. A badly injured animal, blinded to all else but abysmal pain, often reverts to the primitive, wanting only to be left alone with his misery. Injured, panic-stricken, not recognizing you, he might attempt to bite when you wish to help him. Under the stress of fright and pain, this reaction is normal in animals. A muzzle can easily be slipped over his foreface, or a piece of bandage or strip of cloth can be fashioned into a muzzle by looping it around the dog's muzzle, crossing it under the jaws, and bringing the two ends around in back of the dog's head and tying them. Snap a leash onto his collar as quickly as possible to prevent him from running away and hiding. If it is necessary to lift him, grasp him by the neck, getting as large a handful of skin as you can, as high up on the neck as possible. Hold tight and he won't be able to turn his head far enough around to bite. Lift him by the hold you have on his neck until he is far enough off the ground to enable you to encircle his body with your other arm and support him or carry him.

Every dog owner should have handy a first-aid kit specifically for the use of his dog. It should contain a thermometer, surgical scissors, rolls of three-inch and six-inch bandage, a roll of one-inch adhesive tape, a package of surgical cotton, a jar of vaseline, enema equipment, bulb syringe, 10 cc hypodermic syringe, flea powder, skin remedy, tweezers, ophthalmic ointment, paregoric kaopectate, peroxide of hydrogen, merthiolate, army formula foot powder, alcohol, ear remedy, aspirin, milk of magnesia, castor oil, mineral oil, dressing salve, pressure bandages, and any of the new remedies for shock, heat stroke, etc.

I have prepared two charts for your reference, one covering general first-aid measures and the other a chart of poisons and antidotes. Remember that, in most instances these are emergency measures, not specific treatments, and are designed to help you in aiding your dog until you can reach your veterinarian.

Ask your veterinarian to schedule a program of vaccine immunization to protect your puppy against the dread virus diseases and bacterial Leptospirosis. Immunity serums offer no lifetime guarantee, so booster shots should be a part of the immunization program.

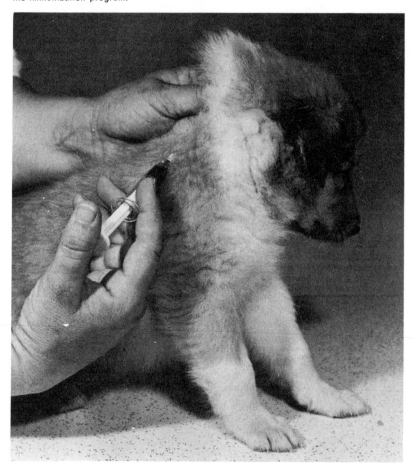

FIRST-AID CHART

Emergency	Treatment	Remarks
Accidents	Automobile, Treat for shock. If gums are white, indicates probable internal injury. Wrap bandage tightly around body until it forms a sheath. Keep very quiet until veterinarian comes.	Call veterinarian immediately.
Bee stings	Give paregoric, 2 teaspoonfuls for grown dog, or aspirin to ease pain. If in state of shock, treat for same.	Call veterinarian for advice.
Bites (animal)	Tooth wounds—area should be shaved and antiseptic solution flowed into punctures with eye dropper. Iodine, merthiolate, etc., can be used. If badly bitten or ripped, take dog to your veterinarian for treatment.	If superficial wounds become infected after first aid, consult veterinarian.
Bloat	Stomach distends like a balloon. Pierce stomach wall with hollow needle to allow gas to escape. Follow with stimulant—2 cups of coffee. Then treat for shock.	Call veterinarian immediately.
Burns	Apply strong, strained tea to burned area, followed by covering of vaseline.	Unless burn is very minor, consult veterinarian immediately.
Broken bones	If break involves a limb, fashion splint to keep immobile. If ribs, pelvis, shoulder, or back involved, keep dog from moving until professional help comes.	Call veterinarian immediately.
Choking	If bone, wood, or any foreign object can be seen at back of mouth or throat, remove with fingers. If object can't be removed or is too deeply imbedded or too far back in throat, rush to veterinarian immediately.	
Cuts	Minor cuts: allow dog to lick and cleanse. If not within his reach, clean cut with peroxide, then apply merthiolate. Severe cuts: apply pressure bandage to stop bleeding—a wad of bandage over wound and bandage wrapped tightly over it. Take to veterinarian.	If cut becomes infected or needs suturing, consult veterinarian.
Dislocations	Keep dog quiet and take to veterinarian at once.	

69

Drowning	Artificial respiration. Lay dog on his side, push with hand on his ribs, release quickly. Repeat every 2 seconds. Treat for shock.	New method of artificial respiration as employed by fire department useful here.
Electric shock	Artificial respiration. Treat for shock.	Call veterinarian immediately.
Heat stroke	Quickly immerse the dog in cold water until relief is given. Give cold water enema. Or lay dog flat and pour cold water over him, turn electric fan on him, and continue pouring cold water as it evaporates.	Cold towel pressed against abdomen aids in reducing temp. quickly if quantity of water not available.
Porcupine quills	Tie dog up, hold him between knees, and pull all quills out with pliers. Don't forget tongue and inside of mouth.	See veterinarian to remove quills too deeply imbedded.
Shock	Cover dog with blanket. Administer stimulant (coffee with sugar). Allow him to rest, and soothe with voice and hand.	Alcoholic beverages are NOT a stimulant.
Snake bite	Cut deep X over fang marks. Drop potassium-permanganate into cut. Apply tourniquet above bite if on foot or leg.	Apply first aid only if a veterinarian or a doctor can't be reached.

The important thing to remember when your dog is poisoned is that prompt action is imperative. Administer an emetic immediately. Mix hydrogen peroxide and water in equal parts. Force this mixture down your dog. In a few minutes he will regurgitate his stomach contents. Once this has been accomplished, call your veterinarian. If you know the source of the poison and the container which it came from is handy, you will find the antidote on the label. Your veterinarian will prescribe specific drugs and advise on their use.

The symptoms of poisoning include trembling, panting, intestinal pain, vomiting, slimy secretion from mouth, convulsions, coma. All these symptoms are also prevalent in other illnesses, but if they appear and investigation leads you to believe that they are the result of poisoning, act with dispatch as described.

POISON	HOUSEHOLD ANTIDOTE
ACIDS	Bicarbonate of soda
ALKALIES	Vinegar or lemon juice
(cleansing agents)	
ARSENIC	Epsom salts
HYDROCYANIC ACID	Dextrose or corn syrup
(wild cherry; laurel leaves)	
LEAD	Epsom salts
(paint pigments)	

PHOSPHORUS	Peroxide of hydrogen
(rat poison)	
MERCURY	Eggs and milk
THEOBROMINE	Phenobarbital
(cooking chocolate)	
THALLIUM	Table salt in water
(bug poisons)	
FOOD POISONING	Peroxide of hydrogen, followed by enema
(garbage, etc.)	
STRYCHNINE	Sedatives, Phenobarbital, Nembutal.
DDT	Peroxide and enema

ADMINISTERING MEDICATION

Some people seem to have ten thumbs on each hand when they attempt to give medicine to their dog. They become agitated and approach the task with so little sureness that their mood is communicated to the patient increasing the difficulties presented. Invite calmness and quietness in the patient by emanating these qualities yourself. Speak to the animal in low, easy tones, petting him slowly, quieting him down in preparation. The administration of medicine should be made without fuss and as though it is some quiet and private new game between you and your dog.

At the corner of your dog's mouth there is a lip pocket perfect for the administering of liquid medicine if used correctly. Have the animal sit, then raise his muzzle so that his head is slanted upward looking toward the sky. Slide two fingers in the corner of his mouth where the upper and lower lip edges join, pull gently outward, and you have a pocket between the cheek flesh and the gums. Into this pocket pour the liquid medicine at the rate of approximately two tablespoonfuls at a time for a full-grown, medium large dog. Keep his head up, and the liquid will run from the pocket into his throat and he will swallow it. Continue this procedure until the complete dose has been given. This will be easier to accomplish if the medicine has been spooned into a small bottle. The bottle neck, inserted into the lip pocket, is tipped, and the contents drained at the ratio mentioned above.

To give pills or capsules, the head of the patient must again be raised with muzzle pointing upward. With one hand, grasp the cheeks of the dog just behind the lip edges where the teeth come together on the inside of the mouth. With the thumb on one side and the fingers on the other, press inward as though squeezing. The lips are pushed against the teeth, and the pressure of your fingers forces the mouth open. The dog will not completely close his mouth, since doing so would cause him to bite his lips. With your other hand, insert the pill in the patient's mouth as far back on the base of the tongue as you can, pushing it back with your second finger. Withdraw your hand quickly, allow the dog to close his mouth, and hold it closed with your hand, but not too tightly. Massage the dog's throat and watch for the tip of his tongue to show between his front teeth, signifying the fact that the capsule or pill has been swallowed.

In taking your dog's temperature, an ordinary rectal thermometer is adequate. It must be first shaken down, then dipped in vaseline and inserted into the rectum for approximately three-quarters of its length. Allow it to remain there for no less than a full minute, restraining the dog from sitting

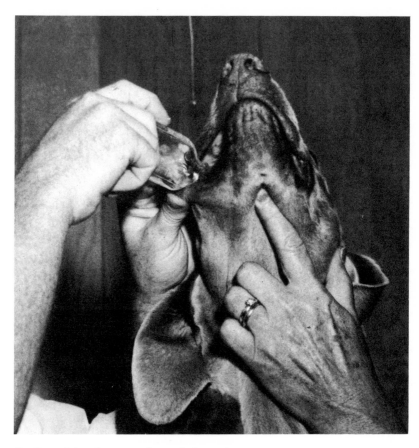

The lip pocket at the corner of your dog's mouth
acts as a funnel, or pocket, into which liquid
medication can be successfully poured. Utilizing
a small bottle as a vehicle for the medicine will
make its administration easier to accomplish.

completely during that time. When withdrawn, it should be wiped with a piece of cotton, read, then washed in alcohol—never hot water. The arrow on most thermometers at 98.6 degrees indicates normal human temperature and should be disregarded. Normal temperature for your grown dog is 101 degrees; normal puppy temperature varies between 101½ to 102 degrees. Excitement can raise the temperature, so it is best to take a reading only after the dog is calm.

In applying an ophthalmic ointment to the eye, simply pull the lower lid out, squeeze a small amount of ointment into the pocket thus produced, and release the lid. The dog will blink, and the ointment will spread over the eye.

Should you find it necessary to give your dog an enema, employ an ordinary

To administer a medical capsule to your dog, force his mouth open with one hand and with the other push the pill or capsule as far back into his throat as possible. Hold his mouth closed and massage his throat until the medication has been swallowed.

human-size bag and rubber hose. Grease the rubber tip with vaseline and insert the hose well into the rectum. The bag should be held high for a constant flow of water. For small dogs a small catheter would be necessary. A quart of warm, soapy water or plain water with a tablespoonful of salt, makes an efficient enema.

When your dog is ill or hurt remember, he needs you, so be calm, be cautious but unafraid, and take care of him as he would take care of you if positions were reversed.

9

THE SHOW DOG

So many things of beauty or near perfection are so often marred and flawed by an improper approach to their finish. A Renoir or an El Greco tacked frameless to a bathroom wall is no less a thing of art, yet loses importance by its limited environment and presentation. Living things, too, need this finish and preparation to exhibit their worth to full advantage. The show ring is a ready frame in which to display your dog. The manner in which he is presented within that frame is up to you.

If you contemplate showing your dog, as so many of you who read this book do, it is of the utmost importance that he be as well and fully trained for exhibition as he is for general gentlemanly conduct in the home. Insufficient or improper training, or faulty handling, can result in lower show placings than your dog deserves and can quite conceivably ruin an otherwise promising show career. In the wider sense, and of even more importance to the breed as a whole, is the impression your dog in the show ring projects to the gallery. Every dog shown becomes a representative of its breed in the eyes of the onlookers. Inside the ring ropes, your dog will be evaluated by the judges as an individual; beyond the ropes, a breed will be judged by the behavior of your dog.

When you enter your dog in a show, you do so because you believe that he or she is a good enough specimen of the breed to afford competition to, and perhaps win over, the other dogs entered. If your animal is as good as you think he is, he certainly deserves to be shown to full advantage if you expect him to win or place in this highly competitive sport. A novice handler with a quality dog which is untrained, unruly, or phlegmatic, cannot give competition to a dog of equal, or even lesser, merit which is well trained and handled to full advantage.

Novice owners frequently bring untrained dogs to shows so that they can become accustomed to the strange proceedings and surroundings, hopefully thinking that, in time, the dog will learn to behave in the wanted manner by himself. Often the novice's training for the show ring begins in desperate and intense endeavor within the show ring itself. Confusion for both dog and handler can be the only result of such a program. Preparation for showing must begin long in advance of actual show competition for both dog and handler.

Let us assume that you have been fortunate enough to breed or purchase a puppy who appears to possess all the necessary qualifications for a successful show career. Training for that career should begin from the moment you bring him home, or if you are the breeder, from the time he is weaned. This early training essentially follows the same pattern as does fundamental training in conduct. Again you begin by establishing between you and the puppy the happy relationship which, in time, becomes the control so necessary to all training. Handle the puppy frequently, brush him, examine his teeth, set him up in a show stance, and stroke his back, slowly. Move him on a loose leash, talking to him constantly in a happy, friendly tone. Make all your movements in a deliberate and quiet manner. Praise and pat the puppy often, establishing an easy and happy *rapport* as you progress. This is simple, early preparation for the more exact training to come.

During this period the owner and prospective handler should take the opportunity to refresh or broaden his own knowledge. Reread the standard, and with this word picture in mind, build a mental reproduction of the perfect dog: his structure, balance, gait, and movement. Critically observe the better handlers at shows to see how they set and gait their dogs. Only by accumulating insight and knowledge such as this can you succeed in the training which will bring out the best features of your own future show dog.

Let us assume that your puppy is old enough to show, or that you have acquired a young dog for whom you plan a show career. Beginning long before the show in which you are going to start him you must prepare him for the serious business (or pleasure, you hope) of showing. I cannot here tell you exactly how to handle or show your dog for the simple reason that the way in which dogs are handled in the ring varies with the breed shown. Indeed, even dogs of the same breed often vary in the way they must be handled in the show ring.

Some dogs are introduced at this stage to the "tidbit." This can be any bit of food which the dog relishes immensely and which is entirely different from the kind of food used in his regular diet. It is generally boiled liver, but it can be any other tasty morsel such as liverwurst, chicken, turkey, or even pheasant if you are that kind of person and have that kind of dog, which I hope you aren't, and don't.

Essentially the tidbit is used as bait, to inveigle your dog to act alert, on his toes and eager. Considering the fact that most dogs are not fed the day before a show and are brought into the ring hungry, it is rather easy to understand how the sight and smell of the tasty tidbit will bring them to full and eager attention.

Allow the pup to taste the tidbit, then hold it away from him, showing it to him but making him stay in the show stance you have set him in. Hold the tidbit high enough so that his head is up and his whole attitude is one of tense but controlled eagerness. Allow him a quick taste of the tidbit occasionally and, when the session is over, give him the tidbit to gulp. Knowing that he will occasionally have a taste and that he will eventually get all of it, keeps the dog constantly interested in the tidbit. Do not allow him to grab it or bite a large chunk from it during showing for he will immediately lower his head to chew it and defeat the whole purpose of its use.

Many dogs are set up by hand, others can be moved into the correct show stance. Try to handle the dog as little as possible. It is better to walk him into position than set him up. Use the command, "*Stand, stay!*" to freeze him.

We will assume that you now have your dog trained to stand easily and naturally on a loose leash for a reasonable period of time. The next step in show training is to teach your dog to move properly when on leash. Keeping the dog on your left side, move him forward at a gait to suit your dog and the breed, checking him sharply when he tends to pull out or break stride. Again, the leash should be kept loose. When you come to the end of the allotted run and turn to start back, do not jerk the dog around; instead give him more leash

Assess your animal, comparing him with the breed standard, evaluating his type against the conformation of the top specimens of the breed. Only in this way can you appraise his faults and virtues.

freedom and allow him to come around easily without a change of leads, meanwhile speaking to him quietly. When he has completed the turn, draw him to you with the leash and continue moving back to the starting point. At the finish, pat and praise him.

While you are teaching your dog the elements of ring deportment, take stock of the pupil himself. To do this correctly, you will need assistance. Have someone else put the dog through his paces, handling him as you have and as he will be handled in the show ring. Observe the dog carefully to determine when he looks his best. Should he be stretched out a bit when posing? Or does he have better balance and outline if his hind legs are not pulled too far back? At what rate of speed, when moving, does he perform his best?

Pretend that you are a judge. Envision the perfect canine specimen of your breed, and employing your knowledge of the standard as a yardstick, study your dog as though he were a strange animal. From this study you will see

The coats of many breeds, such as this Wire Fox Terrier, can be barbered (clipped or plucked) to hide faults and enhance virtues. Though close-coated breeds are trimmed to present a clean outline, their true conformation is very evident.

many things, tiny nuances that will aid you in showing your dog to the best possible advantage in open competition.

Once he has mastered the show training you have given him, you must take every opportunity to allow strangers and friends to go over your dog, much in the manner of a judge, while you pose and gait him, so he will become used to a judge's unaccustomed liberties. It would be well to enter your dog in a few outdoor sanction matches now, to acquaint him with the actual conditions under which he will be shown. During all this time, of course, the character and temperament of your dog, as well as his physical assets, must be taken into consideration, as it must in all types of training, and the most made of the best he has.

Often a handler showing a dog which has not had sufficient training must use other methods to get the most from the animal. We must remember, too, that unless specifically trained to one particular method, a dog may be presented to better advantage when handled in an entirely different manner. It is necessary to attract the attention of some dogs by strange noises, either oral or mechanical. You will also often see handlers squat down on the right side of their animals and set the dog's legs and feet in the desired position. But dogs set up by hand in this manner generally lack the grace and flow of lines that the naturally posed dog shows to such good advantage, except in certain breeds where hand setting is the normal procedure.

There is, of course, that paragon of all show dogs, that canine jewel and handler's delight—the alert, curious animal who takes a keen interest in the world around him and stands in proud and easy naturalness at the end of his long leash, posing every minute he is in the ring. But remember, even this super show dog has had some training in ring manners.

In some instances the dog's master stands outside of the ring in full view of his animal while someone else handles him in the ring. The dog will watch his master, keeping his head and ears up and wearing an alert expression. This is called "double-handling," and is generally frowned upon by other members of the showing fraternity, and the A.K.C.

It is of the utmost importance that you never become blind to your dog's faults, but at the same time realize his good features and attempt to exploit these when in the ring. If your dog is a year old, or older, do not feed him the day before the show. This will make him more eager for the tidbit when in the ring. Make sure your dog is in good physical shape, in good coat, clean and well groomed. If a bath is necessary, give it to him several days before the show so the natural oils will have time to smooth the coat and give it a natural sheen. Be sure he is not thirsty when he enters the ring and that he has emptied himself before showing, or it will cramp his movement and make him uncomfortable.

School yourself to be at ease in the ring when handling your dog, for if you are tense and nervous, it will communicate itself to the dog and he will display the same emotional stress. In the ring, keep one eye on your dog and the other on the judge. One never knows when a judge might turn from the animal he is examining, look at your dog, and perhaps catch him in an awkward moment.

On the morning of the show, leave your home early enough so that you will have plenty of time to be benched and tend to any last minute details which may come up. When the class before yours is in the ring, give your dog a last quick brush, then run a towel over his coat to bring out the gloss. Should his coat be dull, a few drops of brilliantine, rubbed between the palms of your hands and then sparingly applied to the dog's coat, will aid in eliminating the dullness. Some handlers wipe a slightly dampened towel over the coat just before entering the ring to achieve the same effect.*

Bring to the show with you: a container for water, towel, brush, comb, suppositories in a small jar, a bench chain, and a leash for showing. If the dog has not emptied himself, insert a suppository in his rectum when you take him to the exercising ring. If you forget to bring the suppositories, use instead one or two paper matches, wet with saliva, from which you have removed the sulphur tips.

Following is a chart listing the dog-show classes and indicating eligibility in each class, with appropriate remarks. This chart will tell you at a glance which is the best class for your dog.

DOG-SHOW CLASS CHART

Class	Eligible Dogs	Remarks
PUPPY—6 months and under 9 months	All puppies from 6 months up to 9 months.	American and Canadian-bred puppies only can compete in this class.

* The many and varied kinds of coats developed by man to clothe his "best friends," are subject to numerous forms of grooming to present specific breeds at their best.

The ultimate triumph to dog show competitors is to win at one of the country's big, glamorous, much publicized shows such as the Westminster Kennel Club Show held at Madison Square Garden in New York City each year. Here the elite of dogdom compete for the much coveted points and prizes. Our photo depicts the events leading up to the most dramatic moment when one of the six group-winning finalists will be selected as the best-in-show winner. The Great Dane, winner in the Working Group, is being gaited before the critical eyes of the judge while the gallery watches with bated breath.

E. SNAFER

PUPPY—9 months and under 12 months	All puppies from 9 months to 12 months.	Same as above.
NOVICE	Any dog or puppy which has not won an adult class (over 12 months), or any higher award, at a point show.	After three first-place Novice wins, cannot be shown again in the class. American and Canadian breds only can compete in this class.
BRED BY EXHIBITOR	Any dog or puppy, other than a Champion, which is owned and bred by exhibitor.	Must be shown only by a member of immediate family of breeder-exhibitor, *i.e.*, husband, wife, father, mother, son, daughter, brother, sister.
AMERICAN-BRED	All dogs or puppies bred and whelped in the U.S. or possessions, except Champions.	
OPEN DOGS	All dogs, 6 months of age or over, including Champions and foreign-breds.	Canadian and foreign champions are shown in open until acquisition of American title. By common courtesy, most American Champions are entered only in Specials.
SPECIALS CLASS	American Champions.	Compete for B.O.B., for which no points are given.

Each sex is judged separately. The winners of each class compete against each other for Winners and Reserve Winners. The animal designated as Winner is awarded the points. Reserve Winners receive no points. Reserve Winners can be the second dog in the class from which the Winners Dog was chosen. The Winners Male and Winners Female (Winners Dog and Winners Bitch) compete for Best of Winners. The one chosen Best of Winners competes against the Specials for Best of Breed (or Best of Variety), and the Best of Breed winner goes into the Variety Group. If fortunate enough to top this group, the final step is to compete against the other group winners for the Best in Show title.

When Best of Breed is awarded, Best of Opposite Sex is also chosen. A dog which has taken the points in its own sex as Winners, yet has been defeated for Best of Winners, can still compete for Best of Opposite Sex with other animals of its sex appearing in the ring for the Best of Breed award.

Champions are made by the point system. Only the Winners Dog and Winners Bitch receive points, and the amount of points won depends upon the number of dogs of its own sex it has defeated in the classes (not by the number entered). The United States is divided into five regional sections by the A.K.C., and the point rating varies with the region in which the show is held. Consult a show catalogue for regional rating. A dog going Best of Winners is allowed the same number of points as the animal of the opposite sex which it defeats if the points are of a greater amount than it won by defeating members of its own sex. No points are awarded for Best of Breed.

Any breed of dog recognized by the A.K.C. is eligible to compete in a dog show. The winning dogs in all breeds are those that are selected by the judges as being closest to their own specific breed standards of conformation.

To become a Champion a dog must win fifteen points under a minimum of three different judges. In accumulating these points, the animal must win points in at least two major (three points or more) shows, under different judges. Five points is the maximum amount that can be won at any given show. If your dog wins a group and is not a Champion, he is entitled to the highest number of points won by any of the dogs he defeats in the group if the points exceed the amount he has won in his own breed. If the show is a separately staged Specialty, then the Best of Breed winner automatically becomes the Best In Show Dog.

* In December of 1967 the dog show rules relative to the progression of the classes in judging were changed. After Reserve Winners has been chosen in bitches the Winners Dog and Winners Bitch both compete with any champions entered. The judge first chooses Best of Breed, then Best of Winners, and finally Best of Opposite Sex. In the event that one of the class dogs is chosen Best of Breed, it automatically becomes Best of Winners.

The Specials Class (for Champions only), no longer exists as such and has been renamed "For Best of Breed (Variety) Competition". This class is open to the Winners Dog, Winners Bitch, Champions of Record and dogs who have, according to their owners records, completed the requirements for a championship but have not as yet received confirmation of their status from the American Kennel Club. This latter category of dogs can compete for Best of Breed (or Variety) for a period of 90 days from the time they have ostensibly finished their chamionships.

ANATOMY OF THE DOG

THIS SECTION IS PRIMARILY PRESENTED TO EXHIBIT THE STRUCTURAL SIMILARITIES AND DIFFERENCES, WHILE STANDING AND MOVING, BETWEEN VARIOUS CANINE BREED TYPES.

EXTERNAL PARTS OF THE DOG

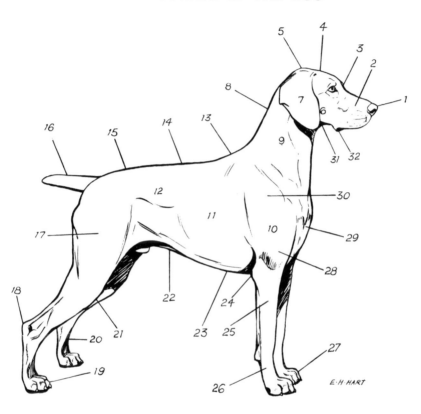

1. Nose.   2. Muzzle   3. Stop   4. Skull   5. Occiput   6. Cheek   7. Ear   8. Crest of Neck   9. Neck   10. Shoulder   11. Ribs   12. Loin   13. Withers   14. Back   15. Croup   16. Tail or Stern   17. Thigh   18. Hock joint   19. Rear feet   20. Metatarsus   21. Stifle   22. Abdomen   23. Chest   24. Elbow   25. Foreleg   26. Pastern   27. Front feet   28. Upper arm   29. Forechest   30. Shoulder blade   31. Throat latch   32. Lip corner.

SKELETON OF THE DOG

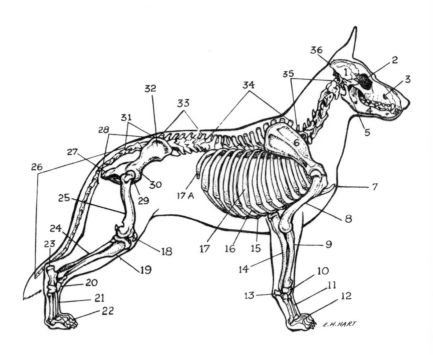

1. Cranium (skull). 2. Orbital cavity. 3. Nasal bone. 4. Mandible (jaw bone). 5. Condyle. 6. Scapula (shoulder blade, including spine and acromion process of scapula). 7. Prosternum. 8. Humerus (upper arm). 9. Radius (front forearm bone — see Ulna). 10. Carpus (pastern joint. Comprising seven bones). 11. Metacarpus (pastern. Comprising five bones). 12. Phalanges (digits or toes). 13. Pisiform (accessory carpal bone). 14. Ulna. 15. Sternum. 16. Costal cartilage (lower, cartilaginous section of ribs). 17. Rib bones. 17a. Floating rib (not connected by costal cartilage to sternum). 18. Patella (knee joint). 19. Tibia (with fibula comprises shank bone). 20. Tarsus (comprising seven bones). 21. Metatarsus (comprising five bones). 22. Phalanges (toes or digits of hind foot). 23. Os calcis (point of hock). 24. Fibula. 25. Femur (thigh bone). 26. Coccygeal vertebrae (bones of tail. Number varies — 18 to 23 normal). 27. Pubis. 28. Pelvic bone entire (pubis, ilium, ischium). 29. Head of femur. 30. Ischium. 31. Sacral vertebrae (comprising five fused vertebra). 32. Ilium. 33. Lumbar vertebrae. 34. Thoracic vertebrae (dorsal, with spinal process or withers). 35. Cervical vertebrae (bones of the neck). 36. Occiput.

MUSCULATURE OF THE DOG

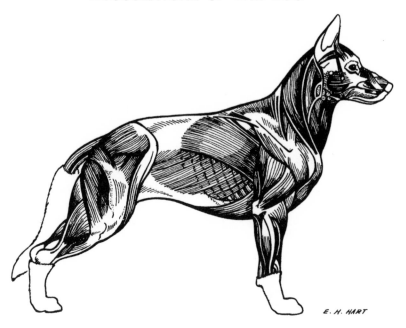

E. H. HART

FRONTS AND REARS OF DOGS

An excellent front for a sight hound (in this case an Afghan Hound).

An excellent front for a Pug Dog and breeds of like conformation.

A poor front for a sight hound; loaded in shoulder, too wide in front, out at elbows, legs set too far apart.

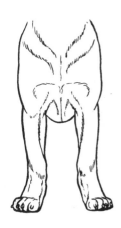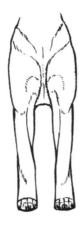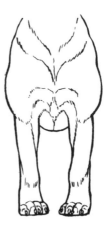

Fiddle front, or east and west.

Too narrow and shallow for some breeds.

Loaded in shoulder. Feet toe in (pigeon toed).

Out at elbow. Ba ribbed. Splay foot. F dewclaws (removed most breeds).

Excellent rear. Hocks parallel and well let down. Good muscula-ture. (German Shep-herd).

Poor rear. Badly cow-hocked. (Drawing is rear of Afghan Hound).

Another poor rear. Cowhocked and has dewclaws, the latter not wanted in most breeds, though standards of Briard and Great Pyre-nees call for double dewclaws.

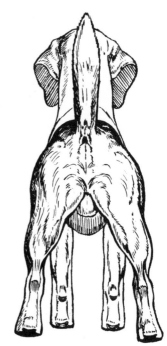

Above are depicted the excellent front and rear end of a Beagle. The same general conformational type is considered excellent for many other breeds including many kinds of hounds and long-legged terriers. Below are two poor hindquarters as seen in profile (German Shepherd model).

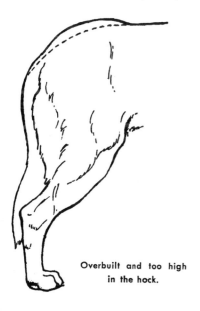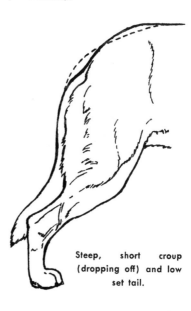

Overbuilt and too high in the hock.

Steep, short croup (dropping off) and low set tail.

THE DOG IN MOTION

The kind of high-headed "Hackney" trot wanted in many breeds.

Correct front movement

Crossing over
(incorrect)

Paddling
(incorrect)

The model is a Scottish Terrier.

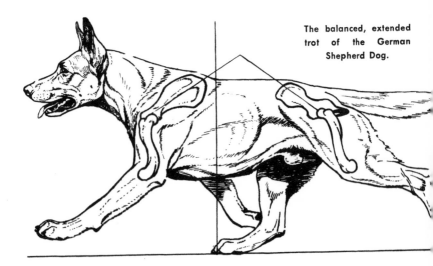

The balanced, extended trot of the German Shepherd Dog.

TEETH AND JAWS OF DOGS

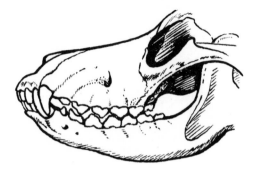

Correct scissors bite.

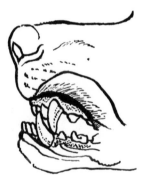

Profile.

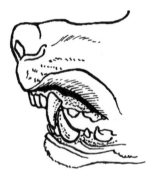

Undershot.

Overshot.

Front.
Correct scissors bite.

Level Bite. (Desired in some breeds such as, Afghans, etc.)

COMMON FAULTS OF DOGS

Roach back. Tail too short (for a Cocker). Legs too short (for dog of normal structure). Loin too long. Hare foot. Angulation in hindquarter too extreme. Head not extreme enough for modern Cocker.

The male below has a poor head for a German Shepherd, snipey in muzzle and with apple skull. Neck is wet and he is too high and square (for his breed). Roached back, lacks bone and body depth, pasterns are too straight (for breed). Mutton (flat) withers, too much tuck up, too little angulation in shoulder and hindquarter. He lacks forechest, is too level in croup, tail too short, and he lacks pigmentation.

Swaybacked. Shoulders too far forward and lacking in angulation (too steep). Lacks angulation behind. Soft in back. (These faults could be applied to many of the Scent Hounds, Terriers, etc.)

Overbuilt. Down in pastern. Poor feet. Lack of hind angulation. Soft back. Too heavy and soft all over. Ears too heavy (for Pug). Incorrect Pug tail carriage.

93

Roached back. Ears set too low (low set ears wanted in many breeds but generally not those with prick or cropped ears). Lack of crest in neck. Tail cut too long (for Schnauzer). Too much tuck-up (wanted in many Sight Hounds). Forechest too prominent. Sickle hocked. Arched in loin.

Too long in body (like so many other breeds the Beagle should be square). Too short and thick in neck. Tail too short and thick. Back not level. Prosternum too prominent leading to exaggerated front (forechest).

SHOULDERS AND FEET OF DOGS

SHOULDER ASSEMBLY ANGULATION
extension of reach is indicated by broken lines

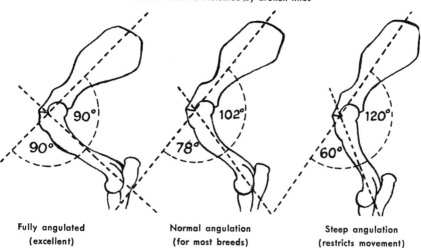

Fully angulated
(excellent)

Normal angulation
(for most breeds)

Steep angulation
(restricts movement)

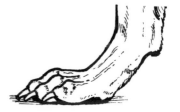

Excellent foot and pastern (for breeds that require let down and spring in pastern)

Hare foot and weak pastern (both incorrect)

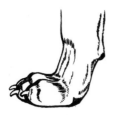

Poor foot and pastern

Excellent tight foot and strong, straight pastern

TAILS OF DOGS

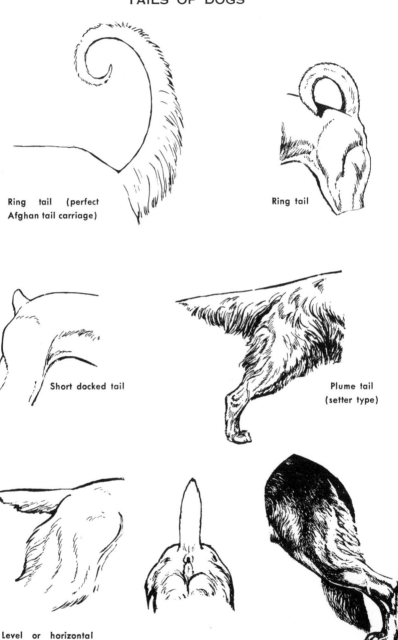

Ring tail (perfect
Afghan tail carriage)

Ring tail

Short docked tail

Plume tail
(setter type)

Level or horizontal
tail
(typical of Cocker)

Gay tail
(typical of Terriers)

Saber (or drop) tail

SECTION II

HISTORY AND STANDARDS OF
DOG BREEDS

Group I: Sporting Dogs

Griffon, Wirehaired Pointing
Pointer
Pointer, German Shorthaired
Pointer, German Wirehaired
Retriever, Chesapeake Bay
Retriever, Curly-Coated
Retriever, Flat-Coated
Retriever, Golden
Retriever, Labrador
Setter, English
Setter, Gordon
Setter, Irish

Spaniel, American Water
Spaniel, Brittany
Spaniel, Clumber
Spaniel, Cocker
Spaniel, English Cocker
Spaniel, English Springer
Spaniel, Field
Spaniel, Irish Water
Spaniel, Sussex
Spaniel, Welsh Springer
Vizsla
Weimaraner

Group II: Hounds

A. Scent Hounds
Basenji
Basset Hound
Beagle
Bloodhound
Bluetick Hound
Coonhound, Black and Tan
Dachshund
Foxhound, American

Foxhound, English
Harrier
Norwegian Elkhound
Otter Hound
Plott Hound
Redbone Hound
Rhodesian Ridgeback
Walker Foxhound

B. Sight Hounds
Afghan Hound
Borzoi
Deerhound, Scottish
Greyhound

Irish Wolfhound
Saluki
Whippet

Group III: Working Dogs

Alaskan Malamute
Belgian Sheepdog
Belgian Malinois
Belgian Tervuren
Bernese Mountain Dog
Bouvier des Flandres
Boxer
Briard
Bullmastiff
Collie
Doberman Pinscher
German Shepherd Dog
Giant Schnauzer
Great Dane
Great Pyrenees

Komondor
Kuvasz
Mastiff
Newfoundland
Old English Sheepdog
Puli
Rottweiler
St. Bernard
Samoyed
Schnauzer, Standard
Shetland Sheepdog
Siberian Husky
Welsh Corgi, Cardigan
Welsh Corgi, Pembroke

Group IV: Terriers

Airedale Terrier
Australian Terrier
Bedlington Terrier
Border Terrier
Bull Terrier
Cairn Terrier
Dandie Dinmont Terrier
Fox Terrier
Irish Terrier
Kerry Blue Terrier

Lakeland Terrier
Manchester Terrier
Norwich Terrier
Schnauzer, Miniature
Scottish Terrier
Sealyham Terrier
Skye Terrier
Staffordshire Terrier
Welsh Terrier
West Highland White Terrier

Group V: Toys

Affenpinscher
Chihuahua
English Toy Spaniel
Griffon, Brussels
Italian Greyhound
Japanese Spaniel
Maltese
Manchester Terrier (Toy)

Papillon
Pekingese
Pinscher, Miniature
Pomeranian
Poodle (Toy)
Pug
Silky Terrier
Yorkshire Terrier

Group VI: Non-Sporting Dogs

Boston Terrier
Bulldog
Chow Chow
Dalmatian
French Bulldog

Keeshond
Lhasa Apso
Poodle
Schipperke

Miscellaneous and Foreign Breeds

Akita
Australian Heeler
Australian Kelpie
Australian Shepherd
Border Collie
Braque Du Bourbonnais
Cavalier King Charles Spaniel
Chinese Crested
English Shepherd
Eskimo
Leonberger
Maremma Sheepdog
Mexican Hairless
Miniature Bull Terrier

Portuguese Cattle Dog
Portuguese Podengo
Portuguese Sheepdog
Portuguese Water Dog
Shih Tzu
Soft-Coated Wheaten Terrier
Spanish Pointer
Spinoni Italiani
Spitz
Tibetan Mastiff
Tibetan Terrier
Toy Fox Terrier
Vallhund
Welsh Sheepdog

GROUP I

Sporting Dogs

glish Setter   The Large Water-Spaniel   The Springer or Cock

IN this initial grouping of dog types, bred by man for specific purposes, are listed, with histories and standards, the gun dogs, the breeds fashioned to hunt game birds in brush and meadow and waterfowl in freezing lake and shore. Some are multiple-purpose breeds who can be trained to fur and feather, bred basically by and for the common man to whom a day in the field was not just a sporting venture and who had to, of necessity, fill the larder with a mixed bag. Other breeds in the sporting group were bred and kept by men of position and means solely as gentlemens' shooting dogs for sport in the autumn fields.

Most of these gundogs share common, early ancestry in the old Spanish Pointers and Spaniels (the latter's family name derived from the country of their origin), root stock of strong genetic influence evidenced by the survival of sporting dog characteristics down through the centuries even when breeding was, in some instances, indiscriminate.

Sporting dogs are generally of good temperament and character and so make excellent family dogs and companions. But it must be remembered that they have been molded to special abilities and only when they are allowed to exercise these man-influenced gifts through contained spontaneity in the field are they, as sporting dogs, complete.

If you have a liking for the outdoors, the scent of leaves, and brush, and smoke, the sound of laughing water and brisk breezes turning rustling leaves when nature wears the vivid, warm colors that precede winter's cold, if you yet carry within you an urge, an excitement for the hunt from some ancient ancestor, then to you is bequeathed the pleasure that this group of canines can impart. For there is nothing to compare to the beauty of the perfect point, the bounding rush through tangled cover to flush the bird to the gun, the rushing wings and echoing shot slapping across water, the splash, the exciting find and retrieve.

These are the times that enrich a man in his heart and soul, that bring exhilaration of the moment and deep and peaceful pleasure in later remembrance. And for these things we recommend the canines known as Sporting Dogs.

Essayons d'Argent

THE WIREHAIRED POINTING GRIFFON

The griffon hound was an ancient breed that is considered to be extinct today. However, it is quite evident that this breed, if not in fact then in romantic theory, was the basis upon which was built the modern breed known as the Wirehaired Pointing Griffon.

It was in Holland, near Haarlem, that E. K. Korthals, a young sportsman, had his dream of reestablishing the extinct griffon hound as a new and better sporting breed. To this end Korthals purchased a bitch that was supposed to be of griffon hound ancestry and, in 1874, began his experiment.

In the next several years this enthusiastic sportsman, utilizing all the vague knowledge of inheritance available in his time, acquired several more dogs of varied pointing and griffon hound ancestry, bred several litters and eventually produced three specimens, Moustache I, Querida, and Lina, which established the Wirehaired Pointing Griffon type and ability in the field.

Korthals later went to Germany and continued his breeding experiments there. He also introduced the breed to France where it was quickly and avidly adopted as "Korthals Pointer" or "Korthals' Patriarchs." Though undoubtedly Dutch, it is regarded now as principally a French breed due to its popularity and the breeding activity carried on in that country.

The breed is a slow and careful worker, keen of nose and with an inbred ability to point and retrieve game. Its all-weather, harsh coat makes it particularly useful in swampy country and inclement weather. The Wirehaired Griffon is also a fine water dog and, in its versatility, can be trained to both fur and feather. Because of its deliberate and thorough way of working it is particularly adapted to elderly, yet still enthusiastic, sportsmen or those who through some physical handicap, can no longer stay with the fast, wide-ranging bird dogs of other modern sporting breeds.

The breeds Korthals used to produce this fine animal probably carried the genetic qualities of setter, spaniel, Otter Hound and Pointer (probably German Shorthaired Pointer) as well as the old griffon strain in their background.

STANDARD OF THE WIREHAIRED POINTING GRIFFON

The Wire-Haired Griffon is a dog of medium size, fairly shortbacked, rather a little low on his legs, he is strongly limbed, everything about him indicating strength and vigor.

His coat is harsh like the bristles of a wild boar and his appearance, notwithstanding his short coat, is as unkempt as that of the long-haired Griffon, but on the other hand he has a very intelligent air.

DESCRIPTION

Head—Long, furnished with a harsh coat, forming a mustache and eyebrows, skull long and narrow, muzzle square.

Eyes—Large, open, full of expression, iris yellow or light brown.

Ears—Of medium size, flat or sometimes slightly curled, set rather high, very lightly furnished with hair.

Nose—Always brown.

Neck—Rather long, no dewlap.

Shoulders—Long, sloping.

Ribs—Slightly rounded.

Forelegs—Very straight, muscular, furnished with rather short wire hairs.

Hindlegs—Furnished with rather short stiff hair, the thighs long and well developed.

Feet—Round, firm and well formed.

Tail—Carried straight or gaily, furnished with a hard coat, without plume, generally cut to a third of its length.

Coat—Hard, dry, stiff, never curly, the undercoat downy.

Color—Steel grey with chestnut splashes, grey white with chestnut splashes, chestnut, dirty white mixed with chestnut, never black.

Height—$21\frac{1}{2}$ to $23\frac{1}{2}$ inches for males, and $19\frac{1}{2}$ to $21\frac{1}{2}$ inches for females.

English Champion Cheyenne Serenade

THE POINTER

Unsurpassed in the field, the Pointer is a specialist in his specific utilitarian area. His business is to hunt, and he tends to his business, when in the field, with every ounce of his lithe, muscular, energetic being. He is every inch a gun dog, clean limbed, hard, and elegant in the "breedy" look that is his heritage.

As a show dog, the Pointer's sculptured beauty, his natural poise, conformation, and satin-smooth coat make him ideal. His temperament, which makes him a perfect kennel dog, is also ideal for the bench.

Among other virtues, the Pointer develops, and so can be trained, early, making him particularly suited for competition in the field in derby and puppy stakes.

In the Pointer, type and ability have always gone hand in hand, hence there has been no great divergence in type between the show and the field dog. He is a good house dog, requires less personal attention than many other breeds and, in the field, will work well for persons other than his owner or handler. As a matter of fact, all he wants to do is hunt and he will hunt for anyone, for this is his greatest interest in life, the object of his breeding and the reason for his birth.

The geneology of the breed points to Foxhound and Bloodhound crosses with probably some Greyhound and early Spaniel infusions. The earliest theory was that Pointers from Spain and Portugal were imported to England

The vivid colors of the autumn woods enchance
the rugged beauty of a hunting scene such as
this. The Pointer, in all his sculptured symmetry,
an extension of his master's will, sharing with
him the zest and excitement of the hunt. The
ages roll back and once again man and dog are
partners in a common pursuit.

and used to produce the local pointing breed. Popular theory today is that the Spanish and Portuguese Pointers were not imported until after the Pointer had been already established as a breed in England and, therefore, were not used in its conception.

It is the author's belief that the original concept was correct. Research done by the author in Spain indicates that the Spanish Pointer is one of the oldest gundog breeds in existence, and probably the basis for most of the modern sporting breeds that point game in the field. (See Spanish Pointer*).

At one time the temperament of the breed was not all it should be, but smart breeders channeled this aggressiveness into competitive spirit to make the Pointer the superlative field-trial dog that he is today. If you wish to see quicksilver, high-energy bird work, poetry in motion in the field, then watch a Pointer do what he was born and bred to do—hunt.

STANDARD OF THE POINTER

General Appearance—The Pointer is bred primarily for sport afield; he should unmistakably look and act the part. The ideal specimen gives the immediate impression of compact power and agile grace; the head noble, proudly carried; the expression intelligent and alert; the muscular body be-

speaking both staying power and dash. Here is an animal whose every movement shows him to be a wide-awake, hard-driving hunting dog possessing stamina, courage, and the desire to go. And in his expression are the loyalty and devotion of a true friend of man.

Temperament—The Pointer's even temperament and alert good sense make him a congenial companion both in the field and in the home. He should be dignified, yet showing at all times a responsive attitude.

Head—Skull long and proportionately wide, but indicating length rather than width. Slight furrow between the eyes, cheeks cleanly chiseled. A pronounced stop midway between nostrils and occiput. Muzzle long, in the same plane as the skull. Jaws ending level and square, with scissors or even bite. The flews clean. Nostrils large, spongy, widely open.

Ears—Set on at eye level. When hanging naturally, they should reach just below the lower jaw, close to the head, with little or no folding. They should be somewhat pointed at the tip—never round—and soft and thin in leather.

Eyes—Of medium size, rounded, pleasant in expression and the darker the better.

Neck—Long, dry, muscular and slightly arched, springing cleanly from the shoulders.

Shoulders—Long, thin, and sloping. The top of blades close together.

Front—Elbows well down, directly under the withers and truly parallel, so as to work just clear of the body. Forelegs straight and with oval bone. Knee joint never to knuckle over. Pasterns of moderate length, perceptibly finer in bone than the leg, and slightly slanting. Chest, deep rather than wide, must not hinder free action of forelegs. The breastbone bold, without being unduly prominent. The ribs well sprung, descending as low as the elbow-point.

Back—Strong and solid, with only a slight rise from croup to top of shoulders. Loin of moderate length, powerful and slightly arched. Croup falling only slightly to base of tail. Tuck-up should be apparent, but not exaggerated.

Tail—Heavier at the root, gradually tapering to a fine point. Length no greater than to reach to the hock joint. Carried straight, ideally on a level with the back.

Hindquarters—Muscular and powerful, with great propelling leverage. Thighs long and well-developed. Stifles well bent. The hocks clean and parallel. Decided angulation is the mark of power and endurance.

Feet—Oval, with long, closely-set, arched toes, well padded, and deep.

Coat—Dense, short, smooth with a sheen.

Color—Liver, lemon, black, orange; either in combination with white or solid-colored. A good Pointer cannot be a bad color. In the darker colors, the nose should be black or brown; in the lighter shades it may be lighter or flesh-colored.

Gait—Smooth, frictionless, with a powerful hindquarters' drive. The head should be carried high, the nostrils wide, the tail moving from side to side rhythmically with the pace, giving the impression of a well-balanced, strongly-built hunting dog capable of top speed combined with great stamina.

Balance and Size—Balance, over-all symmetry, is much more important in the Pointer than size. It is just as vital in a dog bred for field work as it is in an athlete or race horse, and for the same reasons: it indicates muscular co-ordination, endurance, and an equilibrium of power. Whether large or small, a well put-together Pointer, "smooth all over," is to be preferred to an uneven one with contrasting good and bad points. Provided there is balance, considerable variation in size and weight is permissible.

General Appearance—Lack of true Pointer type. Hound or terrier characteristics.

Temperament—Timidity, unruliness.

Head—Blocky or apple head. Short or snipy muzzle or frog face. Bulging cheeks or pendulous flews. Lack of stop, down-face, Roman nose. Undershot or overshot. Small or dry nostrils.

Ears—Low set, round, heavy, folded, leathery or hound ears.

Eyes—Light, hard, almond, or staring eyes.

Neck—Ewe neck. Throatiness. Short, thick neck.

Shoulders—Loaded or bossy shoulders. Set wide apart at top. Straight shoulders, no slope.

Front—Elbows turned either in or out. Forelegs knuckled over. Straight pasterns, terrier front. Bone of forelegs coarse, fine, or round. Narrow chested, shallow, shelly, pigeon-breasted. Chest too wide, resulting in elbows out. Ribs too flat or too barrelled.

Back—Roach or sway back. Unbalanced length of body. Cobbiness. Steep rise, or none at all, in topline. Sagging or long, thin loin. Croup falling away too sharply.

Tail—Rat tail. Set on too high or too low. Carried between the legs, or carried high, flagpole tail.

Hindquarters—Straight stifles. Cow hocks. Lack of angulation or straight in stifle. Any suggestion of weakness in hindquarters.

Feet—Cat-foot. Thin or soft pads. Splayed feet. Flat toes.

Coat—Long hair or curl. Soft or silky coat.

Color—Weak or washed-out colors. Light or flesh-colored nose in a dark-colored dog. Butterfly nose.

Gait—Crossing-over, sprawling or side-tracking. Stepping too high in front—the hackney gait.

SCALE OF POINTS

	Points
Head	10
Ears	3
Eyes	4
Neck	5
Shoulders	8
Front	6
Back	4
Tail	5
Hindquarters	15
Feet	9
Coat and Color	5
Gait	6
Balance and true Pointer type	20
Total	100

Champion Gretchenhof Cimarron

THE GERMAN SHORTHAIRED POINTER

Here is a breed that is the canine embodiment of the word "versatile". Unlike many of the sporting breeds, the German Shorthair makes a wonderful house and watch dog. He is a handy dog for any sportsman for he can be taught to work on fur or feather, can become a night trailing 'coon hound, will work rabbits, 'possum, any kind of feathered game from grouse to duck, and retrieve with style and gaiety in dry brush or water.

Using old German hound stock as a base, the Spanish Pointer, English Foxhound, and Bloodhound were judiciously crossed to produce the "all purpose" breed, which German sportsmen called them before they were adopted by other countries.

The original German Pointer was a rather heavy dog, staunch on point and

with remarkable scenting powers, albeit rather slow in the field. Then, about fifty years ago, German and Austrian sportsmen, wanting more dash and speed, gave their breed an infusion of English Pointer blood. Selective breeding eventually produced a smaller, faster dog of beautiful conformation that still retained the character and superb nose and endurance of the earlier breed.

The most characteristic color of the German Shorthair is liver roan, although he can be solid liver, or liver and white as well.

Fanciers of the breed have been careful to keep him a versatile breed, and there is no such thing as a "bench Shorthair" and "field Shorthair." The same dog can be used in the field that can win on the bench.

The German Shorthaired Pointer works close to the gun and is not as far ranging a dog as his English cousin. This factor worked to his advantage in his homeland where the hunting conditions would not favor a wide-ranging gun dog. It is advantageous, too, to the American hunter who may be disinclined, for various reasons, to follow a lightning, quick-quartering Pointer or Setter in the field.

On the bench, the German Shorthair is in a favorable position among the recognized purebreds. There are many good specimens being shown all across the land and a good Shorthair will usually place high in the Sporting group.

The author has hunted behind several German Shorthaired Pointers and has nothing but admiration for the breed. They are staunch, birdy, and stay close enough to the gun to make any day in the field with them a distinct and memorable pleasure.

STANDARD OF THE GERMAN SHORTHAIRED POINTER

General Appearance—The overall picture which is created in the observer's eye should be that of an aristocratic, well balanced, symmetrical animal with conformation indicating power, endurance and agility and a look of intelligence and animation.

The dog should be neither unduly small nor conspicuously large. It should rather give the impression of medium size, but be like the proper hunter, "with a short back, but standing over plenty of ground." Tall, leggy individuals seldom possess endurance or sound movement.

Dogs which are ponderous or unbalanced because of excess substance should be definitely rejected. The first impression should be that of a keenness which denotes full enthusiasm for work without indication of nervous or flighty character. Movement should be alertly co-ordinated without waste motion.

Grace of outline, clean-cut head, sloping shoulders, deep breast, powerful back, strong quarters, good bone composition, adequate muscle, well-carried tail and taut coat, all of which should combine to produce a look of nobility and an indication of anatomical structure essential to correct gait which must indicate a heritage of purposefully conducted breeding.

Head—Clean-cut, neither too light nor too heavy, in proper proportion to the body. Skull should be reasonably broad, arched on side and slightly round on top. Scissura (median line between the eyes at the forehead) not too deep, occipital bone not as conspicuous as in the case of the Pointer.

The foreface should rise gradually from nose to forehead—not resembling the Roman nose. This is more strongly pronounced in the dog than in the bitch, as befitting his sex. The chops should fall away from the somewhat projecting nose. Lips should be full and deep, never flewy. The chops should not fall over too much, but form a proper fold in the angle. The jaw should be powerful and the muscles well developed.

The line to the forehead should rise gradually and should never possess a definite stop as in the case of the Pointer, but rather a stop-effect when viewed from the side, due to the position of the eyebrows.

The muzzle should be sufficiently long to enable the dog to seize properly and to facilitate his carrying game a long time. A pointed muzzle is not desirable. The entire head should never give the impression of tapering to a point. The depth should be in the right proportion to the length, both in the muzzle and in the skull proper.

Ears—Ears should be broad and set fairly high, lie flat and never hang away from the head. Placement should be above eye level.

The ears, when laid in front without being pulled, should about meet the lip angle. In the case of heavier dogs, they should be correspondingly longer.

Eyes—The eyes should be of medium size, full of intelligence and expressive, good-humored, and yet radiating energy, neither protruding nor sunk. The eyelids should close well.

The best color is a dark shade of brown. Light yellow, china or wall (bird of prey) eyes are not desirable.

Nose—Brown, the larger the better; nostrils well opened and broad. Flesh-colored and spotted noses are not desirable.

Teeth—The teeth should be strong and healthy. The molars should intermesh properly. Incisors should fit close in a true scissor bite. Jaws should be neither overshot nor undershot.

Neck—Of adequate length to permit the jaws reaching game to be retrieved, sloping downwards on beautifully curving lines. The nape should be rather muscular, becoming gradually larger towards the shoulders. Moderate hound-like throatiness permitted.

Breast and Thorax—The breast in general should give the impression of depth rather than breadth; for all that, it should be in correct proportion to the other parts of the body with fair depth of chest.

The ribs forming the thorax should be well-curved and not flat; they should not be absolutely round or barrel-shaped. Ribs that are entirely round prevent the necessary expansion of the chest when taking breath. The back ribs should reach well down.

The circumference of the breast immediately behind the elbows should be smaller than that of the breast about a handsbreadth behind elbows, so that the upper arm has room for movement.

Champion Gretchenhof White Frost

Back and Loins—Back should be short, strong and straight with slight rise from root of tail to withers. Excessively long or hog-backed should be penalized. Loins strong, of moderate length and slightly arched. Tuck up should be apparent.

Assembly of Back Members—The hips should be broad with hip sockets wide apart and fall slightly toward the tail in a graceful curve. Thighs strong and well muscled. Stifles well bent. Hock joints should be well angulated with strong, straight bone structure from hock to pad. Angulation of both stifle and hock joints should be such as to combine maximum combination of both drive and traction. Hocks should turn neither in nor out.

Assembly of Front Members—The shoulders should be sloping, movable, well covered with muscle. The shoulder blades should lie flat. The upper arm (also called the cross bar, i.e., the bones between the shoulder and elbow joints) should be as long as possible, standing away somewhat from the trunk so that the straight and closely muscled legs, when viewed from in front, should appear to be parallel. Elbows which stand away from the body or are pressed right into same indicate toes turning inwards or outwards, which should be regarded as faults. Pasterns should be strong, short and nearly vertical.

Feet—Should be compact, close-knit and round to spoon-shaped. The toes sufficiently arched and heavily nailed. The pad should be strong and hard.

Coat and Skin—The skin should look close and tight.

The hair should be short and thick and feel tough and hard to the hand; it is somewhat longer on the underside of the tail and the back edge of the haunches. It is softer, thinner and shorter on the ears and the head.

Tail—Is set high and firm, and must be docked, leaving approximately two-fifths of length.

The tail hangs down when the dog is quiet, is held horizontally when he is walking, never turned over the back or considerably bent but violently wagged when he is on the search.

Bones—Thin and fine bones are by no means desirable in a dog which should be able to work over any and every country and should possess strength. The main importance accordingly is laid not so much on the size as being in proper proportion to the body. Dogs with coarse bones are handicapped in agility of movement and speed.

Desirable Weight and Height—Dogs: 55 to 70 pounds. Bitches: 45 to 60 pounds.

Dogs: 23 to 25 inches. Bitches: 21 to 23 inches at the shoulders.

Color—Solid liver, liver and white spotted, liver and white spotted and ticked, liver and white ticked, liver roan. Any colors other than liver and white (gray white) are not permitted.

Symmetry and field quality are most essential.

A dog well balanced in all points is preferable to one with outstanding good qualities and defects. A smooth, lithe gait is most desirable.

Faults—Bone structure too clumsy or too light, head too large, too many wrinkles in forehead, dish-faced, snipy muzzle, ears too long, pointy or fleshy, flesh-colored nose, eyes too light, too round or too closely set together, excessive throatiness, cowhocks, feet or elbows turned inward or outward, down on pasterns, loose shoulders, sway-back, black coat or tri-colored, any colors except liver or some combination of liver and white.

Displaying all the ruggedness, intelligence and ability that is the essence of the German Wire-haired Pointer, this portrait of Champion Old-mill Flint is a classic study.

Champion Oldmill Casanova

THE GERMAN WIREHAIRED POINTER

The German Wirehaired Pointer, as indicated by its name, had its origin in Germany, from whence it spread to other Northern European countries. The breed, known as *Drahthaar* in Germany, is translated in English as Wirehaired. Thus, the American name of German Wirehaired Pointer.

The German sportsman demands from his dog that it be able to work as an all-rounder. The dog must be able to find game, and point game as well as retrieve the wounded and killed. It must work the thickets on command, track and trail as well as retrieve in water. The dogs, with appropriate training, must work equally well with game birds, rabbits, fox, deer and boar. In the 1870's, it was recognized that the all-around sporting dog was missing, hence the effort to "create" such an animal. The result was the German Wirehaired Pointer.

It had to be a dog that combined the good abilities of the Pointer, its speed, fine nose and staunch pointing, with the desired traits of liking water, trailing skills, retrieving abilities, intelligence, and ease of training. Furthermore, the dog had to be hardy and persevering. Because of the last requirement, it was considered necessary that the dog be "rough-coated" because a coarse and wiry coat would give the best protection against weather, damage by thorns, bushes and rushes, to make it useful for hunting in any terrain and in all seasons.

In the beginning, the Griffon and Stichelhaar afforded the general type of coat that was considered most desirable; however these breeds had been bred

A winning Wirehaired Pointer in Germany (Odin type).

more for exhibition than performance, and many of the desired abilities were lacking. Here, the Poodle-Pointers were introduced, since they added the abilities of the Pointer, as well as the high degree of intelligence and sporting abilities of the Poodle.* German Shorthaired Pointers were also used to intensify pointing instincts.

On May 15, 1902, the *Verein Deutsch Drahthaar* (German Wirehaired Club) was formed in Berlin. This organization included persons interested in all rough coated sporting dogs. The motto of the club could have been: "Breed as you like, create progress, and tell honestly what you have used." This club was fortunate that the right men were on top. They were experienced and skilled breeders and sportsmen who made great contributions. Lauffo Unkel am/Rhein was President from the start and continued to be for the following thirty-two years.

The purpose of the club was put into words as follows: "The first thing to be obtained is perfection in hunting, next a good and suitable build, and finally beauty." It did not take long before the first goal was reached, because of the liberty that was given in breeding, which included Poodle-Pointers, Stichelhaars, Griffons and Shorthairs. The second and third goals were more difficult to reach. But, after some years, more and more dogs appeared with correct physical structure. The hair was, and still is, the most difficult point.

* *Author's note:* The "Poodle" referred to here by the writer of the above, is the German "Pudel," a heavier boned, sturdier breed than our Poodles, that are used as sporting dogs on the Continent.

118

The necessity to be very critical in choice and to use only the best in breeding was of utmost importance. To control this, rules were made and are still in effect, that the dogs could only be registered in the "*Stammbuch Deutsch Drahthaar*" (German Wirehair Studbook) after the age of one year (later reduced to seven months) and that the dog's coat and conformation must be approved, as well as its abilities in the field. In the German Hunting-dog Studbook, there were more Wirehairs (Drahthaars) entered in 1923 than Shorthairs, and they have led in this ever since.

The fight for recognition was hard and long, and not until 1928, after the Wirehairs had held the leading position in sporting dogs, did the German Wirehaired Club gain membership in the German Kartell for Dogs.

It was finally commonly recognized that the German Wirehaired Club had reached its goal; to develop a rough-coated sporting dog that answered the sportsman's all-around demands. Many sportsmen today have varied sporting grounds, which include common field shooting of birds and rabbits, as well as wooded shooting of birds and fur-bearing animals, plus the shooting of waterfowl over marshes and open water. The Wirehair proved itself to be a dog that could be used for all of these types of hunting.

Today hunting is not for subsistence, nor should it be a contest. There must be responsibility to the nation not to decrease the game, and responsibility to the game that it not suffer needlessly. Hunting is not gentle, but it must not become beastly. The first responsibility demands careful and sensible shooting. The second responsibility demands of the sportsman that he have a dog with sufficient abilities and training to avoid losing wounded or killed game. The searching, finding and retrieving on command, of game is the prime consideration of any sporting dog, and the Wirehair has proven its capabilities in all situations.

Champion Oldmill Flint

The German Wirehaired Pointer is a dog that is essentially Pointer in type, of sturdy build, lively manner, and an intelligent, determined expression. In disposition the dog has been described as energetic, rather aloof but not unfriendly.

STANDARD OF THE GERMAN WIREHAIRED POINTER

Head—The head is moderately long, the skull broad, the occipital bone not too prominent. The stop is medium, the muzzle fairly long with nasal bone straight and broad, the lips a trifle pendulous but close and bearded. The nose is dark brown with nostrils wide open, and the teeth are strong with scissors bite. The ears, rounded but not too broad, hang close to the sides of the head. Eyes are brown, medium in size, oval in contour, bright and clear and overhung with bushy eyebrows. Yellow eyes are not desirable. The neck is of medium length, slightly arched and devoid of dewlap, in fact, the skin throughout is notably tight to the body.

Body and Tail—The body is a little longer than it is high, as ten is to nine, with the back short, straight and strong, the entire back line showing a perceptible slope down from withers to croup. The chest is deep and capacious, the ribs well sprung, loins taut and slender, the tuck-up apparent. Hips are broad, with croup nicely rounded and the tail docked, approximately two-fifths of original length.

Legs and Feet—Forelegs are straight, with shoulders obliquely set and elbows close. The thighs are strong and muscular. The hind legs are moderately angulated at stifle and hock and as viewed from behind, parallel to each other. Round in outline, the feet are webbed, high arched with toes close, their pads thick and hard, and their nails strong and quite heavy. Leg bones are flat rather than round, and strong, but not so heavy or coarse as to militate against the dog's natural agility.

Coat—The coat is weather resisting and to some extent water repellent. The undercoat is dense enough in winter to insulate against the cold but so thin in summer as to be almost invisible. The distinctive outer coat is straight, harsh, wiry and rather flat-lying, from one and one-half to two inches in length, it is long enough to protect against the punishment of rough cover but not so long as to hide the outline. On the lower legs it is shorter, and between the toes, of softer texture. On the skull it is naturally short and close fitting, while over the shoulders and around the tail it is very dense and heavy. The tail is nicely coated particularly on the underside, but devoid of feather. These dogs have bushy eyebrows of strong, straight hair and beards and whiskers of medium length.

A short, smooth coat, a soft, woolly coat, or an excessively long coat is to be severely penalized.

Color—The coat is liver and white, usually either liver and white spotted, liver roan, liver and white spotted with ticking and roaning or sometimes solid liver. The nose is dark brown. The head is brown, sometimes with a white blaze, the ears brown. Any black in the coat is to be severely penalized. Spotted and flesh-colored noses are undesirable and are to be penalized.

Size—Height of males should be from 24 to 26 inches at the withers, bitches smaller but not under 22 inches.

120

Above is a photo of two Pudel Pointers, the breed that was used to form the basic breed type of the German Wirehaired Pointer. This European breed is well liked by Continental sportsmen. Below is another German specimen of the Wirehaired Pointer (Harras type).

One of the few native American breeds, the
Chesapeake Bay Retriever is a powerful and
willing gun dog, noted for its courage, hardiness, and natural retrieving ability.

Ch. Wings of Arundel, C.D., Ch. Wings Teritus, C.D., T.D., and Ch. Ike of Terraqua, C.D.

THE CHESAPEAKE BAY RETRIEVER

The Chesapeake Bay Retriever originated with a shipwreck, when in the year 1807, the English brig, Canton, was wrecked off the coast of Maryland. The crew was rescued, and two Newfoundland pups aboard, who were being taken to England, swam ashore. These dogs, a male and a female, were found to possess exceptional qualities as retrievers, and subsequently were crossed with the native Indian dogs, as well as several other breeds. Only the best retrievers were used for breeding—the rugged dogs who never quit and those who possessed outstanding marking ability. By 1885 this strain was famous and all Chesapeakes trace back to this foundation stock which developed in the Chesapeake Bay area on the eastern shore of Maryland.

Noted for his intelligence, courage and willingness, in appearance the Chesapeake is a fairly heavy-set powerful individual standing about 24 inches high at the withers. Not particularly showy or stylish, the Chesapeake is impressive in his power. Color varies from a dark brown to a dead-grass color (that of straw).

Chesapeakes love children and are ideal playmates for them. Since most Chesapeakes are bodily insensitive the youngsters seldom can hurt them. They not only play with the youngsters, but also protect them. There have been innumerable instances of rescues they have made: saving children from fire, from drowning in water, from approaching automobiles, and from many other hazards.

Hunting is what the Chesapeake was born and bred for, and consequently he is a natural retriever. He has an excellent nose and instinctively uses it in the field. Much as the dog may love the family, when the master collects his gun and hunting gear, his dog is at his side, begging to accompany him.

They are outstanding in their water work. Most Chesapeakes leap into the water after their ducks no matter how far below freezing the temperature may be. Their dense undercoat is a protection against the cold, and ice does not bother them. They have the uncanny ability to remember two or three falls when birds are shot, and go directly to the spot where they fell. Should a bird be crippled they will search and trail it until they find it. No game is lost. A good Chesapeake is a real conservationist.

Pheasants, quail, dove and grouse are all enthusiastically hunted and retrieved by this breed with a minimum of training. Chesapeakes do not range out too far, and their superior scenting powers make it easy for them to locate and flush game. It is a great satisfaction to know that the dog will find and bring back every bird shot. Hunting is much more fun with a dog of which one can be proud.

Obedience competition is a field where the breed excels. Hurdling is not difficult to teach as it seems to come naturally to most Chesapeakes. Owners are proud of the records established by obedience trained Chesapeakes who have been amateur trained and handled to the highest obedience degree obtainable, UDT.

Most Chesapeake owners successfully handle and usually train their own field trial dogs. An amazing number of women today are also successful with Chesapeakes in this type of competition. Perhaps this is because the breed seems to do its best work for its owner, male or female, as it loves to please. Since these dogs possess outstanding marking ability, retrieving double and triple falls is no problem. Teaching a Chesapeake to "handle" is a matter of repeated training on the part of the owner. Of course there are some that are professionally trained but the vast majority running in the trials today are amateur-trained and amateur-handled, including many amateur field champions.

STANDARD OF THE CHESAPEAKE BAY RETRIEVER

Head—Skull broad and round with medium stop, nose medium short-muzzle pointed but not sharp. Lips thin, not pendulous. Ears small, set well up on head, hanging loosely and of medium leather. Eyes medium large, very clear of yellowish color and wide apart.

Neck—Of medium length with a strong muscular appearance, tapering to shoulders.

Shoulders, Chest and Body—Shoulders, sloping and should have full liberty of action with plenty of power without any restriction of movement. Chest strong, deep and wide. Barrel round and deep. Body of medium length, neither cobby nor roached, but rather approaching hollowness, flanks well tucked up.

Back and Quarter Stifles—Back quarters should be as high or a trifle higher than the shoulders. They should show fully as much power as the forequarters. There should be no tendency to weakness in either fore or hind quarters. Hind quarters should be especially powerful to supply the driving power for swimming. Back should be short, well-coupled and powerful. Good hind quarters are essential.

Legs, Elbows, Hocks and Feet—Legs should be medium length and straight,

Champion West River Ripple and Random Lakes Bill's Darky.

showing good bone and muscle, with well webbed hare feet of good size. The toes well rounded and close pasterns slightly bent and both pasterns and hocks medium length—the straighter the legs the better.

Stern—Tail should be medium length—varying from: Males 12 inches to 15 inches, and females from 11 inches to 14 inches; medium heavy at base, moderate, feathering on stern and tail permissible.

Coat and Texture—Coat should be thick and short, nowhere over $1\frac{1}{2}$ inches long, with a dense fine woolly undercoat. Hair on face and legs should be very short and straight with tendency to wave on the shoulders, neck, back and loins only. The curly coat or coat with a tendency to curl not permissible.

Color—Any color varying from a dark brown to a faded tan or, deadgrass. Deadgrass takes in any shade of deadgrass, varying from a tan to a dull straw color. White spot on breast and toes permissible, but the smaller the spot the better, solid color being preferred.

Weight—Males, 65 to 75 pounds; females, 55 to 65 pounds.

Height—Males, 23 inches to 26 inches; females, 21 inches to 24 inches.

Symmetry and Quality—The Chesapeake dog should show a bright and happy disposition and an intelligent expression, with general outlines impressive and denoting a good worker. The dog should be well proportioned, a dog with a good coat and well balanced in other points being preferable to the dog excelling in some but weak in others.

The texture of the dog's coat is very important as the dog is used for hunting under all sorts of adverse weather conditions, often working in ice and snow. The oil in the harsh outer coat and woolly undercoat is of extreme value in preventing the cold water from reaching the dog's skin and aids in quick drying. A Chesapeake's coat should resist the water in the same way that a duck's feathers do. When he leaves the water and shakes himself, his coat should not hold the water at all, being merely moist.

125

Color and coat are extremely important as the dog is used for duck hunting. The color must be as nearly that of his surroundings as possible and with the fact that dogs are exposed to all kinds of adverse weather conditions, often working in ice and snow, the color of coat and its texture must be given every consideration when judging on the bench or in the ring.

Courage, willingness to work, alertness, nose, intelligence, love of water, general quality, and, most of all, disposition should be given primary consideration in the selection and breeding of the Chesapeake Bay Dog.

POSITIVE SCALE OF POINTS

	Points
Head, including lips, ears and eyes	16
Neck	4
Shoulders and body	12
Back quarters and stifles	12
Elbows, legs and feet	12
Color	4
Stern and tail	10
Coat and texture	18
General conformation	12
Total	100

Note.—The question of coat and general type of balance takes precedence over any scoring table which could be drawn up.

APPROXIMATE MEASUREMENTS

Length head, nose to occiput	$9\frac{1}{2}$ to 10
Girth at ears	20 to 21
Muzzle below eyes	10 to $10\frac{1}{2}$
Length of ears	$4\frac{1}{2}$ to 5
Width between eyes	$2\frac{1}{2}$ to $2\frac{3}{4}$
Girth neck close to shoulder	20 to 22
Girth of chest to elbows	35 to 36
Girth at flank	24 to 25
Length from occiput to tail base	34 to 35
Girth forearms at shoulders	10 to $10\frac{1}{2}$
Girth upper thigh	19 to 20
From root to root of ear, over skull	5 to 6
Occiput to top shoulder blades	9 to $9\frac{1}{2}$
From elbow to elbow over the shoulders	25 to 26

GENERAL DISQUALIFICATIONS

1. Black or liver colored.
2. White on any part of body, except breast, belly or spots on feet.
3. Feathering on tail or legs over $1\frac{3}{4}$ inches long.
4. Dewclaws, undershot, overshot or any deformity.
5. Coat curly or tendency to curl all over body.
6. Specimens unworthy or lacking in breed characteristics.

Champion Mark Anthony

THE CURLY-COATED RETRIEVER

The Curly-Coated Retriever is said to be one of the oldest of the existing retriever breeds. He is believed to have been developed from the now extinct English Water Spaniel with probable crossings to the St. John's Newfoundland and the Irish Water Spaniel. During the 1880's it is thought that the Poodle was introduced into the breed, probably to improve the coat and general retrieving ability.

The Curly-Coat may be either black or liver in color. At one time there were some specimens of the breed that were of a golden color, but they have disappeared in more recent times.

The breed name is derived from the unique coat which is a mass of crisp, tight curls from the base of the skull to the tip of the tail. This body covering, combined with his sturdy constitution, makes the Curly-Coat a wonderful water dog. He is impervious to the worst weather, roughest water, and thickest cover.

It is unfortunate that the breed is not better known in the United States. He is, and has been for many years, a popular favorite with gunners in Australia and New Zealand as well as the country of his origin, England.

On the English show bench he has had a certain measure of success. There are several active breeders, and the Curly usually gets a fair share of attention in the Gun Dog (Sporting) group.

The Curly-Coated Retriever was first shown in England at the Birmingham show in 1860. In 1899 the breed was introduced to New Zealand, and in 1907 a dog and a bitch were brought into the United States.

The loyal band of fanciers that have guided the fortunes of the breed have found the Curly-Coat to be an outstanding companion in the field, possessed of great intelligence, tremendous enthusiasm for hunting, and owning one of the softest mouths. He has also acquitted himself just as well as a companion, being faithful, loyal and a most reliable guard dog.

STANDARD OF THE CURLY-COATED RETRIEVER

Head—Long and well proportioned, skull not too flat, jaws long and strong but not inclined to snipiness, nose black, in the black coated variety, with wide nostrils. Teeth strong and level.

Eyes—Black or brown, but not yellow, rather large but not too prominent.

Ears—Rather small, set on low, lying close to the head, and covered with short curls.

Coat—Should be one mass of crisp curls all over. A slightly more open coat not to be severely penalized, but a saddle back or patch of uncurled hair behind the shoulder should be penalized, and a prominent white patch on breast is undesirable, but a few white hairs allowed in an otherwise good dog. Color, black or liver.

Shoulders, Chest, Body and Loins—Shoulders should be very deep, muscular and obliquely placed. Chest, not too wide, but decidedly deep. Body, rather short, muscular and well ribbed up. Loin, powerful, deep and firm to the grasp.

Legs and Feet—Legs should be of moderate length, forelegs straight and set well under the body. Quarters strong and muscular, hocks low to the ground with moderate bend to stifle and hock. Feet round and compact with well arched toes.

Tail—Should be moderately short, carried fairly straight and covered with curls, slightly tapering towards the point.

General Appearance—A strong, smart, upstanding dog, showing activity, endurance and intelligence.

English Champion Harkaway Editha retrieving a rabbit.

SPRINGER SPANIEL.

GERMAN WIREHAIRED
POINTERS (DRAHTHAAR)
IN THE FIELD.

AT LEFT, AN IRISH
SETTER ON POINT.

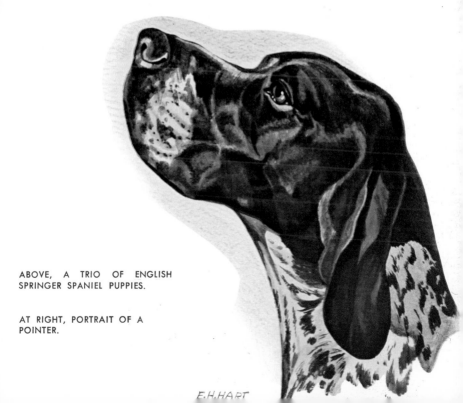

ABOVE, A TRIO OF ENGLISH
SPRINGER SPANIEL PUPPIES.

AT RIGHT, PORTRAIT OF A
POINTER.

E.H.HART

A SPRINGER SPANIEL.

PICTURED BELOW ARE A PAIR OF ENGLISH COCKER SPANIELS.

A GERMAN SHORTHAIRED POINTER
RETRIEVING A DUCK TO HAND.

AN ENGLISH SETTER (FIELD BRED).

HEAD STUDY OF A WEIMARANER.

GERMAN SHORTHAIRED WITH PHEASANT.

GERMAN SHORTHAIRED ON POINT.

A BRITTANY SPANIEL.

A GOLDEN RETRIEVER AT WORK.

IRISH WATER SPANIEL.

A BRACE OF GOLDEN RETRIEVERS.

TEUTONIC GUN DOGS, THE GERMAN WIRE-
HAIRED POINTER AND THE GERMAN SHORT-
HAIRED POINTER.

LABRADOR RETRIEVER (YELLOW COLOR PHASE).

A FLAT-COATED RETRIEVER.

AN ENGLISH COCKER SPANIEL
RETRIEVING TO HAND.

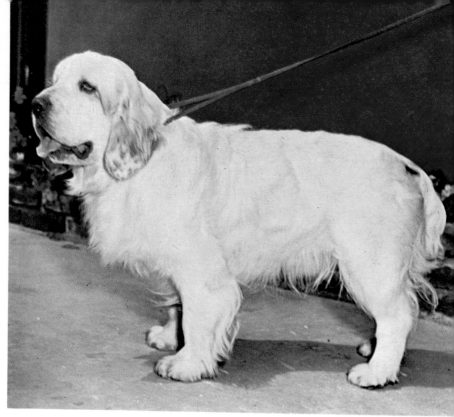

CLUMBER SPANIEL.

AN AMERICAN COCKER
SPANIEL.

AN ENGLISH SETTER (SHOW BRED).

A GORDON SETTER.

HEAD STUDY OF AN IRISH SETTER.

CURLY COATED RETRIEVER.

Champion Mantayo Copper Caliph, C.D.

THE FLAT-COATED RETRIEVER

The best way to describe a Flat-Coated Retriever is to say that he resembles a long-haired Labrador, although he is slightly larger.

The Flat-Coat was developed through crossings with the Labrador Retriever and the St. John's Newfoundland, and although he is the result of a union between these two North American breeds, he was developed and perfected in Great Britain.

In the early days of the breed, the Flat-Coat was known as the "Wavy-Coated Retriever," and there were many experimental crossings carried out to determine what would be the most serviceable gun dog. One of the negative results of these crossings was the creation of great confusion in the matters of proper size, type and color. It was largely due to the efforts of one fancier, Dr. Bond Moore of Wolverhampton, that the Flat-Coat finally came into his own as a specific, pure breed.

In his great insistence on what he felt was correct type, Dr. Moore put down all puppies who were not black in color. Black, he believed, was the only proper color for a Flat-Coat, although the present standard allows for liver as well as black.

The Flat-Coat is considerably more popular in Great Britain than he is in the United States. In recent years, however, there has been an increase in

145

imports and American-breds being shown. Some have done very well, including top wins in the Sporting group being registered on their records.

In obedience, the Flat-Coat has shown himself to be particularly adept. Not a few of the breed have taken some high titles in all-breed obedience competition.

Withal, he still maintains his inbred talent as a great bird dog. His supporters are enthusiastic in their praise of his abilities and anyone who has had the pleasure of working with a Flat-Coat has found him to be second to none in the shooting field.

STANDARD OF THE FLAT-COATED RETRIEVER

GENERAL APPEARANCE

A bright active dog of medium size (weighing from 60 pounds to 70 pounds) with an intelligent expression, showing power without lumber and raciness without weediness.

DETAILED DESCRIPTION

Head—This should be long and nicely molded. The skull flat and moderately broad. There should be a depression or stop between the eyes, slight and in no way accentuated so as to avoid giving either a down or a dish-faced appearance. The nose of good size with open nostrils. The eyes, of medium size, should be dark brown or hazel, with a very intelligent expression (a round prominent eye is a disfigurement), and they should not be obliquely placed. The jaws should be long and strong, with a capacity of carrying a hare or pheasant. The ears small and well set on close to the side of the head.

Neck, Shoulders and Chest—The head should be well set in the neck, which latter should be long and free from throatiness, symmetrically set and obliquely placed in shoulders running well into the back to allow of easily seeking for the trail. The chest should be deep and fairly broad, with a well-defined brisket, on which the elbows should work cleanly and evenly. The fore ribs should be fairly flat showing a gradual spring and well arched in the center of the body but rather lighter towards the quarters. Open couplings are to be ruthlessly condemned.

Back and Quarters—The back should be short, square and well ribbed up, with muscular quarters. The stern short, straight and well set on, carried gaily but never much above the level of the back.

Legs and Feet—These are of the greatest importance. The forelegs should be perfectly straight, with bone of good quality carried right down to the feet which should be round and strong. The stifle should not be too straight or too bent and the dog must neither be cowhocked nor move too wide behind, in fact he must stand and move true all round on legs and feet, with toes close and well arched, the soles being thick and strong and when the dog is in full coat the limbs should be well feathered.

Coat—Should be dense, of fine quality and texture, flat as possible. Color: Black or Liver.

Bramcroft Dauntless making a fine retrieve of a
shackled, live duck at a field trial.

Parbreaker's Daring Doug

One of the top, modern Golden Retriever champions.

THE GOLDEN RETRIEVER

Here is a breed that has been wholeheartedly adopted by American dog fanciers and rightly so, for the Golden Retriever has much to recommend him.

The ancestry of the Golden follows the basic pattern found behind many of the other medium-sized retrieving breeds, namely the usage of prevalent water spaniels, setters, other hunting and water breeds, and the St. John's Newfoundland (also an essential breed in the ancestral backgrounds of the Curly-Coated, Flat-Coated, and Labrador Retrievers). Early Gordon Setters are also named as having been used in the formation of the Golden. It was at one time claimed that the Golden was a direct descendant of the "Russian Tracker," but the interbreeding of canine lines mentioned above is a much more logical explanation.

Lord Tweedmouth was the champion of the Golden Retriever, and he bred these dogs with the usual British thoroughness and care to establish a basic type and performance. His Guisachan estate on the Tweed River in southeast Scotland produced the first true Goldens. To achieve this triumph, his lordship crossed in a local Spaniel type, the Tweed Water Spaniel (very important to the end result), and an experimental cross or two of the Bloodhound and the Irish Setter.

At the present time the Golden Retriever occupies a high place of prominence with American dog lovers. He is a cherished pet and companion. He has the virtues of gentleness, trainability, loyalty and handsomeness. In the field, he is one of the finest performers. His thick undercoat laughs at the foulest weather. He is a most hardy breed and doesn't give up a retrieve even under very trying conditions. He has a soft mouth and has been used with great success on upland birds as well as on all types of waterfowl.

The Golden is particularly adaptable to obedience training and will usually be found competing in all-breed trials with great success.

On the show bench the Golden Retriever is one of the most successful breeds in the Sporting group. There are numerous good specimens being shown all over the United States and group wins by Goldens are most frequent.

It is not difficult to see why the Golden Retriever has been so enthusiastically accepted. His size, appearance, and ease of care combined with his intelligence and level disposition, have earned him the loyalty of many and the admiration of all.

A fine pair of Goldens.

STANDARD OF THE GOLDEN RETRIEVER

A symmetrical, powerful, active dog, sound and well put together, not clumsy or long in the leg, displaying a kindly expression and possessing a personality that is eager, alert and self-confident. Primarily a hunting dog, he should be shown in hard working condition. Over-all appearance, balance, gait and purpose to be given more emphasis than any of his component parts.

Size—Males, 23–24 inches in height at withers; females, 21½–22½. Length from breastbone to buttocks slightly greater than height at withers in ratio of 12–11. Weight for dogs 65–75 pounds; bitches, 60–70 pounds.

Head—Broad in skull, slightly arched laterally and longtidudinally without prominence of frontal or occipital bones. Good stop. Foreface deep and wide, nearly as long as skull. Muzzle, when viewed in profile, slightly deeper at stop than at tip; when viewed from above, slightly wider at stop than at tip. No heaviness in flews. Removal of whiskers for show purposes optional.

Eyes—Friendly and intelligent, medium large with dark rims, set well apart and reasonably deep in sockets. Color preferably dark brown, never lighter than color of coat. No white or haw visible when looking straight ahead.

Teeth—Scissors bite with lower incisors touching inside of upper incisors.

Nose—Black or dark brown, though lighter shade in cold weather not serious. Dudley nose (pink without pigmentation) to be faulted.

Ears—Rather short, hanging flat against head with rounded tips slightly below jaw. Forward edge attached well behind and just above eye with rear edge slightly below eye. Low, houndlike ear-set to be faulted.

Neck—Medium long, sloping well back into shoulders, giving sturdy muscular appearance with untrimmed natural ruff. No throatiness.

Body—Well balanced, short-coupled, deep through the heart. Chest at least as wide as a man's hand, including thumb. Brisket extends to elbows. Ribs long and well sprung but not barrel shaped, extending well to rear of

A practice retrieve.

body. Loin short, muscular, wide and deep, with very little tuck-up. Top line level from withers to croup, whether standing or moving. Croup slopes gently. Slabsidedness, narrow chest, lack of depth in brisket, excessive tuck-up, roach or sway back to be faulted.

Forequarters—Forequarters well co-ordinated with hindquarters and capable of free movement. Shoulder blades wide, long and muscular, showing angulation with upper arm of approximately 90 degrees. Legs straight with good bone. Pastern short and strong, sloping slightly forward with no suggestion of weakness.

Hindquarters—Well-bent stifles (angulation between femur and pelvis approximately 90 degrees) with hocks well let down. Legs straight when viewed from rear. Cow hocks and sickle hocks to be faulted.

Feet—Medium size, round and compact with thick pads. Excess hair may be trimmed to show natural size and contour. Open or splayed feet to be faulted.

Tail—Well set on, neither too high nor too low, following natural line of

A Golden Retriever doing the job it was bred to
do . . . retrieving a wounded duck in water.

croup. Length extends to hock. Carried with merry action with some upward curve but never curled over back nor between legs.

Color and Coat—Dense and water repellent with good undercoat. Texture not as hard as that of a shorthaired dog nor silky as that of a setter. Lies flat against body and may be straight or wavy. Moderate feathering on back of forelegs and heavier feathering on front of neck, back of thighs and underside of tail. Feathering may be lighter than rest of coat. Color lustrous golden of various shades. A few white hairs on chest permissible but not desirable. Further white markings to be faulted.

Gait—When trotting, gait is free, smooth, powerful and well-co-ordinated. Viewed from front or rear, legs turn neither in nor out, nor do feet cross or interfere with each other. Increased speed causes tendency of feet to converge toward center line of gravity.

DISQUALIFICATIONS

Deviation in height of more than one inch from standard either way. Undershot or overshot jaws. This condition not to be confused with misalignment of teeth. Trichiasis (abnormal position or direction of the eyelashes).

152

A fine show and field Labrador Retriever.

THE LABRADOR RETRIEVER

We are dealing with a very substantial and realistic breed in the Labrador Retriever which originally stemmed from a small variety of the Large New-foundland. This small, shortcoated variety, almost always black, was discovered at St. Johns, Newfoundland, and was reared there by the settlers on the coast. At that time they were called "small black water dogs," and later in England, to which they were taken in the fishing boats that plied their trade between Poole and Greenock harbors, were renamed the St. Johns Labrador.

The earliest importers were the Third Earl of Malmesbury, the Fifth Duke of Buccleuch and the Tenth Earl of Home and other sportsmen of that era, anxious to develop the breed for their own private sporting use and interest. In describing some of these early dogs in a letter, Lord Malmesbury wrote . . . "we always call mine Labrador dogs and I have kept the breed as pure as I could from the first I had at Poole . . . The breed may be known by having a close coat which turns off water like oil, and above all a tail like an otter."

The Labrador's unrivaled scenting powers, love of water and its innate gamefinding ability, plus a rugged physique and flawless stamina, were instru-mental, as time went on, in edging out the hitherto popular Curly-Coated and Flat-Coated Retrievers.

A black Labrador with a plump, land-retrieved ringneck, indicating the versatility of the Lab on both land and water.

From the 19th century on, the Labrador was developed to its highest potential in the British Isles for trials, upland shooting (including hare), and one of the most powerful of bench forces at dog shows. The Labrador could well be considered the "national" dog of England, so well represented is he in all walks of life other than those for which he was originally bred. He leads among breeds chosen for Guiding the Blind, his record as a mine detector in both Wars is unassailable, the air force is now using him as liaison dog through parachute jumping, and he has endeared himself to the London Police Brigade, who make use of him in tracking loiterers in Hyde Park and as an honor guard at Buckingham Palace. In the Commonwealth the Labrador is equally at home in India, Africa, Australia and Canada.

The Labrador Club of England was organized in 1916 and the American Club was formed in 1931. The breed's career in this country has been meteoric in its rise to popularity at field trials, rising numerically over all other retriever breeds and it is fast becoming known as an all around gundog and family companion. His enviable position is due not only to his qualities of endurance afield, but because he has an ideal and stable temperament, adaptable to any way of life, fastidious in his manners, and blessed with a short, practical coat which cannot become encumbered with ice or snow, nor marred by thorns or burrs.

His range of coat colors is varied to suit all tastes, from the orthodox black to the shades of yellow, and also a deep rich liver. The three principal breed characteristics of a typical Labrador are:—*Coat, Tail, Expression.*

No matter how good a Labrador may appear to be, he does not represent his breed completely if he does not have these three definite attributes, and he should possess them positively and obviously. The correct Labrador coat texture, regardless of color, is a harsh short outercoat, covering a wooly water resistant undercoat: the tail, aptly named "otter tail," is shaped somewhat like an otter's—very thick at the base, tapering gradually to a modest point at the end; it should not come below the hock when measured for length and may be carried gaily, but not at hound level or over the back. Expression hinges on the size and placement of the eyes, which should be neither too large or too small, too far apart or too close together; to a certain extent on their color, but the character of the dog should emerge with a kindly, soft, warm look that is typical.

STANDARD OF THE LABRADOR RETRIEVER

GENERAL APPEARANCE

The general appearance of the Labrador should be that of a strongly built, short-coupled, very active dog. He should be fairly wide over the loins, and strong and muscular in the hind quarters. The coat should be close, short, dense and free from feather.

DETAILED DESCRIPTION

Head—The skull should be wide, giving brainroom; there should be a slight "stop," i.e., the brow should be slightly pronounced, so that the skull is not absolutely in a straight line with the nose. The head should be clean cut and free from fleshy cheeks. The jaws should be long and powerful and free from snipiness; the nose should be wide and the nostrils well developed. Teeth should be strong and regular, with a level mouth.

The ears should hang moderately close to the head, rather far back, should be set somewhat low and not be large and heavy. The eyes should be of a medium size, expressing great intelligence and good temper, and can be brown, yellow or black, but brown or black is preferred.

Neck and Chest—The neck should be medium length and powerful and not throaty. The shoulders should be long and sloping.

The chest must be of good width and depth, the ribs well sprung and the loins wide and strong, stifles well turned, and the hind quarters well developed and of great power.

Legs and Feet—The legs must be straight from the shoulder to the ground, and the feet compact with toes well arched, and pads well developed; the hocks should be well bent, and the dog must neither be cowhocked nor be too

A hunter and his Labrador, a combination that can transform a sport into a forever heartwarming and memorable experience.

wide behind; in fact he must stand and move true all round on legs and feet. Legs should be of medium length, showing good bone and muscle, but not so short as to be out of balance with the rest of body. In fact, a dog well balanced in all points is preferable to one with outstanding good qualities and defects.

Tail—The tail is a distinctive feature of the breed; it should be very thick toward the base, gradually tapering towards the tip, of medium length, should be free from any feathering, and should be clothed thickly all around with the Labrador's short, thick, dense coat, thus giving that particular "rounded" appearance which has been described as the "otter" tail. The tail may be carried gaily but should not curl over the back.

Coat—The coat is another very distinctive feature; it should be short, very dense and without wave, and should give a fairly hard feeling to the hand.

Color—The colors are black, yellow, or chocolate and are evaluated as follows:

(*a*) Blacks: All black, with a small white spot on chest permissible. Eyes to be of medium size, expressing intelligence and good temper, preferably brown or hazel, although black or yellow is permissible.

(b) Yellows: Yellows may vary in color from fox-red to light cream with variations in the shading of the coat on ears, the underparts of the dog, or beneath the tail. A small white spot on chest is permissible. Eye coloring and expression should be the same as that of the blacks, with black or dark brown eye rims. The nose should also be black or dark brown, although "fading" to pink in winter weather is not serious. A "Dudley" nose (pink without pigmentation) should be penalized.

(c) Chocolates: Shades ranging from light sedge to chocolate. A small white spot on chest is permissible. Eyes to be light brown to clear yellow. Nose and eye rim pigmentation dark brown or liver colored. "Fading" to pink in winter weather not serious. "Dudley" nose should be penalized.

Movement—Movement should be free and effortless. The forelegs should be strong, straight and true, and correctly placed. Watching a dog move towards one, there should be no signs of elbows being out in front, but neatly held to the body with legs not too close together, but moving straight forward without pacing or weaving. Upon viewing the dog from the rear, one should get the impression that the hind legs, which should be well muscled and not cowhocked, move as nearly parallel as possible, with hocks doing their full share of work and flexing well, thus giving the appearance of power and strength.

Height at Shoulders—Dogs, $22\frac{1}{2}$ inches to $24\frac{1}{2}$ inches; bitches, $21\frac{1}{2}$ inches to $23\frac{1}{2}$ inches.

Champion Shamrock Acres Jim Dandy, a yellow Labrador.

THE ENGLISH SETTER

When we think of English Setters our thoughts are linked with fall and a brisk day in the colorful woods behind a good gundog. Indeed, the English Setter with the large amount of white generally found in his silky coat is the perfect dog for the multi-colored background of autumn foliage. Color is not, of course, the breed's main qualification as a gundog. For over a century the quality and usefulness of the English Setter in the field has been known to and acknowledged by all sportsmen.

The English Setter owes its working qualities to its basic origin, a mixture of proven sporting breeds mostly of Spanish origin. The old and breedy Spanish Pointer and Spanish land spaniels bulk large in the English Setter's geneology. Add also some of the genetic worth of the Springer Spaniel and large Water Spaniel of early times and you have the ingredients from which emerged the stylish and worthy English Setter.

In olden times in England it was customary to "net" game and the earliest English Setters were taught to point and then crouch, or "set" so that the net could be thrown over and beyond them to capture the birds. This practice gave rise to the name of the breed.

Major credit for the development of the breed as we know it today must go to Mr. Edward Laverack. In 1824 he received a pair of fine setters from a prominent breeder, the Reverend Harrison, who had been a fancier of the breed for over thirty-five years. Using this pair as foundation stock, Mr. Laverack produced the famous strain of setter that bears his name. Show dogs from this family were the basis for another equally famous family of setters, the Llewellyn strain, bred by Mr. R. L. Purcell Llewellyn. The Laveracks, crossed by this sportsman with north of England dogs (Duke-Rhoebes strain) produced stock of a distinct type that became the most successful field trial animals in sporting history.

The fame of both the Laverack and Llewellyn strains of English Setters soon spread to America from their native England and fine dogs of both strains were imported, generally the Laverack for show purposes and the Llewellyn to work in field trials. The Field Trial English Setter is generally lighter in build and with less lip and squareness of flews than the show dog.

Mild and sweet in temperament, the English Setter makes a marvelous family dog whom the children will all adore. In the outdoors he is a beautiful rugged, keen hunting dog who, in the environment for which he has been bred, has no peers.

STANDARD OF THE ENGLISH SETTER

Head—Long and lean, with a well-defined stop. The skull oval from ear to ear, of medium width, giving brain room but with no suggestion of coarseness, with but little difference between the width at base of skull and at brows and with a moderately defined occipital protuberance. Brows should be at a sharp

The typical chiseled beauty found in the "breedy" heads of Ryman Setters.

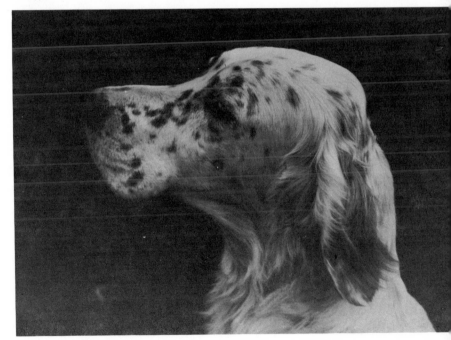

angle from the muzzle. Muzzle should be long and square, of width in harmony with the skull, without any fullness under the eyes and straight from eyes to tip of the nose. A dish face or Roman nose objectionable. The lips square and fairly pendant. Nose should be black or dark liver in color, except in white, lemon and white, orange and white, or liver and white dogs, when it may be of lighter color. Nostrils should be wide apart and large in the openings. Jaws should be of equal length. Overshot or undershot jaw objectionable. Ears should be carried close to the head, well back and set low, of moderate length, slightly rounded at the ends, and covered with silky hair. Eyes should be bright, mild, intelligent, and dark brown in color.

Neck—The neck should be long and lean, arched at the crest, and not too throaty.

Shoulders—Shoulders should be formed to permit perfect freedom of action to the forelegs. Shoulder blades should be long, wide, sloping moderately well back and standing fairly close together at the top.

Chest—Chest between shoulder blades should be of good depth but not of excessive width.

Ribs—Ribs, back of the shoulders, should spring gradually to the middle of the body and then taper to the back ribs, which should be of good depth.

Back—Back should be strong at its junction with the loin and should be straight or sloping upward very slightly to the top of the shoulder, the whole forming a graceful outline of medium length, without sway or drop. Loins should be strong, moderate in length, slightly arched, but not to the extent of being roached or wheel backed. Hip bones should be wide apart without too sudden drop to the root of the tail.

Forelegs—The arms should be flat and muscular, with bone fully developed

A field trial English Setter on point.

Champion Frenchtown Calico Flower.

and muscles hard and devoid of flabbiness; of good length from the point of the shoulder to the elbow, and set at such an angle as will bring the legs fairly under the dog. Elbows should have no tendency to turn either in or out. The pastern should be short, strong and nearly round with the slope from the pastern joint to the foot deviating very slightly forward from the perpendicular.

Hindlegs—The hindlegs should have wide, muscular thighs with well developed lower thighs. Stifles should be well bent and strong. Hocks should be wide and flat. The pastern should be short, strong and nearly round, with the slope from the pastern joint to the foot deviating very slightly forward from the perpendicular.

Feet—Feet should be closely set and strong, pads well developed and tough, toes well arched and protected with short, thick hair.

Tail—Tail should be straight and taper to a fine point, with only sufficient length to reach the hocks, or less. The feather must be straight and silky, falling loosely in a fringe and tapering to the point when the tail is raised. There must be no bushiness. The tail should not curl sideways or above the level of the back.

Coat—Coat should be flat and of good length, without curl; not soft or woolly. The feather on the legs should be moderately thin and regular.

Height—Dogs, about 25 inches; bitches, about 24 inches.

Colors—Black, white and tan; black and white; blue belton; lemon and white; lemon belton; orange and white; orange belton; liver and white; liver belton; and solid white.

Markings—Dogs without heavy patches of color on the body, but flecked all over preferred.

Symmetry—The harmony of all parts to be considered. Symmetrical dogs will have level backs or be very slightly higher at the shoulders than at the hips. Balance, harmony of proportion, and an appearance of breeding and quality to be looked for, and coarseness avoided.

Movement and Carriage—An easy, free and graceful movement, suggesting rapidity and endurance. A lively tail and a high carriage of head. Stiltiness, clumsiness or a lumbering gait are objectionable.

SCALE OF POINTS

Head		*Points*
Skull	5	
Ears	5	
Eyes	5	
Muzzle	5	20

Body		
Neck	5	
Chest and Shoulders	12	
Back, Loin and Ribs	10	27

Running Gear		
Forelegs	5	
Hips, Thighs and Hindlegs	12	
Feet	6	23

Coat		
Length and Texture	5	
Color and Marking	3	8

Tail		
Length and Carriage	5	5

General Appearance and Action		
Symmetry, Style and Movement	12	
Size	5	17
Total	100	100

Champion Buddy D of Han Mar

THE GORDON SETTER

The fourth Duke of Gordon, in the latter part of the 18th century, brought into prominence the black and tan setter of Scotland, which eventually, as a breed, adopted his name. Popular among sportsmen of Scotland for decades, the breed was then very much as it is now in type and usefulness.

Some earlier writers speak of the Gordon as a north British breed, used chiefly on the red grouse of the heather-grown uplands. But when we delve deeply into the breed's background we cannot deny its Scottish ancestry. North British Gordons must have come from Scotland originally.

The Gordon, like other sporting breeds, owes its beginnings to the Spanish Pointer, various early Spaniels, especially those of Spanish origin, and a specific, black, tan and white Spaniel from which came the basic color selected for by Scottish huntsmen.

Gordons have beauty and brains and a head chock full of bird sense. They are easy to train, back well and, though not fast dogs in the field, are steady and will hunt from morning until night without tiring if, of course, they are in hunting condition. Because of their staunchness in the field they have won the name of being a real "meat" dog, or a setter that delivers a full bag for each day's shooting.

Gordon breeders have had the good sense not to make a distinction between the bench and the field dog. The result is consistent quality in the breed, year after year, on the bench and in the field.

The size of the breed varies considerably to suit various terrain in widely spaced sections of the country. But the Gordon's beauty, rich coloring, birdiness, style and sturdiness never vary. His quiet, clean, gentlemanly deportment in the house and his gentleness with youngsters make the Gordon an excellent pet and home companion.

But remember that this beautiful aristocrat of ancient canine lineage is essentially a gentleman's hunting dog, a shooting companion of unexcelled usefulness in the field and is, therefore, always at his best as a hunting dog.

STANDARD OF THE GORDON SETTER

General Impression—A good-sized, sturdily-built dog, well muscled, with plenty of bone and substance, but active, upstanding and stylish, appearing capable of doing a full day's work in the field. Strong, rather short back, well-sprung ribs and short tail, a fairly heavy head, finely chiseled, intelligent, noble and dignified expression, showing no signs of shyness; clear colors and straight or slightly waved coat. A dog that suggests strength and stamina rather than extreme speed.

Size—Shoulder height for males 24 inches to 27 inches; for females 23 inches to 26 inches.

Weight—Males 55 pounds to 75 pounds; females 45 pounds to 65 pounds.

As a guide the greater heights and weights are to be preferred, provided that character and quality are also combined. Dogs over and under these heights and weights are to be discouraged.

Head—Deep rather than broad with plenty of brain room, nicely rounded good size skull, broadest between the ears. The head should have a clearly indicated stop. Below and above the eyes should be lean and the cheek as narrow as the leanness of the head allows. The muzzle fairly long with almost parallel lines and not pointed either as seen from above or from the side. The flews not pendulous but with clearly indicated lips. The nose big, broad with open nostrils and of black color.

Eyes—Of fair size, neither too deep set nor too bulging, dark brown, bright and wise.

Ears—Set low on the head, fairly large and thin.

Neck—Long, lean, arched to the head and without throatiness.

Shoulders—Should be fine at the points, deep and sloping well back, giving a moderately sloping topline.

Chest—Deep and not too broad in front; the ribs well sprung leaving plenty of lung room.

Forelegs—Big boned, straight, not bowed, either in or out with elbows free, well let down and not inclined either in or out.

Hind Legs—The hind legs from hip to hock should be long, flat, and muscular, from hock to heel short and strong. The stifle and hock joints well bent, and not inclined either in or out.

Feet—Both fore and hind feet should have close knit, well-arched toes with plenty of hair between with full toe pads and deep heel cushions.

Tail—Short and should not reach below the hocks, carried horizontal or nearly so, thick at the root and finishing in a fine point. The feather, which starts near the root of the tail, should be slightly waved or straight, have a three square appearance growing shorter uniformly toward the end.

Coat—Should be soft and shining resembling silk, straight or slightly waved—the latter preferred—but not curly, with long hair on ears, under stomach and on chest, on back of the fore and hind legs to the feet.

Color and Markings—Deep, shining coal black with tan markings, either of rich chestnut or mahogany red color. The tan should be shining and not dull, yellowish nor straw color and not mixed with black hairs. Black penciling allowed on toes. The border lines between black and tan colors should be clearly defined. There should not be any tan hairs mixed in the black.

Symmetry and quality are most essential. A dog well balanced in all points is preferable to one with outstanding good qualities and defects. A smooth free movement with high head carriage.

TAN MARKINGS

1. Two clear spots over the eyes not over three-quarters of an inch in diameter.
2. On the sides of the muzzle, the tan should not reach above the base of nose, resembling a stripe around the end of the muzzle from one side to the other.
3. On the throat.
4. Two large, clear spots on the chest.
5. On the inside of the hind legs and inside of thighs showing down the front of the stifle and broadening out to the outside of the hind legs from the hock to the toes. It must, however, not completely eliminate the black on the back of hind legs.
6. On the forelegs from the knees or a little above downward to the toes.
7. Around the vent.

A white spot on the chest is allowed, but the smaller the better.

GORDON SETTER FAULTS

General Impression—Unintelligent appearance. The Bloodhound type with heavy and big head and ears and clumsy body; as well as the Collie type with its pointed muzzle and curved tail, or showing any signs of shyness.

Head—Houndy, pointed, snipy, drooping or upturned muzzle, too small or large mouth.

Eyes—Too light in color, too deep set, or too prominent.

Ears—Set too high or unusually broad or heavy.

Neck—Thick and short.

Shoulders and Back—Irregularly formed.

Chest—Too broad.

Legs and Feet—Crooked legs. Outturned elbows. The toes scattered, flat-footed.

Tail—Too long, badly carried or hooked at the end.

Coat—Curly like wool, not shining.

Color—Yellow or straw colored tan or without clearly defined lines between the different colors. White feet. Too much white on the chest. In the black there must be no tan hairs. It appears often around the eyes.

Champion Cherry Point Brask

THE IRISH SETTER

If there was a pentathlon for dogs, the Irish Red Setter, as he once was called, might well be the winner. Already the breed boasts individuals holding titles for achievement in three divisions: Champion on the Bench; Champion in the Field; holder of highest degree in Obedience. To acquire the fourth and fifth is easy—household companion superb; gentle, intelligent playmate for a child. Yes, the pentathlon could be his.

Agile and very spirited, the graceful Irish Setter was at the beginning a red and white dog, thought to have evolved from setting spaniels of that coloration in or about the eighteenth century. Through succeeding generations, breeders consistently favored in their selections the solid color, until today this dog is an all-red fellow with but a few white hairs, if any, remaining. And what a red it is! Ranging from the deep rich tint of a chestnut in autumn to an even darker and richer mahogany shade, it appears that here Nature has permitted man to develop one animal as eye-catching as some of her most brilliant autumn foliage. Clothed by this mantle of beauty are a temperament and disposition to match, with just a neat little touch of Irish wit and mischief for flavor.

It is perhaps in the specific area of disposition that the gay, red Irish dog excels. Disposition and adaptability. Watch him fly across the fields searching out the birds he so enjoys finding for you, and you can scarcely imagine that this is the same animal which, an hour earlier, was playing some gentle game with your children—HIS children—or maybe receiving visitors for you indoors with the relaxed courtesy of a good host, before lying down quietly to enjoy their presence.

He likes to make decisions of his own; but if his upbringing has been good his reaction to your decision is immediate. This delightful responsiveness shines clearly in his soft fine eyes, projected by the inborn sweetness of the dog's nature. The sweetness, in particular, cannot be missed, for it is written unmistakably in each warm, chiseled line of the Irish Setter's face.

STANDARD OF THE IRISH SETTER

General Appearance—The Irish Setter is an active, aristocratic bird-dog, rich red in color, substantial yet elegant in build. Standing over two feet tall at the shoulder, the dog has a straight, fine, glossy coat, longer on ears, chest, tail and back of legs. Afield he is a swift-moving hunter; at home, a sweet-natured, trainable companion. His is a rollicking personality.

Head—Long and lean, its length at least double the width between the ears. The brow is raised, showing a distinct stop midway between the tip of nose and the well-defined occiput (rear point of skull). Thus the nearly level line from occiput to brow is set a little above, and parallel to, the straight and equal line from eye to nose. The skull is oval when viewed from above or front; very slightly domed when viewed in profile. Beauty of head is emphasized by delicate chiseling along the muzzle, around and below the eyes, and along the cheeks. Muzzle moderately deep, nostrils wide, jaws of nearly equal length. Upper lips fairly square but not pendulous, the underline of the jaws being almost parallel with the top line of the muzzle. The teeth meet in a scissors bite in which the upper incisors fit closely over the lower, or they may meet evenly.

Nose—Black or chocolate.

Eyes—Somewhat almond-shaped, of medium size, placed rather well apart; neither deep-set nor bulging. Color, dark to medium brown. Expression soft yet alert.

Ears—Set well back and low, not above level of eye. Leather thin, hanging in a neat fold close to the head, and nearly long enough to reach the nose.

Neck—Moderately long, strong but not thick, and slightly arched; free from throatiness, and fitting smoothly into the shoulders.

Body—Sufficiently long to permit a straight and free stride. Shoulder blades long, wide, sloping well back, fairly close together at the top, and joined in front to long upper arms angled to bring the elbows slightly rearward along the brisket. Chest deep, reaching approximately to the elbows; rather

narrow in front. Ribs well sprung. Loins of moderate length, muscular and slightly arched. Top line of body from withers to tail slopes slightly downward without sharp drop at the croup. Hindquarters should be wide and powerful with broad, well-developed thighs.

Legs and Feet—All legs sturdy, with plenty of bone, and strong, nearly straight pasterns. Feet rather small, very firm, toes arched and close. Forelegs straight and sinewy, the elbows moving freely. Hind legs long and muscular from hip to hock, short and nearly perpendicular from hock to ground; well angulated at stifle and hock joints, which, like the elbows, incline neither in nor out.

Tail—Strong at root, tapering to fine point, about long enough to reach the hock. Carriage straight or curving slightly upward, nearly level with the back.

Coat—Short and fine on head, forelegs and tips of ears; on all other parts, of moderate length and flat. Feathering long and silky on ears; on back of forelegs and thighs long and fine, with a pleasing fringe of hair on belly and brisket extending onto the chest. Feet well feathered between the toes. Fringe on tail moderately long and tapering. All coat and feathering as straight and free as possible from curl or wave.

Color—Mahogany or rich chestnut red, with no trace of black. A small amount of white on chest, throat, or toes, or a narrow, centered streak on skull, is not to be penalized.

Size—There is no disqualification as to size. The make and fit of all parts and their overall *balance* in the animal are rated more important. Twenty-seven inches at the withers with a show weight of about 70 pounds is considered ideal for a dog; the bitch 25 inches, 60 pounds. Variance beyond an inch up or down to be discouraged.

Gait—At the trot the gait is big, very lively, graceful and efficient. The head is held high. The hindquarters drive smoothly and with great power. The forelegs reach well ahead as if to pull in the ground, without giving the appearance of a hackney gait. The dog runs as he stands: straight. Seen from the front or rear, the forelegs, as well as the hind legs below the hock joint, move perpendicularly to the ground, with some tendency towards a single track as speed increases. But a crossing or weaving of the legs, front or back, is objectionable.

Balance—At his best the lines of the Irish Setter so satisfy in overall balance that artists have termed him the most beautiful of all dogs. The correct specimen always exhibits balance whether standing or in motion. Each part of the dog flows and fits smoothly into its neighboring parts without calling attention to itself.

At the left is Champion Oxton's Irish Perfection, C.D.X., an Irish Setter who has proven himself in the show ring, the obedience ring and in the field, a rare combination of beauty, intelligence and utility.

Wildwood Penelope

THE AMERICAN WATER SPANIEL

The American Water Spaniel is one of the few native American breeds, and unfortunately, one of the most rarely seen.

The breed traces back to somewhere in the mid-nineteenth century. He was developed in the midwestern area of the United States, probably in the vicinity of the State of Michigan. It is generally thought that the American Water Spaniel was developed from the Curly-Coated Retriever, the Irish Water Spaniel and the now extinct, Old English Water Spaniel. There are similarities in his physical appearance to these breeds to adequately substantiate this supposed ancestry.

The American Water Spaniel is a medium-sized shooting dog ranging from 25 to 45 pounds and standing from 15 to 18 inches at the withers.

It is difficult to understand why this breed should not be better known. As a hunting companion he is truly first rate. Equally adept on fur as well as feather, he is extremely rugged and can make retrieves under the most trying conditions, on land as well as in water. His thick, curly coat is made to withstand cold and dampness and his remarkable memory can record the fall of as many as five birds or more which he can then locate exactly and return to the game bag.

His talents are not only limited to the hunting field. Those that know him claim he is an alert guard dog and a very pleasant companion in the home.

The appearances that the breed has made at shows have brought forth favorable comment. This is true for obedience competition as well as the show bench. The breed's inherent good sense stands it in good stead in formal obedience trials.

At one time supporters of the breed were reluctant to have the American Water Spaniel a recognized breed for fear that interest in showing would diminish its usefulness as a shooting dog. But this did not happen and the breed was recognized by the American Kennel Club in 1940 and has been in the AKC Stud Book ever since.

STANDARD OF THE AMERICAN WATER SPANIEL

General Appearance—Medium in size, of sturdy typical spaniel character, curly coat, an active muscular dog, with emphasis placed on proper size and conformation, correct head properties, texture of coat and color. Of amicable disposition; demeanor indicates intelligence, strength and endurance.

Head—Moderate in length, skull rather broad and full, stop moderately defined, but not too pronounced. Forehead covered with short smooth hair and without tuft or topknot. Muzzle of medium length, square and with no inclination to snipiness, jaws strong and of good length, and neither undershot nor overshot, teeth straight and well shaped. Nose sufficiently wide and with well developed nostrils to insure good scenting power.

Faults—Very flat skull, narrow across the top, long, slender or snipy muzzle.

Eyes—Hazel, brown or of dark tone to harmonize with coat; set well apart. Expression alert, attractive, intelligent.

Fault—Yellow eyes to disqualify.

Ears—Lobular, long and wide, not set too high on head, but slightly above the eyeline. Leather extending to end of nose and well covered with close curls.

Neck—Round and of medium length, strong and muscular, free of throatiness, set to carry head with dignity, but arch not accentuated.

Body Structure—Well developed, sturdily constructed but not too compactly coupled. General outline is a symmetrical relationship of parts. Shoulders sloping, clean and muscular. Strong loins, lightly arched, and well furnished, deep brisket but not excessively broad. Well sprung ribs. Legs of medium length and well boned, but not so short as to handicap for field work.

Legs and Feet—Forelegs powerful and reasonably straight. Hindlegs firm with suitable bent stifles and strong hocks well let down. Feet to harmonize with size of dog. Toes closely grouped and well padded.

Fault—Cow hocks.

Tail—Moderate in length, curved in a slightly rocker shape, carried slightly below level of back; tapered and covered with hair to tip, action lively.

Faults—Rat or shaved tail.

Coat—The coat should be closely curled or have marcel effect and should be of sufficient density to be of protection against weather; water or punishing cover, yet not coarse. Legs should have medium short, curly feather.

Faults—Coat too straight, soft, fine or tightly kinked.

Color—Solid liver or dark chocolate, a little white on toes or chest permissible.

Height—15 to 18 inches at the shoulder.

Weight—Males 28 to 45 pounds; females 25 to 40 pounds.

DISQUALIFICATION

Yellow eyes.

Field Champion Ronile Avant Courier

THE BRITTANY SPANIEL

The Brittany Spaniel is a French hunting dog of great and unique ability in the field, for he not only has the spaniel's characteristic ability to retrieve but he is also the only spaniel that points his game—and does so in a very stylish manner.

This is an ancient breed that can be traced back, as can all these gun dog breeds, to early Spanish stock and, once seen in the field, there can be no doubt in the viewer's mind that the Brittany came from the same stock and was originally bred like the various setter breeds.

Wisely, admirers of the breed allow no cleavage in type between bench and field dogs.

The first tail-less ancestor of the Brittany appeared about 100 years ago in Pontou, France. Eventually the breed was adopted by Arthur Enaud, a Gallic sportsman with a deep working knowledge of genetics. He used several European Pointers sparingly and selected rigidly for coat and color as well as type and established the modern version of this delightful and worthwhile breed.

This is a wide-ranging, agile, versatile dog who is sensitive but hardy, rugged, yet light in bone and quick in movement. Since first being imported to America in 1931, the Brittany Spaniel has become a favorite in sporting circles here.

174

STANDARD OF THE BRITTANY SPANIEL

General Description—A compact, closely knit dog of medium size, a leggy spaniel having the appearance as well as the agility of a great ground coverer. Strong, vigorous, energetic and quick of movement. Not too light in bone, yet never heavy boned and cumbersome. Ruggedness, without clumsiness, is a characteristic of the breed. So leggy is he that his height at the withers is the same as the length of his body. He has no tail, or at most, not more than 4 inches.

Weight—Should weigh between 30 and 40 pounds.

Height—17½ to 20½ inches—measured from the ground to the highest point of the back—the withers.

Disqualifications—Any Brittany Spaniel measuring under 17½ inches or over 20½ inches shall be disqualified from bench show competition. Any black in the coat or a completely black nose shall disqualify.

Coat—Hair dense, flat or wavy, never curly. Not as fine as in other spaniel breeds, and never silky. Furnishings not profuse. The ears should carry little fringe. Neither the front nor hind legs should carry heavy featherings.

Note : Long, curly, or silky hair is a fault. Any tendency toward excessive feathering should be severely penalized, as undesirable in a sporting dog which must face burrs and heavy cover.

Skin—Fine and fairly loose. (A loose skin rolls with briars and sticks, thus diminishing punctures or tearing. But a skin so loose as to form pouches is undesirable.)

Color—Dark orange and white, or liver and white. Some ticking is desirable, but not so much as to produce belton patterns. Roan patterns or factors of orange or liver shade are permissible. The orange and liver are found in standard parti-color, or piebald patterns. Washed out or faded colors are not desirable. Black is a disqualification.

Skull—Medium length (approximately 4¾ inches). Rounded, very slightly wedge shaped, but evenly made. Width, not quite as wide as the length (about 4⅜ inches) and never so broad as to appear coarse, or so narrow as to appear racy. Well defined, but gently sloping stop effect. Median line rather indistinct. The occipital crest only apparent to the touch. Lateral walls well rounded. The Brittany should never be "apple headed" and he should never have an indented stop. (All measurements of skull are for a 19½ inch dog.)

Muzzle—Medium length, about two thirds the length of the skull, measuring the muzzle from the tip to the stop, and the skull from the occipital crest to the stop between the eyes. Muzzle should taper gradually in both horizontal and vertical dimensions as it approaches the nostrils. Neither a Roman nose nor a concave curve (dish face) is desirable. Never broad, heavy, or snipy.

Nose—Nostrils well open to permit deep gulping of air and adequate scenting while at top speed. Tight nostrils should be penalized. Never shiny. Color brown, tan, or deep pink. A pure black nose is a disqualification.

Nasal Membranes—Should be as dark as possible—the color of tobacco juice, or bluish purple. Many breeders believe off-color noses are linked with undesirable character faults.

Eyes—Well set into the head. Well protected from briars by a heavy, expressive eyebrow. A prominent, full, or pop eye should be heavily penalized. It is a serious fault in a hunting dog who must face briars. Skull well chiseled under the eyes, so that the lower lid is not pulled back to form a pocket or haw for catching seeds, dirt, and weed dust. Judges should check by forcing head down to see if lid falls away from the eye. Preference should be for darker colored eyes, though lighter shades of amber should not be penalized.

Ears—Set high, above the level of the eyes. Short and leafy, rather than pendulous, reaching about half the length of the muzzle. Should lie flat and close to the head, with the tip rounded very slightly. Ears well covered with dense, but relatively short hair, and with little fringe.

Lips—Tight to the muzzle, with the upper lip overlapping the lower jaw only sufficiently to cover under lip. Lips dry so that feathers do not stick. Drooling to receive a heavy penalty. Flews, to be penalized.

Teeth—Well joined incisors. Posterior edge of upper incisors in contact with anterior edge of lower incisors, thus giving a true scissors bite. Over, or under shot jaw to be penalized heavily.

Neck—Medium length. Not quite permitting the dog to place his nose on the ground without bending his legs. Free from throatiness, though not a serious fault unless accompanied by dewlaps. Strong, without giving the impression of being over-muscled. Well set into sloping shoulders. Never concave or ewe-necked.

Body Length—Approximately the same as the height when measured at the withers. Body length is measured from the point of the forechest to the rear of the haunches. A long body should be heavily penalized.

Withers—Shoulder blades should not protrude much. Not too widely set apart with perhaps two thumbs' width or less between the blades. At the withers, the Brittany is slightly higher than at the rump.

Shoulders—Sloping and muscular. Blade and upper arm should form nearly a 90-degree angle when measured from the posterior point of the blade at the withers to the junction of the blade and upper arm, and thence to the point of the elbow nearest the ribs. Straight shoulders do not permit sufficient reach.

Back—Short and straight. Slight slope from highest point of withers to the root of the tail. Never hollow, saddle, sway or roached backed. Slight drop from hips to root of tail. Distance from last rib to upper thigh short, about three to four finger widths.

Chest—Deep, reaching the level of the elbow. Neither so wide nor so rounded as to disturb the placement of the shoulder bones and elbows, which causes a paddling movement, and often causes soreness from elbow striking ribs. Ribs well sprung, but adequate heart room provided by depth as well as width. Narrow or slab sided chests are a fault.

Flanks—Rounded. Fairly full. Not extremely tucked up, nor yet flabby and falling. Loins short and strong. Narrow and weak loins are a fault. In motion the loin should not sway sideways, giving a zigzag motion to the back, wasting energy.

Hind Quarters—Broad, strong and muscular, with powerful thighs and well bent stifles, giving a hip set well into the loin and the marked angulation necessary for a powerful drive when in motion. Fat and falling hind quarters are a fault.

Tail—Naturally tailless, or not over four inches long. Natural or docked. Set on high, actually an extention of the spine at about the same level.

Front Legs—Viewed from the front, perpendicular, but not set too wide as in the case of a dog loaded in shoulder. Elbows and feet turning neither in nor out. Viewed from the side, practically perpendicular to the pastern. Pastern

The Brittany is the only member of the spaniel family that points. This breed is probably very much like the earliest spaniels from which came the various sporting dogs. Below, the Brittany bench champion, Bonnie Kay's Ricki's Image.

BEST SPORTING

slightly bent to give cushion to stride. Not so straight as in terriers. Falling pasterns, however, are a serious fault. Leg bones clean, graceful, but not too fine. An extremely heavy bone is as much a fault as spindly legs. One must look for substance and suppleness. Height to the elbows should approximately equal distance from elbow to withers.

Hind Legs—Stifles well bent. The stifle generally is the term used for knee joint. If the angle made by the upper and lower leg bones is too straight, the dog quite generally lacks drive, since his hind legs cannot drive as far forward at each stride as is desirable. However, the stifle should not be bent as to throw the hock joint far out behind the dog. Since factors not easily seen by the eye may give the dog his proper drive, a Brittany should not be condemned for straight stifle until the judge has checked the dog in motion from the side. When at a trot, the Brittany's hind foot should step into or beyond the print left by the front foot.

The stifle joint should not turn out making a cowhock. (The cowhock moves the foot out to the side, thus driving out of line, and losing reach at each stride.) Thighs well feathered, but not profusely, half way to the hock. Hocks, that is, the back pasterns, should be moderately short, pointing neither in nor out; perpendicular when viewed from the side. They should be firm when shaken by the judge.

Feet—Should be strong, proportionately smaller than other spaniels, with close fitting, well arched toes and thick pads. The Brittany is not "up on his toes." Toes not heavily feathered. Flat feet, splayed feet, paper feet, etc., are to be heavily penalized. An ideal foot is half way between the hare and cat foot.

A Guide to the Judge—The points below indicate only relative values. To be also taken into consideration are type, gait, soundness, spirit, optimum height, body length and general proportions.

SCALE OF POINTS

	Points
Head	25
Body	35
Running Gear	40
Total	**100**

DISQUALIFICATIONS

Any Brittany Spaniel measuring under 17½ inches or over 20½ inches. Any black in the coat or a nose so dark in color as to appear black. A tail substantially more than 4 inches in length.

Champion Patrice de Sharvogue

Anchorfield Bishop

THE CLUMBER SPANIEL

The aristocratic Clumber Spaniel is the heaviest of all land spaniels. His long, low-slung body suggests crosses with the Basset Hound and the old Alpine Spaniel. This connection is seen in his general conformation and the haws of his eyes, which are considerably more prominent than those of other spaniels.

The Clumber's name was derived from Clumber Park, the home of the Duke of Newcastle. It was here that the Duc de Noailles sent some dogs just before the beginning of the French Revolution. The dogs were bred and perfected in type in their new English home.

The first classes for Clumber Spaniels were offered at English shows in 1859 and the breed became recognized by the American Kennel Club in 1883.

The Clumber has always enjoyed a moderate amount of popularity in England and maintains a few loyal friends among the American dog-loving fraternity.

The slow-moving Clumber makes the ideal hunting companion for a man past his prime who likes to take his gunning easy.

A slow-moving dog afield, he is nevertheless a thorough, efficient worker that can retrieve as well as mark fallen game. Those who have hunted over him prefer his leisurely pace, and he is most useful for older men who still like a day's sport with a gun and a dog.

The Clumber is always white and may have lemon or orange markings on the ears and body, the fewer markings the better. He may also have lemon or orange ticking on the legs and muzzle. His weight range is between 35 and 65 pounds and his height is slightly more than that of an English Springer Spaniel.

Though low on the leg the Clumber is a large and powerful dog. Few in number in the U. S., the Clumber will always have his champions in England.

The grave intelligence and quiet placidity of the Clumber Spaniel is mirrored in this lovely photographic head study.

STANDARD OF THE CLUMBER SPANIEL

General Appearance and Size—General appearance, a long, low, heavy-looking dog, of a very thoughtful expression, betokening great intelligence. Should have the appearance of great power. Sedate in all movements, but not clumsy. Weight of dogs averaging between 55 and 65 pounds; bitches from 35 to 50 pounds.

Head—Head large and massive in all its dimensions; round above eyes, flat on top, with a furrow running from between the eyes upon the center. A marked stop and large occipital protuberance. Jaw long, broad and deep. Lips of upper jaw overhung. Muzzle not square, but at the same time powerful looking. Nostrils large, open and flesh-colored, sometimes cherry-colored.

Eyes—Eyes large, soft, deep set and showing haw. Hazel in color, not too pale, with dignified and intelligent expression.

Ears—Ears long and broad at the top, turned over on the front edge; vine-shaped: close to the head; set on low and feathered only on the front edge, and there but slightly. Hair short and silky, without the slightest approach to wave or curl.

Neck and Shoulders—Neck long, thick and powerful, free from dewlap, with a large ruff. Shoulders immensely strong and muscular, giving a heavy appearance in front.

Body and Quarters—Body very long and low, well ribbed up and long in the coupling. Chest of great depth and volume. Loin powerful and not too much arched. Back long, broad and straight, free from droop or bow. Length an important characteristic; the nearer the dog is in length to being two and one-half times his height at shoulder the better. Quarters shapely and very muscular, neither drooping nor stilty.

Legs and Feet—Forelegs short, straight and immensely heavy in bone. Well in at elbows. Hindlegs heavy in bone, but not as heavy as forelegs. No feather above hocks, but thick hair on back of legs just above foot. Feet large, compact and plentifully filled with hair between toes.

Coat and Feathers—Coat silky and straight, not too long, extremely dense; feather long and abundant.

Color and Markings—Color, lemon and white, and orange and white. Fewer markings on body the better. Perfection of markings, solid lemon or orange ears, evenly marked head and eyes, muzzle and legs ticked.

Stern—Stern set on a level and carried low.

SCALE OF POINTS

	Points
General appearance and size	10
Head	15
Eyes	5
Ears	10
Neck and shoulders	15
Body and quarters	20
Legs and feet	10
Coat and feather	10
Color and marking	5
Total	100

Champion Carmor's Rise and Shine

THE COCKER SPANIEL

The "merry Cocker" is one of the most popular purebreds in the world due to his small size, fine character, beauty, field ability and showmanship. An active, playful, intelligent dog, he is the smallest of the spaniels and his name was derived from his hunting ability on woodcock.

Actually, though an excellent gun dog, the Cocker's popularity grew out of his exceptional qualities as a pet and companion. Combine his bright, adaptable, trustworthy, temperament with handy size and a wide range of color, solid and parti-color, and the reason for this likeable little dog's popularity is easily recognized.

The Spaniels are among the world's oldest dog breeds, coming from ancient Spanish stock and borrowing their family name, Spaniel, from the country of their origin. Like all Spaniels of today, the Cocker has undergone many changes in type over the years. Many famous kennel names were, not so long ago, prominent in Cocker history.

One of the most important dogs in Cocker history was the great Red Brucie, owned by Mr. H. E. Mellenthin in the early 1920's, the foundation dog for his My Own Kennels as well as for the breed in general. Later came Torohill Trader, a black dog whose advanced type helped change the Cocker standard. Both of these dogs were evidently mutants and were the basis upon which the modern Cocker was built.

Today the Cocker Spaniel is, thanks to these early pioneers, one of the best known of purebred dogs. He can be solid black, any shade of tan from silver buff to deep red, black and tan, parti-colored or tricolored.

The Cocker that is seen on the bench owns one of the richest coats in dogdom; long and thick with a high sheen and beautiful deep waves. He is a very successful competitor in Sporting group and all breed competition, accounting for numerous top awards at many of the most important shows in the United States.

The Cocker that is seen in the field is another matter. He is more suited to field work than his bench cousin. With his much less profuse furnishings, longer legs and muzzle, he gives an excellent account of himself whether he is in a field trial or just out for a day's shooting under his owner's gun.

The Cocker can fill any bill, whether as a pet, a show dog, or a gentleman's shooting dog. If you like to hunt and are looking for a dog, check on the Cocker Spaniel. He may be small, but he packs a lot of dog into his little, busy frame.

STANDARD OF THE COCKER SPANIEL

Skull—Well developed and rounded with no tendency towards flatness, or pronounced roundness, of the crown (dome). The forehead smooth, the eyebrows and stop clearly defined, the median line distinctly marked and gradually disappearing until lost rather more than halfway up to the crown. The bony structure surrounding the socket of the eye should be well chiseled; there should be no suggestion of fullness under the eyes nor prominence in the cheeks which, like the sides of the muzzle, should present a smooth, clean-cut appearance.

Muzzle and Teeth—To attain a well-proportioned head, which above all should be in balance with the rest of the dog, the distance from the tip of the nose to the stop at a point on a line drawn across the top of the muzzle between the front corners of the eyes, should approximate one-half the distance from the stop at this point up over the crown to the base of the skull. The muzzle should be broad and deep, with square, even jaws. The upper lip should be of sufficient depth to cover the lower jaw, presenting a square appearance. The teeth should be sound and regular and set at right angles to their respective jaws. The relation of the upper teeth to the lower should be that of scissors, with the inner surface of the upper in contact with the outer surface of the lower when the jaws are closed. The nose of sufficient size to balance the muzzle and foreface, with well-developed nostrils, and black in color in the blacks and black and tans; in the reds, buffs, livers and parti-colors, and in the roans it may be black or brown, the darker coloring being preferable.

Eyes—The eyeballs should be round and full and set in the surrounding tissue to look directly forward and give the eye a slightly almond-shape appearance. The eye should be neither weak nor goggled. The expression should be intelligent, alert, soft and appealing. The color of the iris should be dark brown to black in the blacks, black and tans, buffs and creams, and in the darker shades of the parti-colors and roans. In the reds, dark hazel; in the livers, parti-colors, and roans of the lighter shades, not lighter than hazel, the darker the better.

Ears—Lobular, set on a line no higher than the lower part of the eye, the leather fine and extending to the nostrils; well clothed with long, silky, straight or wavy hair.

Champion Treasure Hill Masterpiece

Neck and Shoulders—The neck sufficiently long to allow the nose to reach the ground easily, muscular and free from pendulous "throatiness." It should rise strongly from the shoulders and arch slightly as it tapers to join the head. The shoulders deep, clean-cut and sloping without protrusion and so set that the upper points of the withers are at an angle which permits a wide spring of rib.

Body—Its height at the withers should approximate the length from the withers to the set-on of tail. The chest deep, its lowest point no higher than the elbows, its front sufficiently wide for adequate heart and lung space, yet not so wide as to interfere with the straight forward movement of the forelegs. Ribs deep and well-sprung throughout. Body short in the couplings and flank, with its depth at the flank somewhat less than at the last rib. Back strong and sloping evenly and slightly downward from the withers to the set-on of tail. Hips wide with quarters well-rounded and muscular. The body should appear short, compact and firmly knit together, giving the impression of strength.

Legs and Feet—Forelegs straight, strongly boned and muscular and set close to the body well under the scapulae. The elbows well let down and turning neither in nor out. The pasterns short and strong. The hindlegs strongly-boned and muscled, with well-turned stifles and powerful, clearly defined thighs. The hocks strong, well let down and parallel when in motion and at rest. Feet compact, not spreading, round and firm, with deep, strong horny pads and hair between the toes; they should turn neither in nor out.

Tail—Set on and carried on a line with the topline of the back, and when the dog is at work its action should be incessant.

Coat—Flat or slightly waved, soft and dense; the ears, chest, abdomen and legs fairly well feathered.

Field Trial Champion Prince Tom III, U.D.

186

Color and Markings—Blacks should be jet black, those showing shadings of brown or liver in the sheen of the coat or feathering should be penalized though not disqualified; solid colors other than black should be of sound shade, but lighter colored feathering, while not favored, does not disqualify; a small amount of white on the chest *and throat* of solid colors should be *penalized*, but does not disqualify; white in any other location on solid colors does disqualify.

In Parti-Colors at least two definite colors appearing in clearly defined markings distinctly distributed over the body are essential. Dogs (excepting black and tans) which are in the opinion of the judge 90 percent or more one solid color and possess limited markings of another color on the skull, neck, toes or other locations are to be disqualified, as they are neither solids nor Parti-Colors. Roans may follow any typical roaning shade or pattern, and are classed as parti-colors.

Black and tans are shown under the variety classification of solid color other than black. The markings of black and tans should be definite. The black should be jet and the tan rich in shade. Tan pigmentation solely under the stern and on the underside of the ears does disqualify. The same penalties apply to white markings on black and tans as apply to solid colors.

Weight—Not under 22 nor over 28 pounds. Weights under or in excess of these limits shall be severely penalized. Puppies are exempt from the minimum limitation.

General Description—Embodying the foregoing we have a serviceable-looking dog with a refinedly chiseled head; standing on straight legs and well up at the shoulders; of compact body and wide, muscular quarters. The Cocker Spaniel's sturdy body, powerful quarters and strong, well-boned legs show him to be a dog capable of considerable speed combined with great endurance. Above all he must be free and merry, sound, well balanced throughout, and in action show a keen inclination to work; equable in temperament with no suggestion of timidity.

Scale of Points

	Points
Skull	8
Muzzle	10
Teeth	4
Eyes	6
Ears	3
Neck and Shoulders	15
Body	15
Legs	9
Feet	6
Stern	3
Coat	6
Color and Markings	3
Action	12
Total	100

A blue roan, bench champion English Cocker.

THE ENGLISH COCKER SPANIEL

The English Cocker Spaniel, a very fine breed for hunting or the home, has had a difficult job freeing itself from both Springer and American Cocker to emerge as a breed in its own right. The heritage lent by the Springer has given the breed its hunting skill and general lovely type and color. But, when the English was brought to America, its type became fused and confused with that of the American Cocker, to the extent where large American Cockers were shown in English classes and small English exhibited as American Cockers. This resulted in the variety being recognized but not as a breed in its own right, until the English Cocker Spaniel Club of America was formed in 1935 and the British standard for the breed adopted.

The breed club wisely militated against interbreeding (or crossbreeding) of English and American Cocker Spaniels, but so much of this had been done that it was almost impossible to find a genetically pure specimen of the English Cocker on this side of the Atlantic. Extensive research, sponsored by Mrs. Geraldine R. Dodge, finally segregated the breeds and found those of pure English ancestry.

The English Cocker loves to hunt and shows it by his joy in field work. He is compact and strong and his coat is more like his Springer ancestor than his Cocker cousin, silky and more easily groomed.

In color the English Cocker may be of a solid color, usually black or red. He can be parti-colored, blue, liver, red, orange, or lemon roan, or black and tan.

He stands higher on the leg than the American Cocker Spaniel and has a longer muzzle.

The English Cocker has found many friends in the United States and enjoys a fine reputation on the bench, in the field, and in the homes of all who know him.

STANDARD OF THE ENGLISH COCKER SPANIEL

General Appearance—The English Cocker Spaniel is an attractive, active, merry sporting dog; with short body and strong limbs, standing well up at the withers. His movements are alive with energy; his gait powerful and frictionless. He is alert at all times, and the carriage of head and incessant action of his tail while at work give the impression that here is a dog that is not only bred for hunting but really enjoys it. He is well balanced, strongly built, full of quality and is capable of top speed combined with great stamina. His head imparts an individual stamp peculiar to him alone and has that brainy appearance expressive of the highest intelligence; and is in perfect proportion to his body. His muzzle is a most distinctive feature, being of correct conformation and in proportion to his skull.

Character—The character of the English Cocker is of extreme importance. His love and faithfulness to his master and household, his alertness and courage are characteristic. He is noted for his intelligence, and merry disposition; not quarrelsome; and is a responsive and willing worker both in the field and as a companion.

Head—The skull and forehead should be well developed with no suggestion of coarseness, arched and slightly flattened on top when viewed both from the stop to the end of the skull as well as from ear to ear, and cleanly chiseled under the eyes. The proportion of the head desirable is approximately one-half for the muzzle and one-half for the skull. The muzzle should be square with a definite stop where it blends into the skull and in proportion with the width of the skull. As the English Cocker is primarily a sporting dog, the muzzle and jaws must be of sufficient strength and size to carry game; and the length of the muzzle should provide room for the development of the olfactory nerve to insure good scenting qualities, which require that the nose be wide and well developed. Nostrils black in color except in reds, livers, parti-colors and roans of the lighter shades, where brown is permissible, but black preferred. Lips should be square, full and free from flews. Teeth should be even and set squarely.

Faults—Muzzle too short or snipy. Jaw overshot or undershot. Lips snipy or pendulous. Skull too flat or too rounded, cheeky or coarse. Stop insufficient or exaggerated.

Eyes—The eyes should be of medium size, full and slightly oval shaped; set squarely in skull and wide apart. Eyes must be dark brown except in livers and light parti-colors where hazel is permissible, but the darker the better. The general expression should be intelligent, alert, bright and merry.

Faults—Light, round or protruding eyes. Conspicuous haw.

Ears—Lobular; set low and close to the head; leather fine and extending at least to the nose, well covered with long, silky, straight or slightly wavy hair.

Faults—Set or carried too high; too wide at the top; insufficient feathering; positive curls or ringlets.

Neck—Long, clean and muscular; arched towards the head; set cleanly into sloping shoulders.

Faults—Short; thick; with dewlap or excessive throatiness.

Body—Close coupled, compact and firmly knit, giving the impression of great strength without heaviness. Depth of brisket should reach to the elbow, sloping gradually upward to the loin. Ribs should spring gradually to middle of body, tapering to back ribs which should be of good depth and extend well back.

Faults—Too long and lacking depth; insufficient spring of rib; barrel rib.

Shoulders and Chest—Shoulders sloping and fine; chest deep and well developed but not too wide and round to interfere with the free action of the forelegs.

Faults—Straight or loaded shoulders.

Back and Loin—Back short and strong. Length of back from withers to tail-set should approximate height from ground to withers. Height of the dog at the withers should be greater than the height at the hip-joint, providing a gradual slope between these points. Loin short and powerful, slightly arched.

Faults—Too low at withers; long, sway or roach back; flat or narrow loin; exaggerated tuck-up.

Forelegs—Straight and strong with bone nearly equal in size from elbow to heel; elbows set close to the body with free action from shoulders; pasterns short, straight, and strong.

Faults—Shoulders loose; elbows turned in or out; legs bowed or set too close or too wide apart; knees knuckled over; light bone.

Feet—Size in proportion to the legs; firm, round and catlike with thick pads and strong toes.

Faults—Too large, too small; spreading or splayed.

Hindquarters—The hips should be rounded; thighs broad; well developed and muscular, giving abundance of propelling power. Stifles strong and well bent. Hock to pad moderately short, strong and well let down.

Faults—Excessive angulation; lightness of bone; stifle too short; hocks too long or turned in or out.

Tail—Set on to conform with the top-line of the back. Merry in action.

Faults—Set too low; habitually carried too high; too short or too long.

Color—Various. In self colors a white shirt frill is undesirable. In parti-colors, the coloring must be broken on the body and be evenly distributed. No large portion of any one color should exist. White should be shown on the

The English Cocker Spaniel is an excellent flushing dog and retriever and will work well with all birds on land or water.

saddle. A dog of any solid color with white feet and chest is not a parti-color. In roans it is desirable that the white hair should be distributed over the body, the more evenly the better. Roans come in various colors: blue, liver, red, orange and lemon. In black and tans the coat should be black; tan spots over the eyes, tan on the sides of the muzzle, on the throat and chest, on forelegs from the knees to the toes and on the hindlegs on the inside of the legs, also on the stifle and extending from the hock to the toes.

Faults—White feet are undesirable in any specimen of self color.

Coat—On head short and fine; on body flat or slightly wavy and silky in texture. Should be of medium length with enough undercoating to give protection. The English Cocker should be well-feathered but not so profusely as to hide the true lines or interfere with his field work.

Faults—Lack of coat; too soft, curly or wiry. Excessive trimming to change the natural appearance and coat should be discouraged.

Weight—The most desirable weights: Males, 28 pounds to 34 pounds; females, 26 pounds to 32 pounds.

Height—Ideal heights at withers: Males, 16 to 17 inches; females, 15 to 16 inches. Deviations to be severely penalized but not disqualified.

Proper physical conformation and balance should be considered more important than weight alone.

Rob Roy and Rob Roy II, sire and son.

Champion Wakefield's Black Knight

THE ENGLISH SPRINGER SPANIEL

The English Springer (or "Springing Spaniel," as he was originally known) is one of the truly handsome and most versatile of all sporting breeds. He is the product, as are all Spaniels, of an intermingling of Spanish breeds and was one of a great many sporting dogs of the loosely defined spaniel variety that were differentiated by weight, size and general appearance. It wasn't until 1902 that the English Springer Spaniel was recognized as a distinct breed by the Kennel Club of England. The parent club of the breed in America was established in 1927.

As a sporting dog the Springer has no peer, and is obsessed with but one purpose in life, to hunt and find game and, while doing this job, to stay within gun range and quarter the ground thoroughly. Because of his size, strength, and compact build, he has a greater turn of speed and endurance in the field than that possessed by most other breeds of spaniels.

Perhaps more than any other individual in North America, Eudore Chevrier, of Winnipeg, has done most for the breed through the large number of typical animals he imported to this continent in 1921.

The English Springer is a medium-sized dog ranging from about 19 to 20 inches at the withers and weighing between 50 and 55 pounds. His attractive, flat coat is usually liver and white or black and white although there is an occasional blue or liver roan.

The English Springer is highly regarded as a specialist on the ringneck pheasant. This wily game bird has a habit of running out from under a point, but the Springer will flush the bird into the air before the hunter's gun.

There is not so great a gap between the Springer on the bench and the Springer in the field as with some other of the gun dog breeds. Both areas of sporting dog endeavor have seen great success scored by the Springer. He has often taken the top prize at important spaniel trials and has frequently gone to the top in all-breed competition at conformation shows.

The English Springer Spaniel is highly regarded at the present day, and he does not come by his popularity without reason. There are few breeds that make such a splendid all-around canine friend as does the English Springer Spaniel.

STANDARD OF THE ENGLISH SPRINGER SPANIEL

General Appearance and Type—The English Springer Spaniel is a medium-size sporting dog with a neat, compact body, and a docked tail. His coat is moderately long, glossy, usually liver and white or black and white, with feathering on his legs, ears, chest and brisket. His pendulous ears, soft gentle expression, sturdy build and friendly wagging tail proclaim him unmistakably a member of the ancient family of spaniels. He is above all a well proportioned dog, free from exaggeration, nicely balanced in every part. His carriage is proud and upstanding, body deep, legs strong and muscular with enough length to carry him with ease. His short level back, well developed thighs, good shoulders, excellent feet, suggest power, endurance, agility. Taken as a whole he looks the part of a dog that can go and keep going under difficult hunting conditions, and moreover he enjoys what he is doing. At his best he is endowed with style, symmetry, balance, enthusiasm and is every inch a sporting dog of distinct spaniel character, combining beauty and utility. To be penalized: Those lacking true English Springer type in conformation, expression, or behavior.

Temperament—The typical Springer is friendly, eager to please, quick to learn, willing to obey. In the show ring he should exhibit poise, attentiveness, tractability, and should permit himself to be examined by the judge without resentment or cringing. To be penalized: Excessive timidity, with due allowance for puppies and novice exhibits. But no dog to receive a ribbon if he

Truly one of the most handsome and versatile of sporting canines, the English Springer Spaniel has long been a favorite on the bench and in the field in many parts of the world. The portrait at right gives some indication of the breed's appeal.

behaves in vicious manner toward handler or judge. Aggressiveness toward other dogs in the ring not to be construed as viciousness.

Size and Proportion—The Springer is built to cover rough ground with ability and reasonable speed. He should be kept to medium size—neither too small nor too large and heavy to do the work for which he is intended. The ideal shoulder height for dogs is 20 inches; for bitches, 19 inches. Length of topline (the distance from top or the shoulders to the root of the tail) should be approximately equal to the dog's shoulder height—never longer than his height—and not appreciably less. The dog too long in body, especially when long in loin, tires easily and lacks the compact outline characteristic of the breed. Equally undesirable is the dog too short in body for the length of his legs, a condition that destroys his balance and restricts the gait.

Weight—Dependent on the dog's other dimensions: a 20-inch dog, well proportioned, in good condition, should weigh about 49–55 pounds. The resulting appearance is a well-knit, sturdy dog with good but not too heavy bone, in no way coarse or ponderous. *To be penalized*—Over-heavy specimens, cloddy in build. Leggy individuals, too tall for their length and substance. Over-size or under-size specimens (those more than one inch under or over the breed ideal).

Color and Coat—Color may be liver or black with white markings; liver and white (or black and white) with tan markings; blue or liver roan; or predominantly white with tan, black or liver markings. On ears, chest, legs and belly the Springer is nicely furnished with a fringe of feathering (of moderate heaviness). On his head, front or forelegs, and below hocks on front of hind-

The Springer works well on upland birds and
retrieves to hand with style and verve.

The Springer's size and strength lend him the ruggedness to work under any conditions. He will retrieve in icy water with all the aplomb he exhibits on dry land.

legs the hair is short and fine. The body coat is flat or wavy, of medium length, sufficiently dense to be water-proof, weather-proof and thorn-proof. The texture, fine and the hair should have the clean, glossy, live appearance indicative of good health. It is legitimate to trim about the head, feet, ears; to remove dead hair; to thin and shorten excess feathering particularly from the hocks to the feet and elsewhere as required to give a smart, clean appearance. *To be penalized*—Rough, curly coat. Over-trimming especially of the body coat. Any chopped, barbered or artificial effect. Excessive feathering that destroys the clean outline desirable in a sporting dog. Off colors such as lemon, red or orange not to place.

Head—The head is impressive without being heavy. Its beauty lies in a combination of strength and refinement. It is important that the size and proportion be in balance with the rest of the dog. Viewed in profile the head should appear approximately the same length as the neck and should blend with the body in substance. The skull (upper head) to be of medium length, fairly broad, flat on top, slightly rounded rather than peaked or angular. The foreface (head in front of the eyes) approximately the same length as the skull, and in harmony as to width and general character. Looking down on the head the muzzle to appear to be about one-half the width of the skull. As the skull rises from the foreface it makes a brow or "stop," divided by a groove or fluting between the eyes. This groove continues upward and gradually disappears as it reaches the middle of the forehead. The amount of "stop" can best be described as moderate. It must not be a pronounced feature as in the Clumber Spaniel. Rather it is a subtle rise where the muzzle blends into

197

the upper head, further emphasized by the groove and by the position and shape of the eyebrows which should be well-developed. The stop, eyebrow and the chiseling of the bony structure around the eye sockets contribute to the Springer's beautiful and characteristic expression. Viewed in profile the topline of the skull and the muzzle lie in two approximately parallel planes. The nasal bone should be straight, with no inclination downward toward the tip of the nose which gives a down-faced look so undesirable in this breed. Neither should the nasal bone be concave resulting in a "dish-faced" profile; nor convex giving the dog a Roman nose. The jaws to be of sufficient length to allow the dog to carry game easily; fairly square, lean, strong, and even (neither undershot or overshot). The upper lip to come down full and rather square to cover the line of the lower jaw, but lips not to be pendulous nor exaggerated. The nostrils, well opened and broad, liver color or black depending on the color of the coat. Flesh-colored ("Dudley noses") or spotted ("butterfly noses") are undesirable. The cheeks to be flat (not rounded, full or thick) with nice chiseling under the eyes. *To be penalized*—Oval, pointed or heavy skull. Cheeks prominently rounded, thick and protruding. Too much or too little stop. Over heavy muzzle. Muzzle too short, too thin, too narrow. Pendulous slobbery lips. Under- or overshot jaws—a very serious fault, to be heavily penalized.

Teeth—The teeth should be strong, clean, not too small; and when the mouth is closed the teeth should meet in an even bite or a close scissors bite (the lower incisors touching the inside of the upper incisors). *To be penalized*—Any deviation from above description. One or two teeth slightly out of line not to be considered a serious fault, but irregularities due to faulty jaw formation to be severely penalized.

Eyes—More than any other feature the eyes contribute to the Springer's appeal. Color, placement, size, influence, expression and attractiveness. The eyes to be of medium size, neither small, round, full and prominent, nor bold and hard in expression. Set rather well apart and fairly deep in their sockets. The color of the iris to harmonize with the color of the coat, preferably a good dark hazel in the liver dogs and black or deep brown in the black and white specimens. The expression to be alert, kindly, trusting. The lids, tight with little or no haw showing. *To be penalized*—Eyes yellow or brassy in color or noticeably lighter than the coat. Sharp expression indicating unfriendly or suspicious nature. Loose droopy lids. Prominent haw (the third eyelid or membrane in the inside corner of the eye).

Ears—The correct ear set is on a level with the line of the eye; on the side of the skull and not too far back. The flaps to be long and fairly wide, hanging close to the cheeks, with no tendency to stand up or out. The leather, thin, approximately long enough to reach the tip of the nose. *To be penalized*—Short round ears. Ears set too high or too low or too far back on the head.

Neck—The neck to be moderately long, muscular, slightly arched at the crest gradually blending into sloping shoulders. Not noticeably upright nor coming into the body at an abrupt angle. *To be penalized*—Short neck, often the sequence to steep shoulders. Concave neck, sometimes called ewe neck or upside down neck (the opposite of arched). Excessive throatiness.

Body—The body to be well coupled, strong, compact; the chest deep but not so wide or round as to interfere with the action of the front legs; the brisket sufficiently developed to reach to the level of the elbows. The ribs fairly long, springing gradually to the middle of the body then tapering as they approach the end of the ribbed section. The back (section between the withers and the loin) to be straight and strong, with no tendency to dip or roach. The loins to be strong, short; a slight arch over loins and hip bones. Hips nicely rounded, blending smoothly into hind legs. The resulting topline slopes very gently from withers to tail—the line from withers to back descending without a sharp drop; the back practically level; arch over hips somewhat lower than the withers; croup sloping gently to base of tail; tail carried to follow the natural line of the body. The bottom line, starting on a level with the elbows, to continue backward with almost no up-curve until reaching the end of the ribbed section, then a more noticeable up-curve to the flank, but not enough to make the dog appear small waisted or "tucked up." *To be penalized*—Body too shallow, indicating lack of brisket. Ribs too flat, sometimes due to immaturity. Ribs too round (barrel-shaped), hampering the gait. Sway-back (dip in back), indicating weakness or lack of muscular development, particularly to be seen when dog is in action and viewed from the side. Roach back (too much arch over loin and extending forward into middle section). Croup falling away too sharply; or croup too high—unsightly faults, detrimental to outline and good movement. Topline sloping sharply, indicating steep withers (straight shoulder placement) and a too low tail-set.

Tail—The Springer's tail is an index both to his temperament and his conformation. Merry tail action is characteristic. The proper set is somewhat low following the natural line of the croup. The carriage should be nearly horizontal, slightly elevated when dog is excited. Carried straight up is untypical of the breed. The tail should not be docked too short and should be well fringed with wavy feather. It is legitimate to shape and shorten the feathering but enough should be left to blend with the dog's other furnishings. *To be penalized*—Tail habitually upright. Tail set too high or too low. Clamped down tail (indicating timidity or undependable temperament), even less to be desired than the tail carried too gaily.

Forequarters—Efficient movement in front calls for proper shoulders. The blades sloping back to form an angle with the forearm of approximately 90 degrees which permits the dog to swing his forelegs forward in an easy manner. Shoulders (fairly close together at the tips) to lie flat and mold smoothly into the contour of the body. The forelegs to be straight with the same degree of size to the foot. The bone, strong, slightly flattened, not too heavy or round. The knee, straight, almost flat; the pastern short, strong; elbows close to the body with free action from the shoulders. *To be penalized*—Shoulders set at a steep angle limiting the stride. Loaded shoulders (the blades standing out from the body by overdevelopment of the muscles). Loose elbows, crooked legs. Bone too light or too coarse and heavy. Weak pasterns that let down the feet at a pronounced angle.

Hindquarters—The Springer should be shown in hard muscular condition, well developed in hips and thighs and the whole rear assembly should suggest strength and driving power. The hip joints to be set rather wide apart and the hips nicely rounded. The thighs broad and muscular; the stifle joint strong and moderately bent. The hock joint somewhat rounded, not small and sharp in contour, and moderately angulated. Leg from hock joint to foot pad, short and strong with good bone structure. When viewed from the rear the hocks to be parallel whether the dog is standing or in motion. *To be penalized*—Too little or too much angulation. Narrow, undeveloped thighs. Hocks too short or too long (a proportion of one-third the distance from hip joint to foot is ideal). Flabby muscles. Weakness of joints.

Feet—The feet to be round, or slightly oval, compact, well arched, medium size with thick pads, well feathered between the toes. Excess hair to be removed to show the natural shape and size of the foot. *To be penalized*—Thin, open or splayed feet (flat with spreading toes). Hare foot (long, rather narrow foot).

Movement—In judging the Springer there should be emphasis on proper movement which is the final test of a dog's conformation and soundness. Prerequisite to good movement is balance of the front and rear assemblies. The two must match in angulation and muscular development if the gait is to be smooth and effortless. Good shoulders laid back at an angle that permits a long stride are just as essential as the excellent rear quarters that provide the driving power. When viewed from the front the dog's legs should appear to swing forward in a free and easy manner, with no tendency for the feet to cross over or interfere with each other. Viewed from the rear the hocks should drive well under the body following on a line with the forelegs, the rear legs parallel, neither too widely nor too closely spaced. Seen from the side the Springer should exhibit a good, long forward stride, without high-stepping or wasted motion. *To be penalized*—Short choppy stride, mincing steps with up and down movement, hopping. Moving with forefeet wide, giving roll or swing to body. Weaving or crossing of fore or hind feet. Cowhocks—hocks turning in toward each other.

In judging the English Springer Spaniel the over-all picture is a primary consideration. It is urged that the judge look for type which includes general appearance, outline and temperament and also for soundness especially as seen when the dog is in motion. Inasmuch as the dog with a smooth easy gait must be reasonably sound and well balanced he is to be highly regarded in the show-ring, however, not to the extent of forgiving him for not looking like an English Springer Spaniel. A quite untypical dog, leggy, foreign in head and expression, may move well. But he should not be placed over a good all-around specimen that has a minor fault in movement. It should be remembered that the English Springer Spaniel is first and foremost a sporting dog of the spaniel family and he must look and behave and move in character.

Springer Spaniel puppies are "lovely to look at and delightful to hold".

THE FIELD SPANIEL

The infrequently seen Field Spaniel is an example of a breed that has experienced great problems but has taken his place in the modern world of dog breeds despite them.

There was a time when fanciers purposely bred him to such a degree of length of body and lowness of leg that he was a grotesque caricature of a spaniel and certainly not the image of a useful dog afield.

Phineas Bullock, an English fancier, was largely responsible for the afore-mentioned type. He made a strong attempt to have this type accepted, but it never truly caught on. Instead the breed eventually turned back to a more sensible type with the help of Mortimer Smith and other fanciers like him.

The present-day Field Spaniel comes to us as a handsome, agile fellow, full of good sense and persevering spirit in the bird field.

He is usually black or liver in color, though he may also be mahogany liver, red, roan, or any of these colors with tan markings in a counter-color pattern like that of the Gordon Setter. These colors in combination with white are permissible but not desirable as they would tend to make the dog resemble a Springer Spaniel too closely.

The Field Spaniel stands about 18 inches at the shoulder and weighs from 35 to 50 pounds.

STANDARD OF THE FIELD SPANIEL

Head—Should be quite characteristic of this grand sporting dog, as that of the Bulldog, or the Bloodhound; its very stamp and countenance should at once convey the conviction of high breeding, character and nobility; skull well developed, with a distinctly elevated occipital tuberosity, which, above all, gives the character alluded to; not too wide across the muzzle, long and lean, never snipy nor squarely cut, and in profile curving gradually from nose to throat; lean beneath the eyes, a thickness here gives coarseness to the whole head. The great length of muzzle gives surface for the free development of the olfactory nerve, and thus secures the highest possible scenting powers.

Eyes—Not too full, but not small, receding or overhung, color dark hazel or brown, or nearly black, according to the color of the dog. Grave in expression and showing no haw.

Ears—Moderately long and wide, sufficiently clad with nice Setter-like feather and set low. They should fall in graceful folds, the lower parts curling inwards and backwards.

Neck—Long, strong and muscular, so as to enable the dog to retrieve his game without undue fatigue.

Body—Should be of moderate length, well-ribbed up to a good strong loin, straight or slightly arched, never slack.

Nose—Well developed, with good open nostrils.

Shoulders and Chest—Former long, sloping and well set back, thus giving great activity and speed; latter deep and well developed, but not too round and wide.

Back and Loin—Very strong and muscular.

Hind Quarters—Strong and muscular. The stifles should be moderately bent, and not twisted either in or out.

Stern—Well set on and carried low, if possible below the level of the back in a straight line or with a slight downward inclination, never elevated above the back, and in action always kept low, nicely fringed with wavy feather of silky texture.

Forelegs—Should be of fairly good length, with straight, clean, flat bone, and nicely feathered. Immense bone is no longer desirable.

Feet—Not too small; round, short soft hair between toes; strong pads.

Coat—Flat or slightly waved, and never curled. Sufficiently dense to resist the weather, and not too short. Silky in texture, glossy and refined in nature, with neither duffleness on the one hand, nor curl or wiriness on the other. On the chest, under belly and behind the legs, there should be abundant feather, but never too much, especially below the hocks, and that of the right sort, viz., Setter-like. The hind quarters should be similarly adorned.

Color—Black, liver, golden liver, mahogany red, roan; or any one of the colors with tan over the eyes, on the cheeks, feet and pasterns. Other colors, such as Black and white, liver and white, red or orange and white, etc., while not disqualifying a dog (provided the architecture is correct), will be considered less desirable, since the Field Spaniel should be clearly distinguished from the Springer Spaniel.

Height—About 18 inches to shoulder.

Weight—From about 35 pounds to 50 pounds.

General Appearance—That of a well-balanced, noble, upstanding sporting dog; built for activity and endurance. A grand combination of beauty and utility, and bespeaking of unusual docility and instinct.

SCALE OF POINTS	Points
Head and jaw	15
Eyes	5
Ears	5
Neck	5
Body	10
Forelegs	10
Hindlegs	10
Feet	10
Stern	10
Coat and feather	10
General appearance	10
Total	100

Champion Shilalah Napper Tandy, C.D.

THE IRISH WATER SPANIEL

The Irish Water Spaniel is an example of true canine uniqueness. He is like no other breed in appearance or in temperament. Nicknamed "the clown of the spaniel family," the Irish Water is one of the finest companions that can be found, indoors or out.

The Irish Water Spaniel is acknowledged to be a very old breed, but as is the case with so many Irish dogs and horses, it is virtually impossible to separate fact from fairy tale, and so the exact date of his origin cannot be firmly established.

His ancestry, like the date of his origin, is also a mixture of fact and folklore. He is believed to be a descendant of old Portuguese water dogs and spaniel root stock that came over to Ireland from the Iberian peninsula when natives of that country conducted periodic raids on Erin's green shores.

One of the chief pioneers of the breed was Justin McCarthy. He owned the great dog, "Boatswain," who sired many fine Irish Waters until his death at age eighteen.

The Irish Water Spaniel was introduced to the United States long before the establishment of the American Kennel Club and was, for many years, the most popular of the retrievers. The breed owed this popularity to its favor among market hunters. Before the turn of the century, when waterfowl were far more plentiful than at the present day, market hunting was a thriving industry and the hard-working Irish Water Spaniel was the gunner's right arm. This dog would not let a single cripple get by him and, due to his size, strength, and great heart, he could go all day long without tiring.

Today the Irish Water Spaniel's popularity has waned in favor of Golden and Labrador Retrievers, but he has a loyal group of friends that hold him in the highest esteem and keep him before the dog-minded public.

As a show dog the Irish Water Spaniel is considered a minor breed in the Sporting group, but there are many good ones shown and specimens of the breed have accounted for a fair number of good wins. Dogs like Ch. Mahoney's O'Toole, who was Best American-Bred in Show at the 1943 Westminster and Ch. Kalibank's Water Gate Wanderer who won the Sporting Group at Westminster in 1959, were examples of this rare, intriguing breed at its best.

This largest of the spaniel family is always liver in color and owns a distinctive, curly coat. His topknot and "rat tail" are the two chief hallmarks of his breed.

Taken in total, it is hard to find a more delightful companion than an Irish Water Spaniel. His Hibernian sense of humor is reflected in his every move and the unswerving allegiance of this breed's fanciers is proof positive that he has something special to offer.

Maurimike's
Kate McCool

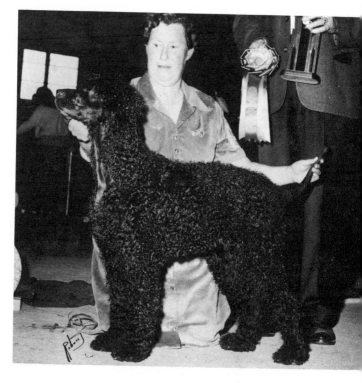

Champion
Maurimike's
Hidden Dell
Irish

STANDARD OF THE IRISH WATER SPANIEL

Head—Skull rather large and high in dome with prominent occiput; muzzle square and rather long with deep mouth opening and lips fine in texture. Teeth strong and level. The nose should be large with open nostrils and liver in color. The head should be cleanly chiseled, not "cheeky" and should not present a short wedge shaped appearance. Hair on face should be short and smooth.

Topknot—Topknot, a characteristic of the true breed, should consist of long loose curls growing down into a well-defined peak between the eyes and should not be in the form of a wig; i.e., growing straight across.

Eyes—Medium in size and set almost flush, without eyebrows. Color of eyes hazel, preferably of dark shade. Expression of the eyes should be keenly alert, inteligent, direct and quizzical.

Ears—Long, lobular, set low with leathers reaching to about the end of the nose when extended forward. The ears should be abundantly covered with curls becoming longer and toward the tips and extending two or more inches below the ends of the leathers.

Neck—The neck should be long, arching, strong and muscular, smoothly set into sloping shoulders.

Shoulders and Chest—Shoulders should be sloping and clean; chest deep but not too wide between the legs. The entire front should give the impression of strength without heaviness.

Body, Ribs and Loins—Body should be of medium length, with ribs well sprung, pear shaped at the brisket, and rounder toward the hindquarters. Ribs should be carried well back. Loins should be short, wide and muscular. The body should not present a tucked-up appearance.

Hindquarters—The hindquarters should be as high as or a trifle higher than the shoulders and should be very powerful and muscular with well developed upper and second thighs. Hips should be wide; stifles should not be too straight; and hocks low set and moderately bent. Tail should be set on low enough to give a rather rounded appearance to the hindquarters and should be carried nearly level with the back. Sound hindquarters are of great importance to provide swimming power and drive.

Forelegs and Feet—Forelegs medium in length, well boned, straight and muscular with elbows close set. Both fore and hind feet should be large, thick and somewhat spreading, well clothed with hair both over and between the toes, but free from superfluous feather.

Tail—The so-called "rat-tail" is a striking characteristic of the breed. At the root it is thick and covered for two or three inches with short curls. It tapers to a fine point at the end, and from the root-curls is covered with short, smooth hair so as to look as if the tail had been clipped. The tail should not be long enough to reach the hock joint.

Coat—Proper coat is of vital importance. The neck, back and sides should be densely covered with tight crisp ringlets entirely free from wooliness. Underneath the ribs the hair should be longer. The hair on lower throat should be short. The forelegs should be covered all around with abundant hair falling in curls or waves, but shorter in front than behind. The hind legs should also be abundantly covered by hair falling in curls or waves, but the hair should be short on the front of the legs below the hocks.

Color—Solid liver; white on chest objectionable.

Height and Weight—Dogs 22 to 24 inches; bitches 21 to 23 inches. Dogs 55 to 65 pounds; bitches 45 to 58 pounds.

General Appearance—That of a smart, upstanding, strongly built but not leggy dog, combining great intelligence and the rugged endurance with a bold,

From left to right, three famous Irish Water Spaniels, Ch. Kalibank's Water Gate Wanderer, Ch. Kalibank's Mister Fitz-Gee, and Ch. Jiggs O'Toole.

Champion Tralee Macroom O'Maille,
and Allanah's Sullivan.

dashing eagerness of temperament.

Gait—Should be square, true, precise and not slurring.

SCALE OF POINTS

		Points
Head		
Skull and topknot	6	
Ears	4	
Eyes	4	
Muzzle and nose	6	20
Body		
Neck	5	
Chest, shoulders, back, loin and ribs	12	17
Driving Gear		
Feet, hips, thighs, stifles and continuity of hindquarter muscles	14	
Feet, legs, elbows and muscles of forequarters	9	23
Coat		
Tightness, denseness of curl and general texture	16	
Color	4	20
Tail		
General appearance and "set on," length and carriage	5	5
General Conformation and Action		
Symmetry, style, gait, weight and size	15	15
		100

THE SUSSEX SPANIEL

The deliberate, slow-going Sussex Spaniel takes his name from the part of England in which he was developed.

Another of the long-bodied, low-slung spaniels, the Sussex is distinguished by his striking golden-mahogany coloring which lends richness to his fine coat.

He has not caught on in the United States since the conditions of hunting and the demands of gunners call for greater speed than the Sussex Spaniel can offer.

Two fanciers that are often mentioned in the history of the breed are a Mr. Fuller, of Brightling, England, and Phineas Bullock, mentioned earlier as a prominent exponent of the Field Spaniel.

The Sussex Spaniel is the only spaniel breed that has a habit of giving tongue on game. This is thought to indicate some kind of hound blood. The breed found great use in England for the purpose of rough shooting where game was plentiful and the need for speed in a sporting dog nonexistent.

He is a happy, willing worker, takes to retrieving readily, and has proven most useful when properly trained for the hunter's individual requirements.

STANDARD OF THE SUSSEX SPANIEL

Head—The skull should be moderately long and also wide, with an indention in the middle and a full stop, brows fairly heavy; occiput full, but not pointed, the whole giving an appearance of heaviness without dullness.

Eyes—Hazel color, fairly large, soft and languishing, not showing the haw overmuch.

Nose—The muzzle should be about three inches long, square, and the lips somewhat pendulous. The nostrils well developed and liver color.

Ears—Thick, fairly large and lobe shaped; set moderately low, but relatively not so low as in the black Field Spaniel; carried close to the head and furnished with soft, wavy hair.

Neck—Is rather short, strong and slightly arched, but not carrying the head much above the level of the back. There should not be much throatiness about the skin, but well-marked frill in the coat.

The quiet companionship found in a duck blind cannot be matched in any other known sport or activity. The good retriever helps weave this magic spell that is cherished in memory when other remembrance fades.

Chest and Shoulders—The chest is round, especially behind the shoulders, deep and wide giving a good girth. The shoulders should be oblique.

Back and Back Rib—The back and loin is long and should be very muscular, both in width and depth; for this development the back ribs must be deep. The whole body is characterized as low, long and level.

Legs and Feet—The arms and thighs must be bony as well as muscular, knees and hocks large and strong; pasterns very short and bony, feet large and round, and with short hair between the toes. The legs should be very short and strong, with great bone, and may show a slight bend in the forearm, and be moderately well feathered. The hindlegs should not apparently be shorter than the forelegs, or be too much bent at the hocks, so as to give a settery appearance, which is so objectionable. The hindlegs should be well feathered above the hocks, but should not have much hair below that point. The hocks should be short and wide apart. (The hock is the joint itself and cannot be short. What is meant is that from the hock to the ground should be short, or that the hind pasterns should be short.—Ed.)

Tail—Should be docked from five to seven inches, set low, and not carried above the level of the back, thickly covered with moderately long feather.

Coat—Body coat abundant, flat or slightly waved, with no tendency to curl, moderately well feathered on legs and stern, but clean below the hocks.

Color—Rich golden liver; this is a certain sign of the purity of the breed, dark liver or puce, denoting unmistakably a recent cross with the black or other variety of Field Spaniel.

General Appearance—Rather massive and muscular, but with free movements and nice tail action, denoting a cheerful and tractable disposition. Weight from 35 pounds to 45 pounds.

POSITIVE POINTS

	Points
Head	10
Eyes	5
Nose	5
Ears	10
Neck	5
Chest and shoulders	5
Back and back ribs	10
Legs and feet	10
Tail	5
Coat	5
Color	15
General appearance	15
Total	100

NEGATIVE POINTS

	Points
Light eyes	5
Narrow head	10
Weak muzzle	10
Curled ears or set on high	5
Curled coat	15
Carriage of stern	5
Topknot	10
White on chest	5
Color, too light or too dark	15
Legginess or light of bone	5
Shortness of body or flat sided	5
General appearance—sour or crouching	10
Total	100

Champion Dein Glynis of Randhaven

THE WELSH SPRINGER SPANIEL

The Welsh Springer Spaniel is thought to have been one of the first of the sporting dogs to be used with the gun. There are old prints that show hunters with medium sized spaniel-type dogs of a red and white color that bear unmistakable resemblance to the Welsh Springer.

This attractive, medium-sized breed is a native of Wales and western England. He has, in recent times, become very widespread in many countries due to his easy adjustment to extremes of temperature and terrain.

The Welsh Springer Spaniel has shown himself to be most adaptable to all sorts of hunting and can retrieve waterfowl as well as he can pursue upland birds. He must, however, be trained early in life as he has an excellent nose and, left to his own devices, he will become a solitary hunter.

The Welsh Springer owns a flat coat that is always white with attractive red markings. He is smaller than the English Springer and longer in body.

While not often seen in the United States he combines many desirable features as a field, pet, and show dog and those that know him best are steadfast in their loyalty to him.

STANDARD OF THE WELSH SPRINGER SPANIEL

The "Welsh Spaniel" or "Springer" is also known and referred to in Wales as a "Starter." He is of very ancient and pure origin, and is a distinct variety which has been bred and preserved purely for working purposes.

Head—Skull—Proportionate, of moderate length, slightly domed, clearly defined stop, well chiselled below the eyes.

Muzzle—Medium length, straight, fairly square; the nostrils well developed and flesh colored or dark.

Jaw—Strong, neither under not overshot.

Eyes—Hazel or dark, medium size, not prominent, nor sunken, nor showing haw.

Ears—Set moderately low and hanging close to the cheeks, comparatively small and gradually narrowing towards the tip, covered with nice setter-like feathering.

A short chubby head is objectionable.

Neck and Shoulders—Neck—Long and muscular, clean in throat, neatly set into long and sloping shoulders.

Forelegs—Medium length, straight well boned, moderately feathered.

Body—Not long; strong and muscular with deep brisket, well sprung ribs; length of body should be proportionate to length of leg, and very well balanced; with muscular loin slightly arched and well coupled up.

Quarters—Strong and muscular, wide and fully developed with deep second thighs.

Hind Legs—Hocks well let down; stifles moderately bent (neither twisted in nor out), moderately feathered.

Feet—Round with thick pads.

Stern—Well set on and low, never carried above the level of the back; lightly feathered and with lively action.

Coat—Straight or flat and thick, of a nice silky texture, never wiry nor wavy. A curly coat is most objectionable.

Color—Dark rich red and white.

General Appearance—A symmetrical, compact, strong, merry, very active dog; not stilty, obviously built for endurance and activity.

Close kin to the English Springer, the Welsh Springer Spaniel exhibits the same stylish technique in the delivery of a bird as does his more popular relative.

Champion Wilson's Pal Joey

THE VIZSLA

The Hungarian Pointer, known by the breed name, Vizsla, is a comparative newcomer to the recognized family of pointing breeds in America. Slightly smaller than the other pointers, he is a self-colored, handsome breed whose ability in the field arouses the interest of all sportsmen who have seen him perform.

Lithe, easily trained, a natural pointer and retriever, the Vizsla, boosted by its champions as the finest of companion-hunting dogs, is unique in the rusty-gold coat-color that is not found in any other recognized pointing breed. Friendly, obedient, gentle, they make excellent house and family dogs when resting between assignments in the field.

The origin of the breed is shrouded in the mists of antiquity, but it is assumed that the ancestors of the Vizsla were hunting and companion dogs brought by the Magyar hordes that a thousand years ago swept over Central Europe to settle in Hungary. Ancient Vizslas probably accompanied their masters with their falcons in the hunts of those distant times. The breed further developed, through judicious selection, on the rich plains of Hungary that abounded in game birds and hare. The huntsman needed, and developed, in this dog of the war lords and nobles, a cautious, swift, close-working dog of superior nose and hunting ability.

Modern wars brought normal breed programs almost to a standstill and the breed became all but extinct. Austria became the recipient of Vizslas brought by their fleeing owners from a Hungary occupied by the Russians in 1945. Some of those animals found their way to other parts of the globe including America, where in 1960, the breed was admitted to A.K.C. registry and has been growing in popularity ever since.

The Vizsla is an all-around hunting dog, on land or in water.

There is a recessive for a setter-like coat carried genetically by certain Vizsla strains in Europe.

STANDARD OF THE VIZSLA

General Appearance—That of a medium-sized hunting dog of quite distinguished appearance. Robust but rather lightly built, his short coat is an attractive rusty-gold, and his tail is docked. He is a dog of power and drive in the field, and a tractable and affectionate companion in the home.

Head—Lean but muscular. The skull is moderately wide between the ears, with a median line down the forehead. Stop moderate. The muzzle is a trifle longer than the skull and, although tapering, is well squared at its end. Jaws strong, with well-developed white teeth meeting in a scissors bite. The lips cover the jaws completely but they are neither loose nor pendulous. Nostrils slightly open, the nose brown. A black or slate-gray nose is objectionable.

Ears—Thin, silky, and proportionately long, with rounded-leather ends; set fairly low and hanging close to the cheeks.

Eyes—Medium in size and depth of setting, their surrounding tissue covering the whites, and the iris or color portion harmonizing with the shade of the coat. A yellow eye is objectionable.

Neck—Strong, smooth, and muscular; moderately long, arched and devoid of dewlap. It broadens nicely into shoulders which are well laid back.

Body—Strong and well proportioned. The back is short, the withers high, and the topline slightly rounded over the loin to the set-on of the tail. Chest moderately broad and deep, and reaching down to the elbows. Ribs well sprung, and underline exhibiting a slight tuck-up beneath the loin.

Legs and Feet—Forelegs straight, strong, and muscular, with elbows close. The hind legs have well-developed thighs, with moderate angulation at stifles and hocks. Too much angulation at the hocks is as faulty as too little. The

Staunch on point, these Hungarian bird dogs are natural pointers and retrievers.

hocks, which are well let down, are equidistant from each other from the hock joint to the ground. Cowhocks are faulty. Feet are cat-like, round and compact, with toes close. Nails are brown and short; pads thick and tough. Dewclaws, if any, to be removed. Hare feet are objectionable.

Tail—Set just below the level of the back, thicker at the root, and docked one-third off.

Coat—Short, smooth, dense, and close-lying, without woolly undercoat.

Color—Solid. Rusty gold or rather dark sandy yellow in different shades, with darker shades preferred. Dark brown and pale yellow are undesirable. Small white spots on chest or feet are not faulted.

Temperament—That of the natural hunter endowed with a good nose and above-average ability to take training. Lively, gentle-mannered, and demonstratively affectionate. Fearless, and with well-developed protective instinct.

Gait—Far-reaching, light-footed, graceful, smooth.

Size—Dogs, 22 to 24 inches shoulder height; 45 to 60 pounds weight. Bitches, 21 to 23 inches shoulder height; 40 to 55 pounds weight. Oversize not to be considered a major fault unless excessive.

American and Canadian Champion Shadowmar Barthaus Dorilio.

THE WEIMARANER

Weimaraners, the "gray ghosts" of dogdom, are direct descendants of the famous Celtic, St. Hubert hounds (St. Hubertus of Brachen) of the 8th century which were introduced to Germany through France. There were *"purebred dogs of completely gray or yellow color"* mentioned in a book on sporting dogs that was published as early as 1820. The animals described were evidently the earliest Weimaraners.

There are numerous theories as to the exact genetic background of the Weimaraner, but it is the author's belief (see "This is The Weimaraner") that the direct line of descent from the St. Hubert hounds was through an ancient German hunting dog, the Leithund, from which developed the red-brown Schweisshund, a typical and true German Bloodhound (the Bloodhound was well established in Europe before the Crusades). When a color mutation occurred in the Schweisshund which caused a dilution of the red-brown resulting in a silvery sheen of taupe, with variations in tone through gray to an almost lavender shade, accompanied by affected pigmentation of the nose, eyes and pads, the earliest Weimaraners came into being. This "Isabellismus" factor was first scientifically recognized and reported upon in 1931 in a paper on genetics written by Dr. N. A. Iljen, though the gray dog of Weimar was recognized as a breed more than a century before. The color change being a genetic recessive the breeding of the silver mutations together produced all silver offspring (occasionally puppies are found in litters with Doberman Pinscher markings or long, setter-like coats, the latter a recessive carried for generations).

These oddly colored, different animals caught the fancy of a few astute dog men particularly in Thuringia near Weimar. Here the gray dogs began to appear in ever increasing numbers and became known, due to the locale, as Weimar hounds, and later as Weimar Pointers, and finally Weimaraners.

In the early days of its existence as a breed, the Weimaraner, sponsored by the nobles of the Court of Weimar, was used as a big game hound, taking scent from the ground and hunting dangerous quarry which it trailed, brought to bay and held for the huntsman. These early gray ghosts were not bird dogs, not pointing dogs, they were hounds like their ancestors. Not long after the breed came into focus, the hunting of big game in Germany with any regularity became a rarity, simply because the larger game died out with the encroachment of civilization. But a good combination fur and feather dog that would mold into one breed all the qualities the sportsman wanted would be of inestimable value. The breed selected by the nobles of Weimar to fill this role was, of course, their Weimaraner.

Selection and the crossing in of native pointing stock was necessary to bring up the head of the breed when "on" game, and to fashion the control, the style and beauty of the point. Thus the Weimaraner developed into a true pointing dog.

Jealously guarded and controlled by a parent club in Germany formed by lovers of the breed, this fine dog of the sporting nobles of Weimar was kept in the hands of a selected few earnest and sincere breeders, the litters culled ruthlessly, and breeding partners intelligently selected to produce the finest stock possible. Bred to a definite standard the Weimaraner emerged and was recognized as a true and definite breed in the 19th century.

Gradually the breed was introduced to other countries. During the early days of the breed in America so many absurd superlatives were attached to the Weimaraner's abilities that he was considered a super-dog. No breed, no matter how great, could live up to the ridiculous publicity heaped upon the Weimaraner. The result was that the breed fell into a short period of decline before interest leveled off and the Weimaraner became recognized by sportsmen for his own very real, inherent abilities in the home and field.

Developed originally as a gentleman's private sporting dog and companion the breed is now being bred also for the intense competition of the field trial, though basically the Weimaraner better fits its traditional role.

The Weimaraner fills a very real need in the hearts of dog lovers and sportsmen. He can, and will if trained, do almost anything any other breed can do and do it well. His temperament and trainability make him an excellent watchdog, home companion and child's pal. He is a superlative obedience competitor and a fine hunting dog on fur or feather.

The Weimaraner is not a kennel dog. He does best when allowed to share in family life as a responsible member of the family. The gray ghost's popularity, his exalted status in the canine family is assured, and it is certain that this breed, bred by nobles for a noble purpose, will always fill the hearts and minds of all men who admire the unique, with a bonus ot grace, intelligence and unusual beauty.

STANDARD OF THE WEIMARANER

General Appearance—A medium sized gray dog with light eyes, he should present a picture of great driving power, stamina, alertness and balance. above all, the dog should indicate ability to work in the field.

Height—At withers: Dogs, 25 to 27 inches; bitches, 23 to 25 inches.

Head—Moderately long and aristocratic, with moderate stop and slight median line extending back over the forehead; rather prominent occipital bone and trumpets set well back, beginning at the back of the eyesockets. Measurement from tip of nose to stop to equal that from stop to occipital bone. The flews should be moderately deep enclosing a powerful jaw. Foreface perfectly straight, delicate at the nostrils. Skin tightly drawn. Neck clean cut and moderately long. Expression kind, keen, intelligent.

Ears—Long and lobular, slightly folded and set high. The ear when drawn snugly alongside the jaw should end approximately two inches from the nose.

Eyes—In shades of light amber, gray or blue gray, set well enough apart to indicate good disposition and intelligence. When dilated under excitement, the eyes may appear almost black.

Teeth—Well set, strong and even; well developed and proportionate to jaw with correct scissors bite, the upper teeth protruding slightly over the lower teeth but not more than one-sixteenth of an inch. Complete dentition is greatly desired.

Nose—Gray.

Lips and Gums—Pinkish flesh shades.

Body—The back should be moderate in length, set in a straight line, strong and should slope slightly from the withers. The chest should be well developed and deep, shoulder well laid on and snug. Ribs well sprung and long. Abdomen firmly held, moderately tucked up flank. The brisket should drop to the elbow.

Coat—Short, smooth and sleek in shades of mouse gray to silver gray, usually blending to a lighter shade on the head and ears. Small white mark allowable on the chest, but not on any other part of the body. White spots that have resulted from injuries shall not be penalized.

Legs—Forelegs—Straight and strong with the measurement from the elbow to the ground approximately equalling the distance from the elbow to the top of the withers.

Hindquarters—Well angulated stifles and straight hocks—well muscled.

Feet—Firm and compact, webbed, toes well arched, pads closed and thick, nails short and gray or amber in color. Dewclaws; allowable only on forelegs, there optional.

Tail—Docked. At maturity it should measure approximately six inches with a tendency to be light rather than heavy and should be carried in a manner expressing confidence and sound temperament.

Gait—The walk is rather awkward. The trot should be effortless, ground covering and should indicate smooth coordination. When seen from the rear, the hind feet should parallel the front feet. When viewed from the side, the top line should remain strong and level.

The unique color that is the heritage of the "Gray Ghosts" of dogdom recommends them to all who like a large sporting dog of novel appearance. These two Weimaraners are typical of this lively and intelligent pointer.

Temperament—The dog should display a temperament that is keen, fearless, friendly, protective and obedient.

Very Serious Faults—Any long haired coat or coat darker than mouse gray to silver gray is considered a most undesirable trait. White, other than a spot on the chest. Eyes any other color than gray, blue gray or amber. Black mottled mouth. Dogs exhibiting strong fear or viciousness.

Serious Faults—Poor gait, very poor feet, cowhocks, faulty backs, either roached or sway. Badly overshot or undershot jaw, snipy muzzle, short ears, yellow in white markings, under size.

Faults—Doggy bitches or bitchy dogs. Improper muscular condition, badly affected teeth, more than four missing teeth. Back too long or too short. Faulty coat, neck too short, thick or throaty, low tail set, elbows in or out—feet east and west.

Minor Faults—Tail too short or too long, pink nose, oversize should not be considered a serious fault, provided the correct structure and working ability is in evidence.

Disqualifying—Cryptorchidism and monorchidism.

GROUP II

Hounds

a. Scent Hounds

nd   The Old English Hound   The Harrier

A S you see, the hounds, designated as Group II by A.K.C. delineation, have here been divided into two sections under the overall Hound Group heading. One of these sections is devoted to the scent hounds and the other section to the sight hounds. The reason for this becomes evident when one studies the breeds involved. Except for the fact that both groups are hunters of game, there is no similarity between them, in their use, their structure, their way of hunting, or their basic beginnings as true breeds.

The true, or scent hounds are, in general, more closely allied to our first group, Sporting Dogs, than they are to the sight hounds, with which they have been linked through group association. Scent hounds find their quarry through body odor picked up by their unbelievably sensitive olfactory senses. They trail the quarry, usually giving tongue as they do, and bring the prey to bay, either on the ground or above it in a tree.

In literature the scent hounds have often played their dramatic parts, even for the pen of the inimitable Bard of Avon, for the bell-like call of a hound's voice in the frosty air of autumn is a thing to remember, to write about with fumbling, inadequate words that never quite reach the truth, a thing to tuck away in the corner of your heart so it can be thought of in the silence of evening with a quiet smile and a contented sigh.

THE BASENJI

This handsome little animal is, for several reasons, one of the most unique of all known purebred dogs. He comes originally from Africa, and not many breeds do; he is so fastidious that he cleans himself in much the same manner as does a house cat; and lastly and most uncommon, he does not bark, this latter rarity giving rise, with good reason, to his title of the "barkless dog of Africa."

Add the last two facts above to the breed's Fox Terrier size and smooth coat and you have, in one package, all the elements necessary for the perfect house dog. The Basenji is certainly tailored to that need, a fact which leads the author to question the breed's inclusion in the hound category despite the fact that they are said to have been hunters on their native heath. Many breeds, not included in the hound group or bred for hunting, will perform the field tasks the natives ask of the Basenji, retrieving, driving game into nets, hunting wounded animals and stalking the vicious reed rats of Africa. But the very unique qualities of the Basenji, as mentioned earlier, combined with his high intelligence, ability to be easily trained, and perky, deer-like beauty, put him in a class by himself. Basenjis were undoubtedly bred to be house dogs in ancient Egypt and, with the decline of Egypt's power, became something less than the early breeders fashioned in the hands of the lower-caste natives.

The Basenji is a still trailer and, in the opinion of the author, as stated above, is not a true hound and not fully admissible to either the scent or sight hound group.

Champion Phemister's Kedar

The breed lapsed into obscurity through the centuries, but was brought to light again in 1895, when an English explorer brought a pair back from Africa to England. Unfortunately these little dogs died before producing any get and it was not until 1937 that the breed was successfully introduced into both England and America. Mrs. Byron Rogers and Alexander Phemister were responsible for the Basenji's foothold in America. The parent club was formed in 1942 and the breed accepted for A.K.C. Stud Book Registration the following year.

The Basenji has gathered a very loyal following in the United States. Most large shows today have good entries.

STANDARD OF THE BASENJI

Characteristics—The Basenji should not bark, but is not mute. The wrinkled forehead and the swift, tireless running gait (resembling a racehorse trotting full out) are typical of the breed.

General Appearance—The Basenji is a small, lightly built, short backed dog, giving the impression of being high on the leg compared to its length. The wrinkled head must be proudly carried, and the whole demeanor should be one of poise and alertness.

Head and Skull—The skull is flat, well chiseled and of medium width, tapering towards the eyes. The foreface should taper from eye to muzzle and should be shorter than the skull. Muzzle, neither coarse, nor snipy but with rounded cushions. Wrinkles should appear upon the forehead, and be fine and profuse. Side wrinkles are desirable, but should never be exaggerated into dewlap.

Nose—Black greatly desired. A pinkish tinge should not penalize an otherwise first class specimen, but it should be discouraged in breeding.

Eyes—Dark hazel, almond shaped, obliquely set and far seeing.

Ears—Small, pointed and erect, of fine texture, set well forward on top of head.

Mouth—Teeth must be level with scissors bite.

Neck—Of good length, well crested and slightly full at base of throat. It should be well set into flat, laid back shoulders.

Forequarters—The chest should be deep and of medium width. The legs straight with clean fine bone, long forearm and well defined sinews. Pasterns should be of good length, straight and flexible.

Body—The body should be short and the back level. The ribs well sprung, plenty of heart room, deep brisket, short coupled, and ending in a definite waist.

Hindquarters—Should be strong and muscular, with hocks well let down, turned neither in nor out, with long second thighs.

Feet—Small, narrow and compact, with well arched toes.

Tail—Should be set on top and curled tightly over to either side.

Coat—Short and silky. Skin very pliant.

Color—Chestnut red (the deeper the better) or pure black, or black and tan, all with white feet, chest and tail tip. White legs, white blaze and white collar optional.

Weight—Bitches, 22 pounds approximately. Dogs, 24 pounds approximately.

Champion Cambria's Taboo

Size—Bitches 16 inches, and dogs 17 inches from the ground to the top of the shoulder. Bitches 16 inches and dogs 17 inches from the front of the chest to the farthest point of the hindquarters.

Faults—Coarse skull or muzzle. Domed or peaked skull. Dewlap. Round eyes. Low set ears. Overshot or undershot mouths. Wide chest. Wide behind. Heavy bone. Creams, shaded or off colors, other than those defined above, should be heavily penalized.

Champion Cambria's Ti-Kobra

The Basset is one of the most unusual of all hound breeds despite its obvious and exaggerated houndiness.

THE BASSET HOUND

The Basset Hound shares a common ancestry with the Bloodhound which he so closely resembles except in size. As a matter of fact the Basset looks much like a Bloodhound with legs cut down to make him handy enough in size to be kenneled under a bureau. He is commonly thought to have originated in France and from there journeyed to England. It is a fact that two distinct types have developed, one in France and the other in England, the latter more Bloodhound-like than the smaller, more agile French-bred Basset. The English Basset is also sounder in limb, though a dog with "full" or "half-crook" legs is desirable.

Short-legged hounds, in early times, were called "Bassets" in France and "Brackets" in England and were used to trail and start game into the open for sight ("gaze") hounds to run down or falcons to catch in the days before firearms, so the breed can boast of ancient lineage. Dogs of the same type were known in Russia and there were wire-haired Bassets bred in France, but they did not become popular.

The breed evidently came from a short-legged mutation in Bloodhounds and the type then bred and selected for over a long period of time. Certainly no breed other than the Bloodhound can surpass the Basset in scenting ability and his deep, hound bellow is much like that of the Bloodhound.

The Basset is used on hare, rabbit and pheasant generally. Sometimes grouse are added to the Basset's game bag. His short legs make him necessarily slow in the field but his voice (if you like the music of the hounds) more than makes up for his lack of speed.

Champion Rocky of Long View Acres

227

Bassets are good natured and more active than they look. The author's son owned one as a boy that we hunted over frequently and with enjoyment. This dog, Bullfiddle's Mister Magoo, weighed 65 pounds and was a fine, beautifully bred show dog (W.D. at Morris and Essex for 4 points, first time shown at 10 months of age). He was also a stubborn dog as Bassets are born to be, for it takes a stubborn dog to push such a big head and body through dense brush with such short legs.

Bassets pack well and are a beautiful sight in the field when run in packs. Of late the popularity of the breed has picked up in America due to the degree of excellence and uniformity produced in the breed by knowledgeable fanciers in this country.

STANDARD OF THE BASSET HOUND

Head—The head should be large, the skull narrow and of good length, the peak being very fully developed, a very characteristic point of the head, which should be free from any appearance of, or inclination, to cheek bumps. It is most perfect when it closest resembles the head of a bloodhound, with heavy flews and forehead wrinkled to the eyes. The expression when sitting or when still should be very sad, full of reposeful dignity. The whole of the head should be covered with loose skin, so loose in fact, that when the hound brings its nose to the ground the skin over the head and cheeks should fall forward and wrinkle perceptably.

Jaws—The nose itself should be strong and free from snipiness, while the teeth of the upper and lower jaws should meet, a pig-jawed hound, or one that is underhung, being distinctly objectionable.

Ears—The ears are very long, and when drawn forward folding well over

228

the nose. They are set on the head as low as is possible and hang loose in folds like drapery, the ends curling inward, in texture thin and velvety.

Eyes—The eyes should be deeply sunken, showing a prominent haw, and in color they should be a deep brown.

Neck and Shoulder—The neck should be powerful with heavy dewlaps set on sloping shoulders.

Forelegs—The forelegs should be short, very powerful, very heavy in bone, close fitting to the chest with a crook'd knee and wrinkled ankle, ending in a massive paw. A hound must *not* be "out at *elbows*" which is a bad fault.

Feet—He must stand perfectly sound and true on his feet which should be thick and massive, and the weight of the forepart of the body should be borne equally by each toe of the fore feet so far as it is compatible with the crook of the legs. *Unsoundness in legs or feet should absolutely disqualify a hound from taking a prize.*

Chest and Body—The chest should be deep and full. The body should be long and low and well ribbed up. Slackness of loin, flatsidedness and a roach or razor back are all bad faults.

Hocks—A hound should not be straight on his hocks, nor should he measure more over his quarters than he does at his shoulder. Cowhocks, straight hocks, or weak hocks, are all bad faults.

Quarters—The quarters should be full of muscle, which stands out so that when one looks at the dog from behind, it gives him a round, barrel-like effect, with quarters "round as an apple." He should be what is known as "a good dog to follow," and when trotting away from you, his hocks should bend well and he should move true all round.

Stern—The stern is coarse underneath, and carried "gaily" in hound fashion.

Coat—The coat should be similar to that of the fox-hound, not too fine and not too coarse, but yet of sufficient strength to be of use in bad weather. The skin loose and elastic.

Color—No good hound is a bad color, so that any recognized fox-hound color should be acceptable to the judge's eye, and only in the very closest competition should the color of a hound have any weight with a judge's decision.

Points of Basset Hound (Smooth)

	Points
Head, skull, eyes, muzzle, flews	14
Ears	10
Neck, dewlap, chest and shoulders	18
Forelegs and feet	18
Back, loins, hocks and hind quarters	18
Stern	5
Coat and skin	5
Color and markings	5
Basset Hound character and symmetry	7
Total	100

Disqualification

Unsoundness in legs or feet should disqualify a hound from taking a prize.

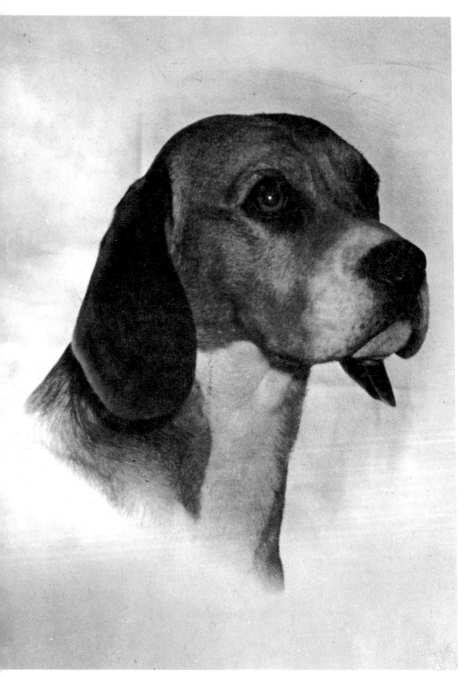

Champion Thornridge Wrinkles

THE BEAGLE

Packs of hounds were used to hunt game by the Greeks 400 years before the birth of Christ, so we can be reasonably certain that the origin of the hound dates from considerably before that ancient time. By 1550 hound breeds were being classified and given specific names according to size and the game they were most used to hunt. Thus larger hounds that were used on deer and boar were called "buck" and "boar" hounds. The smaller breeds, used specifically on hare and rabbits, were called, in French, "*Begles*," which anglicized became, "Beagle."

But these dogs were not our modern-day Beagle. They were, though, an important link in the evolutionary chain that produced Foxhounds, Harriers and, in turn, the Beagle, all three of these modern breeds alike in appearance except for size which is evidently due to selection. The Kerry Beagle, a small Bloodhound type, as well as the Southern English Hound also contributed to the Beagle's heritage. In England the breed was originally quite varied in size and there was also a wire-coated family said to have been keen and hardy hunters in inclement weather.

As a breed the Beagle is a merry and eager little fellow and the finest rabbit hound extant. The author and his son, Allan, hunted, showed, kenneled and bred specimens of this fine breed, among them the famous bench champion, Lynnlann's Button Up, who was also a fine field trial dog and headed the kennel's stud force.

Easy keepers, easy to groom and kennel, eager and splendid hunters and field trial dogs as well as wonderful companions, house dogs, and handsome show dogs, the great popularity of these marvelous little hounds can be easily understood.

Champion Thornridge Toney

The modern Beagle is bred in two sizes. The smaller variety does not exceed 13 inches at the withers. The larger is to exceed 13 inches but should not be taller than 15 inches.

Beagling has become an immensely popular sport in the United States. As mentioned before, the breed is not difficult to keep and so maintaining one or two couples does not amount to the expense connected with keeping larger hounds.

In the show ring the Beagle holds his own. Many good ones are shown all over the country and top wins are a frequent occurrence. Beagle trials are also a popular form of competition with many clubs established for the purpose of furthering the age old sport of pursuing the hare with the "merry Beagle."

Beagle packs are also maintained and run, adding a bit of swank to the many other wonderful attributes of this great little hound.

STANDARD OF THE BEAGLE

Head—The skull should be fairly long, slightly domed at occiput, with cranium broad and full.

Ears—Ears set on moderately low, long, reaching when drawn out nearly, if not quite, to the end of the nose; fine in texture, fairly broad—with almost entire absence of erectile power—setting close to the head, with the forward edge slightly inturning to the cheek—rounded at tip.

Eyes—Eyes large, set well apart—soft and houndlike—expression gentle and pleading; of a brown or hazel color.

Muzzle—Muzzle of medium length—straight and square cut—the stop moderately defined.

Jaws—Level. Lips free from flews; nostrils large and open.

Defects—A very flat skull, narrow across the top; excess of dome, eyes small, sharp and terrier like, or prominent and protruding; muzzle long, snipy or cut away decidedly below the eyes, or very short. Roman nosed, or upturned, giving a dish-face expression. Ears short, set on high or with a tendency to rise above the point of origin.

Body—Neck and Throat—Neck rising free and light from the shoulders, strong in substance yet not loaded, of medium length. The throat clean and free from folds of skin; a slight wrinkle below the angle of the jaw, however, may be allowable.

Defects—A thick, short, cloddy neck carried on a line with the top of the shoulders. Throat showing dewlap and folds of skin to a degree termed "throatiness."

Shoulders and Chest—Shoulders sloping—clean, muscular, not heavy or loaded—conveying the idea of freedom of action with activity and strength. Chest deep and broad, but not broad enough to interfere with the free play of the shoulders.

Defects—Straight, upright shoulders. Chest disproportionately wide or with lack of depth.

Back, Loin and Ribs—Back short, muscular and strong. Loin broad and slightly arched, and the ribs well sprung, giving abundance of lung room.

Defects—Very long or swayed or roached back. Flat, narrow loin. Flat ribs.

Forelegs and Feet—Forelegs—Straight, with plenty of bone in proportion to size of the hound. Pasterns short and straight.

Feet—Close, round and firm. Pad full and hard.

Defects—Out at elbows. Knees knuckled over forward, or bent backward. Forelegs crooked or Dachshundlike. Feet long, open or spreading.

Hips, Thighs, Hindlegs and Feet—Hips and Thighs—Strong and well-muscled, giving abundance of propelling power. Stifles strong and well let down. Hocks firm, symmetrical and moderately bent. Feet close and firm.

Defects—Cowhocks, or straight hocks. Lack of muscle and propelling power. Open feet.

Tail—Set moderately high; carried gaily, but not turned forward over the back; with slight curve; short as compared with size of the hound; with brush.

Defects—A long tail. Teapot curve or inclined forward from the root. Rat tail with absence of brush.

Coat—A close, hard, hound coat of medium length.

Defects—A short, thin coat, or of a soft quality.

Height—Height not to exceed 15 inches, measured across the shoulders at the highest point, the hound standing in a natural position with his feet well under him.

Color—Any true hound color.

General Appearance—A miniature fox-hound, solid and big for his inches, with the wear-and-tear look of the hound that can last in the chase and follow his quarry to the death.

SCALE OF POINTS

		Points
Skull	5	
Ears	10	
Eyes	5	
Muzzle	5	
Head	—	25
Neck	5	
Chest and shoulders	15	
Back, loin and ribs	15	
Body	—	35
Forelegs	10	
Hips, thighs and hindlegs	10	
Feet	10	
Running Gear	—	30
Coat	5	
Stern	5	
	—	10
Total		100

PACKS OF BEAGLES
SCORE OF POINTS FOR JUDGING

Hounds—General levelness of pack	40%	
Individual merit of hounds	30%	
	—	70%
Manners		20%
Appointments		10%
Total		100%

Measuring out Beagles before a field trial. This is an area of beagling that has attracted many sportsmen and in which this wonderful little hound is supreme.

International Champion Kinsman Kricket

Levelness of Pack—The first thing in a pack to be considered is that they present a unified appearance. The hounds must be as near of the same height, weight, conformation and color as possible.

Individual Merit of the Hounds—Is the individual bench show quality of the hounds. A very level and sporty pack can be gotten together and not a single hound be a good Beagle. This is to be avoided.

Manners—The hounds must all work gaily and cheerfully, with flags up— obeying all commands cheerfully. They should be broken to heel up, kennel up, follow promptly and stand. Cringing, sulking, lying down to be avoided. Also a pack must not work as though in terror of master and whips. In Beagle packs it is recommended that the whip be used as little as possible.

Appointments—Master and whips should be dressed alike, the master or huntsman to carry horn—the whips and master to carry light thong whips. One whip should carry extra couplings on shoulder strap.

RECOMMENDATIONS FOR SHOW LIVERY

Black velvet cap, white stock, green coat, white breeches or knickerbockers, green or black stockings, white spats, black or dark brown shoes. Vest and gloves optional.

Ladies should turn out exactly the same except for a white skirt instead of white breeches.

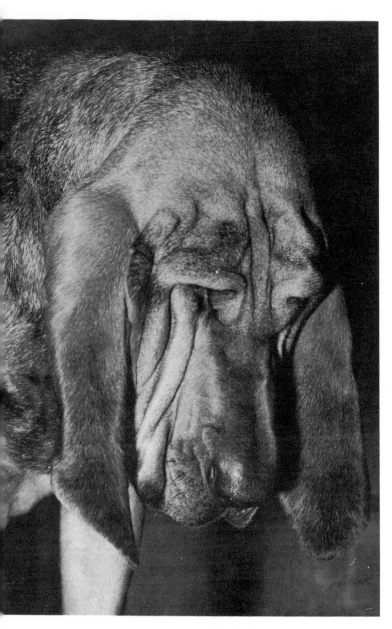

A typical head study of this ancient breed of
hounds that possess scenting powers that have
become legendary. The dog is the Bloodhound,
Champion Lady of Idle Hours.

THE BLOODHOUND

The Bloodhound is the basic breed from whose gene pool most all other scent hounds have drawn their scenting ability. But there is no other dog in existence who can rival the almost uncanny scenting powers of this huge hound.

An ancient breed, its name was probably derived from "blooded hounds," (denoting that they were pure breds) as they were called in the Twelfth century. Unfortunately, due to their publicized man-trailing ability, many uninformed people think that the name denotes a fierceness in the breed's character. The book and play, *Uncle Tom's Cabin*, did much to foster this idea. Nothing could be further from the truth. Bloodhounds never attack their quarry but instead will approach the most vicious criminal (whom they have been trailing for the police) with wagging tail, baying with the enjoyment of the chase. Known to Europe long before the Crusades, the breed was developed from the ancient St. Hubert Hounds, which were crossed into hound stock brought from Normandy to England by William the Conqueror and bred to local scenting canines called "Sleuth" hounds.

The Bloodhound is frequently seen on the show bench today. The breed does rather well in group and best-in-show competition and many of the same dogs that are top winners are accomplished trailers as well.

The author has had the pleasure of helping to train and work with Bloodhounds through his friend, Dr. Leon F. Whitney, of White Isle Kennels Bloodhound fame, and, through the same gentleman, met Captain V. G. Mullikin who, operating in the South, made over 2,500 criminal convictions with his Bloodhounds, including the justly famous "Nick Carter," who once

Champion Eastbourne Tarquin

followed a trail 105 hours old and who has the greatest record of convictions of any dog in the world. The author made a sketch of Nick Carter from life many years ago.

Used in penitentiaries until recently, and still very useful in State Police barracks where they are used mostly to track and find people lost in the woods, the Bloodhound is a big, gentle and affectionate animal who has, through the centuries, given unstintingly of his services to mankind.

STANDARD OF THE BLOODHOUND

General Character—The Bloodhound possesses, in a most marked degree, every point and characteristic of those dogs which hunt together by scent (Sagaces). He is very powerful, and stands over more ground than is usual with hounds of other breeds. The skin is thin to the touch and extremely loose, this being more especially noticeable about the head and neck, where it hangs in deep folds.

Height—The mean average height of adult dogs is 26 inches, and of adult bitches 24 inches. Dogs usually vary from 25 inches to 27 inches, and bitches from 23 inches to 25 inches; but, in either case, the greater height is to be preferred, provided that character and quality are also combined.

Weight—The mean average weight of adult dogs, in fair condition, is 90 pounds, and of adult bitches 80 pounds. Dogs attain the weight of 110 pounds, bitches 100 pounds. The greater weights are to be preferred, provided (as in the case of height) that quality and proportion are also combined.

Expression—The expression is noble and dignified, and characterized by solemnity, wisdom, and power.

Temperament—In temperament he is extremely affectionate, neither quarrelsome with companions nor with other dogs. His nature is somewhat shy, and equally sensitive to kindness or correction by his master.

Head—The head is narrow in proportion to its length, and long in proportion to the body, tapering but slightly from the temples to the end of the muzzle, thus (when viewed from above and in front) having the appearance of being flattened at the sides and of being nearly equal in width throughout its entire length. In profile the upper outline of the skull is nearly in the same plane as that of the foreface. The length from end of nose to stop (midway between the eyes) should be not less than that from stop to back of occipital protuberance (peak). The entire length of head from the posterior part of the occipital protuberance to the end of the muzzle should be 12 inches, or more, in dogs, and 11 inches, or more, in bitches.

Skull—The skull is long and narrow, with the occipital peak very pronounced. The brows are not prominent, although, owing to the deep-set eyes, they may have that appearance.

Foreface—The foreface is long, deep, and of even width throughout, with square outline when seen in profile.

Eyes—The eyes are deeply sunk in the orbits, the lids assuming a lozenge or diamond shape, in consequence of the lower lids being dragged down and everted by the heavy flews. The eyes correspond with the general tone of color of the animal, varying from deep hazel to yellow. The hazel color is, however, to be preferred, although very seldom seen in red-and-tan hounds.

Ears—The ears are thin and soft to the touch, extremely long, set very low, and fall in graceful folds, the lower parts curling inwards and backwards.

Champion St. Hubert Blondel

Wrinkle—The head is furnished with an amount of loose skin, which in nearly every position appears superabundant, but more particularly so when the head is carried low; the skin then falls into loose, pendulous ridges and folds, especially over the forehead and sides of the face.

Nostrils—The nostrils are large and open.

Lips, Flews, and Dewlap—In front the lips fall squarely, making a right angle with the upper line of the foreface; whilst behind they form deep, hanging flews, and, being continued into the pendant folds of loose skin about the neck, constitute the dewlap, which is very pronounced. These characters are found, though in a less degree, in the bitch.

Neck, Shoulders and Chest—The neck is long, the shoulders muscular and well sloped backwards; the ribs are well sprung; and the chest well let down between the forelegs, forming a deep keel.

Legs and Feet—The forelegs are straight and large in bone, with elbows squarely set; the feet strong and well knuckled up; the thighs and second thighs (gaskins) are very muscular; the hocks well bent and let down and squarely set.

Back and Loin—The back and loins are strong, the latter deep and slightly arched.

Stern—The stern is long and tapering, and set on rather high, with a moderate amount of hair underneath.

Gait—The gait is elastic, swinging and free, the stern being carried high, but not too much curled over the back.

Color—The colors are black-and-tan, red-and-tan, and tawny; the darker colors being sometimes interspersed with lighter or badger-colored hair, and sometimes flecked with white. A small amount of white is permissible on chest, feet, and tip of stern.

Barking tree, a sound that, carried by the night air through the autumn woods, is calculated to warm the heart of the coonhunter crashing through brush and bog by flashlight toward the clear bell-like baying. The Redbone Coonhound "doin' what comes naturally" is Champion Moran's Midnight Beauty.

HOUND BREEDS

THE AFGHAN HOUND.

SMALLEST OF THE SIGHT
HOUNDS, THE WHIPPET.

THE POPULAR BEAGLE.

THE AFGHAN, A SIGHT OR GAZE HOUND.

A RHODESIAN RIDGEBACK. EASILY DESCERNIBLE IS THE UNIQUE HAIR FORMATION ON THE BACK FROM WHICH THIS AFRICAN BREED DERIVES ITS NAME.

A BASENJI, THE BARKLESS DOG OF AFRICA.

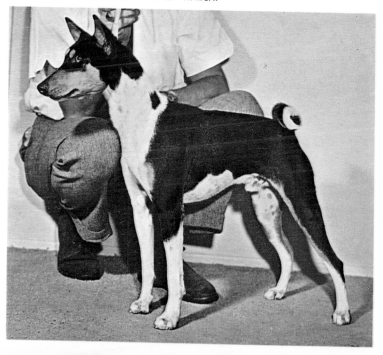

THE THREE COATS OF THE DACHSHUND. AT LEFT THE SMOOTH, BELOW THE WIRE-HAIRED AND, AT THE BOTTOM OF THE PAGE, THE LONGHAIRED DACHSHUND.

THE ARISTOCRATIC BORZOI.

AT RIGHT, AN OTTERHOUND. BELOW, ANCIENT
FRESCOES OF BOAR HUNTING, AND A SALUKI
BEING LED TO THE HUNT.

The author found these frescoes in the National
Archeological Museum in Athens, Greece. They had
decorated walls in the later palace of Tiryns, 1300
to 1200 B.C. Note the Harlequin Markings on some
of the boarhounds.

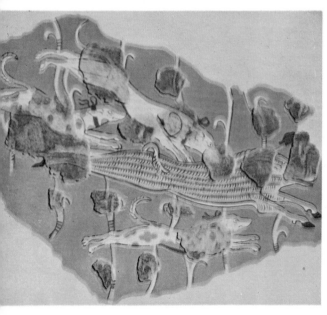

HEAD STUDY OF A
MODERN SALUKI.

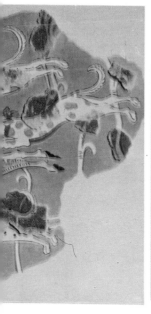

THE LONG-EARED, SHORT-LEGGED, POPULAR
HUNTING HOUND, THE BASSET.

A SOULFUL-EYED BASSET.

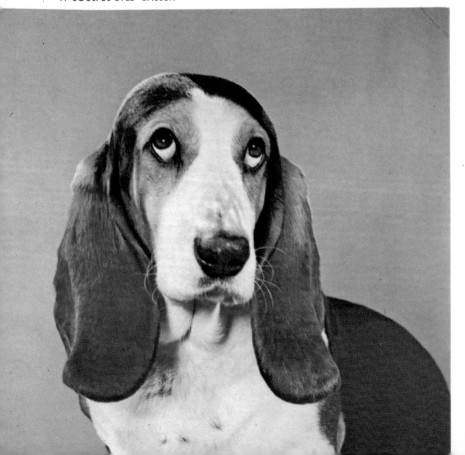

THE   SCOTTISH
DEERHOUND.

BELOW   IS   ANOTHER   COLOR
PHASE OF THE BASENJI.

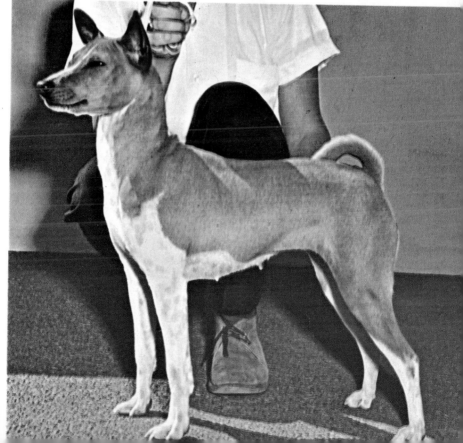

TOP LEFT IS A RHODESIAN RIDGEBACK, AND
BELOW IS A SPECIMEN OF THE BREED THAT IS
THE EPITOME OF ALL SCENT HOUNDS, THE
BLOODHOUND. ABOVE, ON THIS PAGE, IS THE
NORWEGIAN ELKHOUND.

TALLEST OF ALL BREEDS—THE IRISH
WOLFHOUND.

PORTRAIT OF AN AMERICAN FOXHOUND.

BELOW, A BLACK AND TAN COONHOUND.

FLEETEST OF ALL DOGS, THE GREYHOUND

THE COONHOUNDS

There are many breeds of Coonhounds of which only the Black and Tan is registered by the A.K.C. and seen at the familiar A.K.C. shows. Even the Black and Tan used for actual raccoon hunting is not quite the same in type as those who sport A.K.C. registrations. They are undoubtedly a beautiful hound with a bawling, musical, hound voice. In their quality and type they closely resemble the finest type of lithe Bloodhound. The Black and Tan, that is used afield, is shorter in ear and more common in appearance, albeit faster and stronger and is called a "night" dog. The Black and Tan is not as easily broken from running "trash" (animals other than 'coon) as are other Coonhound breeds, but once broken, sticks closely and cleanly to 'coon scent.

The Redbone Hound is one of the most uniform of Coonhounds in type. This is a well balanced, reddish colored, sagacious appearing animal who shows, upon close scrutiny, his Bloodhound ancestry. The coat is short, dense and hard, and the voice as sweet and melodious as a bugle call. Of all Coonhound breeds they are the most dependable night hunters.

The Bluetick Coonhound is the least uniform of the three major types that include the Black and Tan, and Redbone. Breeders tend to diversify, wanting varied sizes and types in their Bluetick Hounds. The author has hunted bear in Maine behind medium sized, houndy Blueticks, and seen a pack of Bluetick lion hounds in Arizona, of which the smallest member stood 25 inches at the shoulder and weighed over 80 pounds. Even the voice of these animals differ, for they drawl, bugle, or chop on the trail. They are nevertheless fine cooners, some of them the best, and a breed that are early starters and grow into real stayers.

The Plott Hound differs from all other hounds in coloring for he is a brindle dog with a black saddle. He has a keen, tough look and less the hound appearance than other breeds in his category. He has a clear, carrying voice, is a sticker, and easily and early trained. He can, like most Coonhounds, be trained to perform excellently on other kinds of game and makes a good cat, wild boar, and bear dog.

The true Treeing Walker is essentially an American Foxhound. The coondog strain comes from animals who took to night running and treeing 'coon and 'possum rather than running fox during the day. Cast out of the fox hunting packs, these animals were picked up by 'coon hunters, their tendency to run 'coon selected for, and they became the Coonhound known as the Treeing Walker. The best of this breed would be identical in type to the American Foxhound whose standard you will find under the history of that particular breed and so will not be repeated here.

The author is a staunch 'coon hunter who has followed many dogs through the masking darkness of many woods and will always thrill to the bawl of true running hounds on a clear crisp night. One of my fondest memories is of a Maine coonhunt with Joe Stetson, of Field and Stream fame, and Dr. George D. Whitney, a Coonhound and Beagle enthusiast from 'way back. But that is another story. To my mind, there is no breed finer for running, treeing and killing 'coon than a truly well bred and trained Redbone Hound.

The exact geneology of these Coonhounds cannot be traced. They are from the same basic stock as all hounds with the Bloodhound's influence predominating, especially in the Redbone. All these breeds are registered by the

U.K.C. (United Kennel Club) and various hound and hunt club stud books.

The standards of all of these Coonhounds, as formulated by their specific breeder's associations for kennel club registry (the A.K.C., the Black and Tan Coonhound and the American Foxhound; the U.K.C., the Redbone, Plott Hound and Bluetick) follows. The American Foxhound standard (parallel to the Treeing Walker) will be found under that breed's history. The author, several years ago, had the privilege of aiding the Coonhound associations in formulating their standards by illustrating the wanted type of each breed of Coonhound.

STANDARD OF THE BLACK AND TAN COONHOUND

The Black and Tan Coonhound is first and fundamentally a working dog, capable of withstanding the rigors of winter, the heat of summer, and the difficult terrain over which he is called upon to work. Judges are asked by the Club sponsoring the breed to place great emphasis upon these facts when evaluating the merits of the dog.

The general impression should be that of power, agility, and alertness. His expression should be alert, friendly, eager, and aggressive. He should immediately impress one with his ability to cover the ground with powerful rhythmic strides.

Head—The head should be cleanly modelled, with medium stop occurring midway between occiput bone and nose. The head should measure from 9 to 10 inches in males and from 8 to 9 inches in females. Viewed from the profile the line of the skull is on a practically parallel plane to the foreface or muzzle. The skin should be devoid of folds or excess dewlap. The flews should be well developed with typical hound appearance. Nostrils well open and always black. Skull should tend toward oval outline. Eyes should be from hazel to dark brown in color, almost round and not deeply set. The ears should be low set and well back. They should hang in graceful folds giving the dog a majestic appearance. In length they should extend well beyond the tip of the nose. Teeth should fit evenly with slightly scissors bite.

Body—Neck, Shoulders and Chest—The neck should be muscular, sloping, medium length, extending into powerfully constructed shoulders and deep chest. The dog should possess full, round, well sprung ribs, avoiding flat-sidedness.

Back and Tail—The back should be level, powerful and strong, with a visible slope from withers to rump. Tail should be strong, with base slightly below level of back line, carried free, and when in action at approximately right angle to back.

Legs and Feet—The forelegs should be straight, with elbows well let down, turning neither in nor out; pasterns strong and erect. Feet should be catlike with compact, well arched toes and thick strong pads.

Hind Quarters—Quarters should be well boned and muscled. From hip to hock long and sinewy, hock to pad short and strong. Stifles and hock well bent and not inclining either in or out. When standing on a level surface the hind feet should set back from under the body, and leg from pad to hock be at right angles to the ground when viewed both from profile and the rear. The stride of the Black and Tan Coonhound should be easy and graceful with plenty of reach in front and drive behind.

Coat and Color—The coat should be short but dense to withstand rough going. As the name implies, the color should be coal black, with rich tan

Grand Mere Black Sally, a Black and Tan Coonhound.

markings above eyes, on sides of muzzle, chest, legs and breeching with black pencil markings on toes.

Size—Measured at the shoulder, males 25 to 27 inches; females 23 to 25 inches. Height should be in proportion to general conformation so that dog appears neither leggy nor close to the ground. Dogs oversized should not be penalized when general soundness and proportion are in favor.

Judges should penalize the following defects: Undersize, elbows out at shoulder, lack of angulation in hind quarters, splay feet, sway or roach back, flatsidedness, lack of depth in chest, yellow or light eyes, shyness and nervousness.

Faults—Dewclaws; white on chest or other parts of body is highly undesirable and if it exceeds 1½ inches in diameter should be disqualified.

DISQUALIFICATION

White on chest or other parts fo the body if it exceeds 1½ inches in diameter.

STANDARD OF THE REDBONE COONHOUND

Color—Solid red preferred, small amount of white on blanket or feet not objectionable.

Head—Ears set moderately low, fine in texture, not stiff and reaching near

Redbone Coonhounds barking "tree".

the end of the nose when stretched out. Ears in proportion to head. *Fault*
Ears not firmly attached to head, seemingly just to skin. Eyes brown or hazel
in color, dark eyes preferred. Set well apart and of pleading expression. Skull
moderately broad, well proportioned with body. Muzzle well balanced with
other features of head, never dished or upturned. Teeth even, neither over-
nor undershot.

Neck—Throat clean, medium in length, strong, slightly arched and held
erect denoting proudness. Slight fold of skin below angle of jaw not objectionable.

Size—Slightly taller at shoulder than at hips. Never opposite, Males 22 to
26 inches. Females 21 to 25 inches.

Body—Deep broad chest, back strong and slightly arched, length well
proportioned to height, thighs and shoulders up, clean and muscular. Well-
sprung ribs, plenty of lung space.

Legs—Legs straight, well boned, pasterns straight, well set, clean and
muscular denoting combination of both strength and speed. Never cow
hocked.

Feet—Cat-paw type, compact, well-padded toes strong and well arched,
stout well-set nails. Feet should set as directly under leg as possible.

Tail—Medium in length, very slight brush, carried gaily but not hooked
over back. Set moderately high.

Coat—Smooth and hard, medium to short in length, sufficient for protection.

Manners—A hound should always indicate a willingness to obey his master's command which denotes intelligence.

Voice—While voice is an important factor in the hound, it should not be considered in bench shows but only on trail or at the tree.

STANDARD OF THE BLUETICK COONHOUND

Head and Neck—Ears well attached slightly below top of skull, should be thin with slight roll, taper well toward a point, and should reach well toward end of nose. Ears set low enough on head and devoid of erectile power. Ear well attached to head to prevent hanging or backward tilt.

Head skull very slightly domed, and broad between ears, never narrow. Length for males from occiput to end of nose, 9 to 10 inches; females, 8 to 9 inches.

Eyes should be rather large, set wide apart at the stop; stop prominent; expression pleading; color, dark brown or black, not lighter than hazel. Lids of eyes should be firm and close, without excess third eyelid showing (no drooping).

Muzzle from stop to end of nose should be square, well proportioned in width with the skull, with depth and flews well covering the lower jaw. Depth of 3 to 4½ inches.

Height at Shoulders—Slightly higher at shoulders than at hips, never lower at shoulders than at hips. Males, 23 to 26 inches at shoulders; females, 21 to 24 inches at shoulders.

Body—Neck should rise free from shoulders, with slight taper, not carried too high or too low, not thick as shoulders; muscular and of moderate length.

Champion "PR" Salt River Blue Rattler, a Bluetick Coonhound.

Throat clean, with very small trace of dewlap (excess dewlap objectionable).

Shoulders clean, gradually sloped and muscular, not broad and protruding, but to appear as part of body, showing freedom of movement and strength.

Chest should show considerable depth, rather than excessive width, allowing plenty of lung space, fairly even with front of shoulders, extending well down to the elbow, in girth for males, 26 to 34 inches; females, 23 to 30 inches.

Ribs should be well sprung with good depth and taper gradually to short ribs, resembling a curve in the chest, rather than a sunken drop-off between chest and stomach. Ribs should gather at the shoulders, sloping well with neck when head is held at alert.

Back should be moderately long and muscular, tapering up to a high gather at the shoulders, sloping well with neck when head is held at alert.

Loins broad, well muscled, and slightly arched. Back lengthy in comparison with height.

Forelegs straight from the shoulder down to the feet, well boned and muscular, with a strong straight pastern. Forelegs should appear straight from either side or front view.

Feet round with well-arched toes (no upward trend of toe claw). Thick tough pads. When standing should appear as a ball rather than to spread.

Hips strong and well muscled, width slightly less than rib spring. Rump should taper slightly with width in proportion to hips.

Thighs of gradual taper with excess muscular development giving abundant propelling power. Breeching full and clean down to hock.

Hocks firm and moderately bent, not excessively bent (as cow hock). Hind legs to appear straight with the body when viewed from behind.

Tail attached slightly below the back line, well rooted and tapering to a moderate length as compared with length of the hound. Carried high with a forward curve as of half moon. Tail well coated (no flag), no rat tail.

Coat medium coarse and laying close to body, to appear smooth and glossy. Neither too rough or too short.

Weight—Males, 55 to 80 pounds; females, 45 to 65 pounds.

Appearance—Appearance of the bluetick coonhound should be that of speedy, well-muscled individual, straight up of racy type, not chunky and clumsily built. Body should be neat, coat glossy; head carried well up, but not goose-necked. Eyes clear and keen. Tail carried gaily above back, not curled or dropped between legs. Feet round and well padded. A pleading hound expression, not wild or cowed acting. Active, ambitious, and speedy on trail.

Voice—The Bluetick should be a free tonguer on trail, with medium bawl or bugle voice when striking and trailing, may change to a steady chop when running, with a steady coarse chop at tree.

Color—Preferred color of the Bluetick is a dark blue thickly mottled body spotted by various-shaped black spots on back and ears and sides. Preference running to more blue than black on body. Head with black predominating, also ears, tan dots over eyes and on cheeks with a dark red ticking on feet and lower legs below body line. Red may be eliminated as to the desire of the breeder, as well as the head coloring and a mound of black on body. The amount of blue ticking should control over the amount of white in the body coat. Off-colors not allowed.

Teeth—Even, neither under- nor overshot.

Breeding—Only recognized pedigree and U.K.C. registered bloodlines acceptable.

Scale of Points

	Points
Head	25
Skull ... 5	
Ears ... 5	
Eyes ... 5	
Muzzle ... 10	
Body	40
Neck ... 5	
Chest and shoulders ... 15	
Back and loins ... 15	
Coat ... 3	
Tail ... 2	
Running Gear	35
Forelegs ... 10	
Hips, thighs, hind legs ... 15	
Feet ... 10	
Total	100

A Plott Hound of the wanted breed type.

STANDARD OF THE PLOTT HOUND

Head—Carried well up, dome moderately flat, moderate width between and above eyes. Ears set moderately high and of medium length, soft and no erectile power. Eyes brown or hazel, prominent, no drooping eyelids. Muzzle moderate length, not square.

Shoulders—Muscular and sloping to indicate speed and strength.

Chest—Deep, with adequate lung space.

Back—Slightly arched, well muscled, not roached.

Hips—Smooth, round, proportionately wide, flanks gracefully arched, muscular quarters and loins.

Tail or Stern—Moderately heavy, strong at root, tapering, rather long without brush, carried free, well up, saberlike.

Front Legs—Straight, smooth, forearm muscular. Straight at knees, perfectly in line with upper leg.

Hind Legs—Strong and muscular above hock, but graceful, slightly bent at hock, no cow hock, speedy shaped and graceful.

Feet—Round solid, cat foot, well padded and knuckled, set directly under leg.

Color and Coat—Smooth haired, fine, glossy, but thick enough for protection in cold wind or water. Brindle or brindle with black saddle. Some white on chest or feet permissible.

Voice—Open trailing, bawl and chop.

Height—Males, 22 to 25 inches at shoulder; females, 21 to 24 inches at shoulder.

Weight—Males, 50 to 60 pounds; females, 40 to 55 pounds.

Characteristics of this Breed—Active, fast, bright, confident, courageous, vicious fighters on game, super treeing instinct, take readily to water, alert, quick to learn, have great endurance and beauty.

SCALE OF POINTS

Points

Head	15
Neck	5
Shoulders	10
Chest and Ribs	10
Back and Loins	15
Hind Quarters	10
Elbows	5
Legs and Feet	15
Coat and Color	5
Stern	5
General Make-up	5
Total	100

THE DACHSHUND

Here is a breed that offers a wide range of fastidious selection in size, coat, and color. One can select either a standard or miniature Dachshund, a smooth, long-coated, or wire-coated dog in either size, and in color, red (tan) in various shades, and black and tan. These usual colors are augmented by other two-colored combinations (black, chocolate, gray, and white). Dappled and brindled Dachshunds are also acceptable and interesting colors.

The name, Dachshund, translated from the original German, means "Badger Hound," and this alone tells us the purpose for which the breed was conceived and used. A type of dog similar in general physical features, but much larger than our modern Dachshund, was used for badger hunting as early as the 15th century. These were probably the ancestors of the modern Dachshund but with the introduction, somewhere along the line, of various terrier breeds.

Again the author takes issue with the classification of this breed as a hound. The character of the Dachshund is much more like a terrier than a hound. The very purpose for which it was bred, to go to ground after its quarry, is more the purpose for which terriers were bred and used than hounds. As a matter of fact, the Dachshunds seen and bred in America are much too small to face as formidable an adversary as a badger.

Knowledgeable German breeders kept the coat varieties separated, set up a standard for the breed, and in 1888, founded the *Deutscher Teckelklub*, the

The smooth champion, Falcon of Heying-Teckel.

parent club for the breed. Hunting Dachshund associations (*Gebrauchsteckelklubs*) kept separate stud books. Incidentally, the wirehaired Dachshund was a later addition to the variety, coming after recognition of the smooth and longhaired varieties.

Dachshunds were imported into this country before the earliest American stud books or dog shows. Like all German breeds their popularity fell drastically in the postwar years, but after World War I was over and some of the bitterness forgotten, the breed again gained and continues to do so.

Sleek and easily kept, good little watchdogs, responsive, friendly, hardy and vigorous, the Dachshund makes a splendid housedog for small apartment or country dwellers. He does not require as much exercise as most longer-legged dogs and, at best, is an elegant, proud, and much-admired little dog.

There is a class, in American dog shows, for "under nine pounds" which permits miniature Dachshunds (the Zwergteckel and Kaninchenteckel of Germany) to compete in open competition.

STANDARD OF THE DACHSHUND (SUMMARY)

General Appearance—Short-legged, long-bodied, low-to-ground; sturdy, well-muscled, neither clumsy nor slim, with audacious carriage and intelligent expression; conformation pre-eminently fitted for following game into burrows.

Head—Long, uniformly-tapered, clean-cut; teeth well fitted, with scissor bite; eyes medium oval; ears broad, long, rounded, set on high and well back; neck long, muscular.

Fore Quarters—Muscular, compact. Chest deep, long, full and oval; breastbone prominent. Broad, long shoulder, and oblique humerus forming right angle; heavy, set close; forearm short, inclined slightly in. Foreleg straight and vertical in profile, covering deepest point of chest. Feet broad, firm, compact, turned slightly out.

Hind Quarters—Well-muscled and rounded. Pelvis, femur and tibia oblique, forming right angles; tarsus inclined forward. Hip should be level with shoulder, back strong, neither sagged nor more than very slightly arched. Tail strong, tapered, well-covered with hair, not carried gaily.

Varieties—Three coat types: *Smooth* or Shorthaired, short and dense, shining, glossy. *Wirehaired*, like German Spiky-Haired Pointer, hard, with good undercoat. *Longhaired*, like Irish Setter. *Miniature*, symmetrical rather slender body conformation below maximum limits of 11.8 and 13.8 inches chest girth, 7.7 and 8.8 pounds weight at minimum age of 12 months.

Color—Solid red (tan) of various shades, and black with tan points, should have black noses and nails, and narrow black line edging lips and eyelids; chocolate with tan points permits brown nose. Eyes of all, lustrous, the darker the better.

Faults—Over- or under-shot, knuckling over, loose shoulders; high on legs, clumsy gait, long, splayed or twisted feet, sagged or roached back, high croup, small, narrow or short chest, faulty angulation of fore or hind quarters, weak loins, narrow hind quarters, bowed legs, cowhocks; weak or dish-faced muzzle, dewlaps, uneven or scanty coat.

STANDARD OF THE DACHSHUND
GENERAL FEATURES
General Appearance—Low to ground, short-legged, long-bodied, but with

Champion William De Sangpur,
a longhaired Dachshund.

compact figure and robust muscular development; with bold and confident carriage of the head and intelligent facial expression. In spite of his shortness of leg, in comparison with his length of trunk, he should appear neither crippled, awkward, cramped in his capacity for movement, nor slim and weasel-like.

Qualities—He should be clever, lively, and courageous to the point of rashness, persevering in his work both above and below ground; with all the senses well developed. His build and disposition qualify him especially for hunting game below ground. Added to this, his hunting spirit, good nose, loud tongue, and small size, render him especially suited for beating the bush. His figure and his fine nose give him an especial advantage over most other breeds of sporting dogs for trailing.

Conformation of Body—Head—Viewed from above or from the side, it should taper uniformly to the tip of the nose, and should be clean cut. The skull is only slightly arched, and should slope gradually without stop (the less stop the more typical) into the finely-formed slightly-arched muzzle (ram's nose). The bridge bones over the eyes should be strongly prominent. The nasal cartilage and tip of the nose are long and narrow; lips tightly stretched, well covering the lower jaw, but neither deep nor pointed; corner of the mouth not very marked. Nostrils well open. Jaws opening wide and hinged well back of the eyes, with strongly developed bones and teeth.

Teeth: Powerful canine teeth should fit closely together, and the outer side of the lower incisors should tightly touch the inner side of the upper. (Scissors bite.)

Eyes: Medium size, oval, situated at the sides, with a clear, energetic, though pleasant expression; not piercing. Color, lustrous dark reddish-brown to brownish-black for all coats and colors. Wall (fish or pearl) eyes in the case of grey or dapple-colored dogs are not a very bad fault, but are also not desirable.

Ears: Should be set near the top of the head, and not too far forward, long but not too long, beautifully rounded, not narrow, pointed, or folded. Their carriage should be animated, and the forward edge should just touch the cheek.

Neck: Fairly long, muscular, clean-cut, not showing any dewlap on the throat, slightly arched in the nape, extending in a graceful line into the shoulders, carried proudly but not stiffly.

Front—To endure the arduous exertion underground, the front must be correspondingly muscular, compact, deep, long and broad. Fore quarters in detail:

(*a*) Shoulder Blade: Long, broad, obliquely and firmly placed upon the fully developed thorax, furnished with hard and plastic muscles.

(*b*) Upper Arm: Of the same length as the shoulder blade, and at right angles to the latter, strong of bone and hard of muscle, lying close to the ribs, capable of free movement.

(*c*) Forearm: This is short in comparison to other breeds, slightly turned inwards; supplied with hard but plastic muscles on the front and outside, with tightly-stretched tendons on the inside and at the back.

(*d*) Joint between Forearm and Foot (wrists): These are closer together than the shoulder joints, so that the front does not appear absolutely straight.

(*e*) Paws: Full, broad in front, and a trifle inclined outwards; compact, with well-arched toes and tough pads.

(*f*) Toes: There are five of these, though only four are in use. They should be close together, with a pronounced arch; provided on top with strong nails, and underneath with tough toe-pads.

Trunk—The whole trunk should in general be long and fully muscled. The back, with sloping shoulders, and short rigid pelvis, should lie in the straightest possible line between the withers and the very slightly arched loins, these latter being short, rigid, and broad.

(*a*) Chest: The breast bone should be strong, and so prominent in front that on either side a depression (dimple) appears. When viewed from the front, the thorax should appear oval, and should extend downward to the mid-point of the forearm. The enclosing structure of ribs should appear full and oval, and when viewed from or above from the side, full-volumed, so as to allow by its ample capacity, complete development of heart and lungs. Well ribbed up, and gradually merging into the line of the abdomen. If the length is correct, and also the anatomy of the shoulder and upper arm, the front leg when viewed in profile should cover the lowest point of the breast line.

(*b*) Abdomen: Slightly drawn up.

Hind Quarters—The hind quarters viewed from behind should be of completely equal width.

(*a*) Croup: Long, round, full, robustly muscled, but plastic, only slightly sinking toward the tail.

(*b*) Pelvic Bones: Not too short, rather strongly developed, and moderately sloping.

(*c*) Thigh Bone: Robust and of good length, set at right angles to the pelvic bones.

(*d*) Hindlegs: Robust and well-muscled, with well-rounded buttocks.

(*e*) Knee Joint: Broad and strong.

(*f*) Calf Bone: In comparison with other breeds, short; it should be perpendicular to the thigh bone, and firmly muscled.

(*g*) The bones at the base of the foot (*tarsus*) should present a flat appearance, with a strongly prominnet hock and a broad tendon of Achilles.

(*h*) The central foot bones (*metatarsus*) should be long, movable towards the calf bone, slightly bent toward the front, but perpendicular (as viewed from behind).

(*i*) Hind Paws: Four compactly-closed and beautifully-arched toes, as in the case of the front paws. The whole foot should be posed equally on the ball and not merely on the toes; nails short.

Tail—Set in continuation of the spine, extending without very pronounced curvature, and should not be carried too gaily.

Note.—Inasmuch as the Dachshund is a hunting dog, scars from honorable wounds shall not be considered a fault.

SPECIAL CHARACTERISTICS OF THE THREE COAT VARIETIES OF DACHSHUNDS

The Dachshund is bred with three varieties of coat: (A) Shorthaired (*or Smooth*); (B) Wirehaired; (C) Longhaired. All three varieties should conform to the characteristics already specified. The longhaired and shorthaired are old, well-fixed varieties, but into the wirehaired Dachshund, the blood of other breeds has been purposely introduced; nevertheless, in breeding him, the greatest stress must be placed upon conformity to the general Dachshund type.

The Wirehaired Dachshund, Champion Vantabe's Draht Timothy.

The following specifications are applicable separately to the three-coat varieties, respectively:

(A) *Shorthaired (or smooth) Dachshund*—Hair: Short, thick, smooth and shining; no bald patches. Special faults are: Too fine or thin hair, leathery ears, bald patches, too coarse or too thick hair in general.

Tail: Gradually tapered to a point, well but not too richly haired; long, sleek bristles on the underside are considered a patch of strong-growing hair, not a fault. A brush tail is a fault, as is also a partly- or wholly-hairless tail.

Color of Hair, Nose and Nails: (*a*) One-Colored Dachshund: This group includes red (often called tan), red-yellow, and yellow, with or without a shading of interspersed black hairs. Nevertheless a clean color is preferable, and red is to be considered more desirable than red-yellow or yellow. Dogs strongly shaded with interspersed black hairs belong to this class, and not to the other color groups. No white is desirable, but a solitary small spot is not exactly disqualifying.

Nose and Nails: Black; red is admissible, but not desirable.

(*b*) Two-Colored Dachshund: These comprise deep black, chocolate, grey, and white; each with rust-brown or yellow marks over the eyes, on the sides of the jaw and underlip, on the inner edge of the ear, front, breast, inside and behind the front leg, on the paws and around the anus, and from there to about one-third to one-half of the length of the tail on the under side. (The most common two-colored Dachshund is usually called black-and-tan.) Except on white dogs, no white is desirable, but a solitary small spot is not exactly disqualifying. Absence, or undue prominence of tan markings is undesirable.

Nose and Nails: In the case of black dogs, black; for chocolate, brown or black; for grey, grey or even flesh color, but the last named color is not desirable; in the case of white dogs, black nose and nails are to be preferred.

(c) Dappled and Striped Dachshund: The color of the dappled (or tiger) Dachshund is a clear brownish or grayish color, or even a white ground, with dark irregular patches of dark-gray, brown, red-yellow or black (large areas of one color not desirable). It is desirable that neither the light nor the dark color should predominate. The color of the striped (brindle) Dachshund is red or yellow with a darker streaking.

Nose and Nails: As for One- and Two-Colored Dachshund.

(B) *Wirehaired Dachshund*—The general appearance is the same as that of the shorthaired, but without being long in the legs, it is permissible for the body to be somewhat higher off the ground.

Hair: With the exception of jaw, eyebrows, and ears, the whole body is covered with a perfectly uniform tight, short, thick, rough, hard coat, but with finer, shorter hairs (undercoat) everywhere distributed between the coarser hairs, resembling the coat of the German spiky-haired pointer. There should be a beard on the chin. The eyebrows are bushy. On the ears the hair is shorter than on the body; almost smooth, but in any case conforming to the rest of the coat. The general arrangement of the hair should be such that the wirehaired Dachshund, when seen from a distance should resemble the smooth-haired. Any sort of soft hair in the coat is faulty, whether short or long, or wherever found on the body; the same is true of long, curly, or wavy hair, or hair that sticks out irregularly in all directions; a flag tail is also objectionable.

Tail: Robust, as thickly haired as possible, gradually coming to a point, and without a tuft.

Color of Hair, Nose and Nails: All colors are admissible. White patches on the chest, though allowable, are not desirable.

(C) *Longhaired Dachshund*—The distinctive characteristic differentiating this coat from the short- or smooth-haired Dachshund is alone the rather long silky hair.

Hair: The soft, sleek, glistening, often slightly-wavy hair should be longer under the neck, on the underside of the body, and especially on the ears and behind the legs, becoming there a pronounced feather; the hair should attain its greatest length on the underside of the tail. The hair should fall beyond the lower edge of the ear. Short hair on the ear, so-called "leather" ears, is not desirable. Too luxurious a coat causes the longhaired Dachshund to seem coarse, and masks the type. The coat should remind one of the Irish Setter, and should give the dog an elegant appearance. Too thick hair on the paws, so-called "mops," is inelegant, and renders the animal unfit for use. It is faulty for the dog to have equally long hair over all the body, if the coat is too curly, or too scrubby, or if a flag tail or overhanging hair on the ears are lacking; or if there is a very pronounced parting on the back, or a vigorous growth between the toes.

Tail: Carried gracefully in prolongation of the spine; the hair attains here its greatest length and forms a veritable flag.

Color of Hair, Nose and Nails: Exactly as for the smooth-haired Dachshund.

Miniature Dachshund—Note.—Miniature Dachshunds are bred in all three coats. They are not under-sized or undeveloped specimens of full-sized Dachshunds, but have been pursposely produced to work in burrows smaller than light- and heavy-weight Dachshunds can enter. The limits set upon their weight and chest circumference have inevitably resulted in a more slender body structure. Depth of chest and shortness of leg proportionate to the regular conformation, would in these diminutive animals, prove impractical for their active hunting purposes.

The German specifications limit Zwergteckel (dwarf dachshunds) to a chest circumference of 13.8 inches (35 centimeters) and to weights for males of 8.8 pounds avoirdupois (4 kilograms, 8 pfunde) and for females of 7.7 pounds (3.5 kg., 7 pfd.), and limit Kaninchenteckel (rabbit dachshunds) to a chest circumference of 11.8 inches (30 cm.) and to weights for both sexes of 7.7 pounds, certified at a minimum age of twelve months. Rather than the ideal, these sizes represent instead the upper limit for miniature registration; and thus in pedigrees provide an index to purity of miniature breeding. For hunting, where Kaninchenteckel originated, in order to move freely through rabbit holes, weights from 6 to below 5 pounds are preferred. In the show ring, weights well below the above maxima, far from being penalized, represent the desired type.

Miniature Dachshunds have not been given separate classification in the United States. A class for "under nine pounds" at American shows permit Zwerg- and Kaninchenteckel to compete as miniatures according to the German specifications. Within the limits imposed, symmetrical adherence to the general Dachshund conformation, combined with smallness, and mental and physical vitality should be the outstanding characteristics of the miniature Dachshund.

GENERAL FAULTS

Serious Faults (which may prevent a dog from receiving any show rating): Over- or under-shot jaws, knuckling over, very loose shoulders.

Secondary Faults (which may prevent a dog from receiving a high show rating): A weak, long-legged, or dragging figure; body hanging between the shoulders; sluggish, clumsy, or waddling gait; toes turned inwards or too obliquely outwards; splayed paws, sunken back, roach (or carp) back; croup higher than withers; short-ribbed or too-weak chest; excessively drawn up flanks like those of a greyhound; narrow, poorly-muscled hind quarters; weak loins; bad angulation in front or hind quarters; cowhocks; bowed legs; "glass" eyes, except for gray or dappled dogs; a bad coat.

Minor Faults (which may prevent a dog from receiving the highest rating in championship competition): Ears wrongly set, sticking out, narrow or folded; too marked a stop; too pointed or weak a jaw; pincer teeth, distemper teeth; too wide or too short a head; goggle eyes, "glass" eyes in the case of gray and dappled dogs, insufficiently dark eyes in the case of all other coat-colors; dewlaps; short neck; swan neck; too fine or too thin hair.

THE FOXHOUNDS
ENGLISH AND AMERICAN

The English Foxhound, highly standardized in England, was and still is, the traditional pack dog for "his lordship's" exciting fox hunts when the ladies and gentlemen of the countryside joined their host in riding to hounds over any and all obstacles atop their favorite hunting horses.

It is quite likely that the breed was developed from early French hounds such as the Whites, Duns and Fallows, and the St. Hubert Hounds who are also in the genetic background of the Bloodhound.

A good English Foxhound is a superb animal showing the regal stamp and symmetry of man's finest breeding touch. English Foxhounds were imported to America in 1738 by the first Lord Fairfax.

The American Foxhound was molded from the English Foxhound by some of our foremost Americans, notably George Washington and many other foxhunting founders of our nation. Lafayette sent our first president some fine French hounds which Washington crossed into his pack of English Foxhounds. Other crosses subsequently occurred from English, French and Irish hound importations producing many familiar name strains such as: Trigg, Birdsong, Walker, July, etc.

Through these crosses a Foxhound was produced of lighter bone and more houndy appearance than the English Foxhound, a dog better fitted for fox-hunting in America's more rugged terrain. Types have varied in different localities but the last few years have seen greater uniformity over a larger area.

An English Foxhound.

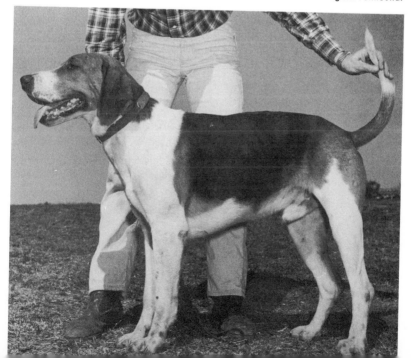

Part of a pack of English Foxhounds.

STANDARD OF THE ENGLISH FOXHOUND

The *Head* should be of full size, but by no means heavy. Brow pronounced, not not high or sharp. There should be a good length and breadth, sufficient to give in a dog hound a girth in front of the ears of fully 16 inches. The nose should be long (4½ inches) and wide, with open nostrils. Ears set on low and lying close to the cheeks. Most English hounds are "rounded" which means that about 1½ inches is taken off the end of the ear. The teeth must meet squarely, either a *pig-mouth* (overshot) or undershot being a disqualification.

The *Neck* must be long and clean, without the slightest throatiness, not less than 10 inches from cranium to shoulder. It should taper nicely from shoulders to head, and the upper outline should be slightly convex.

The *Shoulders* should be long and well clothed with muscle, without being heavy, especially at the points. They must be well sloped, and the true arm between the front and the elbow must be long and muscular, but free from fat or lumber.

Chest and Back Ribs—The chest should girth over 31 inches in a 24-inch hound, and the back ribs must be very deep.

The *Back* and *Loin* must both be very muscular, running into each other without any contraction between them. The couples must be wide, even to raggedness, and the top line of the back should be absolutely level, the *Stern* well set on and carried gaily but not in any case curved *over* the back like a squirrel's tail. The end should taper to a point and there should be a fringe of hair below.

The *Hind Quarters* or propellers are required to be very strong, and as endurance is of even greater consequence than speed, straight stifles are preferred to those much bent as in a greyhound.

Elbows set quite straight, and neither turned in or out are a *sine qua non*. They must be well let down by means of the long true arm above mentioned.

Legs and Feet—Every Master of Foxhounds insists on legs as straight as a post, and as strong; size of bone at the ankle being especially regarded as all important. The desire for straightness had a tendency to produce knuckling-over, which at one time was countenanced, but in recent years this defect has been eradicated by careful breeding and intelligent adjudication, and one sees very little of this trouble in the best modern Foxhounds. The bone cannot be too large, and the feet in all cases should be round and cat-like, with well-developed knuckles and strong horn, which last is of the greatest importance.

The *Color* and *Coat* are not regarded as very important, so long as the former is a good "hound color," and the latter is short, dense, hard, and glossy. Hound colors are black, tan, and white, or any combination of these three, also the various "pies" compounded of white and the color of the hare and badger, or yellow, or tan.

The *Symmetry* of the Foxhound is of the greatest importance, and what is known as "quality" is highly regarded by all good judges.

SCALE OF POINTS *Points*

Head	5
Neck	10
Shoulders	10
Chest and back ribs	10
Back and loin	15
Hind quarters	10
Elbows	5
Legs and feet	20
Color and coat	5
Stern	5
Symmetry	5
Total	100

DISQUALIFICATION

Pig-mouth (overshot) or undershot.

STANDARD OF THE AMERICAN FOXHOUND

Head—Skull—Should be fairly long, slightly domed at occiput, with cranium broad and full.

Ears—Ears set on moderately low, long, reaching when drawn out nearly, if not quite, to the tip of the nose; fine in texture, fairly broad, with almost entire absence of erectile power—setting close to the head with the forward edge slightly inturning to the cheek—round at tip.

Eyes—Eyes large, set well apart—soft and houndlike—expression gentle and pleading; of a brown or hazel color.

Muzzle—Muzzle of fair length—straight and square cut—the top moderately defined.

Defects—A very flat skull, narrow across the top; excess of dome; eyes small, sharp and terrier like, or prominent and protruding; muzzle long and snipy, cut away decidedly below the eyes, or very short. Roman nosed, or upturned, giving a dish-face expression. Ears, short set on high, or with a tendency to rise above the point of origin.

Body—Neck and Throat—Neck rising free and light from the shoulders, strong in substance yet not loaded, of medium length. The throat clean and free from folds of skin, a slight wrinkle below the angle of the jaw, however, is allowable.

Defects—A thick, short, cloddy neck carried on a line with the top of the shoulders. Throat showing dewlap and folds of skin to a degree termed "throatiness."

Shoulders, Chest and Ribs—Shoulders sloping—clean, muscular, not heavy or loaded—conveying the idea of freedom of action with activity and strength. Chest should be deep for lung space, narrower in proportion to depth than the English hound—28 inches (*girth*) in a 23-inch hound being good. Well sprung ribs—back ribs should extend well back—a three-inch flank allowing springiness.

Back and Loins—Back moderately long, muscular and strong. Loins broad and slightly arched.

Defects—Very long or swayed or roached back. Flat, narrow loins.

Forelegs and Feet—Forelegs—Straight, with fair amount of bone. Pasterns short and straight.

Feet—Fox like. Pad full and hard. Well arched toes. Strong nails.

Defects—Straight, upright shoulders, chest disproportionately wide or with lack of depth. Flat ribs.

Defects—Out at elbow. Knees knuckled over forward, or bent backward. Fore legs crooked. Feet long, open or spreading.

Hips, Thighs, Hindlegs and Feet—Hips and Thighs—Strong and muscled. giving abundance of propelling power. Stifles strong and well let down Hocks firm, symmetrical and moderately bent. Feet close and firm.

Defects—Cowhocks, or straight hocks. Lack of muscle and propelling power. Open feet.

Tail—Set moderately high; carried gaily, but not turned forward over the back; with slight curve; with very slight brush.

Defects—A long tail. Teapot curve or inclined forward from the root. Rat tail, entire absence of brush.

Coat—A close, hard, hound coat of medium length.

Defects—A short thin coat, or of a soft quality.

Height—Dogs should not be under 22 or over 25 inches. Bitches should not be under 21 or over 24 inches measured across the back at the point of the withers, the hound standing in a natural position with his feet well under him.

Color—Any color.

Canadian Champion Emden's Huckleberry
Hound, an American Foxhound.

SCALE OF POINTS

		Points	
Head			
Skull		5	
Ears		5	
Eyes		5	
Muzzle		5	
		—	20
Body			
Neck		5	
Chest and shoulders		15	
Back, loins and ribs		15	
		—	35
Running Gear			
Forelegs		10	
Hips, thighs and hindlegs		10	
Feet		15	
		—	35
Coat and Tail			
Coat		5	
Tail		5	
		—	10
Total			100

THE HARRIER

In between the Foxhound and the Beagle, in size and utility, the Harrier has never reached a great degree of popularity, though fanciers of the breed are staunch in their praise of his many merits.

The background of the breed runs parallel to that of the Foxhound and Beagle, and selection for type in all three breeds has been consistent, with the greatest difference in size only. The Harrier is a hare-hunting dog and a specialist at his trade.

The first recorded pack of Harriers was the Penistone, established in 1260 by Sir Elias de Midhope and held together for five centuries, a great tribute to the character and hunting ability of the Harrier. In the British Isles hunting the hare behind a pack of Harriers has been a pleasure of the common man since, unlike fox hunting (where the dogs are followed on finely bred, high headed and expensive horses) the Harrier pack can be followed on foot.

The Harrier differs from the Foxhound in size and in the occasional blue mottled color of coat that is unique with the breed. Though registered with the A.K.C. as early as 1885, subsequent registrations have been few because the breed has been kept mostly for hunting, not for the show bench, and most litters are registered in hunt club hound stud books rather than with the A.K.C.

STANDARD OF THE HARRIER

The points of the modern Harrier are very similar to those of the English

A pack of Harriers with their liveried handlers.

English import, Vale Lune Cockspur.

Foxhound. The Harrier, however, is smaller than the English Foxhound and the most popular size is 19 to 21 inches.

They should be active, well balanced and full of strength and quality, with shoulders sloping into the muscles of the back, clean and not loaded on the withers or point.

The back level and muscular, and not dipping behind the withers or arching over the loin.

The elbow's point set well away from the ribs, running parallel with the body and not turning outwards.

Deep, well-sprung ribs running well back, with plenty of heart room, and a deep chest.

Good straight legs with plenty of bone running well down to the toes, but not overburdened, inclined to knuckle over very slightly but not exaggerated in the slightest degree.

Round cat-like feet, and close toes turning inwards.

Hindlegs and hocks stand square, with a good sweep and muscular thigh to take the weight off the body.

The head should be of a medium size with good bold forehead, and plenty of expression; head must be well set up on a neck of ample length and, not heavy; stern should be set well up, long and well controlled.

279

THE NORWEGIAN ELKHOUND

Of all breeds known to man the Norwegian Elkhound has probably changed least from the pristine dog type through the ages of its development. Dogs like him were in the ancestral design of sheepherding, sled, hunting and hauling dogs which, through centuries of time, mutations, and man's selection, changed drastically in type from the basic canine mold. Only a few remained as they were originally in that dim past predating history, and the Norwegian Elkhound is one of these.

In this case it is all the more remarkable because the type he represents is so far removed in modern times from the hound type with which we are familiar. Perhaps this is due to the many jobs he has done throughout his history. A comrade to the Vikings, a defender of the flocks he herded, from wolves and bear and two-legged predators, a hunter with the nomadic Norsemen; all these has he been, and in all, a fearless animal devoted to his master, his Nordic traits untainted by other blood.

Of all things, despite his unhoundy appearance, the Elkhound is a hunter of big game, especially Elk (in his native Norway), but he can become expert on bear, lynx, bobcat or lion. The Elkhound scents and tracks his game, brings it to bay, avoids destruction through his bouncing agility, and gives high-pitched tongue to bring the hunter. He can be trained to hunt capercailzie, black grouse and other upland birds.

The Elkhound is undoubtedly of Northern basic "Spitz" stock, similar to the sled dogs of the far north but adopted and selected for specialization by men of the North many centuries ago.

STANDARD OF THE NORWEGIAN ELKHOUND

General Description—The Norwegian Elkhound is a typical northern dog,

Norwegian Elkhound puppies.

Champion Carro of Ardmere

of medium size, with a compact, proportionately short body, with a thick and rich, but not bristling, gray coat, with prick ears, and with a tail that is curled and carried over the back. His temperament is bold and energetic.

Head—"Dry" (without any loose skin), broad at the ears; the forehead and back of the head only slightly arched; the stop not large, yet clearly defined. The muzzle is of medium length, thickest at the base and, seen from above or from the side, tapers evenly without being pointed. The bridge of the nose is straight; the lips are tightly closed.

Ears—Set high, firm and erect, are higher than they are wide at the base, pointed (not rounded) and very mobile. When the dog is listening, the orifices are turned forward.

Eyes—Not protruding, brown in color, preferably dark, lively, with a fearless energetic expression.

Neck—Of medium length, "dry" (without any loose skin), strong, and well set up.

Body—Powerful, *compact*, and short, with broad deep chest, well-sprung ribs, straight back, well-developed loins, and stomach very little drawn up.

Legs—Firm, straight and strong; elbows closely set on, hindlegs with little angulation at knees and hocks. Seen from behind, they are straight.

Feet—Comparatively small, somewhat oblong, with tightly closed toes, not turned out. There should be no dewclaws on hindlegs.

Tail—Set high, short, thickly and closely haired, but without brush; tightly curled, not carried too much to one side.

Coat—Thick, rich and hard, but rather smooth-lying. On head and front of legs, short and even; longest on neck and chest, on buttocks, on hindside of

forelegs and on underside of tail. It is made up of longer and harder covering hairs, dark at the tips, and of a light, soft, woolly undercoat.

Color—Gray, with black tips to the long covering hairs; somewhat lighter on chest, stomach, legs, underside of tail, and around anus. The color may be lighter or darker, with a slight shading towards yellow; but a pronounced variation from the gray color disqualifies. Too dark or too light individuals should be avoided; also, yellow markings or uneven coloring. There should be no pronounced white markings.

Height at Shoulder—For dogs, about 20.5 inches; for bitches, about 18 inches.

DISQUALIFICATION

Pronounced variation from gray color.

THE OTTER HOUND

"A Bloodhound in a wire-haired coat," is as good a description as can be found of the Otter Hound. The same ancestry as that which shaped the Bloodhound and the old Vendee Hound of France is the basis for the origin of the Otter Hound. As a matter of fact, though other historians of the breed have credited varied genetic source material to the Otter Hound's background, it is the unbiased truth that the descriptions of the old Vendee Hound and Otter Hound are apparently exact.

The Otter Hound has been a great favorite in England where it is said, "Every sizeable stream has its otter." To hunt these wily animals a very distinct type of hound was first necessary and then evolved to fit the necessity by British sportsmen. The breed's age can be attested to by the fact that King Henry II bore the title of Master of Otter Hounds.

During the last half of the 19th century there were as many as twenty packs of Otter Hounds hunting regularly through the season in England. The best pack, authorities agree, was that of Squire Lomax of Clitheroe.

Essentially bred as a water dog, he has no peer in this element. Courageous, hardy, sagacious and of fine character, the breed is essentially a hard working sporting dog and not a show dog. Shown initially in the United States in 1907, the Otter Hound has never become popular in America, perhaps because he is a specialist without a specialty in this country.

His importance here has been in his role as a progenitor, for the breed gave important genetic material to the foundation stock that eventually produced the popular and utilitarian Airedale Terrier.

Champion Tyburn Trumpeter

In these splendid photos taken in
England we see, above, the
beginning of an Otter hunt, the
hounds eager and ready. The
facing page depicts the end of the
successful hunt, the catch held
high in triumph.

Champion Lugina's Viking of
Adriucha

STANDARD OF THE OTTER HOUND

In general appearance—always excepting the coat—he much resembles the Bloodhound; he should be perfect in symmetry, strongly built, hard and enduring, with unfailing powers of scent, and a natural antipathy to the game he is bred to pursue. The head should be large, broader in proportion than the Bloodhound's, the forehead high, the muzzle a fair length and the nostrils wide. The ears are long, thin and pendulous, fringed with hair. The neck is not naturally long, and looks shorter than it really is from the abundance of hair on it; the shoulders should slope well, the legs be straight and the feet a good size, but compact; the back strong and wide, the ribs, and particularly the back ribs, well let down; the thighs should be big and firm, and the hocks well let down; the stern well and thickly covered with hair and carried well up, but not curled; the colors are generally grizzle or sandy, with black and tan more or less clearly defined.

SCALE OF POINTS

	Points
Skull	10
Jaws	10
Eyes	5
Ears	10
Chest and shoulders	15
Body and loin	15
Legs and feet	10
Coat	10
Stern	5
Symmetry and strength	10
Total	100

THE RHODESIAN RIDGEBACK

The Rhodesian Ridgeback, also known as the African Lion Hound, emerged as a breed from the ancient stronghold of the savage Zulu chiefs of South Africa.

During the 16th and 17th centuries, Europeans migrating to South Africa took with them Terriers, Bloodhounds, Mastiffs and other breeds, and these dogs, inter-bred with the native, half-wild hunting dogs of the Hottentots, became the foundation stock of the Ridgeback of today. In the beginning, the early Boer settlers found it necessary to shoot on sight these fierce maurading native dogs who decimated their flocks of sheep and poultry.

Eventually, however, these "dogs with snakes on their backs"—a phrase deriving from the spinal ridge of backward growing hair on the Ridgeback—came to be recognized as fine hunting dogs with the stamina necessary to withstand the rigors of the African bush, to survive the great temperature changes of the hot tropical days and the freezing nights, and able to go 24 hours or more without water. The dog became a truly utilitarian breed; an animal capable of hunting birds and game, a watchdog who would fearlessly protect his master and his family and livestock in the wilds of the African bush, and a companion during the long, lonely days and nights on the veldt.

One of the pioneer breeders of these African dogs is Louis Pienaar whose kennels on his South African farm, "Montana," have produced some of today's finest show contenders in this breed. According to Pienaar, his father, Gert, was the first white man in Africa to own a dog of this breed which he developed by trading with a Hottentot for two of his outlaw dogs, which he subsequently christened Rogers and Rinkhals. With these two dogs as his foundation stock, he set about standardizing and developing the breed but, unfortunately, he never bothered to register them as purebreds.

In 1897 a visiting missionary saw these animals, bought a pair from Gert Pienaar and introduced them into Rhodesia and Nyasaland, where they became popular with big game hunters for use in the sport of hunting lions and leopards from horseback. They are usually run in packs of three, a leader and two flankers. The Ridgeback is such a fearless, aggressive dog that a pack of three will willingly attack a pride of five lions.

In 1950 the Rhodesian Ridgeback Club of the United States was founded, following the importation of some fine dogs of the breed. The club then applied for official recognition which was granted and the breed duly registered.

In a very short time the breed won many admirers, both in the show ring and as fine, obedient, household companions, fond of children, of good temperament, and with an innate willingness to please its master.

STANDARD OF THE RHODESIAN RIDGEBACK

The peculiarity of this breed is the ridge on the back, which is formed by the hair growing in the opposite direction to the rest of the coat. The ridge must be regarded as the characteristic feature of the breed. The ridge should be clearly defined, tapering and symmetrical. It should start immediately behind the shoulders and continue to a point between the prominence of the hips, and should contain two identical crowns opposite each other. The lower edges of the crown should not extend further down the ridge than one third of the ridge.

Champion Belmore's Mr. Jones of Kraal.

General Appearance—The Ridgeback should represent a strong, muscular and active dog, symmetrical in outline, and capable of great endurance with a fair amount of speed.

Head—Should be of a fair length, the skull flat and rather broad between the ears and should be free from wrinkles when in repose. The stop should be reasonably well defined.

Muzzle—Should be long, deep and powerful, jaws level and strong with well-developed teeth, especially the canines or holders. The lips clean, closely fitting the jaws.

Eyes—Should be moderately well apart, and should be round, bright and sparkling, with intelligent expression, their color harmonizing with the color of the dog.

Ears—Should be set rather high, of medium size, rather wide at base, and tapering to a rounded point. They should be carried close to the head.

Nose—Should be black, or brown, in keeping with the color of the dog. No other colored nose is permissible. A black nose should be accompanied by dark eyes, a brown nose by amber eyes.

Neck and Shoulders—The neck should be fairly strong and free from throatiness. The shoulders should be sloping, clean and muscular, denoting speed.

Body, Back, Chest and Loins—The chest should not be too wide, but very deep and capacious; ribs moderately well sprung, never rounded like barrel hoops (which would indicate want of speed), the back powerful, the loins strong, muscular and slightly arched.

Legs and Feet—The forelegs should be perfectly straight, strong and heavy in bone; elbows close to the body. The feet should be compact, with well-arched toes, round, tough, elastic pads, protected by hair between the toes and pads. In the hind legs the muscles should be clean, well defined, and hocks well down.

Tail—Should be strong at the insertion, and generally tapering towards the end, free from coarseness. It should not be inserted too high or too low, and should be carried with a slight curve upwards, never curled.

Coat—Should be short and dense, sleek and glossy in appearance, but neither woolly nor silky.

Color—Light wheaten to red wheaten. A little white on the chest and toes permissible but excessive white there and any white on the belly or above the toes is undesirable.

Rhodesian Ridgebacks exhibiting the unique ridge specific to the breed.

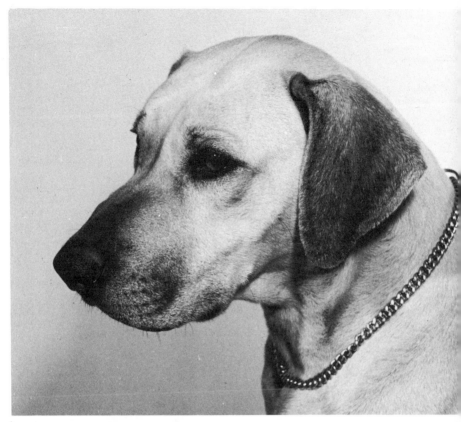
Champion Tayari of Nirvana

Size—A mature Ridgeback should be a handsome, upstanding dog; dogs should be of a height of 25 to 27 inches, and bitches 24 to 26 inches.

Weight—(Desirable) Dogs, 75 pounds; bitches, 65 pounds.

SCALE OF POINTS

	Points
Ridge	20
Head	15
Neck, shoulders	10
Body, back, chest, loins	10
Legs and feet	15
Coat	5
Tail	5
Size, symmetry, general appearance	20
Total	100

GROUP II

Hounds

b. Sight Hounds

The Greyhound   Irish Greyhound

NOTE the general type exhibited by the sight hounds. The cleavage between sight and scent hounds is clear. All coursing, sight or gaze hounds find relationship in this category through a linkage of basic bone structure, muscular development, and general conformation, as well as in the ways in which they have been employed by man. Their inherited hunting aptitudes are as different in usage from those of the scent hounds as they are from the pointing or terrier breeds.

Older than the Pyramids, the sight hounds do not utilize their noses to find game for their scenting powers are almost nil. They depend solely upon their keen eyes to sight the prey and then, through their miraculous speed of foot, to run the quarry down.

This group division boasts the tallest of dogs in the Irish Wolfhound, two of the most ancient of breeds in the Afghan and Saluki, and certainly the fastest breeds in the Greyhound and Whippet, breeds used for racing and coursing. When extended in a full run there is no more breathtaking sight, no greater degree of balance and beauty in movement, than is afforded by the sight hound.

Exhibiting all the archaic beauty of this ancient breed, American and Mexican Champion Crown Crest Zardonx is the epitome of Afghan, wind-blown elegance.

THE AFGHAN HOUND

Ancient carvings by masterful classic sculptors of the past bring undeniable proof of the Afghan Hound's ancient lineage. In a part of ancient Egypt that became the sacred place, Sinai, where Jehovah delivered to Moses the laws of the Ten Commandments (as it is written in the Old Testament), an ancient scribe wrote, about 3500 B.C. at his master's bidding, about the first recorded Afghan Hound. Literal translation refers to the dog as *cynocephalus* or "monkey-faced hound." Illustrations of this breed on Egyptian tombs show that the Afghan's head looked to some extent like that of a baboon.

The Afghan and Saluki undoubtedly share common ancestry and are classic examples of the basic Sight or Coursing Hounds. Under the influence of the desert sheiks these hounds were bred for the hunt as painstakingly as were the great and ancient equines, the Arabian horses. Probably the same records of breeding were kept for both horse and dog, engraved on tablets of ivory.

That he was not a dog of the common man but of royalty cannot be doubted since the common man of those ancient times could not afford to keep a dog or was not allowed to (especially in Egypt where a cult of dog worshippers came into being). The only dogs known, other than breeds owned by people of high rank, were the nondescript pariah dogs who, with the vultures, performed their own necessary task for mankind.

In Afghanistan, from which the breed name was derived in modern times, the Afghan developed the coat that gives it so unique an appearance. As a breed, evidence points to the fact that it was not confined to a specific locale but spread to other ancient lands and, in so doing, came into the hands of men of lesser nobility than it had initially known and became, for them, a guardian of sheep and cattle and a hunter of small game, forsaking in these instances its formerly royal prestige as a hunter of gazelle, deer, and even the formidable leopard of the desert.

Like all breeds of its type, the Afghan hunts by sight, its highly developed vision finding the movement of its prey and then, through sheer speed of foot, it runs the game to ground or at bay. This particular hound, by reason of its "pivotal hipjoints," is especially fast and adept in broken, boulder-strewn country, hurdling formidable obstacles without slackening speed. The Afghan is also fitted, by background and centuries of extreme climatic change, to be comfortable in any temperature.

The breed first appeared in America in the 1930's and commanded immediate attention through its striking appearance. It is, at the moment, an increasingly popular breed.

STANDARD OF THE AFGHAN HOUND

General Appearance—The Afghan Hound is an aristocrat, his whole appearance one of dignity and aloofness with no trace of plainness or coarseness. He has a straight front, proudly carried head, eyes gazing into the distance as if in memory of ages past. The striking characteristics of the breed—exotic or "Eastern" expression, long silky topknot, peculiar coat pattern, very prominent hip bones, large feet, and the impression of a somewhat exaggerated bend in the stifle due to profuse trouserings—stand out clearly, giving the Afghan Hound the appearance of what he is, a King of Dogs, that has held true to tradition throughout the ages.

Head—The head is of good length showing much refinement, the skull evenly balanced with the foreface. There is a slight prominence of the nasal bone structure causing a slightly Roman appearance, the center line running up over the foreface with little or no stop, falling away in front of the eyes so there is an absolutely clear outlook with no interference; the underjaw showing great strength, the jaws long and punishing; the mouth level, meaning that the teeth from the upper jaw and lower jaw match evenly, neither overshot nor undershot. This is a difficult mouth to breed. A scissors bite is even more punishing and can be more easily bred into a dog than a level mouth, and a dog having a scissors bite, where the lower teeth slip inside and rest against the teeth of the upper jaw, should not be penalized. The occipital bone is very prominent. The head is surmounted by a topknot of long silky hair.

Ears—The ears are long, set approximately on level with outer corners of the eyes, the leather of the ear reaching nearly to the end of the dog's nose, and covered with long silky hair.

Eyes—The eyes are almond shaped (almost triangular), never full or bulgy, and are dark in color.

Nose—Nose is of good size, black in color.

Faults—Coarseness; snipiness; overshot or undershot; eyes round or bulgy or light in color; exaggerated Roman nose; head not surmounted with topknot.

Neck—The neck is of good length, strong and arched, running in a curve to the shoulders which are long and sloping and well laid back.

Faults—Neck too short or too thick; a ewe neck; a goose neck; a neck lacking in substance.

Body—The back line appearing practically level from the shoulders to the loin. Strong and powerful loin and slightly arched, falling away toward the stern, with the hip bones very pronounced; well ribbed and tucked up in

Champion
Kurram El Myia

294

flanks. The height at the shoulders equals the distance from the chest to the buttocks; the brisket well let down, and of medium width.

Faults—Roach back, sway back, goose rump, slack loin; lack of prominence of hip bones; too much width of brisket causing interference with elbows.

Tail—Tail set not too high on the body, having a ring, or a curve on the end; should never be curled over, or rest on the back, or be carried sideways; and should never be bushy.

Legs—Forelegs are straight and strong with great length between elbow and pastern; elbows well held in; forefeet large in both length and width; toes well arched; feet covered with long thick hair; fine in texture; pasterns long and straight; pads of feet unusually large and well down on the ground. Shoulders have plenty of angulation so that the legs are well set underneath the dog. Too much straightness of shoulder causes the dog to break down in the pasterns, and this is a serious fault.

All four feet of the Afghan Hound are in line with the body, turning neither in nor out. The hind feet are broad and of good length; the toes arched, and covered with long thick hair; hindquarters powerful and well muscled with great length between hip and hocks; hocks are well let down; good angulation of both stifle and hock; slightly bowed from hock to crotch.

Faults—Front or back feet thrown outward or inward; pads of feet not thick enough; or feet too small; or any other evidence of weakness in feet; weak or broken down pasterns; too straight in stifle; too long in hock.

Coat—Hindquarters, flanks, ribs, forequarters, and legs well covered with thick, silky hair, very fine in texture; ears and all four feet well feathered; from in front of the shoulders, and also backwards from the shoulders along the saddle from the flanks and ribs upwards, the hair is short and close forming a smooth back in mature dogs—this a traditional characteristic of the Afghan Hound.

The Afghan Hound should be shown in its natural state; the coat is not clipped or trimmed; the head is surmounted (in the full sense of the word) with a topknot of long, silky hair—this also an outstanding characteristic of the Afghan Hound. Showing of short hair on cuffs on either front or back legs is permissible.

Faults—Lack of short haired saddle in mature dogs.

Height—Dogs, 27 inches, plus or minus one inch; bitches, 25 inches, plus or minus one inch.

Weight—Dogs, about 60 pounds; bitches, about 50 pounds.

Color—All colors are permissible, but color or color combinations are pleasing; white markings, especially on the head, are undesirable.

Gait—When running free, the Afghan Hound moves at a gallop, showing great elasticity and spring in his smooth, powerful stride.

When on a loose lead, the Afghan can trot at a fast pace; stepping along, he has the appearance of placing the hind feet directly in the foot prints of the front feet, both thrown straight ahead. Moving with head and tail high, the whole appearance of the Afghan Hound is one of great style and beauty.

Temperament—Aloof and dignified, yet gay.

Faults—Sharpness or shyness.

Graced with the special beauty that is the
hallmark of the ancient coursing hounds, the
Borzoi emanates a special charm all its own.

THE BORZOI

The actual heritage of the Borzoi dates back to antiquity, A.D. 1260, with the first written record of coursing (i.e., hunting wolves, fox, hare etc., by sight) in Russia. This was the period of the father of "Ivan the Terrible," first Czar of Russia, and Borzoi was then a descriptive general term including the group of sighthounds recognized today as distinct breeds. (Prior to 1936, in America, the Borzoi was known as the Russian Wolfhound).

What is still sought after and referred to as the "ancient type" (ideal) Borzoi was developed later, around the 16th century. Although there is controversy as to actual origin, it was the opinion of the noted Russian authority, Artem Boldareff, that the Borzoi evolved from the Russian *Laika*, a native northern breed of long coated, Collie type, but taller and more like the Borzoi of today, with a long, gracefully curved tail.

Some authorities claim there was a crossing with the Tartar and Crimean hounds in the 14th century, which is supposed to account for the introduction of black, or black and tan color. To many, this signified the intrusion of foreign blood, hence the reason for early prejudice against black.

The 17th century (1650) witnessed the first written standard which was very close to our present one and it was the dogs from that period and prior to 1860, that the Perchino kennels of Grand Duke Nicholas, and the Woronzova kennels of Mr. Artem Boldareff strove to emulate.

The craze to cross Borzoi (in the 18th century) with foreign dogs of similar build did not reach these two kennels nor the antecedents of their selected stock, so the Borzoi owes its preservation from degeneration, or inevitable extinction, particularly to these two mainstays.

After the 1861 upheaval in Russia, which we leave to the history books, and the subsequent craze to cross, many varieties existed within the breed. The principal hunts that re-formed later, began to develop their own types from the few pure ancient type hounds still available. A scarce few of these ever left Russia, and then usually as a present or a reward from the nobility.

The Prince of Wales exhibited the Borzoi in England in 1889 and in 1890 William Wade of Hulton, Pa., imported what is believed to be the first Borzoi to enter America from England. He started to popularize the breed and in the '90's Mr. Chas. Stedman Hanks of Boston imported directly from the kennels of the Czar.

In 1903, Jos. B. Thomas journeyed to Russia and found the good ancient type that breeders still seek, in the Perchino and Woronzova kennels. Two of his Russian imports were the famous Ch. Bistri of Perchino and Sorva of Woronzova. His Valley Farm kennels brought fame to the Borzoi and provided the foundation stock for Borzois in America. That year the Russian Wolfhound Club of America was formed.

In spite of the tradition in which Borzois were raised (to course, and in some instances to kill ,wolves), it is surprising to note their gentle attitude, especially when raised with children. The well-bred Borzoi is keenly alert, intelligent, has a sweet disposition and a very sensitive character. He is a born aristocrat, affectionate in moderation, and with proper rearing and handling, the most companionable of creatures. In short, the Borzoi embodies all the qualities a dog enthusiast can hope for in one breed. This hound combines beauty,

A vision of style coupled
with elegance and dignity,
this photo brings visual
proof of the aristocratic
beauty of these sight
hounds bred and hunted by
the nobles of old White
Russia.

strength and swiftness, together with graceful bearing, lovable disposition, intelligent alertness and exceptional coursing ability.

It is important to realize he has a mind and temperament all his own which exclusively characterize him. He is rebellious at the thought of being a servant and one accomplishes nothing by harshness, but rather by teamwork, i.e., a Borzoi works with, but not for, one.

While it is a far cry from hunting wolves in Russia, the Borzoi shows his versatility today in field trials, races, obedience trials, and in the show ring, or simply as a loyal companion, feeling comfortably at home in the quiet country or a busy city.

It is the combination of all his qualities that makes the Borzoi truly beloved among those who know him well.

STANDARD OF THE BORZOI

Head—Skull slightly domed, long and narrow, with scarcely any perceptible stop, rather inclined to be Roman-nosed; jaws long, powerful and deep; teeth strong, clean and even, neither pig-jawed nor undershot; nose large and black.

Ears—Small and fine in quality, lying back on the neck when in repose with the tips when thrown back almost touching behind occiput; raised when at attention.

Eyes—Set somewhat obliquely, dark in color, intelligent, but rather soft in expression, never full nor staring, nor light in color, eyelids dark.

Neck—Clean, free from throatiness, somewhat shorter than in the Greyhound, slightly arched, very powerful and well set on.

Shoulders—Sloping, should be fine at the withers and free from coarseness or lumber.

Chest—Rather narrow, with great depth of brisket.

Ribs—Only slightly sprung, but very deep, giving room for heart and lung play.

Back—Rising a little at the loins in a graceful curve.

Loins—Extremely muscular, but rather tucked up, owing to the great depth of chest and comparative shortness of back and ribs.

Forelegs—Bone flat, straight, giving free play for the elbows, which should be turned neither in nor out; pasterns strong.

Feet—Hare-shaped, with well-arched knuckles, toes close and well padded.

Hindquarters—Long, very muscular and powerful, with well bent stifles and strong second thighs, hocks broad, clean and well let down.

Tail—Long, set on and carried low in a graceful curve.

Coat—Long, silky (not woolly), either flat, wavy or rather curly. On the head, ears and front of legs it should be short and smooth; on the neck the frill should be profuse and rather curly. Feathers on hindquarters and tail, long and profuse, less so on the chest and back of forelegs.

Color—Any color, white usually predominating, more or less marked with lemon, tan, brindle, gray or black. Whole-colored specimens of these occasionally appear.

General Appearance—Should be that of an elegant, graceful aristocrat among dogs, possessing courage and combining muscular power with extreme speed.

Size—Dogs, average height at shoulder from 28 to 31 inches; average

Champion Yermaks Rurick

weight from 75 to 105 pounds. Larger dogs are often seen, extra size being no disadvantage when it is not acquired at the expense of symmetry, speed and staying quality. Bitches are invariably smaller than dogs, and two inches less in height, and from 15 to 20 pounds less in weight is a fair average.

Scale of Points

	Points
Head	12
Eyes	5
Ears	3
Neck	5
Shoulders and brisket	10
Ribs, back and loins	15
Hindquarters, stifles and hocks	12
Legs and feet	10
Coat and feather	10
Tail	3
Conformation and gait	15
Total	100

THE SCOTTISH DEERHOUND

The Scottish Deerhound is one of the most ancient of the recognized pure breeds of today. He was once the exclusive property of the nobility of Scotland, since no one lower than an Earl might own one. He is the living link with the days of flashing armor, heralds, minstrels and all the pageantry of the middle ages.

He was bred to chase the wild deer in the Highlands. A stag is nearly twice the height and more than twice the weight of a Deerhound, so the hound had to be brave and fast and strong to overtake and bring down his prey. Guns have replaced dogs in stag hunting, but the breed still retains the speed, staying power, strength, agility, and courage of its forefathers.

In the United States, where hunting of antlered game with dogs is not allowed, he can run such animals as wolves, coyotes, and rabbits.

In the home, he is gentle and fearless, and there is nothing mean about him. He is pleasant to all humans, because he neither expects harm from them nor intends to harm them. His good nature extends to little children, who can do anything they wish with him, and he is a marvel of patience with other dogs.

His great size, 28–32 inches, and the fact that he requires a lot of room for exercise takes him beyond the scope of the large majority of dog owners, and so he is known to only a few. But the breed is ours to cherish and preserve, not for the work they might do but for their gentle dignity, pleasant companionship and loyal love.

If you have enough space to keep a Scottish Deerhound, you could not make a better choice. The breed is too little known (the price they pay for their size), but once you have known them, they make all other dogs seem a bit pale by comparison. Those fortunate enough to know this splendid breed echo in feeling the tribute Sir Walter Scott paid to his beloved Maida: "The most perfect creature of Heaven."

STANDARD OF THE SCOTTISH DEERHOUND

Head—Should be broadest at the ears, narrowing slightly to the eyes, with the muzzle tapering more decidedly to the nose. The muzzle should be pointed, but the teeth and lips level. The head should be long, the skull flat rather than round with a very slight rise over the eyes but nothing approaching a stop. The hair on the skull should be moderately long and softer than the rest of the coat. The nose should be black (in some blue fawns—blue) and slightly aquiline. In lighter colored dogs the black muzzle is preferable. There should be a good moustache of rather silky hair and a fair beard.

Ears—Should be set on high; in repose, folded back like a Greyhound's, though raised above the head in excitement without losing the fold, and even in some cases semi-erect. A prick ear is bad. Big thick ears hanging flat to the head or heavily coated with long hair are bad faults. The ears should be soft, glossy, like a mouse's coat to the touch and the smaller the better. There should be no long coat or long fringe, but there is sometimes a silky, silvery coat on the body of the ear and the tip. On all Deerhounds, irrespective of color of coat, the ears should be black or dark colored.

Neck and Shoulders—The neck should be long—of a length befitting the Greyhound character of the dog. Extreme length is neither necessary nor

A lovely bitch of Blythblue Kennels.

desirable. Deerhounds do not stoop to their work like the Greyhounds. The mane, which every good specimen should have, sometimes detracts from the apparent length of the neck. The neck, however, must be strong as is necessary to hold a stag. The nape of the neck should be very prominent where the head is set on, and the throat clean cut at the angle and prominent. Shoulders should be well sloped; blades well back and not too much width between them. Loaded and straight shoulders are very bad faults.

Tail—Should be tolerably long, tapering and reaching to within 1½ inches off the ground and about 1½ inches below the hocks. Dropped perfectly down or curved when the Deerhound is still, when in motion or excited—curved, but in no instance lifted out of line of the back. It should be well covered with hair, on the inside, thick and wiry, underside longer and towards the end a slight fringe is not objectionable. A curl or ring tail is undesirable.

Eyes—Should be dark—generally dark brown, brown or hazel. A very light eye is not liked. The eye should be moderately full, with a soft look in repose, but a keen, far-away look when the Deerhound is roused. Rims of eyelids should be black.

Body—General formation is that of a Greyhound of larger size and bone. Chest deep rather than broad but not too narrow or slab-sided. Good girth of chest is inidcative of great lung power. The loin well arched and drooping to the tail. A straight back is not desirable, this formation being unsuited for uphill work, and very unsightly.

Scottish Deerhounds, and other sight hounds, pouring out of their truck kennel to course coyotes. The power and flow of their eager action, trapped momentarily by the camera, lends artistry to a simple picture.

Legs and Feet—Legs should be broad and flat, and good broad forearms and elbows are desirable. Forelegs must, of course, be as straight as possible. Feet close and compact, with well-arranged toes. The hind quarters drooping, and as broad and powerful as possible, the hips being set wide apart. A narrow rear denotes lack of power. The stifles should be well bent, with great length from hip to hock, which should be broad and flat. Cowhocks, weak pasterns, straight stifles and splay feet are very bad faults.

Coat—The hair on the body, neck and quarters should be harsh and wiry, about 3 or 4 inches long; that on the head, breast and belly much softer. There should be a slight fringe on the inside of the fore and hindlegs but nothing approaching the "feather" of a Collie. A woolly coat is bad. Some good strains have a mixture of silky coat with the hard which is preferable to a woolly coat. The climate of the United States tends to produce the mixed coat. The ideal coat is a thick, close lying ragged coat, harsh or crisp to the touch.

Color is a matter of fancy but the dark blue-grey is most preferred. Next come the darker and ligher greys or brindles, the darkest being generally preferred. Yellow and sandy red or red fawn, especially with black ears and muzzles, are equally high in estimation. This was the color of the oldest known strains—the McNeil and Chesthill Menzies. White is condemned by all authorities, but a white chest and white toes, occurring as they do in many of the darkest colored dogs are not objected to, although the less the better for the Deerhound is a self-colored dog. A white blaze on the head, or a white collar, should entirely disqualify. The less white the better but a slight white tip to the stern occurs in some of the best strains.

Height of Dogs—From 30 to 32 inches, or even more if there be symmetry without coarseness, which is rare.

Height of Bitches—From 28 inches upwards. There is no objection to a bitch being large, unless too coarse, as even at her greatest height she does not approach that of the dog, and therefore could not be too big for work as overbig dogs are.

Weight—From 85 to 110 pounds in dogs and from 75 to 95 pounds in bitches.

POINTS OF THE DEERHOUND
ARRANGED IN ORDER OF IMPORTANCE

1. *Typical*—A Deerhound should resemble a rough-coated Greyhound of larger size and bone.
2. *Movements*—Easy, active and true.
3. As tall as possible consistent with quality.
4. *Head*—Long, level, well balanced, carried high.
5. *Body*—Long, very deep in brisket, well sprung ribs and great breadth across hips.
6. *Forelegs*—Strong and quite straight, with elbows neither in nor out.
7. *Thighs*—Long and muscular, second thighs well muscled, stifles well bent.
8. *Loins*—Well arched, and belly well drawn up.
9. *Coat*—Rough and hard with softer beard and brows.
10. Feet—Close, compact, with well knuckled toes.
11. *Ears*—Small (dark) with Greyhound-like carriage.
12. *Eyes*—Dark, moderately full.

Ch. Quibba of Enterkine

13. *Neck*—Long, well arched, very strong with prominent nape.
14. *Shoulders*—Clean, set sloping.
15. *Chest*—Very deep but not too narrow.
16. *Tail*—Long and curved slightly, carried low.
17. *Teeth*—Strong and level.
18. *Nails*—Strong and curved.

DISQUALIFICATION
White blaze on the head, or a white collar.

THE GREYHOUND

The Greyhound, a model for the coursing sight hound, is the superlative racing dog (a good one can reach a speed of 37 miles an hour). Like all sight hounds, a dog claiming ancient desert lineage, he was a great hunter of small game especially hare, from which the modern sport of racing developed. He is an elegant dog of graceful, easy movement, slender and fine of line, yet possessed of great strength.

In this country the breed has been used to hunt wolves and coyotes on our Western plains, and has proven to be extremely staunch and courageous in this pursuit. The author once owned a large, fawn specimen of the breed that had been imported from Australia and whose name was Billy Chink. This dog was as courageous as any he has ever known.

Evidence of the esteem in which the breed was held is written in Danish in

Like bolts from a crossbow, these racing Greyhounds streak forward, chasing the mechanical rabbit.

the famous Canute Laws enacted in Parliament held at Winchester in 1016. In part, law number 31 reads: "No meane person may keepe any greihounds, but freemen may keepe greihounds . . ."

The origin of this sight hound's name is buried in the mists of antiquity. Some authorities claim the name to have been derived from the Grecian "Graius" (the breed was popular in ancient Greece), others say it is from the ancient British name for dog, "grech" or "greg." An easier explanation, and one that probably hits closer to the mark, is that the dog was named for the coat color which most often appeared, thus the Greyhound.

Today the Greyhound is enjoyed by thousands on race tracks all over the United States, and as a show dog, he has made an enviable name for himself in all-breed competition.

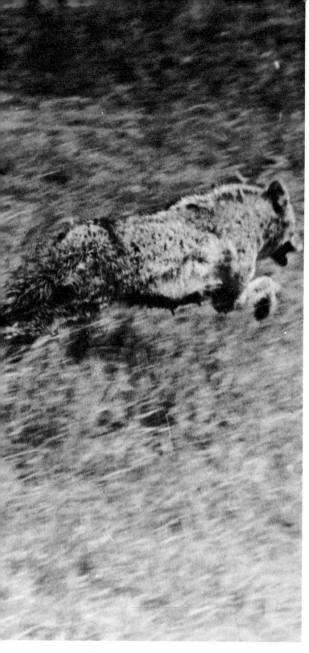

The Greyhound is the fastest of all the sight hound breeds. Not only fancy show and racing dogs, they also serve mankind by ridding sheep and cattle areas of predators. Coursing coyotes, as shown in this remarkable action photo, is the heritage of the Greyhound.

STANDARD OF THE GREYHOUND

Head—Long and narrow, fairly wide between the ears, scarcely perceptible stop, little or no development of nasal sinuses, good length of muzzle, which should be powerful without coarseness. Teeth very strong and even in front.

Ears—Small and fine in texture, thrown back and folded, except when excited, when they are semi-pricked.

Eyes—Dark, bright, intelligent, indicating spirit.

Neck—Long, muscular, without throatiness, slightly arched, and widening gradually into the shoulder.

Shoulders—Placed as obliquely as possible, muscular without being loaded.

Forelegs—Perfectly straight, set well into the shoulder, neither turned in nor out, pasterns strong.

Chest—Deep, and as wide as consistent with speed, fairly well-sprung ribs.

Back—Muscular and broad, well arched.

Loins—Good depth of muscle, well cut up in the flanks.

Hind Quarters—Long, very muscular and powerful, wide and well let down, well-bent stifles. Hocks well bent and rather close to ground, wide but straight fore and aft.

Feet—Hard and close, rather more hare than cat feet, well knuckled up with good strong claws.

Tail—Long, fine and tapering with a slight upward curve.

Coat—Short, smooth and firm in texture.

Color—Immaterial.

Weight—Dogs, 65 to 70 pounds; bitches, 60 to 65 pounds.

SCALE OF POINTS

	Points
General symmetry and quality	10
Head and neck	20
Chest and shoulders	20
Back	10
Quarters	20
Legs and feet	20
Total	**100**

Ch. Tap Dancer of Aroi

Ch. Royaltan Sailing Free

THE IRISH WOLFHOUND

The Irish Wolfhound, tallest and longest-bodied member of the canine race, is an ancient breed with a most romantic history. In A.D. 391 the Roman consul, Quintus Aurelius Symmachus wrote his brother Flavianus thanking him for a gift of seven hounds and said, "All Rome viewed them with wonder."

Wolfhounds were favorites of the ancient Irish kings, in fact among their most valued possessions, and they are frequently mentioned in song and story. About the middle of the 18th century they are credited with having cleared Ireland of wolves and thereafter there was a decrease in the breed's numbers.

In 1862 Capt. George A. Graham, a retired British Army officer, set out to revive the breed. He collected all the specimens he could locate and worked for twenty years to achieve his ideal, a hound that matched the written descriptions and paintings of the ancient hound. In Captain Graham's word, he "recovered" the breed.

Just when the first Irish Wolfhound was exported to the United States isn't known. At Gettysburg battlefield a statue of an Irish Wolfhound overlooks the graves of the members of the 63rd, 69th, and 88th New York Infantry who were killed there. Now, about 100 Wolfhounds, more or less, are registered each year by the American Kennel Club and it is estimated that about 400 are to be found in the United States at any one time, more than in any other country.

Though principally a pet and companion, Wolfhounds are used on coyotes, wolves, and other game in parts of the western U.S. and Canada. They hunt by sight rather than scent and have very keen vision in comparison to most other dogs. They are quiet and affectionate but not "pushy." While most dogs have an affinity for children, Irish Wolfhounds seem to have this trait strongly instilled in them and they get along well with other dogs and animals. The Wolfhound is amiable rather than aggressive but this does not mean that he will accept trespassers. If a deep bark or growl are not sufficient warnings, the hounds take more direct action but they are holders rather than rippers and biters.

The Irish Wolfhound standard approved by the American Kennel Club calls for a male to be at least 32 inches at the withers and weigh 120 pounds, and for females to be at least 30 inches and weigh 105 pounds at the age of 18 months. The standard describes the breed as a "rough-coated, Greyhound-like breed" having "great size and commanding appearance."

STANDARD OF THE IRISH WOLFHOUND

General Appearance—Of great size and commanding appearance, the Irish Wolfhound is remarkable in combining power and swiftness with keen sight. The largest and tallest of the galloping hounds, in general type he is a rough-coated, Greyhound-like breed; very muscular, strong though gracefully built; movements easy and active; head and neck carried high; the tail carried with an upward sweep with a slight curve towards the extremity.

The minimum height and weight of dogs should be 32 inches and 120 pounds; of bitches, 30 inches and 105 pounds; these to apply only to hounds over 18 months of age. Anything below this should be debarred from competition. Great size, including height at shoulder and proportionate length of body, is the desideratum to be aimed at, and it is desired to firmly establish

a race that shall average from 32 to 34 inches in dogs, showing the requisite power, activity, courage and symmetry.

Head—Long, the frontal bones on the forehead very slightly raised and very little indentation between the eyes. Skull, not too broad. Muzzle, long and moderately pointed. Ears, small and Greyhound-like in carriage.

Neck—Rather long, very strong and muscular, well arched, without dewlap or loose skin about the throat.

Chest—Very deep. Breast, wide.

Back—Rather long than short. Loins arched.

Tail—Long and slightly curved, of moderate thickness, and well covered with hair.

Belly—Well drawn up.

Fore-Quarters—Shoulders, muscular, giving breadth of chest, set sloping. Elbows well under, neither turned inwards nor outwards.

Leg—Forearm muscular, and the whole leg strong and quite straight.

Hind-Quarters—Muscular thighs and second thigh long and strong as in the Greyhound, and hocks well let down and turning neither in nor out.

Feet—Moderately large and round, neither turned inwards nor outwards. Toes, well arched and closed Nails, very strong and curved.

Hair—Rough and hard on body, legs and head; especially wiry and long over eyes and under jaw.

Color and Markings—The recognized colors are gray, brindle, red, black, pure white, fawn, or any color that appears in the Deerhound.

314

Fleetwind Rory Shaun

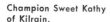

Champion Sweet Kathy
of Kilrain.

Faults—Too light or heavy head, too highly arched frontal bone; large ears and hanging flat to the face; short neck; full dewlap; too narrow or too broad a chest; sunken or hollow or quite straight back; bent forelegs; overbent fetlocks; twisted feet; spreading toes; too curly a tail; weak hindquarters and a general want of muscle; too short in body; lips or nose liver-colored or lacking pigmentation.

THE SALUKI

The Saluki, the royal dog of Egypt, is without doubt the oldest known breed of domesticated dog, "a distinct breed and bred to type as long ago as 329 B.C. when Alexander the Great invaded India." The Saluki is claimed to be as old as the earliest known civilization, the claim being based on the fact that the hounds shown on the earliest carvings look more like Salukis than any other breed: (a Greyhound body with feathered ears, tail, and legs.)

Exactly the same hound appears on the Egyptian tombs of 2100 B.C. and more recent excavations of the still older Sumerian empire, estimated at 7000–6000 B.C. have produced carvings of dogs bearing striking resemblance to the Saluki.

"Whenever one sees the word 'dog' in the Bible it means the Saluki." As the Mohammedan religion classes the dog as unclean, Moslems declared the Saluki sacred and called him *The Noble One* given them by Allah for their amusement and benefit. This permitted them to eat the meat brought down in the chase. The Saluki was the only dog of the time allowed to sleep on the carpet of the Shiek's tent.

So great was the esteem in which the Saluki was held, that his body was often mummified after death like the bodies of the Pharaohs themselves.

The remains of numerous Salukis have been found in the ancient tombs of the Upper Nile region.

As the Saluki was considered sacred he was never sold or allowed to go out of his native haunts. The Arab chiefs attached as much importance to their breeding as they did to the pedigrees of their famous horses.

They did, however, trade among themselves and placed their values in terms of mares, female camels and gennets, according to the Saluki's ability in the chase. It is said that the native women often nursed Saluki pups in order to increase their sustenance.

As the desert tribes are nomadic, the habitat of the Saluki comprised all the region stretching from the Caspian Sea to the Sahara including Egypt, Arabia, Palestine, Syria, Mesopotamia, Anatolia and Persia. Naturally the types varied somewhat in this widely scattered area. However, this difference was mostly in size and coat. Thus the Arabian-bred Saluki, we find of a smaller type with less feathering on the legs and ears than the Persian variety.

As the Crusaders brought "hounds of great swiftness and stamina" from the East to Europe there is little doubt but the Saluki was the progenitor of all the galloping breeds, such as the Whippet, Greyhound and Wolfhound.

The Saluki, having tremendous speed (credited with 42 to 50 miles per hour), was used by the Arabs principally in bringing down the gazelle, the fastest of antelopes. It is recorded that the Pharaohs rode to the chase with their hawks on their wrists and Salukis on the lead.

We also believe the Saluki was used on jackals, foxes and hares. A cut published in 1852 shows a wild boar hunt in Algeria with Salukis tackling a boar.

In England the Saluki is used largely on hares and regular coursing meets are held. The judging is based on the dogs' ability to turn quickly and overtake the hare in the best possible time. The Saluki hunts largely by sight, although he has a fair nose.

A lovely portrait of the tricolor Saluki, Champion Marco Mallmoud, a fine representative of this ancient canine breed.

Champion Ahmed Farouk of Pine Paddocks. The author found evidence of the antiquity of this breed in a fresco in the Egyptian Museum at Cairo.

The sight of the Saluki is remarkable and his hereditary traits often crop out. He loves to lie on the sand and watch an eagle soaring for his prey while paying no attention to the gull.

On his native heath the Saluki gets no pampering. He lives hard and it is a case of survival of the fittest, one reason for his strong constitution and sturdy frame, enabling him to stand any climate in unheated kennels.

The feet of the Saluki are hard and firm and the hair between the toes is a great protection. In all his running and dodging over the roughest kind of ground and rocky country he never damages pads or toes.

The beauty of the Saluki is that of the thoroughbred horse—grace and symmetry of form—clean cut and graceful—short silky hair with the exception of the ears, legs and tail—slender well muscled neck, shoulders and thighs—arched loins—long tail carried naturally in a curve with silky hair hanging from the underside—the arched toes—the rather long head with deep far seeing eyes—an expression of dignity mixed with gentleness.

In color the Saluki can meet the demands of the most fastidious, for while cream and fawn seem to predominate, there is also red, grizzle and tan, white and chestnut, tricolor (black, white and tan), as well as solid black.

In disposition the Saluki shows great attachment to his master and is most gentle with children. He is affectionate without being demonstrative. They are good watch dogs but not aggressive.

The Saluki is little known to people of America although in England they are fast becoming one of the most popular breeds. Today one finds many Salukis in London and Paris promenading in the parks with their owners.

STANDARD OF THE SALUKI

Head—Long and narrow, skull moderately wide between the ears, not domed, stop not pronounced, the whole showing great ability. Nose black or liver.

Ears—Long and covered with long silky hair hanging close to the skull and mobile.

Eyes—Dark to hazel and bright; large and oval, but not prominent.

Teeth—Strong and level.

Neck—Long, supple and well muscled.

Chest—Deep and moderately narrow.

Forequarters—Shoulders sloping and set well back, well muscled without being coarse.

Forelegs—Straight and long from the elbow to the knee.

Hindquarters—Strong, hip bones set well apart and stifle moderately bent, hocks low to the ground, showing galloping and jumping power.

Loin and Back—Back fairly broad, muscles slightly arched over loin.

Feet—Of moderate length, toes long and well arched, not splayed out, but at the same time not cat footed; the whole being strong and supple and well feathered between the toes.

Tail—Long, set low and carried naturally in a curve, well feathered on the underside with long silky hair, not bushy.

Coat—Smooth and of a soft silky texture, slight feather on the legs, feather at the back of the thighs and sometimes with woolly feather on the thigh and shoulder.

Colors—White, cream, fawn, golden, red, grizzle and tan, tricolor (white, black and tan) and black and tan.

General Appearance—The whole appearance of this breed should give an appearance of grace and symmetry and of great speed and endurance coupled with strength and activity to enable it to kill gazelle over deep and rocky mountains. The expression should be dignified and gentle with deep faithful eyes. Dogs should average in height from 23 to 28 inches and bitches may be considerably smaller, this is typical of the breed.

The Smooth Variety—In this variety the points should be the same with the exception of the coat which has no feathering.

THE WHIPPET

This speedy little sight hound, a small replica of the larger Greyhound, from which he was derived, is a graceful little beauty possessing miraculous smoothness of action. He is not of ancient heritage like most of his coursing cousins, but was developed to fill a definite need, as a coursing and racing dog for the English working classes, a sort of "poor man's racehorse," and was particularly developed in the northern and northwestern counties of England.

Crosses of various small native terriers to selected, small Greyhounds, finally produced a dog used for coursing rabbits in an enclosure. At this time it was called a "snap-dog" and used for "snap-dog coursing," in which the winner was the dog that "snapped up" the most rabbits.

Later, the breed, due to its small size and to the fact that it is easy and inexpensive to keep, became the popular racing dog of the working man. Run over a 200 yard straightaway course, the dogs are handicapped according to weight and previous performance. A handler (or slipper) grasps the dog by the neck and root of the tail and practically hurls the dog into its stride at the crack of the starter's gun, toward the animal's owner who stands at the finish line waving a rag or towel which the Whippet has been trained to run to, while the master frantically calls his dog.

The sport still flourishes among the colliermen of Lancashire and Yorkshire and both the sport and the breed were brought to America by English mill operators in Massachusetts.

Introduction of Italian Greyhound breeding added elegance to the breed which resulted in its acceptance and high placing as a show dog.

STANDARD OF THE WHIPPET

General Appearance—The Whippet should be a dog of moderate size, very alert, that can cover a maximum of distance with a minimum of lost motion, a true sporting hound. Should be put down in hard condition but with no suggestion of being muscle-bound.

Head—Long and lean, fairly wide between the ears, scarcely perceptible stop, good length of muzzle which should be powerful without being coarse. Nose entirely black.

Ears—Small, fine in texture, thrown back and folded. Semipricked when at attention. Gay ears are incorrect and should be severely penalized.

Eyes—Large, intelligent, round in shape and dark hazel in color, must be at least as dark as the coat color. Expression should be keen and alert. Light yellow or oblique eyes should be strictly penalized. A sulky expression and lack of alertness to be considered most undesirable.

Teeth—White, strong and even. Teeth of upper jaw should fit closely over the lower. *An undershot mouth shall disqualify.*

Neck—Long and muscular, well-arched and with no suggestion of throatiness, widening gradually into the shoulders. Must not have any tendency to a "ewe" neck.

Shoulders—Long, well laid back with long, flat muscles. Loaded shoulders are a *very* serious fault.

Brisket—Very deep and strong, reaching as nearly as possible to the point of the elbow. Ribs well sprung but with no suggestion of barrel shape. Should

Portrait of an English Champion Whippet. Here
is speed in a small but graceful package.

fill in the space between the forelegs so that there is no appearance of a hollow between them.

Forelegs—Straight and rather long, held in line with the shoulders and *not* set under the body so as to make a forechest. Elbows should turn neither in nor out and move freely with the point of the shoulder. Fair amount of bone, which should carry right down to the foot. Pasterns strong.

Feet—Must be well formed with strong, thick pads and well-knuckled-up paws. A thin, flat, open foot is a serious fault.

Hindquarters—Long and powerful, stifles well bent, hocks well let down and close to the ground. Thighs broad and muscular, the muscles should be long and flat. A steep croup is most undesirable.

Back—Strong and powerful, rather long with a good, natural arch over the loin creating a definite tuck-up of the underline but covering a lot of ground.

Tail—Long and tapering, should reach to a hipbone when drawn through

Champion Whipoo's Wild Honey

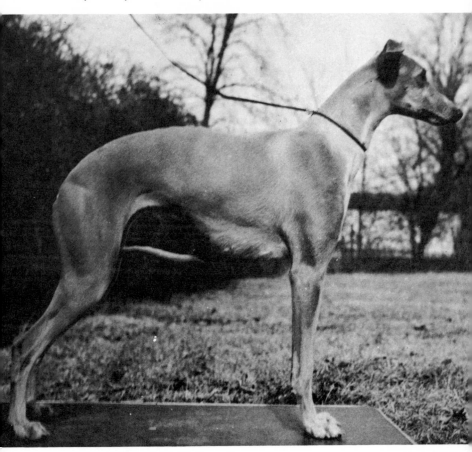

Champion Tinribs Bolney Safe and Sound, one of
the top winning Whippets of England.

between the hind legs. Must not be carried higher than the top of the back
when moving.

Coat—Close, smooth and firm in texture.

Color—Immaterial.

Size—Ideal height for dogs, 19 to 22 inches; for bitches, 18 to 21 inches.
These are not intended to be definite limits, only approximate.

Gait—Low, free moving and smooth, as long as is commensurate with the
size of the dog. A short, mincing gait with high knee action should be severely
penalized.

DISQUALIFICATIONS
Undershot mouth.

GROUP III

Working Dogs

Newfoundland Dog   The Mastiff

MOLDED by man for special tasks through the ages, the human hand and intelligence, turned to the fashioning of working dogs, was never more successful. Here are the breeds that stand beside man in his work to lighten his burden, to guard his possessions, to herd his flocks, and to protect him and his goods from harm.

Dogs in this wide category serve as draft animals, carrying burdens, pulling carts, and dragging sleds through the ice and snow of the forbidding north. Here are dogs that are used to fish as well as hunt, aiding man in the sea as they do on land. In Japan, the Ainus, a primitive tribe, but rich by reason of their dogs, use their canine helpers to drive fish to shallow waters for easy netting. Portuguese fishermen utilize the intelligence of their dogs by training them to dive and retrieve lost nets and other fishing gear.

There are also the specialists within this special service group; dogs that work for utility companies detecting gas leaks, keeping the railroad tracks clear of animals, man included, in isolated stretches of land, rescuing lost travelers in hazardous terrain, finding avalanche victims, so many tasks do these fine animals perform for man that the list becomes unwieldy. And let us not forget the ultimate task, the guiding of the sightless. Man depending completely upon his canine companion and guide and the dog using every sense, every bit of his combined, man-molded abilities and native instincts in this greatest service.

This is the Working Group, an assemblage well-named, for these are certainly the dogs of work, or service, of incalculable usefulness to man throughout the ages. It could be that even man's evolution, in an early time predating history, was slightly altered by his use of the dog as an animal of work. For those of you who admire the animals in this group remember they are not toys, many indeed are as large and can be as dangerous as much respected and feared wild animals of the jungle. These dogs must be trained and controlled and given love and attention and then they will lay down their life for you if need be, for their devotion to man is as old as the ages and will never falter or change. Of all the breeds known to man, to these can most justly be granted the motto, "Ich dien."

Champion Husky-Pak Marclar's Seoux

THE ALASKAN MALAMUTE

The Innuits ("*people*," in the Oranian language) are a very high type of northern Indian who have lived in the far reaches of Alaska for untold centuries. A tribe of Innuits called Mahlemuts settled along the shores of Kotzebuc Sound in the western part of Alaska. These Mahlemuts were far more intelligent and imaginative than most of the peoples native to the grim northland, and they used both these characteristics in molding a breed of northern dog indigenous to their tribe. The dogs they bred were powerful weight pullers, able to work without ceasing in the pitiless, deadly land of the "midnight sun". Sled dogs par excellence, they were also pack animals and hunting dogs of great courage in a land where hunting is less a sport than a necessity and the hunter is in as deadly danger as the hunted.

Unlike many northern peoples who treated their dogs as necessary evils and kept them half wild and dominated by the whip, the Mahlemuts' dogs were part of the household, often living in the dwellings with their master and his family, and treated with kindness and respect for their abilities and their natural necessity to man in the northern lands. Knowing their worth, the Mahlemuts jealously guarded their dogs, allowing no outcrossing to other northern breeds, and this kept their stock pure through the centuries.

326

A canine breed shaped by the icy environment of the Land of the Midnight Sun, the Malamute plays a leading and varied role in the lives of the peoples of the deadly North. This excellent portrait is of the best-in-show winning Malamute, Champion Sno-Crest's Mukluk.

The easy comradeship between man and dog is well illustrated by a piece of film the author saw several years ago in a private showing of a movie taken by a naturalist about the Alaskan tundra. A few feet were devoted to the Mahlemut tribe and it showed a bitch nursing her litter of puppies in a corner of the summer skin dwelling and a naked, native baby crawling across the dirt floor to join the puppies in suckling the bitch. The bitch, the baby, the child's family and the puppies all seemed extremely happy about the entire procedure.

This most noble of all the great family of sled dogs was named after the tribe that had bred him but, with the typical disregard of the white man for phonetics or spelling, the name became bastardized to Malamute. No matter how you spell it, this is a great breed, allied by basic roots to all northern dogs, yet apart from them by nature of its many inbred virtues.

Gentle and sweet in temperament, yet ever able to take care of himself under any circumstances, the Malamute, it has been found, is at home in any climate and makes an ideal and noble companion and house dog. This is one of the finest breeds of dogs known to man, a very worthwhile member of the working group.

STANDARD OF THE ALASKAN MALAMUTE

General Appearance and Characteristics—The Alaskan Malamute is a powerful and substantially built dog with deep chest and strong, compact body, not too short coupled, with a thick, coarse guard coat of sufficient length to protect a dense, woolly undercoat, from 1 to 2 inches in depth when dog is in full coat. Stands well over pads, and this stance gives the appearance of much activity, showing interest and curiosity. The head is broad, ears wedge-shaped and erect when alerted. The muzzle is bulky with only slight diminishing in width and depth from root to nose, not pointed or long, but not stubby. The Malamute moves with a proud carriage, head erect and eyes alert. Face markings are a distinguishing feature. These consist of either cap over head

Champion Tigara's
Dortic Shag-Luck

328

and rest of face solid color, usually grayish white, or face marked with the appearance of a mask. Combinations of cap and mask are not unusual. The tail is plumed and carried over the back, not like a fox brush, or tightly curled, more like a plume waving.

Malamutes are of various colors, but are usually wolfish gray or black and white. Their feet are of the "snowshoe" type, tight and deep, with well-cushioned pads, giving a firm and compact appearance. Front legs are straight with big bone. Hind legs are broad and powerful, moderately bent at stifles, and without cowhocks. The back is straight, gently sloping from shoulders to hips. The loin should not be so short or tight as to interfere with easy, tireless movement. Endurance and intelligence are shown in body and expression. They have a "wolf-like" appearance by their position, but the expression is soft and indicates an affectionate disposition.

Temperament—The Alaskan Malamute is an affectionate, friendly dog, not a "one-man" dog. He is a loyal, devoted companion, playful on invitation, but generally impressive by his dignity after maturity.

Head—The head should indicate a high degree of intelligence, and is broad and powerful as compared with other "natural" breeds, but should be in proportion to the size of the dog so as not to make the dog appear clumsy or coarse.

Skull—The skull should be broad between the ears, gradually narrowing to eyes, rounding off to cheeks, which should be moderately flat. There should be a slight furrow between the eyes, the topline of skull and topline of the muzzle showing but little break downward from a straight line as they join.

Muzzle—The muzzle should be large and bulky in proportion to size of skull, diminishing but little in width and depth from junction with skull to nose; lips close fitting; nose black; upper and lower jaws broad with large teeth, front teeth meeting with a scissors grip but never overshot or undershot.

Eyes—Brown, almond shaped, moderately large for this shape of eye, set obliquely in skull. Dark eyes preferred.

Ears—The ears should be of medium size, but small in proportion to head. The upper halves of the ears are triangular in shape, slightly rounded at tips, set wide apart on outside back edges of the skull with the lower part of the ear joining the skull on a line with the upper corner of the eye, giving the tips of the ears the appearance, when erect, of standing off from the skull. When erect, the ears point slightly forward, but when the dog is at work the ears are sometimes folded against the skull. High-set ears are a fault.

Neck—The neck should be strong and moderately arched.

Body—The chest should be strong and deep; body should be strong and compactly built but not short coupled. The back should be straight and gently sloping to the hips. The loins should be well muscled and not so short as to interfere with easy, rhythmic movement with powerful drive from the hind-quarters. A long loin which weakens the back is also a fault. No excess weight.

Shoulders, Legs and Feet—Shoulders should be moderately sloping, forelegs heavily boned and muscled, straight to pasterns, which should be short and strong and almost vertical as viewed from the side. The feet should be large and compact, toes tight-fitting and well arched, pads thick and tough, toenails short and strong. There should be a protective growth of hair between toes. Hind legs must be broad and powerfully muscled through thighs; stifles moderately bent, hock joints broad and strong, moderately bent and well let down. As viewed from behind, the hind legs should not appear bowed in bone, but stand and move true in line with movement of the front legs, and not too close or too wide. The legs of the Malamute must indicate unusual strength and tremendous propelling power. Any indication of unsoundness in legs or feet, standing or moving, is to be considered a serious fault. Dewclaws on the hind legs are undesirable and should be removed shortly after pups are whelped.

Tail—Moderately set and following the line of the spine at the start, well furred and carried over the back when not working—not tightly curled to rest on back—or short furred and carried like a fox brush, a waving plume appearance instead.

Coat—The Malamute should have a thick, coarse guard coat, not long and soft. The undercoat is dense, from 1 to 2 inches in depth, oily and woolly. The coarse guard coat stands out, and there is thick fur around the neck. The guard coat varies in length, as does the undercoat; however, in general, the coat is moderately short to medium along the sides of the body with the length of the coat increasing somewhat around the shoulders and neck, down the back and over the rump, as well as in the breeching and plume. Malamutes usually have shorter and less dense coats when shed out during the summer months.

Color and Markings—The usual colors range from light gray through the intermediate shadings to black, always with white on underbodies, parts of legs, feet, and part of mask markings. Markings should be either cap-like and/or mask-like on face. A white blaze on forehead and/or collar or spot on nape is attractive and acceptable, but broken color extending over the body in spots or uneven splashings is undesirable. One should distinguish between mantled dogs and splash-coated dogs. The only solid color allowable is the all-white.

Size—There is a natural range in size in the breed. The desirable freighting sizes are: Males, 25 inches at the shoulders—85 pounds. Females, 23 inches at the shoulders—75 pounds. However, size consideration should not outweigh that of type, proportion, and functional attributes, such as shoulders, chest, legs, feet, and movement. When dogs are judged equal in type, proportion, and functional attributes, the dog nearest the desirable freighting size is to be preferred.

IMPORTANT—In judging Alaskan Malamutes their function as a sledge dog for heavy freighting must be given consideration above all else. The judge must bear in mind that this breed is designed primarily as the working sledge dog of the North for hauling heavy freight, and therefore he should be a heavy-boned, powerfully built, compact dog with sound legs, good feet, deep chest, powerful shoulders, steady, balanced, tireless gait, and the other physical equipment necessary for the efficient performance of his job. He isn't intended as a racing sled dog designed to compete in speed trials with the smaller Northern breeds. The Malamute as a sledge dog for heavy freighting is designed for strength and endurance and any characteristic of the individual specimen, including temperament, which interferes with the accomplishment of this purpose is to be considered the most serious of faults. Faults under this provision would be splayfootedness, any indication of unsoundness or weakness in legs, cowhocks, bad pasterns, straight shoulders, lack of angulation, stilted gait or any gait

Champion Tigara's Torch of Arctica

which isn't balanced, strong and steady, ranginess, shallowness, ponderousness, lightness of bone, poor over-all proportion, and similar characteristics.

SCALE OF POINTS

	Points
General appearance	20
Head	15
Body	20
Legs and movement	20
Feet	10
Coat and color	10
Tail	5
Total	100

Champion Liza del Pirata Nero, C.D. (Groenendael).

THE BELGIAN SHEEPDOGS—

GROENENDAEL, TERVUREN, MALINOIS

In the standards that follow only the *Groenendael* and *Tervuren* are written. The Malinois, whose standard is not given, is structurally the same as both of its Belgian sheepherding cousins except that it is shorthaired. In color it is fawn and black like the Tervuren. Some specimens were imported to this country in 1948 but were not adopted by the American fancy with any degree of enthusiasm.

Both the Groenendael and the Tervuren enjoy a common ancestry in both France and Belgium, for they were the basic breeds developed by sheepherders to tend and protect the flocks. Throughout Europe such dogs were called *Chien de Berger*. The animals that were developed specifically in Belgium for sheepherding were eventually called (and registered) *Chien de Berger Belge* in Belgium and France. While journeying through both of these countries, the author often saw representative specimens of Belgian Sheepdogs still doing the task they were bred for, herding sheep. Indeed, the Belgian Sheepdog and the German Shepherd were the recognizable breeds, most frequently seen by the author in many parts of rural Europe tending the flocks.

A blending of the various native Belgian sheepherding breeds was recommended by Professor Reul in 1891 and, even before this, a Monsieur Rose of Groenendael was breeding a self-black strain which became the true Groenendael variety.

About this same time one Monsieur Corbeel, living in the town of Tervuren, owned and bred pure local sheepdogs with long, black-tipped fawn hair. From this stock came the Tervuren, named, of course, after the town from which they originated.

Evidence that both Groenendael and Tervuren are but color phases of the same basic stock is testified to by their parallel physical and mental characteristics and the fact that the black Groenendael sometimes still genetically carry a recessive for fawn.

Belgian Sheepdogs have fine temperaments, are easily trained, and so make excellent house dogs, guard dogs, guides for the blind, and competitors in obedience work.

In 1959 the Groenendael and Tervuren were accepted and listed as different breeds by the A.K.C.

STANDARD OF THE BELGIAN SHEEPDOGS
(GROENENDAEL AND TERVUREN)

Personality—The Belgian Sheepdogs should reflect the qualities of intelligence, courage, alertness and devotion to master. To his inherent aptitude as guardian of flocks should be added protectiveness of the person and property of his master. He should be watchful, attentive and usually in motion when not under command. In his relationship with humans he should be observant and vigilant with strangers but not apprehensive. He should not show fear or shyness. He should not show viciousness by unwarranted or unprovoked attack. With those he knows well, he is most affectionate and friendly, zealous for their attention and very possessive.

General Appearance—The first impression of a Belgian Shepherd is that of a well-balanced square dog, elegant in appearance, with proud carriage of the head and neck. He is a strong, agile, well-muscled animal, alert and full of life. His whole conformation gives the impression of depth and solidity without bulkiness. The male is usually somewhat more impressive and grand than the female. The female should have a distinctly feminine look. Because of frequent comparisons between the Belgian Sheepdog and the German Shepherd Dog, it is to be noted that these two breeds differ considerably in size, substance and structure, the difference being especially noticeable in the formation of the topline and the hindquarters.

Size and Substance—Males 24–26 inches in height, and females 22–24 inches, measured at the withers. The length, measured from point of breastbone to point of rump, should equal the height. Bone structure medium in proportion to height so that he is well balanced throughout and neither spindly or leggy nor cumbersome and bulky.

Stance—The Belgian Sheepdog should stand squarely on all fours. Viewed from the side, the topline, ground level, front legs, and back legs should closely approximate a perfect square.

Expression—Intelligent and questioning, indicating alertness, attention and readiness for action.

Coat—The guard hairs of the coat must be long, well-fitting, straight and abundant. They should not be silky or wiry. The texture should be a medium harshness. The undercoat should be very dense commensurate, however, with climatic conditions. The Belgian Sheepdog is particularly adaptable to extremes of temperature or climate. The hair is shorter on the head, outside the ears and on the lower part of the legs. The opening of the ear is protected by tufts of hair. Ornamentation: especially long and abundant hair, like a collarette, around the neck; fringe of long hair down the back of the forearm; especially long and abundant hair trimming the hindquarters—the breeches; long, heavy and abundant hair on the tail.

Head—Well chiseled, dry, long without exaggeration. Skull and muzzle, measuring from the stop, should be of equal length. Over-all size should be in proportion to the body. Top of skull flattened rather than rounded, the width approximately the same but not wider than the length. Stop moderate. Muzzle moderately pointed, avoiding any tendency to snipiness. The jaws should be strong and powerful. The lips should be tight and black, with no pink showing on the outside. Ears are equilateral triangles in shape, well cupped, stiff, erect, not too large. Set high, the base of the ear should not come below the center of the eye. Eyes brown, preferably dark brown, medium size, slightly almond shaped, not protruding. Light or yellow eyes are a fault. Nose black, without spots or discolored areas. Nostrils well defined. There should be a full complement of strong white teeth evenly set. Either a scissors or even bite is acceptable. Should not be overshot or undershot. Teeth broken by accident

Int. Ch. Gin Du Clos Saint Jacques (Tervuren)

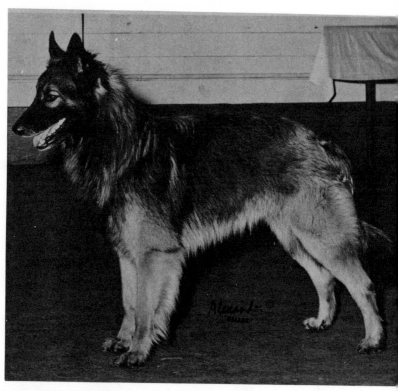

Javelin of Georgjune, C.D.X. (Tervuren)

should not be severely penalized, but worn teeth, especially incisors, are often indicative of the lack of proper bite, although some allowance should be made for age. Discolored (distemper) teeth are not to be penalized.

Torso—Neck round, muscular, rather outstretched, slightly arched and tapered from head to body. Skin well fitting with no loose folds. Topline horizontal, straight and firm from withers to hip joints. The loin section, viewed from above, is relatively short, broad and strong, but blending smoothly into the back. The croup is medium long, sloping gradually. Tail strong at the base, the last vertebra to reach the hock. At rest the dog holds it low, the tip bent back level with the hock. When in action he raises it and gives it a curl, which is strongest toward the tip, without forming a hook. Tail should not be carried too high nor turned to one side. Chest not broad but deep, the lowest point should reach the elbow, forming a smooth ascendant curve to the abdomen. Abdomen moderately developed, neither tucked-up nor paunchy.

Forequarters—Legs straight, parallel, perpendicular to the ground. Shoulders long and oblique, laid flat against the body, forming a sharp angle (approximately 90 degrees) with the upper arm. Top of the shoulder blades should be roughly a thumb's width apart. Arms should move in a direction exactly parallel to the axis of the body. Forearms long and well muscled. Bone

A family of Belgian Tervurens. Beauty and utility combined, this breed gives active service to mankind.

flat rather than round. Pasterns short and strong, slightly sloped. Feet round (cat-footed), toes curved close together, well padded, strong nails. Nail color can vary from black to transparent.

Hindquarters—Legs powerful without heaviness, moving in the same pattern as the limbs of the foreqaurters. Thighs broad and heavily muscled. Stifles clearly defined, with upper shank at right angles to the hip bones. Bone flat rather than round. Hocks moderately bent. Metatarsi short, perpendicular to the ground, parallel to each other when viewed from the rear. Dewclaws, if any, should be removed. Feet slightly elongated, toes curved close together, heavily padded, strong nails. Nail color may vary from black to transparent.

Gait—The gait is lively and graceful, covering the maximum of ground. Always in motion, seemingly never tiring, he shows facility of movement rather than a hard driving action. He tends to single-track at a fast gait, the legs both front and rear converging toward the center line of gravity of the dog. The back line should remain firm and level, parallel to the line of motion with no crabbing. His natural tendency is to move in a circle rather than in a straight line.

Faults—Any deviation from these specifications is a fault. In determining whether a fault is minor, serious, or major, these two factors should be used as a guide: 1. The extent to which it deviates from the Standard. 2. The extent to which such deviation would atually affect the working ability of the dog.

Groenendael—Color: Black. May be completely black or may be black with white, limited as follows: Small to moderate patch or strip on forechest. Between pads of feet. On tips of hind toes. On chin and muzzle (frost—may be white or gray). On tips of front toes—allowable but a fault.

Disqualifications: Viciousness. Color—any color other than black, except for white in specified areas. Ears—hanging (as on a hound). Tail—cropped or stump. Males under 22½ or over 27½ inches in height. Females under 20½ or over 25½ inhces in height.

Belgian Tervuren—Color: Rich fawn to russet mahogany with black overlay. The coat is characteristically double pigmented, wherein the tip of each fawn hair is blackened. On mature males, this blackening is especially pronounced on the shoulders, back and rib section. The chest color is a mixture of black and gray. The face has a black mask, and the ears are mostly black. The tail typically has a darker or black tip. The underpart of the body, tail and breeches are light beige. A small white patch is permitted on the chest, not to extend to the neck or breast. The tips of the toes may be white. White or gray hair (frost) on chin or muzzle is normal. Although some allowance is to be made for dogs under 18 months of age, when true color is attained, washed-out color or color too black resembling the Groenendael is undesirable.

Disqualifications: Ears—hanging, as on a hound. Tail—cropped or stump. Color—white markings anywhere except as specified. Teeth—pronounced undershot. Size—males, under 22½ or over 27½ inches in height; females, under 20½ or over 25½ inches in height.

A Continental Champion Bernese Mountain Dog (smooth)

THE BERNESE MOUNTAIN DOG

A native of Switzerland the Bernese Mountain Dog is one of four breeds from the Alps, but is the only one to enter the United States in numbers sufficient to receive A.K.C. recognition. It is also the only one of the four Swiss mountain breeds not used for sheep or cattle herding. The Bernese, in its native land, was a companion and draft dog, working for the Swiss farmers pulling loads of milk and produce over the steep mountain trails to the market place.

In 1963 the author was in the Swiss Alps, near Lauterbrunnen, attending a rural cattle show for *Simethaler Flekvick*, a fascinating dual breed of Swiss cattle used for both milk and meat. There, midst the farmers, cattle, huge neck bells, and dehorning fires, was a Bernese Mountain Dog. Later, in a little chalet restaurant near the fairgrounds, the author and his wife fed the dog a piece of fresh mountain trout. He took it gently after his master had said he could. This was typical of the breed, gentle and engendering trust, yet under the complete control of his master.

These are strong, faithful, hardy dogs who need no indoor kennels. Farmers who have had the pleasure of owning Bernese Dogs report them to be intelligent, willing and capable in any work they are assigned.

The breed came to Switzerland over 2,000 years ago with the Roman armies. These early specimens were large, mastiff-like animals. Left by the invaders, some of these dogs were given shelter by the natives, bred to local types of sheepherding and draft dogs and became the basis for the breed known as Bernese Mountain Dogs.

The breed almost became extinct by the latter half of the 19th century. Then, after much searching, a few typical specimens were found by Franz Schertenleib of Berne and, through his efforts, the breed came into focus again. In 1907 a specialty club was formed in Switzerland, and in 1937, the breed was introduced to America through the importation of a pair of good specimens.

STANDARD OF THE BERNESE MOUNTAIN DOG

General Appearance—A well-balanced dog, active and alert; a combination of sagacity, fidelity and utility.

Height—Dogs, 23 inches to 27½ inches; bitches, 21 inches to 26 inches at shoulder.

Head—Skull flat, defined stop and strong muzzle. Dewlaps very slightly developed, flews not too pendulous, jaw strong with good, strong teeth. Eyes dark, hazel-brown, full of fire. Ears V-shaped, set on high, not too pointed at tips and rather short. When in repose, hanging close to head; when alert, brought slightly forward and raised at base.

Body—Rather short than too long in back, compact and well ribbed up. Chest broad with good depth of brisket. Loins strong and muscular.

Legs and Feet—Forelegs perfectly straight and muscular, thighs well developed and stifles well bent. Feet round and compact. Dewclaws should be removed.

Tail—Of fair thickness and well covered with long hair, but not to form a

Natural draft dogs, these Bernese, one of the smooth variety the other wearing the longer coat, are shown at the National Festival in Switzerland.

The innate nobility and dignity of this breed from the snow-clad Alps is quite evident in this head study.

flag; moderate length. When in repose, should be carried low, upward swirl permissible; when alert, may be carried gaily, but may never curl or be carried over back.

Coat—Soft and silky with bright, natural sheen; long and slightly wavy but may never curl.

Color and Markings—Jet-black with russet-brown or deep tan markings on all four legs, a spot just above forelegs, each side of white chest markings and spots over eyes, which may never be missing. The brown on the forelegs must always be between the black and white.

Preferable, but not a condition, are—White feet, tip of tail, pure white blaze up foreface, a few white hairs on back of neck, and white star-shaped markings on chest. When the latter markings are missing, it is not a disqualification.

Faults—Too massive in head, light or staring eyes, too heavy or long ears, too narrow or snipy muzzle, under or overshot mouth, pendulous dewlaps, too long or Setter-like body, splay or hare feet, tail curled or carried over back, cowhocks and white legs.

SCALE OF POINTS

	Points
General appearance	15
Size and height	5
Head	15
Body	15
Legs and feet	15
Tail	10
Coat	10
Color and Markings	15
Total	100

Champion Irca de la Thudinie.

THE BOUVIER DES FLANDRES

In the land of its birth, Belgium, a Bouvier des Flandres cannot become a bench show champion unless it holds a working title (as a police, defense or army dog). This is similar to the working degree (*Schutzhund* degree) which a German Shepherd must have in its homeland to be eligible to compete in a dog show, and is one of the most laudable laws a parent club can make to keep its breed a working one with all the intelligence, strength, character and aptitudes necessary to perform its hereditary tasks, intact.

The Bouvier has had many names; Dirty Beard (*Vuilbaard*), Cow Dog (*Koe hond*), Cattle Driver (*Toucheur de Boeuf*), and finally the name it bears today. They were the farmers' herders, cattle drovers, watch dogs, draft dogs, and, in fact, performed any and all the many tasks a dog can do around a farm, though the breed's chief aptitude was cattle-driving. Early Bouviers stood over 26 inches at the shoulder and were very powerful animals.

The breed first came to the attention of dog fanciers when exhibited at the Brussels International show in 1910. A standard was adopted in 1912 and a society of Bouvier breeders was formed that same year in Flanders. The breed was on its way to take its place in the sun of dogdom. Then World War I broke out and the parts of the country where the Bouvier was mostly being bred were bombed out and overrun and most of the dogs were lost.

A very few were saved and one, owned by Veterinarian Captain Darby of the Belgian Army, was the progenitor of a group of dogs that, almost by themselves, revived the breed.

A more comprehensive standard was adopted in Belgium in 1923 and subsequently recognized by the A.K.C. but the breed did not arouse any interest here until close to 1940. In recent years Jacqueline Kennedy, lovely wife of our late President and of French ancestry, bore the maiden name of Bouvier and, because of this, her interest in the Bouvier des Flandres was aroused and, through this interest by such a gracious and beloved lady, the breed will probably find the popularity with dog-conscious people it so well deserves.

The breed descends from the Brabanter, and back to the Tibetan Mastiff, while later progenitors probably crossed with native breeds to fashion the dog most fitted to do the work allotted to it in the particular terrain in which it evolved.

STANDARD OF THE BOUVIER DES FLANDRES

The Bouvier des Flandres is a rough-coated dog of notably rugged appearance as befitting an erstwhile cattle driver and farmers' helper of Flandres, and later an ambulance dog and messenger in World War I. He is a compact-bodied, powerfully built dog of upstanding carriage and alert, intelligent expression.

Head—The head is medium long, with the skull slightly longer than the muzzle.

Skull—Almost flat on top, moderately wide between the ears, and sloping slightly toward the muzzle. The brow is noticeably arched over the eyes. The stop is shallow, and the under-eye fill-in good.

Ears—Rough-coated, set high on the head and cropped to a triangular contour. They stand erect and are carried straight up.

Eyes—Neither protruding nor sunken, the eyes are set a trifle obliquely in the skull and not too far apart. They are of medium size and very nearly oval. Preferred color, a dark nut-brown. Black eyes, although not considered faulty, are less desirable as contributing to a somber expression. Light-colored eyes, and staring or wild expression are faulty.

Muzzle—Wide, deep and well filled out, with width narrowing gradually toward the tip of the nose. Cheeks are clean or flat-sided, the jaws powerful, and the lips dry and tight-fitting. A narrow muzzle, suggestive of weakness, is faulty.

Teeth—Strong and white, with the canines set well apart, the teeth meet in a scissors bite.

Nose—Black and well developed, the nostrils wide open. Across the top the contour is a trifle rounded as opposed to flat. Brown, pink and spotted noses are faulty.

Neck and Shoulders—The neck is well rounded, slightly arched, and carried almost upright, its thickness gradually increasing as it fits gracefully into the shoulders. Clean and dry at the throat. The shoulders are long and sloping.

Body—The brisket is deep, extending down at least to the point of the elbows, and of moderate width.

Back—Short, strong and straight.

Loins—Short, taut, and slightly arched in topline, while the rump is broad and square rather than sloping. Ribs are deep and well sprung. As advantageous for breeding purposes, slightly greater length of loin is permissible in bitches.

Tail—Set high, carried up, and docked to about 4 inches.

Legs and Feet—The leg bones, although only moderate in girth, are made

A group of sound, working and bench type Bouviers in their native land.

to appear heavy because of their covering with thick, rough hair.

Forelegs—Straight as viewed from the front or side, with elbows turned neither in nor out.

Hind Legs—Hindquarters are firm and well muscled, with large, powerful hams. Legs are strong and sturdy, with hocks well let down and wide apart. They are slightly angulated at stifle and hock joints. Viewed from the back, they are absolutely parallel.

Feet—Round, compact, with toes arched and close. The nails are black, the pads thick and tough.

Coat—Rough, touseled and unkempt in appearance, the coat is capable of withstanding the hardest work in the most inclement weather.

Topcoat—Harsh, rough and wiry, and so thick that when separated by the hand the skin is hardly visible.

Undercoat—Fine and soft in texture, and thicker in winter. On the skull the hair is shorter and almost smooth. On the brows it is longer, thus forming eyebrows. Longer growth on muzzle and underjaw form mustache and beard. On the legs it is thick and rough, on the feet rather short. Soft, silky or woolly topcoats are faulty.

Color—From fawn to black; pepper and salt, gray and brindle. A white star on the chest is allowed. Chocolate brown with white spots is faulty.

Height—Dogs, from 23½ to 27½ inches; bitches, a minimum of 22¾ inches.

SCALE OF POINTS

	Points
Coat	20
Head (eyes, ears, skull, foreface)	20
Shoulders and style	10
Hindquarters (hams and legs)	10
Back, loin, brisket, belly	15
Feet and legs	10
Symmetry, size and character	15
Total	100

Champion Barrage of Quality Hill.

THE BOXER

A good Boxer is an eye-arresting dog. Clean in limb and outline, beautifully balanced and attractively colored, he provokes the adjective "clean-cut" as he fills the eye.

The Boxer's geneological background is allied to both the Bulldog and Mastiff type dogs. He descends from the Bullenbeisser, a commonly used hunting dog in Germany during the middle ages. Later, when the baiting of dangerous beasts became a sport, a smaller Bullenbeisser (*the Brabanter Bullenbeisser*) became popular. This was a medium-sized dog, the bull-baiting dog supreme. He was soon adopted by butchers and cattle dealers. The Bullenbeisser goes back through the Mastiff breeds to the basic Molossian dog type. A breed of parallel type to the Boxer developed in Spain, the Spanish Alano, of Andalusia and Extremadura, and the Matin de Terceira or Perro do Presa in the Azores. Another similar breed can be found in the Bouldogue du Mida from the South of France, and the English Bulldog, in an earlier stage of its development, was very similar to the Boxer.

Up until 1830 the breed displayed only brindle and fawn colors with some limited white. But at that date the English Bulldog was brought to Germany

345

Two flashy, fawn Boxers of evident quality. The bitch is Champion Tremblay's Fashion Model, and the dog is Champion Brayshaw's Masquerader. Note the marked secondary sex characteristics of these two animals.

and crossed to dogs of Boxer breeding. It is the Bulldog white, a recessive that runs in certain Boxer strains, that still produces whites (Checks) or dogs carrying too much white.

The modern Boxer traces its lineage back to six specific animals. Three were stud dogs; Wotan, Bosco Immergrun, and Flock St. Salvator. The bitches were Alt 's Flora, her great, great grand-daughter, Meta v.d. Passage, and Mirzl.

The first Boxer was registered in 1904, and the first Boxer champion finished in 1915. But the first true recognition of the breed in America came with the importation, by the Cirrol Kennels in the early 1930's, of the famous Int. Ch. Check v. Hunnenstein. He was the first of his breed to win a best in show in the United States. Mrs. William Z. Breed and John Phelps Wagner imported other great German Boxers and Wagner's famous Mazelaine Kennels came into being. The breed flared into the limelight as a great show dog and, in its sculptured beauty, still remains there.

Fine companions and pets, sturdy and easy to keep clean, the Boxer is a good and dependable family and watch dog.

STANDARD OF THE BOXER

The Boxer is a medium-sized, sturdy dog, of square build, with short back, strong limbs, and short tight-fitting coat. His musculations, well developed, should be clean, hard and appear smooth (not bulgy) under taut skin. His movements should denote energy. The gait although firm is elastic (springy), the stride free and ground-covering, the carriage proud and noble. Developed to serve the multiple purposes of guard, working, and escort-dog, he must combine elegance with substance and ample power, not alone for beauty but to insure the speed, dexterity, and jumping ability essential to arduous hike, riding expedition, police or military duty. Only a body whose individual parts are built to withstand the most strenuous efforts, assembled as a complete and harmonious whole, can respond to these combined demands. Therefore, to be at his highest efficiency he must never be plump or heavy and, while equipped for great speed, he must never be racy.

The head imparts to the Boxer a unique individual stamp peculiar to him alone. It must be in perfect proportion to his body, never small in comparison to the over-all picture. His muzzle is his most distinctive feature, and the greatest value is to be placed on its being of correct form and in absolute proper proportion to the skull.

In judging the Boxer, the first thing to be considered is general appearance, then balance; the relation of substance to elegance and of the desired proportions of the individual parts of the body to each other. Consideration is to be given to an attractive color, after which the individual parts are to be examined for their correct constructions and their functions. Special attention is to be devoted to the head. *Faults*—Head not typical, plump bull-doggy appearance, light bone, lack of balance, bad condition, deficiency in nobility.

Head—The beauty of the head depends upon the harmonious proportion between the muzzle and the skull. The muzzle should always appear powerful, never small in its relationship to the skull. The head should be clean, not showing deep wrinkles. Folds will normally appear upon the forehead when the ears are erect, and they are always indicated from the lower edge of the stop running downward on both sides of the muzzle. The dark mask is confined to the muzzle and is in distinct contrast to the color of the head. Any extension of the mask to the skull, other than dark shading around the eyes, creates a somber undesirable expression. The muzzle is powerfully developed in length, width and depth. It is not pointed, narrow, short, or shallow. Its shape is influenced first through the formation of both jawbones, second through the placement of the teeth, and third through the texture of the lips.

The two jawbones do not terminate in the usual scissor-bite; instead the lower jaw protrudes moderately beyond the upper and bends *slightly* upward. The Boxer is normally undershot. The upper jaw is broad where attached to the skull and maintains this breadth except for a very slight tapering to the front. The lower jaw incisor teeth are in a straight line. In the upper jaw they are slightly rounded. The middle incisors should not project. This formation creates frontal width in both jaws and results in the canine teeth being widely separated from each other. The upper corner incisors should fit snugly back of the lower canine teeth, the pre-molars, anterior palliative foramen (a technical term pertaining to the placing of teeth), and molars fitting in the most normal possible manner, creating a sound, powerful bite.

The lips complete the formation of the muzzle. The upper lip is thick and padded, filling out the frontal space formed by the projection of the lower jaw and it is supported by the jaw's fangs. Therefore, these fangs must stand far apart and be of good length so that the front surface of the muzzle shall become broad and squarish and, when viewed from the side, form a rounded angle with the topline of the muzzle. The lower edge of the upper lip rests on the edge of the lower lip. The repandous (bent upward) part of the under-jaw with the lower lip (sometimes called the chin) must not rise above the front of the upper lip, but much less may it disappear under it. It must be perceptible when viewed from the front as well as the side, without protruding and bending upward in the manner of the English Bulldog. The Boxer must not show his teeth or his tongue when his mouth is closed. Excessive flews are not desirable.

The top of the skull is slightly arched, not rotund, or flat, or noticeably broad, and the occiput must not be too pronounced. The forehead forms a distinct stop with the topline of the muzzle, which must not be forced back into the forehead like that of a Bulldog. It should not slant up, or down (down-faced), or be dished. The tip of the nose lies somewhat higher than the root of the muzzle. The forehead shows a suggestion of furrow which, however, must never be too deep, especially between the eyes. Corresponding with the powerful set of teeth, the cheeks are accordingly well developed, without protruding from the head with too bulgy an appearance, preferably they should taper into the muzzle in a slight, graceful curve. The ears are cut rather long, well trimmed, and carried erect. The dark brown eyes, not too small, not protruding or deep-set, disclose an alert and intelligent expression and must never appear gloomy, threatening, or piercing, they should be encircled by dark hair. The nose is broad and black, very slightly turned up; the nostrils are broad with the nasolabial line running between them.

Faults—Lack of nobility and expression, somber face, unserviceable bite. Pinscher or Bulldog head, badly trimmed ears, visible conjunctiva (haw), driveling, showing teeth or tongue, light so-called "Bird of Prey" eyes. Sloping top line of muzzle, too pointed or too light a bite (snipy).

Neck—Round, of ample length, not too short; strong and muscular and clean throughout, without dewlap, with a distinctly marked nape and an elegant arch running down to the back. *Faults*—Dewlap.

Body—Body is square. Measured in profile, a horizontal line from the front of the forechest to the rear projection of the upper thigh should equal a vertical line dropped from the top of the withers to the ground.

Chest and Front Leg Measurements—The brisket is deep, reaching down to the elbows; the depth of the body at the lowest point of the brisket amounts to half the height of the dog at the withers. The ribs, extending far to the rear, are well arched but not barrel-shaped. The loins are short and muscular; the lower stomach line, lightly tucked up, blending into a graceful curve to the rear. The shoulders are long and sloping, close lying, and not excessively covered with muscle. The upper arm is long, closely approaching a right angle to the shoulder blade. The forelegs, when seen from the front, must be straight, stand parallel to each other, and have strong, firmly joined bones. Chest of fair width, and forechest well defined. The elbows must not press too

Champion Salgray's Flying High.

closely to the chest wall or stand off visibly from it. The forearm is straight, long, and firmly muscled. The pastern (knee) joint of the foreleg is clearly defined but not distended. The pastern is short, slightly slanting, but standing almost perpendicular to the ground. Feet compact, turning neither in nor out, with tightly arched toes and hard soles (cat's paws).

Faults—Too broad and low in front, loose shoulders, chest hanging between the shoulders, hare's feet, hollow flanks, hanging stomach, turned feet, tied-in elbows.

Back—The withers should be clearly defined, the whole back short, straight, and very muscular. *Faults*—Roach back, sway back, thin lean back, long narrow loins, weak union with croup.

Hindquarters—In balance with forequarters; strongly muscled. The thighs broad and curved, the breech musculation strongly developed. The croup very slightly sloped, broad. Tail attachment high, rather than low. Tail clipped, carried upward. The pelvis should be long and especially broad in females. Upper and lower thigh long, leg well angulated. In standing position, the leg below the hock joint should be practically perpendicular to the ground (a slight slope is permissible). Viewed from behind the hind legs are straight. The hocks (metatarsus) clean, strong, and short, supported by powerful rear pads with hock joint clean-cut and clearly defined. The rear toes just a little longer than the front toes, but similar in all other respects.

Faults—Falling off or too rounded or narrow croup, low-set tail, higher in back than in front; steep, stiff, or too slightly angulated hindquarters, light thighs, cowhocks, bowlegs and crooked legs, rear dewclaws, soft hocks, narrow heel, tottering, waddling gait, hare feet, hindquarters too far under or too far behind.

Height—Males, 22 inches to 24 inches at the withers. Females, 21 inches to 23 inches at the withers. Males should not go under 22 inches and females should not go over 23 inches.

Coat—Short, shiny, lying smooth and tight to the body.

Color—The colors are fawn and brindle. Fawn in various shades from light yellow to dark deer red. The brindle variety should have clearly defined black stripes on fawn background. White markings in fawn and brindle dogs are not to be rejected; in fact, they are often very attractive in appearance. The black mask is absolutely required. When white occurs on the muzzle it should be edged by remnants of the black mask. Black toenails are preferred but not essential. Even distribution of head markings is desirable.

Character—The character of the Boxer is of the greatest importance and demands the most solicitous attention. He should be alert and fearless; willing to make friends, but not necessarily effusive. *Faults*—Shyness—A dog should be considered shy if he shrinks away from a friendly approach or displays timidity when approached from the rear, or displays cowardice over sudden and unusual noises. *Viciousness*—A dog should be considered vicious that attempts to attack either his handler or the judge. Belligerency toward other dogs should not be considered viciousness.

DISQUALIFICATION

Boxers with white or black ground color, or entirely white or black or any color other than fawn or brindle. (White markings are allowed but must not exceed one-third ($\frac{1}{3}$) of the ground color.)

Champion Fripon des Hirsutes.

THE BRIARD

Dogs of Briard type have been familiar to the rural districts of Europe for centuries, particularly in Germany and Poland. These breeds are used as sheepherders, drovers, watch dogs and draft animals. The Briard, or Chien Berger de Brie, is descended from a very old breed of French hunting and guard dog owned by the nobles and probably derived from Alaunt and ancient Persian Sheepdog breeding initially.

When the nobility was eliminated by the French Revolution the Briard became a dog of the farmers and was utilized in the tasks of herding, guiding the flocks, and guarding farm property.

In the latter part of the 19th century, Briards found their way into dog shows in France. The *Les Amis du Briard* society was formed in 1900 and established a breed standard which was adopted, with very few changes, by the Briard Club of America.

As a breed the Briard learns rather slowly but once learned, never forgets. The breed has been successfully used not only as sheep and guard dogs but also as police and war dogs. They are well-mannered around the home, only bark when it is necessary and have a tendency to stay within the confines of their owner's land.

351

An unusually sensitive head portrait of a top
winning bench and obedience Briard, Champion
Matador Chez Phydeau, C.D.

The Briard is a large dog between 22 to 27 inches at the withers. His long, coarse coat is made to withstand extremes of weather. It has often been described as "*goatlike*" in texture. The Briard may be any solid color with the exception of white. Most frequently seen colors are black, grey, or tawny.

The Briard has naturally dropped ears, but continental breeders crop the tips thereby making the ear stand erect. This is done for hygienic reasons, but also contributes to a smarter appearance. Unlike most breeds, the Briard must have two dewclaws on each hindleg. Absence of one or both is considered a disqualifying fault in the ring.

STANDARD OF THE BRIARD

General Appearance—A strong and substantially built dog, fitted for field work, lithe, muscular, and well proportioned, alert and active.

Size—Height at shoulders: Dogs, 23 to 27 inches; bitches, 22 to 25½ inches. Young dogs may be below the minimum.

Head—Large and rather long. Stop well marked and placed at equal distance from top of head and tip of nose. Forehead very slightly rounded. Line from stop to tip of nose straight. Teeth strong, white, and meeting exactly even. Muzzle neither narrow nor pointed. Nose rather square than rounded, always black. Hair heavy and long on top of head, the ears, and around the muzzle, forming eyebrows standing out and not veiilng the eyes too much. Eyes horizontal, well opened, dark in color and rather large; intelligent and gentle in expression. Ears placed high, not too large and not carried too flat. In France the tips of the ears are generally cropped, causing the ear to be semi-erect.

Conformation—Neck muscular and distinct from the shoulders. Chest broad and deep. Back straight. Rump slightly sloped. Legs muscular with heavy bones. Hock not too near the ground, making a well marked angle, the leg below the hock being not quite vertical.

Tail—Well feathered, carried low and twisted neither to the right nor to the left, curled at the end, tip when straightened reaching to point of hock.

Feet—Strong, round, with toes close together and hard pads; nails black.

Coat—Long, slightly wavy, stiff and strong.

Color—All solid colors are allowed except white. Dark colors are preferable. Usual colors. Black, and black with some white hairs, dark and light grey, tawny, and combinations of two of these colors, provided there are no marked spots and the transition from one to the other takes place gradually and symmetrically.

Dewclaws—Two dewclaws on each hindleg are required. A dog with only one cannot be given a prize.

Faults—Muzzle pointed. Eyes small, almond-shaped or light in color. Rump straight or too sloped. White spot on the breast (a large white spot is very bad). Tail too short or carried over the back. White nails.

DISQUALIFICATIONS

Size below the limit. Absence of dewclaws. Short hair on the head, face or feet. Tail lacking or cut. Nose light in color or spotted. Eyes spotted. Hair curled. White hair on feet. Spotted colors of the coat.

THE BULLMASTIFF

The breed name of this dog tells us exactly what he is in a no-nonsense way. The Bullmastiff is a cross between the Bulldog and the Mastiff and, in breed type, is very much a smaller edition of the age-old Mastiff.

The known history of the breed begins in 1860 where, in England, poachers were working havoc on the large estates and game preserves. These secret gentlemen of the night were busy breeding poaching dogs, silent animals that could drift like fog in search of game where they were not supposed to hunt. Penalties for poaching were severe but didn't seem to eradicate the practice. The gamekeeper's life then became rather dangerous since poachers would rather shoot and run than accept the penalties incurred from apprehension.

The gamekeepers then, in their turn, decided to employ the canine aids of keen hearing and scent to protect themselves and eliminate poaching. To this end they bred and produced a dog that was fearless, quiet, and would attack on command, but would throw and hold the poacher, not maul him. The dog they produced was the Bullmastiff or the "*Gamekeeper's Night-Dog*," as he was called then.

The breed has proven itself in war as a sentry and guard dog, and are excellent house and estate dogs as well, loyal and affectionate to their human family. They are the kind of watchdogs that can be depended upon not to bite welcome visitors.

The English Kennel Club recognized the breed in 1924 and importations began to many countries. The Bullmastiff was granted recognition in this country by the A.K.C. in 1933.

The Bullmastiff is physically and mentally well suited to the role he was bred for. He stands anywhere from 24 to 27 inches at the withers and can weigh from 100 to 120 pounds. He may be either red, fawn, or brindle in color. Gamekeepers favored the brindle because of the ability of dogs of this color to blend into the darkness and not be seen by their human quarry, but as poaching declined and the Bullmastiff came into his own as a guard dog the other colors, inherited from his Mastiff background, became more frequently seen.

Today the Bullmastiff, while not a popular breed, has made a number of friends and good specimens can be seen at any good-sized show.

STANDARD OF THE BULLMASTIFF

General Appearance—That of a symmetrical animal, showing great strength; powerfully built but active. The dog is fearless yet docile, has endurance and alertness. The foundation breeding was 60% Mastiff and 40% Bulldog.

Head—Skull large, with a fair amount of wrinkle when alert; broad, with cheeks well developed. Forehead flat. Muzzle broad and deep; its length, in comparison with that of the entire head, approximately as 1 is to 3. Lack of foreface with nostrils set on top of muzzle is a reversion to the Bulldog and is very undesirable. Nose black with nostrils large and broad. Flews not too pendulous, stop moderate, and the mouth (bite) preferably level or slightly undershot. Canine teeth large and set wide apart. A dark muzzle is preferable.

International Champion Ritter's Beau

Eyes—Dark and of medium size.

Ears—V-shaped and carried close to the cheeks, set on wide and high, level with occiput and cheeks, giving a square appearance to the skull; darker in color than the body and medium in size.

Neck—Slightly arched, of moderate length, very muscular, and almost equal in circumference to the skull.

Body—Compact. Chest wide and deep, with ribs well sprung and well set down between the forelegs.

Forequarters—Shoulders muscular but not loaded, and slightly sloping. Forelegs straight, well boned and set well apart; elbows square. Pasterns straight, feet of medium size, with round toes well arched. Pads thick and tough, nails black.

Back—Short, giving the impression of a well balanced dog.

Loins—Wide, muscular and slightly arched, with fair depth of flank.

Hindquarters—Broad and muscular with well developed second thigh denoting power, but not cumbersume. Moderate angulation at hocks. Cow-hocks and splay feet are bad faults.

Tail—Set on high, strong at the root and tapering to the hocks. It may be straight or curved, but never carried hound fashion.

Coat—Short and dense, giving good weather protection.

Color—Red, fawn or brindle. Except for a very small white spot on the chest, white marking is considered a fault.

Size—Dogs, 25 to 27 inches at the shoulder, and 110 to 130 pounds weight. Bitches, 24 to 26 inches at the shoulder, and 100 to 120 pounds weight. Other things being equal, the heavier dog is favored.

Champion Twit-Lee's Rajah

The Blue Merle, Champion Belhaven's Blue Lucason.

THE COLLIE

That sheep herding dogs were, next to hunting dogs, the earliest breed of canines developed by man is fairly well established as fact. It is, in most cases, difficult to be more specific than this when we attempt to trace the origin of any given breed, and the Collie is no exception. The truth is that the evolution of the herding dog which eventually came into focus in Scotland as the Collie is hidden in the years.

Evidence of the Collie's existence as a definite breed by the early nineteenth century is established by Thomas Bewick's woodcut of the local Scottish working dogs, engraved in the early 1800's. This woodcut unmistakingly depicts a rough-coated and a smooth-coated Collie. The definite breed characteristics seen in the woodcut lead us to assume that the breed had been already established in the area for at least a century.

From the history of Scotland we can assume that the Collie, as we know the breed today, is a blending of native sheep herding dogs with guard and hunting dogs brought to Scotland by invading Roman Legions. Mute testimony to this invasion is the wall built by the Romans in the Tay locale (Loch Tay) about 500 B.C. The stones of this wall are still to be seen by inquiring tourists. The new breed of dog established by this blending, probably bred true after several generations. Thereafter selection was made, presumably through working ability, and a "master image" began to emerge which became the standard for selection and these end animals became the foundation stock upon which was built the sheepherding dogs of Scotland, the noble and lovely breed known today as the Collie.

Certainly it is true that the lovely Collie is the epitome of the sheepherding dog, the canine who guards and moves the flocks and keeps them from harm, the close companion of the lonely sheepherder.

The origin of the breed name is also lost in the mists of time and open to speculation due to the many and varied words from which the numerous authorities claim the name Collie was derived. It is the author's opinion that the word *collis*, frequently used to identify the sheepherding dogs of the region in the 1800's, is the basic word from which the breed name was derived. The word, when translated, means high ground, or the Scottish Highlands. The Northern hills were the browsing grounds of the Scottish sheep while the lowlands were the coal mining and industrial areas. We know that a sheepherding dog, and undoubtedly a Collie, herded the sheep there in the Highlands, so it would seem that the breed name, signifying a dog of the Highlands, would be the most accurate interpretation of the origin of "Collie."

Early Collies were smaller than the dog we know today. They measured approximately 14 inches at the shoulder. The Thomas Bewick woodcut mentioned earlier, shows the Smooth Collie with a short tail which was probably docked, but both Smooth and Rough are of the same size, the only basic difference being in the coat.

The Smooth Collie was a drover's dog whose job it was to drive cattle and sheep to market. The earlier animals were supposedly larger, fiercer and stronger than the rough-coated sheepherding dogs in the beginning of the

The Sable, Champion Belhaven's Golden Sceptreson.

breed's acceptance. The Smooth variety, most authorities agree, was developed in the North of England, particularly in Northumberland. On the bench, the Smooth is judged by the same standard as the better known Rough Collie with the exception, of course, of the coat.

The Rough Collie is the popular sheepherding dog, and he performs superlatively the job for which sheepherding dogs have been bred ever since man cast aside his spear for the shepherd's staff. There is also the Bearded or Highland Collie who wears a harsh and shaggy coat. This latter variety is recognized in England but not in America.

The Collie, as seen today, is the product of selective breeding through many generations. He is a magnificent animal in the beauty of his heavy coat. As a house dog he is clean and dependable and marvelous with children whom he cares for and watches over as his ancestors did the sheep in their flocks.

STANDARD OF THE COLLIE

ROUGH

General Character—The Collie is a lithe, strong, responsive, active dog, carrying no useless timber, standing naturally straight and firm. The deep, moderately wide chest shows strength, the sloping shoulders and well-bent hocks indicate speed and grace, and the face shows high intelligence. The Collie presents an impressive, proud picture of true balance, each part being in harmonious proportion to every other part and to the whole. Except for the technical description that is essential to this Standard and without which no Standard for the guidance of breeders and judges is adequate. it could be stated simply that no part of the Collie ever seems to be out of proportion to any other part. Timidity, frailness, sullenness, viciousness, lack of animation, cumbersome appearance and lack of over-all balance impair the general character.

Head—The head properties are of great importance. When considered in proportion to the size of the dog the head is inclined to lightness and never appears massive. A heavy-headed dog lacks the necessary bright, alert, full-of-sense look that contributes so greatly to expression. Both in front and profile view the head bears a general resemblance to a well-blunted lean wedge, being smooth and clean in outline and nicely balanced in proportion. On the sides it tapers gradually and smoothly from the ears to the end of the black nose, without being flared out in backskull ("cheeky") or pinched in muzzle ("snipy"). In profile view the top of the backskull and the top of the muzzle lie in two approximately parallel, straight planes of equal length, divided by a very slight but perceptible stop or break. A mid-point between the inside corners of the eyes (which is the center of a correctly placed stop) is the center of balance in length of head.

The end of the smooth, well-rounded muzzle is blunt but not square. The underjaw is strong, clean-cut and the depth of skull from the brow to the under part of the jaw is not excessive. The teeth are of good size, meeting in a scissors bite. Overshot or undershot jaws are undesirable, the latter being more severely penalized. There is a very slight prominence of the eyebrows. The backskull is flat, without receding either laterally or backward and the occipital bone is not highly peaked. The proper width of backskull necessarily depends upon the combined length of skull and muzzle and the width of the backskull is less than its length. Thus the correct width varies with the individual and is dependent upon the extent to which it is supported by length of muzzle. Because of the importance of the head characteristics, prominent head faults are very severely penalized.

Eyes—Because of the combination of the flat skull, the arched eyebrows, the slight stop and the rounded muzzle, the foreface must be chiseled to form a receptacle for the eyes and they are necessarily placed obliquely to give them the required forward outlook. Except for the blue merles, they are required to be matched in color. They are almond-shaped, of medium size and never properly appear to be large or prominent. The color is dark and the eye does not show a yellow ring or a sufficiently prominent haw to affect the dog's expression. The eyes have a clear, bright appearance, expressing intelligent inquisitiveness, particularly when the ears are drawn up and the dog is on the alert. In blue merles, dark brown eyes are preferable, but either or both eyes may be merle or china in color without specific penalty. A large, round, full eye seriously detracts from the desired "sweet" expression. Eye faults are heavily penalized.

Ears—The ears are in proportion to the size of the head and, if they are carried properly and unquestionably "break" naturally, are seldom too small. Large ears usually cannot be lifted correctly off the head, and even if lifted, they will be out of proportion to the size of the head. When in repose the ears are folded lengthwise and thrown back into the frill. On the alert they are drawn well up on the backskull and are carried about three-quarters erect, with about one-fourth of the ear tipping or "breaking" forward. A dog with prick ears or low ears cannot show true expression and is penalized accordingly.

Neck—The neck is firm, clean, muscular, sinewy and heavily frilled. It is fairly long, carried upright with a slight arch at the nape and imparts a proud, upstanding appearance showing off the frill.

Body—The body is firm, hard and muscular, a trifle long in proportion to the height. The ribs are well-rounded behind the well-sloped shoulders and the chest is deep, extending to the elbows. The back is strong and level, supported by powerful hips and thighs and the croup is sloped to give a well-rounded finish. The loin is powerful and slightly arched. Noticeably fat dogs, or dogs in poor flesh, or with skin disease, or with no undercoat are out of condition and are moderately penalized accordingly.

Legs—The forelegs are straight and muscular, with a fair amount of bone considering the size of the dog. A cumbersome appearance is undesirable. both narrow and wide placement are penalized. The forearm is moderately fleshy and the pasterns are flexible but without weakness. The hind legs are less fleshy, muscular at the thighs, very sinewy and the hocks and stifles are well bent. A cowhocked dog or a dog with straight stifles is penalized. The comparatively small feet are approximately oval in shape. The soles are well padded and tough, and the toes are well arched and close together. When the Collie is not in motion the legs and feet are judged by allowing the dog to come to a natural stop in a standing position so that both the forelegs and the hind legs are placed well apart, with the feet extending straight forward. Excessive "posing" is undesirable.

Gait—The gait or movement is distinctly characteristic of the breed. A sound Collie is not out at the elbows but it does, nevertheless, move toward an observer with its front feet tracking comparatively close together at the ground. The front legs do not "cross over", nor does the Collie move with a pacing or

The dainty durability of the female of this beloved old working breed is beautifully illustrated in this picture of Champion Lovely Lady of Glenmist.

rolling gait. Viewed from the front, one gains the impression that the dog is capable of changing its direction of travel almost instantaneously, as indeed it is. When viewed from the rear, the hind legs, from the hock joint to the ground, move in comparatively close-together, parallel, vertical planes. The hind legs are powerful and propelling. Viewed from the side, the gait is smooth not choppy. The reasonably long, "reaching" stride is even, easy, light and seemingly effortless.

Tail—The tail is moderately long, the bone reaching to the hock joint or below. It is carried low when the dog is quiet, the end having an upward twist or "swirl". When gaited or when the dog is excited it is carried gaily but not over the back.

Coat—The well-fitting, proper-textured coat is the crowning glory of the rough variety of Collie. It is abundant except on the head and legs. The outer coat is straight and harsh to the touch. A soft, open outer coat or a curly outer coat, regardless of quantity, is penalized. The undercoat, however, is soft, furry and so close together that it is difficult to see the skin when the hair is parted. The coat is very abundant on the mane and frill. The face or mask is smooth. The forelegs are smooth and well feathered to the back of the pasterns. The hind legs are smooth below the hock joints. Any feathering below the hocks is removed for the show ring. The hair on the tail is very profuse and on the hips it is long and bushy. The texture, quantity and the extent to which the coat "fits" the dog are important points.

Canadian and American Champion Windswept Domino Jac, a tri-color.

Color—The four recognized colors are sable and white, tri-color, blue merle and white. There is no preference among them. The sable and white is predominantly sable (a fawn sable color of varying shades from light gold to dark mahogany) with white markings usually on the chest, neck, legs, feet and the tip of the tail. A blaze may appear on the foreface or backskull or both. The tri-color is predominantly black, carrying white markings as in a sable and white and has tan shadings on and about the head and legs. The blue merle is a mottled or "marbled" color, predominantly blue-gray and black with white markings as in the sable and white and usually has tan shadings as in the tri-color. The white is predominantly white, preferably with sable or tri-color markings. Blue merle coloring is undesirable in whites.

Size—Dogs are from 24 to 26 inches at the shoulder and weigh from 60 to 75 pounds. Bitches are from 22 to 24 inches at the shoulder, weighing from 50 to 65 pounds. An undersize or an oversize Collie is penalized according to the extent to which the dog appears to be undersize or oversize.

Expression—Expression is one of the most important points in considering the relative value of Collies. Expression, like the term "character" is difficult to define in words. It is not a fixed point as in color, weight or height and it is something the uninitiated can properly understand only by optical illustration. In general, however, it may be said to be the combined product of the shape and balance of the skull and muzzle, the placement, size, shape and color of the eye and the position, size and carriage of the ears. An expression that shows sullenness or which is suggestive of any other breed is entirely foreign. The Collie cannot be judged properly until its expression has been carefully evaluated.

SMOOTH

The Smooth Variety of Collie is judged by the same Standard as the Rough Variety, except that the references to the quantity and the distribution of the coat are not applicable to the Smooth Variety, which has a hard, dense, smooth coat.

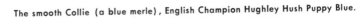

The smooth Collie (a blue merle), English Champion Hughley Hush Puppy Blue.

Champion Dortmund Delly's Colonel Jet

THE DOBERMAN PINSCHER

Early references to this breed classify it as a large terrier, a derivation of the Manchester Terrier, and describe it as being, in type, a large, strong bull terrier. The breed was developed in Thuringen, Germany, toward the close of the 19th century by Louis Dobermann, a dog catcher of Apolda. Using many of the German breeds that came into his hands Herr Dobermann set himself an ideal, bred toward it and eventually reached his goal by producing the Doberman Pinscher (earlier the breed name was spelled with the double "*n*", the same as the name of its originator).

This is a superb animal physically with the clean-limbed and breedy look one associates with thoroughbred horses. Alert, agile, sinewy and quick, the breed possesses much of the temperamental fire of the terrier and many strains are subject to excitability. But, as a check to their impetuosity, is the breed's noted, keen intelligence.

The Doberman exhibits the influence in its breed background of the Rottweiler, Black and Tan Terrier, smooth-haired German Pinscher with a touch of Great Dane, German Shepherd, and Schnauzer.

The Dobe can be considered generally in the category of the "one-man" dog. He is devoted to the hearth and home and is a family guardian par excellence. As a guard, police, and war dog the Doberman has no peer. The early ferocity of the Dobe has been subdued and channeled by correct breeding. Founded in 1921, the Doberman Pinscher Club of America has done a marvelous job of publicizing the breed. His sleek beauty makes the Dobe a dog show favorite. This is proven by the number of top wins the breed has scored at many of the most important shows in the United States.

Many people are not aware of the fact that the Dobe can also be found in a fawn color. The blue color recognized in the standard is the result of dilution factors.

STANDARD OF THE DOBERMAN PINSCHER

General Conformation and Appearance—The appearance is that of a dog of good middle size, with a body that is square, the height, measured vertically from the ground to the highest point of the withers, equalling the length, measured horizontally, from the forechest to the rear projection of the upper thigh. Height, at the withers: Males, 26 to 28 inches, ideal being about 27 inches; bitches, 24 to 26 inches, ideal being about 25½ inches. Compactly built, muscular and powerful, for great endurance and speed. Elegant in appearance, of proud carriage, reflecting great nobility and temperament. Energetic, watchful, determined, alert, fearless, loyal, and obedient.

Faults—Coarseness. Fine greyhound build. Undersized or oversized.

Disqualifying faults—Shyness, viciousness.

Shyness—A dog shall be judged fundamentally shy if, refusing to stand for examination, it shrinks away from the judge; if it fears an approach from the rear; if it shies at sudden and unusual noises, to a marked degree.

Viciousness—A dog that attacks, or attempts to attack either the judge or its handler, is definitely vicious. An aggressive or belligerent attitude towards other dogs shall not be deemed viciousness.

Head—Shape—Long and dry, resembling a blunt wedge, both frontal and profile views. When seen from the front, the head widens gradually towards

The well known Red Dobe, Champion Dictator von Glenhugel.

Tri-International Champion Borong The Warlock

the base of the ears in a practically unbroken line. Top of skull flat, turning with slight stop to bridge of muzzle, with muzzle line extending parallel to the top line of the skull. Cheeks flat and muscular. Lips lying close to jaws, and not drooping. Jaws full and powerful, well filled under the eyes. Nose, solid black in black dogs, dark brown in brown ones, and dark gray in blue ones.

Faults—Head out of balance in proportion to body. Ram's, dishfaced, cheeky, or snipy heads.

Eyes—Almond shaped, *not* round, moderately deep set, *not* prominent, with vigorous, energetic expression. Iris of uniform color, ranging from medium to darkest brown in black dogs, the darker shade being the more desirable. In reds or blues, the color of the iris should blend with that of the markings, but not be of a lighter hue than that of the markings.

Faults—Slit eyes. Glassy eyes.

Teeth—Strongly developed and white. Lower incisors upright, and touching inside of upper incisors—a true scissors bite. 42 teeth—(22 in lower jaw, 20 in upper jaw). Distemper teeth should not be penalized.

Disqualifying Faults—Overshot more than $\frac{3}{16}$ of an inch. Undershot more than $\frac{1}{8}$ of an inch.

Ears—Well trimmed, and carried erect. (In all states where ear trimming is prohibited, or where dogs with cropped ears cannot be shown, the foregoing requirements are waived.) The upper attachment of the ear, when held erect, should be on a level with the top of the skull.

Neck—Carried upright, well muscled and dry. Well arched, and with nape of neck widening gradually toward body. Length of neck proportioned to body and head.

Body—Back short, firm, of sufficient width, and muscular at the loin extending in a straight line from withers to the slightly rounded croup. Withers pronounced, and forming the highest point of body. Brisket full and broad,

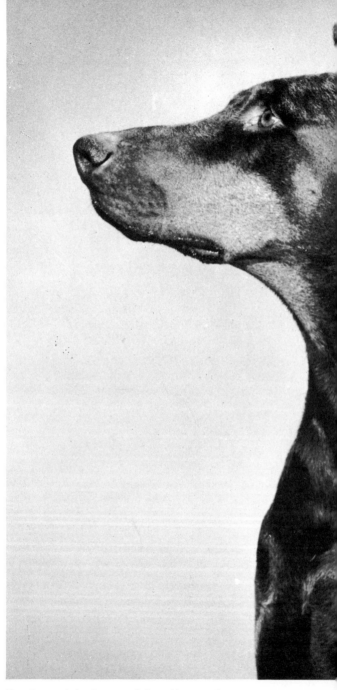

The characteristic alertness of these big, smooth looking, working dogs has been caught by the lens of the photographer.

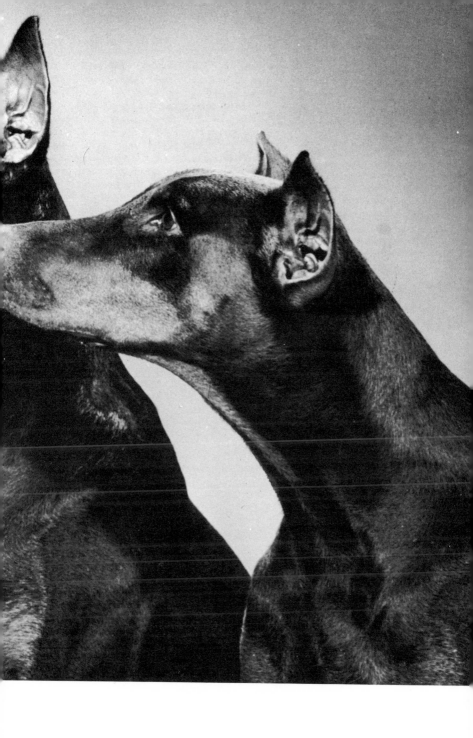

reaching deep to the elbow. Chest broad, and forechest well defined. Spring of ribs pronounced. Belly well tucked up, extending in a curved line from chest. Loins wide and muscled. Hips broad in proportion to body, breadth of hips being approximately breadth of body at rib spring. Tail, docked at approximately second joint, should appear to be the continuation of the spine, without material drop.

Forequarters—Shoulder blade and upper arm should meet at an angle of ninety degrees. Relative length of shoulder and upper arm should be as one to one, excess length of upper arm being much less undesirable than excess length of shoulder blade. Legs, seen from the front and side, perfectly straight and parallel to each other from elbow to pastern; muscled and sinewy, with round, heavy bone. In a normal position, and when gaiting, the elbow should lie close to the brisket. Pasterns firm, with an almost perpendicular position to the ground. Feet well arched, compact, and cat-like, turning neither in nor out.

Hindquarters—In balance with forequarters. Upper shanks long, wide and well muscled on both sides of thigh, with clearly defined stifle. Hocks while the dog is at rest, hock to heel should be perpendicular to the ground. Upper shanks, lower shanks, and hocks parallel to each other, and wide enough apart to fit in with a properly built body. The hip bone should fall away from the spinal column at an angle of about thirty degrees. The upper shank should be at right angles to the hip bone. Croup well filled out. Cat-feet, as on front legs, turning neither in nor out.

Gait—The gait should be free, balanced, and vigorous, with good reach in the forequarters, and good driving power in the hindquarters. When trotting, there should be a strong rear action drive, with rotary motion of hindquarters. Each rear leg should move in line with the foreleg on the same side. Rear and front legs should be thrown neither in nor out. Back should remain strong, firm and level.

Champion
Berman Brier

Coat, Color, Markings—Coat, smooth-haired, short, hard, thick, and close-lying. Invisible gray undercoat on neck permissible. Allowed colors, black, brown, or blue. Markings, rust red, sharply defined, and appearing above each eye, and on muzzle, throat, and forechest, and on all legs and feet, and below tail. White on chest, not exceeding one-half square inch, permissible.

The foregoing description is that of the ideal Doberman Pinscher. Any deviation from the above-described dog must be penalized in proportion to the extent of the deviation, and in accordance with the appended scale of points

SCALE OF POINTS

	Points	
General Conformation and Appearance		
Proportions	8	
Bone, Substance	8	
Temperament, Expression, Nobility ...	8	
Condition	5	
	—	29
Head		
Shape	6	
Teeth	5	
Eyes	3	
Ears	1	
	—	15
Neck	3	
	—	3
Body		
Backline, Withers, Loins, Tail Placement	8	
Chest, Brisket, Rib Spring, Tuck-up	8	
Shape and proportions	4	
	—	20
Forequarters		
Shoulders, Upper arms, Legs, Pasterns	5	
Angulation	4	
Paws	2	
	—	11
Hindquarters		
Upper thigh, Stifle, Hocks	5	
Angulation	4	
Paws	2	
	—	11
Gait	6	
	—	6
Coat, Color, Markings	5	5
	—	—
Total	100	100

DISQUALIFICATIONS

Shyness, viciousness. Overshot more than $\frac{3}{16}$ of an inch; undershot more than $\frac{1}{8}$ of an inch.

371

World Sieger Volker vom Zollgrenzschutz-Haus, Sch. III.

THE GERMAN SHEPHERD DOG

Of all the breeds of dogs known to man there is no breed better fitted for its various but specific utilitarian purposes than the German Shepherd Dog. The breed was formed by a thoughtful blending of at least three types of sheepherding dogs used in diverse sections of Germany during that country's pastoral era. From this mixture of genetic factors there gradually emerged a breed image, based upon a type that could best do the necessary job of herding, that varied only slightly from what could be designated as the canine norm; a feral type, in appearance closely linked to earlier wolf-like dog forms.

Toward the end of the 19th century, Rittmeister Max Emil Friedrich von Stephanitz saw and greatly admired a specimen of the breed and subsequently made it his own. He formed the *Verein fur Deutsche Schaferhunde*, the German breed club, and further refined the breed type toward a working dog ideal. When civilization encroached upon the pasture lands and the native Shepherd dog was threatened with near extinction, von Stephanitz selected within the breed for highly developed protective instinct and subsequently inveigled the politicians and industrialists to accept the German Shepherd Dog for police, war, and protection work.

Since that time the popularity of the breed has fluctuated greatly, due to inordinate exposure on the silver screen and later the TV screen. This led to a period of indiscriminate breeding by uncaring opportunists to fill a widespread demand for puppies. But over the years, in the hands of earnest and capable breeders (particularly in Germany), the German Shepherd has achieved uniformity and a basic breed solidity.

Oddly enough, despite the definite advantages of better feeding, more and advanced medical care, and the financial resources to purchase the finest specimens, Americans cannot produce quality animals in the same number or the same consistency as can Germany, the home of the breed. Undoubtedly, the reason for this lies in the complete control the German breed club exercises over its members, coupled with the insistence, in Germany, on adaptability to training and strict selection for animals that are of sound working type. Indeed, in Germany a Shepherd Dog cannot be shown in adult classes unless it has attained at least one training degree. They also hold important tests and competition for police, guard and herding dogs.

Temperament is of prime importance in the German Shepherd Dog and the correct temperament encompasses incorruptible character, complete trainability, a high degree of intelligence, and an extraordinary willingness to learn and obey.

The German Shepherd is a handsome animal at best, noble, yet of a basic feral type in appearance, intellectually the peer of any breed, and with a love for his master and family that is unsurpassed. The breed is noted for its loyalty and makes the very best of companions. Intelligence, trainability, size and gait make them the ideal dogs for leaders of the blind. As police dogs, commercial guards and general watch dogs they have no equal. Incidently, the author feels that the German Shepherd is perhaps the most widely admired pure bred dog in the world. I have seen them in every country and, in many instances, being used as sheepherding dogs as well as companions, guards and house dogs.

Born to a natural beauty the German Shepherd Dog needs no cropping or docking and is exhibited in the show ring sans artificial trimming or beautification. The gait of the German Shepherd is a floating, ground-covering trot that is the essence of balance, power and beauty in motion.

This, the German Shepherd Dog, is truly a working breed, standing throughout the ages at the side of man, herding, protecting and, above all, worshipping his master.

STANDARD OF THE GERMAN SHEPHERD DOG

General Appearance—The first impression of a good German Shepherd Dog is that of a strong, agile, well-muscled animal, alert and full of life. It should both be and appear to be well balanced, with harmonious development of the forequarter and hindquarter. The dog should appear to the eye, and actually be, longer than the tall, deep-bodied, and presenting an outline of smooth curves rather than corners. It should look substantial and not spindly, giving the impression, both at rest and in motion, of muscular fitness and nimbleness without any look of clumsiness or soft living.

The ideal height for dogs is 25 inches, and for bitches, 23 inches at the shoulder. This height is established by taking a perpendicular line from the top of the shoulder blade to the ground with the coat parted or so pushed down that this measurement will show only the actual height of the frame or structure of the dog. The working value of dogs above or below the indicated heights is proportionately lessened, although variations of an inch above or below the ideal heights are acceptable, while greater variations must be considered as faults. Weights of dogs of desirable size in proper flesh and condition average between 75 and 85 pounds, and of bitches, between 60 and 80 pounds.

The Shepherd should be stamped with a look of quality and nobility—difficult to define but unmistakable when present. The good Shepherd Dog never looks common.

The breed has a distinct personality marked by a direct and fearless, but not hostile, expression, self-confidence and a certain aloofness which does not lend itself to immediate and indiscriminate friendships.

Secondary sex characteristics should be strongly marked, and every animal should give a definite impression of masculinity or femininity, according to its sex. Dogs should be definitely masculine in appearance and deportment; bitches unmistakably feminine without weakness of structure or apparent softness of temperament.

Male dogs having one or both testicles undescended (monorchids or cryptorchids) are to be disqualified.

The condition of the dog should be that of an athlete in good condition, the muscles and flesh firm and the coat lustrous.

The Shepherd is normally a dog with a double coat, the amount of undercoat varying with the season of the year and the proportion of the time the dog spends out-of-doors. It should, however, always be present to a sufficient degree to keep out water, to insulate against temperature extremes and as a protection against insects. The outercoat should be as dense as possible, hair straight, harsh and lying close to the body. A slightly wavy outercoat, often of wiry texture, is equally permissible. The head, including the inner ear, foreface and legs and paws are covered with short hair, and the neck with longer and thicker hair. The rear of fore and hind legs has somewhat longer hair extending to the pastern and hock respectively. Faults in coat include complete lack of any undercoat, soft, silky or too long outercoat and curly or open coat.

Structure—A German Shepherd is a trotting dog and his structure has been developed to best meet the requirements of his work in herding. That is to say a long, effortless trot which shall cover the maximum amount of ground with the minimum number of steps, consistent with the size of the animal. The proper body proportion, firmness of back and muscles and the proper angulation of the fore and hindquarters serve this end. They enable the dog to propel itself forward by a long step of the hindquarter and to compensate for this stride by a long step of the forequarter. The high withers, the firm back, the strong loin, the properly formed croup, even the tail as balance and rudder, all contribute to this same end.

Proportion—The German Shepherd Dog is properly longer than tall with the most desirable proportion as 10 is to 8½. We have seen how the height is ascertained; the length is established by a dog standing naturally and four-square, measured on a horizontal line from the points of the prosternum, or breast bone, to the rear edge of the pelvis, the ischium tuberosity, commonly called the sitting bone.

Angulation (a) Forequarter—The shoulder blade should be long, laid on

Condor vom Sixtberg, Sch. II, A.D.

flat against the body, with its rounded upper end in a vertical line above the elbow, and sloping well forward to the point where it joins the upper arm. The wither should be high with shoulder blades meeting closely at the top, and the upper arm set on at an angle approaching as nearly as possible a right angle. Such an angulation permits the maximum forward extension of the foreleg without binding or effort. Shoulder faults include too steep or straight a position of either blade or upper arm, too short a blade or upper arm, lack of sufficient angle between these two members, looseness through lack of firm ligamentation, and loaded shoulders with prominent pads of flesh or muscles on the outer side. Construction in which the whole shoulder assembly is pushed too far forward also restricts the stride and is faulty.

(b) *Hindquarter*—The angulation of the hindquarter also consists ideally of a series of sharp angles as far as the relation of the bones to each other is concerned, and the thighbones should parallel the shoulder blade while the stiflebone parallels the upper arm. The whole assembly of the thigh, viewed from the side, should be broad, with both thigh and stifle well muscled and of proportionate length, forming as nearly as possible a right angle. The metacarpus (the unit between the hock joint and the foot commonly and erroneously called the hock) is strong, clean and short, the hock joint clean-cut and sharply defined.

Head—Clean-cut and strong, the head of the Shepherd is characterized by nobility. It should seem in proportion to the body and should not be clumsy, although a degree of coarseness of head, especially in dogs, is less of a fault than overrefinement. A round or domey skull is a fault. The muzzle is long and strong with the lips firmly fitted, and its top line is usually parallel with an imaginary elongation of the line of the forehead. Seen from the front, the forehead is only moderately arched and the skull slopes into the long wedge-shaped muzzle without abrupt stop. Jaws are strongly developed. Weak and too narrow underjaws, snipey muzzles and no stop are faults.

(a) *Ears*—The ears should be moderately pointed, open toward the front, and are carried erect when at attention, the ideal carriage being one in which the center lines of the ears, viewed from the front, are parallel to each other and perpendicular to the ground. Puppies usually do not permanently raise their ears until the fourth or sixth month, and sometimes not until later. Cropped and hanging ears are to be discarded. The well-placed and well-carried ear of a size in proportion to the skull materially adds to the general appearance of the Shepherd. Neither too large nor too small ears are desirable. Too much stress, however, should not be laid on perfection of carriage if the ears are fully erect.

(b) *Eyes*—Of medium size, almond shaped, set a little obliquely and not protruding. The color as dark as possible. Eyes of lighter color are sometimes

American Grand Victor

Ch. Jory of Edgetowne

found and are not a serious fault if they harmonize with the general coloration, but a dark brown eye is always to be preferred. The expression should be keen, intelligent and composed.

(c) *Teeth*—The strong teeth, 42 in number—20 upper and 22 lower—are strongly developed and meet in a scissor grip in which part of the inner surface of the upper teeth meets and engages part of the outer surface of the lower teeth. This type of bite gives a more powerful grip than one in which the edges of the teeth meet directly, and is subjected to less wear. The dog is over-shot when the lower teeth fail to engage the inner surfaces of the upper teeth. This is a serious fault. The reverse condition—an undershot jaw—is a very serious fault. While missing premolars are frequently observed, complete dentition is decidedly to be preferred. So-called distemper teeth and dis-colored teeth are faults whose seriousness varies with the degree of departure from the desired white, sound coloring. Teeth broken by accident should not be severely penalized but worn teeth, especially the incisors, are often indica-

English Champion Fenton of Kentwood

Witz v. Haus Schutting, Sch. III

tive of the lack of a proper scissor bite, although some allowance should be made for age.

Neck—The neck is strong and muscular, clean-cut and relatively long, proportionate in size to the head and without loose folds of skin. When the dog is at attention or excited, the head is raised and the neck carried high, otherwise typical carriage of the head is forward rather than up and but little higher than the top of the shoulder, particularly in motion.

Top Line—(*a*) *Withers*—The withers should be higher than and sloping into the level back to enable a proper attachment of the shoulder blades.

(*b*) *Back*—The back should be straight and very strongly developed without sag or roach, the section from the wither to the croup being relatively short. (The desirable long proportion of the Shepherd Dog is not derived from a long back but from over-all length with relation to height, which is achieved by breadth of forequarter and hindquarter viewed from the side.)

(*c*) *Loin*—Viewed from the top, broad and strong, blending smoothly into the back without undue length between the last rib and the thigh, when viewed from the side.

(*d*) *Croup*—Should be long and gradually sloping. Too level or flat a croup prevents proper functioning of the hindquarter, which must be able to reach well under the body. A steep croup also limits the action of the hindquarter.

(*e*) *Tail*—Bushy, with the last vertebra extended at least to the hock joint, and usually below. Set smoothly into the croup and low rather than high. At rest the tail hangs in a slight curve like a sabre. A slight hook—sometimes carried to one side—is faulty only to the extent that it mars, generally, appearance. When the dog is excited or in motion, the curve is accentuated and the tail raised, but it should never be lifted beyond a line at right angles with the line of the back. Docked tails, or those which have been operated upon to prevent curling, disqualify. Tails too short, or with clumpy ends to the ankylosis or growing together of the vertebrae, are serious faults.

Body—The whole structure of the body gives an impression of depth and solidity without bulkiness.

(*a*) *Forechest*—Commencing at this prosternum, should be well-filled and carried well down between the legs with no sense of hollowness.

(*b*) *Chest*—Deep and capacious with ample room for lungs and heart. Well carried forward, with the prosternum, or process of the breast bone, showing ahead of the shoulder when the dog is viewed from the side.

(*c*) *Ribs*—Should be well-sprung and long, neither barrel shaped nor too flat, and carried down to a breast bone which reaches to the elbow. Correct ribbing allows the elbow to move back freely when the dog is at a trot, while too round a rib causes interference and throws the elbow out. Ribbing should be carried well back so that loin and flank are relatively short.

(*d*) *Abdomen*—Firmly held and not paunchy. The bottom line of the Shepherd is only moderately tucked up in a flank, never like that of a Greyhound.

Legs—(*a*) The bone of the legs should be straight, oval rather than round or flat and free from sponginess. Its development should be in proportion to the size of the dog and contribute to the over-all impression of substance without grossness. Crooked leg bones and any malformation such as, for example, that caused by rickets, should be penalized.

(*b*) *Pastern*—Should be of medium length, strong and springy. Much more spring of pastern is desirable in the Shepherd Dog than in many other breeds

The sagacious companion and servant of man, the breed that exemplifies the utilitarian abilities inherent in the working breeds, this is the German Shepherd. The dog is the fine import, now deceased, Ch. Atlas v. Elfenhain.

as it contributes to the ease and elasticity of the trotting gait. The upright terrier pastern is definitely undesirable.

(c) *Metacarpus*—The so-called "hock"—short, clean, sharply defined and of great strength. This is the fulcrum upon which much of the forward movement of the dog depends. Cowhocks are a decided fault but before penalizing for cowhocks, it should be definitely determined, with the animal in motion, that the dog has this fault, since many dogs with exceptionally good hindquarter angulation occasionally stand so as to give the appearance of cowhockedness which is not actually present.

(d) *Feet*—Rather short, compact with toes well-arched, pads thick and hard, nail short and strong. The feet are important to the working qualities of the dog. The ideal foot is extremely strong with good gripping power and plenty of depth of pad. The so-called cat-foot, or terrier foot, is not desirable. The thin, spread or hare-foot is, however still more undesirable.

Pigment—The German Shepherd Dog differs widely in color and all colors are permissible. Generally speaking, strong rich colors are to be preferred, with definite pigmentation and without the appearance of a washed-out color. White dogs are not desirable, and are to be disqualified if showing albino characteristics.

Gait—(a) *General Impression*—The gait of the German Shepherd Dog is outreaching, elastic, seemingly without effort, smooth and rhythmic. At a walk it covers a great deal of ground, with long step of both hind and foreleg. At a trot, the dog covers still more ground and moves powerfully but easily with a beautiful co-ordination of back and limbs so that, in the best examples, the gait appears to be the steady motion of a well-lubricated machine. The feet travel close to the ground, and neither fore nor hind feet should lift high on either forward reach or backward push.

(b) The hindquarter delivers, through the back, a powerful forward thrust which slightly lifts the whole animal and drives the body forward. Reaching far under, and passing the imprint left by the front foot, the strong arched hind foot takes hold of the ground; then hock, stifle and upper thigh come

German Sieger Mutz a.d. Kuckstrasse, Sch. III.

American and Canadian Champion Ulk Wikingerblut, Sch. III, A.D.

into play and sweep back, the stroke of the hind leg finishing with the foot still close to the ground in a smooth follow-through. The over-reach of the hindquarter usually necessitates one hind foot pasisng outside and the other hind foot passing inside the track of the forefeet and such action is not faulty unless the locomotion is crabwise, with the dog's body sideways out of the normal straight line.

(c) In order to achieve ideal movement of this kind, there must be full muscular co-ordination throughout the structure with the action of muscles and ligaments positive, regular and accurate.

(d) *Back Transmission*—The typical smooth, flowing gait of the Shepherd Dog cannot be maintained without great strength and firmness (which does not mean stiffness) of back. The whole effort of the hindquarter is transmitted to the forequarter through the muscular and bony structure of the loin, back and withers. At full trot, the back must remain firm and level without sway, roll, whip or roach.

(e) To compensate for the forward motion imparted by the hindquarter, the shoulder should open to its full extent—the desirability of good shoulder angulation now becomes apparent—and the forelegs should reach out in a stride balancing that of the hindquarter. A steep shoulder will cause the dog either to stumble or to raise the forelegs very high in an effort to co-ordinate with the hindquarter, which is impossible when shoulder structure is faulty. A serious fault results when a dog moves too low in front, presenting an unlevel top-line with the wither lower than the hips.

(f) The Shepherd Dog does not track on widely separated parallel lines as does the terrier but brings the feet inward toward the middle line of the body when at trot in order to maintain balance. For this reason a dog viewed from the front or rear when in motion will often seem to travel close. This is not a fault if the feet do not strike or cross, or if the knees or shoulders are not thrown out, but the feet and hocks should be parallel even if close together.

(g) The excellence of gait must also be evaluated by viewing from the side the effortless, properly co-ordinated covering of ground.

Character—As has been noted before, the Shepherd Dog is not one that fawns upon every new acquaintance. At the same time, it should be approachable, quietly standing its ground and showing confidence and a willingness to meet overtures without itself making them. It should be poised, but when the occasion demands, eager and alert; both fit and willing to serve in any capacity as companion, watchdog, blind leader, herding dog or guardian, whichever the circumstances may demand.

The Shepherd Dog must not be timid, shrinking behind its master or handler; nervous, looking about or upward with anxious expression or showing nervous reactions to strange sounds or sights, nor lackadaisical, sluggish or manifestly disinterested in what goes on about him. Lack of confidence under any surroundings is not typical of good character; cases of extreme timidity and nervous unbalance sometimes give the dog an apparent, but totally unreal, courage, and it becomes a "fear biter," snapping not for any justifiable reason but because it is apprehensive of the approach of a stranger. This is a serious fault subject to heavy penalty.

In summary: It should never beforgotten that the ideal Shepherd is a working animal, which must have an incorruptible character combined with body and gait suitable for the arduous work which constitutes its primary purpose. All its qualities should be weighed in respect to their contribution to such work, and while no compromise should be permitted with regard to its working potentiality, the dog must nevertheless possess a high degree of beauty and nobility.

Evaluation of Faults—Note: Faults are important in the order of their group, as per group headings, irrespective of their position in each group.

Disqualifying Faults—Albino characteristics; cropped ears; hanging ears (as in hound); docked tails.

Very Serious Faults—Major faults of temperament; undershot lower jaw.

Serious Faults—Faults of balance and proportion; poor gait, viewed either from front, rear or side; marked deficiency of substance (bone or body), bitchy male dogs; faulty backs; too level or too short croup; long and weak loin; very bad feet; ring tails; tails much too short; rickety condition; more than four missing premolars or any other missing teeth, unless due to accident; lack of nobility; badly washed out color; badly overshot bite.

Faults—Doggy bitches; poorly carried ears; too fine heads; weak muzzles; improper muscular condition; badly affected teeth.

Minor Faults—Too coarse heads; hooked tails; too light, round or protruding eyes; discolored teeth; condition of coat, due to season or keeping.

Note: Under disqualifying faults—White if indicative of Albino characteristics.

* *Note:* In the author's opinion the long listing of comparative faults is redundant and the wording often vague. Relative proportion and comparison are the only means by which either novice or judge can arrive at a true evaluation of faults or virtues.

Vigilant Anica, C.D.

THE GIANT SCHNAUZER

This is the largest of the three Schnauzers bred in Germany. A hard working breed, very adaptable to a variety of jobs and with an all-weather coat, *the Reisenschnauzer*, or Giant Schnauzer, is the newest of the Schnauzer family. His brother, the Standard Schnauzer, traces his geneology back to dogs seen in Dürer's paintings in 1492, and the statue of the night watchman and his dog in Stuttgart, Wurttemberg, erected in 1620. The type that the Giant comes from is therefore old, tried, and found true.

Bavarian cattlemen journeying to Stuttgart, liked and brought back with them the medium-sized Schnauzer. But they wanted a larger breed for driving cattle to market. Through the use of black Great Danes, some of the local cattle and sheep dogs, and the Bouvier des Flandres, with perhaps a bit of Doberman Pinscher and Rottweiler added, the Giant Schnauzer was produced and then stabilized in type by smart German breeders.

Von Stephanitz, father of the German Shepherd, and a fine canine historian and knowledgeable dog man, places the origin of the Giant Schnauzer in Swabia, southern Bavaria, and it was found in a state of near breed perfection in the region embracing Munich and Augsburg. The author saw several fine specimens of the breed in Munich last year and one in Garmisch-Partenkirchen while viewing a famous German Shepherd kennel in Farchant bei Garmisch.

The breed was, for many years, called the *Munchener* and was widely known as a great cattle and drover's dog. Later, when the breed drew wider attention, it was found that they made excellent police dogs. Giant Schnauzers were introduced into America in the 1920's and admitted to the A.K.C. Stud Book in 1930. They have never been too popular in the United States, though other breeds with much less to offer have surpassed them in registrations and ownership.

STANDARD OF THE GIANT SCHNAUZER

General Impression—The Giant Schnauzer is a robust, sinewy, more heavy

Champion Lasso von Donnerhall

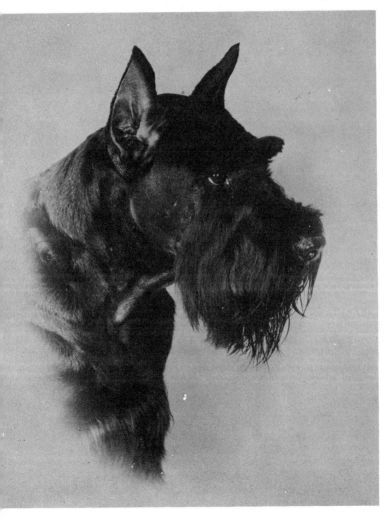

set than slender dog, of somewhat rectangular build. His nature combines high-spirited temperament with extreme reliability.

Head—Strong and elongated, gradually narrowing from the ears to the eyes and thence towards the tip of the nose, in proportion to the size of the body. Its total length (tip of nose to occiput) should compare approximately to one-third the length of the back (withers—first dorsal vertebra—to the beginning of the tail). Upper part of the head (occiput to the base of the forehead) broad between the ears—its width should not be more than two-thirds of the length —with flat, creaseless forehead and well-muscled but not too strongly developed cheeks. Ears, small and V-shaped of moderate thickness, set well on the head and dropping forward closely to the cheek, or cropped, with ears evenly cut, placed high and carried erect in excitement. Eyes medium-sized, dark, oval, turned forward, brows arched and wiry.

The powerful ferreting snout formed by the upper and lower jaw (base of forehead to the tip of nose) should be in proportion to the upper head and should end in a moderately blunt manner, with heavy stubby whiskers. Ridge of the nose straight and running almost parallel to the extension of the forehead. The tip of the nose is black and full. Lips tight and not overlapping, with strongly developed fangs, healthy and pure white.

Neck—Not too short with skin close-fitting at the throat. Nape strong and slightly arched.

Forequarters—Shoulders slanting and flat, but strongly muscled. Forelegs (upper and under arm) seen from all sides are vertical without any curve.

Chest—Moderately broad with visible strong breast bone and reaching at least to the height of the elbow and slowly extending backwards. Back strong and straight with well-developed short thighs. The length of back equal to shoulder height (from withers vertical to floor) built squarely, belly well drawn up towards the back.

Tail—Carried high and cut down to three joints.

Hindquarters—Thighs slanting and flat, but strongly muscled. Hindlegs (upper and lower thighs) at first vertical to the knee, from knee to hock in line with the extension of the upper neckline, from hock vertical to ground.

Paws—Short, round, extremely compact paws, with close arched toes (cat's paws) dark nails and hard soles.

Hair—Close, strong, hard and wiry, on the back seen against the grain—unruly—that is, neither short nor smooth; shorter on ears, forehead, legs and paws.

Height—From 21½ to 25½ inches shoulder height.

Color—All pepper and salt colored or similar equal mixtures, pure black or black with tan.

Faults—Too plump, or too light, low or high-legged build, too heavy around head, creased forehead, sticking-out or badly carried ears, light eye (with yellow or light-grey rings) strongly protruding cheek bones, flabby throat skin; undershot or overshot jaw. Teeth too pointed, too small or too long, sunken or roached back, chest with barrel ribs (tubby) slanting crupper, elbows turned out, heels turned in, hind part overbuilt, too steep, spread open toes, long and flat (hare) paws, too short, sleek, too long, soft, silky, curled, rolled, shaggy hair, all white, spotty, tigered, red and reddish colors.

Small white breast spot, or marking on the breast is not a fault.

Champion Heidere Devil-D of Marydane

THE GREAT DANE

One of the most elegant and distinguished of the giant breeds, the Great Dane's origin is ancient. He is one of the truly old breeds whose genetic basis is in the roots that gave us the Mastiff (Tibetan and then English), some of the large, old hound breeds, and the early Greyhound-type dogs. The Dane was first used in Germany as a boarhound and was, in fact, called a German Boarhound.

Conflict exists as to the true origin of the breed, whether German, Danish, or English. We know that Edwards, writing in 1800, describes the "Great Danish dog . . . is 31″ high, in form between the Greyhound and the Mastiff, usually cropped." He also alludes to ". . . a beautiful variety called the Harlequin Dane." The English adopted the old French designation, *Grand Danois*, meaning "*Big Danish*," but the French also called the breed, "*German Mastiff*" (*Dogue Allemand*). Why the English chose the Danish name with the implications of Danish ancestry is unknown since the breed is essentially a German one, brought to perfection in Germany as the *Deutsche Dogge* and still so called there. There is proof that Great Danes (under different names) were at home in Germany before gunpowder was discovered, and served as boar hunters and protectors of the large Rhineland estates. The popularity of the breed in Germany was enhanced when it was adopted and given great publicity by German Chancellor Bismarck.

The German Dogge Club was founded in Berlin in 1888 and the first standard for the breed established. The American club sponsoring the breed came into being in Chicago in 1889 and became the fourth breed club to join the A.K.C. In 1884 Great Danes had been shown under that name in England, at the Warwick Show. The Great Dane Club of America succeeded the original club in 1891 and a year later, at the Westminster show in New York, a large entry of Great Danes graced the benches.

An outstanding event in early American Dane history was the first Specialty held in 1910 at Woodside, Long Island. Eighty dogs were judged, with the Best of Breed going to an import, Helios von Wurttemburg.

The Great Dane is a breed close to the author's heart. I owned and showed specimens of this fine breed years ago. Great Danes make marvelous house and guard dogs and their nobility and courage were developed long before our time.

STANDARD OF THE GREAT DANE
STANDARD OF POINTS

		Points
1. General Conformation		30
a. General Appearance	10	
b. Color and Markings	8	
c. Size	5	
d. Condition of Coat	4	
e. Substance	3	
2. Movement		28
a. Gait	10	
b. Rear End (Croup, Legs, Paws)	10	
c. Front End (Shoulders, Legs, Paws)	8	
3. Head		20
a. Head Conformation	12	
b. Teeth	4	
c. Eyes (Nose and Ears)	4	
4. Torso		20
a. Neck	6	
b. Loin and Back	6	
c. Chest	4	
d. Ribs and Brisket	4	
5. Tail		2
Total		100

1. General Conformation—30 points.

a. *General Appearance* (10 points)—The Great Dane combines in its distinguished appearance, dignity, strength and elegance with great size and a powerful, well-formed, smoothly muscled body. He is one of the gaint breeds but is unique in that his general conformation must be so well-balanced that he never appears clumsy and is always a unit—the Apollo of dogs. He must be spirited and courageous—never timid. He is friendly and dependable. This physical and mental combination is the characteristic which gives the Great Dane the majesty possessed by no other breed. It is particularly true of this breed that there is an impression of great masculinity in dogs as compared to an impression of femininity in bitches. The male should appear more massive throughout than the bitch, with larger frame and heavier bone. In the ratio between length and height, the Great Dane should appear as square as possible. In bitches, a somewhat longer body is permissible. *Faults*—Lack of unity; timidity; bitchy dogs; poor musculature; poor bone development; out of condition; rickets; doggy bitches.

  b. *Color and Markings* (8 points)—(a) Color: Brindle Danes. Base color

The Dane at the beginning of this section is a fawn. The dog to the left is a black, and on the facing page are a brindle and a harlequin, all legitimate color phases of the breed.

ranging from light golden yellow to deep golden yellow always brindled with strong black cross stripes. The more intensive the base color and the more intensive the brindling, the more attractive will be the color. Small white marks at the chest and toes are not desirable. *Faults*—Brindle with too dark a base color; silver-blue and grayish-blue base color; dull (faded) brindling; white tail tip.

  (b) Fawn Danes. Golden yellow up to deep golden yellow color with a deep black mask. The golden deep yellow color must always be given the preference. Small white spots at the chest and toes are not desirable. *Faults*—Yellowish-gray, bluish-yellow, grayish-blue, dirty yellow color (drab color), lack of black mask.

  (c) Blue Danes. The color must be a pure steel blue as far as possible without any tinge of yellow, black or mouse gray. *Faults*—Any deviation from a pure steel-blue coloration.

Champion Colonel Ace of Guerin

Champion Umpachene Sir Van v. Edelherz

(d) Black Danes. Glossy black. *Faults*—Yellow black, brown black or blue-black. White markings, such as stripes on the chest, speckled chest and markings on the paws are permitted but not desirable.

(e) Harlequin Danes. Base color: pure white with black torn patches irregularly and well-distributed over the entire body; pure white neck preferred. The black patches should never be large enough to give the appearance of a blanket nor so small as to give a stippled or dappled effect. (Eligible but less desirable are a few small gray spots, also pointings where instead of a pure white base with black spots there is a white base with single black hairs showing through which tend to give a salt and pepper or dirty effect.) *Faults*—White base color with a few large spots; bluish-gray pointed background.

c. *Size* (5 points)—The male should not be less than 30 inches at the shoulders but it is preferable that he be 32 inches or more, providing he is well proportioned to his height. The female should not be less than 28 inches at the shoulders, but it is preferable that she be 30 inches or more, providing she is well proportioned to her height.

d. *Substance* (3 points)—Substance is that sufficiency of bone and muscle which rounds out a balance with the frame. *Faults*—Light-weight whippety Danes; coarse, ungainly proportioned Danes; always there should be balance.

e. *Condition of Coat* (4 points)—The coat should be very short and thick, smooth and glossy. *Faults*—Excessively long hair (stand-off coat); dull hair (indicating malnutrition, worms and negligent care).

2. Movement—28 points.

a. *Gait* (10 points)—Long, easy, springy stride with no tossing or rolling of body. The back line should move smoothly, parallel to the ground. The gait of the Great Dane should denote strength and power. The rear legs should have drive. The forelegs should track smoothly and straight. The Dane should track in two parallel straight lines. *Faults*—Short steps. The rear quarters should not pitch. The forelegs should not have a hackney gait (forced or choppy stride). When moving rapidly the Great Dane should not pace for the reason that it causes excessive side-to-side rolling of the body and thus reduces endurance.

b. *Rear End (Croup, Legs, Paws)* (10 points)—The croup must be full, slightly drooping and must continue imperceptibly to the tail root. Hind legs, the first thighs (from hip joint to knee) are broad and muscular. The second thighs (from knee to hock joint) are strong and long. Seen from the side, the angulation of the first thigh with the body, of the second thigh with the first thigh, and the pastern root with the second thigh should be very moderate, neither too straight nor too exaggerated. Seen from the rear, the hock joints appear to be perfectly straight, turned neither towards the inside nor towards the outside. *Faults*—A croup which is too straight; a croup which slopes downward too steeply; and too narrow a croup. Hind legs: Soft, flabby, poorly muscled thighs; cowhocks which are the result of the hock joint turning inward and the hock and rear paws turning outward; barrel legs, the result of the hock joints being too far apart; steep rear. As seen from the side, a steep rear is the result of the angles of the rear legs forming almost a straight line; over-angulation is the result of exaggerated angles between the first and second thighs and the hocks and is very conducive to weakness. The rear legs should never be too long in proportion to the front legs.

Paws, round and turned neither towards the inside nor towards the outside. Toes short, highly arched and well closed. Nails short, strong and as dark as possible. *Faults*—Spreading toes (splay foot); bent, long toes (rabbit paws); toes turned towards the outside or towards the inside. Furthermore, the fifth toe on the hind legs appearing at a higher position and with wolf's claw or spur; excessively long nails; light colored nails.

    c. *Front End* (*Shoulders, Legs, Paws*) (8 points)—*Shoulders*—The shoulder blades must be strong and sloping and seen from the side, must form as nearly as possible a right angle in its articulation with the humerus (upper arm) to give a long stride. A line from the upper tip of the shoulder to the back of the elbow joint should be as nearly perpendicular as possible. Since all dogs lack a clavicle (collar bone) the ligaments and muscles holding the shoulder blade to the rib cage must be well developed, firm and secure to prevent loose shoulders.

    Faults—Steep shoulders, which occur if the shoulder blade does not slope sufficiently; over angulation; loose shoulders which occur if the Dane is flabbily muscled, or if the elbow is turned toward the outside; loaded shoulders.

    Forelegs—The upper arm should be strong and muscular. Seen from the side or front the strong lower arms run absolutely straight to the pastern joints. Seen from the front, the forelegs and the pastern roots should form perpendicular lines to the ground. Seen from the side, the pastern root should slope only very slightly forward. *Faults*—Elbows turned toward the inside or toward the outside, the former position caused mostly by too narrow or too shallow a chest, bringing the front legs too closely together and at the same time turning the entire lower part of the leg outward; the latter position causes the front legs to spread too far apart, with the pastern roots and paws usually

Champion Reggens Madas L of Marydane.

WORKING GROUP

turned inwards. Seen from the side, a considerable bend in the pastern toward the front indicates weakness and is in most cases connected with stretched and spread toes (splay foot); seen from the side a forward bow in the forearm (chair leg); an excessively knotty bulge in the front of the pastern joint.

Paws—Round and turned neither toward the inside nor toward the outside. Toes short, highly arched and well closed. Nails short, strong and as dark as possible. *Faults*—Spreading toes (splay foot), bent, long toes (rabbit paws); toes turned toward the outside or toward the inside; light colored nails.

3. Head—20 points.

a. *Head Conformation* (12 points)—Long, narrow, distinguished, expressive, finely chiseled, especially the part below the eyes (which means that the skull plane under and to the inner point of the eye must slope without any bony protuberance in a pleasing line to the full square jaw), with strongly pronounced stop. The masculinity of the male is very pronounced in the expression and structure of head (this subtle difference should be evident in the dog's head through massive skull and depth of muzzle), the bitch's head may be more delicately formed. Seen from the side, the forehead must be sharply set off from the bridge of the nose. The forehead and the bridge of the nose must be straight and parallel to one another. Seen from the front, the head should appear narrow, the bridge of the nose should be as broad as possible. The cheek muscles must show slightly but under no circumstances should they be too pronounced (cheeky). The muzzle part must have full flews and must be as blunt vertically as possible in front; the angles of the lip must be quite pronounced. The front part of the head, from the tip of the nose up to the center of the stop should be as long as the rear part of the head from the center of the stop to the only slightly developed occiput. The head should be angular from all sides and should have definite flat planes and its dimensions should be absolutely in proportion to the general appearance of the Dane. *Faults*—Any deviation from the parallel planes of skull and foreface; too small a stop; a poorly defined stop or none at all; too narrow a nose bridge; the rear of the head spreading laterally in a wedgelike manner (wedge head); an excessively round upper head (apple head); excessively pronounced cheek musculature; pointed muzzle; loose lips hanging over the lower jaw (fluttering lips) which create an illusion of a full deep muzzle. The head should be rather shorter and distinguished than long and expressionless.

b. *Teeth* (4 points)—Strong, well developed and clean. The incisors of the lower jaw must touch very lightly the bottoms of the inner surface of the upper incisors (scissors bite). If the front teeth of both jaws bite on top of each other, they wear down too rapidly. *Faults*—Even bite; undershot and overshot; incisors out of line; black or brown teeth; missing teeth.

c. *Eyes* (4 points)—Medium size, as dark as possible, with lively intelligent expression; almond-shaped eyelids, well-developed eyebrows. *Faults*—Light colored piercing, amber colored, light blue to a watery blue, red or bleary eyes; eyes of different colors; eyes too far apart; mongolian eyes; eyes with pronounced haws; eyes with excessively drooping lower eyelids. In blue and black Danes, lighter eyes are permitted but are not desirable. In harlequins, the eyes should be dark. Light colored eyes, two eyes of different color and wall-eyes are permitted but not desirable.

c1. *Nose* (no points)—The nose must be large and in the case of brindled and "single-colored" Danes, it must always be black. In harlequins, the nose should be black; a black spotted nose is permitted; a pink colored nose is not desirable.

c2. *Ears* (no points)—Ears should be high, set not too far apart, medium in size, of moderate thickness, drooping forward close to the cheek. Top line of folded ear should be about level with the skull. *Faults*—Hanging on the side as on a foxhound. Cropped ears; high set; not set too far apart, well pointed but always in proportion to the shape of the head and carried uniformly erect.

4. Torso—20 points.

a. *Neck* (6 points)—The neck should be firm and clean, high set, well arched, long, muscular and sinewy. From the chest to the head, it should be slightly tapering, beautifully formed, with well developed nape. *Faults*—Short, heavy neck, pendulous throat folds (dewlaps).

b. *Loin and Back* (6 points)—The withers forms the highest part of the back which slopes downward slightly toward the loins, which are imperceptibly arched and strong. The back should be short and tensely set. The belly should be well shaped and tightly muscled, and, with the rear part of the thorax, should swing in a pleasing curve (tuck-up). *Faults*—Receding back; sway back; camel or roach back; a back line which is too high at the rear; an excessively long back; poor tuck-up.

c. *Chest* (4 points)—Chest deals with that part of the thorax (rib cage) in front of the shoulders and front legs. The chest should be quite broad, deep and well muscled. *Faults*—A narrow and poorly muscled chest; strong protruding sternum (pigeon breast.)

d. *Ribs and Brisket* (4 points)—Deals with that part of the thorax back of the shoulders and front legs. Should be broad, with the ribs sprung well out from the spine and flattened at the side to allow proper movement of the shoulders extending down to the elbow joint. *Faults*—Narrow (slab-sided) rib cage; round (barrel) rib cage; shallow rib cage not reaching the elbow joint.

5. Tail—2 points.

Should start high and fairly broad, terminating slender and thin at the hock joint. At rest, the tail should fall straight. When excited or running, slightly curved (saber like). *Faults*—A too high, or too low set tail (the tail set is governed by the slope of the croup); too long or too short a tail; tail bent too far over the back (ring tail); a tail which is curled; a twisted tail (sideways); a tail carried too high over the back (gay tail); a brush tail (hair too long on lower side). Cropping tails to desired length is forbidden.

FAULTS OF THE GREAT DANE

Disqualification Faults—Deaf Danes. Danes under minimum height. Without visible scrotum. Spayed bitches. Monorchids. White Danes without any black marks (albinos). Merles, a solid mouse-gray color or a mouse-gray base with black or white or both color spots or white base with mouse-gray spots. Harlequins and solid-colored Danes in which a large spot extends coatlike over the entire body so that only the legs, neck and the point of the tail are white. Brindle, Fawn Blue and Black Danes with white forehead line, white collars, high white stockings and white bellies. Danes with predominantly blue gray, yellow or also brindled spots. Docked tails. Split noses.

The faults below are important according to their grouping (very serious, serious, minor) and not according to their sequence as placed in each grouping:

Very serious—Lack of unity. Poor bone development. Poor musculature.

Champion Czardas v. Eppeleinsprung-Noris
(a famous, early import).

Lightweight whippety Danes. Rickets. Timidity. Bitchy dog. Sway back. Roach back. Cowhocks. Pitching gait. Short steps. Undershot teeth.

Serious—Out of condition. Coarseness. Any deviation from the standard on all coloration. Deviation from parallel planes of skull and foreface. Wedgehead. Poorly defined stop. Narrow nose bridge. Snipey muzzle. Any color but dark eyes in fawns and brindles. Mongolian eyes. Missing teeth. Overshot teeth. Heavy neck. Short neck. Dewlaps. Narrow chest. Narrow rib cage. Round rib cage. Shallow rib cage. Loose shoulders. Steep shoulders. Elbows turned inward. Chair legs (Front). Knotty bulge in pastern joint (adult dog). Weak pastern roots. Receding back. Too long a back. Back high in rear. In harlequins, a pink nose. Poor tuckup (except in bitches that have been bred). Too straight croup. Too sloping croup. Too narrow croup. Over-angulation. Steep rear. Too long rear legs. Poorly muscled thighs. Barrel legs. Paws turned outward. Rabbit paws. Wolf's claw. Hackney gait.

Minor—Doggy bitches. Small white marks on chest and toes—Blues, Blacks, Brindles and Fawns. Few gray spots and pointings on Harlequins. In Harlequins, black spotted nose. White tipped tail except on Harlequins. Excessively long hair. Excessively dull hair. Apple head. Small stop. Fluttering lips. Eyes too far apart. Drooping lower eyelids. Haws. Any color but dark eyes in blacks, blues and harlequins. Discolored teeth. Even bite. Pigeon breast. Loaded shoulders. Elbows turned outward. Paws turned inward. Splay foot. Excessively long toe nails. Light nails (except in harlequins). Low-set tail. Too long a tail. Too short a tail. Gay tail. Curled tail. Twisted tail. Brush tail.

Champion Cote de Neige Ariette

THE GREAT PYRENEES

Huge, white and massive, the Great Pyrenees is an eye-catching breed. His name indicates the place where he reached the highest point of his development. The breed has been known by many names, one of which was the Pyrenean Sheep Dog.

Descended from the Tibetan Mastiff the Pyr was used more as a guard dog, to protect the flocks against wolves and bears, by Spanish and French sheepherders. These *"great dogs of the mountains"* were named the official dogs of the Royal Court of France in the 17th century by King Louis XIV. Even earlier, in the first part of the 15th century, the historian, Monsieur Bourdet describes the guard of Pyrenees dogs owned by the Chateau of Lourdes. In the old days, wearing a spiked collar, the Great Pyrenees was an almost unbeatable foe of the huge mountain wolves and bears.

The breed developed over the years inherent traits of loyalty, devotion, love and understanding of man and a desire to protect its master's property. Then the Great Pyrenees almost became extinct when the wolves and bears and wild dogs were driven from the mountains or killed. But, because of their use in other directions, the breed survived and began to prosper.

They make fine house and guard dogs and can be trained to pull sleds or carts. Crossed with black English Retrievers in Newfoundland they produced the picturesque Landseer Newfoundlands, made famous by the great animal painter for which the color variety was named.

The Great Pyrenees was recognized as a breed by the A.K.C. in 1933, but the first pair was sent to these shores as a present to J. S. Skinner by General Lafayette in 1824. The first modern breeding pair was brought to the United States by Mr. and Mrs. Francis V. Crane for their Basquerie Kennels in Holliston, Massachusetts in 1931. This kennel has since become known throughout the world for the many magnificent specimens of the breed it has produced.

STANDARD OF THE GREAT PYRENEES

1. *General Appearance*—A dog of immense size, great majesty, keen intelligence, and kindly expression; of unsurpassed beauty and a certain elegance, all white or principally white with markings of badger, grey, or varying shades of tan. In the rolling, ambling gait it shows unmistakably the purpose for which it has been bred, the strenuous work of guarding the flocks in all kinds of weather on the steep mountain slopes of the Pyrenees. Hence soundness is of the greatest importance and absolutely necessary for the proper fulfilment of his centuries' old task.

2. *Size*—The average height at the shoulder is 27 inches to 32 inches for dogs, and 25 inches to 29 inches for bitches.

The average length from shoulder blades to root of tail should be the same as the height in any given specimen.

Ch. Basquerie Maida

Pyrenees puppies at six weeks of age.

The average girth is 36 inches to 42 inches for dogs, and 32 inches to 36 inches for bitches.

The weight for dogs runs 100 to 125 pounds and 90 to 115 pounds for bitches.

A dog heavily boned; with close cupped feet; double dewclaws behind and single dewclaws in front.

3. *Head*—Large and wedge shaped, measuring 10 inches to 11 inches from dome to point of nose, with rounding crown, furrow only slightly developed and with no apparent stop.

Cheeks—Flat.

Ears—V shaped, but rounded at the tips, of medium size, set parallel with the eyes, carried low and close to the head except when raised at attention.

Eyes—Of medium size set slightly obliquely, dark rich brown in color with close eyelids, well pigmented.

Lips—Close fitting, edged with black.

Dewlaps—Developed but little.

The head is in brief that of a brown bear, but with the ears falling down.

4. *Neck*—Short, stout and strongly muscular.

5. *Body*—Well placed shoulders set obliquely, close to the body.

Back and Loin—Well coupled, straight and broad.

Haunches—Fairly prominent.

Rump—Sloping slightly.

Ribs—Flat-sided.

Chest—Deep.

Tail—Of sufficient length to hang below the hocks, well plumed, carried low in repose, and curled high over the back "making the wheel" when alert.

6. *Coat*—Created to withstand severe weather, with heavy fine white undercoat and long flat thick outercoat of coarser hair, straight or slightly undulating.

7. *Qualities*—In addition to his original age old position in the scheme of pastoral life as protector of the shepherd and his flock the Great Pyrenees has been used for centuries as a guard and watch dog on the large estates of his

Mr. and Mrs. Francis V. Crane, owners of the well known Basquerie Kennels of Great Pyrenees, and some of their famous animals. The Cranes introduced this noble breed to America.

native France, and for this he has proven ideal. He is as serious in play as he is in work, adapting and molding himself to the moods, desires and even the very life of his human companions, through fair weather and foul, through leisure hours and hours fraught with danger, responsibility, and extreme exertion; he is the exemplification of gentleness and docility with those he knows, of faithfulness and devotion for his master even to the point of self-sacrifice; and of courage in the protection of the flock placed in his care and of the ones he loves.

8. *Scale of Points*—(*a*) Head: 25 points comprised as follows:

	Points
Shape of skull	5
Ears	5
Eyes	5
Muzzle	5
Teeth	5

(*b*) General Conformation: 25 points comprised as follows:

	Points
Neck	5
Chest	5
Back	5
Loins	5
Feet	5

(*c*) Coat: 10 points. (*d*) Size and Soundness: 25 points. (*e*) Expression and General Appearance: 15 points. Total number of points 100.

Adopted and accepted as the Standard for The Great Pyrenees by The Great Pyrenees Club of America, January, 1935.

Diszta vom Hochwaldhof (German)

THE KOMONDOR

The Hungarian version of the guardian of sheep and cattle is the Komondor. There are two other working dogs from the same sheep and cattle areas of Hungary but the Komondor is the king. Huge, heavily coated, and solid white, the Komondor (plural of the name is Komondorok) is a direct descendant of the Aftscharka which the Huns found on the steppes of Russia, a breed stemming directly from the Tibetan Mastiff.

Komondorok are used more as guard dogs for the flocks than herding dogs and in this capacity, working for the Magyars, they have a thousand years of training behind them. The Magyars never kept pedigrees, feeling that there was no need since they never allowed the dogs to be bred outside their own race. They were bred for full utility, not for beauty and, as such, breeding of these dogs was neither a hobby nor a commercial venture.

The breed makes wonderful house guards and protectors of property and are truly hardy outdoor animals.

From its native land it spread to many other countries and was introduced from Germany to America in 1935. The A.K.C. gave it breed recognition in 1937.

As a result of the second World War the Komondor remained almost unknown for many, many years, but in recent times the breed has been getting increased attention and show appearances have become more frequent.

The Komondor's coat is unique among dog breeds. It has a natural tendency to mat, and the controlled mattings, or cording, is the way in which these interesting dogs are shown.

The magnificent Komondor has made a number of dedicated friends in the United States and they are sure to help him grow and increase in popularity in the best possible way.

STANDARD OF THE KOMONDOR

General Appearance—The Komondor is characterized by imposing strength, courageous demeanor and pleasing conformation. In general he is a big muscular dog with plenty of bone and substance.

Nature and Characteristics—As a houseguard as well as a guardian of herds he is, when grown up, an earnest, courageous, and very faithful dog. The young dog, however, is just as playful as any other puppy. He is much devoted to his master and will defend him against attack by any stranger. On account of this trait he is not used for driving the herds, but only for guarding them. His special task is to protect the animals, and he lives during the greater part of the year in the open air without protection against strange dogs and all kinds of beasts of prey.

Head—The head of the Komondor is covered all over with long hair, and thus the head looks somewhat short, in comparison to the seemingly wide forehead. If the hair is smoothed it will be seen that the skull is somewhat arched if viewed from the side; the forehead is not wide, but appears, however, wider through the rich growth of hair. The stop is moderate, it is the starting point of the muzzle which is somewhat shorter than the length of the skull. The top line of the muzzle is straight and about parallel with the line of the top of the skull. The muzzle should be fairly square. The lips cover the teeth closely and are black. The muzzle is mostly covered by long hair. The edges of the muzzle are black or steel-blue/gray. The jaws are powerful, and the teeth are level and close together evenly.

Ears—The ears are rather low set and hang along the side of the head. They are medium-sized, and their surface is covered with long hair.

Eyes—The eyes express fidelity. They are medium-sized and almond shaped, not too deeply set and surrounded by rough, unkempt hair. The iris of the eyes is of coffee or darker brown color, light color is not desirable. Blue- white eyes are disqualifying. The edges of the eyelids are slate-grey.

Muzzle— In comparison to the length given in the head description, the muzzle is wide, coarse and not pointed. The nostrils are wide. The color of

400

The Komondor has a unique coat, similar in texture to the Poodle in that it has a tendency to quickly mat if not kept groomed. Komondor owners often allow the coats of their dogs to cord as shown in the lower photo. The woolly coat of the dog in the upper picture shows the effect of care.

the nose is black. Komondors with flesh-colored noses must absolutely be excluded from breeding. A slate-colored or dark brown nose is undesirable but may, however, be accepted for breeding purposes.

Neck—The neck is covered with long hair, is muscular, of medium length, moderately arched. The head erect. No dewlap is allowed.

Body—The body is characterized chiefly by the powerful, deep chest which is muscular and proportionately wide. The height at the top of shoulders is $23\frac{1}{2}$ inches to $31\frac{1}{2}$ inches, the higher, the better. The shoulders slope into the neck without apparent protrusion. The body is moderately long and level. Back and loins are wide. The rump is wide, muscular, moderately sloping towards the root of the tail. The body should be somewhat drawn up at the rear, but not Greyhound-like.

Tail—The tail is as a straight continuation of the rump-line, and reaches down to the hocks slightly curved upwards at its end. It is covered in its full length with long hair, which when the dog is at ease almost touches the ground. When the dog is excited the tail is raised up to the level of the back. The tail should not be docked. Komondors born with short tails must be excluded even for breeding purposes.

Forelegs—The forelegs should be straight, well boned and muscular. Viewed from any side, the legs are like vertical columns. The upper arm joins the body closely, without loose elbows. The legs are covered all around by long, evenly hanging hair.

Hindquarters and Legs—The steely, strong bone-structure is covered with highly developed muscles, and the legs are evenly covered with long hair, hanging down in matted clods. The legs should be straight as viewed from the rear. Stifles well bent. Dewclaws must be removed. The body and the legs should about form a rectangle.

Feet—The feet should be strong, rather large and with close, well arched toes. The hind feet are stronger, and all are covered with long hair. The nails are black or slate-grey. The pads are hard, elastic and black.

Coat—The entire body of the Komondor is covered with a long, soft woolly, dense hair, of different length on the different parts of the body, with inclination to entanglement and shagginess. If the dog is not taken care of, the hair becomes shaggy on the forelegs, chest, belly, rump and on the sides of the thigh and the tail. The longer and the more ragged, the better, though, as above stated, the length of the hair varies on the different parts of the body. The longer hair begins on the head and ears and lengthens gradually on the body, being longest on the thighs and the tail. A somewhat shorter, but still long hair is found on the legs, the muzzle and the cheeks. Too curly hair is undesirable.

Color—The color of the hair is white. Any other color is disqualifying.

Size—The bigger the Komondor, the better, a minimum height of $25\frac{1}{2}$ inches at top of shoulders for males and $23\frac{1}{2}$ inches for females is required.

Faults—Light or flesh-colored nose, albino or blue eyes, highly set and small ears. Short, smooth hair, on the head and legs, strongly curled tail, color:—other than white.

DISQUALIFICATIONS

Blue-white eyes; color other than white.

402

A winning German-bred Kuvasz.

THE KUVASZ

The Turkish word, kawasz, means *"armed guard of the nobility."* In Arabian it is kawwasz, which means *"archer."* Corrupt these words, as the early breeders of the large white Hungarian working dogs did, and you have the breed name Kuvasz (plural form, Kuvaszok).

In ancient times the breed was much larger than today; giants in white coats, closely related to the Komondor, with their lineage derived from the ancient Tibetan Mastiff. They were dogs of the ruling classes and it is recorded that in the latter half of the 15th century Kuvaszok were kept in the kennels of King Matthias I in great numbers at Siebenbuergen. Trainers supervised the dogs' development and selected them for guard dogs and for big game hunting.

The common people were awed by these immense white dogs but later, after the time of Matthias, stock got into the hands of the country people who found that Kuvaszok made fine sheep and cattle guards and herding dogs.

A single specimen of the breed was registered in the A.K.C. stud book in 1931. He had to wait three years before others joined him.

The breed is not as large as in the olden days but is still a big, strong, hardy animal and a very capable working dog.

STANDARD OF THE KUVASZ

General Appearance—Being a working dog of the larger size, the Kuvasz

Kuvaszok in their native Hungary.

should be sturdily built and impress the eye with its strength and activity combined with light footedness. He should move freely on strong legs and any tendency to a weak or hollow back is a decided fault.

Head—Should be in proportion to the body, skull broad and flat with not too decided a stop.

Muzzle—Should be clean cut, rather square in shape and covered with short, fine hair.

Ears—Rather small, set well back folded over level with the top of skull and lying close to the head. They should be covered with fine, short hair but no fringe.

Eyes—Should be of medium size, set slightly obliquely and rather wide apart. They should be as dark as possible.

Nose—Nostrils well developed. The nose together with the flews should be black.

Color—Pure white. Occasionally specimens appear with a yellow saddle but this is a decided fault and such dogs are not to be recommended for breeding purposes.

Coat—Rather long on neck and croup becoming a little shorter and slightly wavy on sides.

Body—Should be well ribbed up with a fairly broad back, neck is fairly short, strong, well set on sloping shoulders with strong muscular loins.

Forelegs—Should have strong bone, be perfectly straight and well muscled, elbows should be in but well let down. Hair short on front and sides of legs. Slightly feathered on back of legs.

Hindquarters—Should be strong, legs should have great freedom of action, lightness of loins and cowhocks are a great defect.

Chest—Should be deep and fairly broad.

Feet—Should be strong and well shaped; splay or turned out feet are objectionable.

Tail—Should be of moderate length reaching a little below the hocks and covered with thick, fairly long hair.

Height—Dogs about 26 inches at shoulder, bitches somewhat less.

Champion Mooreleigh Moby Dick.

THE MASTIFF

There does not appear to be a time in the written history of the human race that Mastiffs were not known. Their history is a continuous one extending through to the present day.

A bas relief, dated about 2200 B.C., serves as a starting point in the history of these dogs as we know them. Later, one notes the Babylonian bas reliefs belonging to the Palace of Assurbanipal (about 700 B.C.) which display scenes of hunting wild horses and lions with Mastiffs.

Many of the Assyrian antiquities show terra-cotta plaques of Mastiffs excavated from the sites of ancient Babylonian cities. It apparently was the Assyrian custom to bury these plaques under the threshold of houses so that the spirits of the dogs might repel the attacks of evil spirits attempting to enter the house. The custom illustrates that even in that early time the Mastiff was prized not only as a most efficient watchdog, but also as a valued friend and ally.

Successors of these Babylonian Mastiffs may later be traced into Egypt and other parts of Mesopotamia. Later, the Mastiff appeared in Greece, where the Molossus of Epirus was clearly a Mastiff. A statue of the Molossus, belonging

to Olympias, the daughter of the Molossian King Pyrrhus I, in the Palazzo Torlonia in Rome, is described by Professor Keller as the true Molossus. The author has seen this statue in Rome and the sculptured dog certainly bears a striking resemblance to the Mastiff of today. The Molossus of Epirus was the most famous and most prized dog of Grecian times. He was used as a guard of the flocks against wolves, as well as house dog, guard, and companion of kings, noblemen and wealthy gentlemen. The following traditional story from Plutarch's Miscellaneous Works is illustrative of the strength and character of the Molossus of Epirus.

"As Pyrrhus (King of Epirus) was journeying through the country he came across a dog guarding the body of his master who had been murdered; and according to the testimony of neighbors, the dog had been there already for three days without moving, or eating, or drinking. Pyrrhus ordered that the man should be buried and he took the dog with him commanding that he should be well treated. A few days afterwards there was a muster and a review of all the soldiers who paraded before the King seated on his throne with the dog near him. The dog lay still until he perceived the murderers of his master when he rushed upon them incontinently with loud barks, and raging fury, turning often towards Pyrrhus in such a way that not only the King but all his attendants conceived a strong suspicion that these must be the men who had killed his master. They were made prisoners, and at their subsequent trial further evidence, both direct and circumstantial, was produced against them, so that in the end they confessed the murder and were put to death."

Although the Mastiff has in modern times been identified with the British Isles, distribution was formerly much wider than is generally imagined and he was to be found through a great part of both Asia and Europe. In fact, Marco Polo informs us that when he visited the Court of the great Mogul Emperor, Kublai Khan, he found that 5,000 Mastiffs were kept for the purpose of hunting lions and other big game.

The Mastiff was found in England when the Romans first landed and it will probably never be definitely ascertained whether the breed was introduced by the Phoenicians or as a result of dog trading with the Continent. English Mastiffs were greatly prized by the Romans who exported large numbers to Rome and other cities, for the purpose of fighting in the arenas.

The breed has been prominent throughout English history. In Norman times the Mastiffs were kept as watchdogs and were the only dogs permitted within the precincts of forests. In the time of Henry V they were greatly esteemed by the knight and warrior classes and accompanied their masters in battle. Henry VIII is said to have presented four hundred Mastiffs to Charles V on the occasion of an alliance with him against Francis I of France, to be used as fighting dogs in his wars.

The dignity that is the emblem of an ancient and noble heritage is etched in every line of the Mastiff's visage. The portrait on the left truly depicts the majestic mein of this breed of the ages.

One of the most celebrated, though far from the most creditable, uses made of Mastiffs was for the so-called sport of bear baiting. This sport appears to have been practiced as early as the time of Edward the Confessor. Lion baiting was also practiced but only on rare occasions.

After the cessation of bear baiting, Mastiffs appear to have declined in popularity and in many instances the breed was hurt by crosses. There does, however, appear to be evidence that many fine specimens could still be found in the possession of wealthy noblemen and gentlemen and that the true Mastiff continued to be bred at Lyme Hall, by the Legh Family; at Chatsworth, by the Duke of Devonshire; at Elvaston, by the Earl of Harrington, and at Trenthan, by the Duke of Sutherland.

The revival of the former popularity of the Mastiff was started about 1867 and with the exception of a brief period between 1883 and 1890 made rapid progress until the World War. It is probable that the Mastiff suffered more than any other breed as a result of the War. The breeding stock was, therefore, scanty at best in 1918.

The history of the Mastiff in America is not well authenticated nor is it as voluminous as one would imagine. One authority states that two dogs came over on the Mayflower—one a Spaniel, and the other a Mastiff. The same authority writes that the early settlers of New Haven, Connecticut, voted to import Mastiffs to guard their settlements.

It was not, however, until the latter part of the 19th century that the breed acquired widespread popularity in the United States. Doubtless, the importations of fine stock made during that period gave impetus to a broader recognition of the outstanding characteristics of the Mastiff.

Unfortunately, the effect of the World War on the Mastiff in England had its counterpart in this country with the result that the early 1920's found the breed almost extinct in its pure form.

English fanciers rallied to save the dog that represented England itself. The Mastiff became well established in Great Britain, and interest was revived in the United States. World War II dealt a serious blow to these great dogs. England was forced to deplete its fine livestock after the German attack on Poland and the resultant major struggle. Mastiff fanciers did their best as Britain entered total war with Hitler. Many Mastiffs were sent to America and there has been a steady increase in their popularity. The largest number of Mastiffs today is in the United States.

At the present time, there is a revival of interest in this magnificent breed of dog which in a relatively few years should go far towards regaining for the Mastiff his erstwhile position of prominence.

"I cannot refrain from quoting a paragraph from the article on the Mastiff in the Cynographia Britannica, published in 1800, which makes one regret the past.

" 'What the Lion is to the Cat the Mastiff is to the Dog, the noblest of the family; he stands alone, and all others sink before him. His courage does not exceed his temper and generosity, and in attachment he equals the kindest of his race. His docility is perfect; the teasing of the smaller kinds will hardly provoke him to resent, and I have seen him down with his paw the Terrier or cur that has bit him, without offering further injury. In a family he will permit the children to play with him, and suffer all their little pranks without offense. The blind ferocity of the Bull Dog will often wound the hand of the master who assists him to combat, but the Mastiff distinguishes perfectly, enters the

Champion Beowulf of Havengore

Champion Sheba of Zimapan

409

field with temper, and engages in the attack as if confident of success; if he overpowers or is beaten, his master may take him immediately in his arms and fear nothing. The ancient and faithful domestic, the pride of our island, uniting the useful, the brave and the docile, though sought by foreign nations and perpetuated on the continent, is nearly extinct where he probably was an aborigine, or is bastardized by numberless crosses, every one of which degenerates the invaluable character of the parent, who was deemed worthy to enter the Roman amphitheatre, and, in the presence of the masters of the world encounter the pard, and assail even the lord of the savage tribes, whose courage was sublimed by torrid suns, and found none gallant enough to oppose him on the deserts of Zaara, or the plains of Numidia.'

"Is it too much to hope that one of these days there may arise a few keen and intelligent breeders who will realize how this splendid dog, once the pride of England, and the envy of the world, has been and still is being sacrificed by the ignorance, jealousy and selfishness of unworthy fanciers; and will strongly take the measures necessary to restore him to his proper place at the head of the canine race?"

STANDARD OF THE MASTIFF

General Character and Symmetry—Large, massive, symmetrical and well knit frame. A combination of grandeur and good nature, courage and docility.

General Description of Head—In general outline giving a massive appearance when viewed from any angle. Breadth greatly to be desired.

Skull—Broad and somewhat rounded between the ears, forehead slightly curved, showing marked wrinkles which are particularly distinctive when at

Ilford Chancellor, an English import and a foundation stud dog.

410

Falcon of Blackroc, imported from England.

attention. Brows (superciliary ridges) moderately raised. Muscles of the temples well developed, those of the cheeks extremely powerful. Arch across the skull a flattened curve with a furrow up the center of the forehead. This extends from between the eyes to halfway up the skull.

Ears—Small, V-shaped, rounded at the tips. Leather moderately thin, set widely apart at the highest points on the sides of the skull continuing the outline across the summit. They should lie close to the cheeks when in repose. Ears dark in color, the blacker the better, conforming to the color of the muzzle.

Eyes—Set wide apart, medium in size, never too prominent. Expression alert but kindly. The stop between the eyes well marked but not too abrupt. Color of eyes brown, the darker the better and showing no haw.

Face and Muzzle—Short, broad under the eyes and running nearly equal in width to the end of the nose. Truncated, i.e., blunt and cut off square, thus forming a right angle with the upper line of the face. Of great depth from the point of the nose to under jaw. Under jaw broad to the end and slightly rounded. Canine teeth healthy, powerful and wide apart. Scissor bite preferred but a moderately undershot jaw permissible providing the teeth are not visible when the mouth is closed. Lips diverging at obtuse angles with the septum and sufficiently pendulous so as to show a modified square profile. Nose broad and always dark in color, the blacker the better, with spread flat nostrils (not pointed or turned up) in profile. Muzzle dark in color, the blacker the better. Muzzle should be half the length of the skull, thus dividing the head into three parts—one for the foreface and two for the skull. In other words, the distance from tip of nose to stop is equal to one-half the distance between the stop and the occiput. Circumference of muzzle (measured midway between the eyes and nose) to that of the head (measured before the ears) as 3 is to 5.

411

Neck—Powerful and very muscular, slightly arched, and of medium length. The neck gradually increases in circumference as it approaches the shoulder. Neck moderately "dry" (not showing an excess of loose skin).

Chest and Flanks—Wide, deep, rounded and well let down between the forelegs extending at least to the elbow. Forechest should be deep and well defined. Ribs extremely well rounded. False ribs deep and well set back. There should be a reasonable, but not exaggerated, cut-up.

Shoulder and Arm—Slightly sloping, heavy and muscular. No tendency to looseness of shoulders.

Forelegs and Feet—Legs straight, strong and set wide apart, heavy boned. Elbows parallel to body. Feet heavy, round and compact with well arched toes. Pasterns strong and bent only slightly. Black nails preferred.

Hindlegs—Hindquarters broad, wide and muscular. Second thighs well developed, hocks set back, wide apart and parallel when viewed from the rear.

Back and Loins—Back muscular, powerful and straight. Loins wide and muscular, slightly rounded over the rump.

Tail—Set on moderately high and reaching to the hocks or a little below. Wide at the root, tapering to the end, hanging straight in repose, forming a slight curve but never over the back when dog is in action.

Coat—Outer coat moderately coarse. Under coat, dense, short and close lying.

Color—Apricot, silver fawn or dark fawn-brindle. Fawn-brindle should have fawn as a background color which should be completely covered with very dark stripes. In any case muzzle, ears and nose must be dark in color, the blacker the better, with similar color tone around the orbits, extending upwards between them.

Size—Dogs, minimum 30 inches at the shoulder; bitches, minimum 27½ inches at the shoulder.

SCALE OF POINTS

	Points
General character and symmetry	10
Height and substance	10
Skull	10
Face and muzzle	12
Ears	5
Eyes	5
Chest and ribs	10
Forelegs and feet	10
Back, loins and flanks	10
Hindlegs and feet	10
Tail	3
Coat and color	5
Total	100

Champion Dryad's Coastwise Show Boat

THE NEWFOUNDLAND

Here is a breed that is as much at home in the water as a polar bear or otter. He has strength and solidity and an enduring look, and well he might have all these things because they are part of his breed heritage. The breed has been used for many tasks; draft dog and pack animal, guard and companion. Today he can serve in the same capacities and, as a watch dog and guard, has that sterling gentleness that makes him a completely safe companion.

Water is this dog's element. His feet are webbed, his coat's oiliness and density is ideal for shedding water and his power makes him master of this domain. The Newfoundland can and does surface dive and swim under water.

The breed's origins are said to be found in Great Pyrenees dogs brought to the coast of Newfoundland by Basque fishermen. Other breeds involved were probably the Talhund and, far back, the ancient pillar of so many breeds, the Tibetan Mastiff. The earliest Newfoundlands were the Landseers (black and white), named for Sir Edwin Landseer, the famous artist who used a dog of this type and color in his painting, "*A Distinguished Member of the Humane Society.*" The solid black color seen today was probably arrived at through selection.

The breed's finest traits are its intelligence, loyalty and sweetness of character. All of these things were stressed in Lord Byron's well known tribute to his beloved Newfoundland, Boatswain. The Newfoundland's work in saving shipwrecked seamen from the tempestuous seas along the stormy,

A group of Landseer Newfoundlands.

rocky coast of Newfoundland is known to all lovers of adventure on the high seas.

While illustrating the book, "This is the Newfoundland," the author came in very close contact with many of the breed which he used as models. They have a kind of character that gets to you. Big, lumbering, good natured, they are nice to have around even if you are a confirmed landlubber.

STANDARD OF THE NEWFOUNDLAND
(By Courtesy of The Newfoundland Club of America)

Symmetry and General Appearance—The dog should impress the eye with strength and great activity. He should move freely on his legs with the body swung loosely between them, so that a slight roll in gait should not be objectionable; but at the same time a weak or hollow back, slackness of the loins or cowhocks should be a decided fault.

Head—Should be broad and massive, the occipital bone well developed, there should be no decided stop, and the muzzle should be short, clean cut, and rather square in shape, and covered with short fine hair.

Coat—Should be flat and dense, of a coarsish texture and oily nature, and capable of resisting the water. If brushed the wrong way it should fall back into its place naturally.

Body—Should be well ribbed up with a broad back. A neck, strong, well set on to the shoulders and back, with strong muscular loins.

414

Forelegs—Should be perfectly straight, well covered with muscle, elbows in but well let down and feathered all down.

Hindquarters and Legs—Should be very strong; the legs should have great freedom of action, and a little feather. Slackness of loins and cowhocks are a great defect; dewclaws are objectionable, and should be removed.

Chest—Should be deep and fairly broad and well covered with hair, but not to such an extent as to form a frill.

Bone—Massive throughout, but not to give a heavy inactive appearance.

Feet—Should be large and well shaped. Splayed or turned out feet are objectionable.

Tail—Should be of moderate length, reaching down a little below the hocks, it should be of fair thickness, and well covered with long hair, but not to form a flag. When the dog is standing still, and not excited, it should hang downwards with a slight curve at the end; but when the dog is in motion it should be carried a trifle up, and when he is excited straight out with a slight curve at the end. Tails with a kink in them, or curled over the back, are very objectionable.

Ears—Should be small, set well back, square with the skull, lie close to the head, and covered with short hair, and no fringe.

Eyes—Should be small, of a dark brown color, rather deeply set but not showing any haw, and they should be rather widely apart.

Champion Dryad's Brown Betty

Color—Dull jet black. A slight tinge of bronze, or a splash of white on chest and toes is not objectionable.

Height and Weight—Size and weight are very desirable so long as symmetry is maintained. A fair average height at the shoulders is 28 inches for a dog, and 26 inches for a bitch, and a fair average weight is, respectively:

Dogs .... 140 to 150 pounds
Bitches .... 110 to 120 pounds

Other Than Black (Landseers)—Should in all respects follow the black except in color, which may be almost any, so long as it disqualifies for the black class, but the colors most to be encouraged are white and black or bronze. Beauty in markings to be taken greatly into consideration.

Black dogs that have only white toes and white breasts and white tip to tail, should be exhibited in the classes provided for "black."

SCALE OF POINTS

Head

	Points	
Shape of skull	8	
Ears	10	
Eyes	8	
Muzzle	8	
Points for head.............................	—	34

Body

Neck	4	
Chest..	6	
Shoulders	4	
Loin and back	12	
Hindquarters and tail	10	
Legs and feet	10	
Coat	12	
Size, height and general appearance...........	8	
Body points..............................	—	66
Total points...		100

MARKINGS OF WHITE AND BLACK DOGS

	Points	
Head	3	
Saddle	5	
Rump	2	
Total..	—	10

"DEFINITION FOR PREFERENCE"

Black head marked with narrow blaze.
Even marked saddle.
Black rump, extending on to tail.
The ten points above are to be considered in differentiating between "Landseers" not added to Standard.

THE SNOW-WHITE SAMOYED.

THE PERSONIFICATION OF ALL UTILITARIAN
CANINES, THE GERMAN SHERHERD DOG.
BELOW, THE BELGIAN TERVUREN.

OF ANCIENT LINEAGE, THE MASSIVE MASTIFF.

THE BRIARD, A WORKING DOG OF FRANCE.

A PEMBROKE WELSH CORGI.

THE PULI, A NATIVE OF HUNGARY.

E·H·HART

AT THE TOP OF THE LEFT HAND PAGE IS
PICTURED A BELGIAN SHEEPDOG. LOWER LEFT
IS A PORTRAIT OF A BRINDLE GREAT DANE.
ABOVE, FROM THE ICY WILDS OF THE ARCTIC,
THE ALASKAN MALAMUTE.

A PAIR OF NEWFOUNDLAND DOGS. AS MUCH AT HOME IN THE WATER AS ON DRY LAND, THE NEWFOUNDLAND CAN SWIM LIKE AN OTTER AND HAS, FOR GENERATIONS, BEEN THE FRIEND AND COMPANION OF MAN.

HEAD STUDY OF A FAWN, MALE BOXER. AT
THE TOP OF THE OPPOSITE PAGE IS A
GREAT PYRENEES, SHEPHERD DOG OF THE
BASQUE COUNTRY. LOWER RIGHT, A SABLE,
ROUGH COLLIE

A BRACE OF ROTTWEILERS.

A ROUGH-COATED ST. BERNARD.

AT TOP OF PAGE IS A SHETLAND
SHEEPDOG. BELOW, THE PORTRAIT
OF A MALE DOBERMAN PINSCHER.

E.H.HART

A PAIR OF KOMONDOROK. THE KOMONDOR
IS THE SHEEPDOG OF HUNGARY.

IN THE BAVARIAN ALPS A MOTHER GERMAN
SHEPHERD LEADS HER SON TO THE FLOCK FOR
HIS FIRST LESSON IN SHEEP HERDING.

A CARDIGAN WELSH CORGI.

A BRACE OF PULIK. THE PULI IS, LIKE THE KOMONDOR, A HUNGARIAN SHEPHERD DOG.

Champion Fezziwig Ceiling Zero.

THE OLD ENGLISH SHEEPDOG

Sometimes called the "Bobtail", this breed is (or was) used mainly as a drover, not a sheep herder. It is probably in the direct line of descent from the ancient Persian Sheepdog with judicious crosses to the Bearded Collie.

The Old English was developed in western England, in Devon, Somerset and Cornwall. Dogs used for herding in England were exempt from taxation and the drovers amputated the tails of their working sheep and cattle dogs to distinguish them from those which were not tax exempt. As a result the standard calls for a bobbed tail, cut off at the first joint when the Old English puppy is just a few days old so that it will be no more than a one to two inch stub upon maturity. This practice has *not* led to some puppies of the breed being born tailless. They are few and far between, a mutation that has been selected for.

The breed can be traced back at least 150 years as a true type. This is not as ancient as the geneology of many of the canine breeds, but figured in dog generations it is still a long, long time. Their long hair, bobbed tails and rolling gait are trademarks of the breed.

These are quiet, lovable, intelligent and affectionate animals. Part the hairs of the Bobtail's face and you will find a pair of beautiful, friendly eyes. They make excellent pets and companions.

Recognized by the A.K.C. in 1888, the breed gained wide recognition by virtue of a Best in Show win at Westminster's Garden Show in 1914. The Bobtail who brought this about was Champion Slumber.

Modern day Old English Sheepdogs do more than their share of winning at the country's leading dog shows. They have a winsome charm and are definitely photogenic, virtues that have led to their use in various visual forms of commercial advertising.

STANDARD OF THE OLD ENGLISH SHEEPDOG

Skull—Capacious and rather squarely formed, giving plenty of room for brain power. The parts over the eyes should be well arched and the whole well covered with hair.

Jaw—Fairly long, strong, square and truncated. The top should be well defined to avoid a deerhound face. (The attention of judges is particularly called to the above properties, as a long, narrow head is a deformity.)

Eyes—Vary according to the color of the dog. Very dark preferred, but in the glaucous or blue dogs a pearl, wall or china eye is considered typical. (A light eye is most objectionable.)

Champion Holloways Pollyanna (imported).

Champion Fezziwig Raggedy Andy.

Nose—Always black, large and capacious.

Teeth—Strong and large, evenly placed and level in opposition.

Ears—Medium sized, and carried flat to side of head, coated moderately.

Legs—The forelegs should be dead straight, with plenty of bone, removing the body a medium height from the ground, without approaching legginess, and well coated all around.

Feet—Small, round; toes well arched, and pads thick and hard.

Tail—It is preferable that there should be none. Should never, however, exceed one and a half or two inches in grown dogs. When not nautral-born bobtails however, puppies should be docked at the first joint from the body and the operation performed when they are from three to four days old.

Neck and Shoulders—The neck should be fairly long, arched gracefully and well coated with hair. The shoulders sloping and narrow at the points, the dog standing lower at the shoulder than at the loin.

Body—Rather short and very compact, ribs well sprung and brisket deep and capacious. Slabsidedness highly undesirable. The loin should be very stout and gently arched, while the hind quarters should be round and muscular and with well-let-down hocks, and the hams densely coated with a thick, long jacket in excess of any other part.

Coat—Profuse, but not so excessive as to give the impression of the dog being over-fat, and of a good hard texture; not straight, but shaggy and free from curl. Quality and texture of coat to be considered above mere profuseness. Softness or flatness of coat to be considered a fault. The undercoat should be a waterproof pile, when not removed by grooming or season.

Color—Any shade of grey, grizzle, blue or blue-merled with or without white markings or in reverse. Any shade of brown or fawn to be considered distinctly objectionable and not to be encouraged.

Size—Twenty-two inches and upwards for dogs and slightly less for bitches. A height of 26 inches or over for dogs or bitches to be considered objectionable and not to be encouraged. Type, character and symmetry are of the greatest importance and are on no account to be sacrificed to size alone.

General Appearance and Characteristics—A strong, compact-looking dog of great symmetry, practically the same in measurement from shoulder to stern as in height, absolutely free from legginess or weaseluess, very elastic in his gallop, but in walking or trotting he has a characteristic ambling or pacing movement, and his bark should be loud, with a peculiar "pot-casse" ring in it. Taking him all round, he is a profusely, but not excessively coated, thick-set, muscular, able-bodied dog with a most intelligent expression, free from all Poodle or Deerhound character. *Soundness should be considered of greatest importance.*

SCALE OF POINTS

	Points
Skull	5
Eyes	5
Ears	5
Teeth	5
Nose	5
Jaw	5
Foreface	5
Neck and shoulders	5
Body and loins	10
Hindquarters	10
Legs	10
Coat (texture, quality and condition)	15
General appearance and movement	15
Total	100

Champion Princess Woodsmoke.

THE PULI

This is the third in the triumverate of Hungarian sheep dogs and is closely allied in geneology to both the Komondor and Kuvasz of his native heath. All stem from the Tibetan Mastiff and through the Aftscharka, a breed found by the Huns on the Russian Steppes. When the Magyars came to Hungary they brought their dogs with them and representatives of the three known Hungarian sheepherding breeds were among them. The one that resembled the Puli was smaller than the other two and there is a school of thought that claims this smaller progenitor of the Pulik (plural form of *Puli*) was genetically closely tied to the ancient Tibetan Terrier.

The Puli is a sheep herder and driver and was selected as a breed for its dark coloration so that it would stand out strongly amongst the sheep. It is a solid colored breed and the black colored specimens show red tints dulling the black. This indicates that the dog is a worker, spending long hours in the bleaching sun and in all kinds of weather. The breed can also sport either a gray or a white coat. The coat is unique, unkempt and often corded in its native country. When brought into the home and thoroughly groomed the coat is wavy and rather Poodle-like.

Pulik make fine guards and companions. Vigorous, hardy and intelligent, they fit into either the home or the hills. In America, tested by the U.S. Department of Agriculture for their sheepherding proclivity, the breed received very favorable notices and they have been tried with success by American sheepmen. It is also claimed that the Puli is a water dog and can be successfully used in duck hunting. The author has found nothing to credit or discredit the breed in this area.

STANDARD OF THE PULI

General Appearance—A dog of medium size, vigorous, alert, and extremely active. By nature affectionate, he is a devoted and home-loving companion, sensibly suspicious of strangers and therefore an excellent guard. Striking and highly characteristic is the shaggy coat which centuries ago fitted him for the strenuous work of herding the flocks on the plains of Hungary.

Champion Cedwood's Jancsi

Head—Of medium size, in proportion to the body. The skull is slightly domed and not too broad. Stop clearly defined but not abrupt, neither dished nor downfaced, with a strong muzzle of medium length ending in a nose of good size. Teeth are strong and comparatively large, and the bite may be either level or scissors. Flews tight.

Ears—Hanging and set fairly high, medium size, and V-shaped.

Eyes—Deep-set and rather large, should be dark brown, but lighter color is not a serious fault.

Neck and Shoulders—Neck strong and muscular, of medium length, and free of throatiness. Shoulders clean-cut and sloping, with elbows close.

Body—The chest is deep and fairly broad with ribs well sprung. Back of

438

medium length, straight and level, the rump sloping moderately. Fairly broad across the loins and well tucked up.

Tail—Occasionally born bobtail, which is acceptable, but never cut. The tail is carried curled over the back when alert, carried low with the end curled up when at rest.

Legs and Feet—Forelegs straight, strong, and well boned. Feet round and compact with thick-cushioned pads and strong nails. Hindquarters well developed, moderately broad through the stifle which is well bent and muscular. Dewclaws, if any, may be removed from both forelegs and hind legs.

Coat—Characteristic of the breed is the dense, weather-resisting double coat. The outer coat, long and of medium texture, is never silky. It may be straight, wavy, or slightly curly, the more curly coat appearing to be somewhat shorter. The undercoat is soft, woolly, and dense. The coat mats easily, the hair tending to cling together in bunches, giving a somewhat corded appearance even when groomed. The hair is profuse on the head, ears, face, stifles, and tail, and the feet are well haired between the toes. Usually shown combed,

A trio of Pulik.

but may also be shown uncombed with the coat hanging in tight even cords.

Color—Solid colors, black, rusty-black, various shades of gray, and white. The black usually appears weathered and rusty or slightly gray. The intermixture of hair of different colors is acceptable and is usually present in the grays, but must be uniform throughout the coat so that the over-all appearance of a solid color is maintained. Nose, flews, and eyelids are black.

Height—Males, about 17 inches, and should not exceed 19 inches. Females, about 16 inches, and should not exceed 18 inches.

Serious Faults—Overshot or undershot. Lack of undercoat, short or sparse coat. White markings such as white paws or spot on chest. Flesh color on nose, flews, or eyelids. Coat with areas of two or more colors at the skin.

THE ROTTWEILER

Here is a breed of ancient lineage which came to Germany with the Roman armies when they stalked down into Central Europe, conquerors with clanking arms, huge armies raising the dust for miles in their might. With them, to feed their hungry hordes, came the herds of sheep and cattle, and with the herds came the dogs to watch and guard and drive this monstrous, living, moving army cafeteria. One of these breeds was the Rottweiler, a drover and Roman camp dog.

The breed as we know it today was developed in the township of Rottweil, a town of butchers and cattle buyers in Germany from which the animal takes its name. He is a superb cattle dog, guard and draft dog. But, when cattle driving became illegal in Germany some 65 years ago and cattle were shipped by rail, the breed declined in popularity. Then, about 1910, the breed was tried on police work and found to be more than adequate in this area. It joined the German Shepherd Dog, Airedale, and the breed that is descended from the Rottweiler (at least in part), the Doberman Pinscher, as the only four breeds completely fitted for police work.

As a breed, the Rottweiler is intelligent, sturdy, courageous and self-reliant. They make excellent, faithful, house and guard dogs.

The Rottweiler was granted A.K.C. recognition in 1935. He has never attained the Doberman's popularity heights, lacking that breed's slick trimness. However, he has dignity and substance and an air of solidity and dependability.

Other colors will occasionally appear in Rottweiler litters, such as blues, tans, mouse colors, etc. The standard indicates that such animals are not pure-bred. The author must differ with this assumption. These colors are the result of the joining of recessives for dilution that must be carried by both the sire and dam to become visible. Long coats are also the result of recessives carried in the germ plasm from some ancient ancestors.

STANDARD OF THE ROTTWEILER

General Appearance and Character—The Rottweiler is a good sized strongly built active dog. He is affectionate, intelligent, easily trained to work, naturally obedient and extremely faithful. While not quarrelsome, he possesses great courage and makes a splendid guard. His demeanor is dignified and he is not excitable.

Head—Is of medium length, the skull broad between the ears. Stop well pronounced as is also the occiput. Muzzle is not very long. It should not be longer than the distance from the stop to the occiput. Nose is well developed, with relatively large nostrils and is always black. Flews which should not be too pronounced are also black. Jaws should be strong and muscular; teeth strong—incisors of lower jaw must touch the inner surface of the upper incisors. Eyes are of medium size, dark brown in color and should express faithfulness, good humor and confidence. The ears are comparatively small, set high and wide and hang over about on a level with top of head. The skin on head should not be loose. The neck should be of fair length, strong, round and very muscular, slightly arched and free from throatiness.

Forequarters—Shoulders should be well placed, long and sloping, elbows

A known and useful breed when the rhythmic and menacing tread of the Roman Legions shook the ground of the known world, the Rottweiler has endured for all these centuries. His beauty is measured in strength and utilitarian value.

441

Rottweiler puppies at eight weeks of age.

well let down, but not loose. Legs muscular and with plenty of bone and substance, pasterns straight and strong. Feet strong, round and close, with toes well arched. Soles very hard, toe nails dark, short and strong.

Body—The chest is roomy, broad and deep. Ribs well sprung. Back straight, strong and rather short. Loins strong and deep, and flanks should not be tucked up. Croup short, broad, but not sloping.

Hindquarters—Upper thigh is short, broad and very muscular. Lower thigh very muscular at top and strong and sinewy at the bottom. Stifles fairly well bent, hocks strong. The hind-feet are somewhat longer than the front ones, but should be close and strong with toes well arched. There should be no dew-claws. Tail should be short, placed high (on level with back) and carried horizontally. Dogs are frequently born with a short stump tail and when tail is too long it must be docked close to body.

Coat—Hair should be short, coarse and flat. The under coat which is absolutely required on neck and thighs should not show through outer coat. The hair should be a little longer on the back of front and hindlegs and on tail.

Color—Black, with clearly defined markings on cheeks, muzzle, chest and legs, as well as over both eyes. Color of markings: Tan to mahogany brown. A small spot of white on chest and belly is permissible but not desirable.

Height—Shoulder height for males is 23¾ to 27 inches, for females 21¾ to 25¾ inches, but height should always be considered in relation to the general appearance and conformation of the dog.

Faults—Too lightly built or too heavily built, sway back, roach back, too long body, lack of spring of ribs. Head too long and narrow or too short and plump. Lack of occiput, snipy muzzle, cheekiness, top line of muzzle not straight, light or flesh colored nose, hanging flews, overshot or undershot, loose skin on head, ears set too low, or ears too heavy, long or narrow or rose ear, or ears uneven in size. Light, small or slanting eyes, or lack of expression, neck too long, thin or weak, or very noticeable throatiness. Lack of bone and muscle, short or straight shoulders, frontlegs too close together or not straight, weak pasterns, splay feet, light nails, weak toes. Flat ribs, sloping croup. Too heavy or plump body. Flanks drawn up. Flat thighs, cowhocks or weak hocks, dew-claws. Tail set too high or too low or that it is too long or too thin. Soft, too short, too long or too open coat, wavy coat or lack of undercoat. White markings on toes, legs, or other parts of body, markings not well defined or smudgy. The one-color tan Rottweiler with either black or light mask or with black streak on back as well as other colors such as brown or blue are not recognized and are believed to be cross bred, as is also a long-haired Rottweiler. Timid or stupid appearing animals are to be positively rejected.

Champion Baron of Rodsden

Champion Andy Boy De Line Farm (shorthaired)

THE ST. BERNARD

Powerful, huge, with a head seemingly containing all the world's dignity and understanding, the St. Bernard, habitat the Swiss Alps, developed from breeds of the heavy "*Molossis*" type (name is from the ancient Grecian City), were brought to Switzerland by invasion. Initially the early breed that was the part progenitor of the St. Bernard was brought by the German conquerors from Asia. Then, through the Talhund, early Great Pyrenees, and back to the Tibetan Mastiff (the familiar geneological background for all breeds of the large, heavy Mastiff type), the St. Bernard as a separate breed was formed.

Their service to mankind is unique and unequaled. In the early 18th century these huge dogs were a part of the Hospice in the Swiss Alps founded by St. Bernard de Menthon. They were trained to find and to help rescue unfortunate people caught in the frequent avalanches of what is now known as St. Bernard pass. From the Hospice that gave them identity and immortality, the breed took its name. One such St. Bernard, Barry, saved the lives of 40 travelers lost in the snow, until he was mistakenly killed by one frightened storm victim who thought the dog was a wolf about to attack him. The dogs were sent out in packs of three or four following storms or avalanches. When a victim was found, two of the dogs would lie on each side of him to bring him warmth, while a third would lick his face to bring him back to consciousness.

The fourth dog would go back to the Hospice to bring help or, in case of an avalanche, bark and find the nearest monk.

Because of Barry's fame the breed was first called "Barry Hounds" (incidentally, Barry was mounted after death and is in the Berne museum). It wasn't until 1865 that the name St. Bernard was adopted, borrowed from the writings of Daniel Wilson who referred to the breed by that name.

The dogs had been of the smooth coated variety initially, but due to losses in storms, particularly two specific seasons of terrible weather, and then a definite weakening of the breed through inbreeding that perpetuated unwanted faults, a change in coat to the long-haired variety occurred through the introduction of Newfoundland blood (1830). This did not destroy the St. Bernard type but did bring new and needed vigor to the breed.

In 1887, at the International Congress in Zurich, a standard for the breed was promulgated. The following year a breed club was organized in America, the oldest breed club in the United States.

STANDARD OF THE ST. BERNARD

SHORTHAIRED

General—Powerful, proportionately tall figure, strong and muscular in every part, with powerful head and most intelligent expression. In dogs with a dark mask the expression appears more stern, but never ill-natured.

Head—Like the whole body, very powerful and imposing. The massive skull is wide, slightly arched and the sides slope in a gentle curve into the very strongly developed, high cheek bones. Occiput only moderately developed.

Champion Danny v. Regensberg (longhaired)

The supra-orbital ridge is very strongly developed and forms nearly a right angle with the horizontal axis of the head. Deeply imbedded between the eyes and starting at the root of the muzzle, a furrow runs over the whole skull. It is strongly marked in the first half, gradually disappearing toward the base of the occiput. The lines at the sides of the head diverge considerably from the outer corner of the eyes toward the back of the head. The skin of the forehead, above the eyes, forms rather noticeable wrinkles, more or less pronounced, which converge toward the furrow. Especially when the dog is in action, the wrinkles are more visible without in the least giving the impression of morosity. Too strongly developed wrinkles are not desired. The slope from the skull to the muzzle is sudden and rather steep.

The muzzle is short, does not taper, and the vertical depth at the root of the muzzle must be greater than the length of the muzzle. The bridge of the muzzle is not arched, but straight; in some dogs, occasionally, slightly broken. A rather wide, well-marked, shallow furrow runs from the root of the muzzle over the entire bridge of the muzzle to the nose. The flews of the upper jaw are strongly developed, not sharply cut, but turning in a beautiful curve into the lower edge, and slightly overhanging. The flews of the lower jaw must not be deeply pendant. The teeth should be sound and strong and should meet in either a scissors or an even bite; the scissors bite being preferable. The undershot bite, although sometimes found with good specimens, is not desirable. The overshot bite is a fault. A black roof to the mouth is desirable.

Nose—Very substantial, broad, with wide open nostrils and, like the lips, always black.

Ears—Of medium size, rather high set, with very strongly developed burr (Muschel) at the base. They stand slightly away from the head at the base, then drop with a sharp bend to the side and cling to the head without a turn. The flap is tender and forms a rounded triangle, slightly elongated toward the point, the front edge lying firmly to the head, especially when the dog is at attention. Lightly set ears, which at the base immediately cling to the head, give it an oval and too little marked exterior, whereas a strongly developed base gives the skull a squarer, broader and much more expressive appearance.

Eyes—Set more to the front than the sides, are of medium size, dark brown, with intelligent expression, set moderately deep. The lower eyelids, as a rule, do not close completely and, if that is the case, form an angular wrinkle toward the inner corner of the eye. Eyelids which are too deeply pendant and show conspicuously the lachrymal glands, or a very red, thick haw, and eyes that are too light, are objectionable.

Neck—Set high, very strong and in action is carried erect. Otherwise horizontally or slightly downward. The junction of head and neck is distinctly marked by an indentation. The nape of the neck is very muscular and rounded at the sides which makes the neck appear rather short. The dewlap of throat and neck is well-pronounced: too strong development, however, is not desirable.

Shoulders—Sloping and broad, very muscular and powerful. The withers are strongly pronounced.

Chest—Very well arched, moderately deep, not reaching below the elbows.

Back—Very broad, perfectly straight as far as the haunches, from there gently sloping to the rump, and merging imperceptibly into the root of the tail.

Hindquarters—Well-developed. Legs very muscular.

446

A brace of fine, longhaired Saints.

Belly—Distinctly set off from the very powerful loin section, only little drawn up.

Tail—Starting broad and powerful directly from the rump is long, very heavy, ending in a powerful tip. In repose it hangs straight down, turning gently upward in the lower third only, which is not considered a fault. In a great many specimens the tail is carried with the edge slightly bent and therefore hangs down in the shape of an f. In action all dogs carry the tail more or less turned upward. However it may not be carried too erect or by any means rolled over the back. A slight curling of the tip is sooner admissible.

Forearms—Very powerful and extraordinarily muscular.

Forelegs—Straight, strong.

Hind Legs—Hocks of moderate angulation. Dewclaws are not desired; if present, they must not obstruct gait.

Feet—Broad, with strong toes, moderately closed, and with rather high knuckles. The so-called dewclaws which sometimes occur on the inside of the hind legs are imperfectly developed toes. They are of no use to the dog and are not taken into consideration in judging. They may be removed by surgery.

Coat—Very dense, short-haired (stockhaarig), lying smooth, tough, without however feeling rough to the touch. The thighs are slightly bushy. The tail at the root has longer and denser hair which gradually becomes shorter toward the tip. The tail appears bushy, not forming a flag.

Color—White with red or red with white, the red in its various shades; brindle patches with white markings. The colors red and brown-yellow are of entirely equal value. Necessary markings are: white chest, feet and tip of tail, nose band, collar or spot on the nape; the latter and blaze are very desirable. Never of one color or without white. Faulty are all other colors, except the favorite dark shadings on the head (mask) and ears. One distinguishes between mantle dogs and splash-coated dogs.

Height at Shoulder—Of the dog should be 27½ inches minimum, of the bitch, 25½ inches. Female animals are of finer and more delicate build.

Considered as faults are all deviations from the standard, as for instance a sway-back and a disproportionately long back, hocks too much bent, straight hindquarters, upward growing hair in spaces between the toes, out at elbows, cowhocks and weak pasterns.

A Saint Bernard sporting the traditional cask, such as the breed wore in their native Alps, filled with brandy to aid avalanche victims that the dogs found and rescued.

Champion Zwinghof Zwingli Zina v. Barri and puppies.

LONGHAIRED

The longhaired variety completely resembles the shorthaired variety except for the coat which is not shorthaired (stockhaarig) but of medium length, plain to slightly wavy, never rolled or curly and not shaggy either. Usually, on the back, especially from the region of the haunches to the rump, the hair is more wavy, a condition, by the way, that is slightly indicated in the shorthaired dogs. The tail is bushy with dense hair of moderate length. Rolled or curly hair on the tail is not desirable. A tail with parted hair, or a flag tail, is faulty. Face and ears are covered with short and soft hair; longer hair at the base of the ear is permissible. Forelegs only slightly feathered; thighs very bushy.

Champion Joli Knika

THE SAMOYED

Almost unchanged through the generations the Samoyed has come down to us from the ancient semi-nomadic Samoyed tribe of Siberia and the Arctic shores of Russia and Nova Zemba. The Samoyed dog was a necessary part of life for these primitives of the Sayantsi family, described as a race in the "transition stages between the Mongol pure and the Finn." The pure white dogs herded the reindeer of the tribe, were sled dogs and household companions of these people who roamed with their herds and families from the White Sea to the Yenisei River. Here, cut off from all contact with other humans or dogs, the Samoyed Dog was bred true, one of the early primitive breeds from which many of our other Spitz-type northern breeds descended.

This handsome, snowy-coated dog developed unique character and temperament due to its centuries of association with man. As a protector, a sled dog, a happy worker no matter what the task, if it is within the Samoyed's canine scope, the breed is outstanding.

The breed owes its establishment both in England and America to the efforts of Mr. and Mrs. E. Kilburn Scott, of Kent, England, who early saw the worth of the Samoyed. The late Queen Alexandra was also an ardent fancier of the breed.

Samoyeds, called the "Reindeer Dog" and the "Smiling Dog", were also used successfully by Arctic explorers and made splendid sled dogs of good temperament and carefree air. Their work in this area is an achievement scarcely equalled in the canine world. Like many another breed of the icy wastes of the Northern frontiers, the Samoyed has no "doggy" odor. Add to this a good natured disposition and even temperament and you will know why the breed is considered a pet par excellence.

STANDARD OF THE SAMOYED

General Conformation—(a) General Appearance—The Samoyed, being essentially a working dog, should present a picture of beauty, alertness and strength, with agility, dignity and grace. As his work lies in cold climates, his coat should be heavy and weather resistant, well groomed, and of good quality rather than quantity. The male carries more of a "ruff" than the female. He should not be long in the back as a weak back would make him practically useless for his legitimate work, but at the same time, a close-coupled body would also place him at a great disadvantage as a draft dog. Breeders should aim for the happy medium, a body not long but muscular, allowing liberty, with a deep chest and well-sprung ribs, strong neck, straight front and especially strong loins. Males should be masculine in appearance and deportment without unwarranted aggressiveness; bitches feminine without weakness of structure or apparent softness of temperament. Bitches may be slightly longer in back than males. They should both give the appearance of being capable of great endurance but be free from coarseness. Because of the depth of chest required, the legs should be moderately long. A very short-legged dog is to be deprecated. Hindquarters should be particularly well developed, stifles well bent and any suggestion of unsound stifles or cowhocks severely penalized. General appearance should include movement and general conformation, indicating balance and good substance.

(b) Substance—Substance is that sufficiency of bone and muscle which rounds out a balance with the frame. The bone is heavier than would be ex-

Nimrod of Snow Shoe Hill

pected in a dog of this size but not so massive as to prevent the speed and agility most desirable in a Samoyed. In all builds, bone should be in proportion to body size. The Samoyed should never be so heavy as to appear clumsy nor so light as to appear racy. The weight should be in proportion to the height.

(c) *Height*—Males, 21 to 23½ inches; females, 19 to 21 inches at the withers. An oversized or undersized Samoyed is to be penalized according to the extent of the deviation.

(d) *Coat (Texture and Condition)*—The Samoyed is a double-coated dog. The body should be well-covered with an undercoat of soft, short, thick, close wool with longer and harsh hair growing through it to form the outer coat, which stands straight out from the body and should be free from curl. The coat should form a ruff around the neck and shoulders, framing the head (more on males than on females). Quality of coat should be weather resistant and considered more than quantity. A droopy coat is undesirable. The coat should glisten with a silver sheen. The female does not usually carry as long a coat as most males and it is softer in texture.

(e) *Color*—Samoyeds should be pure white, white and biscuit, cream, or all biscuit. Any other colors disqualify.

Movement—(a) *Gait*—The Samoyed should trot, not pace. He should move with a quick agile stride that is well timed. The gait should be free, balanced and vigorous, with good reach in the forequarters and good driving power in the hindquarters. When trotting, there should be a strong rear action drive. Moving at a slow walk or trot, they will not single track, but as speed increases the legs gradually angle inward until the pads are finally falling on a line directly under the longitudinal center of the body. As the pad marks converge the forelegs and hind legs are carried straight forward in traveling, the stifles not turned in nor out. The back should remain strong, firm and level. A choppy or stilted gait should be penalized.

(b) *Rear End*—Upper thighs should be well developed. Stifles well bent— approximately 45 degrees to the ground. Hocks should be well developed, sharply defined and set at approximately 30 per cent of hip height. The hind legs should be parallel when viewed from the rear in a natural stance, strong, well developed, turning neither in nor out. Straight stifles are objectionable. Double jointedness or cowhocks are a fault. Cowhocks should only be determined if the dog has had an opportunity to move properly.

(c) *Front End*—Legs should be parallel and straight to the pasterns. The pasterns should be strong, sturdy and straight, but flexible with some spring for proper let-down of feet. Because of depth of chest, legs should be moderately long. Length of leg from the ground to the elbow should be approximately 55 per cent of the total height at the withers—a very short-legged dog is to be deprecated. Shoulders should be long and sloping, with a lay-back of 45 degrees and be firmly set. Out at the shoulders or out at the elbow should be penalized. The withers separation should be approximately 1-1½ inches.

(d) *Feet*—Large, long, flattish—a hare-foot, slightly spread but not splayed; toes arched; pads thick and tough, with protective growth of hair between the toes. Feet should turn neither in nor out in a natural stance but may turn in slightly in the act of pulling. Turning out, pigeon-toed, round or cat-footed or splayed are faults. Feathers on feet are not too essential but are more profuse on females than on males.

Head—(a) *Conformation*—Skull is wedge-shaped, broad, slightly crowned,

Champion Winterland's Kim

A German-bred Samoyed with a magnificent coat.

not round or apple-headed, and should form an equilateral triangle on lines between the inner base of the ears and the center point of the stop.

Muzzle—Muzzle of medium length and medium width, neither coarse nor snipy; should taper toward the nose and be in proportion to the size of the dog and the width of skull. The muzzle must have depth.

Stop—Not too abrupt, nevertheless well defined.

Lips—Should be black for preference and slightly curved up at the corners of the mouth, giving the "Samoyed smile." Lip lines should not have the appearance of being coarse nor should the flews drop predominantly at corners of the mouth.

Ears—Strong and thick, erect, triangular and slightly rounded at the tips; should not be large or pointed, nor should they be small and "bear-eared." Ears should conform to head size and the size of the dog; they should be set well apart but be within the border of the outer edge of the head; they should be mobile and well covered inside with hair; hair full and stand-off before the ears. Length of ear should be the same measurement as the distance from inner base of ear to outer corner of eye.

Eyes—Should be dark for preference; should be placed well apart and deep-set; almond shaped with lower lid slanting toward an imaginary point approximating the base of ears. Dark eye rims for preference. Round or protruding eyes penalized. Blues eyes disqualifying.

Nose—Black for preference but brown, liver, or dudley nose not penalized. Color of nose sometimes changes with age and weather.

Jaws and Teeth—Strong, well set teeth, snugly overlapping with scissors bite. Undershot or overshot should be penalized.

(*b*) *Expression*—The expression, referred to as "Samoyed expression," is

The Samoyed is kin to all the other Arctic breeds of dogs. This photo shows a team doing the work for which they were originally bred.

very important and is indicated by sparkle of the eyes, animation and lighting up of the face when alert or intent on anything. Expression is made up of a combination of eyes, ears and mouth. The ears should be erect when alert; the mouth should be slightly curved up at the corners to form the "Samoyed smile."

Torso—(*a*) *Neck*—Strong, well muscled, carried proudly erect, set on sloping shoulders to carry head with dignity when at attention. Neck should blend into shoulders with a graceful arch.

(*b*) *Chest*—Should be deep, with ribs well sprung out from the spine and flattened at the sides to allow proper movement of the shoulders and freedom for the front legs. Should not be barrel-chested. Perfect depth of chest approximates the point of elbows, and the deepest part of the chest should be back of the forelegs—near the ninth rib. Heart and lung room are secured more by body depth than width.

(*c*) *Loin and Back*—The withers forms the highest part of the back. Loins strong and slightly arched. The back should be straight to the loin, medium in length, very muscular and neither long nor short-coupled. The dog should be "just off square"—the length being approximately 5 per cent more than the height. Females allowed to be slightly longer than males. The belly should be well shaped and tightly muscled and, with the rear of the thorax, should swing up in a pleasing curve (tuck up). Croup must be full, slightly sloping, and must continue imperceptibly to the tail root.

Tail—The tail should be moderately long with the tail bone terminating approximately at the hock when down. It should be profusely covered with long hair and carried forward over the back or side when alert, but sometimes dropped when at rest. It should not be high or low set and should be mobile and loose—not tight over the back. A double hook is a fault. A judge should see the tail over the back once when judging.

Disposition—Intelligent, gentle, loyal, adaptable, alert, full of action, eager to serve, friendly but conservative, not distrustful or shy, not overly aggressive. Unprovoked aggressiveness to be severely penalized.

SCALE OF POINTS

General appearance	20
Head	15
Coat	10
Size	10
Chest and ribs	10
Hindquarters	10
Back	10
Feet	5
Legs	5
Tail	5
Total	100

DISQUALIFICATIONS

Any color other than pure white, cream, biscuit, or white and biscuit. Blue eyes.

THE SHETLAND SHEEPDOG

The Shetland Sheepdog is a miniature Collie and, up to 1914 in England, was known as the "Shetland Collie". The breed comes from the small Shetland Islands where most of the livestock is diminutive, including the Shetland Pony and small Shetland Sheep, the latter bred small because of scarce fodder and lack of space. It is entirely logical that to herd small sheep on a small island a small sheepdog should be used; thus the Shetland Sheepdog.

The breed is originally from the small, old Border Collie breed which was also behind the root-stock of the Collie. Probably some early native breeds were also crossed in to produce the Sheltie. In comparatively modern times, many breeds were introduced in an effort to fix type and size, including spaniels and later strong Collie blood. The goal is to produce a miniature Collie in coat, head and general type, but with slightly more bone, and the size, charm and character of the Sheltie.

The first club for the breed came into being on the Shetland Islands in 1908. A year later the Scottish club was formed. The English club was formed in 1914 and the youngest club is, of course, the American. Each club seemed to have wanted a slightly different type. As a result type has not been completely standardized but is very close to the wanted ideal.

STANDARD OF THE SHETLAND SHEEPDOG

Preamble—The Shetland Sheepdog, like the Collie, traces to the Border Collie of Scotland, which, transported to the Shetland Islands and crossed with small, intelligent, longhaired breeds, was reduced to miniature proportions. Subsequently crosses were made from time to time with Collies. This breed now bears the same relationship in size and general appearance to the Rough Collie as the Shetland Pony does to some of the larger breeds of horses. Although the resemblance between the Shetland Sheepdog and the Rough Collie is marked, there are differences which may be noted.

General Description—The Shetland Sheepdog is a small, alert, rough-coated, long-haired working dog. He must be sound, agile and sturdy. The outline should be so symmetrical that no part appears out of proportion to the whole. Dogs should appear masculine; bitches feminine.

Size—The Shetland Sheepdog should stand between 13 and 16 inches at the shoulder.

Note : Height is determined by a line perpendicular to the ground from the top of the shoulder blades, the dog standing naturally, with forelegs parallel to line of measurement. *Disqualification*—Heights below or above the desired size range are to be disqualified from the show ring.

Coat—The coat should be double, the outer coat consisting of long, straight, harsh hair; the undercoat short, furry, and so dense as to give the entire coat its "stand-off" quality. The hair on face, tips of ears and feet should be smooth. Mane and frill should be abundant, and particularly impressive in males. The forelegs well feathered, the hind legs heavily so, but smooth below the hock joint. Hair on tail profuse. *Note :* Excess hair on ears, feet, and on hocks may be trimmed for the show ring. *Faults*—Coat short or flat, in whole or in part; wavy, curly, soft or silky. Lack of undercoat. Smooth-coated specimens.

Color—Black, blue merle, and sable (ranging from golden through mahogany); marked with varying amounts of white and/or tan. *Faults*—Rustiness in a black or a blue coat. Washed out or degenerate colors, such as pale sable and faded blue. Self-color in the case of blue merle, that is, without any merling or mottling and generally appearing as a faded or dilute tricolor. Conspicuous white body spots. Specimens with more than 50% white shall be so severely penalized as to effectively eliminate them from competition. *Disqualification*—Brindle.

Temperament—The Shetland Sheepdog is intensely loyal, affectionate, and responsive to his owner. However, he may be reserved toward strangers but not to the point of showing fear or cringing in the ring. *Faults*—Shyness, timidity, or nervousness. Stubbornness, snappiness, or ill temper.

Head—The head should be refined and its shape, when viewed from top or side, be a long, blunt wedge tapering slightly from ears to nose, which must be black.

Skull and Muzzle—Top of skull should be flat, showing no prominence at nuchal crest (the top of the occiput). Cheeks should be flat and should merge smoothly into a well-rounded muzzle. Skull and muzzle should be of equal length, balance point being inner corner of eye. In profile the top line of skull should parallel the top line of muzzle, but on a higher plane due to the presence of a slight but definite stop. Jaws clean and powerful. The deep, well-developed underjaw, rounded at chin, should extend to base of nostril. Lips tight. Upper and lower lips must meet and fit smoothly together all the way around. Teeth level and evenly spaced. Scissors bite. *Faults*—Two-angled head. Too prominent stop, or no stop. Overfill below, between or above eyes. Prominent nuchal crest. Domed skull. Prominent cheekbones. Snipy muzzle. short, receding, or shallow under-jaw, lacking breadth and depth. Overshot or undershot, missing or crooked teeth. Teeth visible when mouth is closed.

Eyes—Medium size with dark, almond-shaped rims, set somewhat obliquely in skull. Color must be dark, with blue or merle eyes permissible in blue merles only. *Faults*—Light, round, large or too small. Prominent haws.

Ears—Small and flexible, placed high, carried three-fourths erect, with tips breaking forward. When in repose the ears fold lengthwise and are thrown back into the frill. *Faults*—Set too low. Hound, prick, bat, twisted ears. Leather too thick or too thin.

Expression—Contours and chiseling of the head, the shape, set and use of ears, the placement, shape and color of the eyes, combine to produce expression. Normally the expression should be alert, gentle, intelligent and questioning. Toward strangers the eyes should show watchfulness and reserve, but no fear.

Neck—Neck should be muscular, arched, and of sufficient length to carry the head proudly. *Faults*—Too short and thick.

Body—In over-all appearance the body should appear moderately long as measured from the shoulder joint to ischium (rearmost extremity of the pelvic bone), but much of this length is actually due to the proper angulation and breadth of the shoulder and hindquarter, as the back itself should be comparatively short. Back should be level and strongly muscled. Chest should be deep, the brisket reaching to point of elbow. The ribs should be well sprung, but flattened at their lower half to allow free play of the foreleg and shoulder. Abdomen moderately tucked up. *Faults*—Back too long, too short, swayed or roached. Barrel ribs. Slab side. Chest narrow and/or too shallow.

458

Forequarters—From the withers the shoulder blades should slope at a 45-degree angle forward and downward to the shoulder joints. At the withers they are separated only by the vertebra, but they must slope outward sufficiently to accommodate the desired spring of rib. The upper arm should join the shoulder blade at as nearly as possible a right angle. Elbow joint should be equidistant from the ground or from the withers. Forelegs straight viewed from all angles, musuclar and clean, and of strong bone. Pasterns very strong, sinewy and flexible. Dew-claws may be removed. *Faults*—Insufficient angulation between shoulder and upper arm. Upper arm too short. Lack of outward slope of shoulders. Loose shoulders. Turning in or out of elbows. Crooked legs. Light bone.

Feet (front and hind)—Feet should be oval and compact with the toes well arched and fitting tightly together. Pads deep and tough, nails hard and strong. *Faults*—Feet turning in or out. Splay-feet. Hare-feet. Cat-feet.

Hindquarters—There should be a slight arch at the loins, and the croup should slope gradually to the rear. The hipbone (pelvis) should be set at a 30-degree angle to the spine. The thigh should be broad and muscular. The thighbone should be set into the pelvis at a right angle corresponding to the angle of the shoulder blade and upper arm. Stifle bones join the thighbone and should be distinctly angled at the stifle joint. The over-all length of the stifle should at least equal the length of the thighbone, and preferably should slightly exceed it. Hock joint should be clean-cut, angular, sinewy, with good bone and strong ligamentation. The hock (metatarsus) should be short and straight viewed from all angles. Dewclaws should be removed. Feet (see Forequarters). *Faults*—Croup higher than withers. Croup too straight or too steep. Narrow thighs. Cowhocks. Hocks turning out. Poorly defined hock joint. Feet (see Forequarters).

Tail—The tail should be sufficiently long so that when it is laid along the back edge of the hind legs the last vertebra will reach the hock joint. Carriage of tail at rest is straight down or in a slight upward curve. When the dog is alert the tail is normally lifted, but it should not be curved forward over the back. *Faults*—Too short. Twisted at end.

The charm of the lovely Shetland Sheepdog
is caught by the sensitive lens of the
camera in this delightful portrait of a
family of English Champions.

Gait—The trotting gait of the Shetland Sheepdog should denote effortless speed and smoothness. There should be no jerkiness, nor stiff, stilted, up-and-down movement. The drive should be from the rear, true and straight, dependent upon correct angulation, musculation, and ligamentation of the entire hindquarters, thus allowing the dog to reach well under his body with his hind foot and propel himself forward. Reach of stride of the foreleg is dependent upon correct angulation, musculation and ligamentation of the forequarters, together with correct width of chest and construction of rib cage. The foot should be lifted only enough to clear the ground as the leg swings forward. Viewed from the front, both forelegs and hind legs should move forward almost perpendicular to ground at the walk, slanting a little inward at a slow trot, until at a swift trot the feet are brought so far inward toward center line of body that the tracks left show two parallel lines of footprints actually touching a center line at their inner edges. There should be no crossing of the feet nor throwing of the weight from side to side (often erroneously admired as a "dancing gait" but permissible in young puppies). Lifting of front feet in hackneylike action, resulting in loss of speed and energy. Pacing gait.

SCALE OF POINTS

	Points	
General Appearance		
Symmetry	10	
Temperament	10	
Coat	5	
	—	25
Head		
Skull and stop	5	
Muzzle	5	
Eyes, ears and expression	10	
	—	20
Body		
Neck and back	5	
Chest, ribs and brisket	10	
Loin, croup and tail	5	
	—	20
Forequarters		
Shoulder	10	
Forelegs and feet	5	
	—	15
Hindquarters		
Hip, thigh and stifle	10	
Hocks and feet	5	
	—	15
Gait		
Gait—smoothness and lack of waste motion when trotting	5	
	—	5
Total		100

DISQUALIFICATIONS

Heights below or above the desired range, i.e. 13-16 inches. Brindle color.

Champion Stony River's Miss Aurora

THE SIBERIAN HUSKY

The Siberian Husky belongs to the family of Arctic sled dogs which also includes the Eskimo, Alaskan Malamute, and Samoyed. He is smaller and more refined in build and appearance than either the Alaskan Malamute or the Eskimo, and it is probable that, pound for pound, he is the toughest draft dog that lives.

The origin of the Siberian Husky is obscure, as with the other Arctic dogs. It is tied in with the origin of the Arctic peoples themselves, and this, too, is a mystery.

One theory—and this is held by Dr. Edward M. Weyer, Jr.—is that the Eskimo migrated from Siberia to Alaska, and from thence across the Arctic Circle to Greenland, at least 2,000 years ago. They took with them their dogs, the ancestors of the Malamute and the Eskimo.

Filling in behind the migrating Eskimos were the Chuchis, an Eskimo-like people who settled around the basin of the Kolyma River, and along the foothills of the Cherski Mountains. These people developed the dog which we call the Siberian Husky, but which might more properly be called the Siberian Chuchi.

It is impossible to distinguish this breed from other Arctic dogs in the accounts of early explorers. Baron Wrangell, and others, mention sled dogs,

Champion Markay's Aral's Bourbon

marveled at their endurance and their extraordinary ability to find a trail.

One account tells of relay stations in Siberia where it was possible to exchange sled dogs for the continuation of a journey. This would indicate that Arctic Siberia had an intricate transportation system, via dogs, many decades ago.

Among other distinctive features, it was reported that the dogs have no body odor: that they howl rather than bark: and they are gentle with humans.

In this latter respect, the Siberian Husky appears to have a better reputation than either the Malamute or the Eskimo. This could be from a difference in living habits. The Chuchis and the Samoyeds, that is, the Asiatic Arctic peoples, keep their dogs with them in their dwellings. But the North American Eskimos quite generally do not. The dogs live out in the snow and get only a very minimum of human companionship. This tends to make them wilder and more intractable than their Siberian cousins.*

The origin of the name "Husky" is rather unusual. It is said to have been a term given the Eskimos by the early North American explorers. In recent years, it has come to mean any northern dog which is used for sled work, whether or not he is pure-bred. The Siberian Husky is the only breed in which the term has become part of the proper name.

Shortly after 1900, Americans in Alaska began to hear fabulous accounts of a superior race of sled dogs lying about a thousand miles beyond Alaska, in Siberia. Several teams of these dogs, Siberian Huskies, made their appearance in Alaskan sled races in 1909 and 1910. Thereafter, great numbers of the dogs were imported. They have won nearly all the sled races since, where mere speed under mild weather and trail conditions were not the only factors.

Tales about the dogs and their prowess and gentleness began to reach the United States. By 1930, fair numbers of them were being brought into the country for breeding purposes. Because of this, and because of the remoteness of the original breeding stock, the breed has not suffered from mongrel crosses.

The breed's gentleness has helped him to increasing popularity, too, although it must be admitted he has suffered from suspicion engendered by the actions of other Arctic dogs. His smaller size and great beauty also have combined to make him more popular than other Arctic breeds, save only the Samoyed.

STANDARD OF THE SIBERIAN HUSKY

General Appearance and Conduct—The Siberian Husky is an alert, gracefully built, medium-sized dog, quick and light on his feet, and free and graceful in action. He has a strong, moderately compact body; a deep, strong chest; well-muscled shoulders and hindquarters; and straight, strong legs with medium bone. His coat is dense and very soft, and his brush tail is carried curved over his back when at attention, and trailing when in repose. His head presents a finely chiseled and often foxlike appearance, and his eyes have a keen and friendly expression. His characteristic gait is free, tireless, and almost effortless when free or on loose leash; but showing great strength when pulling; the trot is brisk and smooth, and quite fast. Bitches are smaller than dogs, averaging up to two inches shorter and ten pounds less in weight. Siberians

---

* *Author's note:* The Malamute also has been closely associated with man and is noted for its fine temperament.

range in build from moderately compact (but never "cobby") to moderately rangy; in all builds the bone must be medium, the back powerful (never slack from excessive length), and the shoulder height never exceeding 23½ inches. (Any ranginess is merely a matter of proportion, not of actual height.)

Head. 1. *Skull*—Of medium size in proportion to the body; width between ears medium to narrow, gradually tapering to eyes, and moderately rounded. Muzzle of medium length. Both skull and muzzle are finely chiseled. Lips dark and close-fitting; jaws and teeth strong, meeting with a scissors bite.

Faults—Head clumsy or heavy; muzzle bulky (like the Malamute's); skull too wide between ears; snipiness; coarseness.

2. *Ears*—Of medium size, erect, close-fitting, set high on head, and well covered with hair on the inside. There is an arch at the back of the ears. Ears are slightly taller than width at base, and moderately rounded at tips. When dog is at attention, ears are usually carried practically parallel on top of head, with inner edges quite close together at base.

Faults—Low-set ears; ears too large; "flat" ears; lop ears.

3. *Eyes*—Either brown or blue ("watch" or "China") in color, one blue and one brown eye permissible but not preferable; set only very slightly obliquely in skull. Eyes have a keen, friendly and foxlike expression; this expression is distinctly "interested," sometimes even mischievous.

Faults—Eyes set too obliquely (like a Malamute's).

4. *Nose*—Black for preference; brown allowed in occasional specimens of

Champion Markay's Bonfire and
Champion Markay's Aral's Bourbon.

Siberians in their native element.

reddish coloring; flesh-colored nose and eyerims allowed in white dogs. Some dogs, especially black-and-white ones have what is often termed, a "snow nose," or "smudge nose," i.e. a nose normally solid black, but acquiring a pink streak in winter. This is permissible, but not preferable.

Coat—The Siberian Husky has a thick, *soft*, double coat consisting of a soft, dense, downy under coat of fur next to the skin; and an outer coat of soft, smooth texture, giving a smooth, full-furred appearance and a clean-cut outline (in contrast to the harsh, coarse coat of the Alaskan Malamute or the bear-like Eskimo coat). The coat is usually medium in length; a longer coat is allowed, but the texture must remain the same in any length.

Faults—Any harshness (except while actually shedding); rough or shaggy appearance (like Samoyed, Malamute, or Eskimo); absence of under coat (except when shedding).

Tail—A well-furred brush carried over back in a sickle curve when running or at attention, and trailing out behind when working or in repose. Tail should not "snap" flat to back. Hair on tail is usually of medium length, varying somewhat with the length of the dog's coat.

Color—All colors and white are allowed, and all markings. The commonest colors are various shades of wolf and silver grays, tan (a light sable), and black with white points. A large variety of markings, especially head markings, is found in the Siberian, including many striking and unusual ones not found in any other breed. Frequently found are the cap-like, mask and spectacle markings.

Chest, Ribs and Shoulders—Chest should be deep and strong, but not too broad. Ribs should be well arched and deep. Shoulders well developed and powerful.

Faults—Chest too broad, like Malamute's; weak or flat chest; weak shoulders.

Back, Loins and Quarters—Back of medium length, not too long, nor cobby

A sled team of bench show champions. The wheel dogs are, Ch. Markay's Stardust and Ch. Markay's the Panda Prince. The point pair are Ch. Markay's Bonfire and Ch. Markay's Aral's Bourbon. The lead animal is Ch. Brandy's Star, C.D.

like the elkhound's and strongly developed. Loins well muscled and slightly arched, and should carry no excess weight or fat. Hindquarters powerful, and showing good angulation.

Faults—Weak or slack back; any weakness of hindquarters.

Legs—Straight and well muscled, with good bone (but *never* heavy bone like the Eskimo or Alaskan Malamute). Stifles well bent. Dewclaws occasionally appear on the hind legs. They are not a sign of impure breeding, but, as they interfere with the dog's work, they should be removed, preferably at birth.

Faults—Heavy bone; too-light bone; lack of proper angulation in hind legs.

Feet—Oblong in shape, and not so broad as the Eskimo's or Malamute's; well furred between pads which are tough and thickly cushioned; compact; neither too large (like the Malamute's) nor too small (like many "Samoyeds"). The Siberian's foot, like that of other true Arctic dogs, is a "snowshoe foot," i.e., it is somewhat webbed between the toes, like a retriever's foot. Good feet are very important, and therefore feet should always be examined in the ring.

Faults—Soft or splayed feet; feet too large or clumsy; feet too small or delicate.

Height—Dogs from, 21 to 23½ inches at the shoulder; bitches, from 20 to 22 inches.

Weight—Dogs, from 45 to 60 pounds; bitches, from 35 to 50 pounds.

Disqualification—Weight over 60 pounds in a male or over 50 in a female.

Summary—The most important and characteristic points in a Siberian Husky are *medium* size and bone, *soft* coat, *high-set* ears, freedom and ease of action, and good disposition. Any clumsy, heavy or unwieldly appearance or gait should be penalized.

In addition to the faults stated herein, obvious structural faults common to all breeds (such as cowhocks) are just as undesirable in a Siberian Husky as in any other breed, although not specifically mentioned in this standard.

STANDARD OF POINTS

	Points
General appearance and conduct	20
Head and ears	20
Body and shoulders	20
Legs and feet	15
Coat	15
Tail	10
Total	100

Champion Rick N' Pat's Royal Rogue, C.D.X.

Champion Stone Pine Nickel

THE STANDARD SCHNAUZER

The Standard Schnauzer is the medium sized dog of this triple-sized variety and, of the three, is the prototype animal. He is an old and basic breed in Germany, probably the result of crossings of German Pudel, the old Wire-haired Pinscher, and the German Wolf-Spitz.

When initially introduced to America he was classified as a terrier and made his first appearances in that group in the show ring here from 1899 to 1945. At the latter date he was transferred to the working group on the advice of authorities who contended that he was a working dog who, in the 15th century in Germany, served as a cattle tender, yard and guard dog, and occasionally a ratter.

Although removed from the terrier group the breed is a terrier in appearance, and in Germany are used as ratters, certainly one of the main occupations at which terriers excel. As a matter of fact, the German Schnauzer

German import, Champion Dixi von Hahlweg.

Clubs hold periodic ratting trials, occasionally in conjunction with conformation shows.

The Schnauzer makes an excellent obedience competitor as well as show dog and, in this country and England, is used mostly as a guard and companion.

A standard for the breed was written in 1880, a year after the breed's first appearance at a dog show in Hanover. The Schnauzer Club of America, organized in 1925, became the Standard Schnauzer Club of America in 1933.

STANDARD OF THE STANDARD SCHNAUZER

The Standard Schnauzer is a robust, sinewy, heavy-set dog of the terrier type, sturdily built, square in the proportion of body length to height, with good muscle and plenty of bone. His nature combines high spirited temperament with extreme reliability. His rugged build and dense, harsh coat are accentuated by arched eyebrows, bristly mustache and luxurious whiskers.

Height—At withers, from 18 to 20 inches for males, and from 17 to 19 inches for females. *Faults*—Animals under or over these measurements.

Head—Strong and rectangular, diminishing slightly from the ear to the eyes, and again to the tip of the nose. Total length about one-third the length of the back, measuring from the withers to the beginning of the tail.

Skull—Moderately broad between the ears, width not exceeding two-thirds the length. *Faults*—Too narrow or pronounced.

Forehead—Flat and unwrinkled.

Cheeks—Well muscled, but not too strongly developed. *Faults*—Protruding cheek bones.

Muzzle—Strong and in proportion to the skull ending in moderately blunt manner, with wiry whiskers accenting the rectangular shape of the head. *Faults*—Too long or too short, pointed or lacking whiskers; dish-faced or down-faced.

Nose—Powerful, black and full, with ridge running almost parallel to the extension of the forehead. Lips tight and not overlapping.

An excellent Standard.

Ears—Evenly shaped, set high and carried erect when cropped. If uncropped, they should be small and V-shaped, of moderate thickness and carried rather high and close to the head. *Faults*—low-set, houndy ears and badly cut ears.

Eyes—Medium size, dark brown, oval and turned forward. Vision should not be obstructed from the front or profile by too long an eyebrow. The brow should be arched and wiry. *Faults*—Too large, round, or protruding, light or yellow-ringed eyes.

Jaw—Level, powerful and square. *Faults*—Overhsot or undershot.

Teeth—Sound, strong and white, with canines meeting in scissors bite. *Faults*—Pointed or irregular.

Neck—Nape should be strong, slightly arched and set cleanly on the shoulders. Skin should be tight, fitting closely to the throat. *Faults*—Too short, thick, long and throaty.

Shoulders—Somewhat sloping, strongly muscled. *Faults*—Loose, straight or low shoulders, or steep-set front.

Chest—Moderately broad, with the breast-bone plainly discernible and reaching at least to the height of the elbows, extending slowly backwards. Belly well drawn up towards the back, but no tuck-up. *Faults*—Too broad or too narrow, shallow or false chest.

Back—Strong, stiff, straight and short, with a well developed short loin section, the ribs well sprung. Length of the back from the withers to the set-on of tail should approximate the height at withers. *Faults*—Too long, sunken or roached.

Forelegs—Straight and vertical when seen from all sides, with bone carried well down to the feet; elbows set close to body and pointing directly backward. *Faults*—Legs too high, low, thin, or weak; elbows turned out or in. Pasterns sunken or any weakness of joint, bone or muscular development.

Feet—Small and compact; round with thick pads, strong nails. Toes well arched and pointing straight ahead. *Faults*—Toed-in or toed-out and long or spreading feet.

Hindquarters—Strongly muscled, with thighs slanting and flat, never appearing overbuilt or higher than the shoulders. *Faults*—Hocks let down, cowhocks or any weakness of joint.

Body—Compact, strong, short coupled and substantial so as to permit great flexibility.

Tail—Set moderately high and carried erect. Cut down to two joints and should not be longer than two inches. *Faults*—Too steep, level or too long a croup.

Coat—Hard and wiry, standing up on the back and, when seen against the course of the hair, neither short nor lying flat. The outer coat should be harsh, the under coat soft. It should be trimmed only to accent the body outline and should not be more than an inch long except on the ears and skull. *Faults*—Soft, smooth, curly; too long or short; too closely trimmed, dyed or excessively powdered.

Color—Pepper and salt or similar equal mixtures, light or dark including pure black. *Faults*—Solid colors other than black, also very light or whitish, spotted or tiger colors. A small white spot on the breast is not a fault.

Action—The gait should be sound, strong, quick, free, true and level.

Disqualifications—Shy, savage or highly nervous dogs and dogs which are in excess of or less than the standard in height.

474

Champion Kentwood Rhydlyd (English Cardigan)

THE WELSH CORGIS—

CARDIGAN AND PEMBROKE

These two little dogs, Cardigan and Pembroke Welsh Corgis, are very similar in type and in their utilitarian purposes. Yet, upon closer scrutiny, many small differences can be seen between the two breeds. The most obvious difference is in the tail and ears; the Cardigan has a long tail, the Pembroke sports a stub; the Cardigan's ears are rounded at the tips, the Pembroke's are pointed. The Pembroke has straighter legs and a shorter, higher and more compact body than the Cardigan. They were both bred to be cattle dogs.

It is quite evident that both breeds must share some common ancestry and this comes through the Schipperke and the Wolf-Spitz breeding behind them and the old sheepherding breeds that go back to the Persian Sheepdog. Then, before the middle of the 19th century, the two Welsh Corgi breeds were crossed. Crosses were probably made even earlier but the herders and hillmen who owned these dogs kept no records. Crosses of the two breeds occur even now but the breed clubs, to keep each variety pure, have practically brought a stop to this practice.

Of these two Corgis, the Cardigan is considered to be the oldest and was one of the breeds owned and used as cattle dogs by the ancient Celts. The Cardigan's uses were many, from guardianship of the children to helping in the hunt. The Cardigan did not really herd cattle, he would drive and control their movements by nipping at their heels. This was the manner in which he was used when the Crown owned almost all the land but allowed the Welsh hillmen to graze their herds on the "common" land. When the Crown lands eventually were divided and sold to the crofters and fences appeared, the usefulness of the Corgi was over. The original Corgi, known as the Bronant (an ancient breed), was crossed with a breed known as the Brindle Herder, and then an infusion of Collie blood was added. The principle strains of modern Cardigan Corgis go back to those breedings.

The direct ancestors of the Pembroke Welsh Corgi were brought to England by Flemish Weavers who had been invited by Henry I of England to settle in Wales in 1077. The breed was admitted to English Kennel Club registry in 1928 and within a few years made its debut in this country.

The Cardigan received A.K.C. recognition in 1935 and a year after, the Pembroke was accepted. Both of these breeds make splendid, intelligent guardians and pets and their small size, combined with their other attributes, fit them admirably to the role of house dog.

STANDARD OF THE WELSH CORGI

(CARDIGAN)

Head—To be foxy in shape and appearance. Skull to be fairly wide between the ears and flat, tapering towards the eyes. Muzzle to measure about three inches in length (or in proportion to skull as 3 to 5) and to taper towards the snout. Nose to be rather pointed. Teeth—strong, level and sound.

Eyes—To be of medium size, but giving a sharp and watchful expression, preferably dark in color but clear. Silver eyes permissible in blue merles.

Ears—Proportionate to size of dog and prominent; preferably pointed at the tips; moderately wide at the base; carried erect and set about $3\frac{1}{2}$ inches apart and well back so that they can be laid flat along neck, sloping forward slightly when erect.

Neck—To be fairly long and without throatiness, fitting into well sloped and strong muscular shoulders.

Front—To be slightly bowed, with strong bone; Chest to be moderately broad with prominent breast bone.

Body—To be fairly long and strong, with deep brisket, well sprung ribs and clearly defined waist. Hindquarters to be strong with muscular thighs.

Feet—To be round and well-padded. Legs—short and strong (front forelegs slightly bowed or straight). Dew claws removed.

Tail—To be moderately long and set in line with body (not curled over back) and resembling that of a fox.

Coat—Short or medium, of hard texture. Any color except pure white. Other points being equal, preference to be given in following order: Red (sable, fawn or golden); brindle; black and tan; black and white; blue merles. (White markings are considered to enhance the general appearance.)

Height—To be as near as possible to 12 inches at shoulder.

Weight—Dogs, 18 to 25 pounds. Bitches, 15 to 22 pounds.

General Appearance and Expression—To be as foxy as possible; alertness essential, the body to measure about 34 to 36 inches from point of nose to tip of tail.

Faults—(Examples.) Over or under-shot mouth; high peaked occiput; prominent cheeks, low flat forehead; expressionless eyes, crooked forearms; splayed feet; tail curled over back; silky coat, etc., etc.

Champion Springdale Droednoeth (Cardigan)

STANDARD OF POINTS

	Points
Head	15
Eyes	5
Ears	10
Neck	5
Front	10
Body	10
Feet	10
Tail	5
Coat	10
Height	10
General appearance and expression	10
Total	100

STANDARD OF THE WELSH CORGI
(PEMBROKE)

General Appearance—Low-set, strong, sturdily built, alert and active, giving an impression of substance and stamina in a small space; outlook bold, expression intelligent and workmanlike. The movement should be free and active, elbows fitting closely to the sides, neither loose nor tied. Forelegs should move well forward, without too much lift, in unison with thrusting action of hind legs.

Head and Skull—Head to be foxy in shape and appearance, with alert and intelligent expression, skull to be fairly wide and flat between the ears;

477

(Pembroke) Champion Bundock's Triumph de Rover Run, C.D.X.

(Pembroke) American and Bermudian Champion Zup of Cleden.

moderate amount of stop. Length of foreface to be in proportion to the skull as 3 is to 5. Muzzle slightly tapering. Nose black.

Eyes—Well set, medium size, hazel in color and blending with color of coat.

Ears—Pricked, medium-sized, slightly pointed. A line drawn from the tip of the nose through the eye should, if extended, pass through, or close to, the tip of the ear.

Mouth—Teeth level, or with the inner side of the upper front teeth resting closely on the front of the under ones.

Neck—Fairly long.

Forequarters—Legs short and as straight as possible. "Straight as possible" means straight as soundness and deep broad chest will permit. It does not mean terrier-straight. Ample bone carried right down to the feet. Elbows should fit closely to the sides, neither loose nor tied. Forearm should curve slightly round the chest.

English, Canadian; and American Champion Crawleycrow Pint (Pembroke).

Body—Of medium length, with well-sprung ribs. Not short-coupled or terrier-like. Level top line. Chest broad and deep, well let down between the forelegs.

Hindquarters—Strong and flexible, slightly tapering. Legs short. Ample bone carried right down to the feet. Hocks straight when viewed from behind.

Feet—Oval, the two center toes slightly in advance of two outer toes, pads strong and well arched. Nails short.

Tail—Short, preferably natural.

Coat—Of medium length and dense; not wiry.

Color—Self colors in red, sable, fawn, black and tan, or with white markings on legs, chest and neck. Some white on head and foreface is permissible.

Weight and Size—Dogs, 20 to 24 pounds; bitches, 18 to 22 pounds. Height, from 10 to 12 inches at shoulder.

GROUP IV

Terriers

The Terrier   The Cur Dog

THE Terriers, as their name suggests, go to earth for their prey. They are primarily used to rout out various small animals of vermin and "varmint" classification (including fox) from their lairs in the ground. The name, Terrier, therefore, is derived from the Latin "*terra*", or earth.

This group of dogs has always been composed of the rough-and-ready all-purpose breeds that were easy keepers, scrappy, bright-eyed, intelligent and with courage out of all proportion to their generally small size.

Practically all Terriers are of British origin and though they have been a definite type of canine, they were not given classification until comparatively recent years. This was due to the fact that during the reign of the Danish King Canute in England (1016–1035) Terriers were the only kind of dog working people or peasants were allowed to own. Noblemen and merchants had their breeds of hounds and spaniels and the dog, or dogs, which a person owned became a gauge of his position in the social strata of the age.

The working people didn't care about classifying or giving their game little Terriers specific breed names. All they wanted were vivacious, sturdy little rascals, as tough and scrappy as their owners. These characteristics are still very much a part of each individual breed in one of the most interesting groups in dogdom.

Later in the history of the Terrier breeds they came into the hands of gentlemen fox hunters and were carried in baskets on horseback following the hue and cry of the hunt and then released to dig out the fox when he went to ground.

So their station in life became more exalted and finally from the maze of rough and smooth-coated animals, roughly called Terriers, types and breeds evolved and came into focus. Just as the common people who owned and loved them have been called the "*salt of the earth*," so should these nervy rascals, known as Terriers, who, no matter how trimmed and slick they may have become, still retain the common touch, the down-to-earth characteristics and appeal they always had.

THE AIREDALE TERRIER

This, the largest of the terriers, is also one of the finest all-around breeds of canine developed by man. They are strong water dogs, good hunters, excellent guard and police dogs, useful as guides for the blind and fine war dogs. They excel as big game dogs in Africa, India, Canada and America. The author well remembers the old Oorang Kennels, advertising dogs up to 90 pounds for big game hunting, trained by Sac and Fox Indians under the direction of the great Indian Olympic athlete, Jim Thorpe.

The author's early contacts with the breed as a boy was an enriching experience. I remember the Airedale as a powerful, prideful animal who would step aside for no dog and could lick anything that walked for miles around. During a recent jaunt through Europe I was pleased to see many fine Airedales on the streets indicating from their numbers, the breed's popularity in France, Germany, Holland and even Spain.

Many terriers, specifically an old, extinct black and tan terrier popular in the valleys of the rivers Colne, Calder, Warte, and Aire, combined with the Otterhound, formed the original basis of the breed. Proof of the fine physical finish to which the Airedale was brought by master breeders can be found in the breed's consistent Best in Show wins both here and in England.

Champion Bengal Sabu (imported)

Rural Paladin's Son

Called by several names during its early forming into a breed (*the Working, the Waterside, and the Bingley Terrier*) it took the name by which it is known today after being shown in 1879 at the Bingley, Yorkshire, Airedale Agricultural Society Show.

The patriarch of the breed, Champion Master Briar (end of the 19th century) left prepotent sons who passed on his genetic qualities. In more modern (yet old enough to be called "foundation") breeding, we find Ch. Warland Ditto, the Cragsman King family and the animals of the Warland Kennels.

The Airedale is at its best as a house dog. Sweet in disposition, yet aloof with strangers, dependable and handsome, he makes the finest of companions.

STANDARD OF THE AIREDALE TERRIER

Head—Should be well balanced with little apparent difference between the length of skull and foreface.

Skull—Should be long and flat, not too broad between the ears and narrowing very slightly to the eyes. Scalp should be free from wrinkles, stop hardly visible and cheeks level and free from fullness.

Ears—Should be V-shaped with carriage rather to the side of the head, not pointing to the eyes, small but not out of proportion to the size of the dog. The top line of the folded ear should be above the level of the skull.

Foreface—Should be deep, powerful, strong and muscular. Should be well filled up before the eyes.

Eyes—Should be dark, small, not prominent, full of terrier expression, keenness and intelligence.

Lips—Should be tight.

Nose—Should be black and not too small.

Teeth—Should be strong and white, free from discoloration or defect. Bite either level or vise-like. A slightly overlapping or scissor bite is permissible without preference.

Neck—Should be of moderate length and thickness gradually widening towards the shoulders. Skin tight, not loose.

Shoulders and Chest—Shoulders long and sloping well into the back. Shoulder blades flat. From the front, chest deep but not broad. The depth of the chest should be approximately on a level with the elbows.

Body—Back should be short, strong and level. Ribs well sprung. Loins muscular and of good width. There should be but little space between the last rib and the hip-joint.

Hindquarters—Should be strong and muscular with no droop.

Tail—The root of the tail should be set well up on the back. It should be carried gaily but not curled over the back. It should be of good strength and substance and of fair length.

Legs—Forelegs—Should be perfectly straight, with plenty of muscle and bone.

Elbows—Should be perpendicular to the body, working free of sides.

Thighs—Should be long and powerful with muscular second thigh, stifles well bent, not turned either in or out, hocks well let down parallel with each other when viewed from behind.

Feet—Should be small, round and compact with a good depth of pad, well cushioned; the toes moderately arched, not turned either in or out.

Coat—Should be hard, dense and wiry, lying straight and close, covering the dog well over the body and legs. Some of the hardest are crinkling or just slightly waved. At the base of the hard very stiff hair should be a shorter growth of softer hair termed the undercoat.

Color—The head and ears should be tan, the ears being of a darker shade than the rest. Dark markings on either side of the skull are permissible. The legs up to the thighs and elbows and the under-part of the body and chest are also tan and the tan frequently runs into the shoulder. The sides and upper parts of the body should be black or dark grizzle. A red mixture is often found in the black and is not to be considered objectionable. A small white blaze on the chest is a characteristic of certain strains of the breed.

Size—Dogs should measure approximately 23 inches in height at the shoulder; bitches slightly less. Both sexes should be sturdy, well muscled and boned.

Movement—Movement of action is the crucial test of conformation. Movement should be free. As seen from the front the forelegs should swing perpendicular from the body free from the sides, the feet the same distance apart as the elbows. As seen from the rear the hind legs should be parallel with each other, neither too close nor too far apart, but so placed as to give a strong well-balanced stance and movement. The toes should not be turned either in or out.

Yellow eyes, hound ears, white feet, soft coat, being much over or under the size limit, being under-shot or over-shot, having poor movement, are faults which should be severely penalized.

The use of any and all foreign agents for the improvement of dogs in the Show Ring, such as coloring, dilating the pupil and stiffening the coat, is

Champion Querencia's Suerte
Brava

The largest of the Terrier clan, the Airedale has proven his worth in many fields of endeavor.

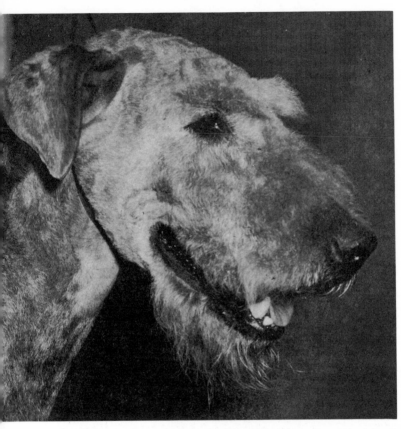

Note the length and strength of the Airedale's jaw.

forbidden under American Kennel Club rules. Such acts are unsportsmanlike and unfair to those exhibitors who live up to the rules.

SCALE OF POINTS

	Points
Head	10
Neck, shoulders and chest	10
Body	10
Hindquarters and Tail	10
Legs and feet	10
Coat	10
Color	5
Size	10
Movement	10
General characteristics and Expression	15
Total	100

THE AUSTRALIAN TERRIER

This is a breed of comparatively recent origin and comes from the land of the marsupials, one of the strangest animal groups known to man. But the Australian Terrier is no marsupial, he is, in fact, a welcome addition to the terrier family. Though one of the smallest of the terriers he has the family spirit and courage, deep affection for his human family, and is rather quiet (despite his terrier spirit) for one of his kind.

When first exhibited in its native land in 1885 at Melbourne, it was called the Australian Rough and was the product of the fusing of local terrier blood, mostly through a dog called, casually, the Broken-Hair or Rough-coated Terrier, with the addition of several terrier breeds of English origin. It was to improve the local Rough-coated breed so that it could compete against

A fine example of this newcomer to the Terrier group.

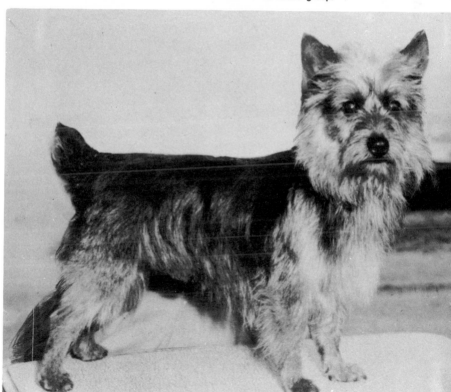

Champion Pleasantpastures Sir Sandy

imported Scotch Terriers that the breedings were made and during the process the Australian Terrier came into being.

The breed has done many jobs in Australia, from hunting snakes and small animals in the bush to guarding mines and tending sheep. Here in America this fine little animal can rest on its laurels and retire to the role of house dog and companion. The Australian Terrier was recognized by the A.K.C. in 1960. This bright-eyed little terrier has proven to be a top contender in obedience competition.

The author's son, Allan, judged this breed (and others) at dog shows in Australia while attending the University of Sydney, and reports that this little terrier is well liked in its native heath.

STANDARD OF THE AUSTRALIAN TERRIER

General Appearance—A small, sturdy, rough-coated terrier of spirited action and self-assured manner.

Head—Long, flat-skulled, and full between the eyes, with the stop moderate. The muzzle is no longer than the distance from the eyes to the occiput. Jaws long and powerful, teeth of good size meeting in a scissors bite, although a level bite is acceptable. Nose black.

Ears—Set high on the skull and well apart. They are small and pricked, the leather either pointed or slightly rounded and free from long hairs.

Eyes—Small, dark, and keen in expression; not prominent. Light-colored and protruding eyes are faulty.

Neck—Inclined to be long, and tapering into sloping shoulders; well furnished with hair which forms a protective ruff.

Body—Low-set and slightly longer from the withers to the root of the tail than from the withers to the ground.

Chest—Medium wide, and deep, with ribs well sprung but not round. Topline level.

Tail—Set on high and carried erect but not too gay; docked leaving 2/5.

Legs and Feet—Forelegs straight and slightly feathered to the carpus or so-called knee; they are set well under the body with elbows close and pasterns strong. Hindquarters strong and well-muscled but not heavy; legs moderately angulated at stifles and hocks, with hocks well let down. Bone medium in size. Feet are small, clean, and catlike, the toes arched and compact, nicely padded and free from long hair. Nails strong and black.

Coat—Outer coat harsh and straight, and about $2\frac{1}{2}$ inches all over the body. Under coat short and soft. The topknot, which covers only the top of the skull, is of finer texture and lighter color than the body hair.

Color—May be blue-black or silver-black, with rich tan markings on head and legs. The blue-black is bluish at the roots and dark at the tips. In the silver-blacks each hair carries black and silver alternating with black at the tips. The tan is rich and deep, the richer the better. Also, sandy color and clear red are permissible but not desirable, other things being equal, as the blue and tan. In the sandies, any suggestion of shading or smuttiness is undesirable.

Gait—Straight and true; sprightly, indicating spirit and assurance.

Temperament—That of a hard-bitten terrier, with the aggressiveness of the natural ratter and hedge hunter, but as a companion friendly, affectionate, and biddable.

Size—Shoulder height, about 10 inches. Average weight 12–14 pounds.

THE BEDLINGTON TERRIER

The Bedlington is one of the most deceptive of all breeds. The dog's lamb-like, quiet appearance masks the courage of a lion, steel-trap jaws, and fighting ability second to none. He is also a marvelous vermin dog.

The name of this breed is borrowed from its point of origin which is a mining shire in the County of Northumberland, England. He was first known as the Rothbury Terrier from the Hannys Hills. Produced by a happy interlocking of local terrier inheritance, the breed was adopted by a colony of nailers and miners in Bedlington, a rough and hearty group of men who took to the Bedlington because of its pluck and toughness.

In the hands of these men he had to constantly prove himself on all types of vermin and "varmints" and, in addition, he fought in the pit against his own kind as well as other terriers, while large sums were wagered on his stoutness and fighting ability. Not really a quarrelsome dog he would, once he had closed with an opponent, fight to the death. His appearance, carefully

Champion Berle's Amo Bon-Wink

Champion Barbeedon's Snowbird Fancy

cultivated for show purposes certainly, as mentioned above, masks the breed's true character.

It is claimed that the Bedlington never sheds and is therefore recommended as a house dog. He has many fine traits other than this one that makes him ideal in the home, namely, his intelligence, hardiness and wish to please. Few Bedlingtons could today face a badger, but, though more in the pet class, they still retain some of their old fire when aroused.

As a show dog this unique terrier has proven himself in the rings of England and America, taking many top wins. The breed came to our shores in the 19th century and has gained a popular following through the years.

STANDARD OF THE BEDLINGTON TERRIER

Skull—Narrow, but deep and rounded, high at the occiput, wedge-shaped, covered with profuse top-knot, which should be nearly white, and, when trimmed, should give a Roman nose appearance.

Jaws—Long and tapering. There must be no "stop" and the line from occiput to nose end straight and unbroken. Well filled up beneath the eye. Close fitting lips, no flew.

Teeth—Level or pincer-jawed. The teeth should be large and strong.

Nose—The nostrils must be large and well defined. Blues and blue and tans have black noses; livers, sandies, etc., have brown noses.

Eyes—Small, bright and well sunk. The ideal eyes have the appearance of being triangular. Blue should have a dark eye; blue and tans have light eyes with amber lights; liver and sandies have a light hazel eye.

Ears—Moderate sized, filbert shaped; set on low and hanging flat to the cheek. They should be covered with short, fine hair, with a fringe of silky hair at the tip.

Legs and Feet—Muscular and moderate length. The hindlegs, by reason of the roach back and arched loin, have the appearance of being longer than the forelegs. The forelegs should be straight, with a moderately wide chest and hare feet.

Body—Muscular, yet markedly flexible. Flat ribbed and deep through the brisket, well ribbed up. The chest should be deep and fairly broad. The back should be roached and the loin markedly arched. Light, muscular, galloping quarters, which are also fine and graceful.

Neck—Long, tapering arched neck, deep at the base. The neck should spring well from the shoulders, which should be flat, and head should be carried high.

Coat—The coat is very distinctive and unlike that of any other terrier, in that it should be thick and linty (not wiry), and when in show condition should not exceed one inch in length. It should be brushed on the body and back from the root of the tail toward the head, and should not lie flat against the body. There should be an absence of hair on the ears except at the tip, where the fringe should be from one-half to one inch long. The hair on the legs should be slightly longer and straighter than that of the body. The top-knot should be highest at the occiput and taper gradually to just in back of the nose. It (the top-knot) should be rounded from side to side from an imaginary line drawn from the outer corner of the eye to the top of the ear on one side to a like line on the opposite side.

Tail—Of moderate length, thick at the root, tapering to a point and gracefully curved, slightly feathered, 9 to 11 inches long, scimitar shaped, carried elevated but not over the back.

Color—Blue, blue and tan, liver, liver and tan, sandy, sandy and tan.

Height—About 15 or 16 inches.

Weight—Dogs, about 24 pounds; bitches, about 22 pounds.

Action—Very distinctive. Rather mincing, light and springy, must gallop like a greyhound, with the whole body.

General—A graceful, lithe but not shelly, muscular dog, with no sign of coarseness or weakness. The whole head should be pear-shaped or wedge-shaped. The expression in repose is mild and gentle. When roused, the eyes should sparkle, and the dog look full of temper and courage.

SCALE OF POINTS

	Points
Head	20
Size	10
Teeth	10
Color	5
Legs and feet	10
Ears	5
Eyes	5
Nose	5
Body	15
Coat	10
Tail	5
Total	100

Champion Braemar Rascal

Champion Alquina's Happy of Rowanoaks

THE BORDER TERRIER

History records that the inhabitants of Northumberland and its Scottish borders were at one time warlike. Civilization gaining ground brought with it law and order, the warlike instincts of the northerners then taking another shape. Sport, in many forms, took the place of raids and to indulge in sport hardy terriers were required. This change of life created two types of dogs— viz., the Border Terrier and the Dandie Dinmont Terrier. The latter leaped into fame when Sir Walter Scott published "Guy Mannering" and gave us "Dandie Dinmont of Charlieshope." He immortalized the Dandie and tells us how they were "regularly entered, first wi' rottens, then wi' stoats or weasels, and then wi' tods and brocks. They fear naething that ever cam' wi' hairy skin on 't!"

Some people hold that the Dandie Dinmont, having become an "exhibition dog," has lost some of its usefulness for sporting purposes. On the other hand, the Border Terrier is bred, by the Border shepherds and country gentlemen,

Cinjola Cha Cha Dancer and Ch. Conjola Buddy Boy Dauntless.

At the right is a photo of the winning Border Terrier, Champion Town Hill Troubador. Above we see a pair of these rugged and untouched little Terriers.

Champion Dalquest Dauntless.
Below, Champion Dalquest Gil-
lian.

496

Champion Koffee Lad.

Below is a head study of the champion, Dalquest Dare's Double.

for work and many hold that the Border Terrier is the *original* Dandie Dinmont. Not being recognized by the Kennel Club, the Border Terrier is rarely exhibited, although at many of the North-Country agricultural shows he is frequently to be seen.* Hexham, the annual venue of the Tyneside Agricultural show, is probably the chief show at which Borders are exhibited, where a generous classification for the real "Native" is always given. That the Border Terrier is a very old breed there is little doubt, and they are still bred on the Borders for bolting (not worrying) foxes. Many of the Fox and Otter Hound packs possess a Border Terrier for this particular purpose, a good Border Terrier will go to ground and face the most savage fox, otter or badger. They have been known to enter holes in rocks and be lost for days, sometimes returning with evidences on their heads and bodies of a bloody struggle. Sandy and Scamp, two Borders owned by Mr. J. T. Dodd, one of the best and oldest authorities on the breed, have been photographed after each dog had had a "go" at a very large otter. Both dogs were fearfully mauled, Sandy losing his nose whilst Scamp's cheek was bitten clean off. My own dog, the aptly named "Harry Hotspur"—a name to conjure with in Border warfare history—knows no fear. Fox, badger or otter are all alike to him.

The Border Terrier should have a good nose, and be able to go to "ground" where other breeds could not enter. Bad weather is nothing to them, wet and cold being all the same, for the breed's hardiness is one of its many assets. No day is too long. Veritable little demons, they live for sport and sport alone.

The Border Terrier is clean in his habits, very intelligent, affectionate and as a companion cannot be surpassed. Of late many fanciers in the south of England have "taken up" this game little Terrier.

* *Author's note :* The Border Terrier Club was formed in England in 1920, after recognition of the breed by the English Kennel Club. The breed in this country is becoming steadily more popular.

497

STANDARD OF THE BORDER TERRIER

Since the Border Terrier is a working terrier of a size to go to ground and able, within reason, to follow a horse, his conformation should be such that he be ideally built to do his job. No deviations from this ideal conformation should be permitted which would impair his usefulness in running his quarry to earth and in bolting it therefrom. For this work he must be alert, active and agile, and capable of squeezing through narrow apertures and rapidly traversing any kind of terrain. His head, "like that of an otter" is distinctive, and his temperament ideally exemplifies that of a terrier. By nature he is good-tempered, affectionate, obedient, and easily trained. In the field he is hard as nails, "game as they come" and driving in attack.

It should be the aim of the Border Terrier breeders to avoid such over-emphasis of any point in the Standard as might lead to unbalanced exaggeration.

General Appearance—He is an active terrier of medium bone, strongly put together, suggesting endurance and agility, but rather narrow in shoulder, body and quarter. The body is covered with a somewhat broken though close-fitting and intensely wiry jacket. The characteristic "otter" head with its keen eye, combined with a body poise which is "at the alert," gives a look of fearless and implacable determination characteristic of the breed. The proportions should be that the height at the withers should be slightly greater than the distance from the withers to the tail; i.e., by possibly 1–1½ inches in a 14 pound dog.

Weight—Dogs, 13–15½ pounds; bitches, 11½–14 pounds, are appropriate weights for Border Terriers in hard-working condition.

Head—Similar to that of an otter. Moderately broad and flat in skull with plenty of width between the eyes and between the ears. A slight, moderately broad curve at the stop rather than a pronounced indentation. Cheeks slightly full.

Ears—Small, V-shaped and of moderate thickness, dark preferred. Not set high on the head but somewhat on the side, and dropping forward close to the cheeks. They should not break above the level of the skull.

Eyes—Dark hazel and full of fire and intelligence. Moderate in size, neither prominent nor small and beady.

Muzzle—Short and "well-filled." A dark muzzle is characteristic and desirable. A few short whiskers are natural to the breed.

Teeth—Strong, with a scissor bite, large in proportion to size of dog.

Nose—Black, and of a good size.

Neck—Clean, muscular and only long enough to give a well balanced appearance. It should gradually widen into the shoulder.

Shoulders—Well laid back and of good length, the blades converging to the withers gradually from a brisket not excessively deep or narrow.

Forelegs—Straight and not too heavy in bone and placed slightly wider than in a Fox Terrier.

Feet—Small and compact. Toes should point forward and be moderately arched with thick pads.

Body—Deep, fairly narrow and of sufficient length to avoid any suggestion of lack of range and agility. Deep ribs carried well back and not oversprung in view of the desired depth and narrowness of the body. The body should be capable of being spanned by a man's hands behind the shoulders. Back strong

Irish Champion Dandyhow Becky Sharp of Ardcairn.

but laterally supple, with no suspicion of a dip behind the shoulder. Loin strong and the underline fairly straight.

Tail—Moderately short, thick at the base, then tapering. Not set on too high. Carried gaily when at the alert, but not over the back. When at ease, a Border may drop his stern.

Hindquarters—Muscular and racy, with thighs long and nicely moulded. Stifles well bent and hocks well let down.

Coat—A short and dense undercoat covered with a very wiry and somewhat broken top coat which should lie closely, but it must not show any tendency to curl or wave. With such a coat a Border should be able to be exhibited almost in his natural state, nothing more in the way of trimming being needed than a tidying-up of the head, neck and feet.

Hide—Very thick and loose fitting.

Movement—Straight and rhythmical before and behind, with good length of stride and flexing of stifle and hock. The dog should respond to his handler with a gait which is free, agile and quick.

Color—Red, grizzle and tan, blue and tan, or wheaten. A small amount of white may be allowed on the chest but white on the feet should be penalized.

SCALE OF POINTS

	Points
Head, ears, neck and teeth	20
Legs and feet	15
Coat and skin	10
Shoulders and chest	10
Eyes and expression	10
Back and loin	10
Hindquarters	10
Tail	5
General appearance	10
Total	100

THE BULL TERRIER

The Bull Terrier looks like a white torpedo—and can be just as dangerous to another dog, if the other dog dares to give him any lip. The breed was formed in a day when "gentlemen" liked a bit of blood with their sport and the Bull Terrier was fashioned to be a fighting dog. As a canine gladiator the Bull Terrier was bred and taught to fight to the death in the pit, where such contests took place, to defend himself and his master courageously, but never to seek or provoke violence for its own sake. For these reasons the breed became known as "*the White Cavalier*."

The tremendous strength, agility and courage of this breed is well known and inherited from his ancestors, the Bulldog and the now extinct white English Terrier. Later, to gain size, there was a cross to the Spanish Pointer.

The Bull Terrier was originally mostly brindle and white and the Colored Bull Terrier still exists and is shown as a separate variety (as of 1936). It was John Hinks of England, about 1860, who developed the all-white dog to meet the demands of the young sporting bucks of that day. The breed moved away from its pit fighting antecedents as it grew more finished in form, leaving a coarser type behind to continue in that savage sport. Thoroughly respectable finally, the white Bull Terrier's popularity was enhanced through the skillful

Ch. Loveland's Egyptian Princess and Ch. White Cavalier of Monty-Ayr.

The white and the colored varieties of the Bull Terrier. Both of these dogs are English champions. On the left is Ormandy's Mr. McGuffin. The colored dog is Romany Rough Weather.

pen of Richard Harding Davis in his well read, "*The Bar Sinister*", one of the best dog stories ever published.

Despite its early use, the Bull Terrier is a friendly animal, rather insensitive to pain and, pound for pound, one of the most powerful dogs on earth.

The author had the privilege of painting the portrait of Ernest Eberhard's famous bitch, Ch. Madame Pompadour of Ernicor, one of the truly great, modern Bull Terriers. She made a splendid model with her white satiny coat and strong musculature. Truly, such an animal would be like a juggernaut in a fight.

STANDARD OF THE BULL TERRIER
WHITE

The Bull Terrier must be strongly built, muscular, symmetrical and active, with a keen determined and intelligent expression, full of fire but of sweet disposition and amenable to discipline.

Head—Should be long, strong and deep right to the end of the muzzle, but not coarse. Full face it should be oval in outline and be filled completely up giving the impression of fullness with a surface devoid of hollows or indentations, i.e., egg-shaped. In profile it should curve gently downwards from the top of the skull to the tip of the nose. The forehead should be flat across from ear to ear. The distance from the tip of the nose to the eyes should be perceptibly greater than that from the eyes to the top of the skull. The underjaw should be deep and well defined. The lips should be clean and tight.

Teeth—Should meet in either a level or in a sissors bite. In the sissors bite the upper teeth should fit in front of and closely against the lower teeth, and they should be sound, strong and perfectly regular.

Ears—Should be small, thin and placed close together. They should be capable of being held stiffly erect, when they should point upwards.

Eyes—Should be well sunken and as dark as possible, with a pierceing glint and they should be small, triangular and obliquely placed; set near together and high up on the dog's head.

Nose—Should be black, with well developed nostrils bent downwards át the tip.

Neck—Should be very muscular, long, arched and clean, tapering from the shoulders to the head and it should be free from loose skin.

Chest—Should be broad when viewed from in front, and there should be great depth from withers to brisket, so that the latter is nearer the ground than the belly.

Body—Should be well rounded with marked spring of rib, the back should be short and strong. The back ribs deep. Slightly arched over the loin. The shoulders should be strong and muscular but without heaviness. The shoulder blades should be wide and flat and there should be a very pronounced backward slope from the bottom edge of the blade to the top edge. Behind the shoulders there should be no slackness or dip at the withers. The underline from the brisket to the belly should form a graceful upward curve.

Champion Madame Pompadour
of Ernicor.

Legs—Should be big boned but not to the point of coarseness; the forelegs should be of moderate length, perfectly straight, and the dog must stand firmly upon them. The elbows must turn neither in nor out, and the pasterns should be strong and upright. The hind legs should be parallel viewed from behind. The thighs very muscular with hocks well let down. Hind pasterns short and upright. The stifle joint should be well bent with a well developed second thigh.

Feet—Round and compact with well arched toes like a cat.

Tail—Should be short, set on low, fine, and ideally should be carried horizontally. It should be thick where it joins the body, and should taper to a fine point.

Coat—Should be short, flat, harsh to the touch and with a fine gloss. The dog's skin should fit tightly.

Champion Kowhai Uncle Bimbo

Color—Should be pure white, though markings on the head are permissible. Any markings elsewhere on the coat shall disqualify.

Movement—The dog shall move smoothly, covering the ground with free, easy strides, fore and hind legs should move parallel each to each when viewed from in front or behind. The forelegs reaching out well and the hind legs moving smoothly at the hip and flexing well at the stifle and hock. The dog should move compactly and in one piece but with a typical jaunty air that suggests agility and power.

Faults—Any departure from the foregoing points shall be in exact proportion to its degree, i.e., a very crooked front is a very bad fault; a rather crooked front is a rather bad fault; and a slightly crooked front is a slight fault.

DISQUALIFICATION
Color—Any markings other than on the head shall disqualify.

COLORED
The standard for the Colored Variety is the same as for the White except for the sub-head "Color" which reads: *Color*—Any color other than white, or any color with white markings. Preferred color, brindle. A dog which is predominately white shall be disqualified.

DISQUALIFICATION
Color—Any dog which is predominately white shall be disqualified.

THE CAIRN TERRIER

As far back in history as the 17th Century, the small dog of Scotland was known as the "terrier." At this period, of course, he was bred to work, not to exhibit. His work consisted chiefly of fox-bolting, as it was called. The farms of the Isle of Skye and the Highlands being infested with foxes, it was the terrier's business to help the crofter exterminate the pest. This he did by following the fox until it went to ground, then plunging in after it and worrying it until it was driven out again to be killed by the crofter.

In these early days, the word "*standard*," as we apply it to dogs, was not known. Beyond the general size requirement, the terrier did not have to conform to any particular type. Consequently, every laird or crofter followed his own idea, some thinking chiefly of speed, others demanding nothing but endurance. It is therefore not surprising that there were many variations in height, weight and color. Broadly speaking, such variations are true of all breeds, as it is only within comparatively recent years that so much stress has been laid upon what we now know as "*points*."

The Cairn represents a modern effort to preserve, in his most typical form, the old fashioned terrier. It is generally accepted that the Cairn comes from

American and Canadian Champion Rossmar's Clanruf of Cairndania.

the same original stock as the dogs now recognized, respectively, as the *"Scottie"* and the *West Highland White*. But in the cases of these two breeds, other influences have been at work which have brought about distinctly different types and characteristics.

It will be noted that the Cairn is a small terrier—in fact, the smallest working terrier of the lot. But he is not in any sense a Toy. Tiny, wiry dogs, with very little substance and suggestive of the Pomeranian, are quite as untypical as the coarse over-grown specimens one sometimes sees under the name of Cairns.

Characteristically, the Cairn is reserved. This is chiefly due to the outdoor life which his forebears led, when they were not pets, but workmen. When he has outgrown the playful blundering of his puppy days, the Cairn does not make friends with anyone and everyone. This, of course, brings about the greater loyalty in the end. Once he has been won, he is single-heartedly devoted to master or mistress, accepting strangers upon no better basis than cold politeness until their claim to his friendship has been proved.

But he is, of course, at his best in the field. He is a natural retriever, he will dig out moles, or he will run rabbits and anything else on four legs until he drops from exhaustion. He takes to the water with delight, and he has often been worked with otter hounds. Here his outer coat serves him well, for a few shakes make him fit to go indoors.

We may not want to work our Cairns, but a real terrier with strength, stamina and spirit, as well as show points, is certainly the goal that all breeders should try for.

Inside the house, the Cairn will lay aside his restless activity. He is quiet, well mannered and thoroughly considerate, even as a young puppy. He can be house broken and taught to refrain from destructive play. He will sleep in the place which is assigned him without complaint and without trespassing upon forbidden chairs or couches, but he will gladly accept a life of cushioned luxury if invited to do so. Nor does this appear to detract in the least from his energy and enthusiasm out of doors. Incidentally, he is a keen motorist.

It is an easy matter to teach a Cairn. The breadth of his skull gives him room for brains and, with a little human encouragement, he will seize the chance to develop those brains to a point limited only by the will and patience of his master. He shows a pathetic pleasure in arriving at an understanding of what is wanted of him and in doing it properly. All these qualities make him an ideal pet for all ages—provided extreme physical punishment is not used. His sensitive nature makes him entirely amenable to sharply spoken reproof, should this be necessary; but to use physical chastisement is almost invariably to spoil a good sport and lose a faithful friend.

As a watch dog, the Cairn has the quick ear and the sharp bark of all terriers. He is not easy to quiet if an intruder is about, but he is quick to recognize any friend of the household, or the daily delivery boy.

It may be fairly claimed for the Cairn that he possesses alertness, gaiety, sporting spirit, stick-to-it-iveness and a guiding intelligence. It is this combination which continues to win him so many friends.

STANDARD OF THE CAIRN TERRIER

General Appearance—That of an active, game, hardy, small working terrier of the short-legged class; very free in its movements, strongly but not heavily built, standing well forward on its fore legs, deep in the ribs, well coupled with strong hind quarters and presenting a well proportioned build with a medium length of back, having a hard weather resisting coat; head shorter and wider than any other terrier and well furnished with hair giving a general foxy expression.

Skull—Broad in proportjon to length with a decided stop and well furnished with hair on the top of the head, which may be somewhat softer than the body coat.

Muzzle—Strong but not too long or heavy. Teeth large—mouth neither over or undershot. Nose black.

Eyes—Set wide apart, rather sunken, with shaggy eyebrow, medium in size, hazel or dark hazel in color depending on body color, with a keen terrier expression.

Ears—Small, pointed, well carried erectly, set wide apart on the side of the head. Free from long hairs.

Tail—In proportion to head, well furnished with hair but not feathery. Carried gaily but must not curl over back. Set on at back level.

Body—Well muscled strong active body with well sprung back of medium length, giving an impression of strength and activity without heaviness.

Shoulders, Legs and Feet—A sloping shoulder, medium length of leg, good bùt not too heavy bone; forelegs should not be out at elbows, and be perfectly straight, but forefeet may be slightly turned out. Forefeet larger than hindfeet. Legs must be covered with hard hair. Pads should be thick and strong and dog should stand well up on its feet.

Coat—Hard and weather resistant. Must be double coated with profuse harsh outer coat with short, soft, close furry undercoat.

Color—May be of any color except white. Dark ears, muzzle and tail tip are desirable.

Ideal Sizes—Involves the weight, the height at the withers and the length of body. Weight for bitches, 13 pounds; for dogs, 14 pounds. Height at the withers—bitches, 9½ inches; dogs, 10 inches. Length of body from 14½ inches to 15 inches from the front of the chest to back of hind quarters. The dog must be of balanced proportions and appear neither leggy nor too low to ground; and neither too short nor too long in body. Weight and measurements are for matured dogs at two years of age. Older dogs may weigh slightly in excess and growing dogs under these weights and measurements.

Condition—Dogs should be shown in good hard flesh, well muscled and neither too fat nor thin. Should be in full good coat with plenty of head furnishings, be clean, combed, brushed and tidied up on ears, tail, feet and general outline. Should move freely and easily on a loose lead, should not cringe on being handled. Should stand up on their toes and show with marked terrier characteristics.

FAULTS

Skull—Too narrow in skull.

Muzzle—Too long and heavy a foreface. Mouth over or undershot.

Eyes—Too large, prominent, yellow, ringed, are all objectionable.

Ears—Too large, round at points, set too close together, set too high on the head; heavily covered with hair.

Legs and Feet—Too light or too heavy bone. Crooked forelegs or out at elbow. Thin ferrety feet; feet let down on the heel or too open and spread. Too high or too low on the leg.

Champion Caithness Rufus

Champion Cairndania Clans-
man's Grey Girl

Champion Redletter Miss Splinters.

Body—Too short back and compact a body, hampering quickness of movement and turning ability. Too long, weedy and snaky a body giving an impression of weakness. Tail set too low. Back not level.

Coat—Open coats, blousy coats, too short or dead coats, lack of sufficient undercoat, lack of head furnishings, lack of hard hair on the legs. Silkiness or curliness. A slight wave permissible.

Nose—Flesh or light colored nose.

Color—White on chest, feet or other part of body.

SCALE OF POINTS

	Points
General appearance (Size and Coat)	30
Skull	5
Muzzle	10
Eyes	5
Ears	5
Body, neck and chest	20
Shoulders, legs and feet	20
Tail	5
Total	100

DISQUALIFICATION

Flesh colored nose.

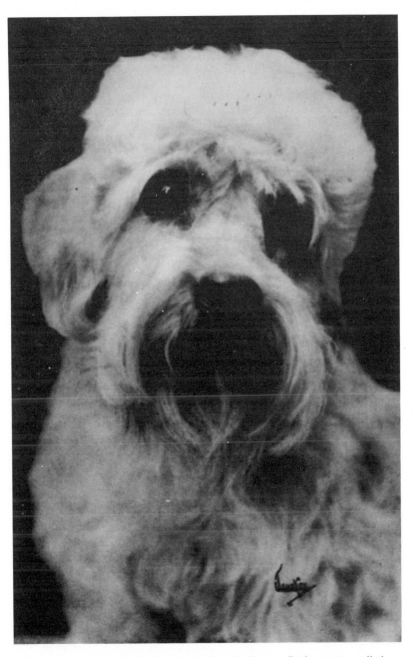

This appealing head study of a famous Dandie Dinmont Terrier portrays all the bewhiskered whimsicality and independence that endears the breed to its admirers.

THE DANDIE DINMONT TERRIER

From the Cheviot Hills between England and Scotland came the Dandie, developed from the rough-coated native terrier used by the Border hunters. From the same section came the Bedlington Terrier and it is entirely possible that these two top-knotted breeds have common ancestry.

The Dandie was first unveiled to the public through Sir Walter Scott's famous novel, "*Guy Mannering*," published in 1814. In the book, Scott's character, a farmer whose name is Dandie Dinmont, kept six small terriers which have, through the magic of Scott's pen, become immortal. These dogs, Auld Pepper, Young Pepper, Auld Mustard, Young Mustard, Little Pepper and Little Mustard, whose pluck and fearlessness are so aptly described in the book, became known as Dandie Dinmont's terriers.

Gainsborough painted an excellent picture of a Dandie in his portrait of Henry, Third Duke of Buccleuch, done in 1770 and Louis Phillippe, King of France, owned a pair of Dandies in 1845. Yes, the Dandie had moved into high places, particularly so considering the fact that in the early 1700's a poacher named Piper Allan developed the Dandie Dinmont as a silent hunter with a

Champion Overhill Conquistador

dark coat, and the breed may very well have poached on the lands of the very nobles into whose laps he eventually landed.

The Dandie was recognized by the A.K.C. in 1886 and is a very adaptable little terrier composed mostly of curved lines (unlike most terriers), is an excellent housedog but sometimes displays a stubborn will of his own.

The Dandie's coat is unusual among terriers, being composed of some soft and some hard hairs. This mixture gives the coat a "crisp" feel. Unusual too is the fact that the coat on different parts of his body is of a different texture; the hair on his body is crisp, on his head it is all soft, and on his tail it is all hard.

The Dandie's head is somewhat large in proportion to his body and the skull is domed, rather than flat as in other terriers. His eyes, which are one of his most famous characteristics, are large, round, and dark hazel in color. They impart an expression that is to be found in no other breed, and in Scotland there is an expression that goes "A Dandie looks at ye as though he's fergat mair than ever ye kent!"

Dandies may be either pepper or mustard in color. Pepper ranges from light silver to dark bluish-black, and mustard ranges from light tan to dark red. The topknot of a pepper is silvery-white and that of a mustard, cream. Peppers should have tan legs and mustards often have grey or black hairs lightly interspersed in their coats.

For those who understand him, the Dandie makes a perfect companion. He is not quarrelsome, but can give an excellent account of himself if picked on. He is always responsive and will appeal to the owner who admires an independent disposition.

STANDARD OF THE DANDIE DINMONT TERRIER

Head—Strongly made and large, not out of proportion to the dog's size, the muscles showing extraordinary development, more especially the maxillary. Skull broad between the ears, getting gradually less towards the eyes, and measuring about the same from the inner corner of the eye to back of skull as it does from ear to ear. The forehead well domed. The head is covered with very soft silky hair, which should not be confined to a mere topknot, and the lighter in color and silkier it is the better. The cheeks, starting from the ears proportionately with the skull have a gradual taper towards the muzzle, which is deep and strongly made, and measures about three inches in length, or in proportion to skull as three is to five. The muzzle is covered with hair of a little darker shade than the topknot, and of the same texture as the feather of the forelegs. The top of the muzzle is generally bare for about an inch from the back part of the nose, the bareness coming to a point towards the eye, and being about one inch broad at the nose. The nose and inside of mouth black or dark colored. The teeth very strong, especially the canine, which are of extraordinary size for such a small dog. The canines fit well into each other, so as to give the greatest available holding and punishing power, and the teeth are level in front, the upper ones very slightly overlapping the under ones. [Many of the finest specimens have a "swine mouth," which is very objectionable, but it is not so great an objection as the protrusion of the under jaw.]

Eyes—Set wide apart, large, full, round, bright, expressive of great determination, intelligence and dignity; set low and prominent in front of the head; color, a rich dark hazel.

Ears—Pendulous, set well back, wide apart, and low on the skull, hanging close to the cheek, with a very slight projection at the base, broad at the junction of the head and tapering almost to a point, the fore part of the ear tapering very little—the tapering being mostly on the back part, the fore part of the ear coming almost straight down from its junction with the head to the tip. They should harmonize in color with the body color. In the case of a Pepper dog they are covered with a soft straight brownish hair (in some cases almost black). In the case of a Mustard dog the hair should be mustard in color, a shade darker than the body, but not black. All should have a thin feather of light hair starting about two inches from the tip, and of nearly the same color and texture as the topknot, which gives the ear the appearance of a distinct point. The animal is often one or two years old before the feather is shown. The cartilage and skin of the ear should not be thick, but rather thin. Length of ear from three to four inches.

Neck—Very muscular, well-developed and strong, showing great power of resistance, being well set into the shoulders.

Body—Long, strong and flexible; ribs well sprung and round, chest well developed and let well down between the fore legs; the back rather low at the shoulder, having a slight downward curve and a corresponding arch over the loins, with a very slight gradual drop from top of loins to root of tail; both sides of backbone well supplied with muscle.

Tail—Rather short, say from eight inches to ten inches, and covered on the upper side with wiry hair of darker color than that of the body, the hair on the under side being lighter in color and not so wiry, with nice feather about two inches long, getting shorter as it nears the tip; rather thick at the root, getting thicker for about four inches, then tapering off to a point. It should not be twisted or curled in any way, but should come up with a curve like a scimitar, the tip, when excited, being in a perpendicular line with the root of the tail. It should neither be set on too high nor too low. When not excited it is carried gaily, and a little above the level of the body.

Legs—The forelegs short, with immense muscular development and bone, set wide apart, the chest coming well down between them. The feet well formed, and not flat, with very strong brown or dark-colored claws. Bandy legs and flat feet are objectionable. The hair on the forelegs and feet of a Pepper dog should be tan, varying according to the body color from a rich tan to a pale fawn; of a Mustard dog they are of a darker shade than its head, which is a creamy white. In both colors there is a nice feather, about two inches long, rather lighter in color than the hair on the fore part of the leg. The hind-legs are a little longer than the fore ones, and are set rather wide apart but not spread out in an unnatural manner, while the feet are much smaller; the thighs are well developed, and the hair of the same color and texture as the fore ones, but having no feather or dewclaws; the whole claws should be dark; but the claws of all vary in shade according to the color of the dog's body.

Coat—This is a very important point; the hair should be about two inches long; that from skull to root of tail, a mixture of hardish and soft hair, which gives a sort of crisp feel to the hand. The hard should not be wiry; the coat is what is termed piley or pencilled. The hair on the under part of the body is lighter in color and softer than on the top. The skin on the belly accords with the color of dog.

512

Champion Ceolaire Bannockburn

The imported Dandie, Champion Salismore Stirrup Cup.

English and American Champion Waterbeck Watermark.

Color—The color is Pepper or Müstard. The Pepper ranges from a dark bluish black to a light silvery gray, the intermediate shades being preferred, the body color coming well down the shoulder and hips, gradually merging into the leg color. The Mustards vary from a reddish brown to a pale fawn, the head being a creamy white, the legs and feet of a shade darker than the head. The claws are dark as in other colors. [Nearly all Dandie Dinmont Terriers have some white on the chest, and some have also white claws.]

Size—The height should be from 8 to 11 inches at the top of shoulder. Length from top of shoulder to root of tail should not be more than twice the dog's height, but preferably one or two inches less.

Weight—From 18 pounds to 24 pounds; the best weight as near 18 pounds as possible. These weights are for dogs in good working condition.

The relative value of the several points in the standard are apportioned as follows:

SCALE OF POINTS

	Points
Head	10
Eyes	10
Ears	10
Neck	5
Body	20
Tail	5
Legs and feet	10
Coat	15
Color	5
Size and weight	5
General appearance	5
Total	100

THE FOX TERRIER

Perhaps the best known of all breeds is the Fox Terrier. Perky, brash, flashy and stylish, this breed is the epitome of the Terrier. In its two varieties, Smooth and Wire, it is popular throughout the world though it originated, as a breed, in England.

Though both varieties were often crossed (a practice discontinued now) and the standards are identical except for the coat, it is claimed by authorities that each came from different source material. The Wire claims the old rough-coated, black-and-tan working terrier as its principal ancestor, while the Smooth descended from crossings of the Bull Terrier, Greyhound, Beagle, and old, smooth black-and-tan terrier. The reason crosses were made between Wire and Smooth was to lend the Wire some of the classical and cleaner-cut outline in head and body of the Smooth. Smooth ancestry can be found in any

Champion Ellastone Gold Nugget (English).

An American Champion Wire, Copper Beech Storm.

English Champion, the Smooth, Watteau Sonata.

extended pedigree of our present Wires. But only in Australia are there any Wire outcrosses to be found in Smooth Fox Terrier breeding.

In 1885 the American Fox Terrier Club was founded and adopted the English standard which was later enlarged upon.

The name of the breed is borrowed from the quarry they pursue, going to earth and driving the fox from his hole. This employment led to the shaping of their type by fox hunters and masters of fox hunt packs who used and bred the fearless little dogs.

The Fox Terrier is an excellent house and watch dog, alert and full of fire. Their energy is boundless and for the person who wants a dog who is on the go from dawn to dark they are excellent. They are fine vermin dogs and are violently affectionate to their family and have, for a number of years, been a prime favorite of American dog fanciers.

STANDARD OF THE FOX TERRIER

The following shall be the standard of the Fox Terrier amplified in part in order that a more complete description of the Fox Terrier may be presented. The standard itself is set forth in ordinary type, the amplification in italics.

Head—The skull should be flat and moderately narrow, gradually decreasing in width to the eyes. Not much "stop" should be apparent, but there should be more dip in the profile between the forehead and the top jaw than is seen in the case of a Greyhound.

The cheeks must not be full.

The ears should be V-shaped and small, of moderate thickness, and drooping forward close to the cheek, not hanging by the side of the head like a foxhound. *The top line of the folded ear should be well above the level of the skull.*

The jaws, upper and lower, should be strong and muscular and of fair punishing strength, but not so as in any way to resemble the Greyhound or modern English terrier. There should not be much falling away below the eyes. This part of the head should, however, be moderately chiseled out, so as not to go down in a straight slope like a wedge.

The nose, towards which the muzzle must gradually taper, should be black. *It should be noticed that although the foreface should gradually taper from eye to muzzle and should tip slightly at its juncture with the forehead, it should not "dish" or fall away quickly below the eyes, where it should be full and well made up, but relieved from "wedginess" by a little delicate chiseling.*

The eyes and the rims should be dark in color, *moderately* small and rather deep set, full of fire, life and intelligence and as nearly as possible circular in shape. *Anything approaching a yellow eye is most objectionable.*

The teeth should be as nearly as possible together, i.e., *the points* of the upper (*incisors*) teeth on the outside of or *slightly overlapping* the lower teeth. *There should be apparent little difference in length between the skull and foreface of a well-balanced head.*

Neck—Should be clean and muscular, without throatiness, of fair length, and gradually widening to the shoulders.

Shoulders—Should be long and sloping, well laid back, fine at the points, and clearly cut at the withers.

Chest—Deep and not broad.

Back—Should be short, straight (i.e., *level*), and strong, with no appearance of slackness. *Brisket should be deep, yet not exaggerated.*

517

Loin—Should be very powerful, *muscular* and very slightly arched. The foreribs should be moderately arched, the back ribs deep *and well sprung,* and the dog should be well ribbed up.

Hindquarters—Should be strong and muscular, quite free from droop or crouch; the thighs long and powerful; *stifles well curved and turned neither in nor out;* hocks *well bent* and near the gound *should be perfectly upright and parallel each with the other when viewed from behind,* the dog standing well up on them like a foxhound, and not straight in the stifle. *The worst possible form of hindquarters consist of a short second thigh and a straight stifle.*

Stern—Should be set on rather high, and carried gaily, but not over the back or curled. It should be of good strength, anything approaching a "pipe-stopper" tail being especially objectionable.

Legs—The forelegs viewed from any direction must be straight with bone strong right down to the feet, showing little or no appearance of ankle in front, and being short and straight in pasterns. Both fore and hindlegs should be carried straight forward in traveling, the stifles not turning outward. The elbows should hang perpendicularly to the body, working free of the sides.

Feet—Should be round, compact and not large; the soles hard and tough; the toes moderately arched, and turned neither in nor out.

Coat—Should be smooth, flat, but hard, dense and abundant. The belly and under side of the thighs should not be bare.

Color—White should predominate; brindle, red, or liver markings are objectionable. Otherwise this point is of little or no importance.

Symmetry, Size and Character—The dog must present a generally gay, lively and active appearance; bone and strength in a small compass are essentials; but this must not be taken to mean that a Fox Terrier should be cloddy, or in any way coarse—speed and endurance must be looked to as well as power, and the symmetry of the foxhound taken as a model. The terrier, like the hound, must on no account be leggy, nor must he be too short in the leg. He should stand like a cleverly made hunter, covering a lot of ground, yet with a short back, as before stated. He will then attain the highest degree of propelling power, together with the greatest length of stride that is compatible with the length of his body. Weight is not a certain criterion of a terrier's fitness for his work—general shape, size and contour are the main points; and if a dog can gallop and stay, and follow his fox up a drain, it matters little what his weight is to a pound or so. *According to present-day requirements, a full-sized, well-balanced dog should not exceed 15½ inches at the withers—the bitch being proportionately lower—nor should the length of back from withers to root of tail exceed 12 inches, while, to maintain the relative proportions, the head should not exceed 7¼ inches or be less than 7 inches. A dog with these measurements should scale 18 pounds in show condition— a bitch weighing some 2 pounds less—with a margin of 1 pound either way.*

Balance—*This may be defined as the correct proportions of a certain point, or points, when considered in relation to a certain other point or points. It is the keystone of the terrier's anatomy. The chief points for consideration are the relative proportions of skull and foreface; head and back; height at withers and length of body from shoulder-point to buttock—the ideal of proportion being reached when the last two measurements are the same. It should be added that, although the head measurements can be taken with absolute accuracy, the height at withers and length of back and coat are approximate, and are inserted for the information of breeders and exhibitors rather than as a hard and fast rule.*

The Smooth, Champion Charneth Choir Boy (English).

Champion Wyrecroft War Bonus (English).

Movement—Movement, or action, is the crucial test of conformation. The terrier's legs should be carried straight forward while traveling, the forelegs hanging perpendicular and swinging parallel with the sides, like the pendulum of a clock. The principal propulsive power is furnished by the hindlegs, perfection of action being found in the terrier possessing long thighs and muscular second thighs well bent at the stifles, which admit of a strong forward thrust or "snatch" of the hocks. When approaching, the forelegs should form a continuation of the straight line of the front, the feet being the same distance apart as the elbows. When stationary, it is often difficult to determine whether a dog is slightly out at shoulder, but, directly he moves, the defect—if it exists—becomes more apparent, the forefeet having a tendency to cross, "weave," or "dish." When, on the contrary, the dog is tied at the shoulder, the tendency of the feet is to move wider apart, with a sort of paddling action. When the hocks are turned in—cowhock—the stifles and feet are turned outwards, resulting in a serious loss of propulsive power. When the hocks are turned outwards the tendency of the hindfeet is to cross, resulting in an ungainly waddle.

N.B.—Old scars or injuries, the result of work or accident, should not be allowed to prejudice a terrier's chance in the show ring, unless they interfere with its movement or with its utility for work or stud.

WIRE-HAIRED FOX TERRIER

This variety of the breed should resemble the smooth sort in every respect except the coat, which should be broken. The harder and more wiry the texture of the coat is, the better. On no account should the dog look or feel woolly; and there should be no silky hair about the poll or elsewhere. The coat should not be too long, so as to give the dog a shaggy appearance, but, at the same time, it should show a marked and distinct difference all over from the smooth species.

SCALE OF POINTS

	Points
Head and ears	15
Neck	5
Shoulders and crest	10
Back and loin	10
Hindquarters	15
Stern	5
Legs and feet	15
Coat	15
Symmetry, size and character	10
Total	100

DISQUALIFYING POINTS

Nose—White, cherry or spotted to a considerable extent with either of these colors.

Ears—Prick, tulip or rose.

Mouth—Much undershot, or much overshot.

THE IRISH TERRIER

Origin of the Irish Terrier is a subject likely to provide debate as long as interest in the breed continues. The famous English authority, F. M. Jowett, says there is direct evidence that a breed of wire-haired black-and-tan terriers existed in Great Britain over 200 years ago and believes this was the foundation of our present Daredevils.

On the other hand, no less a student of dogs in general than James Watson, says there is little use in trying to grope back for any Irish Terrier beginnings. Referring to claims that the breed is mentioned in early Irish manuscripts, he says no one has ever been able to produce these writings, and puts these assertions in the same category with an old-time wit's remark that the reason the Irish Terrier was not mentioned in the manifest of Noah's Ark was that he needed no inside accommodations owing to the ease with which he could swim alongside.

Watson does say, however, that *"From the time the terrier of Northern Ireland became in any way known he was a dog which, from his being the rangiest of the terrier family of that time and the general resemblance in outline of the best specimens to a rough, coarse Greyhound, indicated his descent from the hound dog of Ireland, the Irish Wolfhound."*

Yet while canine historians may disagree as to origin, they are in accord as

Champion Ahtram Golden Smasher

521

The likeable, vivacious, game little Terrier from
the Emerald Isle.

to the breed's characteristics, just as present-day fanciers are unanimous in admiration of its generally likeable qualities even though they may differ over such details as size and conformation.

STANDARD OF THE IRISH TERRIER

Head—Long, but in nice proportion to the rest of the body; the skull flat, rather narrow between the ears, and narrowing slightly towards the eyes; free from wrinkle, with the stop hardly noticeable exeept in profile. The jaw must be strong and muscular, but not too full in the cheek, and of good punishing length. The foreface must not fall away appreciably between or below the eyes; instead, the modeling should be delicate an in contradistinction, for example, to the fullness of foreface of the Greyhound. An exaggerated foreface, which is out of proportion to the length of the skull from the occiput to the stop, disturbs the proper balance of the head, and is not desirable. Also, the head of exaggerated length usually accompanies oversize or disproportionate length of body, or both, and such conformation is not typical. On the other hand, the foreface should not be noticeably shorter than is the skull from occiput to stop. Excessive muscular development of the cheeks, or bony development of the temples, conditions which are described by the fancier as "cheeky," or "strong in head," or "thick in skull," are objectionable. The "bumpy" or "alligator" head, sometimes described as the "taneous" head, in which the skull presents two lumps of bony structure with or without indentations above the eyes, is unsightly and to be faulted. The hair on the upper and lower jaws should be similar in quality and texture to that on the body, and only of sufficient length to present an appearance of additional strength and finish to the foreface. The profuse, goat-like beard is unsightly and undesirable, and almost invariably it betokens the objectionable linty and silken hair in the coat.

Teeth—Should be strong and even, white and sound; and neither overshot nor undershot.

Lips—Should be close and well-fitting, almost black in color.

Nose—Must be black.

Eyes—Dark hazel in color; small, not prominent; full of life, fire and intelligence. The light or yellow eye is most objectionable.

Ears—Small and V-shaped; of moderate thickness; set well on the head, and dropping forward closely to the cheek. The ear must be free of fringe, and the hair much shorter and somewhat darker in color than on the body. A "dead" ear, houndlike in appearance, must be severely penalized. It is not characteristic of the Irish Terrier. An ear which is too slightly erect is undesirable.

Neck—Should be of fair length and gradually widening towards the shoulders; well and proudly carried, and free from throatiness. Generally there is a slight frill in the hair at each side of the neck, extending almost to the corner of the ear.

Shoulders and Chest—Shoulders must be fine, long, and sloping well into the back. The chest should be deep and muscular, but neither full nor wide.

Back and Loin—The body should be moderately long—neither too long nor too short. The short back, so coveted and so appealing in the Fox Terrier, is *not* characteristic of the Irish Terrier. It is objectionable. The back must be symmetrical, strong and straight, and free from an appearance of slackness or "dip" behind the shoulders. The loin strong and muscular, and slightly arched. The ribs fairly sprung, deep rather than round, with a well-ribbed back. The bitch may be slightly longer in appearance than the dog.

Hindquarters—Should be strong and muscular; powerful thighs; hocks near the ground; stifles moderately bent.

Stern—Should be docked, and set on rather high, but not curled. It should be of good strength and substance; of fair length and well covered with harsh, rough hair, and free from fringe or feather. The three-quarters dock is about right.

Feet and Legs—The feet should be strong, tolerably round, and moderately small; toes arched and turned neither out nor in, with black toe-nails. The pads should be deep, not hard, but with a pleasing velvety quality, and perfectly sound; they must be entirely free from cracks or horny excrescences. Corny feet, so-called, are to be regarded as an abominable blemish; as a taint which must be shunned. Cracked pads frequently accompany corny growths, and these conditions are more pronounced in hot and dry weather. In damp weather and in winter such pads may improve temporarily, but these imperfections inevitably reappear and the result is unsound feet, a deplorable fault which must be heavily penalized. There seems to be no permanent cure for this condition, and even if a temporary cure were possible the disease is seldom, if ever, eradicated, and undoubtedly it is transmitted in breeding. The one sure way to avoid corny and otherwise unsound feet is to avoid breeding from dogs or bitches which are not entirely free from this taint. Legs, moderately long, well set from the shoulders, perfectly straight, with plenty of bone and muscle; the elbows working clear of the sides; pasterns short, straight, and hardly noticeable. Both fore and hindlegs should move straight forward when traveling; the stifles should not turn outwards. "Cowhocks" —that is, where the hocks are turned in, and the stifles and feet turned out, are intolerable. The legs should be free from feather, and covered, like the head, with hair of similar texture to that on the body, but not so long.

Coat—Should be dense and wiry in texture, rich in quality, having a broken appearance, but still lying fairly close to the body, the hairs growing so closely and strongly together that when parted with the fingers the skin is hardly visible; free of softness or silkiness, and not so long as to alter the outline of the body, particularly in the hind quarters. At the base of the stiff outer coat there should be a growth of finer and softer hair, differing in color, termed the undercoat. Single coats, which are without any undercoat, and wavy coats, are undesirable; the curly coat is most objectionable. On the sides of the body the coat is never as harsh as on the back and the quarters, but it should be plentiful and of good texture.

Color—Should be whole-colored; the bright red, red wheaten, or golden red colors are preferable. A small patch of white on the chest, frequently encountered in all whole-colored breeds, is permissible but not desirable. White on any other part of the body is most objectionable.

Size and Symmetry—The most desirable weight in show condition is 27 pounds for the dog and 25 pounds for the bitch. The height at the shoulder should be approximately 18 inches. This terrier must be active, lithe and wiry in movement, with great animation; sturdy and strong in substance and bone-structure, but at the same time free from clumsiness, for speed, power and endurance are most essential. The Irish Terrier must be neither "cobby" nor "cloddy," but should be built on lines of speed, with a graceful, racing outline.

524

Champion Cotton Hill's Miss Erin

Champion Suffolk's Own Rory.

The weights herein mentioned are ideal and serve as a guide to both breeder and judge. In the show ring, however, the informed judge readily identifies the over-sized or under-sized Irish Terrier by its conformation and general appearance. The weights named should be regarded as limit weights, as a rule, but it must be considered that a comparatively small, heavily built and "cloddy" dog —which is most undesirable, and not at all typical—may easily be of standard weight, or over it; whereas another terrier which is long in leg, lacking in substance and built somewhat upon the lines of a Whippet— also undesirable and not at all typical—may be of the exact weight, or under it; therefore, although the standard weights must be borne well in mind, weight is not the last word in judgment. It is of the greatest importance to select, in so far as possible, terriers of moderate and generally accepted size, possessing the other various necessary characteristics.

Temperament—The Irish Terrier is game, and asks no quarter. He is of good temper, most affectionate, and absolutely loyal to mankind. Tender and forbearing with those he loves, this rugged, stout-hearted terrier will guard his master, his mistress, children in his charge, or their possessions, with unflinching courage and with utter contempt of danger or hurt. His life is one continuous and eager offering of loyal and faithful companionship, and devoted, loving service. He is ever on guard, and stands between his house and all that threatens.

SCALE OF POINTS

	Points
Head, ears and expression	20
Legs and feet	15
Neck	5
Shoulders and chest	10
Back and loin	5
Hindquarters and stern	10
Coat	15
Color	10
Size and symmetry	10
Total	100

NEGATIVE POINTS

White nails, toes and feet, minus	10
Much white on chest	10
Dark shadings on face	5
Mouth undershot or cankered	10
Coat shaggy, curly or soft	10
Uneven in color	5
Total	50

DISQUALIFYING POINTS

Nose—Any other color than black.

Mouth—Much undershot or overshot.

Ears—Cropped ears.

Color—Any other color than red, golden red, or red wheaten. A small patch of white on the chest is permissible; otherwise parti-colored coats disqualify.

526

THE KERRY BLUE TERRIER

The Kerry Blue Terrier is an Irish breed, called in Eire the Irish Blue Terrier. The breed has been known in Ireland for at least 150 years, mainly in the mountains around Lake Killarney in County Kerry, where Kerries have been used as all-round working and utility terriers. In Ireland and England they are used for hunting small game and birds and are excellent retrievers on both land and water. Tractable and extremely intelligent, they are used successfully as a herd dog for sheep and cattle.

In 1837, Mr. H. D. Richardson of Dublin, famous writer and authority on dogs, mentions what he calls the Harlequin Terrier, a true terrier, bluish slate in color. There is little doubt that the Harlequin Terrier and the Kerry Blue Terrier are one and the same breed.

At a show in Limerick, Ireland in 1887, there was a class listed as Silver-haired Irish Terriers. The dogs shown were slate blue in color.

A class of 20 entries catalogued as Blue Terriers (Working) was seen at the Killarney Show in 1916. This show served to call attention to the breed in England as well as Ireland. In 1920 the All-Ireland Kerry Blue Terrier Club was formed, followed shortly afterward by the Irish Blue Terrier Club.

Kerry Blue Terriers were first shown in England in 1922 at the big Crufts

Champion
Calkerry's
Bronwyn

Champion Kilroy's Sally Blue

Champion Prince Blue Steel of the Chevin
(English).

show, After that show the Kerry Blue Terrier Club of England was organized. The clubs in Ireland and England formulated standards of excellence for the breed that were somewhat similar.

Kerry Blues came to America about the time the breed came into popularity in England and Ireland. In 1923 the first American champion, Ch. Brian of Muchia, was recorded by the American Kennel Club. In New York on February 9, 1926, the Kerry Blue Terrier Club of America was organized; it was incorporated soon afterward. One of its first tasks was to formulate a breed standard for America. It was decided to have the new standard follow along the general lines of the English standard, under which Kerry Blues are trimmed as terriers, rather than the Irish standard under which they are shown untrimmed. Through the years the breed has improved greatly and the Kerry Blues being raised in America today are as good as any in the world.

The modern Kerry Blue Terrier is one of the friendliest dogs in the world. He makes an ideal house pet for he is not a bundle of nerves as are some terriers. Neither is he a yapper and he will not bark without cause.

All Kerry Blue Terrier puppies are born black and at anywhere from 6 to 18 months their coat starts to turn blue. Their ultimate shade may run anywhere from a light silver-blue to a dark slate-blue. Any Kerry that remains black after 18 months is disqualified for the show ring.

The Kerry Blue has one of the softest, silkiest, waviest coats in dogdom. Amazingly, his coat never sheds hair to get all over your clothes, rugs, or furniture—and he has no "doggy" odor.

A Kerry Blue remains playful—a real companion—years longer than most breeds. They are virile and healthy by nature and if given ordinary good treatment will live to a ripe and useful old age.

STANDARD OF THE KERRY BLUE TERRIER

Head—Long, but not exaggerated and in good proportion to the rest of the body. Well balanced, with little apparent difference between the length of the skull and foreface.

Skull—Flat, with very slight stop, of but moderate breadth between the ears, and narrowing very slightly to the eyes.

Cheeks—Clean and level, free from bumpiness.

Ears—V-shaped, small but not out of proportion to the size of the dog, of moderate thickness, carried forward close to the cheeks with the top of the folded ear slightly above the level of the skull. A "dead" ear houndlike in appearance is very undesirable.

Fore-face—Jaws deep, strong and muscular. Fore-face full and well made up, not falling away appreciably below the eyes but moderately chiseled out to relieve the fore-face from wedginess.

Nose—Black, nostrils large and wide.

Teeth—Strong, white and either level or with the upper (incisors) teeth slightly overlapping the lower teeth. An undershot mouth should be strictly penalized.

Eyes—Dark, small, not prominent, well placed and with a keen terrier expression. Anything approaching a yellow eye is very undesirable.

Neck—Clean and moderately long, gradually widening to the shoulders upon which it should be well set and carried proudly.

Shoulders and Chest—Shoulders fine, long and sloping, well laid back and well knit. Chest deep and of but moderate breadth.

Legs and Feet—Legs moderately long with plenty of bone and muscle. The forelegs should be straight from both front and side view, with the elbows hanging perpendicularly to the body and working clear of the sides in movement, the pasterns short, straight and hardly noticeable. Both fore and hind legs should move straight forward when travelling, the stifles turning neither in nor out.

Feet should be strong, compact, fairly round and moderately small, with good depth of pad free from cracks, the toes arched, turned neither in nor out, with black toenails.

Body—Back short, strong and straight (i.e., level), with no appearance of slackness. Loin short and powerful with a slight tuck-up, the ribs fairly well sprung, deep rather than round.

Hindquarters and Stern—Hindquarters strong and muscular with full freedom of action, free from droop or crouch, the thighs long and powerful, stifles well bent and turned neither in nor out, hocks near the ground and, when viewed from behind, upright and parallel with each other, the dog standing well up on them. Tail should be set on high, of moderate length and carried gaily erect, the straighter the tail the better.

Color—The correct mature color is any shade of blue gray or gray blue

Champion Tailteann's Blue Crystal
(Canadian).

from deep slate to light blue gray, of a fairly uniform color throughout except that distinctly darker to black parts may appear on the muzzle, head, ears, tail and feet.

Kerry color, in its process of "clearing" from an apparent black at birth to the mature gray blue or blue gray, passes through one or more transitions—involving a very dark blue (darker than deep slate) shades or tinges of brown, and mixtures of these, together with a progressive infiltration of the correct mature color.

Up to 18 months such deviations from the correct mature color are permissible without preference and without regard for uniformity. Thereafter, deviation from it to any significant extent must be severely penalized.

Solid black is never permissible in the show ring. Up to 18 months any doubt as to whether a dog is black or a very dark blue should be resolved in favor of the dog, particularly in the case of a puppy. Black on the muzzle, head, ears, tail and feet is permissible at any age.

Coat—Soft, dense and wavy. A harsh, wire or bristle coat should be severely penalized. In show trim the body should be well covered but tidy, with the head (except for the whiskers), and the ears and cheeks clear.

General Conformation and Character—The typical Kerry Blue Terrier should be upstanding, well knit and in good balance, showing a well developed and muscular body with definite Terrier style and character throughout. A low-slung Kerry is not typical.

Height—The ideal Kerry should be 18½ inches at the withers for a dog, slightly less for a bitch.

In judging Kerries a height of 18–19½ inches for a dog and 17½–19 inches for a bitch should be given primary preference. Only where the comparative superiority of a specimen outside of the ranges noted clearly justifies it, should greater latitude be taken. In no case should it extend to a dog over 20 inches or under 17½ inches, or to a bitch over 19½ inches or under 17 inches. The minimum limits do not apply to puppies.

Weight—The most desirable weight for a fully developed dog is from 33–40 pounds, bitches weighing proportionately less.

SCALE OF POINTS

	Points
Head	20
Neck	5
Shoulders and chest	10
Legs and feet	10
Body	10
Hindquarters and stern	10
Color	10
Coat	15
General conformation and character	10
Total	100

DISQUALIFICATIONS

1. Solid black.
2. Dewclaws on hindlegs.

THE LAKELAND TERRIER

The Lakeland Terrier originated in the Fell district of Cumberland, near the Scottish border. It is related to several terrier breeds including the Welsh and Airedale, in that all have sprung from the *"old English hard-haired, black and tan terrier."* It also has a dash of Bedlington blood which was introduced to intensify gameness. One of the oldest of working terriers *(which means more than being merely a ratter, but a terrier which goes to ground after fox and badger)*, it has been used for generations in the Lake District for the purpose of exterminating foxes which raid the farmer's sheep fold at lambing time and also make a steady decrease in the poultry census. This breed has had several names, among them Patterdale, Cumberland and Fell Terrier, with the present name being decided upon when breed clubs were formed in the '20's.

Lakeland Terriers are famed for their dead-game grit, a trait not considered desirable in terriers of the fashionable hunting districts of England where the pink-coated, well-mounted members of the hunt follow the fox cross-country after fast-galloping hounds. Such terriers are carried by a hunt servant on

Champion Pitglen Party Piece (imported).

Champion Aristocrat of Greeba (imported).

horseback and it is their purpose to bolt the fox when the hounds check at a drain or burrow. If the terrier kills the fox underground both he and the huntsman are highly unpopular, having deprived the hunt of a further "run". This type of terrier is also used in the slower sport of digging fox and badger, and again must not ruin the sport by killing the quarry, which should be "marked" by shrill barking to guide the diggers, or bolted into their net. It can be seen from this that the dead-game quality of attacking and killing the fox, is desired only in the Lakeland among the working terriers, and this accounts for the Lakeland's reputation for courage and tenacity. Yet in spite of this, he is not quarrelsome with his own kind, saving this energy for his line of work.

The Lakeland has a distinctive expression, differing from the hard-bitten, keen expression so desired in the Welsh and Wire. The most obvious distinction between a Lakeland and a Welsh is in color. The Welsh should be black and tan, or black grizzle and tan, with the tan being preferably a rich mahogany shade. The Lakeland fancier, however, has a much wider choice of colors—red, red grizzle, wheaten, blue and wheaten, red and wheaten, black, liver, and black (or grizzle) and tan. However the tan of the Lakeland is lighter, nearer the wheaten color, and should never be the rich red tan of the Welsh.

Although he is such a sportsman, the Lakeland is quite content to take over the duties of a household, which he does efficiently, both as a guardian and as an entertainer. His quizzical be-whiskered face and his elfin gaiety bring cheer to his adopted family with an ease that professional comedians would envy. His charm and companionability are hard to equal.

STANDARD OF THE LAKELAND TERRIER

General Appearance—The Lakeland Terrier is a small, workmanlike dog of square, sturdy build and gay, friendly, self-confident demeanor. He stands on his toes as if ready to go, and he moves lithe and gracefully, with a straight-ahead, free stride of good length. His head is rectangular in contours, ears V-shaped, and wiry coat finished off with fairly long furnishings on muzzle and legs.

Head—Well balanced; rectangular, the length of skull equalling the length of the muzzle when measured from occiput to stop, and from stop to nose-tip. The skull is flat on top and moderately broad, the cheeks almost straight sided, and the stop barely perceptible. The muzzle is broad with straight nose-bridge and good fill-in beneath the eyes. The nose is black, except that liver-colored noses shall be permissible on liver-colored dogs. Jaws are powerful. The teeth, which are comparatively large, may meet in either a level, edge-to-edge bite, or a slightly overlapping scissors bite. Specimens with teeth overshot or undershot are to be disqualified. The ears are small, V-shaped, their fold just above the top of the skull, the inner edge close to the cheeks, and the flap pointed down. The eyes, moderately small and somewhat oval in outline, are set squarely in the skull, fairly wide apart. Their normally dark color may be a warm brown or black. The expression depends upon the dog's mood of the moment; although typically alert, it may be intense and determined, or gay and even impish.

Neck—Reachy; and of good length; refined but strong; clean at the throat, slightly arched and widening gradually into the shoulders. The withers, that point on the back of the neck where neck and body meet are noticeably higher than the level of the back.

Body—In overall length-to-height proportion, the dog is approximately square. The moderately narrow chest is deep; it extends to elbows which are held close to the body. Shoulder blades are sloping, that is, well laid back, their musculature lean and almost flat in outline. The ribs are well sprung and moderately rounded. The back is short and level in topline. Loins are taut and short, although they may be a trifle longer in bitches than in dogs. Quarters are strong, broad, and muscular.

Legs and Feet—Forelegs are strongly boned, clean and absolutely straight as viewed from the front or side, and devoid of appreciable bend at the pasterns. Hind legs too are strong and sturdy, the second thighs long and nicely angulated at the stifles and the hocks. Hocks are well let down, with the bone from hock to toes straight and parallel to each other. The small feet are round, the toes compact and well padded, the nails strong. Dewclaws, if any, are to be removed.

Tail—Set high on the body, the tail is customarily docked so that when the dog is set up in show position, the tip of the docked tail is on an approximate level with the skull. In carriage it is gay or upright, although a slight curve in the direction of the head is considered desirable. The tail curled over the back is faulty.

Coat and Color—Two-ply or double, the outer coat is hard and wiry in texture, the undercoat soft. Furnishings on muzzle and legs are plentiful as opposed to profuse. The color may be blue, black, liver, black and tan, blue and tan, red, red grizzle, grizzle and tan, or wheaten. Tan, as desirable in the Lakeland Terrier, is a light wheaten or straw color, with rich red or mahogany

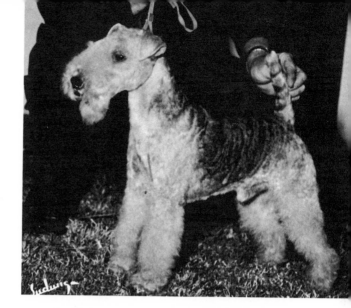

Champion
Westcrag
Warrior
(imported).

tan to be penalized. Otherwise, colors, as specified, are equally acceptable. Dark-saddled specimens (whether black, grizzle, or blue) are nearly solid black at birth, with tan points on muzzle and feet. The black recedes and usually turns grayish or grizzle at maturity, while the tan also lightens.

Size—The ideal height of the mature dog is 14½ inches from the withers to the ground, with up to one half inch deviation either way permissible. Bitches may measure as much as one inch less than dogs. The weight of the well balanced, mature specimen in hard, show condition averages approximately 17 pounds, those of other heights proportionately more or less.

Size is to be considered of lesser importance than other qualities, that is, when judging dogs of equal merit, the one nearest the ideal size is to be preferred. Symmetry and proportion, however, are paramount in the appraisal, since all qualities together must be considered in visualizing the ideal.

Movement—Straight and free, with good length of stride. Paddling, moving close, and toeing-in are faulty.

Temperament—The typical Lakeland Terrier is bold, gay and friendly, with a self-confident, cock-of-the-walk attitude. Shyness, especially shy-sharpness, in the mature specimen is to be heavily penalized.

SCALE OF POINTS

	Points
Head	15
Eyes, ears, expression	15
Neck	5
Body	10
Coat	15
Legs and feet	10
Size and symmetry	10
Movement	10
Temperament	10
Total	100

DISQUALIFICATION

The front teeth overshot or undershot.

THE MANCHESTER TERRIER

One of the most important breeds in terrier history was the old Black-and-Tan or "Rat" Terrier, as he was commonly and appropriately called. Muscular, active, useful, the most accomplished rat killers known, they lent their genetic excellencies, in some degree, to most of the terrier breeds, and these qualities were the fundamental characteristics of this canine family.

The Manchester Terrier of today is the modern, dressed up, sleek and saucy counterpart of the old Black-and-Tan Terrier that was his ancestor. There was one cross made by a fancier named John Hulme, to a Whippet so that the breed could be developed as both a ratter and rabbit coursing terrier, the two "poor men's sports" of that day. From this cross, made in Manchester, came the Manchester Terrier.

Spirited and courageous, early specimens were apt to be short-tempered and snappy, qualities also wanted by their early, rough owners. But as the years

Champion Grenadier Kettledrum

passed and the breed came into other hands, these bad qualities were bred out but the gameness and alertness kept intact.

Up until 1959 the Manchester Terrier and the Toy Manchester Terrier were registered as separate breeds, even though interbreeding of the two varieties was constantly practiced. Since then they have been registered as a single breed of two varieties, which is as it should be since the Toy is simply a smaller Manchester which at first appeared in regular Manchester litters and later was selected for and bred pure. *(See Toy Manchester Terrier)*.

STANDARD OF THE MANCHESTER TERRIER

Head—Long, narrow, tight skinned, almost flat, with a slight indentation up the forehead; slightly wedge-shaped, tapering to the nose, with no visible cheek muscles, and well filled up under the eyes; level in mouth, with tight-lipped jaws.

Eyes—Small, bright, sparkling and as near black as possible; set moderately close together; oblong in shape, slanting upwards on the outside; they should neither protrude nor sink in the skull.

Nose—Black.

Ears (Toy Variety)—Of moderate size; set well up on the skull and rather close together; thin, moderately narrow at base; with pointed tips; naturally erect carriage. Wide, flaring, blunt-tipped or "bell" ears are a serious fault; cropped or cut ears shall disqualify.

Ears (Standard Variety)—Erect, or button, small and thin; smaller at the root and set as close together as possible at the top of the head. If cropped, to a point, long and carried erect.

Neck and Shoulders—The neck should be a moderate length, slim and graceful; gradually becoming larger as it approaches, and blend smoothly with the sloping shoulders; free from throatiness; slightly arched from the occiput.

Chest—Narrow between the legs; deep in the brisket.

Body—Moderately short, with robust loins; ribs well sprung out behind the shoulders; back slightly arched at the loin, and falling again to the tail to the same height as the shoulder.

Legs—Forelegs straight, of proportionate length, and well under body. Hind legs should not turn in or out as viewed from the rear; carried back; hocks well let down.

Feet—Compact, well arched, with jet black nails; the two middle toes in the front feet rather longer than the others; the hind feet shaped like those of a cat.

Tail—Moderately short, and set on where the arch of the back ends; thick where it joins the body, tapering to a point, not carried higher than the back.

Coat—Smooth, short, thick, dense, close and glossy; not soft.

Color—Jet black and rich mahogany tan, which should not run or blend into each other but abruptly forming clear, well-defined lines of color division. A small tan spot over each eye; a very small tan spot on each cheek; the lips of the upper and lower jaws should be tanned, extending under the throat, ending in the shape of the letter V; the inside of the ears partly tanned. Tan spots, called rosettes, on each side of the chest above the front legs, more pronounced in puppies than in adults. There should be a black "thumb mark" patch on the front of each foreleg between the pastern and the knee. There

A quartette of Manchester Terrier champions.

should be a distinct black "pencil mark" line running lengthwise on the top of each toe on all four feet. The remainder of the forelegs to be tan to the knee. Tan on the hind legs should continue from the penciling on the feet up the inside of the legs to a little below the stifle joint; the outside of the hind legs to be black. There should be tan under the tail, and on the vent, but only of such size as to be covered by the tail. White in any part of the coat is a serious fault, and shall disqualify whenever the white shall form a patch or stripe measuring as much as one-half inch in its longest dimension.

Weight (Toy Variety)—Not exceeding 12 pounds. It is suggested that clubs consider dividing the American-bred and Open Classes by weight as follows: 7 pounds and under, over 7 pounds and not exceeding 12 pounds.

Weight (Standard Variety)—Over 12 pounds and not exceeding 22 pounds. Dogs weighing over 22 pounds shall be disqualified. It is suggested that clubs consider dividing the American-bred and Open Classes by weight as follows: over 12 pounds and not exceeding 16 pounds, over 16 pounds and not exceeding 22 pounds.

DISQUALIFICATIONS

Color—White in any part of the coat, forming a patch or stripe measuring as much as $\frac{1}{2}$ inch in its longest dimension.

Weight (Standard Variety)—Over 22 pounds.

Ears (Toy Variety)—Cropped or cut ears.

THE NORWICH TERRIER

This is the breed that went to college. In 1880 the students at Cambridge University in England wanted a sturdy, *"manly little chap"* that was an easy keeper, no bother, small enough to exist in limited quarters and on limited funds. The Norwich Terrier was the answer, and keeping a specimen of the breed became a fad at Cambridge. In fact it was, at the time, suggested that the breed be called the Cambridge or Cantab Terrier.

After World War I some specimens of the breed came to America, called at the time *"Jones Terriers"* after the name of one of the foremost breeders of the little dogs, and were put into the kennels of several Masters of Foxhounds. The dogs proved their excellence at going to ground and had no trouble, despite their short legs, in keeping up with the hunt when not carried.

If you are looking for a small, tough, wire-haired terrier that is game to the core, look no further, the Norwich is your dog. He makes an ideal house dog and his loyalty never falters. Every effort is being made by breeders to keep the breed from being changed in any way by individuals who wish to *"improve"* them for show purposes.

The Norwich is genetically a happy mixture of many small terrier breeds with the Irish Terrier probably most prominent.

Champion Wendover Foxhunter

STANDARD OF THE NORWICH TERRIER

Head—Skull wide, slightly rounded with good width between the ears. Muzzle strong but not long or heavy, with slightly "foxy" appearance. Length about one-third less than the measurement from the occiput to the bottom of the stop, which should be well defined.

Faults—A long narrow head; over square muzzle; highly rounded dome.

Ears—Prick or Drop. If pricked: neat, small and erect. If dropped: neat, small and correctly dropped.

Faults—Oversize; poor carriage.

Eyes—Very bright, dark and keen. Full of expression.

Faults—Light or protruding eyes.

Jaw—Clean, strong, tight lipped, with strong, rather large closely fitting teeth.

Faults—A mouth badly over or undershot.

Neck—Short and strong, well set on clean shoulders.

Body—Moderately short, compact and deep with level top line, ribs well sprung.

Faults—Long weak back, loaded shoulders.

Legs—Short and powerful and as straight as is consistent with the short legs for which we aim. Sound bone, round feet, thick pads.

Faults—Out at elbow, badly bowed, knuckled over. Too light in bone.

Quarters—Strong, rounded, with great powers of propulsion.

Faults—Cow hocks.

Tail—Medium docked, carriage not excessively gay.

Color—Red, wheaten, black and tan or grizzle. White markings on the chest, though allowable, are not desirable.

Faults—White markings elsewhere or to any great extent on the chest.

Coat—As hard and wiry as possible, lying quite close to the body. Coat absolutely straight but in winter longer and rougher, forming almost a mane on the shoulders and neck. Hair on head, ears and muzzle, except for slight eyebrows and slight whiskers, is absolutely short and smooth. These dogs should be shown with as nearly a natural coat as possible. Excessive trimming shall be heavily penalized.

Faults—Silky or curly coat.

Weight—10 to 14 pounds, 11 pounds being the ideal.

Height—10 to 12 inches at the withers, not to exceed.

General Appearance—A small, low, cobby, keen dog, tremendously active. A perfect demon, yet not quarrelsome, and of a lovable disposition, and a very hardy constitution. Honorable scars from fair wear and tear shall not count against.

DISQUALIFICATIONS

Cropped ears shall disqualify.

THE MINIATURE SCHNAUZER

The Schnauzer comes in three sizes, Standard, Giant and Miniature, and though the Miniature is classified as a terrier, the Standard and Giant varieties are listed in the Working Dog category. Of course it is known that both Miniature and Giant were derived from the Standard with different breed crosses brought in to affect the size in either direction, but the problem of where these size variations in the Schnauzer family should really be grouped has not, to the author's mind, been satisfactorily settled. The Minnie, produced by crossing Affenpinschers with selected smaller-than-usual Standard

Champion Dorem Originality

Schnauzers, is then the product of a Toy Dog and a Working Dog. Regardless of type (which is admittedly Terrier), there *seems* to be no reason why he should be classified as a Terrier. As a matter of fact and record, the Standard Schnauzer, which was the mainspring of the Minnie's heritage, at one time was shown out of the Terrier Group until 1945 when the A.K.C. changed its classification to a Working Dog. Practically all the other Terriers in this specific group classification originated in the British Isles with this breed, the Miniature Schnauzer, as one of the very few exceptions.

The Minnie is a trappy, handsome little animal, a good ratter, excellent watch dog and companion. He was recognized as a separate breed in 1899 when he initially appeared in his own classes in Germany, the Schnauzer's native land. They first came to the United States in 1925 and the present club for the breed came into being in 1933.

Hardy and active, less aggressive than the Standard, they are intelligent companions for dog fanciers of all ages.

STANDARD OF THE MINIATURE SCHNAUZER

General Appearance—The Miniature Schnauzer is a robust, active dog of terrier type, resembling his larger cousin, the Standard Schnauzer, in general appearance, and of an alert, active disposition. He is sturdily built, nearly square in proportion of body length to height, with plenty of bone, and without any suggestion of toyishness.

Head—Strong and rectangular, its width diminishing slightly from ears to eyes, and again to the tip of the nose. The forehead is unwrinkled. The topskull is flat and fairly long. The foreface is parallel to the topskull, with a slight stop, and is at least as long as the topskull. The muzzle is strong in proportion to the skull; it ends in a moderately blunt manner, with thick whiskers which accentuate the rectangular shape of the head.

Teeth—The teeth meet in a scissors bite. That is, the upper front teeth overlap the lower front teeth in such a manner that the inner surface of the upper incisors barely touches the outer surface of the lower incisors when the mouth is closed.

Eyes—Small, dark brown and deep-set. They are oval in appearance and keen in expression.

Ears—When cropped the ears are identical in shape and length, with pointed tips. They are in balance with the head and not exaggerated in length. They are set high on the skull and carried perpendicularly at the inner edges, with as little bell as possible along the outer edges. When uncropped, the ears are small and V-shaped, folding close to the skull.

Neck—Strong and well arched, blending into the shoulders, and with the skin fitting tightly at the throat.

Body—Short and deep, with the brisket extending at least to the elbows. Ribs are well sprung and deep, extending well back to a short loin. The underbody does not present a tucked-up appearance at the flank. The topline is straight; it declines slightly from the withers to the base of the tail. The overall length from chest to stern bone equals the height at the withers.

Forequarters—The forequarters have flat, somewhat sloping shoulders and high withers. Forelegs are straight and parallel when viewed from all sides. They have strong pasterns and good bone. They are separated by a fairly deep brisket which precludes a pinched front. The elbows are close, and the ribs

542

Champion Yankee Pride Colonel Stump

spread gradually from the first rib so as to allow space for the elbows to move close to the body.

Hindquarters—The hindquarters have strong-muscled, slanting thighs: they are well bent at the stifles and straight from hock to so-called heel. There is sufficient angulation so that, in stance, the hocks extend beyond the tail. The hindquarters never appear overbuilt or higher than the shoulders.

Feet—Short and round (cat-feet) with thick black pads. The toes are arched and compact.

Action—The trot is the gait at which movement is judged. The dog must gait in a straight line. Coming on, the forelegs are parallel, with the elbows close to the body. The feet turn neither inward nor outward. Going away, the hind legs are parallel from the hocks down, and travel wide. Viewed from the side, the forelegs have a good reach, while the hind legs have a strong drive with good pick-up of hocks.

Tail—Set high and carried erect. It is docked only long enough to be clearly visible over the top line of the body when the dog is in proper length of coat.

Coat—Double, with a hard, wiry outer coat and a close under coat. The body coat should be plucked. When in show condition, the proper length is not less than three-quarters of an inch except on neck, ears and skull. Furnishings are fairly thick but not silky.

Size—From 12 to 14 inches. Ideal size 13½ inches.

Color—The recognized colors are salt and pepper, black and silver, and

Champion Jonaire Pocono Rock n' Roll

solid black. The typical color is salt and pepper in shades of gray; tan shading is permissible. The salt and pepper mixture fades out to light gray or silver white in the eyebrows, whiskers, cheeks under throat, across chest, under tail, leg furnishings under body, and inside legs. The light under-body hair is not to rise higher on the sides of the body than the front elbows. The black and silvers follow the same pattern as the salt and peppers. The entire salt-and-pepper section must be black. Black is the only solid color allowed. It must be a true black with no gray hairs and no brown tinge except where the whiskers may have become discolored. A small white spot on the chest is permitted.

FAULTS

Type—Toyishness, raciness, or coarseness.

Structure—Head coarse and cheeky. Chest too broad or shallow in brisket. Tail set low. Sway or roach back. Bowed or cowhocked hindquarters. Loose elbows.

Action—Sidegaiting. Paddling in front, or high hackney knee action. Weak hind action.

Coat—Too soft or too smooth and slick in appearance.

Temperament—Shyness or viciousness.

Bite—Undershot or overshot jaw. Level bite.

Eyes—Light and/or large and prominent in appearance.

DISQUALIFICATIONS

Dogs or bitches under 12 inches or over 14 inches. Color solid white or white patches on the body.

544

THE SCOTTISH TERRIER

A very, very popular fellow is the low-stationed, stout-hearted Scottie, and for many very good reasons. No other breed is as lovably whimsical as this roguish little "tyke" of the Scottish Highlands. His pluck has earned him the soubriquet "die-hard", and he usually lives up to it. He is companionable, affectionate, and an ideal children's playmate. For his many fine qualities there is no dog that can so endear himself to his owner as the Scottie.

Admirers of the breed argue that all other Scottish breeds must be later offshoots of the Scottie, for to their minds, he must have come first, he must be *"the oldest variety of the canine race indigenous to Britain,"* to quote from Rawdon B. Lee, an English authority on the breed.

In 1880, at the Birmingham Show in England, and at later shows, classes were held for Scottish Terriers. But they were filled with Skyes, Yorkshires and Dandie Dinmonts, not Scotties, and a furore arose, spontaneously begun by indignant breeders of the true Scottish Terriers, at this very wicked deception. Their protests even broke into print and waxed so furious that it was finally brought to a halt only through description of the true type of Scottie, to which all parties agreed, as conceived by Captain Gordon Murray.

Champion Gaidoune Gorgeous Hussy

Subsequently a standard was drawn up by J. B. Morrison to fit the Captain's concept and which was accepted as the standard for the Scottish Terrier.

John Naylor introduced the Scottie here in 1883. The first registration of this breed occurred at about the time the American Kennel Club was being organized.

To the early pioneers of the breed in this country the breed's continued and just popularity in America is an enduring monument.

STANDARD OF THE SCOTTISH TERRIER

Skull—Long, of medium width, slightly domed and covered with short hard hair. It should not be quite flat, as there should be a slight stop or drop between the eyes.

Muzzle—In proportion to the length of skull, with not too much taper toward the nose. Nose should be black and of good size. The jaws should be level and square. The nose projects somewhat over the mouth, giving the impression that the upper jaw is longer than the lower. The teeth should be

Champion
Shieling's
Signature

evenly placed, having a scissors or level bite, with the former being preferable.

Eyes—Set wide apart, small and of almond shape, not round. Color to be dark brown or nearly black. To be bright, piercing and set well under the brow.

Ears—Small, prick, set well up on the skull, rather pointed but not cut. The hair on them should be short and velvety.

Neck—Moderately short, thick and muscular, strongly set on sloping shoulders, but not so short as to appear clumsy.

Chest—Broad and very deep, well let down between the forelegs.

Body—Moderately short and well ribbed up with strong loin, deep flanks and very muscular hindquarters.

Legs and Feet—Both fore and hind legs should be short and very heavy in bone in proportion to the size of the dog. Fore legs straight or slightly bent with elbows close to the body. Scottish Terriers should not be out at the elbows. Stifles should be well bent and legs straight from hock to heel. Thighs very muscular. Feet round and thick with strong nails, fore feet larger than the hind feet.

Champion Walsing Wild Winter of Barberry Knowe (imported).

Champion Bardene Bingo (imported).

Note: The gait of the Scottish Terrier is peculiarly its own and is very characteristic of the breed. It is not the square trot or walk that is desirable in the long-legged breeds. The fore legs do not move in exact parallel planes— rather in reaching out incline slightly inward. This is due to the shortness of leg and width of chest. The action of the rear legs should be square and true and at the trot both the hocks and stifles should be flexed with a vigorous motion.

Tail—Never cut and about 7 inches long, carried with a slight curve but not over the back.

Coat—Rather short, about 2 inches, dense undercoat with outercoat intensely hard and wiry.

Size and Weight—Equal consideration must be given to height, length of back and weight. Height at shoulder for either sex, should be about 10 inches. Generally, a well balanced Scottish Terrier dog of correct size should weigh from 19 to 22 pounds, and a bitch from 18 to 21 pounds. The principal objective must be symmetry and balance.

Color—Steel or iron grey, brindled or grizzled, black, sandy or wheaten. White markings are objectionable and can be allowed only on the chest and that to a slight extent only.

General Appearance—The face should wear a keen, sharp and active expression, Both head and tail should be carried well up. The dog should look very compact, well muscled and powerful, giving the impression of immense power in a small size.

Penalties—Soft coat, round or very light eye, over or undershot jaw, obviously over or under size, shyness timidity or failure to show with head and

Champion Carmichael's Fanfare

Champion Walsing Winning Trick of Edgerstoune (imported).

tail up are faults to be penalized. No judge should put to Winners or Best of Breed any Scottish Terrier not showing real Terrier character in the ring.

SCALE OF POINTS

	Points
Skull	5
Muzzle	5
Eyes	5
Ears	10
Neck	5
Chest	5
Body	15
Legs and feet	10
Tail	$2\frac{1}{2}$
Coat	15
Size	10
Color	$2\frac{1}{2}$
General appearance	10
Total	100

THE SEALYHAM TERRIER

This is a game, strong, sturdy terrier of heavy substance and low to the ground, in which was bred the ability to dig to unearth its quarry, in this instance, badger, otter and fox.

The Sealyham derived its name from the place of its beginning in Haverfordwest, Wales, on the estate of Captain John Edwardes. Between the years 1850 and 1891 the Captain cannily merged many breeds, selecting and discarding and eliminating any dogs that showed the least sign of timidity, and finally producing, a stabilized and finished product, the breed known as the Sealyham Terrier.

The good Captain, engrossed in his breeding experiments, kept no records naming the breeds involved in the heritage of the Sealyham. We can only guess that the Bull Terrier, West Highland White, Dandie Dinmont, and perhaps the Pembroke Corgi contributed to his being.

The breed initially made its appearance on the show bench at Haverfordwest in 1903. The first breed club was founded in January, 1908, and drew up the original standard.

The American Sealyham Terrier Club was founded in 1913, though the breed was recognized by the A.K.C. two years earlier. Many times has the

Champion Barberry Knowe Candidate

Champion Cindy Belle

Sealyham gone Best in Show in America, attesting to the perfection to which it has been brought by earnest breeders.

STANDARD OF THE SEALYHAM TERRIER

The Sealyham should be the embodiment of power and determination, ever keen and alert, of extraordinary substance, yet free from clumsiness.

Height—At withers about 10½ inches. Weight: 21 pounds for dogs, and 20 pounds for bitches. It should be borne in mind that size is more important than weight.

Head—Long, broad and powerful, without coarseness. It should, however, be in perfect balance with the body, joining neck smoothly. Length of head roughly, three-quarters height at withers, or about an inch longer than neck. Breadth between ears a little less than one-half length of head.

Skull—Very slightly domed, with a shallow indentation running down between the brows, and joining the muzzle with a moderate stop.

Cheeks—Smoothly formed and flat, without heavy jowls.

Jaws—Level, powerful and square. Overshot or undershot bad faults.

Teeth—Sound, strong and white, with canines fitting closely together.

Nose—Black, with large nostrils. White, cherry or butterfly bad faults.

Eyes—Very dark, deeply set and fairly wide apart, of medium size, oval in shape with keen terrier expression. Light, large or protruding eye bad faults.

Ears—Folded level with top of head, with forward edge close to cheek. Well rounded at tip, and of length to reach outer corner of eye. Thin, not leathery, and of sufficient thickness to avoid creases. Prick, tulip, rose or hound ears bad faults.

Neck—Length, slightly less than two-thirds of height of dog at withers. Muscular without coarseness, with good reach, refinement at throat, and set firmly on shoulders.

Shoulders—Well laid back and powerful, but not overmuscled. Sufficiently wide to permit freedom of action. Upright or straight shoulder placement highly undesirable.

Legs—Forelegs strong, with good bone; and as straight as is consistent with chest being well let down between them. Down on pasterns, knuckled over, bound, and out at elbow, bad faults. Hindlegs longer than forelegs and not so heavily boned.

Feet—Large but compact, round with thick pads, strong nails. Toes well arched and pointing straight ahead. Forefeet larger, though not quite so long as hindfeet. Thin, spread or flat feet bad faults.

Body—Strong, short coupled and substantial, so as to permit great flexibility. Brisket deep and well let down between forelegs. Ribs well sprung.

Back—Length from withers to set on of tail should approximate height at withers, or 10½ inches. Top line level, neither roached or swayed. Any deviations from these measurements undesirable.

Hindquarters—Very powerful, and protruding well behind the set on of tail. Strong second thighs, stifles well bent, and hocks well let down. Capped or cowhocks bad faults.

Tail—Docked and carried upright. Set on far enough forward so that spine does not slope down to it.

Coat—Weather resisting, comprised of soft, dense undercoat and hard, wiry top coat. Silky or curly coat bad fault.

Color—All white, or with lemon, tan or badger markings on head and ears. Heavy body markings and excessive ticking should be discouraged.

Action—Sound, strong, quick, free, true and level.

Note : The measurements were taken with calipers.

SCALE OF POINTS

		Points
General character, balance and size		15
Head	5	
Eyes	5	
Mouth	5	
Ears	5	
Neck	5	
	—	25
Shoulders and brisket	10	
Body, ribs and loin	10	
Hindquarters	10	
Legs and feet	10	
Coat	10	
	—	50
Tail	5	
Color (body marking and ticking)	5	
	—	10
Total		100

THE SKYE TERRIER

"You can scarcely see the dog for the coat," was a classical remark directed at this very old and unchanged breed of terrier. He comes from the Isle of Skye, the most important of that group of northwestern islands in Scotland, and is the only terrier distinctly belonging to that area that is not common to the rest of the country.

The Skye Terrier has changed very little since it first appeared as a breed and, though most terriers have been formed in type in the last century, the Skye of nearly four hundred years ago was almost the same as the dog of today. In an earlier time there were developed two types which differed only in ear carriage, one type having pendant ears and the other, upright or prick ears.

In the old volume, *"Englishe Dogges"*, written by Dr. John Caius, court physician to Edward VI, Queen Mary, and Queen Elizabeth, the Skye Terrier was described *". . . by reason of the length of heare, makes showe neither of face nor of body."* The Scots, knowing the value of what they had, wanted to keep this breed of theirs' unchanged and stood by the motto of the Skye Club of Scotland: *"Wha Daur Meddle Wi' Me."*

The breed became the pet of nobility and the working terrier of the 19th century, and was one of the most widely known and admired of all terriers. He came to this country in Colonial times and gained A.K.C. recognition in 1887.

Champion Evening Star de Luchar (French import).

Both the prick ear and drop ear are permissible according to the Skye Terrier standard, but the prick eared variety is the most popular.

Though his popularity has lessened since the days when he was one of the most important breeds in American shows, this fearless, hardy terrier still has his staunch adherents to whom no other breed but the Skye appeals.

STANDARD OF THE SKYE TERRIER

Characteristics—An alert terrier with great style, elegance and dignity, gay with friends and reserved with strangers. Fearless, good-tempered, loyal and canny; never shy or ill-tempered. A working terrier, capable of overtaking its game and going to ground, displaying stamina, courage, strength and agility. Must be of a size suitable for its work. Strong in body, quarters and jaws. Of good bone and hard muscle. Neither slight, heavy, lethargic or nervous. Hair on head and body should be of such length and texture to protect it in the brush and in a serious argument.

General Appearance—(Detailed in later sections). Long, low and lank. Level back. Flattish appearance to sides. Strong head. Dark eyes, full of life and intelligence. Ears prick or drop. Graceful neck. Straight front and rear, with hindquarters moderately angulated. Feathered tail. Hard, straight, 5½ inch outercoat, well furnished on ears, face and tail; any color so long as muzzle is dark. A good mover. Ideal height for male 10 inches, for female 9½ inches and length measured chest over tail at rump, twice the height.

Body—Pre-eminently long and low. Back level. Neck long and gracefully arched. Chest deep. Ribs a deep oval giving a flattish appearance to sides.

To be penalized—High on leg or cobbiness. Swayback or roach back. Short neck. Shallow or barrel chest.

Forequarters—Straight front. Good layback of shoulders with tight placement of shoulder blades at withers. Elbows close to body. Legs short, muscular and straight.

To be Penalized—Fiddle front or out at elbows. Straight shoulders. Shoulder blades wide apart at withers. Weak or crooked front legs.

Hindquarters—Full, well developed and moderately angulated. Legs short, muscular and straight, when viewed from behind. No dewclaws.

To be Penalized—Weak hindquarters. Straight stifles. Weak or crooked hind legs as viewed from behind. Cowhocks. Dewclaws on hind legs.

Feet—Large, hare-feet, pointing forward. Pads thick. Nails strong and preferably black.

To be Penalized—Splay, paper or cat-foot.

Movement—The legs should be carried straight forward when traveling. When approaching, the forelegs should form a continuation of the straight line of the front, without paddling or weaving, the feet being the same distance apart as the elbows. The principal propelling power is furnished by the hind legs and should be straight forward without weaving. The whole movement should be fluid without waddle or bounce. Movement is important in a Skye Terrier since conformation may be concealed by a profuse coat. Therefore, the dog must be in motion to reveal its true conformation.

Head—The head should be long and powerful, with slight stop, but never coarse. Strength should not be sacrificed for extreme length. Powerful jaws and mouth, incisor teeth closing level or upper teeth just fitting over lower. Moderate width at back of skull tapering gradually to a strong muscle. Muzzle dark and nose always black.

To be Penalized—Short, weak or coarse head. Snipy muzzle. Wry mouth. Undershot or overshot jaw. Nose any color other than black.

Two famous prick eared champions. The physical individuality possessed by the prick eared Skye Terrier is very much in evidence in this photograph.

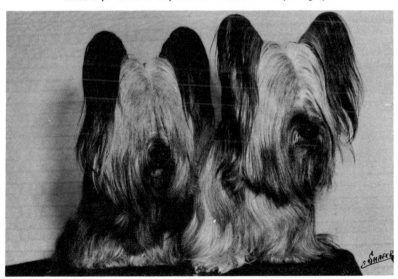

Champion Glamoor Yule Star

Eyes—Brown, preferably dark brown. Medium size, close set, full of life and intelligence.

To be Penalized—Light or yellow colored eyes.

Ears (Prick or drop)—Gracefully feathered and symmetrical. When prick, not large, erect at outer edges and slightly wider apart at peak than at skull; should be placed high on skull. When drop, placed lower on head; larger ears are permitted and they should hang flat against the skull.

To be Penalized—Ears that are not symmetrical. Prick ears that are low set. Semi-prick ears. Drop ears with a lift. Lazy carriage of prick ears.

Ideal Measurements—Dog: height at shoulder, 10 inches. Length, chest

Champion Jacinthe de Ricelaine (French import).

bone over tail at rump 20 inches. Head, 8½ inches. Tail, 9 inches. Bitch: Height at shoulder 9½ inches. Length, chest bone over tail at rump 19 inches. Head, 8 inches. Tail, 8½ inches. A slightly higher or lower dog of either sex is acceptable, providing body, head and tail dimensions are proportionately longer or shorter. It should be noted that the ideal ratio of body length to shoulder height is 2 to 1. The height and length measurements should be taken with the Skye standing in a natural position with the feet well under it. A box caliper is used, vertically and horizontally. For the height, the top bar should be across the back at the highest point of the withers. The head is measured from the tip of the nose to the back of the occipital bone, and the tail from its root to tip.

To be Penalized—Dogs at shoulder 12 inches or higher, and bitches 11¼ inches or higher. Dogs 8 inches or lower, and bitches 7½ inches or lower. These measurements are definite limits and any height over or under is to be considered a very serious fault.

Coat—(Double) Undercoat short, close, soft and woolly. Outercoat 5½ inches, with no extra credit for any greater length. Hard, straight and flat. Body coat hanging straight down each side, parting from head to tail. Hair on head shorter, softer and veiling forehead and eyes, with moderate beard and apron. On ears, overhanging inside, falling down and mingling with side locks, surrounding the ears like a fringe and allowing their shape to appear.

To be Penalized—Any softness or curl of outer coat. A single or sparse coat. Lack of ear or face curtains.

Tail—When hanging, upper section pendulous, and following the line of rump; lower section thrown back in a gentle arc. When raised, a prolongation of the line of the back. Though not preferred, sometimes carried high when happy, excited or angry. When this is a matter of spirit, not conformation, no penalty should follow. Well feathered.

To be Penalized—Tail with twist or curl or continuously carried above the line of the back. Tail poorly feathered.

Color—Any color, including but not limited to black, dark or light blue, gray, fawn or cream. Shade of head and legs should approximate that of body. In dogs of all colors, muzzle, ears and tip of tail are preferably dark.

Scale of Points

	Points
Body—Back and neck. Chest and ribs. Forequarters and hindquarters. Feet. Movement	40
Head—Skull. Jaws and teeth. Eyes and ears	20
Size—Dog: Height at shoulder 10 inches. Length, chest bone over tail at rump 20 inches. Head 8½ inches and tail 9 inches. Bitch: Height at shoulder 9½ inches. Length, chest bone over tail at rump 19 inches. Head 8 inches. Tail 8½ inches. A slightly higher or lower dog of either sex, providing body, head and tail are proportionately longer or shorter	15
Coat—Outercoat hard and straight with a length of 5½ inches, with no extra credit for any greater length. Undercoat short, close, soft and woolly	15
Tail—Carriage and feather	10
Total	100

THE STAFFORDSHIRE TERRIER

Why this breed was given its name instead of the many others that would fit it so much better the author can't imagine. In my youth the breed was known as the Pit Bull Terrier and was the original pit fighting dog, the most courageous animal ever born. The author owned one, a steel-muscled fawn dog with ears clipped close to the skull and a stub of a tail, leaving little for an adversary to grab hold of. He was well scarred and undoubtedly had been used in the pit before I acquired him. He was wonderful with people but death to any animal, especially dogs, cats and rats. Our neighbor, poor soul, was a cat fancier and never did figure out why so many of her cats disappeared. Either my Dad or I could have told her for we wielded the spade that interred all that our dog had left of many of her felines.

The breed was also called American Bull Terrier and Yankee Terrier. The A.K.C. finally recognized it under the name Staffordshire Terrier, a cognomen indicating that the breed came from England. Research does point out that a Bull Terrier, much the same as our Pit Bull Terrier but slightly smaller, was

Champion Lylane Amber, C.D.

developed in Staffordshire by men interested in the so-called *"sport"* of pit fighting.

The White Bull Terrier was an off-shoot of the basic Staffordshire breed with other canine material added (*see Bull Terrier History*). The basis of the Staffordshire's origin was the old Bulldog (which was more like the Staffordshire or Boxer of today than the modern Bulldog) and the extinct white English Terrier. It is quite possible that there was also a cross to the game and scrappy early Fox Terrier.

These dogs, despite their unsavory past, are docile, intelligent, alert companions and guardians. Of course they are "dead game" but they should not be ostracized simply because man used their courage once as a bloody tool for gambling. The breed, though wholly attached to their master and family, if sold, will accept and become attached to their new owners and environment in a comparatively short time. Stafs are amazingly impervious to outwardly inflicted pain.

STANDARD OF THE STAFFORDSHIRE TERRIER

General Impression—The Staffordshire Terrier should give the impression of: Great Strength for his size; a well put-together dog, muscular, but agile and graceful, keenly alive to his surroundings. He should be stocky, not long-legged or racy in outline. His courage is proverbial.

Head—Medium length, deep through, broad skull, very pronounced cheek muscles, distinct stop; and ears are set high.

Ears—Cropped or uncropped, the latter preferred. Uncropped ears should be short and held half rose or prick. Full drop to be penalized.

Eyes—Dark and round, low down in skull and set far apart. No pink eyelids.

Muzzle—Medium length, rounded on upper side to fall away abruptly below eyes. Jaws well-defined. Under jaw to be strong and have biting power. Lips close and even, no looseness. Upper teeth to meet tightly outside lower teeth in front. Nose definitely black.

Neck—Heavy, slightly arched, tapering from shoulders to back of skull. No looseness of skin. Medium length.

Shoulders—Strong and muscular with blades wide and sloping.

Back—Fairly short. Slight sloping from withers to rump with gentle short slope at rump to base of tail. Loins slightly tucked.

Body—Well sprung ribs, deep in rear. All ribs close together. Forelegs set rather wide apart to permit of chest development. Chest deep and broad.

Tail—Short in comparison to size, low set, tapering to a fine point; not curled or held over back. Not docked.

Legs—The front legs should be straight, large or round bones, pastern upright. No resemblance of bend in front. Hindquarters well-muscled, let down at hocks, turning neither in nor out. Feet of moderate size, well-arched and compact. Gait must be springy but without roll or pace.

Coat—Short, close, stiff to the touch, and glossy.

Color—Any color, solid, parti, or patched is permissible, but all white, more than 80 per cent white, black and tan, and liver not to be encouraged.

Size—Height and weight should be in proportion. A height of about eighteen (18) to nineteen (19) inches at shoulders for the male and seventeen (17) to eighteen (18) inches for the female is to be considered preferable.

Faults—Faults to be penalized are Dudley nose, light or pink eyes, tail too long or badly carried, undershot or overshot mouths.

PORTRAIT OF A SCOTTISH TERRIER.

561

A PRICK-EARED SKYE TERRIER.

THE EASILY IDENTIFIED, SMOOTH FOX TERRIER.

FROM THE "DOWN UNDER" CONTINENT COMES
THE APTLY NAMED AUSTRALIAN TERRIER.

THE MINIATURE SCHNAUZER, THIS BREED'S
REPRESENTATIVE IN THE TERRIER GROUP. A
KERRY BLUE TERRIER APPEARS AT THE TOP OF
THE FACING PAGE, AND BELOW HIM IS AN
IRISH TERRIER.

ABOVE IS PICTURED A MINIATURE SCHNAUZER. BELOW, A HEAD STUDY OF A BORDER TERRIER. ON THE OPPOSITE PAGE IS A PAIR OF AIREDALES, THE LARGEST AND MOST VERSATILE OF ALL THE TERRIERS.

TOP LEFT, A STAFFORDSHIRE TERRIER, THE MODERN COUNTERPART OF THE OLD PIT FIGHTING DOG. BELOW HIM IS A HEAD STUDY OF A CAIRN TERRIER. ABOVE IS A PORTRAIT OF THE DROLL DANDIE DINMONT AND, TO THE RIGHT AND CENTER, A BRACE OF WEST HIGHLAND WHITE TERRIERS.

HEAD PORTRAITS OF A PAIR OF FOX TERRIERS
SHOWING THE TWO COATS WORN BY THIS
CANINE VARIETY, THE WIREHAIRED AND THE
SMOOTH.

E·H·HART

AT THE TOP IS THE COLORED BULL TERRIER.

BELOW, THE ALL-WHITE VARIETY OF BULL TERRIER.

THE TRAPPY LITTLE WELSH TERRIER.

A SILVER BRINDLE SCOTTISH TERRIER.

THE CAIRN TERRIER.

HEAD STUDY OF A LAKELAND TERRIER.

A PAIR OF YOUNG AUSTRALIAN TERRIERS.

A FINE AND RUGGED NORWICH TERRIER.

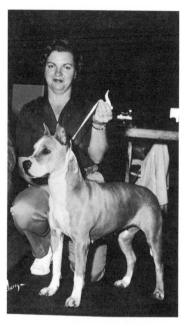

Upper left; Ch. Rip Rock Happy Bold Orin. Above; Ch. Rossmore Victoria. Lower left; Ch. Knight Crusader. Below; Ch. Knight Bomber.

THE WELSH TERRIER

This game little breed came down through the centuries to us almost unchanged from its pristine form. With some few modern touches, he is the personification of the ancient, wire-haired Black-and-Tan Terrier that formed the breed basis for so many of our terrier breeds.

In Wales, his home, the Welsh Terrier went to ground for fox, badger, and otter. For this job he required gameness, sturdiness and agility and he had, and still has, all these attributes in abundance.

Superficially, the Welshman looks like a Fox Terrier-sized Airedale *(or a black and tan Fox Terrier)*, but of course the breed has its own standard that indicates clearly the differences between it and all other terriers.

The Welsh Terrier makes a splendid house dog and is an easy keeper. He was shown earlier under two different names, his own and as an Old English Terrier. As a matter of record, as late as 1893, a dog named Dick Turpin won under *both* breed names. In 1888 Welsh Terriers were brought to America by Mr. Prescott Lawrence and at the Westminster Show of 1901, the breed was given its own classes.

STANDARD OF THE WELSH TERRIER

Head—The skull should be flat, and rather wider between the ears than the Wire-haired Fox Terrier. The jaw should be powerful, clean-cut, rather deeper, and more punishing—giving the head a more masculine appearance than that usually seen on a Fox Terrier. Stop not too defined, fair length from stop to end of nose, the latter being of a black color.

Ears—The ear should be V-shaped, small, not too thin, set on fairly high, carried forward and close to the cheek.

Eyes—The eye should be small, not being too deeply set in or protruding out of skull, of a dark hazel color, expressive and indicating abundant pluck.

Neck—The neck should be of moderate length and thickness, slightly arched and sloping gracefully into the shoulders.

Body—The back should be short, and well-ribbed up, the loin strong, good depth, and moderate width of chest. The shoulders should be long, sloping, and well set back. The hindquarters should be strong, thighs muscular and of good length, with the hocks moderately straight, well let down, and fair amount of bone. The stern should be set on moderately high, but not too gaily carried.

Legs and Feet—The legs should be straight and muscular, possessing fair amount of bone, with upright and powerful pasterns. The feet should be small, round and catlike.

Coat—The coat should be wiry, hard, very close and abundant.

Color—The color should be black and tan, or black grizzle and tan, free from black penciling on toes.

Size—The height at shoulder should be 15 inches for dogs, bitches pro-

Champion Carlano Canakin.

A well set-down Welsh Terrier.

Champion Pool Forge Fast Freight.

portionately less. Twenty pounds shall be considered a fair average weight in working condition, but this may vary a pound or so either way.

SCALE OF POINTS

	Points
Head and jaws	10
Ears	5
Eyes	5
Neck and shoulders	10
Body	10
Loins and hindquarters	10
Legs and feet	10
Coat	15
Color	5
Stern	5
General appearance	15
Total	100

DISQUALIFYING POINTS

(1) Nose: white, cherry or spotted to a considerable extent with either of these colors. (2) Ears: prick, tulip or rose. (3) Undershot jaw or pig-jawed mouth. (4) Black below hocks or white to an appreciable extent.

THE WEST HIGHLAND WHITE TERRIER

This trappy little terrier comes from the same root-stock as the other terriers of Scotland, the Scotties, Cairns and Dandie Dinmonts. It is said to have originated at Poltallock and was bred and owned by the Malcolm family of that section for generations. Small, but game, hardy, and possessed of a large portion of self-esteem, this sparkling little terrier is a true sporting and hunting breed.

At one time the breed was known as the Poltallock Terrier, borrowing the name from its place of origin. It was also called the Roseneath Terrier, taken from the name of the Duke of Argyll's estate in Dumbartonshire. Needless to say, the Duke was also a fancier of this white terrier of Scotland.

The breed was first introduced in the United States by Mr. Robert Goelet who, at great expense, brought in some of the finest champions of England to establish a solid foundation for the breed in America.

Spunky, devoted and gay, the West Highland White Terrier makes a light-hearted pet and companion for the home.

STANDARD OF THE WEST HIGHLAND WHITE TERRIER

General Appearance of the West Highland White Terrier is that of a small,

Champion Elfinbrook Simon

game, hardy-looking terrier exhibiting good showmanship, possessed with no small amount of self-esteem, with varminty appearance strongly built, deep in chest and back ribs, straight back and powerful hindquarters on muscular legs, and exhibiting in a marked degree a great combination of strength and activity. The coat should be about 2 inches long, white in color, hard, with plenty of soft undercoat, and no tendency to wave or curl. The tail should be as straight as possible and carried not too gaily, and covered with hard hair, but not bushy. The skull should be not too broad, being in proportion to the terribly powerful jaws. The ears shall be as small and sharp-pointed as possible and carried tightly up, and must be absolutely erect. The eyes of moderate size, as dark as possible, widely placed with a sharp, bright, intelligent expression. The muzzle should not be too long, powerful and gradually tapering toward the nose; the roof of mouth and pads of feet are usually black in color. The dog should be tidied up. Considerable hair should be left around the head to act as a frame for the face to yield a typical Westie expression.

Color—Pure white; any other color objectionable.

Coat—Very important, and seldom seen to perfection; must be double-coated. The outer coat consists of hard hair, about 2 inches long, and free from any curl. The under coat, which resembles fur, is short, soft and close. Open coats are objectionable.

Size—Dogs should measure about 11 inches at the withers, bitches about 1 inch less.

Skull—Should not be too narrow, being in poportion to his powerful jaw, not too long, slightly domed, and gradually tapering to the eyes, between which there should be a slight indentation or stop, eyebrows heavy. There should be little apparent difference in length between the muzzle and the skull.

Eyes—Widely set apart, medium in size, as dark as possible in color, slightly sunk in the head, sharp and intelligent, which, looking from under the heavy eyebrows give a piercing look. Full eyes and also light colored eyes are very objectionable.

Muzzle—Should be nearly equal in length to the rest of the skull, powerful and gradually tapering towards the nose, which should be fairly wide. The nose itself should be black in color. The jaws level and powerful, the teeth square or evenly met, well set and large for the size of the dog. Teeth much overshot or much undershot should be heavily penalized. Muzzles longer than the skull and not in proportion thereto are objectionable.

Ears—Small, carried tightly erect and never dropped, set wide apart and terminating in a sharp point. The hair on them should be short, smooth and velvety and they should never be cut. The ears should be free from fringe at the top. Round-pointed, broad and large ears are very objectionable as are ears set too closely together or heavily covered with hair.

Neck—Muscular and nicely set on sloping shoulders.

Chest—Very deep, with breadth in proportion to the size of the dog.

Body—Compact, straight back, ribs deep and well arched in the upper half of rib, presenting a flattish side appearance, loins broad and strong, hindquarters strong, muscular and wide across the top.

Legs and Feet—Both fore and hindlegs should be short and muscular. The shoulder blades should be comparatively broad, and well sloped backwards. The points of the shoulder blades should be closely knitted into the backbone, so that very little movement of them should be noticeable when the dog is walking. The elbow should be close into the body both when moving or

Champion Wishing Well's White Frost

Champion Kirk O' The Glen's Snow White

standing, thus causing the foreleg to be well placed in under the shoulder. The forelegs should be straight and thickly covered with short hard hair. The hindlegs should be short and sinewy. The thighs very muscular and not too wide apart. The hocks bent and well set in under the body, so as to be fairly close to each other either when standing, walking, or trotting. The forefeet are larger than the hind ones, are round, proportionate in size, strong, thickly padded, and covered with short hard hair. The hindfeet are smaller and thickly padded. Cowhocks detract from the general appearance. Straight or weak hocks, both kinds, are undesirable, and should be guarded against.

Tail—Five or six inches long, covered with hard hairs, no feather, as straight as possible, carried gaily but not curled over back. Tails longer than 6 inches are objectionable.

Movement—Should be free, straight and easy all round. In front the leg should be freely extended forward by the shoulder. The hind movement should be free, strong and close. The hocks should be freely flexed and drawn close in under the body, so that when moving off on the foot the body is thrown or pushed forward with some force. Stiff, stilty movement behind is very objectionable.

ATTENTION OF JUDGES

1. Under no consideration should a West Highland White Terrier be judged or trimmed as a Scottish Terrier. They are a distinct breed differing in head, body, hindquarters, movement and general overall type. They are *Not* white Scottish Terriers.

2. Any faking such as blackening the nose or bleaching the coat should disqualify the dog.

SCALE OF POINTS

	Points
General appearance	15
Color	7½
Coat	10
Size	7½
Skull	5
Eyes	5
Muzzle	5
Ears	5
Neck	5
Chest	5
Body	10
Legs and feet	7½
Tail	5
Movement	7½
Total	100

FAULTS

Coat—Any silkiness, wave or tendency to curl is a serious blemish as is an open coat, single coat or one having black, gray or wheaten hairs therein.

Size—Any specimens under the minimum or over the maximum weight or height limits are objectionable.

Eyes—Full or light colored.

Ears—Round-pointed, poorly placed, drop, semi-erect or overly large.

Muzzle—Overly long forefaces, teeth too much overshot or too much undershot or defective teeth.

Above are, Lochglen's Play Boy
on the left, and Kirk O' The
Glen's Toorie M'Weyin. Posed
at right is, Ch. Tumbleweed's
Happy Texan.

GROUP V

Toy Dogs

Small Water-Spaniel   The Comforter   The

THESE little dogs, as we know them today, are simply ornamental companions and pets. There has always been a need for such animals, little creatures that can be held close to the heart and will return the love that is given them gladly and without reticence. This is the niche in dogdom that the toy dog fills so admirably.

Though of a size and type to be, as pets, pampered by their owners, they almost all share one common virtue—pluck. They have, as a group, courage much beyond their small size. In many instances these characteristics are a genetic heritage from terrier forebears, or the happy by-products, or skillful results, of selective breeding.

Many of these tiny breeds are sturdier and stronger than they appear and need no special pampering to stay healthy and be content. Most of the toy dogs were fashioned long ago to give pleasure to a kind of people in a kind of habitation long since outmoded and gone. Yet it would seem that those people of the past had some strange ability to look into the future to the present time when small apartments are the habitats of tens of thousands of people in crowded cities where dwelling buildings grow ever higher, reaching toward the sky. For these are the homes for which the Toys were unknowingly molded, the crowded sky-scraping apartment houses with their compact, spaceless living units. Only small dogs can live here, to bring their warm, living, breathing devotion to those who need that companionship, who cannot live without a dog by their side.

So the Toy dog plays his part in the scheme of things; a small animal who can yet bring big happiness to a great many people.

Head study of an Affenpinscher.

THE AFFENPINSCHER

A German breed, the name in its breeders' native tongue, means "*Monkey Terrier*" and it was known as the "*Monkey Dog*" when first introduced in America.

The Affenpinscher is said to have been bred pure in type since the 17th century, and is of the same basic root stock as the Miniature Pinscher, with added introductions of small, wire-haired, terrier-like native breeds to its ancestral background.

The breed is noted for its fearlessness, no matter what the size of the aggressor. Affenpinschers are, of course, quite small but they are sturdily made and need not be babied. This quaint little dog's popularity has been overshadowed by the Brussels Griffon, a breed of which the Affenpinscher is said to have been the progenitor. The little "*Monkey Dog*", bred to the Standard Schnauzer, also produced the Miniature Schnauzer listed in the Terrier Group.

The Affenpinscher was admitted to A.K.C. Stud Book registration in 1936 and enjoyed some measure of popularity which ceased due to the lack of importation of new strains during World War II. Appearing again at the shows, the breed's supporters predict a rise in popular favor in the very near future for this very interesting little dog.

STANDARD OF THE AFFENPINSCHER

As in most Toys, general appearance is one of, if not the most important single point in the Affenpinscher. Details are of secondary importance and anatomical variations are of small concern.

General Appearance—Small, but rather sturdy in build and not delicate in any way. He carries himself with comical seriousness and he is generally quiet and a very devoted pal. He can get vehemently excited, however, when attacked and is fearless toward any aggressor.

Coat—A very important factor. It is short and dense in certain parts and shaggy and longer in others, but should be hard and wiry. It is longer and more loose and shaggy on the legs and around the eyes, nose and chin, giving the typical monkeylike appearance from whence comes his name. The best color is black matching his eyes and fiery temperament. However, black with tan markings, red, grey and other mixtures are permissible. Very light colors and white markings are a fault.

Head—Should be round and not too heavy, with well domed forehead.

Eyes—Should be round, of good size, black and very brilliant.

Ears—Rather small, set high, pointed and erect, usually clipped to a point.

Muzzle—Must be short and rather pointed with a black nose. The upper jaw is a trifle shorter than the lower jaw while the teeth should close together, a slight undershot condition is not material. The teeth, however, should not show.

Neck—Short and straight.

Body—The back should be straight with its length about equal to the height

A top male Affenpinscher in Germany.

Champion Alfa von Elmuer

A trophy winning Affenpinscher.

at the shoulder. Chest should be reasonably deep and the body should show only a slight tuck up at the loin.

Legs—Front legs should be straight as possible. Hind legs without much bend at the hocks and set well under the body.

Feet—Should be round, small and compact. Turned neither in nor out, with preferably black pads and nails.

Tail—Cut short, set and carried high.

Size—The smaller dog, if of characteristic type, is more valuable and the shoulder height should not exceed 10¼ inches in any case.

Thurmer's Botchimee

THE CHIHUAHUA

There are many stories about the origin of the Chihuahua.

I'm inclined to believe the one traced as far back as the 9th Century A.D. when the "Techichi" dog was the beloved pet and companion of the Toltecs of Mexico and were used in their religious rites. They were said to look more like a fawn with longer legs, humped back and thin body, not like our compact Chihuahua of today.

Also we read stories of their running wild on the prairies, even crossing with the wild prairie dog (a genetic impossibility). Even today they are good hunters. If left alone outside they will burrow in the ground, make a nest to whelp puppies. Some will dig a hole in the ground in a flower bed when nearing whelping time. If left to her own devices she would have her puppies there.

The earliest Chihuahua was an import brought from Mexico in 1898. This was an outstanding one in its day. Chihuahuas were first recognized by A.K.C. in 1904, although they were shown in 1901 and registered on their wins.

For many years Chihuahua fanciers tried to form a Club to further the interest and to establish a breed standard. Finally the Chihuahua Club of America was organized in 1923 and a standard agreed upon. The standard of today differs very little.

591

Blood lines are difficult to trace. But the old characteristics are still dominant. Many dark skinned dogs are heavy in "Minatura" blood.

Many kennels of today are noted for different characteristics and bloodlines. Looking at Chihuahuas we can almost tell what and where they came from. It is a hard task to breed good Chihuahuas, to cull out and keep the good ones, to breed correctly. But the reward is so gratifying when we really get down to serious breeding and watch our little ones parade around the ring.

This little dog can adapt to any climate, it is a man's pet as well as a child's and will protect any one who owns it.

STANDARD OF THE CHIHUAHUA

Head—A well rounded "Apple Dome" skull, with or without Molera, Cheeks and jaws lean. Nose moderately short, slightly pointed (self-colored, in blond type, or black). In moles, blues and chocolates, they are self colored. In blond types, pink nose permissible.

Ears—Large, held erect when alert, but flaring at the side at about an angle of 45 degrees when in repose. This gives breadth between the ears.

Eyes—Full, but not protruding, balanced, set well apart—dark, ruby or luminous. (Light eyes in blond types, permissible).

Teeth—Level.

Neck and Shoulders—Slightly arched, gracefully sloping into lean shoulders, may be smooth in the very short types, or with ruff about neck preferred.

Shoulders lean, sloping into a slightly broadening support above straight forelegs that are set well under, giving a free play at the elbows. Shoulders should be well up, giving balance and soundness, sloping into a level back. (Never down or low.) This gives a chestiness, and strength of forequarters, yet not of the "bulldog" chest, plenty of brisket.

Back and Body—Level back slightly longer than height. Shorter backs desired in males. Ribs rounded (but not too much "barrel-shaped.")

Hindquarters—Muscular with hocks well apart, neither out nor in, well let down with firm, sturdy action.

Tail—Moderately long, carried cycle either up or out, or in a loop over the back, with tip just touching the back. (Never tucked under.) Hair on tail in harmony with the coat of the body, preferred furry.

A natural bob-tail or tail-less permissible, if so born, and not against a good dog.

Feet—Small, with toes well split up, but not spread, pads cushioned, with fine pasterns. (Neither the "Hare" nor the "Cat" foot.) A dainty small foot with nails moderately long.

Coat—In the smooth the coat should be soft texture close and glossy. (Heavier coats with undercoats permissible.) Coat placed well over body with ruff on neck, and more scanty on head and ears.

Coat—In the Long Coats, the coat should be of a soft texture, either flat or slightly curly, with undercoat preferred. Ears fringed (heavily fringed ears may be tipped slightly, never down), feathering on feet and legs. Large ruff on neck desired and preferred. Tail full, and long (as a plume).

Color—Any color—solid, marked or splashed.

Weight—Two to six pounds, with two to four pounds preferable. If two dogs are equally good in type, the more diminutive is preferred.

General Appearances—A graceful, alert, swift-moving little dog with saucy expression. Compact, and with terrier-like qualities.

Champion Glavern Mona,
a lovely smooth.

The beautifully balanced
red fawn, Champion
Large's Gaelyn.

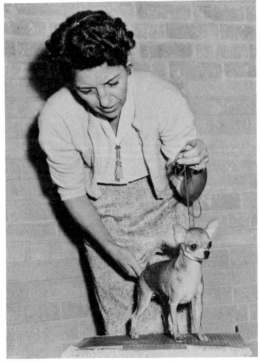

A trio of fine long-coated Chihuahuas.

Disqualifications—Cropped tail, broken down or cropped ears. On long-coated: Too thin coat that resembles bareness.

SCALE OF POINTS

SMOOTH-COATED

	Points
Head, including ears	20
Body	20
Coat	10
Tail	5
Color	5
Legs	15
Weight	10
General Appearance and Action	15
Total	100

LONG-COATED

	Points
Head, including eyes	20
Body	20
Coat	20
Tail	5
Color	5
Legs	10
Weight	5
General Appearance and Action	15
Total	100

THE ENGLISH TOY SPANIEL

This breed embraces four color varieties which were given different names yet all listed as King Charles Spaniels, named after Charles II, King of England, with whom they were favorites. Here, since 1903, they have been named officially English Toy Spaniels. The four color types are; the King Charles, a black and tan; the Prince Charles, tri-color; the Ruby, a chestnut color; and the Blenheim, red and white.

The breed is of ancient origin, said to have come from the Orient in the distant past. There is a tale that specimens of these toy dogs were sent to King James I as gifts from the Emperor of Japan in 1613 and so first came to Western shores. But before this time Dr. Johannes Caius' book, "*Englishe Dogges*", refers to these toy spaniels as "*Spaniell Gentle, otherwise called the Comforter.*"

The original King Charles Spaniels were of the black-and-tan variety. Evidently color mutations occurred and were selected for in more recent times and the other three color varieties became stabilized.

Members of the breed were once, a long time ago, called "Cockers", a term applied to dogs used for hunting woodcock. It was then that the breed was evidently graced with the sporting dog cognomen, "Spaniel". Bred smaller and much less robust and with the blunted muzzle formation selected for, since it seemed more to fit the cute toy type the royal and aristocratic owners wanted, the sporting proclivities of the breed became nil.

The breed is now a pet *("comforter"* or *"sleeve")* dog, a toy bred for the amusement and comfort that a small and cuddly lap dog brings to its owner.

STANDARD OF THE ENGLISH TOY SPANIEL

Note—Under the ruling of the American Kennel Club, passed December 10, 1902, Prince Charles, King Charles, Ruby and Blenheim Spaniels will, after January 1, 1903, be classed together as English Toy Spaniels.

Head—Should be well domed, and in good specimens is absolutely semi-globular, sometimes even extending beyond the half-circle, and absolutely projecting over the eyes, so as nearly to meet the upturned nose.

Eyes—The eyes are set wide apart, with the eyelids square to the line of the face—not oblique or fox-like. The eyes themselves are large and dark as possible, so as to be generally considered black, their enormous pupils, which are absolutely of that color, increasing the description.

Stop—The "stop," or hollow between the eyes, is well marked, as in the Bull-dog, or even more so; some good specimens exhibit a hollow deep enough to bury a small marble in it.

Nose—The nose must be short and well turned up between the eyes, and without any indication of artificial displacement afforded by a deviation to either side. The color of the end should be black, and it should be both deep and wide with open nostrils. A light colored nose is objectionable, but shall not disqualify.

Champion Veldale Volt

Jaw—The muzzle must be square and deep, and the lower jaw wide between the branches, leaving plenty of space for the tongue, and for the attachment of the lower lips, which should completely conceal the teeth. It should also be turned up or "finished," so as to allow of its meeting the end of the upper jaw, turned up in a similar way as above described. A protruding tongue is objectionable, but does not disqualify.

Ears—The ears must be long, so as to approach the ground. In an average-sized dog they measure 20 inches from tip to tip, and some reach 22 inches or even a trifle more. They should be set low down on the head and hang flat to the sides of the cheeks, and be heavy feathered.

Size—The most desirable size is from 9 pounds to 12 pounds.

Shape—In compactness of shape these Spaniels almost rival the Pug, but the length of coat adds greatly to the apparent bulk, as the body, when the coat is wetted, looks small in comparison with that dog. Still, it ought to be decidedly "cobby," with strong stout legs, short broad back and wide chest.

Coat—The coat should be long, silky, soft and wavy, but not curly. There

Champion Tarahall Pouter Pigeon is flanked by his daughter, Champion Tarahall
Penelope (left), and his son, Champion Tarahall Tom Thumb (right).

should be a profuse mane, extending well down in the front of the chest. The feather should be well displayed on the ears and feet, and in the latter case so thickly as to give the appearance of being webbed. It is also carried well up the backs of the legs. In the Black and Tan the feather on the ears is very long and profuse, exceeding that of the Blenheim by an inch or more. The feather on the tail (which is cut to the length of about 1½ inches) should be silky, and from 3 to 4 inches in length, constituting a marked "flag" of a square shape, and not carried above the level of the back.

Colors of the Two Varieties

King Charles and Ruby—The King Charles and Ruby types which comprise one show variety are solid-color dogs. The King Charles are black and tan (considered a solid color), the black rich and glossy with deep mahogany tan markings over the eyes and on the muzzle, chest and legs. The presence of a few white hairs intermixed with the black on the chest is to be faulted,

Champion Joy of Tongemoor

Champion Royal Rogue of Egypt

but a white patch on the chest or white appearing elsewhere disqualifies. The Ruby is a rich chestnut red and is whole-colored. The presence of a few white hairs intermixed with the red on the chest is to be faulted, but a white patch on the chest or white elsewhere appearing disqualifies.

Blenheim and Prince Charles—The Blenheim and Prince Charles types which comprise the other show variety are broken-colored dogs. The Blenheim is red and white. The ground color is a pearly white which has bright red chestnut or ruby red markings evenly distributed in large patches. The ears and cheeks should be red, with a blaze of white extending from the nose up the forehead and ending between the ears in a crescentic curve. In the center of the blaze at the top of the forehead, there should be a clear "spot" of red, the size of a dime. The Prince Charles, a tri-colored dog, is white, black and tan. The ground color is pearly white. The black consists of markings which should be evenly distributed in large patches. The tan appears as spots over the eyes, on the muzzle, chest and legs; the ears and vent should also be lined with tan. The Prince Charles has no "spot," that being a particular feature of the Blenheim.

SCALE OF POINTS

King Charles, or Black and Tan. Prince Charles, White, with Black and Tan Markings. Ruby, or Red.

	Points
Symmetry, condition, size and soundness of limb	20
Head	15
Stop	5
Muzzle	10
Eyes	10
Ears	15
Coat and feathering	15
Color	10
Total	**100**

Blenheim or White with Red Markings

	Points
Symmetry, condition, size and soundness of limb	15
Head	15
Stop	5
Muzzle	10
Eyes	10
Ears	10
Coat and feathering	15
Color and markings	15
Spot	5
Total	**100**

DISQUALIFICATIONS

King Charles and Ruby—A white patch on the chest, or white on any other part.

THE BRUSSELS GRIFFON

A bizarre but fetching appearance, not beautiful but with personality in every whisker, this is the Brussels Griffon. Very intelligent, and sensitive because of it, the Griffon is obedient and manageable.

There are two other varieties of toy Griffons besides the Brussels. There is a Belgian, which differs in coloring; and the Brabancon, who sports a smooth coat unlike the wirehaired coat of the Brussels.

The use of the Pug dog's inheritable factors are obvious in the Brabancon, the quality of coat as well as head features. The Ruby Spaniel, one of the color varieties (*chestnut*) of the English Toy Spaniel, was also used in formulating the Griffon breed. Much of the head shape of the Brussels and Belgian Griffons is attributable to this cross. But the root lines which are the real breed basis of the toy Griffons were due to the breeding of the little German Affenpinschers (*Monkey Dogs*) to the common Belgian street dogs. This latter breed was the peasant's dog, shaggy, tough, unlovely but intelligent. These Griffons D'Ecurie (*Stable Griffons*) paid for their keep by keeping the stables clear of vermin.

Easily trained, all the Toy Griffons are for some unknown reason, stubborn and hard to train to the leash. Toward the end of the 19th century, the breed was introduced from Belgium to England and was introduced to America at the turn of the century.

American and Canadian Champion Buka Proctor

STANDARD OF THE BRUSSELS GRIFFON

General Appearance—A toy dog, intelligent, alert, sturdy, with a thick-set short body, a smart carriage and set-up, attracting attention by an almost human expression.

Head—Skull—Large and round, with a domed forehead.

Ears—Small and set rather high on the head. May be shown cropped or natural. If natural they are carried semi-erect.

Eyes—Should be set well apart, very large, black, prominent, and well open. The eyelashes long and black. Eyelids edged with black.

Nose—Very black, extremely short, its tip being set back deeply between the eyes so as to form a lay-back. The nostrils large, the stop deep.

Lips—Edged with black, not pendulous but well brought together, giving a clean finish to the mouth.

Jaws—Chin must be undershot, prominent, and large with an upward sweep. The incisors of the lower jaw should protrude over the upper incisors, and the lower jaw should be rather broad. Neither teeth nor tongue should show when the mouth is closed. A wry mouth is a serious fault.

Body and Legs—Brisket should be broad and deep, ribs well sprung, back level and short.

Neck—Medium length, gracefully arched.

Tail—Set and held high, docked to about one third.

602

The center Brussels Griffon of this fetching trio of puppies is Champion Barmere's I'm a Pixie. Below is depicted a fine Brussels bitch.

Forelegs—Of medium length, straight in bone, well muscled, set moderately wide apart and straight from the point of the shoulders as viewed from the front. Pasterns short and strong.

Hindlegs—Set true, thighs strong and well muscled, stifles bent, hocks well let down, turning neither in nor out.

Feet—Round, small, and compact, turned neither in nor out. Toes well arched. Black pads and toenails preferred.

Coat—There are two distinct types of coat—rough and smooth. The rough coat should be wiry and dense, the harder and more wiry the better. On no account should the dog look or feel woolly, and there should be no silky hair anywhere. The coat should not be so long as to give a shaggy appearance, but should still be distinctly different all over from the smooth coat. The head should be covered with wiry hair slightly longer around the eyes, nose, cheeks, and chin, thus forming a fringe. The Smooth coat is similar to that of the Boston Terrier or English Bulldog, with no trace of wire hair.

Color—In the rough-coated type, coat is either 1. reddish brown, with a little black at the whiskers and chin allowable, or 2. black and reddish brown mixed, usually, with black mask and whiskers, or 3. black with uniform reddish brown markings, usually appearing under the chin, on the legs, over the eyebrows, around the edges of the ears and around the vent, or 4. solid black. The colors of the smooth-coated type are the same as those of the rough-coated type except that solid black is not allowable. Any white hairs in either the rough or smooth coat are a serious fault, except for "frost" on the black muzzle of a mature dog, which is natural.

Weight—Usually 8 to 10 pounds, and should not exceed 12 pounds. Type and quality are of greater importance than weight, and a smaller dog that is sturdy and well proportioned should not be penalized.

SCALE OF POINTS

		Points
Head		
Skull	5	
Nose and stop	10	
Eyes	5	
Chin and jaws	10	
Ears	5	35
Coat		
Color	12	
Texture	13	25
Body and General Conformation		
Body (brisket and rib)	15	
Legs	10	
Feet	5	
General Appearance (neck, topline, and tail		
carriage	10	40
Total		100

DISQUALIFICATIONS

Dudley, or butterfly nose, white spot or blaze anywhere on coat, hanging tongue, jaw overshot, solid black coat in the smooth type.

Champion Arabella of Finstock, C.D.

THE ITALIAN GREYHOUND

A sleek, tight, silky coat, a marvelous disposition and naturally clean; these are the attributes that have made the Italian Greyhound the pet dog supreme for many centuries. Evidence points to the fact that this breed has been the favorite of people in high places for over 2000 years. He was an effete favorite in ancient Rome and Pompeii, Athens and the English court. We are told that the old Latin motto, *"cave canem,"* did not warn against the guard dogs but really meant that guests should beware that they didn't step on the tiny pet of the house, the slim and elegant Italian Greyhound.

We do not know the exact date that this breed appeared as a distinct type. We do know that the breed is the result of patient and exacting selection and breeding of ever smaller specimens of the ancient Greyhound breed, until the ultimate had been reached, a tiny, perfectly formed Greyhound, the toy Italian Greyhound. Introduced to England, three centuries or more of the sure touch of knowledgeable British breeders brought the breed to the highest state of perfection.

This toy Greyhound, bred to be solely a pet and nothing more, reached its height of popularity in the late Victorian period in England and Scotland and it was also introduced to the United States at this time. Dr. F. H. Hoyt produced many of the top winning Italian Greyhounds in his kennels in Pennsylvania.

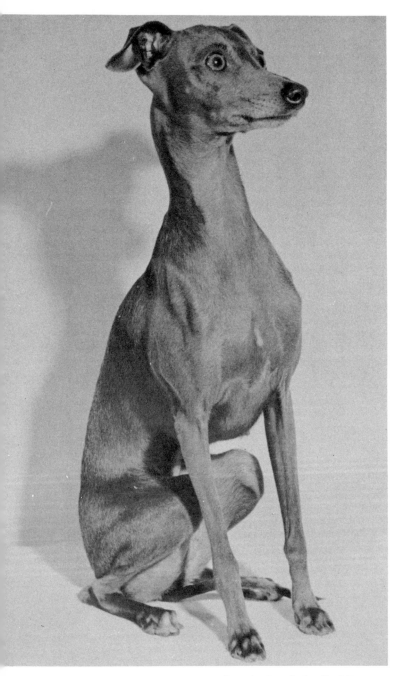

Champion Russo's Casella di Bennato.

Champion Marco Olympia.

Below, Champion Hillengold's Flash, a beautiful blue and white.

STANDARD OF THE ITALIAN GREYHOUND

General Appearance—A miniature English Greyhound, more slender in all proportions, and of ideal elegance and grace in shape, symmetry and action.

Head—Skull, long, flat and narrow. Muzzle, very fine, nose dark, teeth level. Ears, rose shaped, placed well back, soft and delicate. Eyes, rather large, bright and full of expression.

Body—Neck, long and gracefully arched. Shoulders, long and sloping. Chest, deep and narrow. Back, curved and drooping at the hindquarters.

Legs and Feet—Forelegs, straight, set well under the shoulders, fine pasterns, small delicate bones. Hindlegs, hocks well let down, thighs muscular. Feet, the long "hare foot."

Tail—Rather long, fine and with low carriage.

Coat—Skin fine and supple, hair thin and glossy like satin.

Color—All shades of fawn, red, mouse, blue, cream and white are recognized, black and tan terrier markings not allowed.

Action—High stepping and free.

Size—Two classes, one of 8 pounds and under and one over 8 pounds. A good small dog is preferable to an equally good large one but a good larger dog is preferable to a poor smaller one.

607

Champion Marco Andromeda

Scale of Points

	Points
Skull	6
Muzzle	8
Ears	8
Eyes	5
Neck	8
Shoulders	5
Chest	5
Back	8
Forelegs	8
Hindlegs	8
Feet	8
Tail	8
Coat	4
Color	3
Action	8
Total	**100**

A SILKY TERRIER.

T
O
Y

B
R
E
E
D
S

AT THE UPPER LEFT, AN ENGLISH TOY SPANIEL.
BELOW, THE QUAINT, BEWHISKERED, BRUSSELS
GRIFFON. ABOVE, A COURSING HOUND IN THE
TOY GROUP, THE ITALIAN GREYHOUND.

THE AFFENPINSCHER OR "MONKEY DOG", A
PRODUCT OF GERMANY.

TWO TOY POODLES IN DIFFERENT PET CLIPS. THE CHOCOLATE POODLE IN THE FOREGROUND SPORTS THE POPULAR "DUTCH" CLIP. THE SILVER BEHIND HIM IS WEARING A "LAMB" CLIP.

E.H.HART

UPPER LEFT IS A PEKINGESE AND DIRECTLY
BELOW THE PEKE IS A SILVER TOY POODLE IN
AN ENGLISH SADDLE SHOW CLIP. ABOVE IS A
HEAD PORTRAIT OF A CHIHUAHUA.

ABOVE LEFT, THE "LION-HEARTED" DOG OF
CHINA, THE PEKINGESE. UPPER RIGHT IS THE
TOY MANCHESTER TERRIER. IN THE MIDDLE
OF THE PAGE IS A PAIR OF PAPILLONS, THE
"BUTTERFLY" DOGS.

PORTRAIT OF A PERKY POMERANIAN.

AN APRICOT COLORED TOY POODLE PUPPY.

THE TINY YORKSHIRE TERRIER.

THE MINIATURE PINSCHER.

A BRACE OF FLUFFY POMERANIANS.

FROM THE ISLAND OF MALTA COMES
THE TINY, WHITE MALTESE.

E·H·HART

PORTRAIT OF A FAWN PUG.

A TRIO OF YORKSHIRE TERRIERS.

SOFT AND CUDDLY, A PAIR OF PEKE PUPPIES.

JAPANESE SPANIELS, A MOTHER AND HER TWO
PUPPIES.

THE STURDY LITTLE PUG DOG.

A pair of Japanese Spaniel puppies become an integral part of an Oriental motif.

THE JAPANESE SPANIEL

Despite the name of this toy spaniel, it is thought to have come from China and from there introduced to Japan. It wasn't until 1853 that the Western world first saw these little dogs when Commodore Perry brought several back from Japan where they had been gifts to him by the Emperor. Two went to Queen Victoria of England and the others came to the United States.

The Japanese Spaniel (or *Japanese Chin*) probably shares the same ancestral background as the Pug, Pekingese, and other Oriental breeds which spring essentially from the gene-pool provided by the ancient Tibetan Spaniel.

There are several types of Japanese Spaniels that differ only slightly, generally in size and/or coat. Essentially, regardless of slight variations in appearance, the characteristic specimen of the breed must look Oriental and display an aristocratic and stylish mien.

Disregard the connotation of sporting proclivities which the word Spaniel, in the breed's name, may conjure up. It is strictly a toy dog, a bright and alert little pet. Like so many of the small breeds, the Japanese Spaniel is sensitive and displays definite likes and dislikes. The breed was almost wiped out by distemper after being introduced here and it was not until 1912 that the present parent club was established.

STANDARD OF THE JAPANESE SPANIEL

General Appearance—That of a lively, highbred little dog with dainty

The Japanese Spaniel is a dainty and lovely Toy dog.

appearance, smart, compact carriage and profuse coat. These dogs should be essentially stylish in movement, lifting the feet high when in action, carrying the tail (which is heavily feathered, proudly curved or plumed) over the back. In size they vary considerably, but the smaller they are the better, provided type and quality are not sacrificed. When divided by weight, classes should be under and over 7 pounds.

Head—Should be large for the size of the dog, with broad skull, rounded in front.

Eyes—Large, dark, lustrous, rather prominent and set wide apart.

Ears—Small and V-shaped, nicely feathered, set wide apart and high on the head and carried slightly forward.

Nose—Very short in the muzzle part. The end or nose proper should be wide, with open nostrils, and must be the color of the dog's markings, i.e., black in black-marked dogs, and red or deep flesh color in red or lemon-marked dogs. It shall be a disqualification for a Black and White Japanese Spaniel to have a nose any other color than black.

Neck—Should be short and moderately thick.

Body—Should be squarely and compactly built, wide in chest, "cobby" in shape. The length of the dog's body should be about its height.

Tail—Must be well twisted to either right or left from root and carried up over back and flow on opposite side; it should be profusely covered with long hair (ring tails not desirable).

Legs—The bones of the legs should be small, giving them a slender appearance, and they should be well feathered.

Feet—Small and shaped somewhat long; the dog stands up on its toes somewhat. If feathered, the tufts should never increase the width of the foot, but only its length a trifle.

Coat—Profuse, long, straight, rather silky. It should also be absolutely free from wave or curl, and not lie too flat, but have a tendency to stand out, especially at the neck, so as to give a thick mane or ruff, which with profuse feathering on thighs and tail gives a very showy appearance.

Color—The dogs should be either black and white or red and white, i.e., parti-colored. The term red includes all shades of sable, brindle, lemon and orange, but the brighter and clearer the red the better. The white should be clear white, and the color, whether black or red, should be evenly distributed, patches over the body, cheek and ears.

SCALE OF POINTS

	Points
Head and neck	10
Eyes	10
Ears	5
Muzzle	10
Nose	5
Body	15
Tail	10
Feet and legs	5
Coat and markings	15
Action	5
Size	10
Total	100

DISQUALIFICATION

In black and whites, a nose any other color than black.

THE MALTESE

The Maltese is not commonly seen today, but is probably one of the oldest of the breeds. It is often erroneously referred to as the Maltese Terrier, but this is a faulty designation since it is not a terrier.

By reason of its history and characteristics it belongs in the toy dog group but this need not necessarily imply the restrictions that many place on it. The Maltese is usually thought of in terms of plush cushions and over-indulgence. But this diminutive fellow is filled with spunky determination plainly in inverse ratio to his size. We can well wonder at the spirit contained in this tiny creature. He should be completely covered by a cloak of long silky hair parted at the top and extending on both sides of the body to the ground. The carriage of the tail causes it to curl on the hindquarters in the manner of a plume and is exactly the type of tail one would expect in this alert and upstanding little dog.

The Maltese is fearless and will express his feelings in a positive fashion particularly at an intrusion of his domain and this is exactly what his home amounts to. He is intelligent, keen and very much the individualist and his personality does not permit of indiscriminate ownership. He is responsive to his environment in a marked degree and sufficient understanding on the part of his owner makes for a most satisfactory association.

The Maltese is thought to be a descendant of the toy dog of a civilization that preceded the Christian era. It is reasonable to suppose that the traits of the breed endeared it to the hearts of the ladies of that ancient period much as we find it does today. The island of Malta is thought to be the birthplace of the breed.

The color is always pure white and the only contrasting color is furnished by the dark eyes and black nose. In the care of the Maltese considerable attention must be given to the coat to prevent snarling and to keep the animal looking its best. The color and kind of coat are supposed to retard the breed's popularity but I believe those who appreciate the dog's fine qualities will not regard the necessary grooming a bother.

STANDARD OF THE MALTESE

General Appearance—The Maltese is a toy dog covered from head to foot with a mantle of silky white hair that falls in profusion down the sides of the body. He is gentle mannered and affectionate, eager and sprightly in action and, despite his size, possessed of the vigor needed for the satisfactory companion.

Head—Of fair length and in proportion to the size of the dog. The skull is slightly rounded on top, the stop moderate. The drop ears are rather low-set and heavily feathered with long hair that hangs close to the head. Eyes are very dark, round and full; black rims enhance the gentle yet alert expression. The muzzle is medium long, fine, and tapered as opposed to snipy, while the nose is black. The teeth meet in an even edge-to-edge bite, or in a scissors bite, meaning in the latter case that the inner surface of the upper incisors is in contact with the outer surface of the lower incisors when the jaws are closed.

Neck—Sufficient length of neck is desirable as promoting a high carriage of the head.

Above is a photo of Champion Aennchen's Smart Dancer. At the right, Champion Electa Caroline of Oak Manor.

Body—Compact and low-set. Shoulder blades are sloping, the elbows well knit and held close to the body. The back is short and level in topline, the ribs well sprung. The chest is reasonably deep, the loins taut, strong and deep enough to suggest a straight body underline.

Tail—A long-haired plume carried gracefully over the back, its tip lying to the side over the quarter.

Legs and Feet—The forelegs are short, straight, fine-boned and nicely feathered, the pastern joints well knit and devoid of appreciable bend. Hind legs are strong and moderately angulated at stifles and hocks. The feet are small and round, with toe pads black. Scraggly hairs on the feet may be trimmed to give a neater appearance.

Coat and Color—The coat is single, that is, without undercoat. It hangs long and silky over the sides of the body when parted down the back from the nose to the root of the tail. The profuse head hair may be tied up in a topknot on each side of the part, or it may be left hanging. A slight wave in the hair is permissible but any suggestion of kinkiness, curliness or woolly texture is objectionable. Color, white. A light tan or lemon shade on the ears is permissible but not desirable. Pure white is to be preferred.

Size—Weight under 7 pounds, with from 4 to 6 pounds preferred. Overall quality is to be favored over size.

Gait—The Maltese moves with a jaunty, smooth, flowing gait. Viewed from the side the dog gives an impression of rapid movement, size considered. In the stride, the forelegs reach straight and free from the shoulders, with elbows close. A slight toeing-in is acceptable, but weaving or crossing over is faulty. The hind legs, too, move in a straight line. Faulty are cowhocks or any suggestion of hind-leg toeing in or out.

Temperament—For all his diminutive size the Maltese seems to be without fear. His trust and affectionate responsiveness are very appealing. He is among the gentlest mannered of all little dogs, yet he is lively and playful as well as highly intelligent.

SCALE OF POINTS

		Points
Head		
Skull	5	
Eyes	5	
Ears	5	
Muzzle	5	
	—	20
Neck		5
Body		
Back	5	
Chest	5	
Shoulders	5	
Loin	5	
	—	20
Tail		5
Legs and Feet		10
Coat and Color		10
Size		5
Gait		10
Temperament		10
Condition		5
		—
Total		100

Champion Grenadier
Lord Diminutive

THE TOY MANCHESTER TERRIER

This trappy little breed is identical with its larger brother, the Manchester Terrier. Small specimens frequently appeared in litters of Manchester Terriers, were selected for and bred together to finally emerge as a true-producing breed, the Toy Manchester.

Please see information about, and standard of, the Manchester Terrier in the Terrier section of this book for further data.

Champion Iode de Gomaug

THE PAPILLON

The origin of the Continental Toy Spaniel, of which the Papillon is the modern representative, can be traced through the paintings of the Old Masters of every country in Western Europe as far back as the earliest years of the 16th Century. Beginning about 1500, Vecelli (*called Titian*), painted a number of tiny spaniels, rather similar to the hunting spaniels of the day. In this century and the next, dogs—so like the Titian spaniel that it is safe to assume this was a pure breed—made their appearance in Spain, France and the Low Countries.

We can only speculate on the ancestry of the Titian spaniel. Classical Greece and Rome possessed toy dogs but these were a spitz type which seems to have become extinct. During the Dark Ages only hunting and working dogs would have been of value, but with the dawn of the Renaissance, Italy became a prolific source of toy breeds of many varied types; toy greyhounds, dwarf barbets (*a sort of miniature poodle, often clipped lion-fashion*), dogs of Cayenne (*which were curiously pug-like*), and a number of breeds which probably resulted from crosses of various sorts. The toy spaniel was quite different in its characteristics from any of these.

One authority has suggested that the toy spaniel was brought from China, with which country the Venetians had traded since the days of Marco Polo. The Chinese did, in fact, have as late as the 18th Century a parti-colored, long-coated dog not unlike the Titian spaniel, along with those resembling the modern Pekingese.

The name *spaniel* means dog of Spain, for which reason it has often been inferred that the spaniel breeds originated there. The spaniel family, which includes the setters, is as old as such other basic canine patterns as the hounds, the Mastiffs or the Spitzes. It is therefore probable that the hunting spaniels came to Europe along with successive Asiatic tribes. In this case, *spaniel* was a misnomer for the hunting breeds as well as for the toy.

The often repeated story that the conquerors of Mexico brought the Chihuahua to Spain and that the Papillon is descended from it seems to have no historical basis. The Titian Spaniel had been developed as a pure breed prior to the Conquest of Mexico.

The continued popularity of the little spaniel in court circles gave the breeders a ready market for their dogs. Evidently they conducted an intensive breeding program for its refinement. Over the years it developed finer bone, more abundant coat and profuse feathering. The most characteristic change, however, was in the shape of the head. Titian's spaniels had relatively flat heads with little stop; a type of toy spaniel painted shortly after by Veronese and others had high-domed, sometimes bulging heads. By the time of Louis XIV, French and Belgian breeders had perfected the type they sought. Mignard, the official court painter, in his portraits of the child Marie de

Champion Venice of Mariposa, C.D.

Bourbon, the Dauphin and His Family, and several paintings of Henriette d'Orleans, shows us a little spaniel that could scarcely be improved upon today. All of these Continental Toy Spaniels had drooping ears.

Suddenly, toward the end of the 19th Century, the erect ear carriage with its butterfly appearance became highly fashionable. In fact, it so caught the public fancy that the new term of "Papillon" quickly became the name for the entire breed. Several attempts have been made in the past to straighten out the names of the two varieties, without much success. Recently the International Papillon Organization, to which the American but not the English club is affiliated, has given to the drop eared variety the name of "Phalene."

The Titian dogs were red and white. Before long, specimens appeared in all shades from pale lemon to deepest chestnut, while some of the most beautiful examples were black and white or silver-grey and white. All these colors were usually marked with a white blaze and often with the thumb mark on the top of the head. Then, toward the end of the 19th Century through the first two

Champion Picaroon Pan

decades of this one, the vogue was for solid colors or for dogs with only the feet and chest splashed with white.

People often insist on a one word answer to the question, "*Where does the breed come from?*" Baron Albert Houtart of Belgium, author of the most authoritative work on this subject, demonstrated that credit for perfecting the Continental Toy Spaniel belongs equally to France and to Belgium.

The little Papillon has survived rather better than the Royal Families in whose courts he was once such a favorite. Men, women and children, of all ages and in all walks of life, take him into their laps and hearts. Now, as truly as in the past, when he has found his way into a home he is there to stay, as loving as he is beloved.

STANDARD OF THE PAPILLON

General Appearance—The Papillon is a toy dog of fine-boned structure. It

Champion Picaroon Topaz

Champion Danaidae Gille D'Royal.

is gentle, intelligent, dainty, and of lively action. It is not a diminutive form of a breed. There is only one classification—the toy.

Head—The head of the Papillon is well proportioned to the body. It may appear small because it is covered with short hair while the rest of the body is heavily coated. The skull should be of medium width and slightly rounded between the ears. A well-defined stop is formed where the muzzle joins the skull. The muzzle is shorter than the skull and is fine. It is abruptly thinner than the head, becoming more slender down to the nose.

Nose—The nose of the Papillon is small and rounded, and is slightly flat on top. It should be black.

Disqualification—Pink nose, or one with pink spots.

Eyes—The eyes of the Papillon are dark and expressive. The center of the eyes is on a line with the stop. The shape of the eye is round. Rim around the eyes should be black. Eyes must not bulge.

Mouth—The jaws of the Papillon are well adjusted: the lips are tight and thin, and should be black. Teeth should meet in a scissors bite.

Fault—The jaw should not be overshot or undershot.

Ears—The ears of Papillons of either the erect or the drop type should be large and set on the sides of the head. The ears should be fringed.

(1) The erect type of ears is carried obliquely and moves like the spread wings of a butterfly. At rest or when relaxed, their position forms an angle of approximately 45 degrees to the head. The concha is largely open, and the inside is entirely visible and covered with silken hair. The ears should be of fine leather and of sufficient strength to maintain the opened-up position.

(2) The drop type of ears (known on the Continent as Phalene), is similar to the erect type, but the ears are carried drooping, and must be completely down.

Major fault—Ears partly down.

Neck—The neck of the Papillon is slender, and is lost in the collarette.

Body—The body of the Papillon must be slightly longer than high. The Papillon is not a cobby dog. The back is level, the chest is of medium depth and width, the ribs are arched, the loins are tucked up.

Shoulders—The shoulders of the Papillon should be flexible and well-angulated, and are hidden by hair.

Forelegs—The forelegs of the Papillon are fine and straight. It stands with front feet close together. The back of the forelegs is covered with abundant fringes, diminishing to the pastern; the front of the forelegs is covered with short hair.

Hindlegs—The thighs are fairly muscular and well-angulated. The hindlegs are slender and parallel when viewed from behind. They are covered to the hocks with abundant breeches (culottes); the hind pastern is covered with short smooth hair. The stifles are well angulated. The hocks are placed fairly high.

Fault—Cowhocks.

Feet—The feet of the Papillon are thin and elongated (harelike). The toes are close and arched. The hair on the feet is short, but fine tufts may appear between the toes and grow beyond them, forming a point.

Tail—The tail of the Papillon is set high and carried well arched over the body. The plume on the tail usually hangs to the side of the body.

Coat—The Papillon's coat is short and smooth on the head, muzzle, front of legs, and back of legs from the hocks downward. The hair around the neck

Champion Hermione of Mariposa.

forms a collarette. The hair on the neck, shoulders, and breast is abundant in comparison with that on the rest of the body. The back of the forelegs should be well fringed, the length of the fringes shortening down to the pastern. The tail is covered with a long abundant plume.

Quality of Coat—The coat is profuse and shiny, and may be slightly wavy, but not curly. There is no undercoat. The hair on the back is flat. The coat is soft and comparatively fine, but has a resilient quality.

Size—The height of the Papillon at the withers should be 11 inches or under. The weight and height should be in good proportion.

Disqualification—12 inches and over.

Gait—The gait is free, quick, easy, and graceful.

Color and Markings—Papillons are two-colored or tri-colored. The usual two-colors are white and black, white and sable, or white with some shade of red, varying from light tan to deep red. The color is usually in spots or patches thrown in relief against white, which predominates. The size, shape, and placement of the patches are without importance. A tri-colored Papillon is black and white with tan spots. The tan spots may appear over the eyes, on the cheeks, in the ears, and under the tail. The exact placement or omission of the tan spots is of no importance. The black appears in patches on white in the same manner as in the dog of two colors. A saddle is permissible. A blaze is desirable but not essential. Among the allowable colors and markings, there is no preference.

Fault—A coat of solid color.

English Champion Calartha Wee Bo Bo of Ecila.

THE PEKINGESE

The antiquity of this breed is proved by the art and sculpture of ancient dynasties of China. The earliest known record of the Peke dates back to the Tang Dynasty of the 8th century. Even then the breed was fully established in type, indicating that it had been around for a long time before that date.

In ancient times the Peke was considered sacred and the theft of, or injury to one of these animals, which were bred pure and kept only by the imperial family, was punishable by death. The term, *"sleeve dog"*, appended to very small toy dogs, was originated in China and meant specifically a Pekingese tiny enough to be carried around in the voluminous sleeves of the members of the imperial household. A particular strain with golden red coats were called *"Sun Dogs"*.

Another term, *"Lion Dog,"* has been used in reference to the Peke. The official parent club explanation of this appellation is that it refers to the breed's lion-like appearance, but it is the author's opinion that it is, instead, in praise of the Peke's characteristic courage and combativeness, characteristics that typical specimens certainly possess in abundance. These little toy dogs will attack a Great Dane upon the least provocation and will never quit even

638

in the face of impossible odds. They also have stamina and boldness not usually associated with toy breeds.

Pekingese were first exhibited in England in 1893, and in America the parent club for the breed became a member of the A.K.C. in 1909. This is a popular breed of toy in America and deserves its prominence. Pekes are regal, independent, not aggressive, but absolutely fearless and make excellent companions.

STANDARD OF THE PEKINGESE

Expression—Must suggest the Chinese origin of the Pekingese in its quaintness and individuality, resemblance to the lion in directness and independence and should imply courage, boldness, self-esteem and combativeness rather than prettiness, daintiness or delicacy.

Skull—Massive, broad, wide and flat between the ears (not dome shaped), wide between the eyes.

Nose—Black, broad, very short and flat.

Eyes—Large, dark, prominent, round, lustrous.

Stop—Deep.

Ears—Heart shaped, not set too high, leather never long enough to come below the muzzle, nor carried erect, but rather drooping, long feather.

Muzzle—Wrinkled, very short and broad, not overshot nor pointed. Strong, broad under jaw, teeth not to show.

Shape of Body—Heavy in front, well sprung ribs, broad chest, falling away

English Champion Do Do of Shangte

lighter behind, lion-like. Back level. Not too long in body; allowance made for longer body in bitch.

Legs—Short forelegs, bones of forearm bowed, firm at shoulder; hindlegs lighter but firm and well shaped.

Feet—Flat, toes turned out, not round, should stand well up on feet, not on ankles.

Action—Fearless, free and strong, with slight roll.

Coat, Feather and Condition—Long, with thick undercoat, straight and flat, not curly nor wavy, rather coarse, but soft; feather on thighs, legs, tail and toes long and profuse.

Mane—Profuse, extending beyond the shoulder blades, forming ruff or frill round the neck.

Color—All colors are allowable. Red, fawn, black, black and tan, sable, brindle, white and parti-color well defined: black masks and spectacles around the eyes, with lines to ears are desirable.

Definition of a Parti-Color Pekingese—The coloring of a parti-colored dog must be broken on the body. No large portion of any one color should exist. White should be shown on the saddle. A dog of any solid color with white feet and chest is NOT a parti-color.

Tail—Set high; lying well over back to either side; long, profuse, straight feather.

Size—Being a toy dog, medium size preferred, providing type and points are not sacrificed; extreme limit 14 pounds. Anything over must disqualify.

SCALE OF POINTS

	Points
Expression	5
Skull	10
Nose	5
Eyes	5
Stop	5
Ears	5
Muzzle	5
Shape of body	15
Legs and feet	15
Coat, feather and condition	15
Tail	5
Action	10
Total	100

Penalizations—Protruding tongue, badly blemished eye, overshot, wry mouth.

Disqualifications—Weight over 14 pounds; Dudley nose.

The picture to the right is of the red Miniature Pinscher male, Champion Rebel Roc's Casanova von Kurt.

640

THE MINIATURE PINSCHER

The official standard describes this breed as "... *a miniature of the Doberman Pinscher* ..." and this indeed is exactly what a good specimen of the breed is like. Clean limbed, slick and sleek and, in its character suggestive of a much larger breed, the Minnie, despite its lack of size, makes an excellent watchdog.

Oddly enough, though there is definitely no genetic tie between the "Minpin" and the larger Doberman, both breeds developed almost simultaneously. A small pinscher breed had existed in Germany for several centuries and a like type of dog in the Scandinavian countries for an almost equal length of time, but the real development of the Miniature Pinscher began when the Pinscher-Schnauzer Klub was formed in Germany in 1895 and a breed standard evolved. Breed improvement was introduced and immediately the popularity of the "Minpin" began to rise.

The first World War handicapped the progress of all German breeds including the Miniature Pinscher. However, immediately following the cessation of hostilities importations again began to fanciers in other countries.

The breed club in America was formed in 1929 and "Minpins" were given their own dog show classes. The breed's popularity is constantly increasing. The Miniature Pinscher is a born show dog, stylish, smart and full of life. Its intelligence, clean, close coat, lively temperament and fondness for home and hearth, make it an excellent house dog.

STANDARD OF THE MINIATURE PINSCHER

General Appearance—The Miniature Pinscher was originated in Germany and named the "Reh Pinscher" due to his resemblance in structure and animation to a very small specie of deer found in the forests. This breed is structurally a well-balanced, sturdy, compact, short-coupled, smooth-coated toy dog. He is naturally well groomed, proud, vigorous and alert. The natural characteristic traits which identify him from other toy dogs are his precise Hackney gait, his fearless animation, complete self-possession, and his spirited presence.

Faults—Structurally lacking in balance, too long or short-coupled, too coarse or too refined (lacking in bone development causing poor feet and legs), too large or too small, lethargic, timid or dull, shy or vicious, low in tail placement and poor in action (action not typical of the breed requirements). Knotty over-developed muscles.

Head—In correct proportion with the body.

From Top: Tapering, narrow with well-fitted but not too prominent foreface which should balance with the skull. No indication of coarseness.

From Front: Skull appears flat, tapering forward toward the muzzle. Muzzle itself strong rather than fine and delicate, and in proportion to the head as a whole; cheeks and lips small, taut and closely adherent to each other. Teeth in perfect alignment and apposition.

From Side: Well-balanced with only a slight drop to the muzzle, which should be parallel to the top of the skull.

Eyes: Full, slightly oval, almost round, clear, bright and dark even to a true black; set wide apart and fitted well into the sockets.

Ears: Well-set and firmly placed, upstanding (when cropped, pointed and carried erect in balance with the head).

The perky, deer-like quality of the Minpin is personified by this head shot.

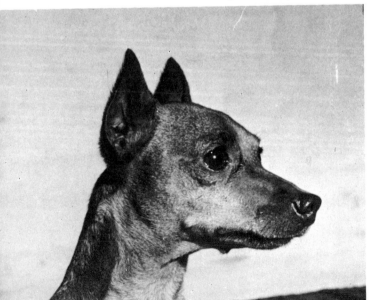

Nose: Black only (with the exception of chocolates which may have a self-colored nose).

Faults—Too large or too small for the body, too coarse or too refined, pinched and weak in foreface, domed in skull, too flat and lacking in chiselling giving a vapid expression. Jaws and teeth overshot or undershot. Eyes too round and full, too large, bulging, too deep-set or set too far apart; or too small, set too close (pig eyes). Light colored eyes not desirable. Ears poorly placed, low-set hanging ears (lacking in cartilage) which detract from head conformation. (Poorly cropped ears if set on the head properly and having sufficient cartilage should not detract from head points, as this would be a man-made fault and automatically would detract from general appearance.) Nose any color other than black (with the exception of chocolates which may have a self-colored nose).

Neck—Proportioned to head and body. Slightly arched, gracefully curved, clean and firm, blending into shoulders, length well-balanced, muscular and free from a suggestion of dewlap or throatiness.

Faults—Too straight or too curved; too thick or too thin; too long or short; knotty muscles; loose, flabby or wrinkled skin.

Body—

From Top: Compact, slightly wedge-shaped, muscular with well-sprung ribs.

From Side: Depth of brisket, the base line of which is level with the points of the elbows; short and strong in loin with belly moderately tucked up to denote grace in structural form. Back level or slightly sloping toward the rear. Length of males equals height at withers. Females may be slightly longer.

From Rear: High tail-set; strong, sturdy upper shanks, with croup slope at about 30 degrees; vent opening not barreled.

Fore Quarters: Forechest well-developed and full, moderately broad, shoulders clean, sloping with moderate angulation, co-ordinated to permit the true action of the Hackney pony.

Hindquarters: Well-knit muscular quarters set wide enough apart to fit into a properly balanced body.

Faults—From top—too long, too short, too barreled, lacking in body development. From side—too long, too short, too thin or too fat, hips higher or considerably lower than the withers, lacking depth of chest, too full in loin, sway back, roach back or wry back. From rear—quarters too wide or too close to each other, over-developed, barreled vent, under-developed vent, too sloping croup, tail set low. Forequarters—forechest and spring of rib too narrow (or too shallow and under-developed), shoulders too straight, too loose, or too short and overloaded with muscles. Hindquarters—too narrow, under- or over-muscled, too steep in croup.

Legs and Feet—Strong bone development and small clean joints; feet catlike, toes strong, well-arched and closely-knit with deep pads and thick, blunt nails.

Fore Legs and Feet: As viewed from the front straight and upstanding, elbows close to body, well-knit, flexible yet strong with perpendicular pasterns.

Hind Legs: All adjacent bones should appear well-angulated with well-muscled thighs or upper shanks, with clearly well-defined stifles, hocks short, set well apart turning neither in nor out, while at rest should stand perpendicular to the ground and upper shanks, lower shanks and hocks parallel to each other.

643

Faults—Too thick or thin bone development, large joints, spreading flat feet. Forelegs and feet—bowed or crooked, weak pasterns, feet turning in or out, loose elbows. Hind legs—thin undeveloped stifles, large or crooked hocks, loose stifle joints.

Tail—Set high, held erect, docked ½ to 1 inch.

Faults—Set too low, too thin, drooping, hanging or poorly docked.

Coat—Smooth, hard and short, straight and lustrous, closely adhering to and uniformly covering the body.

Faults—Thin, too long, dull; upstanding; curly; dry; area of various thickness or bald spots.

Color—
1. Solid red or stag red.
2. Lustrous black with sharply defined tan, rust-red markings on cheeks, lips, lower jaw, throat, twin spots above eyes and chest, lower half of forelegs, inside of hind legs and vent region, lower portion of hocks and feet. Black pencil stripes on toes.
3. Solid brown or chocolate with rust or yellow markings.

Faults—Any color other than listed; very dark or sooty spots.

Disqualifications—Thumb marks or any area of white on feet or forechest exceeding one-half (½) inch in its longest dimension.

Size and Weight—Size to range from 10 inches to 12½ inches at the withers, with a preference of 11 inches to 11½ inches, weight to be governed by size and condition ranging from 6 to 9 pounds for males and 6½ to 10 pounds for females. A squarely built specimen within the size limit, in condition, will conform to weight range. It is recommended that at all dog shows prescribed size and weight will be governed by condition.

Faults—Over-size; under-size; too fat; too lean.

SCALE OF POINTS

	Points
General Appearance and Movement—(*very important*)	30
Skull	5
Muzzle	5
Mouth	5
Eyes	5
Ears	5
Neck	5
Body	15
Feet	5
Legs	5
Color	5
Coat	5
Tail	5
Total	100

DISQUALIFICATIONS

Color—Thumb marks or any area of white on feet or forechest exceeding one-half (½) inch in its longest dimension.

Champion Pixietown Serenade of Hadleigh

THE POMERANIAN

In this instance the name of the breed has nothing whatever to do with its point of origin. It is claimed that the breed was reduced in size to its present smallness in the Duchy of Pomerania. No explanation is made of how it got there and, anyway, the fact is not emphasized or sworn to. Let us just accept the name and, as in the case of other blessings, ask no questions.

We do know that the Pom was once a much larger dog than it is today. In fact, when first noticed in Britain it was not a toy dog at all. Its genetic background at that time was more discernible than now. It is related to, and shares the same basic ancestry as, the Keeshond, Spitz, Norwegian Elkhound, and Samoyed. The background of all these breeds were the sled dogs of the Arctic zones. As a matter of fact the Pom is said to once (*when it weighed up to* 30 *pounds*) have greatly resembled in size, coat and color, the German wolf-spitz breed. Closest to the Pom genetically today is the Spitz. When the English Kennel Club first recognized the breed in 1870 it was called the Spitzdog.

Bred down to true toy size the Pomeranian is one of the best known toys in the world and its very name is synonymous with canine smallness. Classification was accorded the breed in this country in 1900, and in 1911 the American Pomeranian Club held its first specialty show.

Champion Goldenstar of Hadleigh

STANDARD OF THE POMERANIAN

Appearance—The Pomeranian in build and appearance should be a compact, short-coupled dog, well-knit in frame. He should exhibit great intelligence in his expression, docility in his disposition, and activity and buoyance in his deportment, and be sound in action.

Head—The head should be somewhat foxy in outline, or wedge-shaped, the skull being slightly flat, large in proportion to the muzzle, which should finish rather fine, and be free from lippiness. The teeth should be level, and on no account undershot. The head in its profile may exhibit a little "stop," which, however, must not be too pronounced, and the hair on the head and face must be smooth or short-coated.

Eyes—The eyes should be medium in size, rather oblique in shape, not set too wide apart, bright and dark in color, showing great intelligence and docility of temper. In a white dog, black rims around the eyes are preferable.

Ears—The ears should be small, not set too far apart nor too low down, and carried perfectly erect, like those of a fox, and like the head, should be covered with soft, short hair.

Nose—Should be self-colored in Browns and Blue. In all other colors, should be black.

Neck and Shoulders—The neck, rather short, well set in, and lion-like, covered with a profuse mane and frill of long straight hair, sweeping from the under jaw and covering the whole of the front part of the shoulders and chest as well as the top part of the shoulders. The shoulders must be tolerably clean, and laid well back.

Body—The back must be short, and the body compact, being well ribbed up and the barrel well rounded. The chest must be fairly deep and not too wide.

Legs—The forelegs must be well feathered and perfectly straight, of medium length, and not such as would be termed "leggy" or "low on legs," but in length and strength in due proportion to a well-balanced frame. The hindlegs and thighs must be well feathered down to the hocks, and must be neither cow-hocked nor wide behind. They must be fine in bone and free in action. The feet should be small and compact in shape.

Tail—The tail is a characteristic of the breed, and should be turned over the back and carried flat, being profusely covered with long spreading hair.

Coat—Properly speaking there should be two coats, an under and an over coat; the one a soft fluffy undercoat, and the other a long, perfectly straight and glistening coat covering the whole of the body, being very abundant around the neck and forepart of the shoulders and chest, where it should form a frill of profuse, standing-off, straight hair, extending over the shoulders as

Champion Sylvia of Hadleigh

previously described. The hindquarters like those of the collie, should be similarly clad with long hair or feathering from the top of the rump to the hocks. The hair on the tail must be, as previously described, profuse and spreading over the back.

Color—The following colors are admissible: Black, brown, chocolate, red, orange, cream, orange-sable, wolf-sable, beaver, blue, white and parti-colors. The blacks, blues, browns and sables must be free from any white, and the whites must be free from lemon or any other color. A few white hairs in any of the self-colors shall not absolutely disqualify but should carry great weight against a dog. In parti-colored dogs, the colors should be evenly distributed on the body in patches. A dog with a white foot or a white chest would not be a parti-colored dog. Whole colored dogs with a white foot or feet, leg or legs, are decidedly objectionable and should be discouraged and cannot compete as whole colored specimens. In mixed classes where whole colored and parti-colored Pomeranians compete together, the preference should—if in other points they are equals—be given to the whole colored specimens. Sables must be shaded throughout with three or more colors, as uniformly as possible, with no patches of self-color. Oranges must be self-colored throughout and light shadings though not disqualifying should be discouraged.

SCALE OF POINTS

	Points
Appearance	10
Head	5
Eyes	5
Ears	5
Nose	5
Neck and shoulders	5
Body	10
Legs	10
Tail	10
Coat	25
Color	10
Total	100

N.B.—Where classification by weight is made, the following scale, passed by the club as the most suitable division, should be adopted by Show Committees:

1. Not exceeding 7 pounds.
2. Exceeding 7 pounds.

Where classification by color is made, the following division should be adopted:

1. Black.
2. Brown or chocolate.
3. Red, orange or cream.
4. Sables.
5. Any color not mentioned above.

Champion Meisen Frostie Flake

THE POODLE (TOY)

The standard for the Toy Poodle, the history and the clips desired are the same throughout as for Standard and Miniatures (see Poodles, Group VI: Non-Sporting Dogs). The only difference is in size although there is another difference which seemingly is not recognized by the breed club or the A.K.C., and that is the use of the tiny Maltese to bring down and stabilize size in the Toy Poodle. Small specimens from Minnie breeding below the qualified height (over 10 inches, under 15 inches) were undoubtedly used as the basis and later, to keep size from fluctuating too greatly, the Maltese was introduced.

The Poodle can only be shown in competition in solid colors, and this has led to the elimination of many fine "parti-colored" or "phantom" puppies that would have made delightful pets and companions. Many well known and distinguished people have owned parti-colored Poodles by preference and the author has seen tiny parti-colored "sleeve" dogs for which big prices have been paid as a premium for small size.

The partis and phantoms possess all the delightful charm and quick, almost uncanny intelligence for which the Poodle is known. At the moment the author's youngest son owns a gray Toy Poodle, his constant companion and pal. This dog's dam was sired by Count Alexis Pulaski's "Just Johnny" (*Pulaski Caesar Phantom John*), a phantom in color.

The parti-colored Poodle is a basic part of the breed. The Spanish artist,

Champion Legagwann Altair of Old Ivy (black)

Francisco Michaus, in the latter part of the 18th century, painted a parti-color owned by the Spanish royal family, and in a show clip.

Today the Poodle (in all sizes) is the most popular dog in America, and well merits its acclaim. No breed of canine is more intelligent or quicker to learn. The standard for all three sizes of Poodle is the same in all fundamentals except size. Please see "The Poodle," under the non-sporting classification for further information about the breed and the accepted A.K.C. standard.

The silver, Ariane's Petit Zee Zee.

THE PUG

There was a time when this sturdy toy was one of the most popular of breeds. The Pug need not be pampered. They breed true to size and type and are clean, alert and good companions.

Champion Frivolity of Gaifons

The breed was first imported to England by traders from the Dutch East India Company and was originally thought to have been of Dutch origin. Thinking it indigenous to Holland it was sometimes called the Dutch Pug. Actually the origin of the breed is Oriental and initial specimens were acquired by seamen from Dutch trading ships that sailed to the Far East.

The Pug wears Mastiff colors except for the solid black variety which is said to have been the result of an infusion of genetic material from black Japanese Pugs, a breed similar to the Japanese Toy Spaniel.

Where the breed name came from is anybody's guess, but it has been suggested that the pushed-in nose led to the whimsical thought that the typical facial expression was similar to that of a well-punished pugilist or "pug".

Two of the leading sponsors of the breed in England led to a pair of famous breed strains, the Willoughby and the Morrison. The Pug is a good show dog and has proven to be an excellent competitor in the obedience ring. Care must be taken that, with maturity, they do not become too fat and lacking in dash.

STANDARD OF THE PUG

Symmetry—Symmetry and general appearance, decidedly square and cobby. A lean leggy Pug and a dog with short legs and a long body are equally objectionable.

Size and Condition—The Pug should be *multum in parvo*, but this condensation (if the word may be used) should be shown by compactness of form, well-knit proportions, and hardness of developed muscle. Weight from 14 to 18 pounds (dog or bitch) desirable.

Body—Short and cobby, wide in chest and well-ribbed up.

Legs—Very strong, straight, of moderate length, and well under.

Feet—Neither so long as the foot of the hare, nor so round as that of the cat; well-split-up toes, and the nails black.

Muzzle—Short, blunt, square, but not upfaced.

Head—Large, massive, round—not apple-headed, with no indentation of the skull.

Eyes—Dark in color, very large, bold and prominent, globular in shape, soft and solicitous in expression, very lustrous, and, when excited, full of fire.

Ears—Thin, small, soft, like black velvet. There are two kinds—the "Rose" and "Button." Preference is given to the latter.

Markings—Clearly defined. The muzzle or mask ears, moles on cheeks, thumb-mark or diamond on forehead, back-trace should be as black as possible.

Mask—The mask should be black. The more intense and well defined it is the better.

Wrinkles—Large and deep.

Trace—A black line extending from the occiput to the tail.

Tail—Curled tightly as possible over the hip. The double curl is perfection.

Coat—Fine, smooth, soft, short and glossy, neither hard nor woolly.

Color—Silver or apricot-fawn. Each should be decided, to make the contrast complete between the color and the trace and the mask. Black.

SCALE OF POINTS

	Fawn	Points Black
Symmetry	10	10
Size	5	10
Condition	5	5
Body	10	10
Legs and feet	5	5
Head	5	5
Muzzle	10	10
Ears	5	5
Eyes	10	10
Mask	5	—
Wrinkles	5	5
Tail	10	10
Trace	5	—
Coat	5	5
Color	5	10
Total	100	100

International Champion Coolaroo Sir Winston

THE SILKY TERRIER

In Australia most of the breeds have their origin in utility, as cattle dogs, herders or bush dogs. The Silky Terrier, also from "down under", is simply a house dog, a small breed that originated in Sydney (*and for this reason was called the Sydney Silky for many years*) as a companion dog in the homes of flat, cottage and suburban dwellers.

Australian Champion Koolamina Sante

In 1955 the breed was introduced to other countries and is catching hold due to its spunk and quick intelligence. Two separate registration groups in its native land have recognized the Silky Terrier as a distinct breed for almost 30 years and maintained stud book records of the breed.

The Silky was developed from the crossing of Australian Terrier and Yorkshire Terrier. A mutation originally occurred in Australian Terrier breeding and was liked, and the type subsequently enhanced by Yorkie breeding. Selection eventually produced a true-breeding toy. The breed initially exhibited both prick and pendant ear carriage and later "fixed" the upright ear as a breed characteristic. The former double ear carriage and the silky quality of the breed's coat could be an indication of Skye Terrier heritage injected into the breeding picture during the breed's origin.

Though a toy in size the Silky Terrier shows a strong prediliction to terrier character and spirit and its ability in the country of its origin in killing and controlling snakes and rats in the chicken yard indicates further strong terrier influence.

STANDARD OF THE SILKY TERRIER

The Silky Terrier is a lightly built, moderately low-set toy dog of pronounced terrier character and spirited action.

656

Head—The head is strong, wedge-shaped, and moderately long. The skull is a trifle longer than the muzzle, in proportion about 3/5 for the skull, 2/5 for the muzzle.

Skull—Flat, and not too wide between the ears.

Stop—Shallow.

Ears—Small, V-shaped and pricked. They are set high and carried erect without any tendency to flare obliquely off the skull.

Eyes—Small, dark in color, and piercingly keen in expression. Light eyes are a fault.

Teeth—Strong and well aligned, scissors bite. A bite markedly undershot or overshot is a serious fault.

Nose—The nose is black.

Neck and Shoulders—The neck fits gracefully into sloping shoulders. It is medium long, fine and to some degree crested along its top line.

Body—Low-set, about 1/5 longer than the dog's height at the withers. A too short body is a fault. The back line is straight, with a just perceptible rounding over the loins. Brisket medium wide, and deep enough to extend down to the elbows.

Champion Silkallure Roxanne

Tail—The tail is set high and carried erect or semi erect but not over-gay. It is docked and well coated but devoid of plume.

Forequarters—Well laid back shoulders, together with a good angulation at the upper arm, the forelegs set nicely under the body. Forelegs are strong, straight and rather fine-boned.

Hindquarters—Thighs well muscled and strong, but not so developed as to appear heavy. Legs moderately angulated at stifles and hocks, with the hocks low and equidistant from the hock joints to the ground.

Feet—Small, cat-like, round, compact. Pads are thick and springy while the nails are strong and dark colored. White or flesh colored nails are a fault. The feet point straight ahead, with no turning in or out. Dewclaws, if any, are removed.

Coat—Flat, in texture fine, glossy, silky; on matured specimens the desired length of coat from behind the ears to the set-on of the tail is from 5 to 6 inches. On the top of the head the hair is so profuse as to form a topknot, but long hair on face and ears is objectionable. Legs from knee and hock joints to feet should be free from long hair. The hair is parted on the head and down over the back to the root of the tail.

Color—Blue and tan. The blue may be silver blue, pigeon blue or slate blue, the tan deep and rich. The blue extends from the base of the skull to the tip of the tail, down the forelegs to the pasterns, and down the thighs to the hocks. On the tail the blue should be very dark. Tan appears on muzzle and cheeks, around the base of the ears, below the pasterns and hocks, and around the vent. There is a tan spot over each eye. The topknot should be silver or fawn.

Temperament—The keenly alert air of the terrier is characteristic, with shyness or excessive nervousness to be faulted. The manner is quick, friendly, responsive.

Movement—Should be free, light footed, lively, and straightforward. Hindquarters should have strong propelling power. Toeing in or out is to be faulted.

Size—Weight ranges from 8 to 10 pounds. Shoulder height from 9 to 10 inches. Pronounced diminutiveness (such as a height of less than 8 inches) is not desired; it accentuates the quality of toyishness as opposed to the breed's definite terrier character.

Champion Milan Chips of Iradell

A typical top Yorkie from Heskethane.

THE YORKSHIRE TERRIER

Unlike most other breeds the adherents of this little toy dog do not claim for it an origin in the far and dim mists of antiquity. It is a modern breed, manufactured in England, and it made its first appearance in the Leeds show in 1861 as a "Scotch Terrier." It was not until 1886 that the breed was recognized by the Kennel Club of England as a Yorkshire Terrier.

The Yorkshire was developed in Lancashire and Yorkshire and was a dog of the working classes when initially conceived, particularly the weavers. Many of the weavers who came to England from Scotland in the 1850's brought with them their Skye and Paisley terriers. In the area where they settled there were many other small, native English breeds of terrier background. Though of recent origin, the exact breeds that gave the Yorkie its characteristics are not definitely known. There appears to have been many breeds involved in the Yorkie's beginnings, including Skye, Paisley, Manchester and Dandie Dinmont Terriers with some Maltese, combined with selection, for smallness.

Champion Wee
Geordie of
Heskethane

Introduced to the United States in 1880, it did not catch on immediately but did at a later date. Fine show dogs, the Yorkshire coat necessarily takes a lot of care. With its ground-sweeping silken tresses and its festooning ribbons it looks the epitome of the pampered toy dog. It must even wear tiny stockings so it will not ruin its coat by scratching. At heart, though, this little fellow has the spirit and fire of his terrier background.

STANDARD OF THE YORKSHIRE TERRIER

General Appearance—Should be that of a long-coated Toy Terrier, the coat hanging quite straight and evenly down each side, a parting extending from the nose to the end of the tail.

The animal should be very compact and neat, the carriage being very upright, and having an important air. The general outline should convey the existence of a vigorous and well-proportioned body.

Head—Should be rather small and flat, not too prominent or round in the skull, nor too long in the muzzle, with a perfect black nose. The fall on the head to be long, of a rich golden tan, deeper in color at the sides of the head about the ear roots, and on the muzzle where it should be very long. The hair on the chest a rich bright tan. On no account must the tan on the head extend on to the neck, nor must there be any sooty or dark hair intermingled with any of the tan.

Eyes—Medium, dark and sparkling, having a sharp, intelligent expression, and placed so as to look directly forward. They should not be prominent, and the edge of the eyelids should be of a dark color.

Ears—Small V-shaped, and carried semi-erect, or erect, and not far apart, covered with short hair, color to be of a very deep rich tan.

Mouth—Perfectly even, with teeth as sound as possible. An animal having lost any teeth through accident not a fault providing the jaws are even.

Body—Very compact, and a good loin. Level on the top of the back.

Coat—The hair on body moderately long and perfectly straight (not wavy), glossy like silk, and of a fine silky texture. Color, a dark steel blue (not silver blue) extending from the occiput (or back of skull) to the root of tail, and on no account mingled with fawn, bronze or dark hairs.

Legs—Quite straight, well covered with hair of a rich golden tan a few shades lighter at the ends than at the roots, not extending higher on the fore-legs than the elbow, nor on the hindlegs than the stifle.

Feet—As round as possible, and the toe-nails black.

Tail—Cut to medium length; with plenty of hair, darker blue in color than the rest of the body, especially at the end of the tail, and carried a little higher than the level of the back.

Tan—All tan hair should be darker at the roots than in the middle, shading to a still lighter tan at the tips.

Scale of Points

	Points
Formation and terrier appearance	15
Color of hair on body	15
Richness of tan on head and legs	15
Quality and texture of coat	10
Quantity and length of coat	10
Head	10
Mouth	5
Legs and feet	5
Ears	5
Eyes	5
Tail (carriage of)	5
Total	100

Champion Golden
Lad of Heskethane

GROUP VI

Non-Sporting Dogs

The Bull-Dog   The Dalmatian or Coach Dog

THIS is a miscellaneous group of animals, breeds that did not seem to fit into any of the other five groups, yet dogs of character and distinction who share with all breeds the canine's unique love for mankind.

All the dogs described and catalogued here make the finest of companions and house dogs, yet one feels that they mostly deserve inclusion in groups other than this for most have a background of working service for mankind. The Dalmatian was originally a sporting dog and became a stable and coach dog, certainly these are working dog connotations. The Chow Chow was a hunting dog in its native Orient and, by its nature, as excellent a guard dog today as one can find. The Keeshond and Schipperke were watch and vermin dogs on the barges of their respective countries, and the Poodle was, and is still, a jack-of-all-trades and master of many.

These and other breeds in this group can be listed in the sporting, working, or terrier groups, with as much right to inclusion as any of the breeds normally listed in these categories.

But perhaps it is only right to give these few breeds the distinction of separate classification, for they are breeds that are a little different from others, breeds that enter the heart and have greater meaning to those who have been fortunate enough to have known, owned, or bred them.

So let us keep Group VI: Non-Sporting Dogs. The name of the group means nothing and is as good as any other name. It is the dogs that are listed under the name that count and, in this instance, they count for all that has been important in the relationship of man and dog throughout the ages.

THE BOSTON TERRIER

The name of this non-sporting dog indicates the city that was its point of origin. One of the few native American breeds, the Boston Terrier owes its basic characteristics to two English breeds, the Bulldog and the white English Terrier, breeds that were brought to Massachusetts and there crosssed. Selection was subsequently made for certain characteristics and the Boston Terrier came into being.

This resulting breed was a very refined edition of the Bull Terrier and when, in 1891, the American Bull Terrier Club of Boston was formed, their application for registration of their breed was denied by the A.K.C. on the grounds that this was not a *"bull"* terrier breed at all. The suggestion that the breed be called the *"Boston Terrier"* was accepted, the parent club name changed to the Boston Terrier Club and the Boston Terrier received full recognition as a distinct breed in 1893.

The author's parents bred Bostons long years ago. When quite young, I remember a nice stud we had of Peter's King breeding out of a bitch with a half white head. In those days it was difficult to achieve the wanted restricted markings. We also had a bitch of Mosholu breeding that gave us good markings and deep color.

The Boston Terrier, because of its many virtues, has weathered dissension and strife within its own breed club of such proportions as to have wrecked a breed of less endearing personality. The breed has much to recommend it, including sturdiness, agility, looks and the ability to be a fine companion.

STANDARD OF THE BOSTON TERRIER

General Appearance—The general appearance of the Boston Terrier should be that of a lively, highly intelligent, smooth coated, short headed, compactly built, short tailed, well balanced dog of medium station, of brindle color and evenly marked with white. The head should indicate a high degree of intelligence, and should be in proportion to the size of the dog; the body rather short and well knit, the limbs strong and neatly turned; tail short; and no feature be so prominent that the dog appears badly proportioned.

The dog should convey an impression of determination, strength and activity; with style of a high order; carriage easy and graceful.

A proportionate combination of "Color" and "Ideal Markings" is a particularly distinctive feature of a representative specimen, and a dog with a preponderance of white on body, or without the proper proportion of brindle and white on head, should possess sufficient merit otherwise to counteract its deficiencies in these respects.

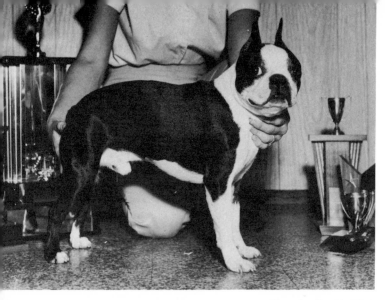

Champion Torch's Pilot

The ideal "Boston Terrier Expression" as indicating a "high degree of intelligence," is also an important characteristic of the breed.

"Color and Markings" and "Expression" should be given particular consideration in determining the relative value of "General Appearance" to other points.

Skull—Square, flat on top, free from wrinkles; cheeks flat; brow abrupt, stop well defined.

Eyes—Wide apart, large and round, dark in color, expression alert but kind

Champion Wood's Lou Lou

and intelligent. The eyes should set square in the skull, and the outside corners should be on a line with the cheeks as viewed from the front.

Muzzle—Short, square, wide and deep, and in proportion to skull; free from wrinkles; shorter in length than in width and depth, not exceeding in length approximately one-third of length of skull; width and depth carried out well to end; the muzzle from stop to end of nose on a line parallel to the top of the skull; nose black and wide, with well defined line between nostrils. The jaws broad and square, with short regular teeth. Bite even or sufficiently undershot to square muzzle. The chops of good depth but not pendulous, completely covering the teeth when mouth is closed.

Ears—Carried erect; small and thin; situated as near corners of skull as possible.

Head Faults—Skull "domed" or inclined; furrowed by a medial line; skull too long for breadth, or *vice versa*; stop too shallow; brow and skull too slanting. Eyes small or sunken; too prominent; light color or wall eye; showing too much white or haw. Muzzle wedge shaped or lacking depth; down faced; too much cut out below the eyes; pinched or wide nostrils; butterfly nose;

Champion Beau Regards Tina Mia

protruding teeth; weak lower jaw; showing "turn up," layback, or wrinkled. Ears poorly carried or in size out of proportion to head.

Neck—Of fair length, slightly arched and carrying the head gracefully; setting neatly into shoulders.

Neck Faults—Ewe-necked; throatiness; short and thick.

Body—Deep with good width of chest; shoulders sloping; back short; ribs deep and well sprung, carried well back to loins; loins short and muscular; rump curving slightly to set-on of tail; flank very slightly cut up. The body should appear short but not chunky.

Body Faults—Flat sides; narrow chest; long or slack loins; roach back; sway back; too much cut up in flank.

Elbows—Standing neither in nor out.

Forelegs—Set moderately wide apart and on a line with the point of the shoulders; straight in bone and well muscled; pasterns short and strong.

Hind Legs—Set true; bent at stifles; short from hocks to feet; hocks turning neither in nor out; thighs strong and well muscled.

667

Feet—Round, small and compact and turned neither in nor out; toes well arched.

Leg and Feet Faults—Loose shoulders or elbows; hind legs too straight at stifles; hocks too prominent; long or weak pasterns; splay feet.

Gait—The gait of the Boston Terrier is that of a surefooted, straight gaited dog, forelegs and hind legs moving straight ahead in line with perfect rhythm, each step indicating grace with power.

Gait Faults—There shall be no rolling, paddling or weaving when gaited and any crossing movement, either front or rear, is a serious fault.

Tail—Set-on low; short, fine and tapering; straight; or screw; devoid of fringe or coarse hair, and not carried above horizontal.

Tail Faults—A long or gaily carried tail; extremely gnarled or curled against body. (Note.—The preferred tail should not exceed in length approximately half the distance from set-on to hock.)

Ideal Color—Brindle with white markings. The brindle to be evenly distributed and distinct. Black with white markings permissible but brindle with white markings preferred.

Ideal Markings—White muzzle, even white blaze over head, collar, breast, part or whole of forelegs, and hind legs below hocks.

Color and Markings Faults—All white; absence of white marking; preponderance of white on body; without the proper proportion of brindle and white on head; or any variations detracting from the general appearance.

Coat—Short, smooth, bright and fine in texture.

Coat Faults—Long or coarse; lacking lustre.

Weight—Not exceeding 25 pounds, divided by classes as follows: Lightweight: Under 15 pounds. Middleweight: 15 and under 20 pounds. Heavyweight: 20 and not exceeding 25 pounds.

Disqualifications—Solid black; black and tan; liver or mouse colors. Dudley nose. Docked tail or any artificial means used to deceive the judge.

SCALE OF POINTS

	Points
General appearance	10
Skull	10
Eyes	5
Muzzle	10
Ears	2
Neck	3
Body	15
Elbows	4
Forelegs	5
Hind legs	5
Gait	10
Feet	5
Tail	5
Color	4
Ideal markings	5
Coat	2
Total	100

The Bulldog has, for hundreds of years and in almost every land, been the personification of unflinching courage and determination. In building this breed, beauty was not part of the breeders' aim. Savagery, tenacity due to lack of sensitivity to pain, was once a necessary part of his make-up. In those old days when the breed acquired its name, it played one of the chief roles in the so-called "sport" of bull baiting, which was popular among certain classes in England for over 700 years until it became illegal in 1835.

The Bulldog was also used in bear baiting and pit fighting (*dog pitted against dog*). He was bred with a short neck, tremendously powerful body and limbs, an undershot jaw and set-back nose so he could hang onto the bull and at the same time breathe with ease.

When these barbarous sports were outlawed the Bulldog, who represented the English grit and ability to persist until a job was done, as the lion is a symbol of the majesty of Great Britain, was in danger of oblivion. Luckily, far-sighted dog lovers rescued the breed and bred it toward the present ideal.

The Bulldog was probably originally fashioned from the small Bullenbeisser. This latter kind of dog was the progenitor of all the Mastiff-like breeds. They were used as guard, attack, fighting, and wild animal baiting dogs, in ancient Assyria, Greece, Egypt, and Rome, and were in common use among the early half-savage Teutonic and Celtic tribes. The early Bullenbeissers were large massive animals, but a smaller, lighter Bullenbeisser was developed. The English masters of the art of livestock breeding used this smaller Bullenbeisser from which to fashion the Bulldog.

Clever selective breeding has developed one of the friendliest and most companionable of breeds in the Bulldog. Homely, lovable, and good natured to an almost impossible degree, but still endowed with an abundance of grit, the "*Sourmug*" will probably last as long as any breed in existence because of his numerous virtues.

The Bulldog Club of America was formed in 1890, but Bulldogs had first appeared in shows about ten years previously.

STANDARD OF THE BULLDOG

General Appearance, Attitude, Expression, Etc.—The perfect Bulldog must be of medium size and smooth coat; with heavy, thick-set, low-swung body, massive short-faced head, wide shoulders and sturdy limbs.

The general appearance and attitude should suggest great stability, vigor and strength.

The disposition should be equable and kind, resolute and courageous (not vicious or aggressive), and demeanor should be pacific and dignified.

These attributes should be countenanced by the expression and behavior.

Gait—The style and carriage are peculiar, his gait being a loose-jointed, shuffling, sidewise motion, giving the characteristic "roll." The action must, however, be unrestrained, free and vigorous.

Proportion and Symmetry—The "points" should be well distributed and bear good relation one to the other, no feature being in such prominence from either excess or lack of quality that the animal appears deformed or illy proportioned.

Influence of Sex—In comparison of specimens of different sex, due allowance should be made in favor of the bitches, which do not bear the characteristics of the breed to the same degree of perfection and grandeur as do the dogs.

Size—The size for mature dogs is about 50 pounds; for mature bitches about 40 pounds.

Coat—The coat should be straight, short, flat, close, of fine texture, smooth and glossy. (No fringe, feather or curl.)

Color of Coat—The color of coat should be uniform, pure of its kind and brilliant.

The various colors found in the breed are to be preferred in the following order:

(1) Red brindle, (2) all other brindles, (3) solid white, (4) solid red, fawn or fallow, (5) piebald, (6) inferior qualities of all the foregoing.

Note—A perfect piebald is preferable to a muddy brindle or defective solid color.

Solid black is very undesirable, but not so objectionable if occurring to a moderate degree in piebald patches. The brindles to be perfect should have a fine, even and equal distribution of the composite colors.

In brindles and solid colors a small white patch on the chest is not con-

English and American champion, Eastgate Stalwart Bosun.

sidered detrimental. In piebalds the color patches should be well defined, of pure color and symmetrically distributed.

Skin—The skin should be soft and loose, especially at the head, neck and shoulders.

Wrinkles and Dewlap—The head and face should be covered with heavy wrinkles, and at the throat, from jaw to chest, there should be two loose pendulous folds, forming the dewlap.

Skull—The skull should be very large, and in circumference, in front of the ears, should measure at least the height of the dog at the shoulders.

Viewed from the front, it should appear very high from the corner of the lower jaw to the apex of the skull, and also very broad and square.

Viewed at the side, the head should appear very high, and very short from the point of the nose to occiput.

The forehead should be flat (not rounded or "domed"), neither too prominent nor overhanging the face.

Cheeks—The cheeks should be well rounded, protruding sideways and outward beyond the eyes.

Stop—The temples or frontal bones should be very well defined, broad, square and high, causing a hollow or groove between the eyes. This indentation, or "stop," should be both broad and deep and extend up the middle of the forehead, dividing the head vertically, being traceable to the top of the skull.

Eyes and Eyelids—The eyes, seen from the front, should be situated low down in the skull, as far from the ears as possible, and their corners should be in a straight line at right angles with the stop. They should be quite in front of the head, as wide apart as possible, provided their outer corners are within the outline of the cheeks when viewed from the front.

They should be quite round in form, of moderate size, neither sunken nor bulging, and in color should be very dark.

The lids should cover the white of the eyeball, when the dog is looking directly forward, and the lid should show no "haw."

Ears—The ears should be set high in the head, the front inner edge of each ear joining the outline of the skull at the top back corner of skull, so as to place them as wide apart, and as high, and as far from the eyes as possible.

In size they should be small and thin. The shape termed "rose ear" is the most desirable. The "rose ear" folds inward at its back lower edge, the upper front edge curving over, outwards and backwards, showing part of the inside of the burr. (The ears should not be carried erect or "prick-eared" or "buttoned" and should never be cropped.)

Face—The face, measured from the front of the cheek bone to the tip of the nose, should be extremely short, the muzzle being very short, broad, turned upwards and very deep from the corner of the eye to the corner of the mouth.

Nose—The nose should be large, broad and black, its tip being set back deeply between the eyes.

The distance from bottom of stop, between the eyes, to the tip of nose should be as short as possible and not exceed the length from the tip of nose to the edge of under lip.

The nostrils should be wide, large and black, with a well-defined line between them. (The parti-color or "butterfly nose" and the flesh-color or

672

Two photos that convey the ugly charm and lovability of the "sourmug".

Champion Ne Mac's Frankie O'Fearnaught

Champion Broadford Foden Esquire.

"Dudley nose" are decidedly objectionable, but do not disqualify for competition.) Amended at a special meeting of Club, held September 5, 1914, to read: Any nose other than black is objectionable and "Dudley" or flesh-colored nose absolutely disqualified from competition.

Chops—The chops or "flews" should be thick, broad, pendant and very deep, completely overhanging the lower jaw at each side.

They join the under lip in front and almost or quite cover the teeth, which should be scarcely noticeable when the mouth is closed.

Jaws—The jaws should be massive, very broad, square and "undershot," the lower jaw projecting considerably in front of the upper jaw and turning up.

Teeth—The teeth should be large and strong, with the canine teeth or tusks wide apart, and the six small teeth in front, between the canines, in an even, level row.

674

Neck—The neck should be short, very thick, deep and strong and well arched at the back.

Shoulders—The shoulders should be muscular, very heavy, wide-spread and slanting outward, giving stability and great power.

Chest—The chest should be very broad, deep and full.

Brisket and Body—The brisket and body should be very capacious, with full sides, well rounded ribs and very deep from the shoulders down to its lowest part, where it joins the chest.

It should be well let down between the shoulders and forelegs, giving the dog a broad, low, short-legged appearance.

The body should be well ribbed up behind with the belly tucked up and not rotund.

Back—The back should be short and strong, very broad at the shoulders and comparatively narrow at the loins. There should be a slight fall in the back, close behind the shoulders (its lowest part), whence the spine should rise to the loins (the top of which should be higher than the top of the shoulders), thence curving again more suddenly to the tail, forming an arch (a very distinctive feature of the breed), termed "roach-back" or, more correctly, "wheel-back."

Forelegs—The forelegs should be short, very stout, straight and muscular, set wide apart, with well developed calves, presenting a bowed outline, but the bones of the legs should not be curved or bandy, nor the feet brought too close together.

Elbows—The elbows should be low and stand well out and loose from the body.

Hindlegs—The hindlegs should be strong and muscular and longer than the forelegs, so as to elevate the loins above the shoulders.

Hocks should be slightly bent and well let down, so as to give length and strength from loins to hock.

The lower leg should be short, straight and strong, with the stifles turned slightly outward and away from the body. The hocks are thereby made to approach each other, and the hindfeet to turn outward.

Feet—The feet should be moderate in size, compact and firmly set. Toes compact, well split up, with high knuckles and with short stubby nails.

The front feet may be straight or slightly out-turned, but the hind feet should be pointed well outward.

Tail—The tail may be either straight or "screwed" (but never curved or curly), and in any case must be short, hung low, with decided downward carriage, thick root and fine tip.

If straight, the tail should be cylindrical and of uniform taper.

If "screwed" the bends or kinks should be well defined, and they may be abrupt and even knotty, but no portion of the member should be elevated above the base or root.

SCALE OF POINTS

	Points
Proportion and symmetry	5
Attitude	3
Expression	2

Gait	3	
Size	3	
Coat	2	
Color of coat	4	
General properties	—	22
Skull	5	
Cheeks	2	
Stop	4	
Eyes and eyelids	3	
Ears	5	
Wrinkle	5	
Nose	6	
Chops	2	
Jaws	5	
Teeth	2	
Total, head	—	39
Neck	3	
Dewlap	2	
Shoulders	5	
Chest	3	
Ribs	3	
Brisket	2	
Belly	2	
Back	5	
Forelegs and elbows	4	
Hindlegs	3	
Feet	3	
Tail	4	
Total, body, legs, etc.	—	39

Total 100

DISQUALIFICATION

Dudley or flesh colored nose.

The black Chow Chow, Champion Pandee's
Alpha Sing, a Best-In-Show winner.

Champion Loy-Jean's
Beau Monty

This is a breed of many names in its native China. There it appears in two coats, the rough with which we are familiar, and the smooth, a variety not seen or evidently wanted in the western world.

The classification of the Chow in the non-sporting group is rather odd considering its background of service in China and its evident origin. Its genetic background is one with the northern sled dogs, a modern example of the most ancient of the breeds of the far north, probably in a direct line from the impossibly ancient northern Tibetan and Siberian sled dogs. Or possibly he was a contemporary of those ancient breeds and came down pure from that time of antiquity. This would explain the strange "blue-black" tongue that is unique with this breed.

The many names mentioned above that the breed enjoys in China are: lang kou (*wolf dog*), hsiung kou (*bear dog*), hei shet kou (*black-tongued*) and Kwantung Kou (*dog of Canton*). The popular name Chow-Chow was evolved from a pidgin-English term for any kind of goods, animate or inanimate, brought from the Orient during the latter part of the 18th century.

In China the Chow was used as a hunting dog and is credited with keen scenting powers. He is said to be a clever hunter and (of all things) staunch on point like a setter! This last the author would have to see to believe. But the breed was supposed to be the hunting dog of Emperors and Oriental aristocrats.

The Chow is certainly a breed that can be labeled "one-man". In his own home with his own people he will stoically accept advances from friends of the family. But away from his master, he will resent any attempt by strangers or even acquaintances to become chummy. They characteristically possess the bland aloofness of the Orient.

The breed first drew notice in this country at the 1890 Westminster show and with the beginning of the 20th century has made breed progress in America.

STANDARD OF THE CHOW-CHOW

General Appearance—A massive, cobby, powerful dog, active and alert, with strong, muscular development, and perfect balance. Body squares with height of leg at shoulder; head, broad and flat, with short, broad, and deep muzzle, accentuated by a ruff; the whole supported by straight, strong legs. Clothed in a shining, off-standing coat, the Chow is a masterpiece of beauty, dignity, and untouched naturalness.

Head—Large and massive in proportion to size of dog, with broad, flat skull; well filled under the eyes; moderate stop; and proudly carried.

Expression—Essentially dignified, lordly, scowling, discerning, sober, and snobbish—one of independence.

Muzzle—Short in comparison to length of skull; broad from eyes to end of nose, and of equal depth. The lips somewhat full and overhanging.

Teeth—Strong and level, with a scissors bite; should neither be overshot, nor undershot.

Nose—Large, broad, and black in color. *Disqualification*—Nose spotted or distinctly other color than black, except in blue Chows, which may have solid blue or slate noses.

Chow-Chow puppies look like fuzzy, Oriental teddy bears.

Tongue—A blue-black. The tissues of the mouth should approximate black.
Disqualification—Tongue red, pink, or obviously spotted with red or pink.

Eyes—Dark, deep-set, of moderate size, and almond-shaped.

Ears—Small, slightly rounded at tip, stiffly carried. They should be placed wide apart, on top of the skull, and set with a slight, forward tilt. *Disqualification*—Drop ear or ears. A drop ear is one which is not stiffly carried or stiffly erect, but which breaks over at any point from its base to its tip.

Body—Short, compact, with well-sprung ribs, and let down in the flank.

Neck—Strong, full, set well on the shoulders.

Shoulders—Muscular, slightly sloping.

Chest—Broad, deep, and muscular. A narrow chest is a serious fault.

Back—Short, straight, and strong.

Loins—Broad, deep, and powerful.

Tail—Set well up and carried closely to the back, following line of spine at start.

Forelegs—Perfectly straight, with heavy bone and upright pasterns.

Hindlegs—Straight hocked, muscular, and heavy boned.

Feet—Compact, round, cat-like, with thick pads.

Gait—Completely individual. Short and stilted because of straight hocks.

Coat—Abundant, dense, straight, and off-standing; rather coarse in texture with a soft, woolly undercoat. It may be any clear color, solid throughout, with lighter shadings on ruff, tail, and breechings.

DISQUALIFICATIONS

Nose spotted or distinctly other color than black, except in blue Chows, which may have solid blue or slate noses. Tongue red, pink or obviously spotted with red or pink. Drop ear or ears.

Champion Starcrest Spy of
Poppyland

THE DALMATIAN

On the Adriatic Sea in Western Yugoslavia is a province of Austria, named Dalmatia. It was here that the spotted dog first came into focus and from this province took its breed name. Though the spotted dogs had been known for centuries they had so frequently been in the hands of the nomad Romanies (Gypsies) that they had been accredited with a dozen nationalities and names until the name Dalmatian became fixed and stable. In England alone he had been called the Plum Pudding Dog, Spotted Dick, the English Coach Dog, the Fire House Dog, and the Carriage Dog. He is still frequently termed the Coach Dog in America.

The breed has been connected with varied uses and is said to have been a shepherd, draft, guard and sentry dog. When first brought to England, the Dalmatian was introduced as a sporting dog and primarily as a pointer. But the native English sporting dogs were far superior in that area and the Dalmatian fell into disuse. Then its marked fondness for horses and stables was noted and the breed became the carriage dog supreme. Later it was adopted by the fire departments and stayed as a fixture even when the fire horses had vanished and the departments became mechanized.

The breed is by instinct, training and breeding the perfect coach dog. He can do the various work such a job entails and do it with the flair that has earned him the right to be called the only true carriage dog in the world.

The Dalmatian is a good watch dog and guard and a fine family dog. He is sturdy, neat and clean, and an easy keeper. His spotted markings are peculiarly his own. He makes a nice picture in the show ring and is a prominent contender in obedience competition. Anyone who has seen the fantastic act of the performing Dalmatians trained by Willi Necker, during the Westminster Dog Show at Madison Square Garden, can never doubt the breed's intelligence.

A symphony of shadows.

Champion Coachman's Callisto.

STANDARD OF THE DALMATIAN

Head—Should be of a fair length, the skull flat, rather broad between the ears, and moderately well defined at the temple, i.e., exhibiting a moderate amount of stop, and not in one straight line from the nose to the occiput bone, as required in a Bull Terrier. It should be entirely free from wrinkle.

Muzzle Should be long and powerful; the lips clean, fitting the jaws moderately close.

Eyes—Should be set moderately well apart, and of medium size, round, bright and sparkling, with an intelligent expression, their color greatly depending on the markings of the dog. In the black-spotted variety the eyes should be dark (black or brown); in the liver-spotted variety they should be light (yellow or light brown). Wall eyes are permissible.

The rim around the eyes in the black-spotted variety should be black; in the liver-spotted variety, brown—never flesh-colored in either.

Ears—Should be set on rather high, of moderate size, rather wide at the base and gradually tapering to a rounded point. They should be carried close to the head, be thin and fine in texture, and always spotted, the more profusely the better.

Nose—In the black-spotted variety should always be black; in the liver-spotted variety, always brown.

Neck and Shoulders—The neck should be fairly long, nicely arched, light and tapering, and entirely free from throatiness. The shoulders should be moderately oblique, clean and muscular, denoting speed.

Body, Back, Chest and *Loins*—The chest should not be too wide, but very deep and capacious, ribs moderately well sprung, never rounded like barrel hoops (which would indicate want of speed); back powerful; loin strong, muscular, and slightly arched.

Legs and Feet—Of great importance. The fore legs should be perfectly straight, strong and heavy in bone; elbows close to the body; feet compact, well-arched toes, and tough, elastic pads. In the hind legs the muscles should be clean, though well defined; the hocks well let down.

Nails—In the black-spotted variety, black and white; in the liver-spotted variety, brown and white.

Gait—Length of stride should be in proportion to the size of the dog; steady in rhythm of 1, 2, 3, 4 as in the cadence count in military drill. Front legs should not paddle, nor should there be a straddling appearance. Hind legs should neither cross nor weave; judges should be able to see each leg move with no interference of another leg. Drive and reach are most desirable.

Tail—Should not be too long, strong at the insertion, and gradually tapering towards the end, free from coarseness. It should not be inserted too low down, but carried with a slight curve upwards, and never curled. It should be spotted, the more profusely the better.

Coat—Short, hard, dense and fine, sleek and glossy in appearance, but neither woolly nor silky.

Color and Markings—These are most important points. The ground color in both varieties should be pure white, very decided, and not intermixed. The color of the spots in the black-spotted variety should be black, the deeper and richer the black the better; in the liver-spotted variety they should be brown. The spots should not intermingle, but be as round and well defined as possible, the more distinct the better; in size they should be from that of a dime to a half dollar. The spots on the face, head, ears, legs, tail and extremities to be smaller than those on the body.

Size—Height of dogs and bitches between 19 and 23 inches; weight, between 35 and 50 pounds.

General Appearance—The Dalmatian should represent a strong, muscular and active dog, symmetrical in outline and free from coarseness and lumber, capable of great endurance, combined with a fair amount of speed.

SCALE OF POINTS

	Points
Head and eyes	10
Ears	5
Neck and shoulders	10
Body, back, chest and loins	10
Legs and feet	10
Gait	10
Coat	5
Color and markings	25
Tail	5
Size, symmetry, etc.	10
Total	100

684

THE FRENCH BULLDOG

The French Bulldog is a small, compact, heavy-boned, alert, lively, intelligent dog that adapts himself to the small city apartment or the country home. He is the ideal house pet and companion to adults and children alike. The "Frenchie"—as he is familiarly called—is a good watch dog but does not disturb the neighborhood by needless barking. He easily learns his house manners, tricks and obedience work. He is devoted to his own family but is friendly and good-natured with others.

The variety of allowed colors—all shades of brindle, fawn, cream, white, Pied (white with brindle markings)—gives us a wide choice. There are lightweights, under 22 pounds, and heavyweights, 22 to 28 pounds. The

Champion Hover's Le Petit Roi Blanc, C.D.

short hair and clean habits make the Frenchie easy to keep perfectly groomed at all times. The French Bulldog needs no docking of tail or cropping of ears. He is born with his erect "bat" ears and short tail. Indeed the Breed Standard forbids mutilation.

To France goes the credit for developing this breed from the Toy Bulldogs taken to France when the Nottingham lace workers migrated to the coast of Normandy taking with them the small English Bulldogs that in some instances weighed as little as ten pounds.

The country justly credited with producing the French Bulldog has thrown little light on the breeding operations that resulted in a type of dog with at least three features distinctly different from the originating breed. The bat ear, unlike other erect or semi-erect ears, has a well rounded-top not unlike the ears of a bat. They are set on the head so that, looking from the front the whole orifice shows. The Frenchie alone possesses the bat ear.

The other peculiarly distinctive features relate to the skull formation. First, the skull between the ears should be flat or level. Second (*and here lies the total difference from the English Bulldog*), the portion of the skull directly above the eyes and best designated as forehead, should be curved giving this part of the head the slightly rounded appearance that accounts for the quaint and unusual appearance of the French Bulldog.

It was at the Westminster Show in February 1896 that the French Bulldog was introduced to American dog fanciers. In those days the rose ear was recognized in France and the English judges favored it while the American fanciers felt the bat ear belonged on the French Bulldog.

The emphatic and positive declaration of the American Club and its courageous fight for the bat ear is its proudest achievement. Today if there is one point beyond all others that French Bulldog fanciers throughout the world agree on, it is that the dog should have a bat ear.

The French Bulldog thrives and develops best when raised in a home where close human companionship brings out the sparkling personality and innate cleverness that characterize the breed. He respects and tries to please his human family without loss of dignity or individuality. His versatility is such that the Frenchie house pet and watch dog can also be the show dog and obedience trial star.

STANDARD OF THE FRENCH BULLDOG

General Appearance—The French Bulldog should have the appearance of an active, intelligent, muscular dog, of heavy bone, smooth coat, compactly built, and of medium or small stature.

Proportion and Symmetry—The points should be well distributed and bear good relation one to the other, no feature being in such prominence from either excess or lack of quality that the animal appears deformed or poorly proportioned.

Influence of Sex—In comparison of specimens of different sex, due allowance should be made in favor of the bitches, which do not bear the characteristics of the breed to the same marked degree as do the dogs.

Weight—A lightweight class under 22 pounds; heavyweight class, 22 pounds, and not over 28 pounds.

Head—The head should be large and square. The top of the skull should be flat between the ears; the forehead should not be flat but slightly rounded.

The stop should be well defined causing a hollow or groove between the eyes. The muzzle should be broad, deep and well laid back; the muscles of the cheeks well developed. The nose should be extremely short; nostrils broad with well defined line between them. The nose and flews should be black, except in the case of the lighter colored dogs, where a lighter color nose is acceptable. The flews should be thick and broad, hanging over the lower jaw at the sides, meeting the underlip in front and covering the teeth which should not be seen when the mouth is closed. The underjaw should be deep, square, broad, undershot and well turned up.

Eyes—The eyes should be wide apart, set low down in the skull, as far from the ears as possible, round in form, of moderate size, neither sunken nor bulging, and in color dark. No haw and no white of the eye showing when looking forward.

Neck—The neck should be thick and well arched, with loose skin at throat.

Ears—The ears shall hereafter be known as the bat ear, broad at the base, elongated, with round top, set high in the head, but not too close together, and carried erect with the orifice to the front. The leather of the ear fine and soft.

Body—The body should be short and well rounded. The chest, broad, deep and full, well ribbed with the belly tucked up. The back should be a roach back, with a slight fall close behind the shoulders. It should be strong and short, broad at the shoulders and narrowing at the loins.

Legs—The forelegs should be short, stout, straight and muscular, set wide apart. The hindlegs should be strong and muscular, longer than the forelegs, so as to elevate the loins above the shoulders. Hocks well let down.

Feet—The feet should be moderate in size, compact and firmly set. Toes compact, well split up, with high knuckles and short, stubby nails; hindfeet slightly longer than forefeet.

Tail—The tail should be either straight or screwed (but not curly), short, hung low, thick root and fine tip; carried low in repose.

Ch. Bedal's Menjou
Le Chef D'Oeuvre

Ch. Terrette's Chef
D'Oeuvre Anjou, C.D.

Ch. Hampton's
Beau Garcon

left
Ch. Hampton's Valentine

right
Ch. Hampton's Le Comte de
Paris

Color, Skin and Coat—Acceptable colors are: All brindle, fawn, white, brindle and white, and any color except those which constitute disqualification. The skin should be soft and loose, especially at head and shoulders, forming wrinkles. Coat moderately fine, brilliant, short and smooth.

Disqualifications—Other than bat ears; black and white, black and tan, liver, mouse or solid black (black means black without any trace of brindle) eyes of different color; nose other than black except in the case of the lighter colored dogs, where a lighter color nose is acceptable; hare lip; any mutilation; over 28 pounds in weight.

SCALE OF POINTS

	Points	
Proportion and symmetry	5	
Expression	5	
Gait	4	
Color	4	
Coat	2	
Total, general properties	—	20
Skull	6	
Cheeks and chops	2	
Stop	5	
Ears	8	
Eyes	4	
Wrinkles	4	
Nose	3	
Jaws	6	
Teeth	2	
Total, head	—	40
Shoulders	5	
Back	5	
Neck	4	
Chest	3	
Ribs	4	
Brisket	3	
Belly	2	
Forelegs	4	
Hindlegs	3	
Feet	3	
Tail	4	
Total, body, legs, etc.	—	40
Grand total		100

A BOSTON TERRIER.

NONSPORTING

A DARK BRINDLE FRENCH BULLDOG. TOP RIGHT, ON THE FACING PAGE, IS A STANDARD POODLE PUPPY, HIS CREAM COAT IN A PUPPY CLIP. BELOW HIM IS A DALMATIAN, THE BREED KNOWN TO MANY AS A COACH DOG.

A BULLDOG, DAM AND DAUGHTER.

PORTRAIT OF AN APRICOT COLORED MINIATURE
POODLE IN A SHOW CLIP.

THE SCHIPPERKE, OF BELGIUM.

A KEESHOND, FROM HOLLAND.

THE CHINESE CHOW CHOW.

AT TOP A PAIR OF BOSTON TERRIERS. BELOW,
A WHITE STANDARD POODLE.

A CAVALIER KING CHARLES SPANIEL.

HEAD STUDY OF A TOY FOX TERRIER, ALSO
KNOWN AS AN AMERTOY.

ONE OF THE NATIVE SHEEPHERD-
ING BREEDS FROM THE LAND OF
THE MARSUPIALS, THIS IS AN
AUSTRALIAN SHEPHERD. TO THE
RIGHT IS A BEDOUIN SHEPHERD.

The author took this photo of a
desert dog in Jordan. It is bred
true to type by the Bedouins to
herd flocks and drive Camels. Note
the tiny, cupped, prick ear; identical to that probably worn by the
prototype dog, Tomarctus, fifteen
million years ago.

A CHINESE CRESTED DOG.

THE SMALL AND CHARMING SHIH TZU OF CHINESE ORIGIN.

THE TIBETAN TERRIER, A NATIVE OF THE FABULOUS MOUNTAINS OF "SHANGRI-LA."

THE SPITZ BELONGS TO A BASIC GROUP OF
CANINES THAT EXHIBIT GREAT VARIATION IN
SIZE.

FROM THE LAND OF THE RISING SUN COMES
THE AKITA, ONE OF JAPAN'S MOST POPULAR
BREEDS.

A SOFT-COATED WHEATEN TERRIER.

THE KEESHOND

Sometimes called the Dutch Barge Dog this breed is so closely associated with its native country that it was the symbol of the political party called the Patriots in the years immediately following the French Revolution. The Keeshond was the dog of the people and as such, symbolized the Patriotten in their struggle against the Prinsgezinden (*partisans of the Prince of Orange*). The leader of the Patriots was Kees de Gyselaer of Dordrecht. He had a Dutch Barge Dog which he had named for himself, Kees. This dog, becoming the dog of the Patriots, the symbol of the common man, gave the breed its name.

The Keeshond, as a breed, is kept as a pet and house dog throughout Holland and has served for centuries on the rijnaken, small vessels used on the Rhine River. As a barge dog, they were simply pets and watch dogs. The author thought that he would find Holland and the Rhine literally overrun with Keeshonden. To be frank, I saw very few in two visits to the Rhine and a drive throughout the Netherlands. The breed is probably more of a show dog today.

Champion Theo v. Hargert

Its connection with the Patriot party almost caused its undoing for it symbolized the losing political party and few people wanted a living symbol in their home of the party that had opposed the Prince of Orange. The breed was at low ebb until adopted by the Baroness van Hardencroek who built the breed to prominence again.

The Keeshond is evidently a descendent of that hardy group of northern dogs that has given us the Spitz, Samoyed, Husky, Norwegian Elkhound, etc. It is probably in a direct line of descent from the Finnish Spitz.

The author well remembers his first contact with the breed many years ago. In the process of judging the group, I had my first opportunity of putting my hands on a Keeshond and was surprised and impressed by the sturdy, compact body and hard musculature of the breed.

Keeshonden are not hunting dogs or specialists in anything but their permanent role as house and companion dogs. With their native intelligence and fine temperament, they are superb at their jobs.

STANDARD OF THE KEESHOND

1. *General Appearance and Conformation*—The Keeshond is a handsome dog, of well-balanced, short coupled body, attracting attention not only by his alert carriage and intelligent expression; but also by his luxurious coat, his richly plumed tail, well curled over his back, and by his fox-like face and head with small pointed ears. His coat is very thick round the neck, fore part of the shoulders and chest, forming a lion-like mane. His rump and hindlegs, down to the hocks, are also thickly coated forming the characteristic "trousers." His head, ears and lower legs are covered with thick short hair.

The ideal height of fully matured dogs (over two years old), measured from

Nine-week-old Keeshond puppies.

Champion Ruttkay Muundawg

Champion Ruttkay Pixie van Reuzenwerk

top of withers to the ground, is: for males, 18 inches; bitches, 17 inches. However, size consideration should not outweigh that of type. When dogs are judged equal in type, the dog nearest the ideal height is to be preferred. Length of back from withers to rump should equal height as measured above.

2. *Head*

Expression—Expression is largely dependent on the distinctive characteristic called "spectacles,"—a delicately pencilled line slanting slightly upward from the outer corner of each eye to the lower corner of the ear, coupled with distinct markings and shadings forming short but expressive eyebrows. Markings (or shadings) on face and head must present a pleasing appearance, imparting to the dog an alert and intelligent expression.

Fault—Absence of "spectacles."

Skull—The head should be well proportioned to the body, wedge-shaped

Champion Rhapsody of Westcrest

when viewed from above. Not only in muzzle, but the whole head should give this impression when the ears are drawn back by covering the nape of the neck and the ears with one hand. Head in profile should exhibit a definite stop.

Fault—Apple head, or absence of stop.

Muzzle—The muzzle should be dark in color and of medium length, neither coarse nor snipy, and well proportioned to the skull.

Mouth—The mouth should be neither overshot nor undershot. Lips should be black and closely meeting, not thick, coarse or sagging; and with no wrinkle at the corner of the mouth.

Fault—Overshot or undershot.

Teeth—The teeth should be white, sound and strong (but discoloration from distemper not to penalize severely); upper teeth should just overlap the lower teeth.

Eyes—Eyes should be dark brown in color, of medium size, rather oblique in shape and not set too wide apart.

Fault—Protruding round eyes or eyes light of color.

Champion Ruttkay Moore's
Fancy Pants

Ears—Ears should be small, triangular in shape, mounted high on head and carried erect; dark in color and covered with thick, velvety, short hair. Size should be proportionate to the head—length approximating the distance from outer corner of the eye to the nearest edge of the ear.

Fault—Ears not carried erect when at attention.

3. *Body*

Neck and Shoulders—The neck should be moderately long, well shaped and well set on shoulders; covered with a profuse mane, sweeping from under the jaw and covering the whole of the front part of the shoulders and chest, as well as the top part of the shoulders.

Chest, Back and Loin—The body should be compact with a short straight back sloping slightly downward toward the hindquarters; well ribbed, barrel well rounded, belly moderately tucked up, deep and strong of chest.

709

Legs—Forelegs should be straight seen from any angle, and well feathered. Hindlegs should be profusely feathered down to the hocks,—not below, with hocks only slightly bent. Legs must be of good bone and cream in color.

Fault—Black markings below the knee, penciling excepted.

Feet—The feet should be compact, well rounded, cat-like, and cream in color. Toes are nicely arched, with black nails.

Fault—White foot or feet.

Tail—The tail should be set on high, moderately long, and well feathered, tightly curled over back. It should lie flat and close to the body with a very light gray plume on top where curled, but the tip of the tail should be black. The tail should form a part of the "silhouette" of the dog's body, rather than give the appearance of an appendage.

Fault—Tail not lying close to the back.

Action—Dogs should show boldly and keep tails curled over the back. They should move cleanly and briskly; and the movement should be straight and sharp (not lope like a German Shepherd).

Fault—Tail not carried over back when moving.

4. *Coat*—The body should be abundantly covered with long, straight, harsh hair; standing well out from a thick, downy undercoat. The hair on the legs should be smooth and short, except for a feathering on the front legs and "trousers," as previously described, on the hindlegs. The hair on the tail should be profuse, forming a rich plume. Head, including muzzle, skull and ears, should be covered with smooth, soft, short hair,—velvety in texture on the ears. Coat must not part down the back.

Fault—Silky, wavy or curly coats. Part in coat down the back.

5. *Color and Markings*—A mixture of gray and black. The undercoat should be very pale gray or cream (not tawny). The hair of the outer coat is black tipped, the length of the black tips producing the characteristic shading of color. The color may vary from light to dark, but any pronounced deviation

The Keeshond has a Dutch charm all its own. The breed's basic sturdiness is derived from its close association, genetically, with the hardy sled dog breeds.

Champion Ruttkay Heir Apparent

from the gray color is not permissible. The plume of the tail should be very light gray when curled on back, and the tip of the tail should be black. Legs and feet should be cream. Ears should be very dark,—almost black.

Shoulder line markings (light gray) should be well defined. The color of the ruff and "trousers" is generally lighter than that of the body. "Spectacles" and shadings, as previously described, are characteristic of the breed and must be present to some degree. There should be no pronounced white markings.

Very Serious Fault—Entirely black or white or any other solid color; any pronounced deviation from the gray color.

SCALE OF POINTS

		Points
1. *General Conformation and Appearance*		20
2. *Head*—		
Shape	6	
Eyes	5	
Ears	5	
Teeth	4	20
3. *Body*—		
Chest, back and loin	10	
Tail	10	
Neck and shoulders	8	
Legs	4	
Feet	3	35
4. *Coat*		15
5. *Color and Markings*		10
Total		100

THE LHASA APSO

From beneath the shadows of towering Mount Everest in the land of the Abominable Snowman, ancient Lamas and hoary monasteries, that mysterious country, Tibet, sent us Apso Seng Kye, the *"Bark Lion Sentinel Dog,"* known to the western world as the Lhasa Apso.

The breeds native to that far-away exotic country have two things in common, the heavy coat of hair that protects and insulates in a country of interchangeable intense cold and heat, and the tail carriage, upturned and curled over the back. All four Tibetan breeds; the Mastiff, Spaniel, Terrier, Lhasa Apso, share this typical pair of characteristics.

While the fierce and powerful Tibetan Mastiff prevents intruders from entering the dwelling, the Lhaso Apso serves as a special guard within the house. Their intelligence, keen hearing and inbred discrimination make them particularly adept at this occupation.

Two beautiful specimens of the breed were imported to this country from

Champion Licos Kulu La

Champion Hamilton Torma

Asia as foundation animals. Today the breed is becoming increasingly popular and has spread to fanciers in Mexico as well as the United States.

These are hardy dogs, easily trained, very responsive to the ones they love, and excellent watch dogs.

STANDARD OF THE LHASA APSO

Character—Gay and assertive, but chary of strangers.

Size—Variable, but about 10 inches or 11 inches at shoulder for dogs, bitches slightly smaller.

Color—Golden, sandy, honey, dark grizzle, slate, smoke, parti-color, black, white or brown. This being the true Tibetan Liondog, golden or lion-like colors are preferred. Other colors in order as above. Dark tips to ears and beard are an asset.

Body Shape—The length from point of shoulders to point of buttocks longer than height at withers, well ribbed up, strong loin, well developed quarters and thighs.

Coat—Heavy, straight, hard, not woolly nor silky, of good length, and very dense.

Mouth and Muzzle—Mouth level, otherwise slightly undershot preferable. Muzzle of medium length; a square muzzle is objectionable.

Head—Heavy head furnishings with good fall over eyes, good whiskers and beard; skull narrow, falling away behind the eyes in a marked degree, not quite flat, but not domed or apple shaped; straight foreface of fair length. Nose black, about 1½ inches long, or the length from tip of nose to eye to be roughly about one-third of the total length from nose to back of skull.

Eyes—Dark brown, neither very large and full, nor very small and sunk.

Ears—Pendant, heavily feathered.

Legs—Forelegs straight; both fore and hindlegs heavily furnished with hair.

Feet—Well feathered, should be round and cat-like, with good pads.

Tail and Carriage—Well feathered, should be carried well over back in a screw, there may be a kink at the end. A low carriage of stern is a serious fault.

713

THE POODLE

The Pudel (*Canis Familiaris Aquatius*), or "water dog" in Germany; the Caniche (*chien canard*), or "duck dog" in France; in England, the Poodle, doubtless derived from the German pudel or pudelin, the latter meaning to "splash in water"; all these names have been given to the breed we know as the Poodle. Note that they all connote a major tendency in the breed to be near, or to be useful or retrieve, in water.

The similarity in type between the Poodle and the water dogs and water spaniels of an earlier date (*discounting the finish brought by expert breeding and selection*) as well as later breeds such as the Irish Water Spaniel, indicates the breed's origin and linkage to the sporting breeds.

The Miniature, Champion Lorac's Magic Gay Blade.

The Toy, Champion Loramar's I'm A Dandee.

In many parts of the world the breed is still used as a gun dog and retriever in water. Last year the author, attending the German Shepherd Sieger show in Germany, was shown a brace of native Pudels used exclusively as sporting dogs. They were clipped all over leaving about an inch of heavy, curled coat for protection and were much coarser and heavier on bone than the breed as we know it here.

The Poodle's unusual intelligence was quickly assessed and utilized by show business people. Playing the clown in vaudeville acts combined with the clips which the breed sports, in and out of the show ring have, over the years, induced many people to treat the breed with ridicule. Far from being ridiculous, the Poodle is the most easily taught, most intelligent and widely capable in the performing of many tasks, as any breed on earth.

Poodles come in three sizes and many colors (*see discussion of parti-colored and phantom Poodles in Toy Dogs—Poodles*). They can be clipped in many ways to suit the individual. They love water, have keen scent, are good retrievers, and their phenomenal intelligence and quick response make them capable of doing almost anything a dog can do, sporting or working.

In the show ring the breed, in all sizes, has done much winning due to the close proximity to the standard that selection and knowledgeable breeding has brought it.

STANDARD OF THE POODLE

General Appearance, Carriage and Condition—That of a very active,

intelligent and elegant-looking dog, squarely built, well-proportioned, moving soundly and carrying himself proudly. Properly clipped in the traditional fashion and carefully groomed, the Poodle has about him an air of distinction and dignity peculiar to himself.

Head and Expression—(*a*) Skull: moderately rounded, with a slight but definite stop. Cheek-bones and muscles flat. Muzzle: long, straight and fine, with slight chiseling under the eyes. Strong without lippiness. The chin definite enough to preclude snipiness. Teeth white, strong and with a scissors bite. Nose sharp with well-defined nostrils. (*b*) Eyes: set far apart, very dark, full of fire and intelligence, oval in appearance. (*c*) Ears: set low and hanging close to the head. The leather should be long, wide and heavily feathered.

Neck and Shoulders—Neck well proportioned, strong and long to admit of the head being carried high and with dignity. Skin snug at throat. The neck should rise from strong muscular shoulders which slope back from their point of angulation at the upper foreleg to the withers.

Body—The chest deep and moderately wide. The ribs well sprung and braced up. The back short, strong and slightly hollowed, the loins short, broad and muscular. (Bitches may be slightly longer in back than dogs.)

Tail—Straight, set on rather high, docked, but of sufficient length to insure a balanced outline. It should be carried up and in a gay manner.

Legs—The forelegs straight from the shoulder, parallel and with bone and muscle in proportion to size of dog. The pasterns should be strong. The hind legs very muscular, stifles well bent and hocks well let down. The thigh should be well developed, muscular and showing width in the region of the stifle to insure strong and graceful action. The four feet should turn neither in nor out.

Feet—Rather small and oval in shape. Toes arched, close and cushioned on thick, hard pads.

The three sizes in which Poodles are bred are
pictured on the left hand page. Toy;
Ch. Fieldstreams Valentine. Miniature;
Ch. Coppoquin Bon Jongleur.Standard;
Ch. Puttencove Moonshine. Below is the
Miniature (silver) Ch. Ledahof Silverlaine.

Coat—Quality: very profuse, of harsh texture and dense throughout.

Clip—A Poodle may be shown in the "Puppy" Clip or in the traditional "Continental" Clip or the "English Saddle" Clip. A Poodle under a year old may be shown in the "Puppy" Clip with the coat long except the face, feet and base of tail, which should be shaved. Dogs one year old or older must be shown in either the "Continental" Clip or "English Saddle" Clip.

In the "Continental" Clip the hindquarters are shaved with pompons on hips (optional). The face, feet, legs and tail are shaved leaving bracelets on the hind legs, puffs on the forelegs and a pompon at the end of the tail. The rest of the body must be left in full coat.

In the "English Saddle" Clip the hindquarters are covered with a short blanket of hair except for a curved shaved area on the flank and two shaved bands on each hind leg. The face, feet, forelegs and tail are shaved leaving puffs on the forelegs and a pompon at the end of the tail. The rest of the body must be left in full coat.

Color—The coat must be an even and solid color at the skin. In blues, grays, silvers, browns, cafe-au-laits, apricots and creams the coats may show varying shades of the same color. This is frequently present in the somewhat darker feathering of the ears and in the tipping of the ruff. While clear colors are definitely preferred such natural variation in the shading of the coat is not to be considered a fault. Brown and cafe-au-lait Poodles have liver-colored noses, eye-rims and lips, dark toenails and dark amber eyes. Black, blue, gray, silver, apricot, cream and white Poodles have black noses, eye-rims and lips, black or self-colored toenails and very dark eyes. In the apricots while black is preferred, liver-colored noses, eye-rims and lips, self-colored toenails and amber eyes are permitted but are not desirable.

Gait—A straightforward trot with light springy action. Head and tail carried high. Forelegs and hind legs should move parallel turning neither in nor out. Sound movement is essential.

Champion Silver Swank of Sassafras (Toy)

Champion Puttencove Privateer (Standard)

SIZE

Standard—The Standard Poodle is over 15 inches at the withers. Any Poodle which is 15 inches or less in height shall be disqualified from competition as a Standard Poodle.

Miniature—The Miniature Poodle is 15 inches or under at the withers, with a minimum height in excess of 10 inches. Any Poodle which is over 15 inches, or 10 inches or less at the withers shall be disqualified from competition as a Miniature Poodle.

Toy—The Toy Poodle is 10 inches or under at the withers. Any Poodle which is more than 10 inches at the withers shall be disqualified from competition as a Toy Poodle.

SCALE OF POINTS

	Points
General appearance, carriage and condition	20
Head, ears, eyes, and expression	20
Neck and shoulders	10
Body and tail	15
Legs and feet	15
Coat—color and texture	10
Gait	10
Total	100

719

Major Faults

Eyes—Round in appearance, protruding, large or very light.
Jaws—Undershot, overshot or wry mouth.
Cowhocks.
Feet—Flat or spread.
Tail—Set low, curled or carried over the back.
Shyness.

Disqualifications

Parti-colors—The coat of a parti-colored dog is not an even solid color at the skin but is variegated in patches of two or more colors. Any type of clip other than those listed in section on coat.

Any size over or under the limits specified in section on size.

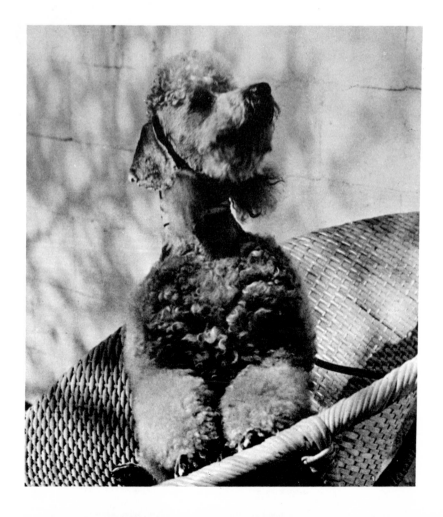

Above is a splendid studio portrait of the all-
white Standard Poodle, Champion Puttencove
Playboy. Generally only show dogs are kept in
the classic English saddle or Continental clips.
Most pet Poodles are given more easily cared
for clips. One of the most popular pet clips is
the Royal Dutch (and variations) modeled by the
Silver Miniature at the left.

THE SCHIPPERKE

The black, tail-less Schipperke is related to the larger Belgian Sheepdogs and are the barge dogs of their native Belgium. Essentially they are a diminutive of the "*Leauvenaar*", a black sheep dog of the provinces with which they share inheritance with the Groenendael. Because they were barge dogs, and due to the fact that Holland and Belgium were sometimes united previous to 1832, they were often confused with the Keeshond. The name of the breed means, in Flemish, "*Little Skipper*." These little dogs have the distinction of having taken part in the world's first specialty show in 1690 in Brussels, held in the Grand Palace specifically for Guild workmen and their dogs.

Actually, though essentially a barge dog, the little Schip was always as well distributed in the homes of landlubbers of the working and middle classes as on the barges. He is often referred to as "le meilleur chien de maison" (*the best house dog*). As a breed, the Schip is exceptionally hardy, intelligent, very quick and full of pep. They make admirable pets, are good vermin dogs, and live exceptionally long and active lives. The breed is allowed a tail about an inch long but many of these foxy little tykes are born completely tailless, a condition called for in the standard.

Made fashionable in 1885 through adoption of the breed by Queen Marie Henriette, they were first imported to America by Walter J. Comstock, of Rhode Island, in 1888. The present Schipperke Club of America was founded in 1929 and has been active on behalf of this fine little breed ever since.

The Schip has a large bump of curiosity which sometimes leads him into trouble with other dogs. Not a powerful fighter, he has the kind of courage that will cause him to ignore his own size limitations. He is also sometimes jealous of other pets in the household due to the vast love he has for his human family. Incidentally, the Schip has an instinctive love of horses.

722

STANDARD OF THE SCHIPPERKE

The name Schipperke is Flemish for Little Captain and is correctly pronounced Skeeper-ker (last r almost silent). This standard is an interpretation of the standard of the country of the Schipperke's origin—Belgium.

Appearance and General Characteristics—Excellent and faithful little watchdog, suspicious of strangers. Active, agile, indefatigable, continually occupied with what is going on about him, careful of things that are given him to guard, very kind with children, knows the ways of the household; always curious to know what is going on behind any closed door or about any object that has been moved, betraying his impressions by his sharp bark and upstanding ruff, seeking the company of horses, a hunter of moles and other vermin; can be used to hunt, a good rabbit dog.

Head—Fox-like, fairly wide, narrowing at the eyes, seen in profile slightly rounded, tapering muzzle not too elongated nor too blunt, not too much stop.

Nose—Small and black.

Eyes—Dark brown, small, oval rather than round, neither sunken nor prominent.

Expression—Should have a questioning expression: sharp and lively, not mean or wild.

Ears—Very erect, small, triangular, placed high, strong enough not to be capable of being lowered except in line with the body, nearer together at the tips than at the base when erect.

Teeth—Meeting evenly.

Neck—Strong and full, slightly arched, rather short.

Shoulders—Muscular and sloping.

Chest—Broad and deep in brisket.

Body—Short, thick set and cobby. Broad behind the shoulders, seeming higher in front because of the ruff. Back strong, short, straight and level or slightly sloping down toward rump. Ribs well sprung.

Loins—Muscular and well drawn up from the brisket but not to such an extent as to cause a weak and leggy appearance of the hind quarters.

Forelegs—Straight under the body, with bone in proportion, but not coarse.

Hindquarters—Somewhat lighter than the foreparts, but muscular, powerful, with rump well rounded, tail-less (about an inch allowed). Hocks well let down.

Feet—Small, round and tight (not splayed) nails straight, strong and short.

Coat—Abundant and slightly harsh to the touch, short on the ears and on the front of legs and on the hocks, fairly short on the body, but longer around neck beginning back of the ears, and forming a ruff and jabot extending down between the front legs, also longer on rear where it forms a culotte the points turning inward. Undercoat dense and short on body, very dense around neck making ruff stand out. Culotte should be as long as the ruff.

Color—Solid black.

Weight—Up to 18 pounds.

Faults—Light eyes, large round prominent eyes, ears too long or too rounded, narrow head and elongated muzzle, too blunt muzzle, domed skull, smooth short coat with short ruff and culotte, lack of undercoat, curly or silky coat, body coat more than 3 inches long, slightly over or undershot, swayback, bullterrier shaped head, straight hocks.

Disqualifications—Drop or semi-erect ears. Born with white (a few white hairs are objected to but are not disqualifying). Badly over or undershot.

Miscellaneous
AND
Foreign Breeds

The Greenland Dog   The Spanish Pointer

PRACTICALLY every country in the world has fashioned the living canine clay they found pertinent to their locale into specific and parallel lines. Except for the dogs of the Northland, America has no truly native breeds, for even those we name native borrow their ancestry from breeds formed and indigenous to other lands. If we had shaped breeds from the dogs of our aboriginals, the American Indians, then would we have had animals that we could truly call native. Perhaps the reason for our lack in this area is due to the fact that our continent was so late in joining the brotherhood of nations that had existed for over 1,400 calendar years and more in other parts of the world.

The breeds you will find here come from many lands. Some can be seen in our show rings, in miscellaneous classes, as though standing in the wings waiting for their cue to join, on the stage, that vast group of many and varied breeds already basking in the spotlight of recognition. Others you may never see, unless you travel to the lands to which they are native, as I have. And, in all those countries you will find the parallel breeds, the native sheepherding dogs, the basic gun dogs, the guard and house dogs. Here I have listed just a few of the many breeds popular in foreign lands, bred to a standard of perfection, and recognized by the native kennel clubs as true and purebred breeds.

You will also find a few breeds that have been with us for a very long time but have never received American Kennel Club recognition. These breeds, known in the United States much longer than many, or most, of the officially recognized breeds, must be given notice and place in such a book as this.

Here are dogs that provide a variety of uses for men of many lands and many climes, that bring with them some exotic aura of their native habitat to intrigue us. Dogs that generally have specific chores to do, and were bred to do, for mankind, and who do them well.

THE SPANISH POINTER

If you trace back in the geneology of most of the sporting dogs you will find a genetic basis of old Spanish Pointer and Spanish Spaniel. These were the prototype sporting dogs. Yet today in Spain there are few specimens of these breeds left.

There are many dogs in Spain, wandering freely through the streets of towns, living in homes or on the beaches or with the Guardia Civil, but they are not purebreds. Generally only in a few of the larger cities, such as Madrid or Barcelona, can purebred dogs of any breed be found. The author saw Spanish Pointers in Spain, sometimes in very unlikely places, such as Ronda, sitting on a plateau in the forbidding Sierra Bermejas. In almost every instance these Pointers were owned by a family who had been breeding them for generations and kept their own breed records. This latter practice is a necessity since there is no central registry, no responsible canine body, that can be remotely called equivalent to our American Kennel Club. There are no dog magazines in Spain.*

Spanish Pointers are still used for sport afield. As a matter of fact, the Spaniard is an ardent hunting enthusiast and in the butcher shops, especially in the fall, one can usually purchase partridge, black partridge, pheasant, grouse, and other game birds as well as wild rabbits. The Pointer of Spain is handsome, stylish, powerful, and he works game much as the German Short-hair does, thoroughly quartering the area but without the tremendous speed of an English Pointer. He is steady on point and a fine retriever. As a house-dog, he is clean, quiet and an intelligent and dependable watch dog. The author has hunted the native grouse behind a Spanish Pointer in the mountains above Malaga and found this Iberian gundog a delightful companion and steady and staunch in the field.

In an attempt to locate other native Spanish breeds, such as the *Spanish Spaniel* and the *Ibiza Hound*, the author asked the help of Senor Ricardo Perla Cuevas, leading veterinarian of Fuengirola in the county of Malaga. Dr. Cuevas gave me the information earlier used here in reference to dogs in Spain. Incidentally, the Ibiza Hound, a scent hound that in appearance is much like a cross between a Foxhound and a Borzoi, can only be found in the Balearic Islands and then only infrequently.

It is truly a shame that this country of Spain, which has given so much in an earlier time to the geneology of our modern dog, should have become almost barren of interest in, and completely apathetic to, the pure-bred canine cause. It is no wonder that the A.K.C. will not recognize or register dogs born in Spain. In a country of such beauty and inspiration, the habitat of such charming, gay and gracious people, we can only hope that in time this anti-pathy toward the purebred dog will be rectified.

* *Author's note :* The only registering body in Spain is the Real Sociedad Central de Fomento de las Razas Canines en Espana, in Madrid.

726

THE MEXICAN HAIRLESS AND CHINESE CRESTED

Both these breeds are small, in the Toy Group, and practically hairless. Rare and certainly unusual dogs in appearance, hairless dogs have been known in many parts of the world, but only these two breeds have been, through selection and proper breeding procedures, stabilized as to type and registered as specific breeds.

The Mexican Hairless is not native to Mexico. The breed was brought to that country by traders in the last half of the 16th century. It probably originated in the Orient as did the Chinese Crested, the result of mutations in some other Chinese toy breed and, through selection for this hairless trait, perpetuated by clever Oriental breeders.

The Mexican Hairless is not completely without coat. They carry a tuft of coarse hair on the skull and a small amount on the lower half of the tail.

The Chinese Crested exhibits hair on the head, feet and tail and certain of its premolar teeth are, as a breed, missing. Both breeds are about the size of Toy Fox Terriers.

In Mexico the breed known in the United States as Mexican Hairless are called Chinese Dogs. The breed known as Chinese Crested Dogs in this country can also be bred in a coated variety called Powder Puffs. The Chinese Crested should weigh a maximum of 15 pounds, though larger dogs are sometimes seen. The most popular size for the Mexican Hairless is under 10 pounds.

The Mexican Hairless Dog (Xoloizcuintle).

Chinese Crested Dog.

STANDARD OF THE MEXICAN HAIRLESS

The Mexican Hairless is a small, active dog, about the size of a small Fox Terrier, symmetrical and well proportioned, with a rather broad chest and ribs and with slender legs.

Head—Should be slender and skull narrow, cheeks lean, muzzle long and pointed. There should be a tuft of coarse hair on top of the skull, in the center but a bit forward, in some cases shadowing the brow.

Eyes—Should not be too deep set but balanced and not bulging—eye rims pink or dark and the eyes themselves hazel, yellow or dark.

Neck—Should be of good length, slender and well arched into flat shoulders and the chest rather broad, legs fairly long and slender, ribs well rounded and chest rather deep.

Back—Should be level, rump slightly rounded.

Skin—Smooth and soft, not wrinkled, any color, hot to touch, no hair whatever. Muscles and sinews well developed. A nervous tremor of muscles and sinews is characteristic like that of a nervous race horse.

Feet—Should be hare feet, nails black in dark skin or pale in pale skin dogs.

Tail—Long smooth tail, carried out similar to that of Manchester Terrier. A little fuzz or hair on lower half of tail permitted.

728

Absence of tuft on top of the head is undesirable but not a disqualification. Cut or broken ears or tail are disqualifications, likewise a fuzz or any hair, except as above described.

STANDARD OF THE CHINESE CRESTED DOG

The following standard has been prepared by members of the American Hairless Dog Club for the Chinese Crested Dog:

There are two distinct types of this dog which are purebred and recognized by the American Hairless Dog Club. The Deer Type: very slender, long slender legs, fine bone; somewhat similar to the Italian Greyhound. The Cobby type: heavier body, medium length legs, medium-boned; somewhat similar to the Terrier.

General Appearance—A small, active and graceful dog; medium to fine-boned; rather narrow in shoulders, body and quarter; smooth hairless body, with hair on feet, head and tail.

Head—Long skull, slightly rounded, slight stop; moderately long muzzle; cheeks lean.

Crest—Flat, high or long-flowing; sparse crest acceptable, full crest preferred.

Ears—Large upstanding ears, with or without ear fringe.

Eyes—Medium size, set wide apart.

Teeth—Level or scissors bite. Canine teeth or tusks extended towards front. Fewer teeth than most dogs. Premolars absent.

Neck—Long graceful neck, slightly arched, carried high. Sloping gracefully to shoulders.

Body—Should be medium to long. Rump slightly rounded. Chest deep and fairly broad. Belly moderately tucked up.

Tail—Up, or carried high, usually over back. Plume on lower two-eighths of tail. Sparse plume acceptable. Full plume preferred. The hair in the plume may be either long or short.

Forelegs—In Deer type: long straight legs, small delicate bones. Cobby type: straight legs, medium length, slightly heavier bone.

Hind Legs—In Deer type: hocks well let down.

Feet—Hare foot, long with nails moderately long. Nails: color of toes or black or white. Sox should not come above first joint from floor.

Color—Any color, plain or spotted.

Skin—Smooth and soft. Warm to touch.

Weight—In size they vary considerably but should not be over 15 pounds.

Disqualifications—Broken down or cropped ears; cropped tail; no visible crest; jaw much overshot or undershot.

APPENDIX

Mexican Hairless—A number of authorities agree that hairless dogs were brought to Mexico from the Orient about the end of the 16th century. The hairless dogs were apparently concentrated in the present State of Guerrero, in the region of Acapulco, but no distinct breed of hairless dog exists in this region today.

The Mexicans have always called hairless dogs "Chinese" dogs, the name "Mexican Hairless" being given to the breed by the American Kennel Club. The Mexican Kennel Club has registered only five hairless dogs in its entire history!

THE SPITZ

This is a breed which you will not find listed by, or registered with, the A.K.C., yet the Spitz has been, and still is, a very popular house dog and companion.

Intelligent, rugged and healthy, and a keen watchdog, a good specimen can be bought cheaply because of the distinction it lacks as an A.K.C. recognized breed. Spitz are, though, registerable in the United Kennel Club Stud Book. Bright and pretty in its all-white coat, handy in size (from 16 to 25 pounds), the Spitz is a larger edition of the toy Pomeranian.

In the typical white or occasional pale cream coat with which we are familiar, and also in wolf-gray and black, the Spitz has been a breed favorite in Germany for centuries and the progenitor of many well known breed favorites on the show bench and in the homes of dog fanciers throughout the world.

The Spitz sports a heavy coat that somehow manages to stay fairly clean even when the necessary grooming and bathing of such coats in other breeds is here ignored. In the Mid-Victorian era the breed was everywhere to be seen but today has lost ground to other popular breeds. The breed is decidedly not friendly to humans or animals to which it takes a dislike and will exhibit its feelings with little reluctance. This uncertainty of temper may have reduced it in favor among many fanciers.

A Spitz mother and her pure white whelps.

English Shepherds, Stodghill Bhodark and Bozo.

THE ENGLISH SHEPHERD AND THE
BORDER COLLIE

These two well-known breeds are much alike in conformation, size and working abilities. The greatest difference is in color. The *English Shepherd* is black and tan and marked like a Rottweiler (a minimum of white permitted). The *Border Collie* is colored and marked the same as the breed we know as the Collie, with preferably even white markings on the legs and a full white collar. Colors buff, sable, merle, tri-color, but generally one of the many densities of sable.

The coats of these dogs are dense but not as full as the show Collie's. In type they are truly ancient, brought to England by Caesar in his disastrous campaign on British soil. When the Roman troops withdrew they left, among other chattels, their camp dogs. They used sheepherding dogs close in type to the English Shepherd and Border Collie as well as drover and guard dogs, of which one type eventually became the Rottweiler. Evidently one species of sheepherding dog was crossed to the Rottweiler and retained the dominant black and tan coloration, but returned to the basic shepherd type. This is the English Shepherd who then blends two distinct early geneological lines, going back to the ancient Persian Sheepdog and the Tibetan Mastiff.

A Border Collie taking care of the flock. This
pastoral scene could probably have been duplicated long before the camera that took this
picture was invented.

The Border Collie is descended, like most true sheepherding breeds, from the Persian Sheepdog. It, or a breed like it, was probably the progenitor of the Collie and the Shetland Sheepdog.

These two breeds are not registered by the American Kennel Club and not recognized as true breeds by show-conscious dog fanciers. But they have been bred pure for centuries, not for show but for utilitarian purposes. As sheepherding dogs they have no peers. As house dogs they are splendid, intelligent, quiet animals who will keep the children from danger just as they would the sheep in their flocks.

They made their appearance on the American scene at a very early date, brought over by the earliest English settlers to guard their flocks in the New World.

STANDARD OF THE ENGLISH SHEPHERD

The English Shepherd is a medium size strong built active dog, They are affectionate, intelligent, natural, obedient, not quarrelsome or possessive but of great courage and extremely faithful. They are not easily excitable and usually dignified in manner. English Shepherds have the intelligence to adapt themselves to a variety of jobs and have proved themselves useful as watch dogs in the large cities and as retrievers and trailers in the hunting field. They attack an animal from the rear and can kill an animal much larger than they are themselves. The only thing an English Shepherd will attack bulldog fashion is another dog or a wolf, and they are much used to protect young calves, sheep and chickens from wolves, because they are alert and on the job, and not afraid. Also much used to protect young children. How could a dog trained by time to wait so tenderly upon a little lamb fail to catch the eye of a little child, or respond with a tender glance to the call of a man or woman? This temperament and this intelligence makes the English Shepherd the ideal family pet. They are the finest of all cattle dogs because they are natural low heelers and will go to the back or side of the farm after the milk cows. Also have the grit it takes to pen the roughest, wildest cattle.

General Appearance and Size—The English Shepherd is a medium size long haired dog. He is sturdy and has plenty of bone. Height: Not less than 18 inches or over 22 inches. The length from breast bone to tip of back quarter should equal the height. Weight: not less than 40 pounds or over 60 pounds, but the most desirable size is 20 inches high and 50 pounds. Dogs too small are more desirable than dogs too large.

Head—Medium length, the muzzle from tip of nose to stop should approximately equal length of skull from stop to occiput. The skull should be broad between the ears, but not so broad as to appear clumsy (very few are broad enough). Stop well pronounced.

Nose—Large and black.

Jaws—Not long but deep and powerful.

Teeth—Strong and incisor bite, the lower incisor must touch the inner surface of the upper incisor.

Eyes—Prominent but not protruding. They should be brown and express

733

good humor, faithfulness and confidence. (A strong eye is very desirable, that is a dog that keeps an eye on the job at hand also keeps an eye on his master).

Ears—Wide apart, stand slightly outward at the base with a sharp bend and lie close to the head which keeps the rains and sleet out of their head. When dog is relaxed, ears lay close to head, when they are alert the ears raise up a little.

Neck—Well muscled, round, and rather outstretched.

Body—Perfect balanced.

Ribs—Well arched but not barrel shaped.

Chest—Deep, broad enough for strength, but not so broad as to make the dog appear slow and clumsy.

Loin—Short, strong and deep.

Tail—Strong at base and long enough to touch the hock. Hair on the lower side of the tail should be half as long again as the hair on the body. When dog is at work the tail is carried on the level with the body (down a little is better than too high). When dog is relaxed the tail is carried on about a 45 degree angle with a little curve near the end of the tail. A natural born bob tail is permissible but not desirable, should breed a natural bob to a long tail dog.

Running Gear—Shoulders, long and oblique (sloping) forming a sharp angle with the upper arm.

Forearm—Forearm strong and moderately heavy from elbow to pastern. The forearm is perfectly straight viewed from the front. Hindquarters and thighs: strongly muscled. Hock points, well bent. The angulation shows plenty of springing power. The hind legs viewed from the back should be straight.

Dew Claws—Are desirable because they show pure breeding, but it is permissible for breeders to clip them off as soon as pups are born.

Feet—Should be well padded and large so as to take hard use on mud or snow as well as rough ground. The toes are well split up and strongly arched.

Coat—The hair should be from $1\frac{1}{2}$ to 2 inches long, glossy and water repellent. Slightly curly, wavy hair is desirable, kinky hair is a fault because it catches too many burrs.

Color—The most desirable color for an English Shepherd is a true, Black-tan (glossy black with tan markings) Tan dot over each eye, tan around the mouth, under the tail, tan bar across the chest, tan on all four feet, runs down to the ground. Now on the back legs the tan is only on the front side of the back legs and the black runs down to the ground on the back side of the back legs. The markings may be a mahogany brown to a golden tan. A small amount of white on the chest is permissible and the dog is still to be classified as a true black-tan. A tri-color with a white ring neck is also good. Black with white markings are also acceptable as long as the white doesn't cover up more than one-third the dog. The best white markings are, a white chest, a white tipped tail, white feet and a ring neck. (In mating black and white dogs together you have to be careful or you will get too many pups with too much white that will have to be sold at a discount.) Sable colored dogs are permissible for English Shepherds but are not desirable. The most desirable color for English Shepherds is a True black-tan and the black should come down to the ground on the back side of the back legs. What is meant by black-tan is a glossy black with tan trim.

THE ESKIMO AND OTHER SLED DOGS
OF THE NORTH

These breeds, not including the Alaskan Malamute, Siberian Husky, and Samoyed, comprise a vast family of animals much the same in general type and exactly the same in their constant, uncomplaining service to mankind.

The true *Eskimo* dog weighs from 65 to 85 pounds or more, is powerful, has erect ears, heavy coat, and a wolf-like appearance. They originated in Greenland, Labrador and the northeastern section of the country. He is, like his close relatives listed in our first paragraph, descended from the Spitz and the Wolf-Spitz, back to basic canine blood.

There are many other sled dogs very similar in type to the Eskimo but, through selection and perhaps the introduction of some foreign canine characteristics, differing slightly in various northern districts. Dogs, therefore,

An Eskimo Dog of North Greenland type.

from the Aleutians and Alaska would present a somewhat different appearance than those bred in Greenland or along the Hudson Bay.

A rather distinct breed is the *North Greenland Eskimo Dog*. They are a heavy, deep-jawed, pale buff colored dog with a marked depth and breadth of muzzle. An example of the true type North Greenland Eskimo Dog was the famous "Polaris", that came from the animals which Admiral Robert E. Peary used as sled dogs when he discovered the North Pole. The dog enjoyed much deserved publicity and eventually became the property of Dr. Wilfred Grenfell in Labrador.

These breeds were generally molded as a result of the "survival of the fittest", and their service to mankind cannot be weighed or ever duplicated. As a matter of fact, without these northern dogs to pull the sleds, carry packs, and to aid them in the hunt, even those races most suited to the climate, the Eskimos and northern Indians, could not exist in that land of white hell. The Eskimo and other Arctic breeds are singularly free from the usual doggy odors.

In their native land many of these dogs exhibit the tell-tale signs of arctic wolf ancestry. The Alaskan Malamute and Siberian Husky are free of this feral taint and have been bred pure, but wolf crosses are frequently found in the other, miscellaneous breeds that are used by the natives of the land of the midnight sun.

The basic wolf ancestry, or the evidence of the occasional crossing of dog to wolf, is frequently discernable in many of the Arctic Eskimo dogs.

736

THE AUSTRALIAN SHEPHERD

The Australian Shepherd was first seen arriving with large bands of sheep in California from Australia. Not knowing the origin and history of these small dogs, ranchers and farmers in that area were quite taken with the working ability of the Australian Shepherd. These blue dogs with eyes of blue and brown were seen working silently and smoothly, bunching, driving and penning sheep. Quite fleet of foot and never seeming to tire the Australian Shepherd soon became a dog to talk about. Some of the ranchers and farmers in the California area were so taken with the working ability of the Australian Shepherd on sheep, they decided to try them on other livestock. Doing so they found this breed more than capable. With their natural working ability, the Australian Shepherd soon became a favorite. They were found to be easily trained, natural watch dogs and very good companions for children as well as adults. Never seeming to tire, this breed of dog could be called on at any time to help out and were soon found to be happiest when hard at work, wanting only to please their master. Being a very sturdy dog the Australian Shepherd required no special care. Weather was the least of their worries. It was not odd

A blue-merle Shepherd from "Down Under", Harper's Old Smokey.

to see them asleep in the snow even though warm quarters were near by. All they ask for a hard day's work are food, a place to sleep, a pat on the head and a word of praise. This breed could be corrected severely and would not sneak or run, rather, in just a matter of minutes, be ready once again to please. Unlike many dogs, the Australian Shepherd needed no special training. A kind word and a pat on the head would make them turn out double-fold for their master. No job was too hard or too long as long as they knew they were pleasing the one they worked for.

The true origin and history of the Australian Shepherd is not known. They are said to be a cross between the Kelpie and Scottish Border Collie (quoted from two Australian farmers). They, in Australia, are known as the "Shepherd Dog" and are used for livestock working, companionship and as watch dogs.

Their first and basic ability is for use on livestock of all kinds. Since arriving in California the Australian Shepherd has been used for many things. They are noted for their guarding and herding ability, were used in World War II as messenger dogs, have been used for hunting and tracking, as trick dogs. They are very good varmint dogs; have appeared in movies and on many TV programs. Many are now being used as pets and watch dogs in the city.

The Australian Shepherd has many colors but their unusual gentleness and patience are their trade marks . . . that and their grace of movement, conformation and alertness. Though the blue color is the most desired, dogs of other colors are not considered less pure-bred.

AUSTRALIAN SHEPHERD—TENTATIVE STANDARD

Color—Blue, i.e., salt and pepper of black and white is desired; buff, i.e., brown and white; all white pups should be destroyed at birth; as they will develop blindness or deafness.

Coat—Moderate length, water resistant with an undercoat. The head, ears, feet and front of legs should have short hair.

Height—Preferred height 18 inches to 24 inches at withers; length in proportion to height.

Head—The head shall be in proportion with the body. The skull flat or slightly domed with a moderate stop. The jaw shall not be massive nor too pointed.

Eyes—Shall be almond shaped of average size, set well apart, neither prominent nor sunken. They must have an alert, intelligent expression. In color may be blue, brown, or one blue and one brown, or, flecked or, halves.

Teeth—Should be sound and strong, Lower incisors shall close just behind the upper incisors. Overshot or undershot jaws are serious faults. Tip of nose may extend beyond teeth.

Ears—Moderate length, erect, three-fourths to one-half, fox.

Muzzle—Moderately strong, clean, with black nostrils. Puppy pink nostrils often turn black in adult dogs.

Neck—Should be strong, well set on the shoulders, slightly arched, free from throatiness and with a fair ruff.

Shoulders—Muscular, finely boned and sloping with close-set withers.

Chest—Deep rather than wide, ribs well sprung and not barrel.

Forelegs—Muscular, flat dense boned and perfectly straight when viewed from the front. When viewed from the side the pastern should show a slight angle with the forearm. Elbows set parallel with the body and well under the body.

Back and Loins—Moderate length, straight with broad, strong loins.

Hindquarters—Should show breadth and strength. The haunch bone should be long rather than short and laid at a corresponding angle to the shoulders. The rump rather long and sloping to the legs; the stifles well turned, the hocks fairly well let down and placed slightly under the body. Cow-hocks and bow-hocks are definitely defects.

Feet—Should be oval, strong, deep in pads and close knit, with well arched toes and strong, short nails.

Tail—Should be natural bob or, on long tails, should be docked for working dogs.

Disposition—Australian Shepherds are sensitive, easily trained, natural guardians with strong herding instinct.

Distinctive Characteristics are—(1) Unusual gentleness and patience; (2) Peculiar bark-howl combination; and (3) in a fight their quick snapping usually makes them the victor.

Harper's Gwen Fre-Ho Genie, sports a natural bob tail.

THE TOY FOX TERRIER

You will not find this perky little fellow registered with the A.K.C. and therefore the breed is not eligible to be shown. However, the Toy Fox Terrier has been a big favorite as a pet and house dog for many years, its type unchanged. It is also called the American Toy Foxterrier or the Amertoy.

A very quick and active intelligence, friendliness and basic cleanliness make the Toy Fox an excellent bet for the individual looking for a pint sized pleasing canine package.

In type this little fellow should be as close to the recognized Smooth Fox Terrier type as possible (*see Fox Terrier—Smooth—in Terrier section*). The major difference is in the ears which in the Toy are larger and generally upright or pricked.

Bred by selecting for undersized animals in normal Fox Terrier litters and then adding judicious doses of Chihuahua and Toy Manchester Terrier, the Toy Fox is a bright-eyed type weighing from 3 to 8 pounds. A good specimen of the breed can be bought cheaply because they are not eligible for A.K.C. registration though the Toy Fox Terrier can be registered with the U.K.C.

Toy Fox Terriers

VALLHUND

This fine Swedish herding dog is very closely allied to the Welsh Corgi and mirrors the Corgi type. The Vallhund is of ancient descent and has for centuries been used as a drover's dog in its native land. Once almost extinct, breeders suddenly realized its value and selected breeding, notably in the cattle-rearing provinces of southwest Sweden (particularly around Västgötland and Halland), brought it back again to prominence. The breed was officially recognized in Sweden in 1942, and has gained steadily in public recognition ever since.

Height, 14 to 15 inches. Weight, 21 to 25 pounds. Colors are usually gray or light red, with darker mask, saddle and ears, Coat harsh, short, close. Body length much greater than height. Ears erect and sharp pointed. Tail usually only a stump.

Vallhund

WELSH SHEEPDOG

This is the champion Sheepdog of North Wales, an area where Sheepdog Trials are popular and enthusiastically patronized. The Welsh Collie is the result of blending the genetic qualities of the Working Collie and the now practically extinct Black-and-Tan Welsh Shepherd Dog. The Welsh Sheepdog (or Collie) of today has been bred for a considerable time as a pure bred dog. It is only just that perhaps the finest sheepherding dog in the world should be native to the area in which Shepherding trials orginated in 1873. This is a highly adaptable and very sensitive breed that is very easily trained to many tasks, if handled gently and without harsh rebuke to which they are extremely sensitive. At Sheepdog Trials they give their dramatic performances with almost uncanny skill.

The Welsh Sheepdog stands about 18 inches high and weighs approximately 35 pounds. The coat is fairly long but smooth and close to the body, and exceedingly weather-resistant. Colors are, all black, black and tan, tricolor, or black with white markings.

Welsh Sheepdog

741

LEONBERGER

The St. Bernard monks, in order to give greater vitality and strength to their dogs, brought into the breeding of the great rescue dogs, that borrowed their name from the Hospice where they were bred, several Newfoundlands of outstanding virtues. From the offspring of these breedings they selected the best of those that most closely mirrored the St. Bernard type. The other puppies were given by the monks to patrons in Switzerland about 1832. It was from these discarded animals of the St. Bernard-Newfoundland cross that the Leonberger was bred to become a distinct and recognized breed.

Height about 27 inches. Weight, about 100 pounds. Color, any dark shade with occasional white markings. The coat is fairly long and soft.

SPINONI ITALIANI (SPINONE)

This Italian Pointer is descended from the Spanish Pointer and its forebears, as are practically all Pointer and Spaniel breeds. This is an all-purpose gun dog and has been for centuries in its native land, a dog that will fill the hunter's bag, even though it may be a mixed bag of both fur and feather. Staunch on point, strongly modelled, the Italian Kennel Club has pushed this deserving breed to the fore in Italy. Not fast like the English Pointer, this dog quarters well, is staunch on point and is easy to follow.

Height, 24 inches, bitches, 22 inches. Weight, 70 to 75 pounds. Coat short, tough, and wiry. All Pointer and Spaniel colors allowed, from all white to roan.

TIBETAN MASTIFF

This animal, more closely than any other living breed of dog, mirrors the conformation of the ancient prototype Mastiff that was the progenitor of all the large, Mastiff type breeds. It has changed little over the centuries, is still a surly and ferocious watchdog or guard dog, spending most of its life on the end of a stout chain. Outside of Tibet and India it has not become very popular. The importance of this dog lies in its almost unchanged similarity to the ancient root-breed.

Height, about 28 inches. Weight, approximately 130 pounds. Coat is long or medium, thick and weather resistant. Ears are hanging (pendant), set rather high. Tail plumed and carried over back, but not curled. Colors are: black; black and tan; black and red; mixtures of the previously mentioned shades or colors.

BRAQUE DU BOURBONNAIS

This breed was used in France 500 years ago as an all-purpose gun dog, and is still, today, one of the most popular sporting dogs of the French outdoors man. It has great adaptability in the field and possesses great endurance and an aptitude to discriminate and hunt for either fur or feather, on dry land or in the water, abilities evidently inherited from its direct and ancient ancestor, the French Braque.

Height about 27 inches. Solidly built and colored white for easy recognition in the field. Ears large, triangular, pendant, colored chestnut, as is the muzzle. Coat tight and smooth, showing chestnut ticking. Tail conspicuous by its absence, or very short and not to exceed 3 inches in length.

Leonberger

Head portrait of a Spinoni Italiani, the dock-tailed, wire-haired, strong and stylish Pointer of Italy.

Hovawart (similar to Leonberger. Bred and shown in Germany)

PORTUGUESE CATTLE DOG

In the mountains of Northern Portugal the official Portuguese Cattle Dog was evolved, a breed used by the drovers extensively for both driving and guarding the herds from wolves. This dog is a true and efficient working dog, large in size as are most dogs bred in mountain terrain.

Height, 24 inches, bitches slightly smaller. The coat is an all-weather coat, short and harsh with a heavy undercoat. All shades of brindle and gray (generally solid in color) tint the coat, usually accompanied by a black muzzle. The skull is broad, slightly convex, tapering to a rather pointed muzzle; the ears are set low and well apart and hanging; eyes almond shaped and dark; body powerful, lithe, longer than the height at shoulder (approximately as 8 is to 10); tail low set, thickly feathered, 14 inches in length.

PORTUGUESE PODENGO

This is the most commonly seen of the nine native Portuguese breeds. The Podengo is comparable to the Beagle in America in usage and popularity. It differs from the Beagle in that it comes in three sizes (unless we assume that the Beagle, Harrier, and Foxhound are simply three varieties in size of the same basic type). There is a Grande, or large, Podengo; a Medio, or medium-sized; and the Pequeno, or small variety. The large and the small types are well distributed throughout the country and are great favorites with all the people of Portugal. There is a Spanish Podengo that shares similar ancestry with the Portuguese Podengo, but the breeds are now distinct and separate.

The Grande is from 22 to 27 inches high; the Medio, 16 to 20 inches; the Pequeno, 12 to 16 inches. The coat is short, tight, harsh and comes in all colors, including fawn, gray, from black to white, varied head markings; a full tail with brush similar to a Beagle's. The head is fox-shaped with a pointed muzzle and large, erect ears that are wide at the base.

Portuguese Podengo

PORTUGUESE SHEEPDOG

These are huge, massively built Sheepdogs native to the Estrela Mountains. Exhibited in bench shows in Portugal, these big dogs mostly live above an altitude of 2,000 feet. Though called a "sheep dog" they are generally used as a protector of the flocks. Like the Portuguese people and their neighbors, the Spaniards, these big dogs are independent; but they give their complete loyalty to their masters. They are also quite ferocious and cannot be handled by strangers. This latter characteristic makes the breed excellent watchdogs.

Height, up to 28 inches, bitches smaller. The coat can be either short or rough (longhaired), similar to the St. Bernard. Though sometimes seen in fawn colored coats, or grey and fawn, the breed is generally marked like a Doberman in black and tan, or red and tan. The tail is plumed and should reach to the hocks or lower.

PORTUGUESE WATER DOG

This is an extremely old and cherished breed in Portugal. It was once found all along the whole coast, but is now confined mostly to the southern

Portuguese Water Dog

shores of the Algarve region of Portugal. This is truly a water dog and was highly valued by the fishermen for whom it served in many capacities. These marvelous dogs were particularly helpful in retrieving lost tackle, broken tackle and nets, and as a bearer of messages from boat or fleet to shore. The breed shares basic heritage through the Spanish Spaniels and Water Dogs, with the Poodle, one of the world's most popular breeds. As a matter of fact the Portuguese Water Dog is clipped in a fashion that closely mimics a Poodle clip. The long, Poodle-type coat is clipped close on the body and hind legs and most of the tail (which is long and held high and curling toward the body). The front part of the body is left untrimmed, with top-knot on head. The Muzzle is clipped and a tuft is left at the end of the tail. Colors are: black, chocolate, pearl grey, and any of these same colors with a white trim. Height is approximately 21 inches and weight about 46 pounds.

MAREMMA SHEEPDOG

From Tuscany to Abruzzes, the Maremma is the most common and popular shepherd dog of Central Italy. They are used as both shepherds and guards and lead a rather Spartan life in their native habitat. The breed is recognized by both the Italian and English Kennel Clubs as a pure breed and was first introduced to the English fancy in 1931. Resembling a Kuvasz, the Maremma Sheepdog (also sometimes called, Abruzzi Sheepdog, and Cane da Pastor Maremmano, the latter translating from the Italian to Maremma Shepherd Dog) is a handsome and useful breed.

Appenzell Mountain Dog of
Switzerland (similar to the
Bernese Mt. Dog).

Below is an Australian
Heeler (blue merle).

Height, 24 to 26 inches. Weight, about 70 to 80 pounds (Pyrenean Mountain Dog massiveness is to be avoided). Color: generally white, occasionally biscuit color, fawn, lemon or belton. The coat is soft, medium in length, lustrous and lays flat. Nose, black; eyes, opaque; slightly arched in loin; tail full and carried low. In both head and body the Maremma is much like the Kuvasz but should exhibit more refinement throughout.

AUSTRALIAN HEELER

Slightly larger than the Kelpie, the Australian Heeler was bred from basic Kelpie stock to which was added both Collie and Dingo breeding. Collie merling factors have been incorporated in the breed affecting both the Kelpie black (blue merle) and the Dingo red (red merle). This blending results in the blue and red speckling or flecking that is the basic color of the breed, and is not derived from Dalmatian breeding in the background as is supposed.

The Heeler is exclusively a cattle or drover dog and has stirred up keen interest in Australia when exhibited at bench shows "down under."

Height, 20 inches, bitches 19 inches. Weight, between 32 and 35 pounds. Color, blue speckled or red speckled . . . these flecks show the Dalmatian blood, as do the black head patches (see author's comment above). Coat short and harsh and weather-resistant. Head long and fairly narrow; ears set high and erect; back short; legs fairly long with compact feet; tail long and carried low when standing, horizontal when the dog is moving or excited.

AUSTRALIAN KELPIE

Strongly entrenched in Australia, the Kelpie has many specialty clubs to promote him on the show bench and as a working sheepherder. Recognized by the Kennel Control Council of Australia as a pure breed, the Kelpie has been bred to type since 1865.

The breed was developed from crossings of the small Collies owned by Scots settlers, to the native wild Dingo. There have been two types of Kelpies, the standard dog and a variety known as the Barb. The latter is a larger dog than the standard Kelpie, is solid black in color, and weighs as much as 55 pounds. The standard dog weighs from 25 to 30 pounds, stands 18 to 20 inches at the shoulder, and sports a variety of colors; black and tan, red, red and tan, chocolate, slate, blue and fawn, and occasionally fawn. The Kelpie's coat is short, its ears are pointed and erect, and its tail is occasionally docked.

THE CAVALIER KING CHARLES SPANIEL

One of the most aristocratic of dog breeds, the Cavalier has for many years been a favored pet in England and its colonies.

The Cavalier is somewhat larger and racier than the English Toy Spaniel, but both breeds are of the same colors. The Cavalier has a longer, more spaniel-like foreface. His silky coat is also like that of the larger members of the spaniel family.

He is an excellent housepet, clean in his habits and not given to excessive barking.

STANDARD OF THE CAVALIER KING CHARLES SPANIEL

The following standard, drawn up by the English Cavalier King Charles Spaniel Club and approved by the English Kennel Club, has been adopted as the standard for the Cavalier King Charles Spaniel Club, U.S.A.

The standard should be well studied, as it is carefully drawn up and means what it says. Even very slight deviations from the standard may produce a completely different dog, i.e., eyes. If the dog has not got large and dark eyes, widely spaced, he will have a hard or mean expression foreign to the breed.

Again, when a dog is nervous or sulky, he loses breed character. Particular attention must be paid to keeping the Cavalier what he sets out to be—a gay, active, fearless, dog.

General Appearance—An active, graceful, well-balanced dog. Absolutely fearless and sporting in character and very gay and free in action.

Head and Skull—Head almost flat between the ears, without dome. Stop shallow; length from base of stop to tip about 1½ inches. Nostrils should be well developed and the pigment black. Muzzle well tapered and to the point. Lips well covering but not hound-like.

Eyes—Large, dark and round, but not prominent. The eyes should be spaced well apart.

Ears—Long and set high, with plenty of feathering.

Mouth—Level.

Neck—Should be well set on.

Forequarters—Shoulders not too straight. Legs: moderate bone, straight.

Body—Should be short, coupled with plenty of spring of rib. Back level. Chest moderate, leaving ample heart room.

Hindquarters—Legs: moderate bone, straight.

Feet—Compact and well cushioned.

Coat—Long, silky, and free from curl. A slight wave is permissible. There should be plenty of feather.

Tail—The docking of tails is optional. The length of the tail should be in balance with the body.

Cavaliers showing some of the typical breed colors, black and tan, and two Blenheims with a tricolor between them.

Color—Black and tan—raven black with tan markings, above eyes, on cheeks, inside ears, on chest and legs and underside of tail. Tan should be bright.

Ruby—Whole-colored rich red. *Blenheim*—Rich chestnut markings, well broken up on a pearly-white ground. The markings should be evenly divided on the head, leaving room between the ears for the much valued lozenge mark or spot, a unique characteristic of the breed. *Tricolor*—black and white, well spaced and broken up, with tan markings, over the eyes on cheeks, inside ear, inside legs and on underside of tail. Black and white permissible, but not desirable.

Weight and Size—Weight: 10 to 18 pounds. A small, well balanced dog, well between these weights is desirable.

Faults—Light eyes. Undershot and crooked mouths and pig jaws. White marks on whole-colored specimens. Coarseness of type. Putty noses. Flesh marks. Nervousness.

The Miniature Bull Terrier
Champion Willing of Upend.

THE MINIATURE BULL TERRIER

The Miniature Bull Terrier differs from the larger type principally in size. He should stand no more than 14 inches at the withers and weigh not in excess of 20 pounds. Outside of this the standard is the same for both sizes.

At one time the Miniature looked more like a white English Terrier than a Bull Terrier, but today he is almost an exact replica of his larger cousin. He was originally used as a ratter, and is now the same staunch, steely, good companion as is the standard sized dog.

749

Sumi San of Darli, Lin Sing of Buddletown, and Ya Mada San of Darli, Shih Tzus all.

THE SHIH TZU

During the Manchu Dynasty of Imperial China, the Shih Tzu was considered the royal dog of the Emperor's household. He was produced by crossing the native Pekingese with Lhasa Apsos that went to China either as gifts from the Dalai Lama or as war booty.

The name "Shih Tzu" is Chinese for "Tibetan Lion dog," and it is said that the Chinese groomed and clipped their dogs so that they resembled miniature lions.

The Shih Tzu is relatively new to America, but he has made many friends and is proving himself to be a first-class pet and companion. Some of the finest Shih Tzus are bred in Sweden where they have achieved quite a bit of popularity.

The breed is quiet and nice to have around, displaying the serenity of the larger breeds of dogs. When viewed face on and close-up, the wise little face has the appearance of an animated shrunken head from the Amazon

STANDARD OF THE SHIH TZU

By permission of the Kennel Club I am enabled to print the English standard for the Shih Tzu (also used by the A.K.C.):

General Appearance—Very active, lively and alert, with a distinctly arrogant carriage. The Shih Tzu is neither a terrier nor a toy dog.

Head and Skull—Head broad and round; wide between the eyes. Shock-headed with hair falling well over the eyes. Good beard and whiskers; the hair growing upwards on the nose gives a distinctly chrysanthemum-like effect. Muzzle square and short, but not wrinkled like a Pekingese; flat and hairy. Nose black from preference and about one inch from tip to top.

Eyes—Large, dark and round but not prominent.

Ears—Large, with long leathers, and carried dropping. Set slightly below the crown of the skull; so heavily coated that they appear to blend with the hair of the neck.

Mouth—Level or slightly underhung.

Forequarters—Legs short and muscular with ample bone. The legs should look massive on account of the wealth of hair.

Body—Body between withers and root of tail should be longer than height at withers; well-coupled and sturdy; chest broad and deep, shoulders firm, back level.

Hindquarters—Legs short and muscular with ample bone. They should look straight when viewed from the rear. Thighs well-round and muscular. Legs should look massive on account of the wealth of hair.

Feet—Firm and well padded. They should look big on account of the wealth of hair.

Tail—Heavily plumed and curled well over back; carried gaily, set on high.

Coat—Long and dense but not curly, with good undercoat.

Color—All colors permissible, but a white blaze on forehead and a white tip to the tail are highly prized. Dogs with liver markings may have dark liver noses and slightly lighter eyes. Pigmentation on muzzle as unbroken as possible.

Weight and Size—Up to 18 pounds, ideal weight 9–16 pounds, type and breed characteristics of the utmost importance and on no account to be sacrificed to size alone.

Faults—Narrow heads, big jaws, snipyness, pale pink noses and eyerims small or light eyes, legginess, sparse coats.

THE SOFT-COATED WHEATEN TERRIER

Of the four native terrier breeds of Ireland, the Soft-Coated Wheaten is probably the oldest. He was kept strictly as a working terrier, and was indispensible around the farm and homestead.

The Wheaten's distinctive, golden coat never sheds and he is a good deal more sensible than many of the other terrier breeds.

Dogs shown in America are not trimmed, but the coat may be tidied to show the outline of the body. The Wheaten is steadily making more and more friends wherever he is seen and, as a breed, he has a wealth of attributes to recommend him as a top-drawer, all-around dog.

STANDARD OF THE SOFT-COATED WHEATEN TERRIER

The Soft-Coated Wheaten Terrier is a hardy, short-coupled dog of medium station, graceful and lively in movement.

Head—Only moderately long, its length equally divided between the skull and foreface. The topskull is flat, cheeks clean-sided and the stop defined. Eyes are small to medium in size, dark hazel or deep brown in color. Ears set high and dropped. Jaws are strong, the bite either level or scissors.

Dog of Hong Kong

Above is the Akita, Banko-Maru, a large and noble breed from Japan. At the right is a group of three Soft-Coated Wheaten Terriers, of ancient heritage. Their ancestors were probably the progenitors of all the Terriers of Ireland. At the far right is an Oriental Pariah Dog.

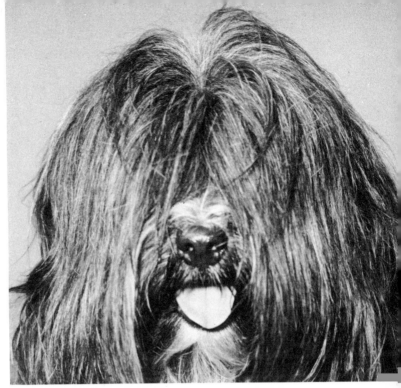

Tibetan Terrier, Kenspa Ponya Lamleh of Kalai

Neck—Moderately long, clean at the throat.

Body—Compact. The back is short, the shoulders sloping, the chest deep and ribs well sprung. Forelegs are straight, hind legs well muscled and powerful, bent at the stifles and well let down in the hocks. The docked tail is carried above the horizontal, its bone neither too thick and stubby nor spindly thin.

Coat—Abundant, moderately long and slightly wavy, its texture soft and silky. Color, wheaten.

Size—Height of dogs, 18 to 19 inches; bitches a little less. Weight; dogs from 35 to 45 pounds; bitches somewhat less.

Serious Faults—Undershot or overshot jaws. Any color except wheaten. Hair woolly or coarse in texture, in mature specimens. Dewclaws on hind legs.

THE TIBETAN TERRIER

The Tibetan Terrier is a small breed similar to the Lhasa Apso that has been purebred in this remote country for hundreds of years.

Originally kept by monks in Tibetan monasteries, these dogs were never sold, but given as gifts to persons of high rank or as special tokens of esteem. Very few of these dogs ever found their way out of Tibet until recently. The breed is still very rare, but their small size and desirable combination of canine virtues is finding them an ever growing group of supporters among dog lovers everywhere.

STANDARD OF THE TIBETAN TERRIER

The description and standard of the Tibetan Terrier as set down by the Tibetan Terrier Club of England, and adopted by the Tibetan Terrier Club of America in 1957, is as follows:

Skull and Head—Skull of medium length, not broad or coarse, narrowing slightly from ear to eye, not domed but not absolutely flat between the ears. The malar bones are curved, but should not be overdeveloped so as to bulge. There should be a marked stop in front of the eyes, but this must not be exaggerated. The head should be well furnished with long hair, falling forward over the eyes. The lower jaw should carry a small but not over-exaggerated amount of beard. Jaws between the canines should form a distinct curve. The length from the eye to top of nose should be equal of that from eye to base of skull; not broad or massive.

Nose—Black.

Eyes—Large, dark, neither prominent nor sunken; should be set fairly wide apart. Eyelids dark.

Ears—Pendant, not too close to the head, "V" shaped, not too large; heavily feathered.

Mouth—Level by preference but a slight undershot should not be penalized.

Forequarters—Legs straight, heavily furnished.

Body—Compact and powerful. Length from point of shoulder to root of tail equal to height at withers. Well ribbed up. Loin slightly arched.

Hindquarters—Heavily furnished, hocks well let down.

Feet—The feet should be large, round, and heavily furnished with hair between the toes and pads. *The dog should stand well down on its pads.*

Tail—Medium length, set on fairly high and carried in a gay curl over the back. Very well feathered. There is often a kink near the tip.

Coat—Double coated. The undercoat fine wool, the top coat profuse, fine, but not silky or woolly; long; either straight or waved.

Color—White, golden, cream, gray or silver, black, parti-color and tricolor; in fact almost any color but chocolate.

Weight and Size—Average weight 22 to 23 pounds . . . but may be from 18 to 30 pounds. Height from 14 to 16 inches.

Faults—Poor coat; mouth very undershot or overshot; a weak snipy foreface.

THE AKITA

The Akita has been purebred in his native Japan for about three-hundred years. He was used as a hunter, guard and fighting dog. Of great size and noble bearing, the Akita is of the family of northern dog breeds and has the typical erect ears, rather pointed but strong muzzle, and a plume-like tail, curled and carried over the back.

Akitas were introduced to the United States by servicemen returning from Japan after World War II and have become rather popular, particularly in the California area.

They are staunch guard dogs, alert, and highly intelligent and are sure to become one of the more important guard dogs in time to come.

STANDARD OF THE AKITA

Head—Expresses dignity, friendliness and noble character; has a massive broad skull, rather flat on top with a stop well marked but not abrupt. The ears are erect and rather small, with wide base and are carried slightly forward over the eyes.

The head should be free from wrinkle. The muzzle is of moderate length, deep and square with powerful jaw and level bite.

Nose—Black and rather large.

Eyes—Medium size, dark brown and rather triangular in shape.

The Akita has a thick muscular neck without excessive dewlap. The neck widens gradually toward the shoulders, which are muscular and powerful, with the shoulder blades laid well back. The wide, deep chest reaches down to the elbows and ribs are well sprung. The back is straight and firm with loin well muscled and slightly tucked up. Bitches are a little longer in loin than dogs.

Forelegs—Set wide apart, are straight and strong with heavy bone. The feet are cat-like with toes well arched, close together. The hindquarters are muscular and powerful with hocks bent but straight in line.

Tail—The breed is distinguished by a large tail, set high and carried over the back in a three quarters, full or double curl. When hanging down, the tip of the tail should brush the hocks.

Coat—These dogs have a double coat, the outer coat being straight and harsh with the undercoat being thick and furry. The outer coat is of medium length, shorter and softer on the head and legs and longer and harsher on the body and tail.

Color—The coat may be of almost any color from cream to black, including all shades of brown, red, gray and silver, as well as brindle. Some of the solid color dogs have a variety of shadings and coats may be silver-tipped. No more than one-third of the coat may be white and the white may appear only on the muzzle as a blaze, on the chest or forelegs as a collar, or on the hindpaws and tip of tail.

GLOSSARY OF
DOG TERMINOLOGY

Almond eyes: Eye shaped like an almond.

Angulation: The angle formed by the meeting of two bones in a point. In dogs, shoulder bones and hindquarter bones.

Apple head: Rounded skull, shaped like an apple.

Apron: Hair frill falling below neck and chest.

Balanced: An animal that is symmetrical and shows equalization of proportions.

Barrel: Rounded section of the ribs.

Barrel-legged: Bowed legs (front).

Bat ear: Erect ear rounded at top.

Bay: The voice of the hunting hound while trailing.

Belton: Mingling of hair colors that produces roan.

Bench-legged: Also fiddle-fronted. Legs bent, toes facing out.

Bench show: A dog show at which the dogs are kept on benches while not being shown in competition. Some shows are not benched.

Best in show: Show award to the dog winning best of all breeds.

Birdy: A dog with strong bird hunting instincts.

Bird dog: A sporting dog bred and trained to hunt game birds.

Bitch: The female canine.

Bite: The position of the upper and lower teeth as they meet.

Blaze: Stripe running up the center of the dog's face.

Blocky: Square formation of head or body.

Bloom: The appearance of prime condition.

Blue: Color. Dilute black due to recessives.

Blue merle: Marbled mixture of black, gray and white hairs.

Bobtail: A tail docked (or cut) very short.

Bone: Relating to substance and girth of leg bone.

Brace: A matched pair of dogs.

Breeching: Tan hair on the inside of the thighs.

Breed: A specific strain or family of related dogs similar in type and use, usually developed under the influence of man.

Brindle: Striped coat effect caused by mixture of black hairs on lighter colored base.

Brisket: Chest between the forelegs in front.

Broken color: Solid color broken by patches of another color.

Broken-haired: Rough, wire coat.

Brood bitch: A bitch used for breeding.

Brush: A bushy tail. (Fox brush).

Bullbaiting: An ancient sport for which the Bulldog was bred.

Butterfly nose: A nose which is spotted with flesh color.

Button ear: The ear flap folding forward, the tip lying close to the skull and pointing towards the eye.

Bye: In field-trials; the odd dog left after braces are drawn.

Canine: Classification of the group of animals to which belong dogs, foxes, wolves, jackals.

Canines: Two upper and two lower large fang teeth.

Castrate: Removal of testicles of a male animal.

Cat-foot: Compact foot like that of a cat.

Catch dog: A dog used to catch and hold quarry so that it can be taken alive.

Champion: A dog that has won a specific number of points according to A.K.C. rules at dog shows or field trials.

Character: The complex of mental and temperamental traits of a dog.

Cheeky: Cheeks rounded and bulky.

Chest: Forepart of the body.

China eye: A light blue or white eye.

Chiseled: Delineation of skull formation giving character to the face.
Choke collar: Collar that forms running noose.
Chops: Pendulous flesh of the jaw.
Chorea: Nervous muscular jerking movement. Often distemper, hepatitis residual.
Clip: To trim the coat with scissors or clippers.
Cloddy: Low and thickset.
Close-coupled: Short in body length.
Coat: The hair covering the animal's body.
Cobby: Short in length; compact.
Collar: The marking around the neck.
Companion Dog (CD); Companion Dog Excellent (CDX): Obedience-test titles.
Condition: Inner health manifested by outward appearance.
Conformation: Arrangement of the parts in conformance with breed-standard ideals.
Couple: Two hounds.
Coupling: A leash ring for holding two dogs together.
Coursing: The sport of chasing prey with sight hounds.
Cow-hocked: When the hocks turn in toward each other.
Crest: The top arched part of the neck.
Cropping: The trimming of the ears to make them stand erect.
Crossbred: A dog whose sire and dam are of two different breeds.
Croup: Section from hip bones (pelvis) to tail set.
Crown: The topskull.
Cry: "Voice" of a hound.
Cryptorchid: The adult whose testicles have not descended into the scrotum.

Dam: The female parent (mother).
Dappled: Mottled marking of varied colors.
Derby: Field-trial competition for young, novice sporting dogs.
Dewclaw: An extra claw (sometimes two) on the inside of the rear legs.
Dewlap: Loose hanging skin under the throat.
Diehard: Nickname of Scottish Terrier.
Dish-faced: A concave top of muzzle line from stop to nose tip.
Disqualification: A fault that, according to its breed standard, makes a dog ineligible to win a prize in organized competition.
Distemper teeth: Teeth discolored as a result of distemper or other disease which occurred when mature teeth were appearing.
Dock: To cut the tail in accordance with the breed standard.
Dog: The male of the species.
Dog show: A competitive exhibition of purebred dogs.
Domed: Convex topskull.
Double coat: Outer coat and undercoat.
Down in pastern: Weak pastern joint. Obviously over-angulated.
Drag: A trail prepared by dragging a bag impregnated with scent along the ground.
Drawing: Selection by lot of dogs to be run in pairs in a field-trial stake.
Drop ear: Ear hanging straight down.
Dropper: A bird-dog cross.
Dry neck: No dewlap.
Dry: Tight, not over-heavy in bone.
Dual champion: A dog that has won bench and field-trial championship.
Dudley nose: Flesh-colored nose.

Ewe neck: Concave curvature of the top neckline. Lack of crest.
Eyeteeth: Upper canines or fangs.

Fall: Hair overhanging the face as in the Old English Sheepdog.
Fancier: A person active in some phase of the dog game other than commercial.
Fangs: See Canines.
Feathering: Long fringe of hair on ears, legs, tail, or body.
Feet east and west: Toes of the front feet turned out away from each other.
Fetch: Retrieve by dog; also command.
Fiddle-front: Forelegs out at elbows, pasterns close, and feet turned out. Resembling the shape of a violin.
Flag: A long-haired, fringed tail. Tail held high.
Field trial: A competition for sporting dogs to test hunting ability.
Flank: Side of body between the last rib and the hip.
Flare: Blaze that widens as it approaches topskull.
Flat bone: Ellpitical rather than round bone (in leg).
Flat-sided: Ribs flat instead of rounded.
Flews: Pendulous upper lips.

Flush: To drive birds from cover.
Forearm: The bone of the foreleg between the elbow and the pastern.
Foreface: The muzzle.
Foster mother: A female with milk used to nurse whelps that are not her own.
Foul color: A color or marking not characteristic for the breed. (Also foul marked).
French front: See Fiddle front. Position of feet of French dancing master.
Frill: See Apron.
Fringes: See Feathering.
Frogface: Nose extended and accompanied by receding jaw, usually overshot.
Front: Forelegs, chest, brisket, shoulder, neck. Also front assembly.
Furrow: A slight indentation down center of skull to stop.
Futurity stake: A class at dog shows or field trials for young dogs which have been nominated at or before birth.

Gait: The manner in which the dog walks or runs. (Also, movement).
Game: Prey or quarry. Also plucky, when used to describe disposition.
Gay tail: The tail carried up, generally too high.
Gazehounds: Sight Hound. A dog who hunts by sight and the running down of the quarry.
Geneology: Pedigree. Lineage.
Genitalia: Reproductive organs.
Goose rump: Too steep in croup.
Grizzle: Bluish-gray or roan color.
Groom: The act of cleaning, brushing and caring for a dog's coat.
Groups: The breeds as grouped by the A.K.C.
Gun dog: A dog that works to the gun.
Guns: Men who do the shooting at field trials.
Gun-shy: A dog who fears sound and sight of guns.

Hackles: Hair on neck and back when raised in fright or anger.
Handler: A person who handles a dog in the show ring or field trial. Usually also the dog's trainer.
Hard-mouthed: the dog that bites or mutilates the game he retrieves.
Harefoot: An elongated foot like a rabbit's foot.
Harlequin: Pied coloration. (Great Danes).
Haw: Red membrane exposed due to droop of lower eyelid.
Heat: Seasonal menstrual period of bitch. Estrum.
Heel: The hock joint; also a command.
Height: Vertical measurement from the withers to the ground. (Height at shoulder).
Hie on: A hunting command to urge the dog on.

Honorable scars: Scars from injuries suffered as a result of work.
Hound: A dog of a breed used for hunting furred game by scent or sight.
Hound-marked: Three-color—white, tan, and black—the predominating color usually being mentioned first. (Beagle).
Hucklebones: Top of the hipbones (pelvic bones),

Inbreeding: The mating of closely related dogs.
Incisors: Upper and lower front teeth between the canines.
Interbreeding: The breeding together of dogs of different varieties.
Isabella: Fawn, mouse, or light red color, due to dilute color recessives.

Judge: Official licensed by the A.K.C. to judge dogs at shows and trials.

Kennel: Building or enclosure where dogs are kept.
Kink tail: Sharply bent tail.
Knuckling over: Weak pastern with joint bending forward.

Leather: The skin of the ear.
Level bite: When the edges of the front teeth (incisors) of the upper and lower jaws meet. Also pincer bite.
Line breeding: The mating of related dogs of the same breed that show common ancestry.
Litter: Offspring of dog at one birth.
Liver: Deep reddish brown coat color.
Loaded shoulders: When the shoulder blades are shoved outward from the body by over-development of the muscles.
Loin: That part of the body on either side of the vertebral column between the last ribs and the hindquarters as seen in profile.
Lumbering: Awkward, disconnected gait.
Lurcher: A crossbred hound.

Mane: Long and profuse hair on top and sides of the neck, as a Pekingese.
Mantle: Dark-shaded portion of the coat on shoulders, back, and sides.
Mask: Dark shading of color on the foreface.
Match show: An informal dog show at which no championship points are awarded.
Merle: A mixture of gray, white and black hairs in varied intensities (as in the Collie).
Miscellaneous class: Class at dog shows for breeds not yet recognized by the A.K.C.
Mongrel: A dog of mixed-breed origin.
Monorchid: A degree of cryptorchidism.
Mutton withers: Flat formation of withers.
Mute: To trail without baying or barking (a hound).
Muzzle (anatomical): Foreface.
Muzzle band: White marking around muzzle.

Nose: Ability to detect by means of scent.

Occiput: Back point of the skull between ears.
Open bitch: A bitch that can be bred.
Open class: A class at dog shows in which all dogs of a breed, champions and imported dogs included, may compete.
Orange belton: Reddish roan color. Mixture of red and white hairs.
Out at elbows: Elbows turning out from the body.
Outcrossing: The mating of unrelated individuals of the same breed.
Overhang: Pronounced brow.

Overshot: The front incisors of the upper jaw overlapping those of the lower jaw.

Pace: A gait which promotes a slight rolling motion to the body. The left foreleg and left hind leg advance in unison, then the right foreleg and right hind leg; the same as a pacing horse; Usually considered faulty.

Pack: Many hounds kept together in one kennel, or run on hunt. Mixed pack is composed of dogs and bitches.

Paddling: Moving with forefeet wide, inducing body swing.

Pads: Soles of the canine's feet.

Parti-color: Variegated in patches of two or more colors.

Pastern: Region of the foreleg between the carpus or wrist and the digits or foot.

Pedigree: Written record of a dog's geneology for three generations or more.

Pied: Comparatively large patches of two or more colors. Piebald, parti-colored.

Pigeon breast: A narrow chest with protruding breastbone.

Pile: Dense undercoat of soft hair.

Plume: A feathered tail carried over the back.

Poach: To trespass on private property when hunting.

Point: Pause of hunting dog pointing at hidden game.

Points: Color on face, ears, legs, and tail when correlated—usually white, black or tan.

Police dog: Any dog of any breed trained for police work.

Pompon: A rounded tuft of hair on the tip of the tail left when the coat is clipped (Poodle).

Premium list: An advance-notice brochure sent to prospective exhibitors and containing details regarding a forthcoming show.

Prick ear: Carried erect and usually pointed at the tip.

Professional handler: A person licensed by the A.K.C. to show and handle dogs for a fee.

Puppy: A dog under twelve months of age.

Purebred: A dog whose sire and dam belong to the same breed, and are themselves of unmixed descent since recognition of the breed.

Quality: High degree of excellence.

Racy: Tall, of comparatively slight or light conformation.

Rat tail: Hairless, rat-like stern.

Register: To record a dog's breeding particulars with a registration body.

Retrieve: The act of bringing back shot game by dog to the handler.

Ring tail: Tail that curves almost in a circle.

Roach back: A convex curvature or arch of the back toward the rear.

Roan: A fine mixture of vari-colored hairs.

Roman nose: Nasal top line that forms a convex line. Ram's nose.

Rose ear: A small drop ear which folds over and back.

Rounding: Trimming the ends of the ear. (English Foxhounds).

Rudder: The tail or stern.

Ruff: Thick, longer hair growth around the neck.

Sable: Black tipped hairs over a lighter ground color.

Saddle: A black marking over the back, shaped like a saddle or saddle blanket. (Airedale Terrier).

Scent: The odor left by an animal (including man) in passing.

Scissors bite: A very silght overlapping of the upper teeth over the lower teeth when the mouth is closed. In most breeds, much desired.

Screw tail: Naturally short tail twisted in spiral formation.
Second thigh: That part of the hindquarter from the stifle to the hock. Lower thigh.
Self color: One color over entire body except for lighter shadings.
Seeing Eye dog: A dog trained by the institution, The Seeing Eye, as guide dog for the blind. (Usually German Shepherds).
Semi-prick ears: Ears carried erect but with tips bent. (Collie).
Septum: The cleft extending vertically between the nostrils.
Shelly: A shallow, narrow body lacking in bone and bulk.
Short-coupled: Short in length in comparison to height. Square, height to length. Comparatively short in distance from sternum to outer edge of thigh.
Shoulder-height: Height of dog's body as measured from the withers to the ground. See Withers.
Sickle tail: Stern carried out and up in a semicircle.
Sire: The male parent.
Sled dogs: Dogs used to draw sleds. Usually northern "Sled Dog" breeds.
Smooth coat: Short, close-lying hair.
Snipy: A pointed, weak muzzle, lacking breadth and depth.
Soundness: Free from flaws or defects, firm and strong.
Spay: To surgically cut a bitch's fallopian tubes to prevent conception or pregnancy.
Splashed: Irregularly patched, color on white or white on color. (St. Bernard),
Splay foot: A flat foot with spreading toes. Usually also shallow pads.
Spread: Width between the forelegs.
Spring of ribs: Degree of rib cage width in proportion to rest of body.
Squirrel tail: Carried up and forward. Usually considered faulty.
Stake: Designation of a class, used in field-trial competition.
Stance: Placement of legs and attitude in standing.
Standard: A description of the ideal type for each recognized breed.
Standoff coat: Coat that stands away from the body. (Pomeranian).
Staring coat: Harsh, dry coat.
Stern: Tail.
Sternum: Breastbone. (Actually cartilage rather than bone).
Stifle: The joint of the hind leg between the thigh and the second thigh. The knee.
Stilted: Choppy, straight-hocked gait.
Stop: The step up from nose to skull; indentation between the eyes.
Straight-hocked: Lacking angulation of the hock. Also straight behind.
Straight shoulders: The shoulder blades connected rather straight up and down; not well-angulated.
Stud book: A record of the breeding particulars of dogs of recognized breeds.
Substance: Strong, firm bone and body. Lack of substance is opposite.
Swayback: Concave curvature of the back line between the withers and the hip bones or pelvis.

Team: Usually four dogs.
Thigh: The hindquarter from hip to stifle.
Throatiness: An excess of loose skin under the throat, Wet.
Ticked: Small, isolated areas of black or colored hairs on a white ground.
Topknot: A tuft of longer hair on top of the head. (Dandie Dinmont Terrier).
Trace: A dark stripe down the back of the Pug dog.
Trail: To hunt by following scent left by quarry on ground.
Triangular eye: A three-cornered eye.
Tricolor: Three colors in one coat: white, black and tan.
Trim: To shape the coat by plucking or clipping.
Tucked up: Small-waisted. The upward sweep of dog's bottom line.
Tulip ear: The ear carried erect with slight drop forward of the flap along the sides.
Type: The characteristic qualities distinguishing any breed.

Undershot: The front teeth (incisors) of the lower jaw overlapping or projecting beyond the front teeth of the upper jaw.

Upper arm: The humerus or bone of the forelegs, sloping from shoulder blade to forearm.

Varmint: Small destructive wild animal.

Walleye: An eye with a pale whitish iris. A pearl eye.

Weaving: When in motion, the crossing of the forefeet or the hind feet, one over the other, imparting a "weaving" movement.

Wheaten: Pale yellow or fawn color.

Whelps: Unweaned puppies.

Whip tail: Carried out straight and stiff.

Whiskers: Longer coarse hairs on muzzle sides and underjaw.

Winners: An award given at dog shows to the best dog (winners dogs) and best bitch (winners bitches) competing in regular classes.

Wirehair: A coat of hard, crisp, wiry texture.

Withers: The highest part of the body on topline between neck and back.

Wrinkle: Loose, folding skin on forehead and foreface.

GLOSSARY OF
GENETIC TERMS
AND SYMBOLS

GENE (*noun; ajd. genotypic*). A single unit of inheritance (Mendel's "Determiners"); a microscopic part of a chromosome.

CHROMOSOMES (*noun; adj. autosomal*). Small microscopic bodies within the cells of all living things. When division of cells begins the chromosomes appear as short strings of beads or rods.

DOMINANT (*adj.*). A trait or character that is seen. Indicates that a trait contributed by one parent conceals that contributed from the other parent. For example, dark eyes are dominant over light eyes.

RECESSIVES (*adj.*). A trait or character that is concealed by a like dominant character. Exception: when no dominant is present and recessive genes pair for a certain trait. For example, the Weimaraner color, fawn Great Danes, etc. Paired recessives = Visibility.

FACTOR (*noun*). A simple Mendelian trait: may be considered synonymous with gene.

HETEROZYGOUS (*adj.*). Possessing contrasting genes (or allelomorphs). Where dominant and recessive genes are both present for any trait or traits.

HOMOZYGOUS (*adj.*). Pure for a given trait, or possessing matched genes for that trait. The opposite of heterozygous. (Thus inbred strains are said to be homozygous, and out-crossed animals to be heterozygous. Degree must be substantiated.)

GENOTYPE (*noun; adj. genotypic*). The hereditary composition of an individual. The sum total of every animal's dominant and recessive traits.

PHENOTYPE (*noun; adj. phenotypic*). The external appearance of an individual. The outward manifestation of all dominant genetic material (or double recessive. See Recessive).

ALLELOMORPHS (*noun; adj. allelomorphic*). Genes, factors, traits or types which segregate as alternatives. Contrasting gene pattern.

ALLELE (*noun*). A gene, factor, trait, which differs from its sister gene. See Allelomorph.

AUTOSOMES (*noun; adj. atuosomal*). Paired, ordinary chromosomes, similar in both sexes, as differentiated from the sex chromosomes.

CROSSING-OVER (*noun*). An exchange of inheritance factors or genes between related chromosomes.

HYPOSTASIS (*noun; adj. hypostatic*). The masking of the effect of another factor, not an allelomorph. For example, the masking of the ticking factor in dogs by solid color.

EPISTASIS (*noun; adj. epistatic*). Similar to hypostasis. Like dominance but epistasis occurs between factors not alternative or allelomorphic.

♂ Indicates a male. The symbol represents the shield and spear of Mars, the God of War.

♀ Indicates a female. This symbol represents the mirror of the Goddess of Love, Venus.

✕ Means "with", "between", etc. A mating between any male and female.

F_1 Represents the first filial generation. The progeny or "get" produced from any specific mating.

F_2 Is the symbol used to denote the second filial generation, that is, the progeny, or young, produced from a mating of a male and female from the F_1 breeding above.

GET. Puppies or offspring.

DNA. Deoxyribonucleic acid. Chemical compound in chromosomes that is, with protein, the material of heredity.

RNA. Ribonucleic acid. An approximate image of DNA.

BIBLIOGRAPHY

Arenas, N., and Sammartino, R., "Le Cyle Sexuel de la Chienne." Etude Histol Bull. Histol. Appl. Physiol. et Path., 16:299 (1939).
Ash, E. C., Dogs: Their History and Development, 2 vols., London, 1927.
Anrep, G. V., "Pitch Discrimination in the Dog." F. Physiol., 53-376-85 (1920).
Barrows, W. M., Science of Animal Life. New York, World Book Co., 1927.
Burns, Marca, 1952. The Genetics of the Dog, Comm., Agri. Bur., Eng. 122 pp.
Castle, W. E., Genetics and Eugenics, 4th ed. Cambridge, Mass., Harvard University Press, 1930.
Darwin, Charles, The Origin of Species and The Descent of Man, Modern Library, 1936.
———— and Wallace, A. R., Evolution By Natural Selection, Cambridge Univ. Press, London, 1958.
Darwin, C., The Variation of Animals and Plants Under Domestication, New York, D. Appleton Co., 1890.
Davenport, C. B., Heredity in Relation to Eugenics. New York, Henry Holt & Co., Inc., 1911.
De Vries, Hugo, The Mutation Theory (vols. I & II), Open Court Pub. Co., 1909.
Dorland, W. A. N., A.M., M.D., F.A.C.S., The American Illustrated Medical Dictionary. Philadelphia, W. B. Saunders Co., 1938.
Duncan, W. C., Dog Training Made Easy. Boston, Little, Brown & Co., 1940.
Dunn, L. C., and Dobzhansky, T., Heredity, Race and Society. New York, New American Library of World Literature, 1946.
Elliot, David D., Training Gun Dogs to Retrieve. New York, Henry Holt & Co., 1952.
Evans, H. M., and Cole, H. H., "An Introduction to the Study of the Oestrus Cycle of the Dog." Mem. Univ. Cal., Vol. 9, No. 2.
Fisher, Sir Ronald Aylmer, The Genetical Theory of Natural Selection, Clarendon Press, Oxford, 1930.
Hart, Ernest H., Artificial Insemination (article) Your Dog, 1948.
———— Doggy Hints, Mens Mg., Zenith Pub. Co. (article).
———— Budgerigar Handbook, T.F.H. Pub. Co., Inc., N.J., 1961.
———— This Is The Puppy, T.F.H. Pub. Co., Inc., N.J., 1962.
———— This Is The Weimaraner, T.F.H. Pub. Co., Inc., N.J., 1965.
———— This Is The Great Dane, T.F.H. Pub. Co., Inc., N.J., 1967.
———— Dog Breeders' Handbook, T.F.H. Pub. Co., Inc., N.J., 1966.
———— The Poodle Handbook, T.F.H. Pub. Co., Inc., N.J., 1966.
———— The Cocker Spaniel Handbook, T.F.H. Pub. Co., Inc., N.J., 1967.
———— Your German Shepherd Puppy, T.F.H. Pub. Co., Inc., N.J., 1967.
———— How To Train Your Dog, T.F.H. Pub. Co., Inc., N.J., 1967.
———— and Goldbecker, W., This Is The German Shepherd, T.F.H. Pub. Co., Inc., N.J., 1955.
Hermansson, K. A., "Artificial Impregnation of the Dog." Svensk. Vet. Tidshr., 39:382 (1934).
Humphrey, E. S., Articles on "The German Shepherd Dog." The Bulletin Shep. Dog Cl. of Amer. (1923-1927).
———— "Mental Tests for Shepherd Dogs." J. of Hered., 25:129 (1934).
————, and Warner, Lucien, Working Dogs. Baltimore, Johns Hopkins Press, 1934.
Keeler, C. E., and Trimble, H. C., "Inheritance of Dewclaws." J. of Hered., 29:145 (1938).
Kelly, G. L., and Whitney, L. F., Prevention of Conception in Bitches by Injections of Estrone. J. Ga. Med. Assoc., 29:7 (1940).
Kraus, C., "Beitrag zum Prostatakrebs und Kryptorchismus des Hundes." Frankfurter Zeitsch. Path., 41:405 (1931).
Krushinsky, L. A., "A Study of the Phenogenetics of Behaviour Characters in Dogs." Biol. Journ. T., VII, No. 4, Inst. Zool., Moscow State Univ. (1938).
Laughlin, H. H., "Racing Capacity of Horses." Dept. of Genetics 37-73. Yearbook, Carn. Inst., No. 30, The Blood Horse, 1931.
MacDowell, E. C., "Heredity of Behaviour in Dogs." Dept. of Genetics, Yearbook, Carn. Inst., No. 20, 1921, 101-56.
Morgan, T. H., Evolution and Adaptation, Macmillan, N.Y. and London, 1903.
———— The Mechanism of Mendelian Heredity, Henry Holt, 1933.

Muller, Friedrich, *Geschichte des Verein jur Deutsche Schaferhunde.* 1899-1949. S.V., Augsburg, 1949.
Nagel, W. A., *Der Farbensinn des Hundes. Zbl. Phsysiol.,* 21 (1907).
Otto, E. von, Grey Pointers of Weimar, *Huntsport und Fagd.* 1930.
Pearson, K., and Usher, C. H., "Albinism in Dogs." *Biometrica,* 21:144-163 (1929).
Razran, H. S., and Warden, C. J., "The Sensory Capacities of the Dog (Russian Schools)." *Psychol. Bulletin* 26, 1929.
Roesbeck, Dr., *40 Jahre Arbeit fur den Deutschen Schaferhunde,* S. V., Augsburg, 1939.
Schwabacher, J., *"The Popular Alsatian,* rev. ed., Popular Dogs Publishing Co., Ltd., 1950.
Stephanitz, Max von, *The Shepherd Dog in Word and Picture.* Jena, Anton Kampfe, 1923.
———— "What Is Nobility?" *Koerbook.* S. V., Augsburg, 1930.
Stetson, J., "Heartworm Can Be Controlled." *Field and Stream* June 1954 (article).
Telever, J., 1934. When Is the Heat Period of the Dog?
The Complete Dog Book, The American Kennel Club Edition, Garden City Books, Garden City, N.Y.
Whitney, L. F., *The Basis of Breeding.* N. H. Fowler, 1928.
———— *How To Breed Dogs.* New York, Orange Judd Pub. Co., 1947.
———— *Feeding Our Dogs.* New York, D. van Nostrand Co., Inc., 1949.
———— *Complete Book of Dog Care,* Garden City, L.I., Doubleday & Co., Inc., 1953.
———— and Whitney, G. D., *The Distemper Complex.* Orange, Conn., Practical Science Pub. Co., 1953.

768

INDEX